BROADLAND

BROADLAND

Shaping marsh and fen

TOM WILLIAMSON & ALISON YARDY

With: Keith Bacon, Michael Brandon-Jones, Di Cornell,
Jacky Heath, Ian Hinton, Tim Holt-Wilson, Carol Horner,
Charlotte Jarvis, Ann Nix, Michael Nix, Jo Parmenter,
Claire Penstone-Smith, Tim Pestell and Sophie Tremlett

UNIVERSITY OF HERTFORDSHIRE PRESS

First published in Great Britain in 2024 by
University of Hertfordshire Press
College Lane
Hatfield
Hertfordshire
AL10 9AB
UK

© individual contributors 2024

The right of Tom Williamson and Alison Yardy to be identified as the editors of this work have been asserted by them in accordance with the Copyright, Designs and Patents Act 1988.

All rights reserved. No part of this book may be reproduced or utilised in any form or by any means, electronic or mechanical, including photocopying, recording or by any information storage and retrieval system, without permission in writing from the publisher.

British Library Cataloguing in Publication Data
A catalogue record for this book is available from the British Library

ISBN 978-1-912260-67-6
Design by Arthouse Publishing Solutions
Printed in Great Britain by Henry Ling Ltd

CONTENTS

List of illustrations vii
Abbreviations xi
Contributors xiii
Acknowledgements xv

1 Introducing Broadland 1
2 The uplands 35
3 The marshes 103
4 The valleys 167
5 Drainage by wind and steam 227
6 Waterways and industry 277
7 Recreation, tourism and conservation 327
8 Conclusion 363

Bibliography 371
Index 385

ILLUSTRATIONS

Figures

1.1	View across the Halvergate Marshes	1
1.2	View near Upton	2
1.3	Principal watercourses and settlements in Broadland	3
1.4	Flint nodules in the ruins of St Saviour's church, Surlingham	8
1.5	Exposure of strata at the Bramerton pit	10
1.6	Fluvial origins of rocks in the Wroxham Crag	13
1.7	Outwash sands at the Welcome Pit, Burgh Castle	16
1.8	Dry valleys in the Herringfleet Hills	19
1.9	Breydon Water and the coastal spit at Great Yarmouth	23
1.10	Broadland: relief	25
1.11	The watercourses of northern Broadland in the early Middle Ages	27
1.12	Aerial view of the Bure valley	29
1.13	Broadland: geology	31
2.1	A late prehistoric trackway at Belton	39
2.2	The Middle Bronze Age enclosure at Ormesby St Michael	40
2.3	Cropmarks of a field system at Cantley and Beighton	42
2.4	A double-ditched enclosure at Beighton	45
2.5	The Middle Saxon log boat found at Ludham Bridge	47
2.6	The distribution of selected place-name elements in Broadland	48
2.7	Two churches in one churchyard at South Walsham	52
2.8	Extract from William Faden's 1797 map of Norfolk	54
2.9	Church sites and geology in the Bure valley	56
2.10	The field pattern in Rollesby and Repps-with-Bastwick	60
2.11	Churches and parishes discussed in this section	63
2.12	St Mary's, East Somerton	66

VIII BROADLAND

2.13 St John the Baptist, Barnby   69
2.14 St Edmund's, Fritton   70
2.15 The tower of St Mary the Virgin, Burgh St Peter   73
2.16 Detail from Henry Bright's 'St Benet's Abbey'   75
2.17 The locations of the Broadland monastic foundations discussed
      in the text   76
2.18 The location of St Benet's Abbey   78
2.19 The income of monasteries in East Anglia in 1291   80
2.20 Lidar imagery of the siting of monastic houses   84
2.21 The Trinitarian cross on the tomb of Sir Roger de Boys   86
2.22 Danegelt House, Geldeston   95
2.23 The Bell, St Olaves   96
2.24 The late-seventeenth-century Thurne Manor   98
2.25 The Croft, Rollesby   99
2.26 Camberley Cottage, Happisburgh   101
3.1   Typical view across the Halvergate Marshes   105
3.2   The Roman fort at Burgh Castle   106
3.3   The distribution of salterns recorded by Domesday   108
3.4   The pattern of relict saltmarsh channels on Halvergate   111
3.5   Aerial view of the Halvergate Fleet   112
3.6   The complex pattern of parish boundaries on the Halvergate Marshes   115
3.7   The holdings of Benet's Abbey and the Cathedral Priory on Halvergate   119
3.8   The distribution of medieval mounds on the Halvergate Marshes   121
3.9   The medieval mound near Ash Tree Farm   122
3.10 Detail from an estate map from the 1730s showing land in
      Halvergate parish   124
3.11 Earthworks of a probable medieval saltern   126
3.12 Lidar image showing the 'Northern Rond' and medieval mound sites   127
3.13 The relationship between former creeks, medieval mounds and parish
      boundaries   129
3.14 Possible courses of the rivers Ant and Bure before changes in the
      thirteenth century   130
3.15 Detail from a map of 1721, showing drainage windmill in Stokesby   136
3.16 Drainage 'Levels' on the Halvergate Marshes in the late
      nineteenth century   138
3.17 The proliferation of drainage dykes in South Walsham Detached   144
3.18 The modern pattern of drainage dykes on the Halvergate Marshes   145
3.19 Patterns of ownership on the Halvergate Marshes in c.1840   150
3.20 Owner-occupied land on the Halvergate Marshes in c.1840   156
3.21 A lost marsh farm in Acle Detached   160

3.22	Raven Hall, a seventeenth-century farmhouse on Haddiscoe Island	161
3.23	Cattle grazing on the Halvergate Marshes	162
4.1	Dawn at Upton Broad	168
4.2	Beds of reed on Hickling Broad	168
4.3	Aerial view of grazing marshes at Thurne	169
4.4	Catfield Fen	169
4.5	The 'doles' at Upton in 1839	177
4.6	Narrow strips of grazing marsh, former 'doles', near Rockland Broad	178
4.7	Typical 'carr' in the Ant valley	181
4.8	Detail from the enclosure map for Thurne, 1820	187
4.9	The development of 'Broad Waters' in Woodbastwick Fen	193
4.10	The distribution and extent of poor's allotments in the Ant valley	194
4.11	Barton Broad from the air	196
4.12	Rockland Broad	196
4.13	Sprat's Water, Carlton Colville	198
4.14	The location of broads, lost or extant, in northern Broadland	200
4.15	The location of broads, lost or extant, in southern Broadland	201
4.16	Surlingham Broad, as depicted on the enclosure map of 1822	207
4.17	The drainage mill in Catfield Middle Fen	209
4.18	Crested buckler-fern (*Dryopteris cristata*)	212
4.19	Fen meadow on the Upton Marshes nature reserve	214
4.20	Tufted sedge (*Carex elata*)	216
4.21	Marsh marigold (*Caltha palustris*)	222
5.1	Drawing of Herringfleet smock drainage mill, showing internal workings	228
5.2	Brograve Level Mill, one of the oldest in Broadland, was built in 1771	231
5.3	Pettingill's Mill, shortly before it finished work in the 1940s	232
5.4	The archaic lower gearing at Tunstall Black Mill in 1938	235
5.5	'Mill at Reedham' by Thomas Lound (1802–1861)	236
5.6	Herringfleet Mill, built around 1820: the only extant smock drainage mill in Broadland	238
5.7	Palmer's Mill, a rare surviving example of a 'hollow post mill'	241
5.8	The distribution of drainage windmills in the late eighteenth century	243
5.9	The distribution of drainage mills *c.*1840	244
5.10	The distribution of drainage mills *c.*1885	245
5.11	Drawing of Stracey Arms drainage mill, showing internal features	247
5.12	Thurne Mill or Morse's Mill	250
5.13	Turf Fen Mill, beside the Ant in Irstead	254
5.14	Hardley Mill	254
5.15	Berney Arms Mill, the tallest in Broadland	257

5.16 Boardman's Mill, one of only three 'skeleton' or 'trestle' mills surviving in Broadland — 259
5.17 The steam engine house at Strumpshaw — 264
5.18 Polkey's Mill and steam engine house, Reedham Marshes — 264
5.19 A mixture of technologies: Calthorpe Mill and engine house, Acle, and Stokesby Commission Mill — 271
6.1 A wherry under sail on the river Yare — 278
6.2 A keel, laden with timber, on the river Yare in 1829 — 278
6.3 Principal improvements made to the course of the river Ant — 287
6.4 The New Cut — 289
6.5 Map of public staithes in Broadland — 290
6.6 A former warehouse at Stokesby Staithe — 298
6.7 The granary at Stalham Staithe — 298
6.8 The staithes discussed in the chapter — 300
6.9 Gay's Staithe, Irstead, from John Payne Jennings' *Sun pictures* — 301
6.10 The 'Black Shed' at Barton Turf staithe — 304
6.11 The development of Stalham Staithe — 308
6.12 Nineteenth-century malthouse at Ludham — 311
6.13 The remains of Somerleyton brickworks — 315
6.14 The cement works at Berney Arms — 316
6.15 Beccles, as shown on the first edition 25-inch Ordnance Survey map — 317
6.16 Sign on the wall of a house in Northgate Street, Beccles — 317
6.17 The medieval bridge at Potter Heigham — 320
6.18 Buckenham ferry, as painted by Joseph Stannard — 322
6.19 Willows lining the road to Halvergate village — 324
6.20 Railway lines and navigations in Broadland — 325
7.1 Boathouses at the northern end of Hickling Broad — 328
7.2 St Benet's Abbey from the air — 330
7.3 Fritton Decoy, photographed by John Payne Jennings, *c.*1890 — 332
7.4 Wildfowl decoys in Broadland — 335
7.5 Peter Henry Emerson, 'Snipe Shooting' (1886) — 340
7.6 Maurice Bird punting on Hickling Broad in *c.*1900 — 342
7.7 Riverside chalets on the Thurne, upstream from Potter Heigham Bridge — 350
7.8 Peter Henry Emerson, 'Reed Cutters' (1892) — 356
7.9 Wroxham and Hoveton from the air — 361
8.1 The Suffolk Wildlife Trust's Carlton Marshes reserve — 368

Tables

1.1 Environments represented in the Ludham Research Borehole (1959) — 11

ABBREVIATIONS

BM	British Museum, London
CERC	Church of England Record Centre, London
CUC	Catfield United Charities
ENRCB	East Norfolk Rivers Catchment Board
IDB	Internal Drainage Board
NHER	Norfolk Historic Environment Record, Norwich
NRO	Norfolk Record Office, Norwich
SHER	Suffolk Historic Environment Record, Bury St Edmunds
SRO	Suffolk Record Office, Ipswich
SSSI	Site of Special Scientific Interest
TNA	The National Archives, Kew
WMA	Water Management Alliance archive, Kings Lynn

CONTRIBUTORS

Keith Bacon completed his MA and PhD at the University of East Anglia. His research interests include enclosure and landholding in east Norfolk and the history of emigration and access. He is a trustee of a number of Broads-based charities and organisations.

Diana Cornell is a retired teacher and independent researcher with a particular interest in Broadland's history. She is a Founder Trustee of The Museum of the Broads.

Jacky Heath read biology at York University before taking her MSc in clinical biochemistry at Surrey. She later gained a Diploma in field archaeology and landscape history at the University of East Anglia and has a particular interest in the use of tithe maps in the study of landscape history.

Ian Hinton took his PhD at the University of East Anglia after taking early retirement. He is currently Chair of the Norfolk Historic Buildings Group and editor of its journal. His book *The Alignment and Location of Medieval Rural Churches* was published in 2012.

Tim Holt-Wilson is an independent researcher who has written widely on the geology, geomorphology and geodiversity of Norfolk and Suffolk. He is actively involved in earth heritage conservation, and a variety of outreach projects, throughout East Anglia.

Charlotte Jarvis studied landscape history at the University of East Anglia. She has wide interests in the landscapes and gardens of Norfolk, and a particular interest in the origins and development of the broads, the subject of her MA dissertation.

Ann Nix has an MSc in human ecology and is a retired local and naval history librarian. She is an independent researcher with a variety of interests, and is currently researching her great uncle's experiences in the Indian army during the First World War.

Michael Nix has a PhD in maritime history from the University of Leicester and researches, amongst other subjects, the history of the textile industry. His book *Norwich Textiles: A Global Story 1750–1840*, published in 2023, won the history and tradition category in the East Anglian Book Awards.

Jo Parmenter took her PhD at the University of East Anglia and is a botanist and ecologist with a lifelong interest in the flora of Broadland. She combines a now part-time career in ecological consultancy with roles with various conservation charities and botanical recording for the Botanical Society of the British Isles.

Tim Pestell is Senior Curator of Archaeology at Norwich Castle Museum and Art Gallery and has published extensively on medieval monasticism in East Anglia and early medieval archaeology.

Sophie Tremlett is an archaeologist. For the last 20 years she has worked on aerial archaeology projects in Norfolk and Suffolk as part of Norfolk County Council's Environment Team.

Claire Penstone-Smith, Michael Brandon-Jones and Carol Horner are all members of the Neatishead, Irstead and Barton Turf Community Heritage Group with a particular interest in researching the history of these three Broadland villages.

ACKNOWLEDGEMENTS

This book is one of the outputs of the 'Water, Mills and Marshes' Landscape Partnership project, and our greatest debt is to the project's principal funder, the National Lottery Heritage Fund. We would like to thank the volunteer researchers, surveyors and aerial archaeology investigators involved in the project, especially the late David Stannard, Jacky Heath, Alice Leftley, Suzanne Longe, Karen Michlmayr, Mark Nicholson and Susan York; Andrew Farrell at the Broads Authority; and Andrew Tullett, Sophie Cabot and others at Norfolk County Council, who were involved in its administration and organisation. Our thanks also to Jack Powell, for his work on GIS; to Heather Hamilton for assistance with Historic Environment Record data; to local landowners, in particular Barry Brooks and Beckhithe Farms, for allowing access to their property; to Kate Skipper, for research assistance; and to Acle Community Archive Group, Richard Ademek, Peter Allard, Mike Barnes, Tony Bradstreet, Rob Driscoll, Clare Everitt, Dick Foyster, David High, Sheila and Paul Hutchinson, the Museum of the Broads, Paul Reynolds, Richard Seago, Anne Whelpton, the Wherry Maud Trust, the Norfolk and Suffolk Record Offices, the Norfolk Wildlife Trust, the Suffolk Wildlife Trust and the Broads Authority for information, help and advice. Much of the archive research on public staithes was funded by the Broads Authority and undertaken by Philippa Parker and the late Ivan Ringwood.

The maps and diagrams are by the authors, but mostly tidied up and made presentable by Rik Hoggett, with the exception of: 1.6, by Tim Holt-Wilson and P. Riches; 2.17, 2.19 and 2.20, by Tim Pestell; 2.18, by Sue White; 5.1, by the late John Reynolds (and originally published in his *Windmills and Watermills* (London, 1970)); and 5.11, which is © John Brandrick.

The photographs are by the authors, except 5.6, 5.13, 5.14, 5.15 and 5.16, Alamy Photos; 1.1, 2.16, 3.9, 3.23, 6.4, 6.6, 6.7, 6.10, 6.13, 6.16, 6.19 and 7.7, by

Liz Bellamy; 1.2, by Liz Dack; 1.12, 2.7, 7.2 and 7.9, by John Fielding; 4.17, by Tim and Geli Harris; 2.11, 2.12, 2.13, 2.14, 2.15, 2.22, 2.23, 2.24, 2.25 and 2.26, by Ian Hinton; 5.12, by Debra Nicholson; 4.1 and 4.2, by Richard Osbourne; 4.3 and 6.17, by Mark Oakden/TourNorfolk.co.uk; 2.2, 5.17 and 5.18, by Mike Page; 3.22, by Lisa Drewe/Islandeering; 4.12, 4.18, 4.19, 4.20 and 4.21, by Jo Parmenter; 2.21, by Tim Pestell; 2.5, by Heather Wallis; and 1.4, 1.5, 1.7 and 1.9, by Tim Holt-Wilson.

Figure 1.8 is from the British Geological Survey; 6.18, from the Yale Centre for British Art; 3.10, 3.15, 3.21, 4.5, 4.6, 4.8, 4.16 and 6.11 are courtesy of Norfolk Record Office; 5.5 is © Norfolk Museums Service; 5.19, 6.9 and 7.3 are reproduced courtesy of Norfolk County Council Library and Information Service; 5.3 is reproduced courtesy of Norfolk County Council; 3.2, 3.5, 4.11 are © Historic England Archive; and 7.6 was scanned by James Parry and is reproduced with the permission of Felicity Tredwell.

Figures 2.1, 2.3 and 2.4 feature archaeological mapping © Norfolk County Council, licensed to Historic England, with base mapping derived from Ordnance Survey MasterMap © Crown copyright and database rights 2023 Ordnance Survey 100019340.

All lidar imagery, whether reproduced directly or used to generate maps or diagrams, is derived from UK Environment Agency open-source data. Geological mapping is based on British Geological Survey data.

INTRODUCING BROADLAND

Broadland, also referred to as 'the Broads' or 'the Norfolk Broads', is a unique area of wetlands that constitutes the only National Park in eastern England. The famous 'broads' themselves are shallow freshwater lakes, now around 40 in number but formerly more, which occupy the floodplains of a network of interconnected, tidal, mainly navigable waterways in eastern Norfolk and north-eastern Suffolk. These are the rivers Yare, Bure (also known in the past as the 'North River'), Waveney, Ant, Thurne and Chet, together with their various tributaries, such as the picturesquely named Muck Fleet. Lakes and waterways are set in a complex and varied landscape of fen and marsh. In some places the scenery is wild and rather enclosed in

Figure 1.1 View across the Halvergate Marshes towards Mutton's Mill.

Figure 1.2 View near Upton: the wetter, wilder landscapes found on the peat soils of the river valleys.

character, elsewhere more open and managed, with extensive level panoramas and wide skies (Figures 1.1 and 1.2). Particular structures contribute to the landscape's distinctive character, most notably the towers of numerous drainage windmills, all now redundant and many derelict or ruined, that punctuate the low horizon. Such scenes proved irresistible to John Sell Cotman, John Crome, Henry Bright, Joseph Stannard and other painters of the Norwich School, which flourished in the area in the early nineteenth century.

Since the late nineteenth century, when the Broads were 'discovered' by the writer George Christopher Davies, the area has boasted a significant tourist industry. Generations of visitors have been attracted by the beauty of its landscape and its rural tranquillity, and by the simple pleasures of exploring by boat its intricate network of waterways, which has a total length of over 200 kilometres. But the area is valued for other reasons, most importantly for its wealth of wildlife. Many rare species, both flora and fauna, survive here, and many hundreds of hectares are now managed primarily for nature conservation. We should not, however, exaggerate the unspoiled rural character of Broadland. Major concentrations of commercial boatyards, supplying craft for hire, along with facilities and 'attractions' for visitors, have developed at a number of places, most notably, perhaps, Wroxham. The area is, moreover, bounded to the west by the great city of Norwich, with a current population of more than 380,000; and

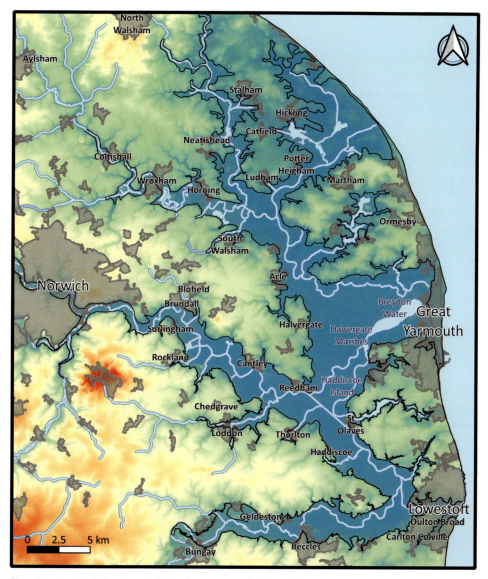

Figure 1.3 Broadland, showing principal watercourses and settlements.

to the east by the holiday resorts of Great Yarmouth (where the Broadland rivers have their collective outfall to the sea) and Lowestoft, both with sprawling suburbs (Figure 1.3). One of the strange things about Broadland, and worrying for the future development of its landscape, is that the boundaries of the Broads National Park – within which insensitive development can be most easily restricted – scarcely anywhere extend far beyond the floodplain fens and marshes. This said, for the most part Broadland still remains a remote and rural area, and in places a rather wild one.

In some ways, as we shall see, Broadland has actually become *more* rural over the last century or so. Its waterways were vital arteries for trade long before they became a playground for holiday makers, and a range of industries – now largely vanished – was drawn to their margins. It has also, over this same period of time, become rather wilder in appearance, as traditional methods of managing the fens have steadily declined, creating in many places wetter and more wooded environments. In recent decades, moreover, powerful organisations have in places attempted to accelerate this process, creating artificial wildness where, for centuries, there was managed, productive marshland, in order to promote biodiversity. The Broadland we see today is different to that of a century ago, and not merely because of the more obvious accretions and additions, of boatyards and motor cruisers and riverside holiday chalets. Different again was the Broadland of the seventeenth century, of the fifteenth, or the thirteenth. Landscapes are always changing, in subtle as much as in obvious ways, and Broadland is no exception. And what to the casual visitor may seem a timeless scene – reedbeds, woodland, ruined drainage mill, distant church – is in reality an amalgam of elements bequeathed by successive generations, each of which has its own definable history.

As with all valued landscapes, recognising this propensity to change raises difficult philosophical questions. What are we doing when we strive to 'preserve' an area or a place – to halt change, or at least to limit or control it – given that change is normal, and has served to produce what we value in the first place? These are issues to which we shall return: at this stage we would merely note that a thorough understanding of a landscape's history, of the origins and character of its essential features, is essential for managing it for the benefit and enjoyment of present and future generations. Perhaps more importantly, a knowledge of history is vital, in Broadland as elsewhere, for the successful conservation of the habitats so vital for sustaining biodiversity, for these are, for the most part, 'semi-natural' in character: that is, they were created and maintained by forms of human exploitation such as mowing, grazing and reed-cutting. But this book is aimed not primarily at landowners and land managers, but rather at all those who love Broadland, whether local residents or visitors, and who simply want to understand more about its landscape. Why do some of the wetlands take the form of open grazed pastures, while others comprise wilder and wetter landscapes of reedbeds, fen and alder? When were the iconic drainage mills erected and how did they work? Why are there so many churches in Broadland and why do so many stand alone in the fields, remote from the dwellings of parishioners? These are the kinds of question we try to answer in the chapters that follow.

Many books have been written on Broadland over the last century and a half, and a significant number of these are concerned, in whole or part, with the development of its landscapes. Perhaps the most famous is *The Making of the*

Broads, published in 1960, in which Joyce Lambert, Joseph Jennings and their collaborators established beyond reasonable doubt that the broads – that is, the freshwater lakes – were artificial, the consequence of medieval peat-digging.[1] It is a conclusion that has stood the test of time, although modified and nuanced in a number of significant ways in Chapter 4 of this volume. Ted Ellis's 'New Naturalist' volume *The Broads* followed in 1965 and, while mainly concerned with natural history, included a chapter by Lambert and Jennings on their recent research on the origins of the broads, as well as considerations of 'Man in Broadland' by the archaeologist Raynbird Clarke and of 'Native River Craft of the Broads' by H. Bolingbroke.[2] Important publications in 1971 and 1973 by Robert Malster – *Wherries and Waterways* and *The Broads* – threw important new light on, in particular, the commercial and industrial history of the broads and rivers, while Martin George's monumental *The Land Use, Ecology and Conservation of Broadland* of 1992 and Brian Moss's *The Broads* of 2001 – although focused primarily on matters ecological – of necessity include good overviews of the area's history.[3] Malster's *The Norfolk and Suffolk Broads* (2003) expanded on his earlier work with a greater emphasis on the physical environment; David Cleveland's *A Look Back at The Broads* (2019) shed new light on, in particular, the area's history as a holiday destination; in 2014 the noted cultural geographer David Matless published his *In the Nature of Landscape: Cultural Geography on the Norfolk Broads*, a book that explores both past and contemporary engagements with, and understandings of, the Broadland landscape; and in 1997 one of the present writers (Williamson) published a volume specifically entitled *The Norfolk Broads: a Landscape History*.[4] Why, the reader might be wondering, given this mass of publications, is another book on Broadland's landscape required?

The answer is that new research, in part facilitated by new digital technologies, has thrown a great deal of new light on Broadland's history. Lidar, a form of remote sensing that uses pulsed lasers to map variations in the Earth's surface, has revolutionised the identification and mapping of earthworks, while Geographical Information Systems (GIS) – computer mapping – allows novel and powerful ways of interrogating spatial data. Some of the work presented here was undertaken as part of a major community project, 'Water, Mills and Marshes', principally financed

---

1 J.M. Lambert, J.N. Jennings, C.T. Smith, C. Green and J.N. Hutchinson, *The making of the Broads: a reconsideration of their origin in the light of new evidence* (London, 1960).
2 E.A. Ellis (ed.), *The Broads* (London, 1965).
3 R. Malster, *Wherries and waterways* (Lavenham, 1971). R. Malster, *The Broads* (Chichester, 1993). M. George, *The land use, ecology and conservation of Broadland* (Chichester, 1992). B. Moss, *The Broads: the people's wetland* (London, 2001).
4 R. Malster, *The Norfolk and Suffolk Broads* (Chichester, 2003). D. Cleveland, *A look back at the Broads* (Manningtree, 2019). D. Matless, *In the nature of landscape: cultural geography on the Norfolk Broads* (Oxford, 2014). T. Williamson, *The Norfolk Broads: a landscape history* (Manchester, 1997).

by the National Lottery Heritage Fund and organised by Norfolk County Council, which among other things encouraged the research of local historians and other independent scholars. But some, including that presented by Jarvis, Bacon and Parmenter, was undertaken some time earlier as part of research degrees at the University of East Anglia, and has until now remained unpublished and inaccessible to the general public. While much of this book is written by the main authors, in part it is thus an edited work, with a range of able contributors, whose names are given at the beginning of the relevant sections. Such a format is the consequence of the sheer diversity of subjects that any serious examination of Broadland's landscape must address, more than any individual researcher could confidently command, ranging from fen vegetation to prehistoric archaeology, from vernacular architecture to geology. Different contributors have addressed their areas of interest in their own particular way and, to an extent, have similarly defined their geographical focus, but without, we hope, any loss of overall coherence.

As we shall emphasise throughout, Broadland's landscape is in many ways one created by humans. But the raw materials from which it was fashioned were natural, while much that is distinctive about the area arises directly from the character of the natural topography, which is everywhere level, or muted. We begin our story, accordingly, with an examination of rocks and geomorphology, with deep geological time.

Geology and topography
by Tim Holt-Wilson

Broadland is famous for its wetland landscapes and biodiversity. Its geodiversity is not so well known. By geodiversity we mean the abiotic, physical aspects of the Earth – geological (rocks, minerals, sediments, fossils), geomorphological (natural landforms and generative processes such as erosion and deposition), pedological (soil) and hydrological (water) features. Broadland has an abiotic story that is well worth telling, and this account is intended only as an introduction, showing how the present landscape has evolved against a backdrop of deep time. Our subject will be the landscape as scoped and then interpreted within a framework of causal sequences (over time) and spatial arrangements (through space). We will draw on the disciplines of geology, geomorphology and palaeontology to explain the origins of the physical landscape we see today.

The essential geological structure of Broadland is quite simple. Much of the geology is 'soft' and easily eroded, so the topography is subdued. The uplands are underlain by glacial and periglacial sediments of Middle and Late Pleistocene age; the valleys have cut down to expose earlier strata, principally the Crag, marine and estuarine deposits of Late Pliocene and Early Pleistocene age and – in a few places – the Chalk, dating from the much earlier Cretaceous period. The valley floors are occupied by layers of marine and freshwater alluvium, including peat, built up since the end of the last glacial period (about 10,000 years ago). Lying as it does on the western margin of the North Sea, the Broads landscape is a liminal one, its character shaped by gentle rises and falls of sea level over millennial timescales, and by occasional storm surges over the span of a few days. Much of the Broadland landscape is thus, in geological terms, very recent. As John W. Robberds noted in 1826, 'the eastern vallies of Norfolk … offer some highly important and instructive facts, relating to one of the most recent formations of land that can be found on the face of the globe'.[5] Later researchers have used an increasingly sophisticated range of techniques to elucidate the story of the area: the complexities of its glacial and post-glacial stratigraphy; the phasing of marine and freshwater origins for its sediments; the development of its valleys; and the formation of its broads and wetlands.

The oldest bedrock in the Broads area is the Chalk, a soft limestone of Late Cretaceous age, about 70 million years old. This outcrops in places along the sides of the Yare valley near Norwich (around Whitlingham and Postwick) and in the Bure valley near Wroxham (as at 'Little Switzerland' in Horstead). Elsewhere it is blanketed by layers of much more recent deposits. Local observations and information from boreholes enabled early geological investigators such as William Smith (d. 1839) and Richard C. Taylor (d. 1851) to ascertain that the upper surface of the Chalk slopes gently from east to west. For instance, at Bramerton it lies at about 2 metres above sea level, while at Great Yarmouth it lies at 176 metres below sea level, indicating a regional dip of its upper surface of about 4.6 metres per kilometre.[6] The Chalk has contributed to the economy and culture of Broadland as well as to its physical landscape. Where readily accessible, it was quarried and mined in past centuries for the production of lime, and to obtain the flint nodules contained within it.[7] East Anglia is a region poor in useable building stone, so flint has usefully supplied constructional materials for traditional walling, whether in the form of natural nodules and cobbles (raw or split, Figure 1.4) or specially knapped shapes (flushwork). It could also be used to make gunflints and – in earlier periods – stone tools.

Following the end of the Cretaceous period the Chalk was uplifted by tectonic forces in the Earth's crust. Within 5 million years, marine deposits of Palaeocene (*c.*60 million years ago) and Eocene age (*c.*53 million years ago) had been deposited on an eroded chalk basement. These are buried deeply and have been encountered only in boreholes, as at Ludham, Ormesby and Somerton. A long period of

---

5   J.W. Robberds, *Geological and historical observations on the eastern vallies of Norfolk* (Norwich, 1826).
6   P.F. Riches, P.E.P Norton, D.C. Schreve and J. Rose, 'Bramerton Pits SSSI', in I. Candy, J.R. Lee and A.M. Harrison (eds), *The Quaternary of East Anglia* (Cambridge, 2007), pp. 73–84, at p. 73. R.S. Arthurton, S.J. Booth, A.N. Morigi, M.A.W. Abbott and C.J. Wood, *Geology of the country around Great Yarmouth. Memoir for the 1:50,000 Geological Sheet 162 (England and Wales)* (London, 1994), p. 112 and Fig. 15.
7   J. Jones and J. Jones, 'Lime burning in Norfolk', *Journal of the Norfolk Industrial Archaeology Society*, 2/2 (1977), pp. 21–31.

Figure 1.4 Flint nodules in the ruins of St Saviour's church, Surlingham. The use of flint quoins here is unusual, and perhaps due to the proximity of quarries yielding boulders from chalk of the Paramoudra Chalk sub-division (Campanian stage) and the Norwich Crag basement bed.

landscape change – some 50 million years – separated the Eocene from the next stratified sequence of deposits in the Broads area, the Crag. Almost all evidence of intervening formations has been removed by erosion. About 2 million years ago, the Broads area was situated on the edge of the North Sea basin and formed part of the south-western side of a bight with a northwards exit to the Atlantic.[8] Crag sediments were deposited on an eroded surface of Chalk in the west and on (now-buried) Eocene rocks in the east. The lowermost (basement) bed of the Crag preserves evidence of this relationship at sites such as Bramerton, Horstead and Whitlingham. It includes large flints, too heavy to have been moved far by the waves, which provided a useful building material in past centuries (Figure 1.4). The chalk surface is typically an undulating one, with small-scale ups and downs indicating local erosional irregularities.

---

8   G. Kuhlmann, *High resolution stratigraphy and paleoenvironmental changes in the southern North Sea during the Neogene; an integrated study of Late Cenozoic marine deposits from the northern part of the Dutch offshore area* (Utrecht, 2004), p. 80.

The Crag of East Anglia is divided into four formations: Coralline, Red, Norwich and Wroxham. Only the two youngest of these, Norwich and Wroxham, are found in the Broads area. Both formations were deposited in near-shore environments and comprise a variety of sands, silty clays and gravels representing various advances and retreats of the coast across the area between around 2.4 and 0.6 million years ago. The gravel fraction of the sediment includes a high percentage of flint, evidence that the Crag sea and East Anglian rivers were scouring the Chalk bedrock and/or eroding and recycling pre-existing, flint-rich gravel deposits. Some horizons of the Crag are very fossiliferous, yielding abundant mollusc shells, often broken, and occasional vertebrate bones, particularly from basement beds or in gravelly layers. At Horstead the 'entire skeleton of the Great Mastodon' was found in 1821, 'lying on its side stretched out between the chalk and the gravel'.[9] Assemblages of pollen and other microfossils provide detailed information about changing onshore and offshore palaeoenvironments.[10] They have also allowed distinct time horizons ('chronostratigraphic stages') to be designated in the Crag. Four Broadland rivers and parishes have contributed their names to British stages of the Early Pleistocene: the Antian, Bramertonian, Thurnian and Ludhamian.

The Norwich Crag is named after its type locality at Bramerton, in the Yare valley near Norwich.[11] Here, the geological sequence is still accessible in two old quarries dug into the southern slopes of the valley: Common Pit and Blake's Pit (Figure 1.5). The Crag basement bed rests on chalk and is overlain by a sequence of sands, silts and shell beds of the Norwich Crag and later strata. The site is designated as an SSSI, as a key locality of national importance for Pleistocene studies. Fossils include mollusca typical of temperate seas and the bones and teeth of mammals including seal, *Enhydra reevei* (sea otter) and *Gazella borbonica* (European gazelle), as well as the most primitive microtine rodent assemblage known from the British Isles.[12] Fossil pollen from the lower part of the exposure indicates a deciduous forest environment, with alder, oak and hornbeam suggestive of warm

---

9   H.B. Woodward, *The geology of the country around Norwich* (London, 1881), p. 57.
10 B.M. Funnell, 'The Palaeogene and Early Pleistocene of Norfolk', in G.P. Larwood and B.M. Funnell (eds), *The geology of Norfolk, Transactions of the Norfolk and Norwich Naturalists' Society*, 19/6 (1961), pp. 340–64. M.J. Head, 'Marine environmental change in the Pliocene and Early Pleistocene of Eastern England: the dinoflagellate evidence reviewed', in T. van Kolfschoten and P.L. Gibbard (eds), *The dawn of the Quaternary: proceedings of the SEQS-EuroMam Symposium, Kerkrade, 16–21 June 1996* (Utrecht, 1998), pp. 199–226. R.G. West, 'Vegetational history of the Early Pleistocene of the Royal Society borehole at Ludham, Norfolk', *Proceedings of the Royal Society of London*, B, 155 (1962), pp. 437–53.
11 C. Reid, *The Pliocene deposits of Britain* (London, 1890).
12 D.F. Mayhew and A.J. Stuart, 'Stratigraphic and taxonomic revision of the fossil vole remains (Rodentia, Microtinae) from the Lower Pleistocene deposits of eastern England', *Philosophical Transactions of the Royal Society of London*, B, 312 (1986), pp. 431–85. P.F. Riches, 'The palaeoenvironmental and neotectonic history of the Early Pleistocene Crag Basin in East Anglia', PhD thesis (University of London, 2012).

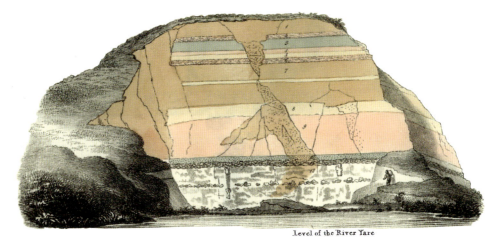

Figure 1.5 Exposure of strata at the Bramerton pit, as illustrated in R.C. Taylor, 'On the Crag-strata at Bramerton near Norwich', *Transactions of the Geological Society*, Second Series, 1 (1824), pp. 371–3.

conditions; this period has been named the Bramertonian stage. A layer further up the sequence yielded evidence for a flora dominated by pine and heathland plants, representing a transition to colder conditions.

Other Broadland localities provide further insights into the onshore and offshore life of the period. In 1959 a research borehole was drilled at Ludham water works and the core samples recovered were analysed for sediments and microfossils. On the basis of this work, six pollen assemblages and seven foraminiferal assemblages were recognised and arranged into a sequence of zones spanning part of the Red Crag, Norwich Crag and Wroxham Crag (Table 1).[13] Augmented by the results of the later Ormesby borehole, these zones provide a framework for understanding the changing environments of the Broads area during the Early Pleistocene.[14] The presence of *Pterocarya* (wingnut) in the lowermost (Red Crag) sediments is typical of the warmer conditions prevailing in much of the Pliocene. As time went on, however, such warmth-loving plants were eliminated by climatic cooling.

In the Waveney valley, the old Aldeby brickyard was active in the nineteenth century, extracting fine-grained sediment to make red bricks, and H.B. Woodward described how 'Mammalian remains have been found in the pebbly gravel overlying the clay-beds'.[15] They included *Delphinus delphis* (common dolphin), *Trichecus huxleyi* (a walrus) and *Uria aalge* (common guillemot). 'At Aldeby … Messrs. Crowfoot and Dowson have now obtained sixty-six species of mollusca

---

13 Funnell, 'Palaeogene and Early Pleistocene'. West, 'Vegetational history'.
14 Arthurton *et al.*, *Geology*, pp. 33–5, 114.
15 Woodward, *Geology*, p. 39.

Table 1.1 Environments represented in the Ludham Research Borehole (1959), with synthesis of zonal information.

Age (approx)	Formation	Stage	Environment
1.8 million	Wroxham Crag	Pastonian	Temperate, mixed coniferous/deciduous forest of pine, spruce, oak and alder; some elm and hornbeam and a little hemlock. Water-plant pollen indicates proximity of freshwater conditions.
1.9 million	Norwich Crag	Baventian/Pre-Pastonian A	A cold stage more severe than the Thurnian, with boreal, oceanic heath vegetation including pine and birch.
2 million	Norwich Crag	Antian/Bramertonian	Temperate mixed coniferous/deciduous forest similar to the Ludhamian, with frequent birch.
2.4 million	Norwich Crag	Thurnian	Cold boreal, oceanic heath vegetation including heather and crowberry and a few trees, mostly pine and birch.
2.5 million	Red Crag	Ludhamian	Temperate, mixed coniferous/deciduous forest of pine, spruce, hemlock, oak and alder; wingnut also present.

Sources: West, 'Vegetational history'; R.G. West, *The pre-glacial Pleistocene of the Norfolk and Suffolk coasts* (Cambridge, 1980).

… . Of these about nine-tenths are recent. They are in a perfect state … ', wrote Sir Charles Lyell in 1871.[16] Aldeby was one of the sites at which researchers first showed that the relative percentages of modern versus extinct mollusc genera and species could be used for rough dating purposes. More recent investigations by Norton and Beck have used fossil pollen and mollusca to provide us with a picture of the local environment in the Baventian cold stage, about 1.9 million years ago.[17] Onshore, the landscape was a predominantly open one with grasses, sedges and heather-type plants, and patchy woodland of birch, pine, spruce and alder. Marine molluscan evidence confirms the cold conditions, with species such as *Serripes groenlandicus* (Greenland cockle) and *Macoma calcarea* (a tellin) typical of cold, northern seas.

The Wroxham Crag is the most recent Crag formation in the Broads area and was deposited over a long time period between 1.85 and 0.5 million years ago. It is named after several sites in the Wroxham area, and includes what used to be known as the Bure Valley Beds and the Weybourne Crag.[18] It is more extensively

---

16 C. Lyell, *The student's elements of geology* (London, 1871).
17 P.E.P. Norton and R.B. Beck, 'Lower Pleistocene molluscan assemblages and pollen from the Crag of Aldeby (Norfolk) and Easton Bavents (Suffolk)', *Bulletin of the Geological Society of Norfolk*, 22 (1972), pp. 11–31.
18 J. Rose, 'Palaeogeography of eastern England during the Early and Middle Pleistocene', in I. Candy, J.R. Lee and A.M. Harrison (eds), *The Quaternary of northern East Anglia: field guide* (London, 2008), pp. 13–14.

exposed at the surface in Broadland than is the Norwich Crag, particularly along the valleys of the Ant and Bure and their tributaries, and contains a higher proportion of sand and gravel. Like the Norwich Crag it is rich in flint pebbles, but is distinguished from it by having a higher proportion (30–40 per cent) of exotic rock types: non-flint, silica-rich pebbles (specifically quartzes and quartzites) and other lithologies originating outside East Anglia. Evidently, the Crag seas and East Anglian rivers were now drawing on different sources of sediment than they had been in Norwich Crag times. The first appearance of the fossil mollusc *Macoma balthica* (Baltic tellin) has been cited as another indicator distinguishing the two formations.[19] Interestingly, at Aldeby the Wroxham Crag sands and gravels include a horizon of iron oxide reddening and clay enrichment that provides evidence for soil-forming processes. The sea must have retreated temporarily, long enough to allow a soil to develop – clear evidence for fluctuating sea levels in the period.[20]

The two classic Wroxham Crag sites are Dobb's Plantation Pit (Wroxham) and How Hill (Ludham). The former is located on the side of the valley of Dobb's Beck, a small tributary of the Bure. The deposits comprise shelly sands with abundant *Macoma balthica* resting on chalk bedrock. The basement bed has yielded fossils of fish (shark, ray, snapper, batfish) and mammal (elephant, rodent and deer).[21] A range of exotic pebbles is also present, including quartzites and cherts. How Hill is located on a low shoulder of the Ant valley side near Crome's Broad. A series of trial pits exposed sands, gravels and silty clays typical of tidal, near-shore conditions. The pebbles were found to be about 50 per cent flint, with the bulk of the remainder being quartz and quartzites. There were also minor – though significant – quantities of rarer rock types, including Carboniferous, Jurassic and Cretaceous cherts, Cretaceous sandstone and Palaeozoic volcanic rocks, probably from Wales, indicating far-travelled input from rivers.[22] The Dobb's Plantation site is thought to be about 1.9 million years old, and that at How Hill between 1.8 and 0.9 million years old.

The presence of quartzites, cherts and other exotic rock types in the later Crag deposits requires explanation. To understand it, we need to widen our geographic frame of reference to include much of southern Britain. During Norwich Crag times there were three now-vanished rivers contributing sediment to the Crag sea:

---

19 *Ibid.*
20 J. Rose, 'Early and Middle Pleistocene landscapes of eastern England', *Proceedings of the Geologists' Association*, 120 (2009), pp. 3–33.
21 P.G. Cambridge, 'A Section in the "Bure Valley Beds" near Wroxham (TG273158)', *Bulletin of the Geological Society of Norfolk*, 30 (1978), pp. 79–91.
22 J. Rose, N. Gulamali, B.S.P. Moorlock, R.J.O. Hamblin, D.H. Jeffery, E. Anderson, J.A. Lee and J.B. Riding, 'Pre-glacial Quaternary sediments, How Hill, near Ludham, Norfolk, England', *Bulletin of the Geological Society of Norfolk*, 45 (1996), pp. 3–28.

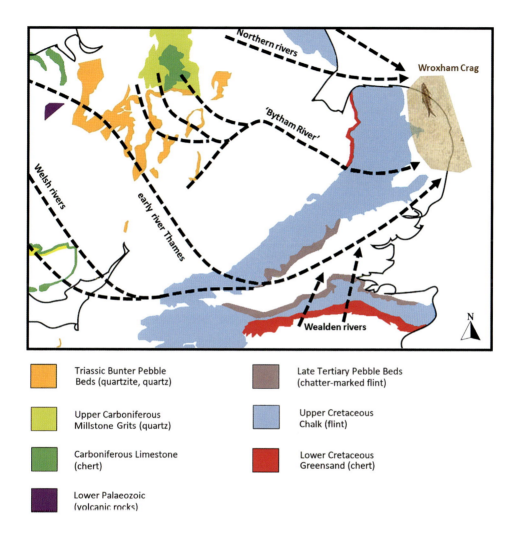

Figure 1.6 Fluvial origins of far-travelled rocks to the Wroxham Crag sea, c.1 million years BP (after P. Riches).

a northern river system (including an 'Ancaster River') flowing across Lincolnshire with its headwaters in the southern Pennines; a central river system (including a 'Bytham River') draining the north Midlands; and a southern river system (including the ancestral Thames) draining the south Midlands and parts of Wales, Wessex and the Weald (Figure 1.6). Like rivers today, they mostly transported fine-grained particles in suspension. However, by Wroxham Crag times they had become powerful enough to transport coarse, gravelly material from their headwaters as far as the Crag sea. It is likely that the cooling climate of the later Early Pleistocene led to glaciation in the uplands of Britain, causing the westwards expansion of river catchments and the movement of greater quantities of coarse sediment as bedload. Inland tectonic uplift would also have contributed to more dynamic river regimes.[23] The Broads area thus became the recipient of a range of lithologies gathered from as far afield as the Pennines, Wales, Wessex and the Weald by powerful meltwater rivers (Figure 1.6).

The 'Bytham' is the only one of these cold-phase rivers to have left direct evidence of its presence in Broadland. Boreholes along the Waveney valley have revealed a deposit of sands and gravels rich in quartzose lithologies that rests on Wroxham Crag and crosses the area at depth in a south-west–north-east direction.[24] This is known as the Ingham Formation, and ties in with a suite of similar river sediments to the east, exposed in a number of places between Bungay and Bury St Edmunds. Their composition and topographical situation allows us to identify them as sediments of the 'Bytham', deposited during times when the Wroxham Crag sea had retreated, probably in cold periods when absolute sea levels were lower.

Warm-phase river sediments have also been preserved in the Broads area dating from later in the Early Pleistocene. These can be attributed to the Cromer Forest Bed formation, and comprise fine-grained onshore (river and estuarine) sediments deposited at the same time as the Wroxham Crag was being formed offshore.[25] At Norton Subcourse quarry, organic-rich river deposits were found sandwiched between the Wroxham Crag and the Ingham Formation.[26] They contain fossils characteristic of warm, temperate conditions perhaps 0.68 million years ago. Plant fossils indicate a floodplain environment with backwater pools containing diverse pond weeds and yellow water-lily, with fringing pine, oak and elm forest. Bones of hippopotamus (probably *H. antiquus*) and *Equus altidens* (gracile horse) were found, along with an abundant assemblage of small mammals including *Mimomys savini* (ancestral water vole) and *Sorex minutissimus* (least shrew). Hyaena coprolites indicate the presence of scavenging carnivores. Other places with organic-rich river deposits of the period in the vicinity of the Broads include Pakefield, where early human artefacts, around 0.7 million years old, have been found, and Happisburgh (Site 3), where artefacts and human

---

23 J. Rose, I. Candy, B.S.P. Moorlock, H. Wilkins, R.J.O. Hamblin, J.R. Lee, J.B. Riding and A.N. Morigi, 'Early and Middle Pleistocene river, coastal and neotectonic processes, southeast Norfolk, England', *Proceedings of the Geologists' Association*, 113/1 (2002), pp. 47–67, at pp. 63–4; Rose, 'Palaeogeography', p. 19.

24 B.S.P. Moorlock, R.J.O. Hamblin, S.J. Booth and A.N. Morigi, *Geology of the country around Lowestoft and Saxmundham. Memoir for 1:50,000 Geological Sheets 176 and 191* (London, 2000). Rose et al., 'Pre-glacial Quaternary sediments'.

25 Simon Parfitt, pers. comm. Rose, 'Early and Middle Pleistocene landscapes'.

26 S.G. Lewis, S.A. Parfitt, R.C. Preece, J. Sinclair, G.R. Coope, M.H. Field, B.A. Maher, R.G. Scaife and J.E. Whittaker, 'Age and palaeoenvironmental setting of the Pleistocene vertebrate fauna at Norton Subcourse, Norfolk', in D.C. Schreve (ed.), *The Quaternary mammals of southern and eastern England: field guide* (London, 2004).

footprints may date back over 0.78 million years.[27] It is clear that the valleys and estuarine margins of the 'Bytham River' and its tributaries were favourable areas for human settlement during the warmer phases of what is known as the 'Cromerian Complex', a sequence of four warm/cold climatic oscillations in the late Early Pleistocene.[28]

Work by Elvin Thurston has revealed further elements of the Broads landscape at this time.[29] Using borehole data he plotted the upper surface of the Wroxham Crag in east Norfolk and showed that it can be mapped as a stepped sequence of three level benches: the oldest at 16 metres above current sea level, another at 12 metres and the lowest at 4 metres, all buried and invisible beneath today's land surface. The risers of this 'staircase' are a series of bluffs facing roughly north-east – that is, towards the North Sea – which are dissected by sinuous, north-eastward-trending depressions in several places. The benches probably formed in response to pulses of uplift of the coastal seabed between 0.87 and 0.63 million years ago. Episodes of cold climate led to increased erosion on land and increased transport of sediment by rivers, and, as more sediment entered the North Sea, this caused gentle crustal downwarping and episodic compensatory uplift of the adjacent land area. So each cold phase led to a pulse of uplift, a phased north-eastwards retreat of the coastline across a bench and the creation of a relict coastal bluff or cliff overlooking it. The sinuous depressions must be former river valleys; one of them corresponds neatly with the location of the warm-phase river deposits identified at Norton Subcourse.[30] Thurston's study is an excellent example of deep-level landscape archaeology.

Glacial conditions first directly affected the Broads area in the Middle Pleistocene, perhaps 600,000 years ago. An ice sheet advanced from the north, depositing a stiff, grey-brown, sandy clay known as the Corton Till of the Happisburgh Formation (a till is a mixed deposit of clay and stones deposited by

---

27　S.A. Parfitt, R.W. Barendregt, M. Breda, I. Candy, M.J. Collins, G.R. Coope, P. Durbidge, M.H. Field, J.R. Lee, A.M. Lister, R. Mutch, K.E.H. Penkman, R.C. Preece, J. Rose, C.B. Stringer, R. Symmons, J.E. Whittaker, J.J. Wymer and A.J. Stuart, 'The earliest record of human activity in Northern Europe', *Nature*, 438 (December 2005), pp. 1008–12. S.A. Parfitt, N.M. Ashton, S.G. Lewis, R.L. Abel, G.R. Coope, M.H. Field, R. Gale, P.G. Hoare, N.R. Larkin, M.D. Lewis, V. Karloukovski, B.A. Maher, S.M. Peglar, R.C. Preece, J.E. Whittaker and C.B Stringer, 'Early Pleistocene human occupation at the edge of the boreal zone in northwest Europe', *Nature*, 466 (July 2010), pp. 229–33. N. Ashton, S.G. Lewis, I. De Groote, S.M. Duffy, M. Bates, R. Bates, P.G. Hoare, M. Lewis, S.A. Parfitt, S. Peglar, C. Williams and C.B. Stringer, 'Hominin footprints from Early Pleistocene deposits at Happisburgh, UK', *PLoS ONE*, 9/2, e88329 (7 February 2014).

28　R.C. Preece and S.A. Parfitt, 'The Cromer Forest-Bed: new thoughts on an old problem', in S.G. Lewis, C.A. Whiteman and R.C. Preece (eds), *The Quaternary of Norfolk and Suffolk: field guide* (London, 2000), pp. 1–27.

29　E. Thurston, 'Neotectonics and the preglacial landscape of eastern Norfolk, UK', *Proceedings of the Geologists' Association*, 128 (2017), pp. 742–56.

30　*Ibid.*, Fig. 10.

Figure 1.7 Outwash sands of the Corton Sand Member, Happisburgh Formation, at the Welcome Pit, Burgh Castle. There are many intersecting beds, evidence for cross-cutting relationships between successive multiple stream channels on the glacial outwash plain. The scale represents one metre.

glacial ice).[31] This till and its associated meltwater sands and gravels are found at the surface on many areas of higher ground north of a line running roughly from Norwich to Lowestoft, resting on the Norwich Crag, Wroxham Crag and Ingham formations. Collectively, they are informally known as the North Sea Drift, and include erratics (far-travelled rocks) from as far away as Scandinavia; some of these can be seen built into rubble walls of medieval churches, as at Hassingham, and some vernacular buildings. The ice sheet advanced as far south as the Waveney valley; indeed, its meltwaters are thought to have partly flowed along the old 'Bytham River' channel. They drained eastwards out into the North Sea basin, depositing as they did so a stack of fine-grained outwash deposits known as the Corton Sands (Figure 1.7), which contribute much to the sandy soils of the Lothingland and Flegg uplands.[32]

---

31 J.R. Lee, M.A. Woods and B.S.P. Moorlock (eds), *British regional geology: East Anglia*, 5th edn (Keyworth, 2015).
32 C.A.H. Hodge, R.G.O. Burton, W.M.C. Corbett, R. Evans and R.S. Seale, *Soils and their use in Eastern England* (Harpenden, 1984).

About 450,000 years ago a second glacial episode impacted the Broads area, during the Anglian stage of the Middle Pleistocene. Its deposits are found all across the uplands south of the Yare valley, with a significant outlier to the west of Acle. They comprise a blue-grey, clay-rich, chalky till (the Lowestoft Till) and associated meltwater sands and gravels belonging to the Lowestoft Formation.[33] The high percentage of Cretaceous chalk and Jurassic mudstone within the till indicates that the ice sheet came from the British mainland, to the north-west. It has left a legacy of clay-rich, brown-earth soils in upland areas south of the Yare valley.[34]

The influence of the Happisburgh and Lowestoft ice sheets on the Broads area was profound. They laid the framework for today's landscape: the configuration of uplands and lowlands and the pattern of river valleys. When the Lowestoft ice sheet retreated about 425,000 years ago it left an uneven, unvegetated landscape in which lakes and rivers could develop. The valleys of the Broads were initiated at this time. The Bure began as a corridor draining meltwaters from the uplands of the Cromer Ridge, the Yare was a conduit for water draining from much of central Norfolk, while the Waveney conveyed meltwaters from the Norfolk/Suffolk borderlands as far west as Harleston.[35]

The warm period that followed the end of the Anglian stage is known as the Hoxnian interglacial (between 424,000 and 374,000 years ago). It saw the arrival of early humans – probably *Homo heidelbergensis* – in East Anglia, evidence for which has been found in the form of distinctive Acheulean-style handaxes. The most important site is at Whitlingham Sewage Farm (Kirby Bedon), where Yare valley gravels resting on Norwich Crag were excavated in 1926. Large numbers of handaxes and flakes were found in fresh condition in a near-primary context, including distinctive ficron-shaped specimens, suggesting that this was a manufacturing site where flint nodules in the gravel were being exploited.[36] Other handaxe findspots are scattered around the area, including at Aldeby, Geldeston, Langley, Surlingham and Wroxham, often associated with river gravels. As most represent single finds it is likely that they were manufactured elsewhere and entrained by rivers during one of the post-Anglian cold periods. The Whitlingham site is tentatively dated

---

33 Lee et al., *British regional geology*.
34 Hodge et al., *Soils and their use*, p. 132.
35 A. Straw, 'The glacial geomorphology of central and north Norfolk', *East Midlands Geographer*, 5 (1973), pp. 333–54. A. Straw and K.M. Clayton, *The geomorphology of the British Isles. Eastern and central England* (London, 1979). P. Coxon, 'The geomorphological history of the Waveney valley', in P. Allen (ed.), *Field guide to the Gipping and Waveney valleys, Suffolk. May 1982* (Cambridge, 1984), pp. 105–6. R.G. West, *From Brandon to Bungay. An exploration of the landscape history and geology of the Little Ouse and Waveney rivers* (Ipswich, 2009).
36 J.J. Wymer, *Palaeolithic sites of East Anglia* (Norwich, 1985).

to the end of the Hoxnian, around 300,000 years ago.[37] Later, the Broads area was sporadically occupied by *Homo neanderthalensis*. Their distinctive, flat-butted (*bout coupé*) handaxes have been found at North Cove in the Waveney valley and at Mousehold Heath, just to the west of our area.[38] With their mobile, hunter-gatherer mode of life, these hominins made little impact on the Broads landscape.

A succession of warm and cold climatic oscillations characterised the second half of the Pleistocene. The colder periods are termed glacials and the warmer ones interglacials. In cold periods, slopes became modified by solifluction (soil-flow processes), as frozen surface layers thawed in summer and slowly crept downslope. The outcome can be seen in the gently sloping profiles of valley sides and in spreads of material called 'head' found at the foot of slopes, as at Haddiscoe. Fine, aeolian (wind-blown) material called 'loess' was deposited across the northern and central parts of Broadland by dust-storms whipped up on poorly vegetated land surfaces. A substantial proportion of the fine material in the topsoil at Stalham, for example, is of aeolian origin.[39] Rivers with multiple braided channels seasonally transported meltwaters and a chaotic bedload of sand and gravel; the results are present as gravelly spreads, ridges and hummocks underlying present floodplains, as at Beccles and the Barsham Marshes.[40] These rivers flowed out into the North Sea basin at a much lower level than today. Evidence of this has been found beneath Breydon Water and Great Yarmouth, where boreholes have revealed that the Broads rivers once had their collective outflow through a steep-sided valley cut into Crag bedrock at a depth of 25 metres below current sea level. This valley is now filled with sands and gravels of the Yare Valley Formation.[41] During the height of the last cold period, the Devensian (about 22,000 years ago), absolute sea levels were 120 metres lower than today, and the North Sea area was a barren, undulating plain, now named Doggerland, crossed by rivers and seasonally populated by meltwater lakes. Broadland lay on the western margin of this plain.[42] Offshore, we can recognise the deposits of a 'Greater Broadland' in the brackish-water lagoonal clays of the Brown Bank Formation.[43]

---

37 P. Pettitt and M.J. White, *The British Palaeolithic: human societies at the edge of the Pleistocene world* (Abingdon, 2012).
38 Wymer, *Palaeolithic sites*, p. 61.
39 Hodge *et al.*, *Soils and their use*, p. 204.
40 K. Krawiec, B.R. Gearey, H.P. Chapman, E.-J. Hopla, M. Bamforth, C. Griffiths, T.C.B. Hill and I. Tyers, 'A late prehistoric timber alignment in the Waveney valley, Suffolk. Excavations at Barsham Marshes', *Journal of Wetland Archaeology*, 10 (2011), pp. 46–70. B. Gearey, A. Howard and H. Chapman, *Down by the river: archaeological, palaeoenvironmental and geoarchaeological investigations of the Suffolk river valleys* (Oxford, 2016).
41 Arthurton *et al.*, *Geology*, pp. 69–70. Moorlock *et al.*, *Geology*, pp. 71–2.
42 V. Gaffney, S. Fitch and D. Smith, *Europe's lost world: the rediscovery of Doggerland* (York, 2009).
43 T.D.J. Cameron, A. Crosby, P.S. Balson, D.H. Jeffery, G.K. Lott, J. Bulat and D.J. Harrison, *The geology of the southern North Sea* (London, 1992), p. 113. L. Tizzard, A. Bicket and D. De Loecker, *Seabed prehistory. Investigating the palaeogeography and early Middle Palaeolithic archaeology in the southern North Sea* (Salisbury, 2015), p. 58.

Figure 1.8 The dry valley landscape developed on the sandy soils of the Herringfleet Hills, looking south-west towards the Wheatacre Marshes.

By contrast, during warm periods absolute sea levels were higher and wet conditions extended for some distance up the Broads valleys. Fine-grained peat and alluvial deposits formed on valley floors, while forest, scrub and grassland developed in upland areas. The last interglacial before the present one, known as the Ipswichian, is dated between 128,000 and 115,000 years ago. There are Ipswichian sites in the middle reaches of the Yare, Wensum and Waveney valleys, but none are currently known from the Broadland area itself. This is probably because later over-deepening of valleys in Devensian times eroded any floodplain deposits from the period.

The warm–cold oscillations in the later Pleistocene led to the formation of dry valleys: shallow, waterless vales on sandy soils along the upland margins. The Herringfleet Hills have many fine examples, with the break of slope fretted by small but steeply incised valley landforms (Figure 1.8). There are many hypotheses for how such features were formed.[44] In a Broadland context, however, we can plausibly envisage a situation in which springs were active in periods of high water table, carving out small tributary valleys that later

---

44 A.S. Goudie, *The landforms of England and Wales* (Oxford, 1990), p. 178.

became inactive when large-scale cold-phase incision in the main valleys lowered the water table, leaving the tributaries hanging high and dry. These landforms will have been refreshed in periglacial conditions, when springtime snowmelt poured off the uplands. River terraces are another category of landform resulting from climatic oscillations. These are spreads of sand, gravel and alluvium that occur discontinuously as benches flanking valley sides, and are the remnants of former floodplains isolated by later downcutting by rivers, a process driven by falls in base level and/or uplift of the landmass. River terraces are well represented in the middle reaches of the Waveney valley, where a stacked sequence of three has been recognised above Geldeston; they do not have surface expression to the east, as they are buried beneath layers of peat and alluvium.[45]

The story of the past 10,000 years in the Broads is more easily explained than that of earlier periods, in large measure because of the abundance of surviving evidence. This is the period known as the Holocene. Thick layers of sediment underlie the valley floors and represent a readily available geological archive of local environmental change. Using geomorphology and geoarchaeology, we can readily study the interaction of land and sea along the North Sea boundary and the impact of human activity on the landscape. The climate warmed up by fits and starts at the end of the Devensian, beginning a process of overall sea-level rise which, with minor pauses and reverses, has continued to the present. Gradually Doggerland became inundated. There was a period between 12,000 and 9,000 years ago when sea levels stabilised at about 45 metres below present level.[46] At this time, the Broads rivers were tributaries of a single 'palaeo-Yare' that flowed through the Great Yarmouth area; its meandering course can be detected offshore by bathymetric survey and sediment cores, and onshore in the deposits of the aforementioned Yare Valley Formation. Sea level had risen to approximately its present height by about 6,300 years ago (i.e. early Neolithic times).[47] As levels rose, first freshwater swamp and later brackish water conditions progressively extended up the Broads valleys, and deposits of peat were succeeded by estuarine alluvium. A generalised Holocene sequence of five freshwater and brackish-water sedimentary units has been identified, comprising Lower Peat, Lower Clay, Middle Peat, Upper Clay and Upper Peat. This ensemble is termed the Breydon Formation.[48] The peats

---

45   Moorlock *et al.*, *Geology*, pp. 68–9.
46   S.E. Limpenny, C. Barrio Froján, C.J. Cotterill, R.L. Foster-Smith, B. Pearce, L. Tizzard, D.L. Limpenny, D. Long, S. Walmsley, S. Kirby, K. Baker, W.J. Meadows, J. Rees, J. Hill, C. Wilson, M. Leivers, S. Churchley, J. Russell, A.C. Birchenough, S.L. Green and R.J. Law, *The east coast regional environmental characterisation* (Lowestoft, 2011).
47   Limpenny *et al.*, *East coast*, pp. 129, 131.
48   Arthurton *et al.*, *Geology*, p. 72.

were deposited in swamp woodland and fen; the clays were deposited in saltmarsh and estuarine flat. The sequence rests on a local basement of either Chalk, London Clay, Crag, glacial deposits or valley gravels. Which elements of the sequence are represented in which part of a valley depends on local factors operating at the time of deposition, especially the site's position within the catchment and distance from the sea.

On the seaward side of the Broads, at Great Yarmouth, the geological succession shows Lower Peat followed by Lower Clay. A further peat layer – the Middle Peat – was deposited from about 4,700 years ago, when freshwater swamp conditions returned. This change is likely to have been brought about by the growth of a spit over the mouth of the estuary, so impeding the tidal influx of seawater. Marine conditions had resumed by about 2,200 years ago (i.e. the Late Iron Age), forming what has come to be known as the Great Estuary, lying at the confluence of the Broads rivers, now the great level expanse of drained marshland lying to the west of Great Yarmouth. This event may have been brought about when the sea breached sandbars across the estuary mouth.[49] The Upper Clay was then deposited, including layers of sand and cockle shells. Only a remnant of the estuary survives today as the tidal lagoon of Breydon Water, but its approximate former extent can be judged by the areas of level marshland that extend up Broads valleys. Marine conditions extended for some distance up the river valleys during this 'Romano-British marine transgression', although attenuated with increasing distance from the sea: saltmarshes fed by tidal channels were present, rather than mud flats and estuarine lagoons. The 'Upper Clay' accordingly becomes thinner higher up the valleys, although it reaches as far up the Waveney valley as Beccles.[50] Evidently the Great Estuary was deep enough for warships of the Roman North Sea fleet to make their base at Burgh Castle: 'In the marshes ... have frequently been discovered parts of anchors, rings and other pieces of iron ... which were evidently appurtenances of ships.'[51] The estuary began to silt up in late Roman times, probably as a result of the regrowth of a spit across its mouth, and much of its area began slowly to turn into saltmarsh, the traces of which can still be discerned today in the wriggling pattern of former creeks underlying the grazing marshes (see pp. 109–112). The soils are stoneless, clay-rich, marine alluvium.[52] They have sometimes in the past been exploited for making bricks, as at Caister brickpits.[53]

---

49   Moss, *The Broads*, p. 49.
50   Moorlock *et al.*, *Geology*, p. 80.
51   J.H. Blake, *The geology of the country near Yarmouth and Lowestoft. Explanation of Sheet 67* (London, 1890), p. 76.
52   Hodge *et al.*, *Soils and their use*, p. 263.
53   NHER 8688.

Geological core samples have been taken from the sediments beneath Burgh Common, Fleggburgh, in the Muckfleet valley. They give us a picture of the environmental succession in a backwater valley of the Broads.[54] The local basement is glacial till, probably of the Happisburgh Formation, lying at a depth of 7.4 metres below the present floodplain. It is overlain by a thick (4.25 metre) layer of brushwood peat. This must represent a floodplain forest environment of Early and Middle Holocene date, one not influenced by the Early Holocene marine incursion that deposited the Lower Clay at Great Yarmouth. The arrival of the Great Estuary in the later Holocene is indicated by a sequence of alluvial clays 2.5 metres thick, including a horizon rich in cockle shells. Finally, the deposition of fibrous Upper Peat indicates the development of reedswamp in the Muckfleet valley – the same environment that is present at the site today.

Greater thicknesses of Upper Peat are preserved in the upper reaches of other valleys. For instance, core samples taken close to the river Bure at Larkbush, south of Hoveton Great Broad, revealed a continuous peat sequence over 6.5 metres deep, with no evidence of Upper Clay intervening between peat units.[55] Cored transects across Great Broad itself have revealed the presence of steep-sided basins cut into the Upper Peat – classic evidence for the medieval peat extraction industry that led directly to the formation of this broad after the diggings became flooded (see p. 199).[56] Today, the Upper Peat often hosts reedswamp and carr woodland, and soils developed on it are typically dark and rich in organic matter, with recognisable plant remains at depth.[57]

The eastern side of the Broads area is defined by a series of uplands, including the Isle of Flegg and Lothingland, which are dissected by small westward-draining valleys such as those occupied by Fritton Decoy and Oulton Broad. About 2,000 years ago the coastline lay perhaps one kilometre to the east of its present position.[58] Coastal retreat has since truncated this upland area: it has beheaded the valley now occupied by Oulton Broad, so giving it the misleading appearance of being a former outlet of the river Waveney.[59] It has also eroded the headwaters of the river Thurne and Hundred Stream, leaving them vulnerable to sea surges along the coastal strip between Eccles-on-Sea and Winterton-on-Sea. A frail line of shingle banks and sand dunes is all that stops the sea from regularly breaking through in this area, which lies more or less at sea level. Sediment cores show that this was

---

54 I would like to thank Dr Jo Parmenter for access to this unpublished information.
55 Lambert et al., *Making of the Broads*, p. 24 and Fig. 20.
56 Wessex Archaeology, 'Bringing the Bure back to LIFE: Hoveton Wetland Restoration Project', Report No. 112861.01 (September 2016), pp. 11–12.
57 Hodge et al., *Soils and their use*, p. 90.
58 Arthurton et al., *Geology*, pp. 86, 87.
59 Blake, *Geology*, p. 73.

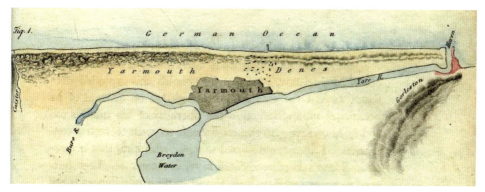

Figure 1.9 Breydon Water and the coastal spit at Great Yarmouth, as illustrated in R.C. Taylor, *On the geology of east Norfolk; with remarks upon the hypothesis of Mr. J.W. Robberds, respecting the former level of the German Ocean* (London, 1827). North is to the left.

an open marine inlet in Great Estuary times: at Winterton Holmes a sequence of sand washed over by storm surges (one metre thick) rests on estuarine Upper Clay (three metres thick) overlying brushwood peat.[60] The coastal strip is maintained by sediment supplied by longshore drift, which transports material southwards from the eroding soft-rock cliffs of north-east Norfolk. This drift has created the cuspate foreland of Winterton Ness and the spit upon which Great Yarmouth is located (Figure 1.9). The formation of the latter, as we have seen, led to the silting up of the Great Estuary and the growth of the Upper Peat in the valleys of the rivers feeding into it.

The hydrology of Broadland owes much to the influence of the Chalk, which outcrops towards the west in the Yare and Bure valleys and is important more widely as an aquifer supplying lime-rich water to seeps, springs and flushes as well as baseflow up through valley floors. The Lowestoft Till also contributes lime-rich water, as it has a high chalk content (between 56 and 84 per cent). To the east, the Chalk aquifer is confined by London Clay, which impedes the upwelling of water, and by Crag strata, although the latter also provides an aquifer that was widely exploited in the past and is still used by local farmers. The mosaic of sandy and clayey strata in the Crag and glacial deposits creates complex patterns of localised water discharge into valleys.[61] Groundwater in some areas of marshland near the coast has high chloride concentrations where drainage has lowered the water table and allowed sea water to seep into the land, as in the Thurne catchment.[62] Occasional sea floods also contribute to the salination of groundwater in this area.

---

60 British Geological Survey Borehole TG42 SE2: http://scans.bgs.ac.uk/sobi_scans/boreholes/519477/images/12117425.html (accessed October 2022).
61 Arthurton *et al.*, *Geology*, pp. 61, 70, 80, 96, 99.
62 I.P. Holman and S.M. White, *Synthesis of the Upper Thurne research and recommendations for management: report to the Broads Authority* (Cranfield, 2008), p. 6.

As we have seen, the physical landscape of the Broads has been actively shaped by naturally driven processes during the Holocene. It has also been shaped by human activity, notably the creation of the marshes and broads by drainage and peat extraction; the installation of coastal protection works; aquifer depletion by over-abstraction of groundwater; and the pollution of waters by nitrates and phosphates. We might argue that these changes are instances of an 'Anthropocene', transitioning out of the Holocene: a new geological epoch characterised by marked feedbacks between humanity and geology and the 'hybridisation' of nature by human intervention.[63] Some anthropogenic modifications, such as the construction of embankments, are likely to be readily reversible by natural processes, while others, such as the mercury pollution of river Yare sediment, will be present over geological timescales.[64] We have seen how Broadland has been formatively shaped by the comings and goings of rivers, ice sheets and the North Sea, and by global geophysical processes. Anthropogenic climate change will become the most immediate future driver of landscape change in the area. With absolute sea levels predicted to rise by as much as one metre within the next century, estuarine conditions will reappear in the most low-lying areas of the Broads, and the Great Estuary will return.[65]

The three landscapes of Broadland: the 'uplands', the marshes and the valleys

The geology of Broadland has had a determining influence on the way successive human societies have inhabited the land. It imposed constraints on where people might settle, encouraged certain forms of land use above others and provided particular kinds of fuel and building materials, as well as the raw materials for industries such as lime-burning and brick-making. Above all, the area's geology – the dominance of soft, easily eroded rocks such as chalk, and of poorly consolidated clays, sands and gravels – engendered subdued relief, with extensive tracts of ground now lying at or below sea level and a network of interconnected navigable tidal watercourses, which were used initially for commercial trade (Chapter 6) and subsequently to develop a tourist industry (Chapter 7) (Figure 1.10).

The exploitation of the lowest land, and thus its ecological development, has been critically shaped over the centuries by changes in the relative levels

---

63 P. Höfele, O. Müller and L. Hühn, 'Introduction: the role of nature in the Anthropocene – defining and reacting to a new geological epoch', *The Anthropocene Review*, 9/2 (2022), pp. 129–38, at p. 130.
64 George, *Land use*, pp. 158, 159.
65 Intergovernmental Panel on Climate Change, 'Summary for policymakers', in H.O. Pörtner *et al.* (eds), *IPCC special report on the ocean and cryosphere in a changing climate. Intergovernmental Panel on Climate Change, 2019.* https://www.ipcc.ch/srocc/chapter/summary-for-policymakers/ (accessed October 2022).

INTRODUCING BROADLAND 25

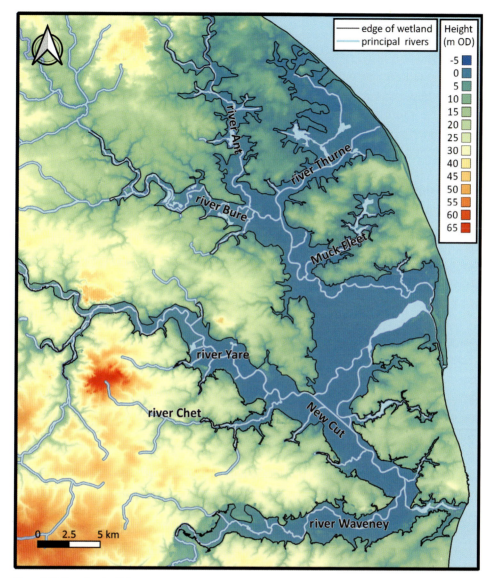

Figure 1.10 Broadland: relief.

of water and land that remain imperfectly understood. The scale and timing of fluctuations were, and are, in part the consequence of the complex interplay of *eustatic* factors – global changes in sea levels – and *isostatic* ones – the sinking of the land surface in south-east England resulting from post-glacial uplift in the north and west. But they were also the result of very local influences, and in particular of whether the Broadland rivers discharged into an open estuary or through an outfall constricted by a spit of sand and gravel. As already described, by Mesolithic times rising sea levels led to more sluggish rivers and the accumulation of peat in the valleys – the 'Lower Peat' – which formed as plants died and only partially decayed *in situ*. But as sea levels continued to rise estuarine conditions penetrated further inland, covering the peat with alluvial clay. From around 3000 BC the build-up of a substantial spit of sand and gravel across the mouth of the estuary led to reduced tidal flows and the renewed accumulation of peat (the 'Middle Peat'), a phase followed in turn, from around 100 BC, by the disintegration of the spit, the re-establishments of the estuary and the deposition of the 'Upper Clay' some way up the valleys (the 'Romano-British transgression'). By Anglo-Saxon times, however, the shingle spit was forming again and this reduced tidal flows, accelerated silting and significantly lowered water levels within the former estuary. By the time of the Norman Conquest they may have been as much as 1.5 metres lower than today, although saltwater continued to flow along the creeks running through what must have been relatively dry, raised saltmarsh occupying the great expanse of level land lying to the west of Great Yarmouth.[66]

From the twelfth century, as global sea levels continued to rise, local water levels began to rise again, the effects compounded in the late thirteenth and fourteenth centuries by an increased incidence of storms and sea surges associated with a general climatic deterioration.[67] There were particularly serious floods in Broadland in 1287, the effects of which were described by the chronicler John of Oxnead.[68] It was probably in this period, as we shall see, that areas of saltmarsh within the former estuary first began to be embanked, protecting them from flooding and allowing their conversion to 'fresh' marsh. Scattered documentary references also suggest the construction of banks and dykes higher up the river valleys.[69] Natural processes ensured that sea levels continued to rise, albeit at a slower rate from the seventeenth century, but local hydrology was by now increasingly influenced by human activities, by

---

66 Moss, *The Broads*, pp. 45–9. B. Cornford, 'Past water levels in Broadland', *Norfolk Research Committee Bulletin*, 28 (1982), pp. 14–18. J.M. Lambert and J.N. Jennings, 'Alluvial stratigraphy and vegetational succession in the region of the Bure valley broads: detailed vegetational and stratigraphical relationships', *Journal of Ecology*, 39 (1951), pp. 120–48. B.P. Coles and B.M. Funnell, 'Holocene palaeoenvironments of Broadland, England', in S.-D. Nio, R.T.E. Shüttenhelm and Tj.C.E. Van Weering (eds), *Holocene Marine Sedimentation in the North Sea Basin*, Special Publications of the International Association of Sedimentologists, 5 (1981), pp. 123–31. B.M. Funnell, 'History and prognosis of subsidence and sea-level change in the lower Yare valley, Norfolk', *Bulletin of the Geological Society of Norfolk*, 31 (1979), pp. 35–44. M. Godwin, 'Microbionization and microbiofacies of the Holocene deposits of east Norfolk and Suffolk', PhD thesis (University of East Anglia, 1993).

67 M. Bailey, '"Per Imperetum Maris": natural disaster and economic decline in eastern England, 1275–1350', in B. Campbell (ed.), *Before the Black Death: the crisis of the early fourteenth century* (Manchester, 1991), pp. 184–209.

68 H. Ellis (ed.), *Chronica Johannis de Oxenedes* (London, 1859).

69 Cornford, 'Past water levels'.

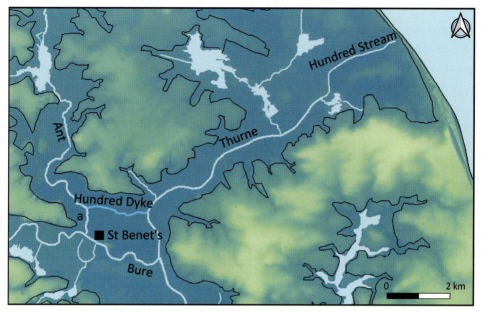

Figure 1.11 The watercourses in northern Broadland, as discussed in the text. In the early Middle Ages the Thurne flowed north to the sea along what is now the Hundred Stream. It formed, in effect, the lower reaches of the Ant, which then flowed east along the Hundred Dyke. The present lower course of the river ('a'), connecting it to the Bure, was probably created by St Benet's Abbey to reduce flooding, as the old outfall along what is now the Hundred Stream was blocked by the accumulation of sand and shingle.

embanking, mechanical drainage and the dredging of, and alterations made to the courses of, the rivers.

So extensive are the areas of low and level ground in Broadland that the courses of several rivers appear to have been radically altered, by human agency or natural processes, in relatively recent times. The Thurne, perhaps uniquely for a British river, has its source a few hundred metres from the sea, from which it flows away to the south-west, joining the Bure at Thurne Mouth. There is no doubt, however, that the low-lying marshes where its headwaters now lie originally formed an open estuary, a diminutive companion to the 'Great Estuary' to the south, and sharing the same fate: it was closed by the formation of a spit of sand and gravel across its mouth. That is why the valley of the Thurne contains much less peat, and much more alluvial clay, than those of Broadland's other rivers. Even after the estuary was closed and had silted up, some kind of outfall to the sea continued to exist here well into the Middle Ages. The line of the Thurne is continued directly to the sea by a watercourse called the Hundred Stream (Figure 1.11), so named because it formed the boundary between the hundreds (ancient administrative units) of Happing and West Flegg. Now a minor drainage dyke, it is bounded by widely spaced banks, denoting a former watercourse of some importance.

This outfall seems originally to have taken the waters of the river Ant to the sea, for, rather than turning south near Ludham Bridge to flow into the Bure at Ant Mouth, that river originally continued in an easterly direction, joining the present course of the Thurne around 1.5 kilometres north of its confluence with the Bure. Again, the old course is marked by what was evidently once a major watercourse, followed by an ancient territorial boundary – the hundredal boundary between Happing and Tunstead – and which is still known as the Hundred Dyke. The modern course of the Ant below its junction with this feature, in contrast, is not even followed by a parish boundary. The change was almost certainly made by St Benet's Abbey, in the twelfth or thirteenth century, in order to alleviate problems of flooding caused to its properties in the area, and perhaps to parts of the monastic precinct itself, by the progressive blockage of the old outfall along the Hundred Stream by the ongoing accumulation of sand and shingle. What is now the lower course of the Thurne, the 1.5 kilometres above its confluence with the Bure, was presumably created around the same time, to provide an exit for water draining off the adjacent areas of higher ground, although, as we shall see, there is another, more intriguing, possibility (see p. 131).

Extensive coastal wetlands like these, even when embanked and drained, remained vulnerable to flooding. Some major flooding events have been caused, throughout history, by increased and sudden flows of water from the surrounding uplands following periods of heavy rain or a rapid thaw of snow. Others, as in 1912 and 1953, were the consequence of 'surges', when strong winds in the North Sea funnelled water southwards, causing abnormally high tides to flow up the Yare and raising water levels in its tributary rivers. Most, however, were the result of the sea breaking through the line of dunes between Waxham and Winterton, which had sealed the mouth of the old estuary just described, something that occurred most recently in 1938. The events of 1608, 1617, 1622, 1718 and 1720 led to the establishment of relatively short-term 'Sea Breach Commissions', empowered to levy a rate on holders of land in the marshes, in order to repair the dunes. That set up in 1802, in contrast, remained in place until 1932.[70] A severe storm in 1791 had torn nine 'breaches' in the dunes, leading to widespread floods, one wherryman describing how he had been 'prevented from navigating the North River [the Bure] for a fortnight' because the banks were invisible, 'the tops of the reeds being his only guide'.[71] The breaches were only finally repaired, and the marshes protected from further flooding, in 1806, as the result of a scheme of

---

[70] D. Matless, 'Checking the sea: geographies of authority on the east Norfolk coast, 1790–1932', *Rural History*, 30 (2019), pp. 215–40. B. Cornford, 'The Sea Breach Commission in east Norfolk 1609–1743', *Norfolk Archaeology*, 37 (1979), pp. 137–45. George, *Land use*, pp. 314–16. NRO MSC 6/6. NRO NRS 4193 (255).

[71] NRO EAW 2/118.

Figure 1.12 The Bure valley. Wroxham, Hoveton Great Broad and Salhouse Broads in the foreground; Decoy Broad and Hoveton Little Broad in the middle distance; the village of Horning beyond.

works directed by William Smith, a leading civil engineer now more famous for his work as a geologist.[72]

Geology and topography provide the framework we employ through the next three chapters for analysing the history of the landscape and environment. The most obvious and important division in Broadland's landscape is between the higher, drier ground and the low-lying wetlands, of marsh and fen. But topographically, to an extent geologically, and certainly in historical terms, the wetlands can themselves be subdivided. Firstly, we have the landscape of the drained marshes lying to the west of Great Yarmouth, the former 'Great Estuary' of Roman times: a vast level expanse, gradually reclaimed and drained from the natural saltmarsh that formed as the estuary silted up. Often loosely described as the 'Halvergate Marshes', it comprises more than 70 square kilometres of estuarine clay and alluvium, with only small and scattered pockets of peat around its margins. When drained and embanked from the tides and the waters of the Bure, Yare and Waveney that meander across it, the soils of the marshes afforded good pasture land and were even, on occasions, used as arable. Even before reclamation, however, the area provided an important source of grazing and,

---

[72] NRO MSC 6/6.

more importantly, its tidal creeks afforded opportunities for the production of salt. This was always relatively valuable land that, from Late Saxon times, hosted a thin scatter of small settlements.

The wetland landscapes of the river valleys feeding into the former estuary are rather different, although the change is a gradual one. Progressing up the valleys, the areas of peripheral peat steadily increase and completely occupy the floodplains of the Yare between Buckenham and Whitlingham, of the Bure above its confluence with the Ant and of the Ant upstream of How Hill. The deposits of peat, as we shall see, were traditionally characterised by waterlogged fens, rather than by grazing marshes, and are today mostly rather wild landscapes, of reedbeds, wet woodland and open water – for it is here, on the peat, that the 'broads' or lakes from which the area takes its popular name are mainly to be found (Figure 1.12). Where areas of alluvium occur in the valleys, moreover, they developed in rather different ways from the more extensive deposits of the Halvergate Marshes. Their narrow width ensured both that they were often more subject to waterlogging, from water flowing off the adjacent uplands and from springs and seepage lines in the Chalk or Crag, and that they could be easily exploited by farms located at their margins, on the adjacent areas of higher, drier ground, often (as we shall see) as common land. Both factors ensured that, in marked contrast to the situation on the Halvergate Marshes, the alluvial deposits of the valley floors have always been devoid of settlements.

The two broad divisions of the wetlands flow seamlessly into each other and it is difficult, and perhaps unnecessary, to draw a firm boundary between them. On the Bure a line of division might reasonably be drawn at Wey Bridge (Acle Bridge), and on the Yare at Reedham Ferry. But along the wide valley of the Waveney, largely peat-free below Oulton and Burgh St Peter, a boundary is harder to define and while we will mostly, when discussing the Halvergate Marshes, limit our attention to the area lying to the north of Haddiscoe Bridge, we will on occasions, and without apology, venture some way to the south of it.

Broadland is not, of course, the only wetland landscape in England or, indeed, northern Europe, and aspects of its history invite comparisons with the Fenland of western East Anglia and with many parts of the Netherlands. These regions, likewise, display marked contrasts between the development of areas overlying peat and those over estuarine clays, with the former being shaped by large-scale peat extraction, and have a history of reclamation involving wind drainage. But in detail their histories, and even more their modern landscapes and environments, display many differences. In part these are a consequence of the extent and the particular morphological and hydrological characteristics of the wetlands themselves. But in part they arise from their wider social and geographical contexts – from the character of the surrounding areas of higher, drier ground.

INTRODUCING BROADLAND 31

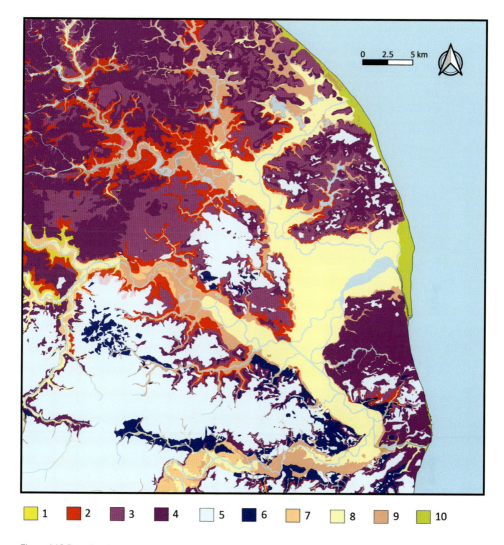

Figure 1.13 Broadland: geology. Key: 1. Chalk 2. Crag 3. Happisburgh Formation ('North Sea Drift') and related Middle Pleistocene glacial deposits: silts and clays 4. Happisburgh Formation ('North Sea Drift') and related Middle Pleistocene glacial deposits: predominantly sand and gravel 5. Lowestoft Formation: chalky boulder clay 6. Lowestoft Formation sands and gravels, and related deposits from the Anglian period 7. River terrace deposits 8. Alluvium and estuarine clay 9. Peat 10. Recent coastal sands and gravels.

It is impossible to understand Broadland if we neglect its 'uplands' – a useful if, to those coming from hillier terrain, rather odd term for the only slightly higher land lying beyond the rivers and floodplains. Uplands and wetlands have always been intimately connected. In innumerable ways the development of the marshes and fens was shaped by the communities living around them. The landscape of the uplands displays, moreover, a number of distinctive and unusual features, particularly in terms of buildings and settlement, that have a determining influence on the appearance and the visitor's experience of the lower ground. These distinctive features are, in large measure, the consequence of environmental factors, of climate and – in particular – of the basic geological structures already highlighted.

The geology of the 'uplands', in spite of superficial complexity, is comparatively straightforward and its key influences on the development of settlement and the local economy may be briefly summarised as follows (Figure 1.13). In places on the lower slopes of the valleys the Crag and, to a more limited extent, the Chalk are exposed, providing an aquifer – a reliable source of water – and, in the case of the Chalk especially, a source of useful raw materials. Across most of Broadland, however, these formations are buried beneath glacial deposits. To the north and west of the river Yare these are mainly the clays, silts, sands and gravels of the Happisburgh Formation. These deposits are often interdigitated in a complex manner but extensive and continuous areas featuring sand and gravel alone occur in Lothingland, to the south of Yarmouth, and in various places across the north and west of Broadland, flanking the higher reaches of the Bure, Ant and Yare. Over these varied Middle Pleistocene deposits significant quantities of wind-blown silt, *loess*, were, as noted in the previous section, widely deposited during the last glaciation. Where these overlie the silts and clays, loamy soils of exceptional fertility are found, which – being easy to cultivate – were especially attractive to early farmers.[73] But where they overlie the sands and gravels, less fertile, more acidic soils developed, giving rise in places to areas of heathland. For the most part, fertile soils of the former kind predominate in the central and north-eastern parts of Broadland: between the Yare and the Bure; between the Thurne and the Ant; and, in particular, on the 'Island' of Flegg, to the north of Great Yarmouth.

Where the Happisburgh deposits comprised sands and gravels, the choices and opportunities of early farmers were limited in another way. The water table often lay at a considerable depth, out of reach of all but the deepest wells. But the silts and clays of the Formation also provided uncertain supplies of water, for much of the precipitation they received ran off into surface watercourses. The best supplies were obtained where gravels lay thinly over clays and silts, close to the margins of the former. Here the water accumulating at the junction of permeable and impermeable deposits was within the reach of shallow wells.

The uplands in the south and south-east of Broadland – the areas lying between the Yare and the Waveney, and to the south of the latter river – are characterised by the rather later glacial deposits of the Lowestoft Formation, overwhelmingly dominated by chalky boulder clay. This gives rise to stiff and poorly draining soils,

---

[73] Hodge *et al.*, *Soils and their use*, pp. 346–51.

fairly fertile but generally much less attractive to farmers before later Saxon times than those found further north.[74] Moreover, such soils make good pasture as well as productive arable, and much land here was laid to grass in the early modern period and used for grazing cattle.[75] Perhaps the most important feature of the boulder clay, however, is that across an extensive and continuous area it provided a ready supply of water almost everywhere. The clay contains thin layers of sand and forms a kind of damp sponge blanket laid across the upland, a 'perched' water table, easily accessed by shallow wells in a way that the more deeply buried 'true' aquifer, of the Chalk and Crag, could not be. Settlements could therefore be established almost anywhere and farms and cottages are today more widely and evenly scattered across the landscape than elsewhere in Broadland, although no part of the area displays the kinds of highly clustered settlement pattern, with farms and cottages all huddled together in nucleated villages, that are found in many parts of England – across much of the Midlands or, to a lesser extent, in western East Anglia.

We do not mean to suggest that all aspects of Broadland's character can be explained, in a simple way, as a direct consequence of its rocks and landforms. Rather, these are best understood as a kind of prism through which wider currents of demographic, economic, social and cultural history were refracted: a template giving a distinctive local expression to national and international forces of change. Yet these influences were themselves to an extent shaped or framed by wider geographies, and Broadland's development over time shared many themes with a far broader area of eastern England. We might highlight, in particular, proximity to the North Sea and the connections to northern Europe that this engendered, and a climate especially well suited to cereal cultivation. In medieval times these together ensured relatively high population densities and a vibrant economy, including in East Anglia an important textile industry; well into the seventeenth century Norwich, on the western fringes of Broadland, remained England's second largest city. But industry stagnated thereafter and, through the eighteenth and nineteenth centuries, East Anglia became a more rural and, relative to the northern districts of England especially, less populous area. The low gradients of its rivers militated against the use of water power for industrial production; reserves of coal and metal ores were absent. The local economy expanded, but on the basis of agriculture and the activities connected to it. The Industrial Revolution largely passed East Anglia by. But its importance as a grain-growing region increased and it was instead the acknowledged birthplace of 'agricultural improvement'. This, and the wider economic expansion it engendered, had a significant impact on the landscape.

74　Hodge et al., *Soils and their use*, pp. 117–23, 132–8.
75　S. Wade Martins and T. Williamson, *Roots of change: farming and the landscape in East Anglia, c.1700–1870* (Exeter, 1999), pp. 22–5.

In the course of the three chapters that follow we explore the development of Broadland's landscape within the framework of this simple, yet useful, tripartite division, examining in turn the 'uplands', marshes and valleys, before going on to consider particular features or aspects they share in common, or which were created by the complex connections between them.

2

THE UPLANDS

Before the Middle Ages
by Sophie Tremlett

The settlement of the Broads landscape spans many thousands of years. The archaeological evidence that can inform us about this process is by its nature incomplete and skewed by spatial and temporal biases relating to deposition, preservation and discovery. Much of the evidence forming the basis of the rapid overview presented here is derived from the Broads 'uplands' and valley sides, rather than from the fens, marshes and rivers for which the area is better known. This bias does at least partly reflect a genuine pattern in the occupation and use of the Broads landscape, with human populations across millennia favouring valley sides and uplands for settlement, agriculture and the construction of funerary monuments. The fact remains, however, that we know relatively little about how the lower-lying landscapes of the Broads were utilised prior to the medieval period. We can assume that they must have been significant for transport, hunting, fishing, grazing and the procurement of a range of materials, and that the relative importance of different resources and opportunities would have fluctuated across different periods.

Sites such as Happisburgh and Pakefield on the modern coastline attest to the presence of early humans in the area long before the end of the last glaciation. Subsequent episodic occupation would have taken place when the climate allowed and the landmass was accessible. As the climate warmed and sea levels rose during the Late Glacial/Early Holocene and Mesolithic periods (from around 10,000 BC to 4000 BC), we can envisage a rich and varied landscape of uplands, river valleys, marshes and coast that would have provided a range of opportunities for the groups of people that gradually occupied the area. Excavations at Carrow Road football ground, Norwich, revealed a rare example of a stratigraphically intact site dating from the Late Glacial/Early Holocene period. Here, on the western edge of

Broadland, *in situ* clusters of worked flint show that groups were making what were probably short-term visits to an island or sandbar adjacent to the river Wensum.[1] The Broads area at this time was experiencing fluctuating climatic conditions, shifting vegetation patterns and rising sea levels. The gradual submersion of 'Doggerland' – that once linked eastern England to north-west Europe and now lies under the North Sea – is perhaps the most striking demonstration of the changing conditions for early inhabitants. By *c.*6000 BC the land bridge to the continent had been cut off, making Britain an island.[2] The periodic marine transgressions already described (above, pp. 20–2), related to changing climate and sea levels, would also have had a significant impact on the landscape, particularly along the coast and river valleys.[3]

In the Mesolithic period the area would have been occupied by relatively small, mobile 'hunter gatherer' groups, moving through the landscape to exploit different resources. The traces of such groups consist primarily of surface finds of flint tools and debris from their manufacture. These have most often been found during fieldwalking surveys or by chance during the excavation of sites dating to other periods. At some locations artefact scatters are dense enough to be regarded as flint-working sites.[4] Unfortunately, sealed, stratigraphically intact deposits, or finds other than flint tools, are scant. Finds from elsewhere, where preservation has been more favourable, demonstrate the wide range of bone, wood, leather and other organic materials that would have been used for shelter, hunting and foraging. The burning of woodland to manage vegetation and the construction of boats for transport and/or fishing may also have taken place.[5]

The Neolithic period (broadly 4000 BC to 2200 BC) brought the adoption of farming and the transition to a more settled society. Some of the social and economic developments during this period are likely to have taken place gradually, with change occurring over many centuries, while others may have been more rapid. The light, loess-rich, easily farmed soils of the central and northern part of the Broads area may have been particularly attractive for Norfolk's early farmers. Finds of flint and stone tools – including axeheads – are widespread. Other developments associated with the Neolithic, such as the use of pottery and the creation of large monuments, make this period far more visible in the archaeological record than

---

1 NHER 26602.
2 R. Bradley, *The prehistory of Britain and Ireland*, 2nd edn (Cambridge, 2019), p. 10.
3 P. Murphy, 'The archaeology of the Broads: a review', report. https://www.broads-authority.gov.uk/__data/assets/pdf_file/0021/198003/BroadsArchaeologyReviewFINALRptwithIll.pdf, 2014, p. 4 (accessed July 2022).
4 For example, Spixworth (NHER 24651), Woodbastwick (NHER 8473) and Rackheath (NHER 24651).
5 V. Fryer, P. Murphy and P. Wilshire, 'Vegetation history and early farming', in T. Ashwin and A. Davison (eds), *An historical atlas of Norfolk*, 3rd edn (Chichester, 2005), pp. 10–11. J.J. Wymer, 'Late glacial and Mesolithic hunters', in T. Ashwin and A. Davison (eds), *An historical atlas of Norfolk*, 3rd edn (Chichester, 2005), pp. 15–16.

earlier phases. For the first time, traces of human occupation in the Broads can be seen readily in the landscape, in the form of earthworks and cropmarks, as well as buried features and artefact scatters.

Settlements of this period remain hard to identify without excavation. For the Early Neolithic, the archaeological evidence tends to comprise clusters of pits, as at Broome Heath in the Waveney valley, Eaton Heath in the Yare valley and Hopton-on-Sea, overlooking a tributary of Fritton Decoy.[6] Far more visible are the remains of funerary sites and what are assumed to be ceremonial monuments: causewayed enclosures, cursus monuments and henges. None of these are common in the Broads landscape, but one of Norfolk's suggested causewayed enclosures, known only from cropmarks, is located in the Bure Valley at Buxton with Lammas, in the extreme north-west of the Broads area.[7] Nationally, such sites appear to have been constructed during a short period of only a few hundred years (c.3800 to 3500 BC). They are usually interpreted as places for communal gatherings and social activities such as feasting and the performance of rituals.[8] Cursus monuments, which were constructed later in the Neolithic period (from around 3500 to 3000 BC), and which again are presumed to have had a communal and/or ritual function, are even rarer, and there are no convincing examples known from the Broads area.

Long barrows – Neolithic burial mounds, roughly rectangular in shape – and related funerary sites are rather more common, although still far from numerous. Only a small proportion of the population, presumably a social elite, would have been interred within them, the majority of individuals receiving some other, less visible form of burial. A surviving long barrow still stands on Broome Heath, but the Broads sites are predominantly known from cropmarks, with only the outer ditches enclosing the mound usually visible. Whether all such rectangular enclosures originally surrounded long mounds, or whether some represent funerary or 'mortuary' enclosures that never possessed an inner mound – a related monument type – is not known. A few of these sites have been excavated in the Broads area in recent years: at Flixton, Broome and Rackheath, for example. No mounds or human remains were recovered at any of these sites, but all three have been interpreted as having a funerary function.[9] An inhumation excavated within

---

[6] G.J. Wainwright, 'The excavation of a Neolithic settlement on Broome Heath, Ditchingham, Norfolk', *Proceedings of the Prehistoric Society*, 38 (1972), pp. 1–97. G.J. Wainwright, 'The excavation of prehistoric and Romano-British settlements on Eaton Heath, Norwich', *The Archaeological Journal*, 130 (1973), pp. 1–43. M. Pitts, 'Ceremony and settlement in rural Norfolk', *British Archaeology* (May–June 2021), pp. 8–9.

[7] NHER 7690. A. Oswald, C. Dyer and M. Barber, *The creation of monuments. Neolithic causewayed enclosures in the British Isles* (Swindon, 2001), p. 153.

[8] Historic England, *Causewayed enclosures: introductions to heritage assets* (Swindon, 2018).

[9] S. Boulter, *Living with monuments. Excavations at Flixton Volume II*, East Anglian Archaeology 177 (Cirencester, 2022), pp. 141–3. D. Robertson, 'A Neolithic enclosure and Early Saxon settlement: excavations at Yarmouth Road, Broome, 2001', *Norfolk Archaeology*, 44/2 (2003), pp. 222–50. G. Trimble, 'Land at North Rackheath, Norfolk. An archaeological evaluation', Pre-Construct Archaeology report R14843 (Pampisford, 2022).

a barrow on Broome Heath in 1858 may have been from the surviving long barrow, but this is not certain, and the burial could in any case have been a later, potentially post-Roman insertion into an earlier funerary monument.[10] Other, less typical forms of Neolithic monument have also been recorded from the area, including a C-shaped earthwork on Broome Heath, a (probably) Late Neolithic timber circle at Flixton and a Late Neolithic or Early Bronze Age palisaded enclosure to the south of Norwich.[11] Several possible henges or small henge-like ('hengiform') monuments, typically dated to the Late Neolithic to Early Bronze Age, are also recorded. These, comprising a roughly circular enclosure defined by a bank with an internal ditch, are mostly known from cropmarks visible on aerial photographs, and their date and function are uncertain, but they include the confirmed henge and timber circle at Arminghall, in the Yare valley.[12] There is evidence for flint-mining taking place to the south of Norwich and this would also have been a significant resource for those living in the Broads area.[13]

The archaeological record of the Early Bronze Age (*c*.2350 BC to 1501 BC) in the Broads shares much in common with that of the Neolithic, in that settlement evidence remains elusive and hard to characterise. It has been noted that Early Bronze Age settlement sites may have been used on a cyclical basis, and that there is a tendency for them to be visible as spreads of material (pottery and worked flint, for example) rather than as sub-surface features.[14] One such settlement may have been located at Bacton, on the northern fringes of the Broads area, at the headwaters of the river Ant. Significant quantities of both Neolithic and Bronze Age worked flints have been recovered from the site.[15] Other settlements of this period are marked by pit groups. At Great and Little Plumstead, a streamside settlement of Late Neolithic or Early Bronze Age date was represented by fence lines, post- and stake-holes and a buried soil.[16] Undoubtedly, the most visible features of this period to have survived in the landscape are round barrows (circular burial mounds), which have been recorded in considerable numbers across the Broads uplands and valley fringes. As with Neolithic burial mounds, upstanding examples are rare; a surviving round barrow on Broome Heath, together with a surviving Neolithic long barrow, appears to have once been part of a group of mounds, the others since

---

10 M. Barber and A. Oswald, *An enclosure on Broome Heath, Ditchingham, Norfolk* (London, 1995), p. 5.
11 Wainwright, 'Neolithic Settlement on Broome Heath', pp. 1–97. S. Boulter and P. Walton Rogers, *Circles and cemeteries: excavations at Flixton Volume I*, East Anglian Archaeology 147 (Bury St Edmunds, 2012), pp. 12–19, 48–51. NHER 39268.
12 NHER 6100.
13 NHER 9547, for example.
14 T. Ashwin, 'Neolithic and Bronze Age Norfolk', *Proceedings of the Prehistoric Society*, 62 (1996), pp. 41–62, at p. 52.
15 NHER 6899.
16 NHER 37644. D. Gurney and K. Penn, 'Excavations and surveys in Norfolk 2003', *Norfolk Archaeology*, 44/3 (2004), pp. 573–89, at p. 577.

Figure 2.1 A trackway, probably of late prehistoric date, at Belton with Browston; it appears to respect the position of several probably Bronze Age round barrows, now visible principally as the cropmarks of ring ditches (mound in red, ditches in green).

lost to demolition and quarrying.[17] At most of the Broads sites the mounds have been levelled and only the outer ring ditch is visible as a cropmark. In several cases distinct clusters of such features occur, indicating the development of a cemetery; one example at Broome may have encompassed as many as 16 barrows.[18] In some cases, as at Broome Heath, Bronze Age burial mounds may have been constructed with reference to earlier funerary or ceremonial monuments; at Cantley, scattered ring ditches surround what may have been a large barrow comprising multiple ditch circuits, or possibly a henge-like monument of Late Neolithic or Early Bronze Age date.[19] At Flixton, in the Waveney valley, as many as 16 ring ditches, interpreted as the remains of Bronze Age round barrows, were excavated in the vicinity of a long barrow, a possible 'long mortuary enclosure' and a timber circle, among other, non-monumental, evidence of Neolithic activity.[20] Certainly, Bronze Age barrows seem to have persisted as significant landmarks within later landscapes. There are examples of later prehistoric trackways (Figure 2.1), field systems of Iron Age

---

17   Barber and Oswald, *An Enclosure on Broome Heath*, p. 5.
18   J. Albone, S. Massey and S. Tremlett, 'The archaeology of Norfolk's Broads Zone: results of the National Mapping Programme', 2007, p. 15. https://historicengland.org.uk/research/results/reports/113-2007?searchType=research+report&search=broads.
19   *Ibid.*, pp. 14–15. NHER 64965.
20   S. Boulter, *Living with monuments*, pp. 144–5, Fig. 3.14.

Figure 2.2 Part of the Middle Bronze Age enclosure at Ormesby St Michael during excavation in 2010.

or Roman date and medieval parish boundaries all being laid out with reference to what must at the time have been upstanding mounds.[21] There is also evidence for round barrows being reused as the foci for funerary activity and other, more mundane functions in later periods. One of the ring ditches at Flixton became a focus for burial in the Early Saxon period, its mound subsequently being reused for the site of a windmill in the later medieval or early post-medieval period.[22]

From the end of the Early Bronze Age (c.1500 BC), major changes took place in settlement, land division and burial practices.[23] Reflecting this, several substantial Middle Bronze Age enclosures have been identified in Norfolk in recent years. One was constructed at Ormesby St Michael, in a low-lying position on the edge of what is now Ormesby Broad (Figure 2.2). Excavation revealed that it contained at least two contemporary structures. Further possible examples in the Broads area, identified on aerial photographs, are known from Ashby with Oby, Mautby, Freethorpe, South Walsham and Gorleston-on-Sea. Even when excavated, how the enclosures were utilised is not entirely clear-cut, and they do not appear to have been used solely or even primarily for settlement; the farming of livestock

---

21 J. Albone, S. Massey and S. Tremlett, 'The archaeology of Norfolk's Coastal Zone: results of the National Mapping Programme', 2007, pp. 48–9. http://historicengland.org.uk/research/results/reports/114-2007?searchType=research+report. Albone et al., 'Broads Zone', pp. 29–30. NHER 18332.

22 Boulter and Walton Rogers, *Circles and cemeteries*, p. xi, Fig. 3.2 and *passim*.

23 Bradley, *Prehistory of Britain and Ireland*, p. 207.

may have been an equally significant factor in the construction of at least some examples.[24] Alongside the construction of enclosures, the Middle Bronze Age may also have seen the development of field systems in the Broads area, as evidenced at Ormesby St Michael. While some land division may have taken place in the earlier Bronze Age, evidence nationally and regionally suggests that this process intensified during the Middle Bronze Age.[25] While few field systems in Broadland are securely dated to the Bronze Age through excavation and scientific dating, several identified on aerial sources are thought to be potentially or even probably from this period.[26]

The character of Iron Age (*c*.800 BC to AD 42) settlement in East Anglia is still relatively poorly understood. Certainly, there is a scarcity of large, defended sites comparable to the hillforts of Wessex. There is, instead, evidence for extensive unenclosed settlements.[27] The Iron Age settlement pattern in Norfolk has been described as 'spurgy': that is, with activity and occupation spread over extensive areas and shifting over time.[28] In Broadland, the archaeological traces of this pattern can be difficult to identify in the absence of excavation; multiple enclosures potentially relating to Iron Age settlement have been identified on aerial sources, but in few cases can they be definitively dated and there is little to differentiate them from examples of Roman date.[29] Other settlement sites – at Acle, for example – are known only from surface finds and their physical character is unknown.[30] Middle Iron Age round houses were excavated at Harford Farm, on the route of the Norwich Southern Bypass overlooking the rivers Tas and Yare.[31] At Langley, cropmarks of a square enclosure, defined by a ditch and containing a single ring

---

24 N. Gilmour, S. Horlock, R. Mortimer and S. Tremlett, 'Middle Bronze Age enclosures in the Norfolk Broads: a case study at Ormesby St Michael, England', *Proceedings of the Prehistoric Society*, 80 (2014), pp. 141–57.

25 R. Johnston, R. May and D. McOmish, 'Understanding the chronologies of England's field systems', in S. Arnoldussen, R. Johnston and M. Løvschal (eds), *Europe's early fieldscapes: archaeologies of prehistoric land allotment* (New York, 2021), pp. 185–207. S. Griffiths, R. Johnston, R. May, D. McOmish, P. Marshall, J. Last and A. Bayliss, 'Dividing the land: time and land division in the English North Midlands and Yorkshire', *European Journal of Archaeology*, 25/2 (2022), pp. 216–37.

26 For example, Albone *et al.*, 'Coastal Zone', pp. 45–7.

27 S. Tremlett, 'Iron Age landscapes from the air: results from the Norfolk National Mapping Programme', in J. Davies (ed.), *The Iron Age in northern East Anglia: new work in the land of the Iceni* (Oxford, 2011), pp. 25–39, at pp. 26–7.

28 J.D. Hill, 'Settlement, landscape and regionality: Norfolk and Suffolk in the pre-Roman Iron Age of Britain and beyond', in J. Davies and T. Williamson (eds), *Land of the Iceni: the Iron Age in northern East Anglia* (Norwich, 1999), pp. 185–207. J.D. Hill, 'The dynamics of social change in later Iron Age eastern and south-eastern England c. 300 BC–AD 43', in C. Haselgrove and T. Moore (eds), *The later Iron Age in Britain and beyond* (Oxford, 2007), pp. 16–40.

29 Albone *et al.*, 'Coastal Zone', pp. 51–4, p. 60.

30 NHER 40570.

31 T. Ashwin, 'Excavations at Harford Farm, Caistor St Edmund (Site 9794), 1990', in T. Ashwin and S. Bates, *Excavations on the Norwich Southern Bypass, 1989–91 Part I: excavations at Bixley, Caistor St Edmund, Trowse, Cringleford and Little Melton*, East Anglian Archaeology 91 (Dereham, 2000), pp. 52–140.

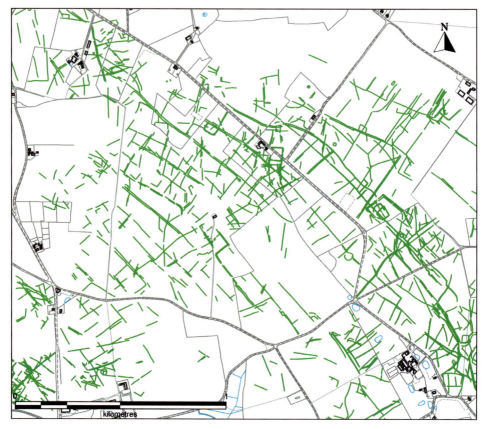

Figure 2.3 Extensive field system, probably of Late Iron Age and/or Roman date, visible as cropmarks at Cantley and Beighton (ditches in green).

ditch and a possible rectilinear structure, may be the site of an Iron Age farmstead.[32] At Hopton-on-Sea, on the eastern fringes of Broadland, aerial photographs have revealed what appears to be a large, complex nucleated settlement made up of multiple enclosures. Several round houses are evident, suggesting a prehistoric date, and the entire area seems to be overlain by a regular, apparently planned, field system of probable Roman date.[33]

At some stage, probably in the later Iron Age and/or Roman period, large-scale field systems were established across extensive tracts of the Broads uplands. They are dramatically visible on aerial photographs as cropmarks.[34] Where comprehensive and large-scale survey has mapped and characterised these features, they appear as highly organised, generally 'co-axial' (brickwork-pattern)

---

32   NHER 19407.
33   Tremlett, 'Iron Age landscapes from the air', pp. 25–39; p. 30, Fig. 4.
34   Tremlett, 'Iron Age landscapes from the air'; Albone *et al.*, 'Broads Zone', pp. 26–40.

field systems, running along the interfluves between the principal rivers (Figure 2.3). They are particularly prominent in the area between the rivers Bure and Yare; at their most extensive, in the parishes of Cantley and Beighton, they can be traced virtually unbroken across an area of several square kilometres. They are usually defined along their long axis by double-ditched boundaries or – more probably – trackways. Frequently, small rectilinear enclosures can be seen attached to the major boundaries, which perhaps played a role in stock management. It is possible that the main alignment of the field systems linked upland heaths or wood-pastures to the north and east of what is now Norwich to the rich lower-lying grazing land of the Halvergate Marshes. This suggests an origin before the formation of the 'Great Estuary', and parallels with similar examples known from elsewhere and stratigraphic relationships with enclosures and possible settlements of probable Iron Age and Roman date suggest that parts at least are likely to have originated in the Iron Age, with further elements perhaps being added in the Roman period. In lower-lying areas, at Geldeston, Beccles and Barsham, preserved timber alignments and/or trackways of Late Iron Age date have been excavated, demonstrating the extension of activity onto the floodplain of the river Waveney.[35]

The Roman period is usually considered to begin with the Claudian invasion of AD 43 and the creation of the Roman province of Britannia. In Norfolk and north Suffolk, however, the territory of the Iceni tribe remained largely independent until the defeat of Boudica's rebellion in AD 63, rather later than neighbouring parts of the country. In common with the Icenian territory as a whole, there is relatively little archaeological evidence of a military presence in Broadland in the early Roman period.[36] The character and date of a circular structure and possible military site at Reedham remain enigmatic.[37] At East Ruston a square enclosure with an inner palisade, visible as cropmarks, could feasibly be a small military camp overlooking the river Ant, but this is far from certain. Fieldwalking has recovered Roman pottery from the site, among finds of other periods.[38]

As described in the previous chapter, the coast and marshes of the Broads in the Roman period were radically different from those of today. A natural sand barrier on the site of the modern spit now occupied by Great Yarmouth had disintegrated, resulting in marine incursion and the creation of what is often termed the 'Great Estuary'. This large expanse of water covered much of what is now Halvergate Marshes; a remnant still survives as Breydon Water. It turned

---

35 Murphy, 'Archaeology of the Broads', p. 7.
36 J. Plouviez, 'The Roman period', in D. Dymond and E. Martin (eds), *An historical atlas of Suffolk*, 3rd edn (Ipswich, 1999), pp. 42–3. D. Gurney, 'Roman Norfolk (c. AD 43–110)', in T. Ashwin and A. Davison (eds), *An historical atlas of Norfolk*, 3rd edn (Chichester, 2005), pp. 28–9.
37 NHER 10418.
38 NHER 45242. Albone *et al.*, 'Broads Zone', p. 17.

Flegg and Lothingland, to its north and south respectively, into peninsulas – or, in the case of Flegg, possibly an island – and estuarine conditions extended as far inland as Acle.[39] The estuary would have provided ready access and harbourage for sea-borne trade and transport, while the river valleys would have facilitated access westwards, for example to the towns at Brampton, Caistor St Edmund and Scole.

The uplands surrounding the estuary and river valleys appear to have been relatively densely populated and intensively exploited. A network of roads and tracks would have facilitated access into and across the area. Not only is Roman material culture – pottery, building material, coinage – more plentiful and better suited to survival than that from most other periods, but settlements and fields of this period are better represented in the archaeological record. Cropmarks visible on aerial photographs, combined with the results of fieldwalking and metal-detecting, have been particularly useful for identifying probable Roman period settlements and possible estate centres. While structural evidence for villa buildings is scarce, there is better evidence for what may have been the central places of large agricultural estates. Typically defined by a rectilinear, often double-ditched boundary (when visible as cropmarks), these are likely to have acted as centres for agricultural production, processing and surplus management and distribution. It is probable that they possessed fewer of the trappings of a 'Roman' lifestyle, and consumed fewer luxury goods, than would be expected at a typical villa.[40] At Beighton, a large square double-ditched enclosure appears to overlie a smaller enclosure of earlier, possibly Iron Age date (Figure 2.4).[41] Another probable example is visible at Strumpshaw, close to the cropmarks of a timber building that may have been an aisled barn.[42] Smaller farmsteads also existed, although these can be harder to distinguish from sites of other periods in the cropmark evidence. Two adjacent early Roman examples excavated at Hopton-on-Sea, on the eastern coastal fringes of the Broads, proved to have been short-lived, abandoned after approximately 60 years of use, although the surrounding landscape continued to be farmed.[43] To the south of Lowestoft, a small farmstead was established at Bloodmoor Hill, on the site later occupied by a more substantial Early Saxon settlement and cemetery.[44] A temple site visible as cropmarks at Aldeby, and

---

39 P. Murphy, 'Coastal change and human response', in T. Ashwin and A. Davison (eds), *An historical atlas of Norfolk*, 3rd edn (Chichester, 2005), pp. 6–7. Albone *et al.*, 'Coastal Zone', p. 74. Murphy, 'Archaeology of the Broads', p. 4.
40 C. Evans, 'Late Iron Age and Roman resource assessment', in *East of England Research Framework*, 2021. https://researchframeworks.org/eoe/resource-assessments/late-iron-age-and-roman/.
41 NHER 49574 and 21762. Albone *et al.*, 'Broads Zone', p. 18.
42 NHER 64926 and 49574.
43 Pitts, 'Ceremony and settlement'.
44 S. Lucy, J. Tipper and A. Dickens, *The Anglo-Saxon settlement and cemetery at Bloodmoor Hill, Carlton Colville, Suffolk*, East Anglian Archaeology 131 (Cambridge, 2009).

Figure 2.4 Double-ditched enclosure at Beighton, probably the site of a Roman agricultural estate centre (ditches in green).

evidence for industries such as metal-working, pottery manufacture and salt-making, throw light on other facets of life during this period.[45]

In the later Roman period, Saxon Shore Forts were constructed at Caister-on-Sea and Burgh Castle, on either side of the entrance to the Great Estuary. They became part of a chain of such fortifications, stretching around the coast from Brancaster in Norfolk to Portchester in Hampshire. The chief purpose of the earliest forts, including Caister-on-Sea, may have been to control and safeguard shipping and trade, but they were eventually used to defend the coast from attacks by raiders from Germany and the Netherlands.[46] Reedham has been suggested as the

---

45   NHER 45036. Albone *et al.*, 'Broads Zone', p. 18. Gurney, 'Roman Norfolk'.
46   D. Gurney, *Outposts of the Roman Empire: a guide to Norfolk's Roman forts* (Norwich, 2002), pp. 5–10.

possible site of a *pharos* or lighthouse associated with these forts.[47] Within the wider region of East Anglia, the later Roman period saw a steep decline in the number of small farming settlements, probably due to changes in the way the countryside was organised and farmed.[48] It is likely that this contraction also took place in Broadland, although the scarcity of securely dated – in effect, excavated – sites from much of the area means that such generalised models must be treated with caution.

With the end of Roman rule and influence, traditionally taken to be in AD 410, the population, settlement pattern and economy of the Broads area underwent considerable change. Settlement density – and presumably population levels – declined significantly, and this in turn must have led to changes in land use and vegetation.[49] Proximity to the exposed eastern coast meant that raiding by groups of 'barbarians' from the continent also occurred on a significant scale, followed by migration. Much of the evidence for the Early Saxon period is derived from cemetery sites, most of which are known only from surface and metal-detected finds, but these demonstrate the presence of European migrants buried with continental grave goods.[50] Notable excavated examples in the Broads area include the cemeteries at Bloodmoor Hill, to the south of Lowestoft, and at Flixton, in the Waveney valley.[51] Settlements are less easy to identify, due to the scarcity and generally low quality of ceramics, and the difficulty of identifying sites of this period from the air,[52] but several examples have been excavated in the Broads area. That at Bloodmoor Hill has been interpreted as possibly representing an early form of estate centre. It was occupied for more than 200 years and produced considerable evidence for metal-working.[53] At Broome in the Waveney valley, seven or eight post-built buildings and a sunken-featured building were uncovered during excavations in advance of quarrying.[54] This small settlement is typical for the period, with its combination of building types and location in a river valley. At Horning a possible defensive linear earthwork, forming a barrier across the peninsula of land between the rivers Ant and Bure, may also date to this period (see p. 79).[55] It is one of several such earthworks known in East Anglia.

---

47 *Ibid.*, p. 13.
48 A. Smith, 'The east', in A. Smith, M. Allen, T. Brindle and M. Fulford, *The rural settlement of Roman Britain* (London, 2016), pp. 208–41.
49 Williamson, *The Norfolk Broads*, p. 19.
50 K. Penn, 'Early Saxon settlement (c. AD 410–650)', in T. Ashwin and A. Davison (eds), *An historical atlas of Norfolk*, 3rd edn (Chichester, 2005), p. 30.
51 Lucy *et al.*, *Bloodmoor Hill*; Boulter and Walton Rogers, *Circles and cemeteries*.
52 Albone *et al.*, 'Coastal Zone', pp. 81–2.
53 Lucy *et al.*, *Bloodmoor Hill*, pp. 425, 430–4.
54 Robertson, 'Excavations at Yarmouth Road'.
55 E. Rose, 'A linear earthwork at Horning', in Norfolk Archaeological Unit, *Trowse, Horning, deserted medieval villages, Kings Lynn*, East Anglian Archaeology 14 (Dereham, 1982), pp. 35–9.

Figure 2.5 The Middle Saxon log boat found at Ludham Bridge, during excavation. It was situated within a partially silted up channel; the possibly contemporary animal skulls found close to it may be part of a 'closing' deposit.

During the Middle Saxon period (approximately AD 650–850), the origins of many facets of medieval society and the medieval landscape can be seen emerging – the kingdom of East Anglia, the first monastic sites and many place-names can be dated to this period. In the Broads area there is evidence of an increasing population. At Witton, on the northern edge of the Broads, it has been possible to not only identify settlement sites but also model the increasingly large area of land being exploited.[56] The fortuitous discovery of a preserved dug-out log boat of Middle Saxon date on the bank of the river Ant provides tangible evidence of what were presumably well-used waterways (Figure 2.5).[57] Artefacts of preserved wood of Middle Saxon date recorded at a number of locations in and around the Broads suggest that the lower-lying valleys and marshes were seeing increasing use in this period, perhaps as the Great Yarmouth sand spit developed and the Great Estuary began to recede.[58] By the Late Saxon period, most of the villages and towns of the Broads that we know today had been established.

---

56   K. Wade, 'The late Saxon period', in A.J. Lawson (ed.), *The archaeology of Witton near North Walsham*, East Anglian Archaeology 18 (Dereham, 1983), pp. 73–7.
57   Murphy, 'Archaeology of the Broads', p. 8. Heather Wallis, pers. comm.
58   Heather Wallis, pers. comm.

48 BROADLAND

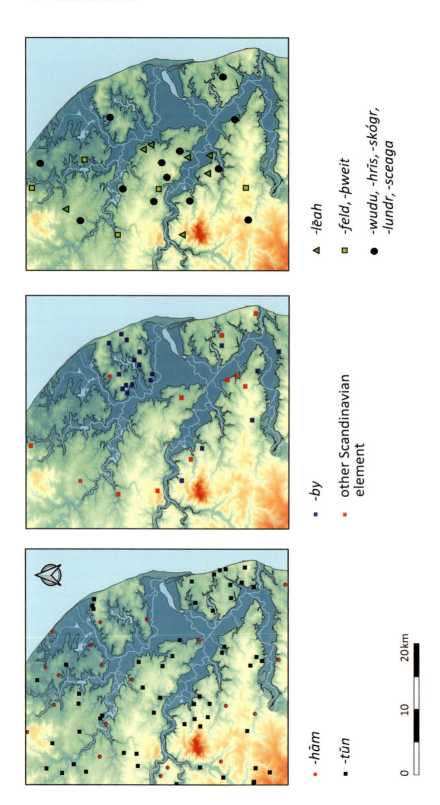

Figure 2.6 The distribution of place-name elements in Broadland. Left, names featuring the Old English elements *hām* (-ham) and *tūn* (-ton). Centre, names featuring Scandinavian elements. Right, names featuring elements relating to woodland or its clearance.

Villages and fields

There was remarkably little continuity between the Roman landscape of Broadland and that of the Middle Ages. Few, if any, elements of the prehistoric and Roman field systems discussed in the previous section appear to have survived into the medieval period to influence the layout of fields and roads or the course of parish boundaries. The decline in population and contraction of settlement that occurred in the late Roman and immediate post-Roman periods appears to have been severe. Known settlements of fifth- and sixth-century date are few in number and are mainly found on the lower ground, avoiding the uplands, where place-names such as Southwood, Lingwood, Strumpshaw, Lound and Blofield, all containing Old English or Old Norse second elements referring to woods (*wudu*, *sceaga*, *lundr*) or to grazing land adjacent to it (*feld*), suggest that grazed woodland, interspersed with tracts of open, heathy land, had replaced cultivated fields (Figure 2.6).[59] Some areas of Anglo-Saxon woodland also existed on lower ground, to judge from the Old English element *leah*, meaning 'wood' or 'clearing', in the names of Acle, Cantley, Langley and Fishley. Woodland in such locations, lying closer to the main areas of early Anglo-Saxon settlement, may have been more intensively managed. Certainly, many areas of semi-natural 'coppice-with-standards' woodland could be found in such locations, close to major watercourses, in post-medieval times, including Acle Wood and Catfield Wood, destroyed in the nineteenth century, or South Walsham Wood, which remains extant.

It is noticeable that almost all Broadland villages with names featuring the suffix *-ham*, excluding examples ending in 'ingham', are to be found close to the principal rivers. Such names are generally considered to indicate places settled early in the Anglo-Saxon period, a proportion of which developed, in the Middle Saxon period, as major centres of royal, ecclesiastical or lordly power.[60] Places with names featuring the element *tun*, in contrast – suggesting subsidiary and/or later settlements – are more widely scattered. Many examples, such as Moulton or Beighton, are to be found on higher ground, and presumably represent places established as settlement and cultivation re-expanded at the expense of woodland and pasture in the course of the eighth, ninth and tenth centuries (Figure 2.6). There are hints of the early importance, and especially the early ecclesiastical importance, of some of the Broadland *hams*. Medieval tradition held that the church at Reedham, which incorporates much material quarried from a derelict

---

[59] M. Gelling and A. Cole, *The landscape of place-names* (Stamford, 2000). D. Hooke, *Trees in Anglo-Saxon England* (Woodbridge, 2010). D. Hooke, 'The woodland landscape of early medieval England', in N. Higham and M.J. Ryan (eds), *Place-names, language and the Anglo-Saxon landscape* (Woodbridge, 2011), pp. 143–74. O. Rackham, *Ancient woodland: its history, vegetation and uses in England* (London, 1980), pp. 127–30.

[60] M. Gelling, *Signposts to the past: place-names and the history of England*, 3rd edn (Chichester, 1997), pp. 108–16.

Roman building, was originally founded in the seventh century by St Felix, the first bishop of the East Angles.[61] The churches at Martham and Ludham stand in yards extending over about two and roughly three acres (0.8 and 1.2 hectares) respectively, significantly larger than those in neighbouring parishes, a sign that they may have been 'minsters': that is, important early churches built at major estate centres and served by communities of priests.[62] The extensive *parochiae* attached to such churches gradually fragmented in Late Saxon times to create the medieval pattern of local parishes, as minor lords and prosperous freemen erected churches to serve their families and dependents. Other riverside settlements, with different kinds of name, have similar indications of ancient significance. The name of Loddon is probably derived from the Celtic *Ludne*, 'muddy river', presumably a description of the river Chet. At the time of Domesday it lay within Lodningas Hundred, the name of which incorporates that of an early tribal group similarly named after the river. Loddon church was the only other in Broadland associated by legend with Felix. It stands in a vast churchyard covering more than 4 acres (*c.*2.5 hectares).[63]

The most noticeable feature of Broadland place-names is the large number that incorporate Scandinavian elements, mainly *by*, 'a small settlement', but also *Þveit*, 'meadow, clearing' (Crostwight, Thwaite) and *lundr*, 'wood' (Lound) (Figure 2.6). Such names reflect the presence of Scandinavian settlers in the area in the later ninth or tenth centuries, when much of eastern England was conquered by Danish armies. How intensive Danish settlement was and how far Scandinavian place-names can provide a guide to its spatial distribution remain debated, but the remarkable concentration of names featuring the element *by* strongly suggests large-scale occupation, perhaps a consequence of formal agreement, of the discrete and circumscribed territory of the 'island' of Flegg.[64] Eastern England in general, and Broadland in particular, were also characterised, by the time that Domesday Book was compiled in 1086, by large numbers of free men and sokemen – peasant farmers with only limited obligations to manorial lords – and this has often been associated with the Danish settlements that occurred some two centuries earlier.[65] But in detail the distributions of Domesday's free peasants and of Scandinavian

---

61 As described in the Liber Albus of Bury St Edmunds, BM Add. Mss. 14847.
62 R. Morris, *Churches in the landscape* (London, 1989), pp. 93–167. J. Blair, *The church in Anglo-Saxon society* (Oxford, 2005).
63 Liber Albus, BM Add. Mss. 14847.
64 L. Abrams and D. Parsons, 'Place-names and the history of Scandinavian settlement in England', in J. Hines, A. Lane and M. Redknap (eds), *Land, sea and home: settlement in the Viking period* (Leeds, 2004), pp. 379–431. D. Boulton, 'Differing patterns of Viking settlement in East Anglia: an analysis of Scandinavian and Anglo-Scandinavian place-names in their geographical and archaeological contexts', PhD thesis (University of East Anglia, 2020).
65 R.H.C. Davis, 'East Anglia and the Danelaw', *Transactions of the Royal Historical Society*, 5 (1955), pp. 23–39. F.M. Stenton, *Anglo-Saxon England* (Oxford, 1943). R.G. Lennard, *Rural England, 1086–1135: a study of social and agrarian conditions* (London, 1959).

place-names are poorly correlated and the less manorialised character of eastern England is probably, in the main, a consequence of environmental factors. The east of the country was, and is, better suited to arable agriculture than the west, and harvests here more dependable, allowing small farmers greater scope for retaining their freedom as, over time, the power of local lords increased. It is noticeable that eastern areas of England were also the most densely settled at the time of Domesday, presumably for the same reasons.[66] The fertile and easily worked soils, formed in loess overlying glacial silts and clays, that are found widely across the central and north-eastern parts of Broadland were, at the time of Domesday, characterised by particularly complex and confused tenurial structure, with large numbers of free men and, in most townships, numerous small manors. They also had one of the highest population densities in England. These characteristics, which persisted through the twelfth and thirteenth centuries, have left an indelible mark on the landscape.

Broadland's settlement pattern presents a number of challenges to the landscape historian. Not only are houses and cottages scattered, to varying extents, across the landscape, but the principal elements – churches, former manor houses and other dwellings – are oddly related to each other. There are a few major nucleations of settlement, mainly small market towns and/or places that have probably developed, in the manner just described, from ancient centres of royal or lordly power, such as Ludham or Stalham. But in many parishes any clusters of houses are only loosely grouped, typically taking the form of lines of dwellings strung out along the junction of the uplands and wetlands. In addition, there are numerous outlying farms and 'halls', sometimes interspersed with small hamlets. Equally striking is the way that only a handful of churches stand, like that at Ludham, in the middle of the main cluster of houses in a parish. Some are to be found on the edge of it but many are located at a distance, accompanied only by a manorial 'hall' or a parsonage, or else standing completely alone in the fields, as at Thurne or Stokesby.

Parish churches are, moreover, extraordinarily numerous in the area, and their associated parishes correspondingly small. Before modern changes Southwood, for example, covered 439 acres (177 hectares), Burlingham St Peter 410 acres (166 hectares), Billockby a mere 396 acres (160 hectares). Indeed, in some villages there were, in medieval times, two or more churches, originally serving separate parishes. In South Walsham and Rockland St Mary they even shared the same churchyard (Figure 2.7). More usually they stood within reasonable proximity – those in Surlingham, for example, some 300 metres apart, on either side of a minor valley. Domesday suggests that many, perhaps most, such multiple churches

---

66 T. Williamson, *England's landscape: East Anglia* (London, 2006), pp. 51–5, 87–92.

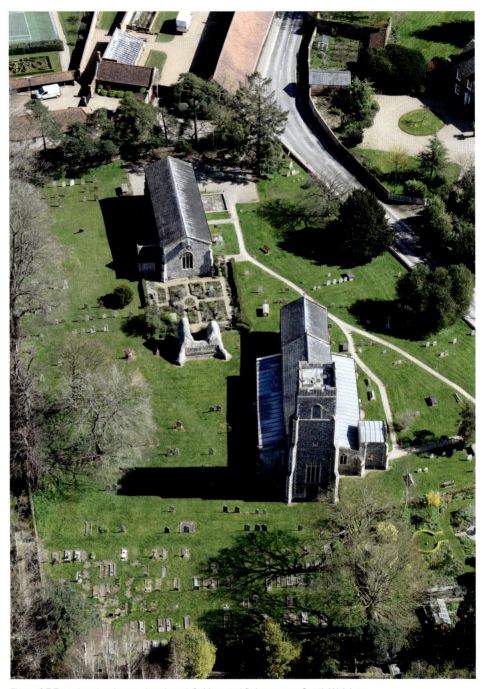

Figure 2.7 Two churches in one churchyard: St Mary and St Lawrence, South Walsham.

already existed by 1086 and in places such as Barton Turf list two churches, where only one is later recorded. In most cases, one of the churches became redundant and ruinous before the eighteenth century and the two parishes were merged. But occasionally both survived, serving separate ecclesiastical units, so that the churches of West and East Somerton stand 550 metres apart, those of Burlingham St Peter and Burlingham St Andrew 280 metres. All these curious features of settlement can be found, to varying extents, across much of Norfolk and northern and eastern Suffolk,[67] but they are more prominent in Broadland than elsewhere, ultimately reflecting the high population density in the Late Saxon period and the social and tenurial idiosyncrasies already noted.

In East Anglia as a whole, as in most other parts of England, the present pattern of settlement began to form from the eighth or ninth centuries, in the Middle Saxon period. Numerous archaeological field surveys in Norfolk and Suffolk have revealed that most isolated or partly isolated churches are surrounded by scatters of pottery of this date.[68] The churches, or rather their wooden predecessors, were originally built in small settlements that were sometimes the only one within the area that became the parish, although elsewhere accompanied by another and occasionally more. But from the tenth or eleventh century, as the population continued to grow and the area under cultivation expanded, farms increased in number and dispersed more widely across the landscape, usually hugging the edges of greens and commons that represented the tattered remnants of formerly more extensive and continuous pastures. In some cases the original settlement by the church failed to grow, remaining as a small group of houses or simply as a 'hall–church complex', a pairing of church and manorial site that reflected the fact that it was the lord who had originally built and endowed the church, placing it beside his residence for convenience and as a symbol of status. Sometimes, however, the original settlement site was abandoned altogether, as all the inhabitants decamped to a common edge, leaving the church isolated.

Only one large-scale, systematic fieldwalking survey has been carried out in Broadland, by the archaeologist Alan Davison in the 1980s.[69] But this, together with chance discoveries, suggest that the area broadly conforms to this wider East Anglian pattern. Archaeological finds from in and around parish churches at Hickling, Claxton and elsewhere suggest that most mark the sites of relatively

---

67   Williamson, *East Anglia*, pp. 51–5, 87–92.
68   A. Davison, *The evolution of settlement in three parishes in south-east Norfolk*, East Anglian Archaeology 49 (Dereham, 1990). P. Wade-Martins, *Village sites in the Launditch hundred*, East Anglian Archaeology 10 (Gressenhall, 1980). E. Martin, 'Rural settlement patterns in medieval Suffolk', *Annual Report of the Medieval Settlement Research Group*, 15 (2001), pp. 5–7. P. Warner, *Greens, commons and clayland colonization* (Leicester, 1987). A. Rogerson, 'Fransham: an archaeological and historical study of a parish on the Norfolk boulder clay', PhD thesis (University of East Anglia, 1995).
69   Davison, *Evolution of settlement*.

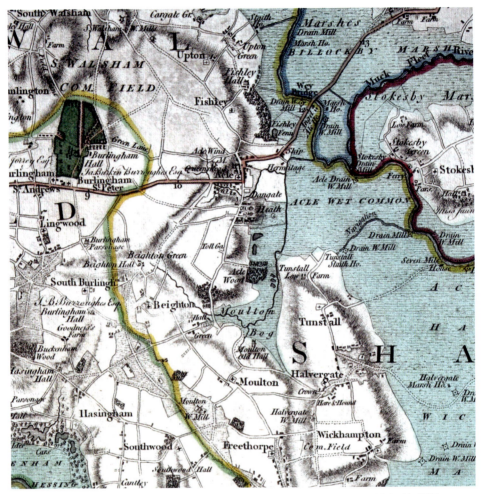

Figure 2.8 Extract from William Faden's *Topographical Map of the County of Norfolk*, published in 1797, showing typical features of the settlement pattern of Broadland. Note, in particular, the isolated churches and the clusters of farms and cottages on the margins of areas of common land.

small eighth- or ninth-century settlements.[70] Seventeenth- and eighteenth-century maps indicate that most farms and cottages stood on the margins of greens and commons, spreading there – again, to judge from the available archaeological evidence – from the tenth or eleventh centuries onwards (Figure 2.8). Not surprisingly in this fertile and populous area, this medieval settlement pattern developed from one that was already unusually dense. The multiple churches found in some villages almost certainly indicate discrete Middle and Late Saxon settlements, and finds of seventh-, eighth- or ninth-century date have also been made at a distance from any medieval church. Alan Davison's survey of Hales,

---

70   NHER 8393. NHER 38081.

Loddon and Heckingham located a number of such sites. Of particular interest was his discovery that the small Middle Saxon settlement beside Heckingham church was accompanied by at least two others lying within 300 metres, all strung out along rising ground overlooking the valley of the river Chet to the north.[71] If one of these had also acquired a church, then the kind of arrangements seen at Surlingham or Burlingham, with two or more medieval churches standing in close proximity, would have resulted. Some of these early sites may survive in the modern landscape not as churches or 'hall–church complexes' but as isolated manorial sites that early maps suggest lay at some distance from both churches and commons. Chamery Hall in South Walsham, standing alone around a kilometre west-south-west of the two parish churches in their shared yard, and more than 300 metres from the nearest common, is a good example. Its name derives from the fact that it was the manor of the Chamberlain of St Benet's Abbey, identifiable with the abbey's main holding here in 1066.[72]

Many of Broadland's parish churches, and thus the early settlements they mark, are located on low-lying sites, less than 10 metres above and within 200 metres of a floodplain – like most of the Middle and Late Saxon settlements discovered in Davison's survey of Loddon and Heckingham. The result, as at much-photographed Irstead, can be highly picturesque. In general, churches so placed are more common in the north and west of Broadland than in the south and east. They are numerous in the valleys of the Bure (Horstead, Belaugh, Wroxham, Horning, Ranworth, South Walsham, Acle), the Ant (Irstead, Catfield, Sutton) and in the upper reaches of the Yare (Surlingham, Buckenham, Hassingham). There is a rather thinner scatter around the fringes of the Halvergate Marshes (Reedham, Runham, Limpenhoe, Burgh Castle, Burgh St Peter, Oulton, Haddiscoe Thorpe, Wickhampton) and in the valley of the Chet (Chedgrave, Heckingham), with a few in the valley of the Thurne (Potter Heigham, Ludham, Bastwick). In contrast, churches standing beside river or floodplain are much rarer in the valleys of the lower Yare or Waveney, in Lothingland or on Flegg. Here, most churches serving parishes extending down to the fens or marshes stand more than 200 metres, and sometimes more than a kilometre, away from their edge.

Villages with 'low-lying' churches include most of the 'hams' and other places of early importance noted earlier and it is possible that such locations reflect a desire to place significant settlements close to navigable rivers. But for the most part the pattern is probably associated with a desire to access fresh water with minimal effort. 'Low-lying' churches are found in areas where water could be easily accessed on the floodplain margins from shallow wells sunk in the Crag,

---

71 Davison, *Evolution of settlement*, pp. 18, 38–9.
72 NHER 14469. F. Blomefield and C. Parkin, *An essay towards a topographical history of the county of Norfolk*, 11 vols (London, 1810), vol. 11, pp. 140–1.

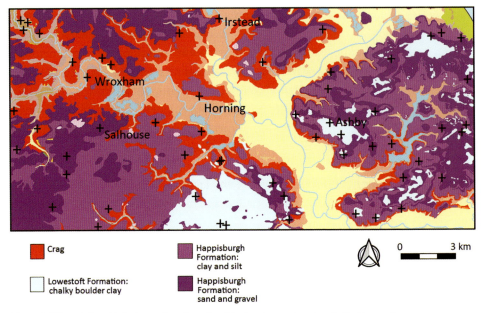

Figure 2.9 The relationship between the sites of parish churches and geology in the Bure valley.

but where on the adjacent slopes it was out of reach because the Crag lies thicker. Early settlements were only established on the higher ground, away from rivers, where some kind of perched water table existed: where sands and gravels of the Happisburgh Formation lay thinly over clays, usually near the margins of the former, or on the chalky tills of the Lowestoft Formation, where one was more widely available. In such circumstances churches often occupy upland sites even if, as is usually the case, the Crag aquifer could have been exploited from a low-lying one (Figure 2.9). The settlements in which they were erected would here have been more centrally positioned in relation to their arable fields. Much of the land close to those on low-lying sites, in contrast, would have comprised marsh and fen. As so often, the key and characteristic features of a local landscape are shaped by the hidden hand of geology.

The drift of farms to the margins of common land, which produced the basic framework of rural settlement across most of East Anglia, has never been adequately explained. As the landscape began to fill up with small peasant farms, a location beside a common, close to the grazing and other resources that it offered, evidently made more sense than it had done earlier in the Saxon period, when settlements were fewer and probably occupied by extended kin groups. Inhabitants had perhaps then been able to share the daily tasks of farming, including management and supervision of livestock and their movement to and from common pastures, in a way that the individual peasant living at the time of the Norman Conquest, occupying his own holding, could not. This may have made it more important to place the farmstead in convenient proximity to the surviving remnants of the common 'waste'. Whatever the explanation, most of the new farms were sited according to the same hydrological rules as the earlier sites. They thus spread along the lower margins of the Crag, often in loose scatters around the edges of the common fens or marshes but sometimes, in the valley of the Bure especially, remaining close to the church, leading to the formation of relatively compact waterside villages such as Belaugh or Coltishall. On the higher ground in the northern and central parts of Broadland, on the deposits of the Happisburgh Formation, the spreading farms and cottages tended to hug the margins of pockets of gravel overlying clays and silts, although also extending onto areas where the latter alone were exposed and water supplies were less dependable, creating sprawling, loosely nucleated villages such as Filby or Ormesby. On the boulder clays to the south, largely unconstrained by any restrictions on access to water, farms dispersed to a greater extent, creating loose girdles around greens or heaths, or lining roads leading to them. In some places, expanding settlements were drawn to aquifers different from those which the original Saxon settlements, marked by churches, had exploited. Stokesby church, for example, stands quite alone on a patch of boulder clay, at a height of 25 metres above sea level; the village lies 400 metres away, clustered around a common, on an outcrop of Crag beside the river Bure.

Rising population and the spread of farms across the landscape, continuing through the eleventh, twelfth and thirteenth centuries, were accompanied by the development of 'open fields': areas of arable in which the lands of different farms lay intermingled as unhedged strips.[73] The configuration of parish boundaries on the fertile soils in the north and centre of Broadland, often apparently picking their way around groups of former strips, suggest that open fields had reached the margins of some townships by the time that parochial bounds were fixed, probably in the twelfth century. Broadland's open fields differed in a number of important respects from the more familiar examples found in the Midlands and, to an extent, in the western parts of East Anglia. In these latter areas settlement generally took the form of nucleated villages and farms were comparatively large because the practice of primogeniture ensured that they passed intact from generation to generation, and lords and communities strove to limit an active market in land. The arable strips were extensively intermingled, for the lands of each farm were scattered relatively evenly across the territory of each township. Farming, including the sequence of cropping, was organised on highly communal lines and each year a half or a third of the arable, lying in a continuous block, lay 'fallow' or uncropped, and was grazed in common by the village livestock, the dung from which replaced

---

[73] B.M.S. Campbell, 'Population change and the genesis of commonfields on a Norfolk manor', *Economic History Review*, 33 (1980), pp. 174–92.

the nutrients depleted by repeated cropping.[74] Little of this pertained in Broadland, for a complex mixture of social and environmental reasons. Here, rather than being widely scattered and extensively intermingled, the strips of each holding were usually fairly clustered, in the vicinity of the farmhouse itself. Farming was much less controlled by community regulation and, on the fertile loams especially, was organised on remarkably 'modern' lines. Year-long fallows were often done away with altogether and common grazing limited to the weeds and residues left after the harvest. Fertility was maintained by hand-spreading manure from livestock mainly kept in farmyards and fed on leguminous fodder crops. This was intensive, individualised farming, which also involved repeated cultivations and careful weeding. The high yields per acre thus produced were desperately needed in this crowded landscape: partible inheritance had fragmented holdings to such an extent that most, by the thirteenth century, covered less than six acres.[75]

Of course, not all of the medieval landscape on the higher ground comprised arable land. There were areas of enclosed, coppiced woodland that in the north of Broadland were, as we have seen, often located towards the edge of the wetlands, but which in the south were usually on higher ground, on the heavy, poorly draining soils of the boulder-clay plateau. Such woodland was, and is, particularly extensive around the watershed between the Yare and Waveney, in the area between Kirby Cane and Hales.[76] There were also numerous areas of common land – 'greens' – of various sizes on the clays, of which the magnificent Hales Green is the largest surviving example, and heaths on the glacial sands and gravels. These provided grazing but also, in the case of the heaths especially, fuel in the form of gorse and heather. Much of this land had been tree-covered – had comprised grazed woodland – in the Saxon period. But as trees were felled, died of old age or were barked by livestock, regeneration was prevented by the intensity of grazing. The name of Mousehold Heath, which extended across some 6,000 acres (*c.*2,430 hectares) from Norwich to the edge of Ranworth, incorporates the Old English word *holt*, 'wood'. As late as the thirteenth century it still carried significant tracts of woodland but by the sixteenth century was largely treeless.[77]

From the late Middle Ages the size of farms gradually increased in Broadland, although even in the nineteenth century relatively small agricultural holdings continued to characterise this area of fertile soils, alongside larger units of

---

74 D. Hall, *Medieval fields* (Princes Risborough, 1982). D. Hall, *The open fields of Northamptonshire* (Northampton, 1995). T. Williamson, R. Liddiard and T. Partida, *Champion. The making and unmaking of the English midland landscape* (Liverpool, 2013).

75 B.M.S. Campbell, 'Agricultural progress in medieval England: some evidence from eastern Norfolk', *Economic History Review*, 36 (1983), pp. 26–46.

76 G. Barnes and T. Williamson, *Rethinking ancient woodland: the archaeology and history of woods in Norfolk* (Hatfield, 2015), pp. 38–48.

77 O. Rackham, *The history of the countryside* (London, 1986), pp. 299–303.

production. As late as 1851 over 40 per cent of holdings in the area covered less than 50 acres (20 hectares).[78] Away from the marshes and the fens, moreover, soils and climate ensured the continued dominance of arable farming and, except where tracts of common existed, most of the land remained under the plough. On the higher, heavier land on the chalky boulder clay lying to either side of the Waveney valley, it is true, significant areas were laid to pasture and used for cattle farming from the fifteenth century, but this process was reversed in the decades around 1800, a time when parliamentary acts also saw the enclosure and cultivation of most of the upland commons, including the great Mousehold Heath.[79] Extensive areas of open heather and grassland were replaced by regular landscapes of straight-sided arable fields defined by neat hawthorn hedges. Enclosure acts also removed many areas of open field, which had survived better in Broadland than in the neighbouring areas of East Anglia. But in many parishes, especially on the heavier soils of the south, open arable had already been significantly reduced in extent, or even completely extinguished, through gradual, 'piecemeal' enclosure. Individuals gradually bought and sold land until they possessed a number of contiguous strips, which they could then fence or hedge and remove from the routines of communal cultivation; or large landowners gradually bought up the strips of small freeholders, enclosing in a similar manner as they did so. Piecemeal enclosure, because it involved the gradual hedging or fencing along the margins of groups of strips, tended to preserve in simplified form the essential layout of the old open landscape. Open-field plough strips – and thus the hedged boundaries created in this manner – were seldom dead straight. They were usually slightly curving or sinuous in plan, sometimes taking the form of a shallow 'reversed S', caused by the way that the ploughman moved to the left with his team as he approached the headland at the end of the strip in order to avoid too tight a turning circle.[80] In addition, because open-field strips running end to end seldom came to be enclosed in line by this method, field patterns produced by piecemeal enclosure often exhibit numerous small 'kinks', tiny dog-legs, where the boundary of one field runs not to the corner of the next field but to a point some way along the boundary line, a strip or two strips' distance away (Figure 2.10).

On the boulder-clay soils in the south of Broadland these sinuous patterns came to dominate the landscape, except where islands of rectilinear fields were created by the parliamentary enclosure of areas of common land. But, across much

---

78 Wade Martins and Williamson, *Roots of change*, p. 77.
79 Ibid., pp. 47–52. M. Turner, 'Parliamentary enclosure', in T. Ashwin and A. Davison (eds), *An historical atlas of Norfolk*, 3rd edn (Chichester, 2005), pp. 130–2. K.P. Bacon, 'Landholding and enclosure in the hundreds of East Flegg, West Flegg and Happing in Norfolk, 1695 to 1832', PhD thesis (University of East Anglia, 2003), pp. 208–9, 233–40.
80 S.R. Eyre, 'The curving ploughland strip and its historical implications', *Agricultural History Review*, 3 (1955), pp. 80–94. T. Williamson, 'Understanding enclosure', *Landscapes*, 1 (2000), pp. 56–79.

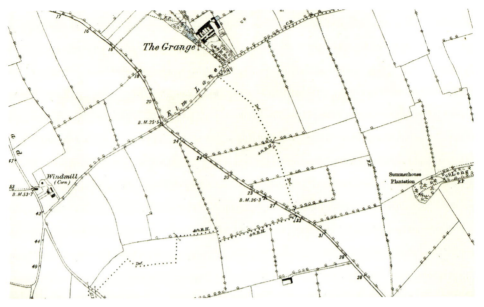

Figure 2.10 The field pattern on the boundary between Rollesby and Repps-with-Bastwick in 1883. Note the complex mixture of ruler-straight boundaries, dating to the later eighteenth and nineteenth centuries, and gently curving ones, sometimes featuring small kinks, created by the 'piecemeal' enclosure of open fields.

of the area, by the middle of the nineteenth century ruler-straight and sinuous boundaries were intimately intermixed, in part because the process of enclosure, begun 'piecemeal', was completed by parliamentary act and in part because the boundary patterns created by the former process were often tidied and rationalised by owners over subsequent decades (Figure 2.10). Such subtle variations, clear on late-nineteenth-century maps, are no longer so evident because of a subsequent phase of large-scale hedge removal and field amalgamation that has ensured that, in many places, especially on the loamy soils in the centre and north of Broadland, the landscape bordering the marshes and fens now comprises huge arable fields with few trees or hedges. Already, in the 1930s, Mosby was able to describe how there was a tendency in the area 'to enlarge the fields by removing the intervening hedge. Where this has been done the farmers, particularly those who use a tractor plough, have reduced their labour costs.'[81] But the rate of removal increased markedly in the post-war period, and especially in the 1960s and 1970s, before slowing in the last decades of the twentieth century.[82]

The principal changes in settlement morphology in the post-medieval period were the consequence of parliamentary enclosure, which tended to convert loose girdles of farms and cottages around the larger commons into a scatter of isolated

---

81 J.E. Mosby, *The land of Britain: Norfolk* (London, 1938), pp. 203–4.
82 W. Baird and J. Tarrant, *Hedgerow destruction in Norfolk, 1946–1970* (Norwich, 1970). G. Barnes and T. Williamson, *Hedgerow history: ecology, history and landscape character* (Macclesfield, 2006), pp. 21–3.

dwellings surrounded by fields, as, for example, when the great tract of common lying between Moulton, Hassingham and Beighton was enclosed. But the new allotments were often built on and, where commons were small, they might within a few decades become largely or even entirely filled with houses, as in the cases of Upton Green or Barton Common. Only at a few places, most notably Stokesby and Martham, do houses still hug the margins of surviving commons, with the church standing at a distance. The buildings making up Broadland villages are mainly of post-medieval date, though a few of the outlying 'halls' are older. Although this was a wealthy area in the Middle Ages, farms were small and wealth too thinly spread to generate substantial timber-framed houses worth preserving into later times. Most villages were rebuilt wholesale through the seventeenth, eighteenth and nineteenth centuries. Red brick and pantiles abound, with some thatch, and shaped 'Dutch' gables ornament the larger residences (see p. 99).

Methodist and especially Primitive Methodist chapels of early-nineteenth-century date feature prominently in many villages, with a few examples more remotely located, such as the Wesleyan chapel of 1814 that stands alone in the huge fields in the far north-western corner of Wickhampton parish.[83] Their prominence reflects the continuing importance of small freehold farmers in the area, able and willing to donate the land on which to erect them. Conversely, there are comparatively few large mansions, great parks or other signs of landed wealth. This is especially true on the fertile soils in the north of the area, where high land values precluded the possibility of amassing a really extensive property. In some parishes, such as Wickhampton or Tunstall, there were no resident gentry in the eighteenth and nineteenth century; in most they were present but owned only a proportion of the land and resided in diminutive mansions set in ornamental grounds covering less than 15, and usually less than 10, hectares. Broadland's landscape was not, for the most part, shaped by great landed estates.

Yet we must not exaggerate the extent of this. Wealthy landowners did exist in the area and, over time, exercised increasing control over the wilder parts of the wetlands, managing them for shooting and private recreation. Moreover, there were, and still are, some large estates, although, with the exception of that at Woodbastwick – its mansion demolished in 1971 – their halls and parks lay back from the marshes and rivers. The largest, by the nineteenth century, was the Beauchamp-Proctors' Langley estate, covering over 6,700 acres (2,700 hectares), which was focused on the eighteenth-century mansion of Langley Hall in its park landscaped by Capability Brown.[84] The estate was broken up in the 1920s, although the hall remains, now used as a school. Honing Hall and Beeston Hall, in contrast, still survive in private

---

83   C. Stell, *Nonconformist chapels and meeting-houses in eastern England* (London, 2002), p. 241.
84   M. Fenwick, 'Langley', in S. Bate (ed.), *Capability Brown in Norfolk* (Aylsham, 2016), pp. 65–100.

ownership, standing in parks designed in the eighteenth century by Humphry Repton and Nathaniel Richmond respectively.[85] So too, in the south of Broadland, does Somerleyton Hall, lavishly rebuilt in the 1840s for the great entrepreneur Sir Morton Peto and provided with new gardens designed by William Andrews Nesfield and a picturesque 'model' village on the edge of its large park.[86]

Raveningham Hall, set in its fine eighteenth-century park, also survives, but Burlingham Hall was finally demolished in 1952, after being used as a school, following a period of dereliction. Its 3,000-acre (*c*.1,200-hectare) estate had been bought by Norfolk County Council in 1919 and divided up into smallholdings, concentrating on vegetable- and fruit-growing, as part of a government scheme to revitalise the rural economy and resettle veterans of the First World War.[87] This was one aspect of a more general change. In the agricultural depression of the late nineteenth and early twentieth century many small farms in Broadland responded to low cereal prices by diversifying into horticulture, market gardening and fruit-growing, especially in the area around Hickling, Stalham and Martham. But in the middle decades of the twentieth century such activities declined and average farm size increased. Away from the fens and marshes the countryside is now intensively arable, and for the most part managed in large, efficient holdings.

To an extent – although *only* to an extent – the landscape of the 'uplands' thus possesses its own distinctive character, born principally of the long interaction of local societies with the environment. That character impinges on the experience of visitors in a number of ways – most strongly, perhaps, through the large numbers, and unusual locations, of parish churches. But, for many, it is the architectural heritage that makes the greatest impression, a subject addressed in the following sections.

The churches of Broadland
by Ian Hinton

> Bor, ha' yew noticed yew hin't far t'saarch
> in Norfick, if yew wanter see a chaarch?
> Jus yew go up ena little hill
> an yew'll see savrel chaarches, that yew will.
> ('Norfolk Churches' – John Kett, 1927–2020)

85　P. Dallas, R. Last and T. Williamson, *Norfolk gardens and designed landscapes* (Oxford, 2013), pp. 77–8, 217–18.
86　T. Williamson, I. Ringwood, and S. Spooner, *Lost country houses of Norfolk: history, archaeology and myth* (Woodbridge, 2015), pp. 116–17.
87　Q. Bone, 'Legislation to revive small farming in England 1887–1914', *Agricultural History*, 49 (1975), pp. 653–61. S. Wade Martins and T. Williamson, *The countryside of East Anglia: changing landscapes, 1870–1950* (Woodbridge, 2008), pp. 55–60. C.W. Rowell, 'County council smallholdings, 1908–1958', *Agriculture*, 60 (1959), pp. 109–14.

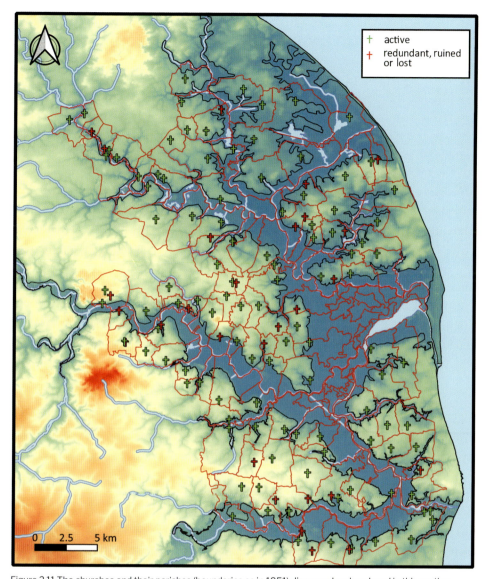

Figure 2.11 The churches and their parishes (boundaries as in 1851) discussed and analysed in this section.

Broadland can almost certainly boast the highest density of rural parish churches in the country. The Broads National Park and its adjacent parishes have an area of approximately 600 square kilometres and by the thirteenth century contained 136 known churches – one church for every 4.5 square kilometres. This compares with a density of one for every 8.7 square kilometres in Norfolk as a whole and one per 7.5 square kilometres in Suffolk.[88] Elsewhere the figures can be much lower, with

---

88   N. Pevsner and E. Radcliffe, *The buildings of England: Suffolk* (London, 1991).

one per 20 square kilometres in Cornwall[89] and a mere one for every 86 square kilometres in Cumbria.[90] One hundred of the medieval churches in the sample examined for this chapter (see Figure 2.11) are still in use, but no fewer than 36 (27 per cent) are redundant, ruined or lost.[91]

Fifty-six of these churches are listed in the Domesday survey of 1086, although two of them only in passing.[92] The Domesday survey was essentially a record of assets as taxable resources, so is not a complete list. Eleven churches that it fails to mention are known to have existed at this date because they are referred to in pre-Conquest wills or charters.[93] As described earlier, churches in Broadland, as elsewhere in East Anglia, seem generally to mark the sites of Middle and Late Saxon settlements, perhaps implying the existence of a burial ground, if not of an actual church, from an early date. It has been suggested that, by the time of the Norman Conquest, there may have been as many churches in the county of Norfolk, and by extension in Broadland, as there are today.[94] Yet of the architectural features generally accepted as indicating a pre-Conquest date, none are found in Broadland churches, the overwhelming majority of which must, at the time of the Norman Conquest, have been timber structures.[95]

Almost one-third of Broadland churches are now largely isolated, many with only the 'Big House' or an individual farm for company. Around 20 stand entirely by themselves, such as that at Braydeston, whose closest neighbour is 600 metres away and is another church – St Peter in the neighbouring parish of Blofield. There is no evidence to support the common belief that isolated churches were the result of the Black Death destroying villages beside them in the fourteenth century. Churches are isolated because as settlement moved, or expanded elsewhere, in the course of the Middle Ages, in the manner already described, community investment in the building and the presence of a burial ground kept them fixed in position.

Parish churches were originally built by landowners. This process started at the top, with the Saxon kings, ealdormen and senior thegns building churches on their estates – the minster churches referred to earlier – and, over time, lower-order thegns and even families of aspiring freemen doing the same on their own smaller

---

89   N. Pevsner and E. Radcliffe, *The buildings of England: Cornwall* (London, 2002).
90   N. Pevsner, *The buildings of England: Cumberland and Westmorland* (London, 1997).
91   N. Batcock, *The ruined and disused churches of Norfolk*, East Anglian Archaeology 51 (Dereham, 1991).
92   D. Butcher, *Norfolk and Suffolk churches: the Domesday record* (Oulton, 2019), pp. 44–56. A. Powell-Smith (ed.), 'Open Domesday'. https://opendomesday.org (accessed August 2022).
93   C. Hart, *The early charters of eastern England* (Leicester, 1966), pp. 83, 92. W. Page, 'Houses of Benedictine monks: the abbey of St Benet of Holm', in W. Page (ed.), *A history of the county of Norfolk*, vol. 2 (London, 1906), pp. 330–6. R. Hoggett, 'Changing beliefs: an archaeology of the East Anglian conversion', PhD thesis (University of East Anglia, 2007), p. 130.
94   S. Cotton, 'Domesday revisited – where are the 11th-century churches?', *Norfolk Archaeological Research Group News*, 21 (1980), pp. 11–17.
95   H.M. and J. Taylor, *Anglo-Saxon architecture* (Cambridge, 1980).

properties.[96] Building a church was an act of piety but also an assertion of status, for possessing one was a mark of lordship, a necessary precondition for recognition as a thegn. Landowners endowed churches with glebe land and retained important rights over them, including that of nominating the priest. Broadland, with its generally good soils, was able to support a multitude of small estates, many of whose owners evidently established and endowed churches in the period leading up to, and perhaps continuing for a time after, the Norman Conquest. Indeed, there are 12 cases where individual townships contained more than one parish church – in the case of Ormesby as many as four, and at South Walsham, Gillingham, Kirby Bedon and Rockland two churches stand in the same, or adjacent, churchyards.[97] These curious phenomena can be found elsewhere in East Anglia, but are particularly prominent here.

This profusion of early churches, steadily rebuilt in stone in the century or so following the Conquest, bequeathed a problem of over-endowment to later generations that might be exacerbated by changing economic or demographic circumstances: Broadland has more than its fair share of lost and ruined churches (Figure 2.12). The parish of Carleton St Peter, for example, now has around 15 households, compared with 38 recorded at the time of Domesday. In 1603, despite attendance being compulsory, the four churches in Ormesby, together with Scratby church, had only 220 communicants; as early as 1205, there was only one priest in Ormesby, three of the churches being served by curates.[98] It is not surprising, then, that 36 medieval churches have been lost from the landscape. Some were associated with small townships that have themselves ceased to exist. Domesday records churches at *Ierpestuna* and *Thurketliarte* in Clavering Hundred and *Let(h) a* in Blofield Hundred, all places that seem to have disappeared before 1200.[99] Two small settlements in which churches are also recorded – Windle and Winston, both now within the parish of Gillingham – disappeared in around 1440, while that recorded at Worlingham Parva, a tiny parish in the Waveney valley comprising no more than 15 fields, was presumably lost when the living was consolidated with Worlingham Magna in 1492; it was rediscovered by excavation in 1980.[100] Holverston parish was united with Rockland St Mary in 1358 because of falling

---

96 B.M.S. Campbell, 'Medieval land use and values', in T. Ashwin and A. Davison (eds), *An historical atlas of Norfolk*, 3rd edn (Chichester, 2005), pp. 48–9. B.M.S. Campbell, 'The complexity of manorial structure in medieval Norfolk: a case study', *Norfolk Archaeology*, 39 (1986), pp. 225–61.

97 N. Groves, 'Two sisters: two churches', in A. Longcroft and R. Joby (eds), *East Anglian studies: essays presented to J.C. Barringer on his retirement* (Norwich, 1995), pp. 108–15. P. Warner, 'Shared churchyards, freemen church-builders and the development of parishes in eleventh-century East Anglia', *Landscape History*, 8 (1986), pp. 39–52.

98 A. Dyer and D. Palliser (eds), *The diocesan population returns for 1563 and 1603* (Oxford, 2005), p. 449.

99 Batcock, *Ruined and disused churches*, p. 55.

100 B. Tooley and I. Hinton, *Barnby and North Cove: a history of two villages* (Barnby, 2002), p. 40. Blomefield and Parkin, *Topographical history*, vol. 11, p. 238.

Figure 2.12 St Mary's, East Somerton, one of many lost or ruined churches in Broadland.

population.[101] The church was still in use in the mid-sixteenth century, but had been demolished by 1700 and today Holverston Hall stands alone.[102] There were 5 other parish churches within 1.5 kilometres of the site of Holverston church and 20 within 3.5 kilometres – only a brisk 30-minute walk away.

Losses continued into the post-medieval period, especially where there were multiple churches in a village. Problems of maintenance often ensured that one was eventually abandoned and its fabric used to help repair the other. This was particularly likely to happen where, as was often the case, the tithes and the right to appoint the priest had been donated by a medieval landowner to a monastic house, in part so that the monks would in return say masses to speed the donor's passage through purgatory. Following the Dissolution the abolished institutions were no longer in a position to maintain the building, leading, for example, to the loss of St Mary at Kirby Bedon and St Edmund at West Caister. Problems of over-provision were exacerbated by the appearance of rival religious groups with their own places of worship. The Toleration Act of 1689 removed the obligation to attend a Church of England service and allowed meetings to be held by most nonconformist groups, including the Baptists, Congregationalists and Presbyterians. This, followed by the rise of Methodism in the eighteenth century and, in particular, the appearance of the Primitive Methodists in the nineteenth, might reduce the size of church congregations, in many instances dividing rural populations by social status. In general terms, church redundancies in Broadland have been fairly evenly spread over the centuries, with 16 in the four centuries up to 1600, another 12 in the seventeenth and eighteenth centuries and 10 in the nineteenth and twentieth.[103] Six of the latter were declared redundant in the second half of the twentieth century, including Buckenham St Nicholas, Moulton St Mary and Hales St Margaret.

The small stone churches erected in the wake of the Norman Conquest were almost all subsequently extended and altered because of growing demands and changing liturgical requirements.[104] Without excavation, it is often difficult to see evidence of the principal changes, because it is obscured by still later alterations, or by the repointing or refacing of walls, but the broad pattern of development is clear. Most churches initially had short chancels, often with apsidal ends, as seen in the best surviving example of a twelfth-century church in the area, at Hales. The majority, however, were lengthened and rebuilt in the thirteenth or fourteenth centuries in order to cater for the requirements of new ceremonial forms associated with the doctrine of Transubstantiation, codified at the Fourth Lateran Council of 1215. Clear

---

101 Blomefield and Parkin, *Topographical history*, vol. 5, p. 488. Batcock, *Ruined and disused churches*, pp. 158–9.
102 Batcock, *Ruined and disused churches*, p. 159.
103 Batcock, *Ruined and disused churches*, pp. 3, 50–5.
104 S. Heywood, 'Stone building in Romanesque East Anglia', in D. Bates and R. Liddiard (eds), *East Anglia and its North Sea world in the Middle Ages* (Norwich, 2013), pp. 230–56.

structural evidence for this change is rare in Broadland, present only in the case of Barnby and, on the western periphery of the area, Yelverton and Framingham Earl.

Medieval churches, as most readers will be aware, were ranged roughly east–west, but in England as a whole one in six churches has a chancel on a slightly different alignment from its nave, usually by only a few degrees, something that presumably dates to this period of rebuilding.[105] Twenty-one of the standing churches in Broadland exhibit this phenomenon (22 per cent). It was suggested by ecclesiologists in the nineteenth century that this was a form of religious symbolism – it represented the Crucifixion, with Christ's head leaning to the left – hence the term 'weeping chancels'. In reality, in only about half the cases does the chancel 'lean' to the left, the remainder being aligned the other way. Broadland is typical here, with 11 leaning to the left and 10 to the right. Lamas St Andrew, on the northern edge of the Broadland area, has the largest leftward variation of any of the 2,100 churches that were measured in a structured nationwide survey – a difference of 14 degrees.[106] Here, as in the majority of cases, the chancel is aligned more closely to the east than the nave, probably indicating the real reason for the difference – a desire to improve on an original, less accurate orientation. Interestingly, 'weeping chancels' were never mentioned by Guillaume de Durandus, who wrote extensively on liturgical matters at the end of the thirteenth century, in spite of the fact that he managed to find symbolism in the most mundane aspects of church buildings, such as window splays.[107]

A growing population during the twelfth and thirteenth centuries also had an effect on church buildings, necessitating an increase in the size of naves. Evidence for the eastward extension of naves can be clearly seen at Ashby St Mary, Carleton St Peter, Coltishall and South Burlingham. More usually, the nave was widened, something that also reflected the increasing importance of processions in services during the thirteenth and fourteenth centuries (this also led to a need for a place to store the processional banners when not in use, and Broadland has four of only 25 banner-stave lockers remaining in the whole country, at Catfield, Halvergate, Strumpshaw and Barnby, the latter still with its original fretwork door).[108] Aisles were added to 24 Broadland churches, around one in six. This is a low proportion by national standards – over half the churches in the remainder of Norfolk were provided with aisles. As population, or church attendance, fell in later years, some were demolished, possibly when expensive maintenance was required, as at Claxton,

---

105 I. Hinton, 'Aspects of the alignment and location of medieval rural churches', PhD thesis (University of East Anglia, 2012), pp. 37–41 (337 churches with differently aligned chancels of the 2096 churches surveyed – 16 per cent).
106 Hinton, 'Aspects of alignment', p. 37.
107 W. Durandus, *The symbolism of churches and church ornaments*, 1286, trans J. Neale and B. Webb (London, 1906).
108 F. Bond, *English church architecture*, vol. 1 (Oxford, 1913), p. 95.

Figure 2.13 St John the Baptist, Barnby, Suffolk: the smallest surviving parish church in Broadland.

Horning and Mautby. Extra width could also be achieved by rebuilding one of the nave walls further out but, while this avoided the construction of an internal arcade, it necessitated an almost complete rebuilding of the church, including replacing the entire roof, effectively taking the building out of use for an extended period of time. Not surprisingly, extensions of this kind are even rarer than the addition of aisles, with only six clear instances – at Beeston St Lawrence, Blundeston, Burlingham St Peter, Fritton St Edmund, Norton Subcourse and Wheatacre. The failure of most Broadland parishes to increase nave size almost certainly reflects, once again, early over-provision. In a landscape over-burdened with churches, local lords and congregations had neither the need nor the means to increase accommodation: the greater extent to which chancels were rebuilt may in part reflect the fact that these were the responsibility of church and incumbent, rather than of the parish. Indeed, Broadland churches are slightly smaller on average than those found in other parts of eastern England, with an average floor area of 229 square metres – some 10 per cent smaller than the 256 square metres average for the rest of Norfolk, for example.[109] There are some large churches, either urban, such as Beccles, or with probable origins as early minsters, such as Martham St Mary, which covers some 505 square metres. The smallest church is Barnby, with a ground area of 95 square metres (Figure 2.13) – less than one-fifth of Martham's size – but even this small building is the result of both eastward extension, as noted earlier, and westward,

---

109 Hinton, 'Aspects of alignment', Data Appendix.

Figure 2.14 St Edmund's, Fritton, Norfolk, one of over 30 surviving round-towered churches in Broadland.

as described below. Sixty-five of the 100 active churches have a ground area of less than 250 square metres, or half that of Martham.

The majority of churches originally had no bell tower, acquiring one only in the course of the twelfth, thirteenth or fourteenth centuries. When adding a tower, it was usual to build it as a free-standing structure and then extend the nave westwards to meet it when complete, as this allowed the church to continue in use during the building work, which might take more than a decade. The building techniques for flint walls changed in around 1300 from a regularly coursed style to a far more random method, making any such change made around this time relatively easy to identify. But frequently the only evidence for extension are the quoin stones embedded in the wall marking the original termination of the building or the infilled original opposed doorways in the north and south walls of the nave, for in all but one example of a westward nave extension in Broadland these were also moved, the exception being Toft Monks, where only the position of the south door was changed. It is difficult to see why the doorways needed to be relocated in this way, unless it was to maintain a respectful distance from the high end of the church, the chancel; the spatial relationship between the two mirrors that between the opposed entrances of the cross passage, and the parlour, in a medieval house (see p. 92). Obvious evidence of westward extension to embrace a new tower can be seen at Acle, Aldeby, Barnby, Belaugh, Braydeston, Buckenham, Carleton St Peter, Fritton St Edmund, Hoveton, Toft Monks and West Somerton. Only two churches in Broadland have central towers – so-called 'centrally planned' churches: Aldeby (a priory church: see p. 83) and Oulton St Michael, where the transepts have been demolished and the central tower partly rebuilt in brick. Gillingham St Mary appears to have a central tower, but close examination of the wall thicknesses shows that it originally formed the west end of the church, a structure of uncertain purpose having later been added to its western face.

Round-towered churches are particularly associated with Norfolk. Just over 70 per cent of the 186 examples in England are to be found in the county, with a further 30 in the adjacent parts of northern and eastern Suffolk (Figure 2.14).[110] Broadland lies at the heart of their national distribution, with 32 standing examples and a further 5 known among the lost churches – Burlingham St Peter, Great Hautbois, Kirby Bedon St Mary, Ormesby St Peter and Little Worlingham – making 37 in all, around a quarter of the total of medieval churches in the area. There has been much discussion over the years as to why round towers were built, and why mainly in East Anglia. The most outlandish antiquarian suggestions were that they were the exposed walls of wells revealed by land shrinkage, or the erosive effects of Noah's flood![111] It has also been suggested that they were built for defence against the Vikings, and that they were a specifically Saxon style, but it has been shown that they were still being erected as late as the thirteenth or fourteenth century, being clearly added to existing buildings that were then extended westwards to meet them, in the manner just described (as at Acle, Buckenham, Fritton St Edmund, Toft Monks or West Somerton). More plausibly, it has been argued that round towers were built because there were no local sources of the freestone required for the corners of square ones.[112] There are, however, numerous cases – both in Broadland and more widely – of perfectly serviceable corners to towers, naves and chancels being constructed using large flints, erratics or conglomerate, as at Surlingham, Kirby Bedon St Mary, Ashby St Peter and Barnby.[113] Some architectural historians have, in addition, noted the existence of similar round towers in parts of north Germany and Schleswig-Holstein, and have suggested their concentration in East Anglia reflects the trading and cultural links with these areas.[114] Perhaps a shortage of local freestone at a time of prolific construction encouraged emulation of a foreign style that became a local fashion that was sometimes, but by no means invariably, adopted by church builders: but the issue remains unresolved.

---

110 The Round Tower Churches Society, https://roundtowers.org.uk (accessed August 2022).
111 https://roundtowers.org.uk (accessed August 2022); W.J. Goode, *East Anglian round towers and their churches* (Kings Lynn, 1982); S. Hart, *The round tower churches of England* (Norwich, 2003), pp. 8–20.
112 Hart, *Round tower churches*, pp. 9–14.
113 Heywood, 'Stone building', p. 263.
114 S. Heywood, 'The round towered churches of East Anglia', in J. Blair (ed.), *Minsters and parish churches: the local church in transition, 960–1200* (Oxford, 1988), pp. 169–77.

Additions and alterations might be funded jointly, by congregations, or by the pious donations of individual benefactors, especially as the belief in purgatory increased in importance from the thirteenth century. Donors' names were added to the Roll of Benefactors read out in the church each Whit Sunday, occasioning prayers for their souls. Over a hundred such donations are known of in relation to churches in Broadland.[115] The largest focus was on the church tower, some for a new tower to be built and others for its 'embattlement', raising its height with an additional stage, or for the provision of new bells. Another common target for donations were new porches, which were frequently added to churches from the fifteenth century onwards. Many of the services of the church – baptism, confirmation, marriage, the churching of women after childbirth and funerals – began at the church door, so protection from the elements for the participants was a pragmatic solution to the challenges posed by the British climate. In Broadland 96 of the 100 active churches (96 per cent) have a porch and 15 of these have porches on both their north and south sides (15 per cent), broadly in line with the pattern for East Anglia as a whole.

The successive development of architectural styles made windows a particular object for donations, as a new window in a different style would have been a particularly noticeable feature. By the end of the twelfth century the pointed Gothic arch had been introduced, replacing the round-headed 'Romanesque' windows and doors of the Norman style. Initially, during the Early English period, the arches were tall and two-centred and windows comprised single narrow lancet openings, followed by two-light openings with Y-shaped tracery. The Decorated style that developed from this towards the end of the thirteenth century was characterised by larger windows with elaborate tracery, often consisting of flame shapes – hence the term 'flamboyant'. Other variations had regular reticulated shapes to the tracery and in some later cases the arches were ogee-shaped. In the decade or so before the Black Death of 1349 the Perpendicular style began to appear in some larger churches, so called because the window mullions ran right to the top of the windows, the extra load-bearing capability that this provided enabling thinner stonework and larger openings. Tall, thin mullions often required horizontal transoms for additional strength and, overall, the tracery was less complex than in the previous style. The added strength also allowed the arched tops of the windows to become flatter, using three- or four-centred arches. In general, there were short, perhaps 20-year, transitional intervals between each architectural phase, but the change from Decorated to Perpendicular in East Anglia seems to have been spread out over a longer period.

---

115 P. Cattermole and S. Cotton, 'Medieval parish church building in Norfolk', *Norfolk Archaeology*, 28 (1983), pp. 235–79.

Figure 2.15 The unusual stepped brick tower of St Mary the Virgin, Burgh St Peter, built in the 1790s.

The donations of generations of churchgoers are evident in the windows of some of the churches of Broadland. Buckenham St Nicholas is a good example, with Early English, Decorated and Perpendicular windows side by side, while Moulton St Mary has one grand three-light Perpendicular window in its south wall among the remaining much older, and smaller, Y-tracery versions. Postwick church has two three-light windows in the south wall of the nave, one a grand flamboyant Decorated-period example and the other late Perpendicular. Some churches had few later windows added, retaining some or all of their fenestration from the twelfth or thirteenth centuries: Ashby St Peter and Clippesby, for example, have lancet windows and South Burlingham Y-tracery examples.

Numerous minor alterations were made to Broadland churches in the course of the post-medieval period but, perhaps unsurprisingly, there was little substantial rebuilding. The principal exceptions were three chancels reconstructed in brick in the eighteenth and nineteenth centuries – at Repps, Surlingham and Thorpe next Haddiscoe – and the idiosyncratic stepped brick tower of Burgh St Peter, rebuilt by Samuel Boycott, patron of the living, in the 1790s (Figure 2.15).

In an area of low-lying, damp land where reeds and sedge are abundant, thatch was an obvious choice as a roofing material. The drawings of Norfolk churches made by John Berney Ladbrooke in the 1820s show that 55 examples in the Broadland portion of the county were then thatched, of which 9 had only a thatched nave and 8 only a thatched chancel.[116] The rest had coverings of local tile. By 2022, the total had fallen to 28, 8 of which were nave only, and with no separately thatched chancels. The majority of changes were to slate (14), with 7 now using peg tiles, 1 pantiles and 1 lead; 4 of the chancels are now without roofs. The development of the Victorian railway network allowed slate, with a lower maintenance requirement, to be brought to Broadland from the north and west of Britain, but at least 2 of the churches in the area used some slate imported from Norway – Kirby Bedon St Andrew and Runham. In the case of the former, three different types of slate were used.[117]

As noted earlier, Broadland has no local building stone other than flint and the erratics brought in by the various glaciations. The transport of freestone from Cambridgeshire, Lincolnshire and Northamptonshire, for use as quoins and in other applications where shaping was required, doubled the cost of the stone itself.[118] Proximity to the North Sea and the network of navigable rivers made it possible to bring it from French quarries, although the transportation costs were even higher, tripling that of stone from Caen.[119] To an extent the dominance of flint, together with the occasional survival of roofs of reed thatch, shapes the character of Broadland churches, but the former in particular is much more widely shared and local distinctiveness derives, above all, from the great density of churches and their often remote location, their small size and often humble character, and their frequent possession of round towers. It is, perhaps, worth noting that the most frequently visited of Broadland's churches, St Helen at Ranworth, with its soaring square tower, ample nave and chancel, and large Perpendicular windows, is a rather atypical beast.

The character of Broadland's churches arises in part from local materials; in part, perhaps, in the case of round towers, from the area's connections with continental Europe; but primarily from social and economic history. The early abundance of churches, arising from the dense population and numerous small estates of the later Saxon period, for the most part hampered extravagant expansion or rebuilding, even as demographic growth continued through the thirteenth and early fourteenth centuries. The large church congregations of the high medieval period then declined, initially as a consequence of the Black Death but continuing thereafter with changes in landholding and farming practices, compounded by the rise of alternatives to the established church and, latterly, a more general decline in organised religious observance. Retrenchment, abandonment and parochial amalgamation have dominated the later history of Broadland's churches. Around a

---

116 J.B. Ladbrooke, *Views of Norfolk churches*, 7 vols (Norwich, undated *c*.1832).
117 T. Holt-Wilson, 'Kirby Bedon slate roof', *Norfolk Historic Buildings Group Newsletter*, 46 (2022), p. 19.
118 B. Haward, *Master Mason Hawes of Occold, Suffolk and John Hore Master Carpenter of Diss* (Ipswich, 2000), p. 48.
119 L. Salzman, *Building in England down to 1540: a documentary history* (Oxford, 1992), p. 11.

quarter of the churches present in the twelfth century are now redundant, in ruins or have disappeared completely. Many of those that remain are remote from the communities they serve and face the dual threat of the rising maintenance costs associated with all ageing buildings that require specialist repairs and the declining income resulting from dwindling congregations. A significant number may, indeed, face a future reliant on charitable intervention.

The monastic foundations of Broadland
by Tim Pestell

Medieval monasteries make a significant impact on the visitor's experience of the Broadland landscape. The great fourteenth-century gatehouse of St Benet's Abbey, beside the Bure, with an eighteenth-century drainage mill built into it, has been an icon of Broadland since at least the early nineteenth century, when it became a favoured subject for artists of the Norwich School (Figure 2.16). The former 'holm',

Figure 2.16 Detail from Henry Bright's 'St Benet's Abbey on the Bure', c.1854.

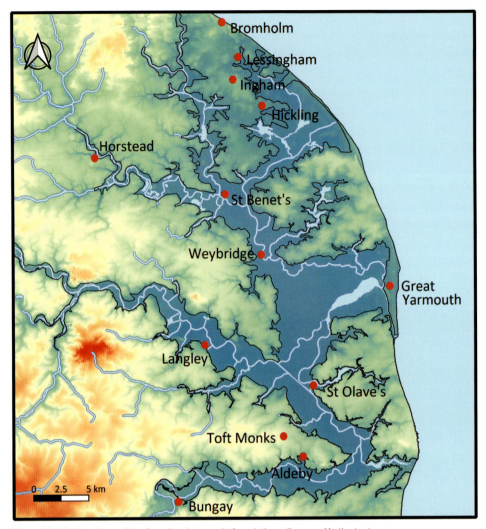

Figure 2.17 The locations of the Broadland monastic foundations discussed in the text.

or island, to its east contains the lower walls of the abbey church and extensive earthworks. The site of the Premonstratensian abbey of Langley, featuring the remains of the church and the great monastic barn, and that of the Augustinian priory of St Olave's, with its ruined refectory, complete with vaulted undercroft, are also much visited. Such survivals represent the tip of a much larger iceberg: indeed, it may occasion some surprise to consider just how many other communal religious institutions there once were in the area (Figure 2.17). This, of course, depends on where the edge of the Broads proper is defined and Norwich, with its cathedral priory, cell of St Leonard's, nunnery at Carrow and full complement of friaries and hospitals is better approached through the lens of urban monastic settlement. However, somewhere like Bromholm, at the northern extremity of

Broadland, is well placed to claim inclusion. By this slightly subjective reckoning, we have no fewer than 13 monastic houses in the area. Medieval monasteries are closely associated with other wetland areas of England, such as the Fenland of western East Anglia or the Somerset Levels. This chapter will examine the monastic houses of Broadland and consider the extent to which they were distinctive or particularly influenced by local topography and society.

The total of 13 monastic houses includes three of the more problematic 'alien priories', founded in Horstead, Lessingham and Toft Monks during William Rufus' reign, between 1087 and 1100.[120] These are perhaps better considered as land grants to continental monasteries, being a feature of the first wave of religious patronage after the Conquest; it was this foreign ownership that later led to them being considered 'alien' and dissolved in 1415.[121] A typical lack of infrastructural development separates them from other monastic foundations and they would seem to have been treated more typically as granges, directing their produce or income to the continental mother house. However, they often seem to have possessed financial endowments comparable to those of 'developed' monasteries. Thus Lessingham, a cell of Bec, had a value of £16 13s 9¼d in the 1291 *Taxatio Ecclesiastica* and its associated parish church a further £6 13s 4d, whereas nearby Hickling, founded in 1185 and with a fully developed monastic church, had its landholdings in 32 Norfolk parishes valued at only £15 12s 9d. Of our other aliens, Horstead, granted to the nuns of Caen Holy Trinity, was worth £25 2s 5½d, while Toft Monks, a cell of Préaux, was even wealthier, with an assessed value of £40 16s 10½d.[122]

Two other types of medieval religious community in Broadland that it could be argued require consideration are hospitals and colleges. Examples of the former were founded in Horning (belonging to St Benet's), West Somerton, Herringby, Great Hautbois, Gorleston and Beccles, while an important college was established at Mettingham. The charitable obligations of monasteries could lead to some overlap with hospitals, yet the diversity of religious expression in the latter institutions, often with communities that were not bound by a rule of life, means that it is hard to include them in a consideration of monasticism *per se*.[123] The same may be said of colleges, although again it could be a short step from one becoming monastic, as we shall see later in the case of Ingham.

Let us begin with our poster boy for Broadland monasteries, St Benet's Abbey, the area's only pre-Conquest monastery with a regular community living by the Benedictine Rule. Throughout the Anglo-Saxon period the English Church was

---

120 D. Knowles and R.N. Hadcock, *Medieval religious houses: England and Wales* (Harlow, 1971), pp. 88, 89 and 93.
121 C.W. New, *History of the alien priories in England* (Chicago, 1916).
122 T. Astle, S. Ayscough and J. Caley (eds), *Taxatio Ecclesiastica Angliae et Walliae Auctoritate P. Nicholai IV c.1291* (London, 1802).
123 See also C. Rawcliffe, *The hospitals of medieval Norwich* (Norwich, 1995).

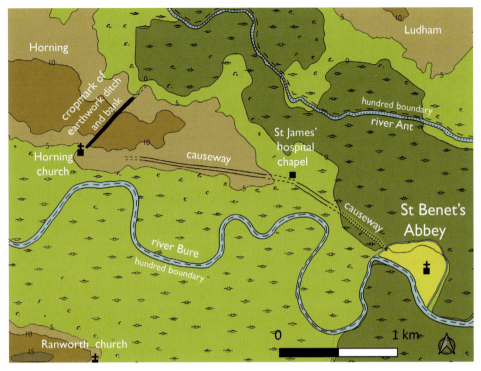

Figure 2.18 The location of St Benet's Abbey in relation to its surrounding landscape.

characterised by many communities of priests living together in institutions described as minsters, or in Latin *monasteria*, that could vary in size and in the type or strictness of their rules. It was, for instance, not uncommon for Anglo-Saxon priests to be married and for the lands attached to a church to be personally held and passed down to sons.[124] As noted earlier (see p. 50), many Anglo-Saxon minsters were placed in association with secular power centres, typically those of large estates. This is important because in many instances this pre-existing Anglo-Saxon ecclesiastical landscape came to shape post-Conquest Norman monasticism, with existing communities being refounded to live according to 'regularised' monastic rules.

Such regularisation may have occurred in the case of St Benet's Abbey. Here, the eleventh-century monastery was positioned on its small island 'holm' at the end of a promontory, extending into the low-lying marsh between the rivers Ant and Bure (Figure 2.18). Its location might be interpreted as the idealised arrangement of a monastery, sitting on a marshland island in splendid isolation, its monks able to live out a contemplative life free from the concerns of the secular world. Such tropes of wild isolation, expressed most powerfully in Felix's *Life*

---

124 Blair, *Church in Anglo-Saxon society*, pp. 354 and 361–3.

of St Guthlac, written *c*.720–49, were of course the voice of ecclesiastics and the world view they themselves wanted to project.[125] Yet it fails to explain why this particular holm or island was chosen. The answer seems to be suggested by wider archaeological evidence, as aerial photographs show that the St Benet's peninsula was once cut off from the upland by a massive linear earthwork.[126] While undated, its presence emphasises that the wider parish's name of Horning – meaning 'a horn-shaped piece of land' – was a reference to this peninsula, and that this once held a strategic importance that justified the investment required to build such a defensive structure.[127] It has close parallels with various early medieval ditches and banks elsewhere, but, most intriguingly, with the arrangement at Horningsea in Cambridgeshire.[128] Here, another peninsula jutting out into a fen was defended by a ditch and bank, behind which stood Horningsea church, described by the *Liber Eliensis*, an Ely Abbey cartulary chronicle written between 1169 and 1174, as 'a minster of royal standing'.[129] Not only are the place-names and topography similar; equally striking is the location of a church at one end of the ditch-line. At Horningsea, the church of Fen Ditton stands at the west end of the Fleam Dyke, while it is Horning church that sits at the southern end of *its* earthwork. Together, these hints suggest that King Cnut, intimately involved in the Benedictine foundation of St Benet's, may have been using royal estate land where an earlier Anglo-Saxon religious community once existed. A final suggestion of this being part of an earlier, larger, block of land comes from wider parish boundaries that form a straight line within Tunstead Hundred, deflected only at the centre by Beeston St Lawrence. The land to the north was possibly attached to another early estate based on North Walsham.[130]

St Benet's foundation created a focus for pious donations of land and by the time of Domesday Book the monastery's possessions were extensive, although fundamentally local and almost exclusively within Broadland – unlike those of Bury St Edmunds, to which half of St Benet's monks were apparently sent when

---

125 B. Colgrave (ed.), *Felix's life of Saint Guthlac* (Cambridge, 1956).
126 Rose, 'Linear earthwork at Horning', pp. 35–9.
127 E. Ekwall, *The concise Oxford dictionary of English place-names*, 4th edn (Oxford, 1960), p. 251.
128 For the ditch and bank see Royal Commission on Historical Monuments (England), *An inventory of historical monuments in the county of Cambridgeshire, volume 2: north-east Cambridgeshire* (London, 1972), pp. 144–7. For work on the ditches more generally T. Malim *et al.*, 'New evidence on the Cambridgeshire dykes and Worsted Street Roman road', *Proceedings of the Cambridge Antiquarian Society*, 85 (1997), pp. 27–122.
129 J. Fairweather (ed.), *Liber Eliensis. A history of the Isle of Ely* (Woodbridge, 2005), p. 128.
130 A discussion of this estate can be found in K. Wade, 'A model for Anglo-Saxon settlement expansion in the Witton area', in A.J. Lawson, *The archaeology of Witton near North Walsham*, East Anglian Archaeology 18 (Dereham, 1983), pp. 77–8. See also K. Penn, 'The early church in Norfolk: some aspects', in S. Margeson, B. Ayers and S. Heywood (eds), *A festival of Norfolk archaeology* (Norwich, 1996), pp. 40–6, at p. 45. T. Pestell, *Landscapes of monastic foundation: the establishment of religious houses in East Anglia c.650–1200* (Woodbridge, 2004), pp. 142–3. Given the probable estate centre and minster at nearby Happisburgh, there is clearly much of this early landscape still left to resolve.

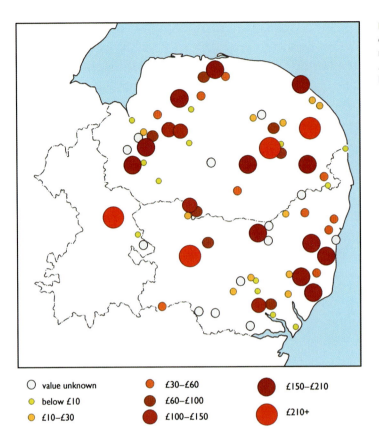

Figure 2.19 The distribution of monasteries in East Anglia in 1291, weighted by income.

Bury was regularised as a Benedictine community.[131] By 1086 Bury was already well into its meteoric rise to become one of the principal abbeys of medieval England, its holdings extending far from its west Suffolk home as the fame of its patron saint grew. Similarly, the other major pre-Conquest Benedictine monasteries in eastern England show more widespread geographical landholdings, principally put together in the tenth century by the aggressive acquisitions of Bishops Æthelwold and Oswald. In comparison to Ely, Peterborough, Crowland, Thorney and Ramsey, St Benet's was always a smaller, poorer, cousin, but within the context of Broadland it was the major player. At one level this speaks of the wider political capital of the Fenland monastic houses during the tenth-century Benedictine Reformation; at another it displays the enthusiasm with which the later, eleventh-century, foundation of St Benet's was greeted in east Norfolk.

We can view this patronage in another way, by considering the locations and the values of those monasteries that had been founded by 1291, again using the *Taxatio*

---

[131] T. Licence, 'The origins of the monastic communities of St Benedict at Holme and Bury St Edmunds', *Revue Bénédictine*, 116 (2007), pp. 42–61.

Ecclesiastica (Figure 2.19). Firstly, East Anglian monasteries are clustered to either side of the central watershed that snakes up through the centre of the region. But whereas in Norfolk they are present to east and west in roughly equal numbers, in Suffolk there was a contrast between the east, where there was a significant density of houses, and the west, dominated by the centrally placed Bury St Edmunds, the presence of which evidently retarded the foundation of other monasteries. Secondly, within Broadland itself St Benet's was clearly the pre-eminent house: the only foundations of comparable wealth, such as Norwich Cathedral Priory and Wymondham Abbey (another Benedictine monastery apparently based upon an earlier Anglo-Saxon minster), lay a little outside the area.[132] Within Broadland only the northern outlier of Bromholm was at all comparable in wealth, a situation that had much to do with its destination as a pilgrimage site from the thirteenth century. Most exceptional in Broadland is the relative wealth of Langley Abbey, a Premonstratensian house founded in 1195 and barely a century later valued at £178 5s ¾d, indicating an unusually rich endowment relative to its date of foundation.[133]

As Figure 2.19 clearly shows, within East Anglia as a whole monastic foundations seem to cluster in particular areas, rather than to be evenly spaced across the landscape, a situation that suggests certain localities were considered particularly numinous or otherwise suitable for placing a monastery. Nowhere is this more evident than in the Nar Valley of west Norfolk, where no fewer than five monasteries lay within four miles (*c.*6.5 kilometres) of each other, strung around the marshy edges of this eastern extremity of the Fens. Was the favouring of this landscape for monastic settlement solely a result of its 'marshiness'? Or were other factors at play?

Perhaps the most important element in establishing a new monastery was the role of its founder or founders. Their desires helped to determine which monastic order was chosen, with preferences often coming and going in wider waves of fashion. More importantly, this initial benefaction was usually fundamental in determining the eventual size of the overall endowment, which was characteristically made up of land but often (for the Augustinians especially) included the ownership of churches, creating the income that would determine the future monastery's wealth and success. The location of the initial endowment was also typically related to that of the founder's own landholdings, from which it was taken, and thus where the founder and nascent community could agree that the house should be sited.

Given the need for a reasonable landed endowment to make any monastic enterprise viable, if we look at where the larger single lordships were in Norfolk we gain an idea of where landowners might have had the resources of land with which

---

132 Pestell, *Landscapes of monastic foundation*, pp. 194–5.
133 W. Page (ed.), *The Victoria history of the county of Norfolk* (London, 1906), vol. 2, pp. 418–19.

to endow a new monastery. This is easier said than done, but two sources that provide some insights are Domesday Book and the 1316 *Nomina Villarum*. Both can be used to assess the distribution of free men and sokemen and conversely, by implication, areas most dominated by lordly estates.[134] Broadly speaking, this suggests that west Norfolk was, in particular, characterised by the sorts of larger landholdings that might be needed by a founder and this seems evidenced by the 1291 *Taxatio* values, which indicate a clear concentration in this broad area not only of monasteries but also of the richer examples. Equally, it remains the case that the Broadland monasteries also form a dense cluster, despite being in an area where the character of landholding might have made the provision of a good foundation more difficult. The devil, of course, is in the detail, as even in districts with an *average* lower number of rich lordships there will be exceptions, and these richer lords were precisely those within society more likely to create such foundations. It is therefore worth examining some of Broadland's foundations in more detail, to illuminate such specifics.

One constant theme of Broadland is water and the importance of rivers as both means of communication and as barriers. Two houses that reflect this particular feature were founded at Acle and Herringfleet, better known as Weybridge and St Olave's Priories respectively. Weybridge was founded by Hugh Bigod, earl of Norfolk, perhaps some time between 1207 and 1225. Despite the earl's wealth, the house appears to have always been small and impoverished, having a value of £8 7s 1¾d in 1291.[135] Perhaps most crucially, the first head was recorded as a 'warden or keeper', with the provision that, should the means of the house increase sufficiently, the secular habit and life should be converted into a religious one, led by a prior or abbot.[136] Weybridge's progression to an Augustinian priory could not mask the frailty of its existence, reflected also by the lack of surviving infrastructural remains on the site bar some earthworks.[137] Its location by Acle-Dam or Wey Bridge across the Bure on the main route from Norwich to Yarmouth was surely not coincidental, the crossing being a fording site until the first bridge was built in *c.*1101.[138] St Olave's Priory, also Augustinian, was another thirteenth-century foundation, established by Roger Fitz Osbert about 1216 with both he and his son Peter directing that their remains be buried in the priory church. Most notably, the site was near to the position of a ferry across the river Waveney. A

---

134 For the *Nomina Villarum* see Campbell, 'Complexity of manorial structure', pp. 225–61. For the distribution of freemen and sokemen see T. Williamson, *The origins of Norfolk* (Manchester, 1993), pp. 116–21.
135 Page, *Victoria history*, vol. 2, p. 406.
136 *Ibid.*
137 Although, curiously, a printed calendar of 1505 survives from the priory and is now in Norwich Castle Museum (accession 1944.134).
138 Blomefield and Parkin, *Topographical history*, vol. 11, p. 92. R. Taylor, *Index monasticus* (London, 1821), p. 27. For the bridge see B. Grint, unpublished notes in the Norfolk HER.

bridge was subsequently constructed adjacent to the priory, suggesting that this had previously been the ferry's crossing point.

That both Weybridge and St Olaves should be located beside important crossing points is unlikely to be coincidence. A number of monasteries have been noted as having a relationship with bridges because, as permanent institutions, they could serve as their custodians;[139] a lack of documentation for both Weybridge and St Olaves makes it difficult to know what precise relationship either had with their adjacent crossing points but the association seems to reflect the Augustinians' less enclosed outlook as a monastic order, compared with the Benedictines. Similarly, both houses were founded in the early thirteenth century, when the mendicant orders, with their active relationships with the laity, were becoming popular.

Another small priory, Aldeby, was also placed adjacent to a river, lying to the north of the Waveney on the Norfolk–Suffolk border. In this case the location would appear to have had little to do with routeways; the small Benedictine monastery was granted to the monks of Norwich Cathedral Priory some time between 1107 and 1116 and was attached to the parish church. It was founded by Agnes de Beaufour or Bellofago, whose husband Hubert de Rye endowed it with tithes.[140] More significantly, Hubert seems to have been an active supporter of Herbert de Losinga's construction of the new cathedral in Norwich, the priory's *First Register* describing how Hubert and Agnes laid its second foundation stone. The association may well have been encouraged by the fact that Agnes's father was Ralph de Beaufour, a former sheriff of Norwich and possibly the brother of William Bellofago, Losinga's predecessor and bishop of Thetford between 1085 and 1091.[141] The priory is of interest as it was never rich, yet its church was arranged with an axial tower to give a cruciform plan, suggestive of a higher, monastic, status. Its location is also interesting, as it stands overlooking an inlet on the peninsula of land formed by the river Waveney as it winds its way down towards Breydon Water and Yarmouth (Figure 2.20 (a)).

The Cathedral Priory's presence in Broadland is perhaps most notable in the cell founded by Losinga at Yarmouth itself. This appears to have been based on an earlier Anglo-Saxon church. The wealth of the town, and of the priory cell, almost certainly rested on the fishing trade and the right to tolls and tax earned from this.[142] So jealously were St Nicholas's church rights exercised that not even a chapel was established in the town until the nineteenth century. Losinga's establishment, effectively exercising influence over the town, was part of a wider

---

139   J. Bond, *Monastic landscapes* (Stroud, 2004), pp. 296–301.
140   H.W. Saunders (ed.), *The first register of Norwich cathedral priory* (Norwich, 1939), pp. 50–1. B. Dodwell (ed.), *The charters of Norwich cathedral priory* (London, 1974), No. 20.
141   Ralph holding Aldeby at Domesday: *Little Domesday Book* fol. 225b.
142   T. Pestell, 'Monastic foundation strategies in the early Norman diocese of Norwich', *Anglo-Norman Studies*, 23 (Woodbridge, 2001), pp. 199–229, at pp. 216–19.

84 BROADLAND

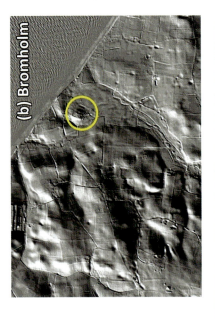
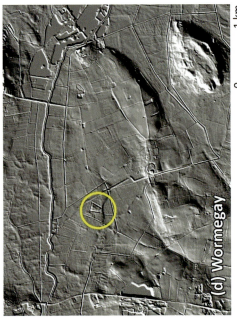
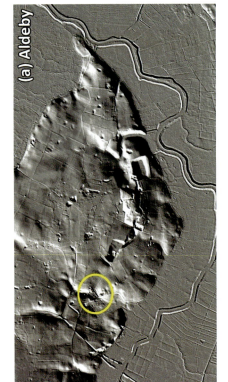
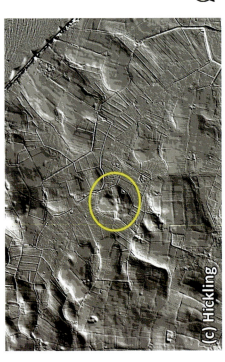

Figure 2.20 Lidar imagery of the siting of monastic houses: (a) Aldeby; (b) Bromholm; (c) Hickling; (d) Wormegay.

process Neil Batcock has described as 'episcopal imperialism', and was matched by his foundation of a similar priory cell in Kings Lynn, based on St Margaret's church.[143] Although Aldeby Priory was, at one level, an expression of private faith by Agnes and Hubert, its foundation also probably expressed a political affiliation, and its highly visible location, on a major watercourse, represented another beacon of Norwich Cathedral Priory's presence on the Norfolk–Suffolk border.

The activities of Losinga and Norwich Cathedral Priory illustrate clearly the ultimately political role monasteries might be imbued with, and their close identification with founders and their families. A more traditional relationship in this sense is the twinning of a seigneurial seat with a monastery, often involving a castle, as would appear to have been the case at Bungay. Here, a nunnery was founded by Roger de Glanville and his wife the countess Gundreda on 7 August 1183, under Prioress Anastasia.[144] Gundreda's role was probably crucial, not only in selecting Benedictine nuns for the project but because the endowments seem to have been drawn from her dowry, albeit with husband Roger also granting the church at Roughton. Although there is no evidence that Gundreda ever entered the nunnery as a widow, it is possible that its creation was in part an insurance policy to provide for her when her husband went (and probably died) on Crusade.[145] In fact, the foundation was not a true twinning of castle and monastery, of the type discussed by Thompson, through which Norman baronial families actively sought to dominate a surrounding region under their lordship.[146] Instead, Bungay castle had been built by Roger Bigod c.1100 and was retained by the Bigod family even as the Glanvilles took over the town's principal parish church and constructed a nunnery on the site. However, this was no subversion of Bigod power, but rather an expression of familial links, for Gundreda was the widow of Roger's son Hugh Bigod, earl of Norfolk, before her marriage to Roger de Glanville.

On the other side of Broadland the intimately personal role of the founder is perhaps best seen at Ingham Priory, a Trinitarian house founded in 1360. This was a period characterised by a general decline in the foundation of conventional monasteries of the traditional orders, with patronage of urban friaries becoming more fashionable from the thirteenth century. Ingham is also typical of the

---

143 N. Batcock, 'The parish church in Norfolk in the 11th and 12th centuries', in J. Blair (ed.), *Minsters and parish churches. The local church in transition 960–1200* (Oxford, 1988), pp. 179–90, at p. 188.
144 Ellis, *Chronica Johannis de Oxenedes*, p. 69.
145 R. Mortimer, 'The family of Rannulf Glanville', *Bulletin of the Institute of Historical Research*, 54/129 (1981), pp. 1–16, at pp. 4–5 and 12–13. Mortimer notes Roger went on Crusade with his nephew Rannulf, distinguishing himself at the Siege of Acre in 1190 and taking some Saracens prisoners in a raiding reconnaissance before the gates of Jerusalem in April 1192. For the complex ownership of Bungay see also D. Crouch, *The reign of King Stephen: 1135–1154* (London, 2000), p. 120.
146 M. Thompson, 'Associated monasteries and castles in the Middle Ages: a tentative list', *Archaeological Journal*, 143 (1986), pp. 305–21.

Figure 2.21 The Trinitarian cross on the tomb of Sir Roger de Boys, Ingham Church.

tendency, by the fourteenth century, for families (often at lower levels of society) to found colleges of priests as chantries that were focused on saying masses for the souls of their patrons. Ingham provides an interesting case study of how these trends might intersect.

The Trinitarians were an unusual choice for a patron, being both a poorly known monastic order and one present on only a small scale in England. The order was dedicated to redeeming captives of the Crusades, a purpose to which a third of its revenues was directed.[147] This focus was a development of the earlier concern of the Knights Templars and Hospitallers to retrieve their own members captured on crusade and the Trinitarians, framing themselves as a quasi-military order, were represented by a symbol that combined the red cross of the Templars and blue cross of the Hospitallers (Figure 2.21). By 1360 the age of crusading was long over and the Trinitarians had accordingly shifted their focus to maintaining hospitals. This was not the case with Ingham. Instead, in 1355 Innocent VI issued a mandate to grant a licence for

> Miles de Stapilton, knight … to rebuild and enlarge the church … and elect therein a college, in honour of the Holy Trinity and All Saints, of 13 religious, one of whom is to be the prior or warden and another sacristan, making it a conventual church with due statutes and ordinances.[148]

---

147 The Trinitarians have received scant scholarly attention. The largest treatment remains P. Deslandres, *L'Ordre des Trinitaires pour le Rachat des Captifs*, 2 vols (Paris, 1903). A more recent summary is T. Knecht, *Histoire de L'Ordre de la Sainte Trinité et de la Redemption Des Captifs* (Cerfroid, 1993).

148 W.H. Bliss and C. Johnson (eds), *Calendar of papal registers: papal letters III 1342–62* (London, 1897), p. 561.

By 1362 Ingham comes into focus as a Trinitarian priory, royal letters patent granting Sir Miles and Joan his wife 'Licence for ½ mark paid to the king by the Prior of Ingham, for the alienation in mortmain … of an acre of land in Ingham for the enlargement of their manse'.[149] It is the personal circumstances of the founders that arguably provide the *raison d'être* for Ingham. Stapleton was a junior son of a major Yorkshire landowning family but rose to prominence on the back of a distinguished military career in the service of Edward III. His accomplishments were acknowledged when he became one of the elite founding Knights of the Garter, standing on the 'King's side' at the order's creation. It was his marriage to Joan, daughter and heiress of Sir Oliver de Ingham, seneschal of Gascony, that brought him to Norfolk.

Ingham Priory's foundation seems to reflect his arrival in both society and Norfolk, and to have drawn on Joan's social connections as well as his own. The first brethren appear to have been drawn from Easton Priory in Wiltshire, judging by their names – Richard Marleburgh (Marlborough) and John Pevesey (Pewsey) – reflecting the fact that the Ingham family held lands in the area. At the same time, the Stapletons held land around Knaresborough in Yorkshire, where St Robert, a famous hermit, had lived and whose shrine was cared for by another of the few Trinitarian monasteries in the country. Particular aspects of Sir Miles's activities and social milieux may have encouraged an enthusiasm for the Trinitarians. It is perhaps not without significance that the Black Prince had a special devotion to the Holy Trinity, and that fellow Garter knights the third Earl of Arundel and Edward, fifth Lord Despencer, had established, respectively, a college and chapel dedicated to the Holy Trinity. Sir Miles also appears to have cultivated a crusading image in courtly circles, using a Saracen's head as his crest in tournaments, and it was through the ransoming of noble captives that many of his knightly contemporaries came to make money in the wars with France; both, perhaps, encouraged an affinity with the Trinitarians, deeply involved in the redemption of those captured in the Holy Land.[150] We can see here something of the complex, multiple messages and meanings that contemporaries could have read into the foundation of monastic houses and which must frequently have

---

149 'in mortmain': after the passing of the Statutes of Mortmain in 1279 and 1290 donations of land into the 'dead hand' of the Church required special royal dispensation. R.F. Isaacsons (ed.), *Calendar of patent rolls, Edward III: volume 12, 1361–64* (London, 1912), p. 164.

150 T. Pestell, 'Of founders and faith: the establishment of the Trinitarian Priory of Ingham, Norfolk (England)', in G. De Boe and F. Verhaeghe (eds), *Religion and belief in medieval Europe: papers of the Medieval Europe Brugge 1997 Conference 4* (Zellik, 1997), pp. 65–78. More recently, Sally Badham has reviewed the funeral monuments and sees the priory more directly associated with wife Joan's agency: S. Badham, 'Beautiful remains of antiquity. The medieval monuments in the former Trinitarian Priory church at Ingham, Norfolk. Part 1: the lost brasses', *Church Monuments*, 21 (2006), pp. 7–33, at pp. 13–14. The arguments are too complex to respond to here but ignore several features that make Joan's prime role equivocal.

been made manifest in the decorative arts within them, most of which have now been lost.[151]

I now want to return to my starting point, the question of what the Broads as an area might have had to offer founders and foundations, by returning to the Glanville family, who, prodigiously, founded four monasteries in 60 years in a grand statement of arrival, if not piety. In 1113 William de Glanville chose to establish a Cluniac monastery at Bromholm in Bacton parish on the north-east Norfolk coast, on the northern edge of Broadland. The site chosen for this cell of Castle Acre was a prominent gravel 'holm' rising out of the surrounding low-lying coastal plain. As lidar data makes clear (Figure 2.20 (b)), the holm stands within an extinct watercourse that once either flowed out to sea or channelled ultimately into the river Ant and the wider broads basin. The priory achieved national renown as a site of pilgrimage after it acquired a relic of the True Cross c.1223, bringing the house numerous visitors and considerable wealth.[152] A century earlier, the foundation was arguably located to eschew interaction with the laity, expressing the idea of a community set apart from secular society on an island forming a spiritual space.

However, it is unclear how isolated the priory ever really was. Bacton appears to have been a polyfocal parish with several berewicks, or dependent settlements, including Keswick, which, with its church, lay immediately to the east. Bromholm therefore appears to have been founded in a well-settled area. Fieldwalking and an intensive programme of metal-detection has shown that the holm itself was unsettled virgin ground before the priory was founded.[153] Yet, if the ruined buildings seem prominent today, one needs only to think of the impression the priory must have made upon a twelfth-century audience looking at the impressive monastic church with its stylish Transitional architecture, probably gleaming white from an external render and with bells ringing throughout the day and much of the night in its calls to prayer. As a marker in the landscape, it must have projected a less than subtle message of the Glanvilles' place in the world order and, while the priory's location physically separated its inmates from the rest of society (at least initially), they were clearly an intimate part of it.

We may conclude by looking at this concept of removal from society through a consideration of what is as quintessential a Broadland monastery as St Benet's Abbey: Hickling Priory. Sitting on a small marshland island (Figure 2.20 (c)), this

---

151 One may immediately think of the remarkable thirteenth-century wall paintings in Horsham St Faith Priory's refectory, illustrating its founder's vow to St Faith to found a monastery made while on pilgrimage: E.W. Tristram, 'The wall paintings at Horsham St Faith, near Norwich', *Norfolk Archaeology*, 22 (1926), pp. 257–9.

152 The best exploration remains F. Wormald, 'The rood of Bromholm', *Journal of the Warburg Institute*, 1 (1937), pp. 31–45.

153 T. Pestell, 'Using material culture to define holy space: the Bromholm Project', in A. Spicer and S. Hamilton (eds), *Defining the holy. Sacred space in medieval and early modern Europe* (Aldershot, 2005), pp. 161–86.

Augustinian house was founded in 1185 by Theobald de Valognes.[154] This location may have been enough to have attracted a monastic foundation, but might there have been other reasons for the choice of site? Detailed fieldwalking has shown that the island was unoccupied before the priory was founded. Yet, Hickling presents us with tantalising suggestions of an interesting Anglo-Saxon past. The place-name, meaning 'Hicel's people', is reminiscent of early tribal origins and a possible early estate centre would not be contradicted by the large size of the parish, its 4,244 acres (1,718 hectares) on a par with North Walsham (at 4,252 acres (1,721 hectares)) which, as we have seen, was probably another early estate or territory. Domesday Book frustratingly provides little help, recording a church with an entirely average endowment of 20 acres worth 20d, although a chapel of St Mary was sited within the churchyard, an arrangement that is reminiscent of some Anglo-Saxon minsters.[155] A possible explanation for Theobald's choice may come from another house that just misses out on being considered here as a 'Broadland' monastery, sitting as it does too far along the Waveney valley on the Norfolk–Suffolk border at Mendham. Here, clear evidence for an Anglo-Saxon minster survives in the will of Bishop Theodred of London, who in 951 gave lands at Shotford and Mettingham to its community.[156] The house seems to have survived until at least 1086, judging from Domesday Book, but in 1155 a Cluniac priory was founded in Mendham as a cell to Castle Acre.[157] This appears to have been a case where Norman regularisation of an earlier ecclesiastical community involved relocation to a new site, an island set in marshland. The new priory was overlooked from the high ground of the mainland by the old church and village and, as at Bromholm, this intervisibility in the landscape must have been a key element in the choice of site. Yet another example of such relocation occurred at Wormegay in west Norfolk. Here, an Augustinian priory was founded between 1166 and 1175 by Reginald de Warenne, who also seems to have built a castle on a small island in the fens where the parish church was already located.[158] Archaeological evidence shows there to have been high-status Anglo-Saxon occupation and possibly a minster here.[159] The new priory was not, however, placed beside or on the site of the existing church, but on another small island adjacent to it (Figure 2.20 (d)). Yet again, we see an act of deliberate placement, with a 'removed' monastery intervisible with its secular patrons and local community. It may well be that

---

154 A.H. Chifferiel, *Records of Hickling Priory and Hickling district in the hundred of Happing* (privately printed, 1911).
155 Blomefield and Parkin, *Topographical history*, vol. 9, p. 307.
156 D. Whitelock (ed. and trans.), *Anglo-Saxon wills* (Cambridge, 1930), No. 1.
157 Knowles and Hadcock, *Medieval religious houses*, p. 100.
158 *Ibid.*, p. 180.
159 A. Rogerson, 'Six middle Anglo-Saxon sites in west Norfolk', in T. Pestell and K. Ulmschneider (eds), *Markets in early medieval Europe trading and 'productive' sites 650–850* (Macclesfield, 2003), pp. 110–21, at pp. 119–20.

Theobald's landholdings at Hickling provided both a suitable local endowment as well as a historically numinous landscape for his new monastic statement.

What might the foregoing discussion tell us about the monastic houses of Broadland? Certainly that there was a great variety and – perhaps disappointingly, in the context of this book – that there is nothing that makes the way monastic houses were founded here particularly unique, with a representative selection of monastic orders, including even the exotic Trinitarians. There is, then, no Broadland equivalent to the 'Cistercian landscape' seen in parts of Yorkshire. However, there certainly does seem to have been a favouring of the marshland locations that Broadland provided, as is also seen in the Fens and on the fen-edge in the Nar Valley. The slight clustering of monasteries in Broadland, despite the general absence of many large or single-lordship vills, is a hint that topography and *concepts* of isolation or marshy spiritual fastnesses may have made it a desirable place for foundations. Metal-detecting in particular has shown the deep Anglo-Saxon origins of many monastic houses in western Norfolk, such as Wormegay, Pentney or West Acre. The Broadland area currently has a more impoverished archaeological record, and it will be interesting to see whether future research reveals a similar palimpsest, building on an earlier Anglo-Saxon religious landscape – or whether monastic Broadland was actually more of a medieval creation.

Vernacular houses in Broadland
by Ian Hinton

Traditionally, a vernacular building was defined as one constructed of local materials, using local techniques and in a local style. Vernacular architecture was generally accepted as starting at the point when the first buildings capable of surviving to the present were erected, and ending when houses were based on architects' designs, adopted forms and features selected from pattern books, or were built using materials from further afield and/or with universal or common techniques, after which they were described as 'polite'. The higher the social status, the earlier the vernacular period started and finished. In the case of farmhouses occupied by yeomen, the vernacular period by this definition probably finished in the second half of the seventeenth century; with smaller cottages perhaps a century later. Gentry houses can rarely be considered vernacular as they were often individually designed in styles that were national, rather than regional or local. More recently it has been proposed that 'vernacular' status has more to do with use. Matthew Johnson has argued that vernacular houses should not be looked at for what they are, but for what they mean and how they reflect the needs of the occupants.[160] He suggests, for instance, that when a house becomes just a house

---
160 M. Johnson, *Housing culture: traditional architecture in an English landscape* (London, 1993).

– for example, when services are split off and farm storage is moved elsewhere – it is no longer part of the domestic or farming micro-economy, and therefore becomes less 'vernacular', even though it may still be built of local materials and in a local style. Both these views of what constitutes vernacular architecture are useful, but the former is perhaps most readily applicable in the present context. Many of the older houses in Broadland were initially built with local materials, and with features of construction distinctive to East Anglia and, to a lesser extent, to Broadland itself. Many were altered along less locally distinctive lines from the later seventeenth century but their 'massing', layout and interior may still preserve vernacular features, and even the alterations may display some locally distinctive characteristics, as does the style of smaller cottages, few if any examples of which appear to pre-date the eighteenth century.

This difference in the antiquity of farmhouses and cottages in Broadland is a good expression of the concept of the 'vernacular threshold', concerning the character of the transition to buildings sufficiently durable to survive to the present, which was first developed by Ronald Brunskill in 1971. He emphasised that the vernacular buildings that exist in our modern landscape are not necessarily representative of the wider stock that was built at various times in the past; not all buildings survive and survival rates differ based on the size and type of house. Basically, the larger and more important the building, and the more durable the materials with which it is built, the more likely it is to survive.[161] Constructional techniques were also important. Indeed, the first crossing of the 'threshold', which occurred in south-east England in particular in the thirteenth century, was probably a consequence of more sophisticated framing, using complex mortice-and-tenon joints, and of the erection of houses on stone or rubble plinths, which protected them from the rot that had limited the life of their forebears, constructed with earth-fast posts. But less material factors also influenced a house's survivability. Christopher Currie has argued that survival was dependent on a building's potential for adaptation in the face of changing fashions and living standards.[162] Studies carried out in Devon and Essex suggest that the taller medieval houses – particularly in terms of eaves height – have survived in greater numbers than examples of the same construction but with lower eaves, because floors could be inserted into the open halls of the former more easily than with the latter when this became fashionable in the sixteenth century.[163]

Regional building styles were well established by the fifteenth century. Cruck frames were common in the north and west of Britain, but in the east and south-

---

161 R. Brunskill, *Illustrated handbook of vernacular architecture* (London, 1971).
162 C. Currie, 'Time and chance: modelling the attrition of old houses', *Vernacular Architecture*, 19 (1988), pp. 1–9.
163 D. Stenning, 'Small aisled halls in Essex', *Vernacular Architecture*, 34 (2003), pp. 1–19.

east box framing was universal.[164] Within these broad patterns, more local traditions were also being formalised, including, for example, the use of 'close studding' in East Anglia and much of south-east England – that is, the profligate use of vertical timbers, often for visual effect. Regional variation becomes clearer in buildings surviving from the sixteenth and seventeenth centuries, depending in particular upon the local materials available: in Norfolk, for example, the use of timber is predominant in the south, flint and clunch in the north and west.

But there was much less regional variation in the layout of rural houses. Until the middle of the sixteenth century the 'open-hall house' was the norm, consisting of a main central room (the hall) that was open to the roof. It had an open fire in its centre for cooking and heating and was essentially a public space. It was flanked at one end by the parlour, which served as a withdrawing room for the owner and family, and at the other by service rooms, used for the preparation of food, the storage of utensils, brewing and dairying. Both these cells had first-floor chambers that were used either as sleeping accommodation or for storage, and were accessed by stairs or a ladder. Access to the house itself was via opposed doors at the service-room end, often screened off from the hall by a partition, thus creating a cross passage. Some smaller buildings had just two cells – that is, an open hall and the two service rooms with a chamber above them. From the middle of the sixteenth century, however, open-hall houses began to be replaced by, or converted into, buildings with one and a half or two storeys throughout, with an off-centre chimney stack, sometimes timber-framed at first but soon of brick. Initially the opposed doors and cross passage were retained, but in many regions, including East Anglia, it soon became normal to enter the house via a lobby next to the chimney stack, placed between hall and parlour. The unheated service rooms at one end of the building were retained, as processes such as brewing and butter-making required cool conditions. Those open-hall houses that were capable of being adapted had floors and chimney stacks inserted but the majority of houses of this style were built new. Fully floored buildings were the norm by 1600.

The replacement of the central fire of the open hall by a brick stack, often with two hearths, or four if the upper rooms were heated, was accompanied by another improvement. At the beginning of the sixteenth century, windows were always unglazed in the sorts of houses being discussed here. Rudimentary weather-proofing was provided by sliding shutters, or the window could be covered by a form of oiled cloth. Towards the end of the century, as glass became cheaper, its installation in windows became more common in the houses of yeomen. Further changes followed. The two unheated service rooms were often incorporated into

---

164 Cruck buildings rely on the giant curved frames of the crucks to support the roof: the walls were not a structural element.

the domestic arrangements and usually heated through the addition of a new stack attached to the gable end, probably because many of their functions, including brewing and dairying, requiring a cool environment, were now carried out in outbuildings. This additional end stack, coupled with the original off-centre stack, can be seen in dozens of houses in Broadland, for example at Burlingham Old Rectory, Raven Hall, Haddiscoe and Beech Grove Farm in Loddon.

In 1953 W.G. Hoskins coined the term 'The Great Rebuilding' for what he believed had been a revolution in housing that took place between the accession of Elizabeth I in 1558 and the outbreak of the Civil War in 1642, and especially in the years between 1575 and 1625. It involved both the modernisation of existing houses along the lines just described, where this was feasible, or their replacement by new buildings, where it was not. The 'rebuilding' reflected farming prosperity, a new desire for comfort and an increase in furnishings and possessions.[165] Hoskins' concept has been discussed many times since, many researchers agreeing with it in broad terms but suggesting variations in timing by region or social class.[166] Detailed studies of Norfolk parishes lying at no great distance from Broadland, however – Hempnall, Walsingham, New Buckenham and Binham – have demonstrated that in these places, at least, a 'Great Rebuilding' did indeed happen roughly in the period proposed by Hoskins, albeit at slightly different times, depending on the local economic situation.[167]

A lack of comparable studies in Broadland makes it hard to assess how the area fits into these wider narratives, debates and concepts. The experience of local historic buildings groups has shown repeatedly that internal details are the principal indication of the true origin and development of a building, and that without a detailed survey it is difficult to unravel its history, particularly in the case of the oldest examples. Any suggestions about an area's vernacular buildings based on the default source, national and county databases, must of necessity be considered partial and provisional. For the 124 Broadland parishes considered here, the national Statutory List of Buildings of Special Architectural or Historic Interest includes 326 houses, of which 152 were assessed as having been built before 1700.[168] Many of these assessments are historic and most, if not all, were

---

165 W.G. Hoskins, 'The rebuilding of rural England 1570–1640', *Past and Present*, 4 (1953), pp. 44–59.
166 See in particular Currie, 'Time and chance'. R. Machin, 'The Great Rebuilding: a reassessment', *Past and Present*, 77 (1977), pp. 35–56. E. Mercer, *English vernacular houses* (London, 1975). P. Smith, 'Time and chance: a reply', *Vernacular Architecture*, 21 (1990), pp. 4–5. N. Alcock, 'The Great Rebuilding in its later stages', *Vernacular Architecture*, 14 (1983), pp. 45–8. J.T. Smith, 'Short-lived and mobile houses in late seventeenth-century England', *Vernacular Architecture*, 16 (1985), pp. 34–5.
167 See I. Hinton (ed.), *The buildings of Hempnall*, Norfolk Historic Buildings Group Journal, 7 (2020), pp. 35–42, for a fuller discussion of the picture in Norfolk.
168 British Listed Buildings, 'Listed buildings in Norfolk'. https://britishlistedbuildings.co.uk/england/norfolk#.Y0nRBkzMLqV (accessed 5 October 2022).

made using external surveys only, although the Norfolk Historic Environment Record (NHER) contains some entries based on more detailed examinations. This source lists 167 houses of the sixteenth and seventeenth centuries within the Norfolk portion of Broadland, of which 23 may be adapted or extended medieval-period buildings.[169]

Perhaps the most striking feature of the area, as suggested by these sources, is the relative paucity of early buildings. While most parishes in the Broadland area contain at least one house built before the end of the seventeenth century, few contain more than a handful. This contrasts sharply with the situation in parishes on the clay soils lying to the south and south-west, in south Norfolk and north-east Suffolk, in which official lists commonly record five, ten or more. The rather small number of probable medieval houses is particularly striking. Where early houses do exist they have often later been clad in brick, either as a repair or as a statement of wealth, and have had larger glazed windows inserted and other alterations made to them. But most of the housing stock that existed before the later seventeenth century has evidently been replaced entirely with brick buildings, initially displaying a traditional three-cell plan but increasingly, in the course of the eighteenth or nineteenth centuries, built in the new symmetrical style with a chimney stack at either end, central front door and large, equally spaced windows. There are many examples of such post-vernacular, Georgian- and Victorian-period farmhouses in Broadland that appear to have replaced earlier houses, where the farms are older than the house, as at Grove House, Irstead, Allens Farm, Neatishead and Ivy House, East Somerton. It is true that similarly low densities of early buildings appear also elsewhere in East Anglia – in western Norfolk or the Suffolk Sandlings, for example. But much of the Broads area is, as we have noted, characterised by soils of particular fertility, which might have been expected to have generated a stock of durable houses worth retaining or adapting. Indeed, by and large the density of buildings pre-dating *c*.1650 is lowest in those parts of Broadland – the centre and north – where such soils are most extensive.

In part, the answer to this apparent conundrum may lie in the area's idiosyncratic social structure. As we have seen, Broadland – its northern and central parts especially – was characterised in the Middle Ages by large numbers of small farms, and while later sources, such as the 1522 Subsidy Returns, suggest high or average per-acre wealth, population densities were also generally high and wealth thus spread thinly.[170] Only gradually did changes in landholding ensure the emergence of greater numbers of larger farms, and thus perhaps the construction in significant numbers of larger dwellings, with greater long-term 'survivability'. It

---

169   https://www.heritage.norfolk.gov.uk/ (accessed 5 October 2022).
170   J. Pound, 'Sixteenth-century Norfolk: population and wealth', in T. Ashwin and A. Davison (eds), *An historical atlas of Norfolk*, 3rd edn (Chichester, 2008), pp. 100–2.

Figure 2.22 Danegelt House, Geldeston, one of a handful of surviving medieval houses in Broadland.

is noteworthy that, of the few examples in Broadland of medieval open-hall houses retained and adapted for more modern living in the early modern period, most have floors squeezed uncomfortably into the hall space, because of its low height, and ranges with two full floors added to one end, as at Rush Fen Cottage and Danegelt House in Geldeston, and Dawn Cottage in Repps (Figure 2.22). Given the size of most Broadland farms in the fifteenth and sixteenth centuries, it seems likely that such diminutive structures were the norm, and were usually completely rebuilt, rather than adapted, as open halls went out of use.

The effects of these social influences may have been exacerbated by the materials that were readily and cheaply available to house builders. Medieval East Anglia was not a particularly well-wooded region: at the time of Domesday many Broadland vills had no woodland and the amounts recorded in most others were low, except in the south of the area, on the edge of the clay plateau.[171] A substantial amount of timber was required to build a house. Oliver Rackham's study of Grundle House in Stanton (Suffolk) shows that the timber used in its construction equated to 50 years' growth on 5.7 acres of woodland, or one year's growth on 286 acres (116 hectares).[172] It should be noted that Grundle House is around four times the size of the typical vernacular house in the Broads (approx. 50 feet by 16 feet, 15 metres by 5 metres) but the paucity of woodland may, nevertheless, have encouraged the use of less durable materials, higher up the social scale, than was the case elsewhere. It is true that Broadland houses surviving from before the mid-seventeenth century

---

171 O. Rackham, 'The ancient woods of Norfolk', *Transactions of the Norfolk and Norwich Naturalists' Society*, 27 (1986), pp. 161–7.

172 O. Rackham, 'Grundle House: on the quantities of timber in certain East-Anglian buildings', *Vernacular Architecture*, 3 (1972), pp. 3–8.

Figure 2.23 The Bell, St Olaves, unusual in Broadland for its exposed timber frame and first-floor jetty.

are broadly similar to those found in neighbouring areas: built with timber frames using close vertical studding, infilled with wattle and daub and originally rendered over with lime mortar and often colour-washed, although a few, such as Castell Farm in Raveningham and The Bell at St Olaves, had exposed timbers, as was the usual fashion in the southern parts of East Anglia (Figure 2.23). These two houses, together with Mitre House in Acle, are jettied – the first floor overhangs the ground-floor walls – a fashion that continued into the later sixteenth century and in Norfolk perhaps first appeared in the mid-fifteenth (in New Buckenham in south Norfolk, newly built jettied buildings encroaching on the marketplace have been dated dendrochronologically to 1470).[173] The jetty at the Mitre was later underbuilt almost flush in brick, a not uncommon occurrence and one that may have served to conceal other Broadland examples. Some quite large and sophisticated timber-framed buildings clearly existed in Broadland. But the fact that surviving examples are few in number suggests that many of the farms and most cottages erected in the area before the late seventeenth century may have been less substantially constructed, perhaps with walls of clay. Mass clay walling, often using material excavated from the subsoil of the land around the house, needs to be distinguished from clay lump construction, using large blocks of unfired clay and straw, usually the size of eight normal bricks. The latter method was used only from the end of the eighteenth century, for the construction of farm buildings and small cottages.[174]

---

173 A. Longcroft (ed.), *The historic buildings of New Buckenham*, Norfolk Historic Buildings Group Journal, 2 (2005).
174 J. McCann, 'Is clay lump a traditional building material?', *Vernacular Architecture*, 18 (1987), pp. 1–16.

The former, in contrast, has been used in East Anglia for centuries and as late as *c.*1800 around a third of parsonages described in glebe terriers in Norfolk were so constructed.[175]

On balance, it thus seems probable that a housing stock dominated by relatively small and poorly built structures was replaced wholesale by brick buildings from the later seventeenth century, a process perhaps facilitated and made more complete by the low transport costs provided by the Broads waterways – as we shall see, building materials were one of the main cargoes transported by keels and wherries (see p. 313). Brick construction was not new in eastern England. References to the domestic manufacture of bricks do not really start until the early fifteenth century,[176] but the use of bricks in grand houses, such as Little Wenham Hall in Essex, can be dated to the later thirteenth century, when they were imported from the Low Countries.[177] Initially, bricks were relatively thin and irregularly sized, but by the later seventeenth century even those used at vernacular level were generally thicker and more regular. Brick bonds – the pattern of bricks laid lengthwise (stretchers) and those laid through the wall (headers) – also became more regular. The earliest walls have irregular bonds, sometimes composed entirely of headers, but by the early seventeenth century English bond, in which there were alternate courses of headers and stretchers, was widely employed at vernacular level and by the middle of the century this was being superseded by Flemish bond, with alternating headers and stretchers in the same course, although English bond continued to be used in certain situations that required particular strength.

Brick was used in Broadland in combination with timber framing from as early as the sixteenth century; brick gable ends might, in particular, be combined with timber-framed side walls, as at Castell Farm in Raveningham. From the middle of the seventeenth century timber framed buildings of all kinds often had their walls replaced with brick or had an outer skin of brick applied to them, either as a necessity, because of a failing timber frame, or as a fashionable or decorative feature. Where houses already possessed brick gable ends, the change is usually revealed by a vertical discontinuity between the courses of brickwork in the side and the end walls. There are examples of this at Orchard House in Bramerton, Holverston Hall, Old Hall Farm in Hemblington and Durrants Farmhouse, Sutton, as well as examples of joins with wrap-round gables at Church Cottages in Wickhampton, South Burlingham Hall and Berry Hall Farm in Barton Turf.

---

175 R. Lucas, 'Some observations on descriptions of parsonage houses made in Norfolk glebe terriers', *Transactions of the Ancient Monuments Society*, 39 (1996), pp. 83–95, at p. 92.
176 R. Symonds, 'Bricks through history', https://www.brocross.com/Bricks/Penmorfa/Bricks/Bits/BRICKS%20THROUGH%20HISTORY.pdfhttp://www.brocross.com. (Accessed 20 May 2024).
177 Salzman, *Building in England*, pp. 140–3. J. Wight, *Brick building in England: from the Middle Ages to 1550* (London, 1972), p. 31.

Figure 2.24 The late-seventeenth-century Thurne Manor, built entirely of brick but still with a lobby-entry plan.

By the last decades of the seventeenth century timber framing had been abandoned and, while houses such as Thurne Manor continued to be constructed to the old three-cell plan, with a lobby entry, they were built of brick from the start (Figure 2.24). Whether as modifications and additions, or in houses entirely built of brick, brickwork offered a number of novel decorative opportunities. The use of poorly controlled clamps (basically bonfires) or small kilns to fire bricks often meant uneven temperatures, resulting in the production of some bricks of darker colours. These were used in so-called diaperwork, with diamond-shaped patterns picked out in darker bricks, as at the adjacent Church Farm and Old World Cottages in Rollesby. To a lesser extent, burnt brick headers were also set in a simple chequerboard pattern, a practice that continued into the eighteenth century. A chequerboard pattern in different coloured bricks can be seen at the Dutch House in Ludham and bricks patterned with flint at the Old Rectory at Martham. At Manor Farm in Stokesby the diaperwork was created using red bricks set in the flint wall. In the gable-end wall of Burlingham Old Rectory darker bricks were laid to give the appearance of full-height pilasters in a red-brick wall. Gables might also receive decorative attention. Stepped capping, often called 'crow steps', are in fact a happy coincidence of decoration and practicality, as they provide a way to finish the gable wall without having to cut the bricks so that the ends of the horizontal courses match the slope of the roof. Notable examples include Cottage Farm in North Cove, Park Farm, Somerleyton and Manor Farm in Stokesby. The

Figure 2.25 The Croft, Rollesby. Thatch continued to be used for the roofs of new houses well into the eighteenth century.

use of 'tumbling-in', a method of angling the brickwork courses so as to present the end of the brick at the top of the gable wall, became common later, around the start of the eighteenth century, and is often seen in Broadland. Although not classed by many as a 'vernacular' form, curvilinear-shaped gables – often called 'Dutch' gables – became popular in the late seventeenth century, often being used on houses in towns or the larger villages, with five examples in Coltishall alone perhaps an indication of their purpose of fashionable display (see Figure 6.16). But there are also more remotely located rural examples, such as Kirby Row Farm in Kirby Cane and Rockland Old Hall.

The wave of building and rebuilding in brick that occurred in Broadland from the second half of the seventeenth century was not directly matched by the adoption of tiles as a roof covering. Well into the eighteenth century cottages and even farms newly built in brick were provided with thatched roofs (Figure 2.25). Thatching has distinct regional variations, both in style and material. There is a broad distinction between the angular thatching of the Northern and Eastern traditions and the rounded Southern style, the boundary roughly following the northern section of the old Roman road of Watling Street and thus, perhaps suggestively, the old boundary of the Danelaw. Broadland thatching follows the Eastern tradition, lacking the widespread use of boarded gable ends seen in the north, with its Danish parallels, and characterised instead by steep-pitched, angular roofs similar to those found in Germany and the Netherlands.[178] There are also differences within the east of England, especially in the treatment of the ridge and the gable ends. Rolled gables are seen only in Essex and parts of Hertfordshire; gables that show the new and old cut ends are a feature of the Suffolk–Essex border; while there are wooden boarded gable ends in a small area of mid-Suffolk around Stowmarket. North Suffolk and south Norfolk roofs usually have the thatch oversailing the gable walls, but the Broads area has a large number of upstanding brick gable ends against which the thatch finishes, requiring flashing with lead or mortar.[179] Not surprisingly, reed is exclusively used in the Broads area, resulting in a plain roof, in contrast to the longstraw roofs often found elsewhere in East Anglia, which use hazel spars on the ridge and eaves. Both types use sedge for the ridge.

Forty-four of the 167 sixteenth- and seventeenth-century houses noted in the NHER are still thatched. At least as many again have roofs that must previously have been thatched, to judge from their steep angle, necessary for thatch to function effectively as a waterproof covering, or tall upstanding gable ends. In addition, many seventeenth- and eighteenth-century houses in the area that now have a shallow roof angle display traces of the original steeper roof within the gable walls. Thirty-six of the currently thatched houses, including Burlingham Old Rectory, Tabard Cottage in Catfield and Raven Hall in Haddiscoe, have upstanding gables in the Broads tradition. Eight, including Lavender House in Brundall and Dawn Cottage in Repps, have oversailing thatch, although there are two houses that use both methods, one at each end: Clarkes Farm in Martham and Thatched House Farm in Norton Subcourse.

New thatched roofs, as noted earlier, continued to be constructed in Broadland well after 1700, appearing on some 'polite' buildings with symmetrical façades such as High Hill House in Hickling and the Manor House in Ludham. But by this time thatch was being replaced by pantiles for new roofs, and on many existing ones. Pantiles – distinctive S-shaped tiles found across the east of England from Suffolk to Yorkshire – originated in Holland and were first imported into East Anglia in the late seventeenth century, with production beginning here in the early eighteenth.[180] The tiles were usually red but some – known as 'smut' tiles – were black and some of these, by the later eighteenth century, were glazed. Pantiles have better resistance to fire than thatch and do not need to be replaced every few decades; they are also lighter than regular plain tiles as they overlap only the course immediately below, so fewer are used.

---

178 Thatch Advice Centre, 'Regional Thatch – East Anglia'. https://www.thatchadvicecentre.co.uk/thatch-information/thatched-roofs/regional-thatching-styles/regional-thatch-east-anglia (accessed 8 October 2022).
179 *Ibid.*
180 R. Lucas, 'Dutch pantiles in the county of Norfolk: architecture and international trade in the 17th and 18th centuries', *Vernacular Architecture*, 38 (1998), pp. 75–94.

Figure 2.26 Camberley Cottage, Happisburgh. Small one-and-a-half storey brick cottages, with roofs of thatch or pantile, dominate the older housing stock in most villages in the Broadland area.

While a small number of farmhouses or former farmhouses survive in Broadland from before 1650, and a reasonable number from the later seventeenth century, the earliest cottages are of eighteenth-century date, for the reasons already explained (Figure 2.26). Almost all are single storey or one-and-a-half storey buildings, of brick with pantiled roofs, but a few are thatched, such as 1–3 Station Road, Belton, Grange Farm Cottage in Bramerton and Toad Hole Cottage, at How Hill, now preserved as a museum. There are also examples of terraced groups of thatched cottages on Norwich Road in Ludham and Lower Street in Horning, for example.

If one of the sixteenth- or seventeenth-century houses in Broadland were to be placed elsewhere in Norfolk, in north-east Suffolk or more widely in eastern England, it would not appear particularly out of place. Houses from this period, right across this region, display broad similarities in size and layout manifest in such things as off-centre chimney stacks and front doors and small, slightly irregularly spaced windows. Nevertheless, considered as a group, and within the broader context of smaller houses erected before the nineteenth century, local houses display distinctive features that contribute significantly to the character of the Broadland landscape. The paucity of visible timber framing, a predominance of brick as the main construction material, roofs featuring thatch or pantile and, in the riverside villages especially, an abundance of single storey or one-and-a-half storey cottages, all make a significant impact. A desire to improve one's home has existed since houses were first built and extensions, modifications and the addition of ornamentation to ensure that they remained relevant to current needs and tastes are universal. But the character of vernacular buildings and of the architectural heritage more generally varies from area to area because of the differing abilities of people, living at different times in the past, to achieve such desires in forms capable of surviving to the present, as well as being shaped by the raw materials for construction available locally, or which could be imported at a reasonable cost. The last century or so has seen a steady increase in the appreciation of age in a building, contrasting with the Georgian and Victorian periods, when efforts were made to disguise or replace older houses. This, together with the protection afforded by statutory listing and planning processes, should ensure their continued survival, in Broadland as elsewhere.

3

THE MARSHES

Introducing the marshes

'Halvergate Marshes' is a useful shorthand term for the great triangle of level land lying to the west of Great Yarmouth, if strictly speaking an inaccurate one, given that the marshes extend into many other parishes. Traditionally used as pasture but now in part under the plough, the marshes are crossed by the rivers Bure, Yare and Waveney as they approach the sea. The Yare and Waveney join at the south-western end of Breydon Water, an extensive (*c*.400-hectare) area of tidal mudflats. A single river, the Yare, exits its north-eastern end, and is immediately joined by the river Bure. Its path to the sea then seemingly blocked by the town of Great Yarmouth, the river runs south for four kilometres before making its outfall.

The marshes, which almost everywhere lie a metre or more below high tide level, are dissected by a complex network of water-filled ditches or 'dykes', some serpentine or curving but others linear in character. These serve to drain the marsh, the water making its way to a major watercourse, where it is lifted over one of the 'walls' or embankments that preserve the marshes from inundation. In earlier centuries this was done by windmills, but these were joined in the nineteenth century by steam pumps and in the course of the twentieth both were superseded by ones powered by internal combustion engines or electricity. Long, continuous stretches of dyke usually mark the junction of upland and wetland – 'landspring dykes', intended to intercept water flowing off the higher ground or emanating from springs or seepage lines. The dykes also function as 'watery fences' to restrict the movement of livestock (there are accordingly no hedges on the marshes, and field gates stand solitary and erect in the flat landscape) and provide livestock with drinking water, although in certain conditions, in marshes lying beside the lower reaches of the rivers, their contents might be too saline for this purpose. In 1876 it was reported that tenants on the Skeetholme marshes, just outside Yarmouth, were carting water from the town because that in the dykes was too salty for the cattle.[1]

Attention to drainage works has always been of paramount importance in this watery world. The 'walls' need regular maintenance, with the clay required for this purpose traditionally being dug from the *soke dykes* that run alongside and behind them. All the dykes need to be kept free of vegetation ('croming') and, every few years, cleared of silt ('bottom finding' or 'bottomfying'), something now done by machines but until relatively recently by hand. Because the material removed from the dykes is spread on the ground beside them, moreover, each portion of marsh has tended, over time, to become slightly lower in the centre than towards the edges, so that numerous shallow spade-dug 'foot drains' have been excavated to assist the flow of water into the dykes, and more generally to help drain concavities in the land surface. All this work and investment reflects the fact that the marshes provide lush grazing in a district in which good-quality pasture has always been in short supply. But the quality of the herbage varies, and over the centuries writers have repeatedly emphasised the poorer character of the land lying towards the margins of the Halvergate 'triangle'. Here the flow of water from the adjacent uplands and the presence of springs ensure pockets of damper ground and, in places, the build-up of deposits of peat; 'in general the further the marsh is situated from the "land" the greater its grazing value'.[2] Today the most waterlogged areas are marked by the presence of patches of wet woodland or 'carr', and more subtly by concentrations of rigidly linear dykes. These indicate where areas of common land existed until they were enclosed in the seventeenth, eighteenth or nineteenth centuries, in contrast to the situation elsewhere on the marshes, where the land parcels are more irregular in shape and were generally held 'in severalty' – as private property – from an early date.

The marshes are a striking landscape, loved by many, loathed by a few, with wide panoramas of level green pastures and a skyline punctuated by the towers of drainage windmills, some derelict, some restored, although none now working (Figure 3.1). It is a lonely landscape. There are a handful of marsh farms, mostly accessed by private tracks. There are few footpaths and fewer public roads, the latter including the A47 or 'Acle Straight', a turnpike constructed in the 1830s, which crosses the northern part of the marsh in two spectacularly straight alignments; and the 'Halvergate Branch', equally straight, which leads off it near to where these alignments meet, close to Stracey Arms Mill. Equally linear are the two railway

---

1 NRO DCN 59/15/6.
2 Mosby, *Norfolk*, p. 198.

Figure 3.1 Typical view across the Halvergate Marshes.

lines that cross the marshes *en route* for Great Yarmouth. But all these are minor intrusions into what feels like an older, remoter landscape.

As we saw in Chapter 1, the marshes were once an open estuary, something recognised by the agricultural writer William Marshall as early as 1787:

> The marshes were a new world to me – They form a vast level, containing many thousand acres, of a black and somewhat moory soil; formed, perhaps, originally of sea mud; it being highly probable that the whole level has once been an estuary of the German Ocean.[3]

The two Roman Saxon Shore Forts erected on the northern and southern margins of the marshes, at Burgh Castle and Caister, indicate that the area was still an

---

3   W. Marshall, *The rural economy of Norfolk* (London, 1787), vol. 2, p. 276.

Figure 3.2 The Roman Saxon Shore fort at Burgh Castle, overlooking Breydon Water and the wide expanse of the Halvergate Marshes, the former 'Great Estuary'.

estuary in the later Roman period (Figure 3.2). But during the following centuries tidal penetration was reduced by the growth, across the estuary mouth, of the great spit of sand and shingle on which the town of Yarmouth now stands, and this – combined with wider changes in relative land/sea levels – ensured that mudflats gradually gave way to saltmarsh, crossed by rivers and dissected by tidal creeks. By the tenth century much of the land surface probably lay above the level of all but the highest tides.[4] And it is at this point, when human activity first begins to leave enduring traces, that our story really begins.

---

4   Coles and Funnell, 'Holocene palaeoenvironments'. Funnell, 'Lower Yare Valley, Norfolk'. Godwin, 'Holocene deposits of East Norfolk and Suffolk'.

The saltmarsh landscape

Domesday Book is a difficult source but it suggests that by the end of the Anglo-Saxon period the saltmarshes were dry enough to be exploited for much of the year and offered two key resources. Firstly, the flows of saline water along the tidal creeks provided the raw material for salt-making. Salt was of immense value in the early Middle Ages, both as a seasoning and a preservative, and may have had a particular importance locally because of the scale of the herring-fishing industry.[5] So important and profitable was salt-making that some Norfolk manors lying many kilometres away possessed one or more salterns – salt-making sites – within the area of the marshes. Domesday thus records, in its entry for the St Benet's Abbey estate in South Walsham, two salterns; there were also half shares of salterns listed on two of the other holdings in the vill, at least one of which was partly controlled by the abbey. South Walsham village lies some six kilometres from the edge of the marshes and far beyond the range of saline water, and the salt-making sites recorded by Domesday in fact lay in what later became an isolated 'island' of that parish in the middle of the marshes, one of several such detached parochial properties within their area. Two other places lying well back from the edge of the marshes in which Domesday records salterns, Cantley and North Burlingham, likewise had detached portions and these, like South Walsham's, were located towards the northern edge of the marshes. What is particularly striking is that all the places where Domesday records particularly large numbers of salterns lay in this same area, immediately to the north of the marshes: Herringby with 5½, Runham with 18½, Mautby with 23½ and Caister with a staggering 46, although some of these may have been located on the seashore, which bounds the parish to the east. Moreover, where salterns are recorded in vills located away from the marsh edge that did not later, as parishes, possess detached portions in the marshes, these were all located to the north, on the Island of Flegg – in Rollesby, Burgh St Margaret, Filby, Thrigby, Winterton and Somerton. In contrast, salterns were recorded in only three townships holding land in the centre and south of the marshes – Gorleston, Burgh Castle and Fritton (Figure 3.3). Evidently, early medieval salt production was strongly concentrated in the northern part of the Halvergate Marshes, for reasons to which we shall return.

The saltmarshes also provided grazing for sheep. Although their herbage was perhaps not particularly lush, periodic inundation created saline conditions that ensured the destruction of the parasite that, in other waterlogged contexts, caused foot rot in sheep. Where townships beside the marsh included a manorial demesne (only the lord's livestock were recorded) Domesday often notes very large numbers of sheep compared with elsewhere in eastern Norfolk or northern

---

5   J. Campbell, 'Domesday herrings', in C. Harper-Bill, C. Rawcliffe and R. Wilson (eds), *East Anglia's history: studies in honour of Norman Scarfe* (Woodbridge, 2002), pp. 5–17.

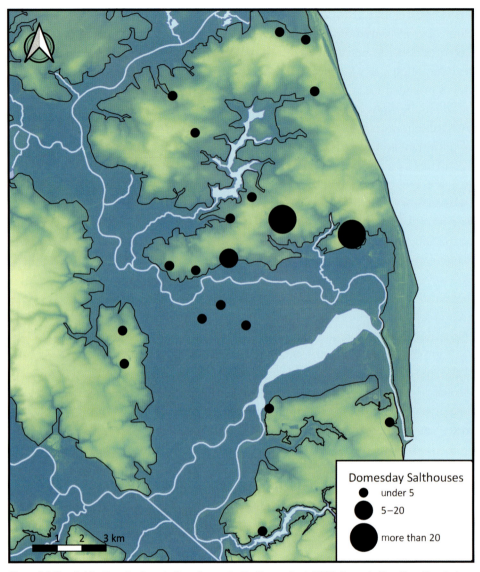

Figure 3.3 The distribution of *salinae* (salterns) recorded by Domesday in 1086. Recorded by vill and located within detached portions of eponymous parishes where relevant. Note the marked concentration towards the north of the marshes.

Suffolk. Acle had 120 sheep, Stokesby 180, South Walsham 220, Tunstall 268, Cantley 400, Runham 480 and Halvergate – the parish later to possess the largest tract of land on the marshes – no fewer than 960. The Domesday entry for Heckingham refers to a 'marsh for 60 sheep'. Salt and sheep continued, to judge from the available evidence, to be the principal produce of the marshes through the three centuries following the Norman Conquest. In the 1140s, for example, St Benet's Abbey leased its demesne lands in South Walsham, described as a marsh with 300 sheep and saltpans.[6] In 1147 Phillip Basset granted to St Benet's Abbey the marsh of Fuelholm (in what is now the detached section of Postwick parish) together with '300 sheep, saltpans and all things pertaining to it'; around 1180 the same property was granted to 'Geoffrey, son of Master Nicholas', again with saltpans and unspecified numbers of sheep.[7] The flocks were often large and kept on the marshes for much if not all of the year. At the start of the thirteenth century that belonging to Norwich Cathedral Priory was kept constantly on Fowlholme, the detached portion of Acle parish lying at the northern end of Breydon Water, except for ten weeks after harvest, when it was fed and folded on the stubbles at Martham, a practice intended to provide manure for the crops rather than reflecting a need for additional feed.[8] Sometimes the dung, rather than the sheep, was moved to the arable fields: the sheep were either penned in folds by night or housed in roofed shelters called cotes, and the dung carefully collected and transported to where it was needed by boat, a practice recorded, for example, on the earl of Norfolk's demesne marshes in Acle, Halvergate and South Walsham, where 1,800 sheep were being grazed in 1278.[9] Sheep remained the principal stock grazed on the marshes into the fourteenth century – St Benet's had over 1,500 on their marsh holdings in 1343.[10]

More information about this early medieval landscape is provided by the remarkable pattern of meandering linear depressions that furrow the surface of the marshes, which represent the tidal creeks and saltmarsh channels that existed before the area was embanked and drained (see Figure 3.12). Most of the drainage dykes that exhibit a curving and sinuous, as opposed to a ruler-straight, form appear to fit neatly into this pattern of relict features, and are evidently elements of the same network, indicating that they evolved out of – were made by adapting – the natural pattern of saltmarsh drainage. The relict creeks and channels survive in variable condition. Over the centuries some examples were deliberately levelled because they formed damp, poorly draining areas of land where the grass was infested with reeds and rushes. More systematic destruction occurred in the course of the twentieth century, as portions of marsh were ploughed up and converted to arable. Nevertheless, most of the original pattern can be reconstructed, using aerial photographs and lidar images (Figure 3.4).

We might begin by emphasising the distinction between the major relict creeks, once significant tidal watercourses navigable by boats, and the smaller

---

6 J.R. West (ed.), *St Benet of Holme 1020–1210: the eleventh and twelfth century sections of Cott.Ms Galba E ii, the register of the abbey of St Benet of Holme* (Norwich, 1932), p. 84.
7 Ibid., p. 85.
8 Cornford, 'Past water levels', p. 18.
9 Campbell, 'Agricultural progress', p. 35.
10 Ibid.

saltmarsh channels. Although it is hard to draw a clear division between the two categories, in broad terms we might say that former creeks are, or were, defined by low, parallel banks enclosing level ribbons of ground more than ten metres wide, while the smaller saltmarsh channels were narrower and with less substantial banks, some displaying a simple U-shaped profile. The banks flanking the creeks are in part usually artificial embankments but in part represent natural features called *levées*. During particularly high tides the creeks would fill, the water flowing over their edges and across the adjacent areas of marsh. The heavier particles of silt and stone suspended in the water would not have been carried far from the channel, but would instead have been deposited beside it, eventually forming low banks of slightly firmer ground. Lidar images show that the margins of the largest former creeks are bounded by multiple parallel banks, indicating changes in the configuration of the channel over time and in some cases, perhaps, the traces left by major flood events.

Today the most obvious of these major ancient creeks is the feature known as the 'Halvergate Fleet', although strictly speaking this name applies to the diminutive watercourse that now runs within it. The Fleet – from the Old English word *fleot*, 'a watercourse or stream' – is a flat-bottomed marshy depression mainly between 50 and 70 metres in width, which runs across the marshes to the north of Breydon Water in a series of bold, smooth curves ('a' on Figure 3.4). It is flanked by low embankments, now discontinuous, the northermost one carrying a track that, before the construction of the Acle Straight turnpike road in the 1830s (the modern A47), formed a routeway for vehicles crossing the marshes *en route* for Great Yarmouth. On or beside both embankments, north and south, are a scatter of marsh farms and drainage mills. The presence of the latter – Stone's Mill, Mutton's, High's and Howard's – reflects the fact that until comparatively recently the Fleet performed an important role in the local drainage system, as a receptacle for water pumped from the surrounding marshes (Figure 3.5).

The Halvergate Fleet in the strict sense – that is, the minor watercourse running within the former creek – follows the inner edge of one embankment, but crosses at intervals to follow the other. Minor drainage dykes also run along the inside edge of the embankments, and sometimes along their outsides. Minor watercourses, in other words, mirror the line of the embankments. Today the Fleet takes a clear, well-defined form for some seven kilometres from its beginning, on the western fringes of the marshes, not far from Wickhampton church, to a point close to Breydon Water, at TG 47652 07153. Beyond this it disappears as an obvious physical feature, and the Fleet watercourse itself makes an abrupt right-angle turn, running south-east and then south for *c*.250 metres to a sluice on the edge of Breydon Water – an arrangement that must be of some antiquity, for the

THE MARSHES 111

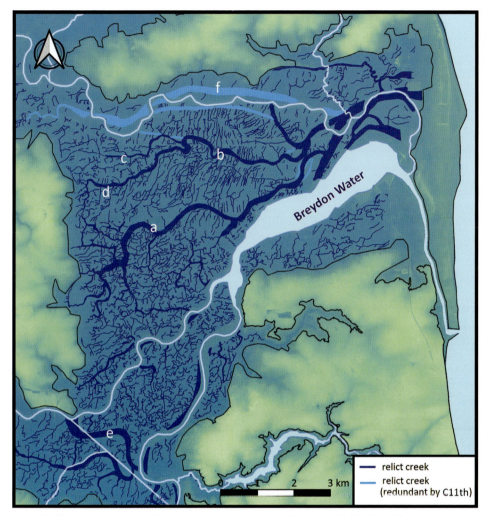

Figure 3.4 The pattern of relict saltmarsh creeks and channels on Halvergate. Plotted from lidar images and aerial photographs, and including channels surviving as drainage dykes. 'a' is the Halvergate Fleet, 'b' the 'Northern Rond'. For the other letters, see text.

line of the watercourse is followed by the boundary between detached portions of Reedham and Freethorpe parishes. But the original line of the Fleet can still be traced beyond this point, in the pattern of dykes, in the line of parish boundaries and in places as a single slight embankment, for more than three kilometres to the north-east, running with the same bold curves as before and still roughly parallel with the edge of Breydon Water.

In the period before the later eighteenth century many other former creeks seem to have survived in a form broadly resembling that of the Halvergate Fleet – that is, as broad ribbons of poorly draining ground, flanked by low banks. William Marshall was able, as late as 1787, to describe how

Figure 3.5 The Halvergate Fleet, a major 'rond' or former tidal creek, looking east: Breydon Water and Great Yarmouth in the far distance.

> The Marshes, taken collectively, are, though nearly *level*, not perfectly *smooth*; being furrowed into inequalities by swamps; which, in their natural state, seem to have been the main drains of the mud-banks. These swamps, or 'reed-ronds', in some places of considerable width, are now the main drains to the Marshes; from the grassy drier parts of which they are detached by banks of soil; which at once serve the purposes of roads, fences and embankments.[11]

'Rond' is today a term used to describe the strips of reedswamp lying between a river and its embankment or 'wall'. In earlier periods it was more widely applied

---

11   Marshall, *Rural economy*, vol. 2, p. 277.

to the ribbons of poorly draining, reed-infested land marking the former course of the tidal creeks.

In the course of the late eighteenth and nineteenth centuries, as the drainage of the marsh was progressively improved, the relict creeks gradually became less obvious features, as their banks were neglected or levelled and as concerted efforts were made to convert the reed-infested ronds into good-quality pasture. But fragments survive in places and, as noted, most are still clear on aerial photographs and lidar images. Their course is also marked by continuous, broadly curving lines of modern drainage dyke and parish boundary, sometimes displaying sharp kinks at intervals where, as in the case of the Halvergate Fleet, a later drainage channel crossed from one side of a lost rond to another.

Of particular note on Figure 3.4 is a major lost creek that meanders from east to west across the marshes in the area between the Halvergate Fleet and the river Bure, a striking feature that has been labelled the 'Northern Rond' ('b' on Figure 3.4). Towards the west it comprises two tributary channels. The northern ('c' on Figure 3.4), the less substantial of the two, is clearly visible from a point in the marshes to the south of Stracey Arms, touching the straight branch road leading south-west from the Acle Straight towards Halvergate at TG 4362 0844, although it can be traced, less clearly, running for some distance further to the west. The southern, more substantial tributary ('d') begins close to the villages of Halvergate and Tunstall.

After the confluence of the two tributaries at TG 4585 0880 Northern Rond proceeds east across the marshes in a series of curves, some rather sharper than those exhibited by the Halvergate Fleet. The two nearly converge around TG 4903 0838 and beyond this point the pattern is confused, with multiple channels, some of which appear to pass *under* the river Bure. This poorly defined and somewhat braided pattern perhaps reflects the fact that, because it lay closer to the sea, this was an area of less vegetated saltmarsh and mudflat, and the creek pattern less fixed and stable than it was to the west.

It would be tedious to discuss in detail the course of the other major creeks but two characteristics shared with the Northern Rond should be briefly noted. Firstly, like modern saltmarsh channels they generally display a dendritic pattern, with a number of defined 'tributaries', especially in their upper reaches. The Halvergate Fleet itself has a number of lesser creeks running into it, especially towards its western end. Secondly, relict creeks often join, and have their line continued by, the existing rivers. A major lost creek thus joins the river Yare near Reedham and the river Waveney near Fritton Marshes, shadowing, as it were, in serpentine form the ruler-straight course of the New Cut, the ship canal dug in 1832–3 to link the two rivers ('e' on Figure 3.4). Rivers and creeks thus, in places, appear to be parts of the same drainage system, although elsewhere, as the relationship of the braided channels to the Bure, noted above, suggests, rivers seem to have changed their course since the basic pattern of creeks was established. Before embanking and drainage, this was a wilder, less stable landscape than today, in which watercourses might shift suddenly following some major flooding event. And details of the creek pattern itself, with channels seeming in places to under- or overlie one another, suggests that not all its elements are contemporary. So, too, does the fact that a number of major creeks (such as 'f', shadowing the course of the Bure in the far north of the marshes) are very faint, almost invisible on the ground and only really revealed by lidar. These must have ceased to function long before the marshes were embanked, and almost certainly by the time of Domesday. The pattern of relict channels does not represent a single chronological horizon, but instead incorporates a number of phases. This said, there is an overall coherence to the pattern formed by the more clearly defined relict creeks and channels that suggests they are broadly contemporary.

The portions of marsh lying between the larger creeks must have resembled islands when the tide was high. This perhaps explains the examples of local place-names incorporating the element *holm*, from the Scandinavian *holmr*, 'island'. In particular, the areas of marsh called Fowlholme and Skeetholme, in the detached portion of Acle parish to the north-west of Yarmouth, are surrounded by relict creeks (the first element of the former name is probably Old English 'foul'; that of the latter, the Scandinavian *skitr*, 'dung').[12] The group of 12 marshes called Dirt Holme in Wickhampton occupy most of an oval of ground almost surrounded by major and minor creeks. These and other names contain echoes of the way that shepherds and saltworkers must have experienced the great saltmarshes, wet and muddy and full of birds and, in places, their excrement. Fuelholm in Postwick Detached features the Old English *fule*, 'wild bird'. The name of Stergott Marsh, likewise in Postwick Detached, derives from the Scandinavian *storr*, 'sedge, bent grass', and Old English *gota*, 'a watercourse, a stream'. The latter element is probably behind the various 'Goat Marshes' found in the detached portion of Reedham parish lying immediately to the north of Breydon Water, although here possibly used in the later Middle English sense of 'sluice'. Gallow Gate (a group of marshes in Wickhampton and Reedham, and a single marsh in Acle) and Gallants, in Reedham, seem to feature the Old English *galla*, 'wet ground with bare areas'. The presence of Scandinavian elements in several of these names is noteworthy, perhaps reflecting the period – the tenth and eleventh centuries – when the marshes first became dry enough to be settled and exploited on a significant scale.

By the end of the Middle Ages the marshes were divided between no fewer than 38 different parishes, 30 in Norfolk and 8 in Suffolk. Their holdings were

---

12 For the interpretation of all these names see A.H. Smith, *English place-name elements*, 2 vols (Cambridge, 1956) and P. Cavill, *A new dictionary of English field-names* (Nottingham, 2018).

THE MARSHES

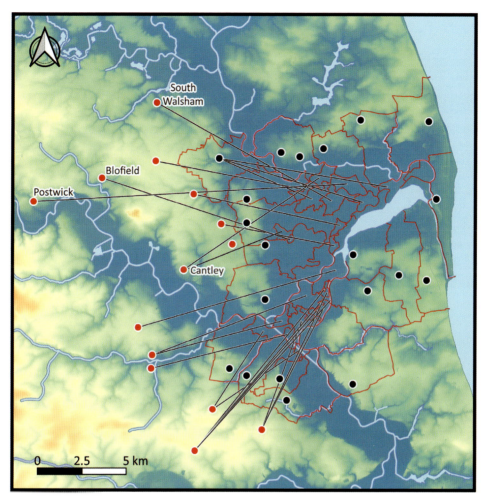

Figure 3.6 The complex pattern of parochial organisation which existed on the marshes before modifications in the nineteenth and early twentieth centuries. Circles mark the parish church of parishes possessing a share of the marsh. Lines show connections to detached portions.

interdigitated in a complex manner (Figure 3.6). In many cases, parishes located on the adjacent 'upland' simply extended down onto the lower ground to embrace a portion of the marshes, in the case of Halvergate, Wickhampton and Reedham reaching far into their centre. Acle extended less far but it had, in addition, three sizeable detached portions, one lying on the eastern side of the marshes, near Great Yarmouth. Runham likewise possessed a section immediately adjoining its 'upland' portion, and also a detached parcel lying close to Yarmouth. Eleven further parishes held isolated blocks of land in the marshes, but themselves lay at a distance from their margins. Chedgrave, Raveningham and Toft Monks each had two such isolated sections, Stockton no fewer than four. In most cases only 5 or 6 kilometres separated the main parish and its detached portion but in a few the distance was rather greater. Eleven kilometres separated the churches of South Walsham from the parish's detached marshland holding; the largest of the two belonging to Cantley, and that of Postwick, lay 9 and 15 kilometres from their respective churches while Blofield's detached portion, a tiny 35 acres (14 hectares) of marsh sandwiched between a second detached portion of Cantley and Wickhampton, lay nearly 11 kilometres away.[13] Such complicated arrangements of intermingled and detached parochial territories are known from elsewhere in England and usually indicate the presence of some important resource, often a dwindling reserve of woodland and pasture, which many were keen to retain or acquire a share of.[14] The complex pattern of boundaries may thus have arisen as a tract of common land, jointly exploited by communities living over a wide area, was divided up and discrete shares assigned to those families who had formerly exploited it collectively. But such arrangements might also arise as wealthy individuals or institutions subsequently acquired blocks of such desirable land through grant or purchase. These, often with little in the way of permanent residents, would be tacked on to a parish dominated by the lord in question, or would be included in one created subsequently, as his heirs erected and endowed a church to serve their estate. Like the main property, these isolated portions would pay the tithe required to maintain the church and support its priest.

It seems, in fact, that the complex pattern of parishes on the Halvergate Marshes arose through both these processes. Most of the parishes with detached portions lay close to the marshes, separated from them only by a parish that itself extended directly out onto them. Loddon was thus divided from the marshes by Norton Subcourse, Chedgrave by Hardley, Toft Monks by Haddiscoe, North Burlingham and Beighton by Acle, Moulton by Halvergate and Raveningham by Norton Subcourse. Places lying immediately adjacent to the marsh appear to have been able to assert rights over their nearest portion, while those lying at one remove had to settle for a detached block lying more remotely. Precisely how, or when, the marsh was parcelled out in this way remains unclear, but it was probably a gradual process of negotiation and perhaps dispute extending over a period of time. In such a process the character of land ownership in various places may also have been an important factor in shaping the configuration of territories.

We have already noted how Domesday reveals that eastern Norfolk and Suffolk were, at the time of the Norman Conquest, characterised by large numbers of free peasants, sokemen and, in particular, free men (see above, p. 50). The latter

---

13   Blofield's detached portion had disappeared by the time the Ordnance Survey 6-inch map was surveyed in 1884, but is shown on the 1845 tithe map, NRO PD 317/52. The adjacent portion of Cantley had been absorbed into Halvergate by the time the tithes were commuted in 1840, although it was still referred to as Cantley Level: NRO PD 354/27. It had still formed part of Cantley parish in 1769: NRO MC 2000/1, 898X7.
14   A. Winchester, *Discovering parish boundaries* (Princes Risborough, 1990).

effectively owned their own small properties and paid their own taxes directly to the state, although most were 'commended' to some powerful individual – that is, had sworn him loyalty in return for support and protection.[15] There were, however, also numerous manors of conventional form, estates comprising a demesne, the property of a wealthy landowner, on which a body of tenants were obliged to provide regular labour as rent for their own farms, and to pay other dues. In some Broadland townships by 1066 all the land was held by free peasants, often commended to a variety of different lords. In others, one or more manors existed, of varying size, usually alongside groups of free men. But there was a strong tendency for the latter, in the wake of the Norman Conquest, to lose their independence. The informal, personal bond of commendation was now interpreted, by a new elite, in such a way that the lands of the commended man came to be seen as the property of his lord. Those free men commended to a lord in the same township were thus increasingly drawn into the economy of his manor, obliged to render rent and other dues there. The lands of those living more distantly from their lord might become an outlying portion of his manor, the main part of which was located in a neighbouring township, and ultimately parish.[16]

It is necessary to make this brief excursion into medieval social history because these circumstances help explain certain aspects of the pattern of early territorial organisation on the marsh. Some parishes had much larger shares of the marsh than others, and in broad terms these, at the time of the Conquest, tended to be places with large manors, strong lords and few free men. In particular, Halvergate and Acle, with the largest shares of marsh (in each case extending over more than 5 square kilometres), were both, unusually for the area, under the control of a single lord immediately before the Conquest, in both cases the powerful Ralph, earl of East Anglia. It is easy to see how such a man, or his predecessors, might have managed to assert claims over particularly extensive tracts of marshland. At the other extreme, Beighton (with around 0.37 square kilometres of marsh), Moulton (with 0.36) or Stockton (with 0.54) were not only more distantly located but also less strongly manorialised, with multiple holdings and in most cases large numbers of free peasants, and without the kind of dominant lord found in Halvergate or Acle.

Such correlations are not absolute but may imply that, in general, the patterns of division within the marsh were fixed not long before the Conquest. Yet some aspects indicate a rather longer chronology. The detached portions of Beighton and Moulton lie adjacent and separated by a straight and arbitrary boundary. They appear to be a single unit subdivided, an impression reinforced by the fact that the

---

15   Williamson, *Norfolk*, pp. 116–25.
16   *Ibid.*, pp. 162–5.

two portions are almost equal in area. The several detached sections of Stockton and Toft Monks lie interdigitated, in a complex manner, on the eastern side of Haddiscoe Island, similarly suggesting subdivision of what was once a single block of land. In both cases the adjacency of the detached parcels mirrors that of the main body of the parishes in question, lying several kilometres away. This in turn suggests that the paired parishes may once have formed single territorial units that were later subdivided, along with their marshland holdings. But if so their division, in both cases, must have occurred well before the time of Domesday, which lists them as separate places and provides no hint of any ancient connection between them. In all probability, the basic pattern of parish boundaries evolved out of patterns of ownership that developed in stages during the two centuries leading up to the Norman Conquest.

Such processes account for most of the parochial complexity of Halvergate, but not all. It is hard to explain in this manner the detached sections of Postwick, Cantley, Blofield or South Walsham, the main parishes of which are located many kilometres away. When the tithes were commuted in 1838 it was reported that the 'tract of marshland formerly called Stargote Marsh', while 'reputed and taken as parcel of the parish of Postwick … is tithe free by prescription', while the detached section of South Walsham had anciently rendered a 'modus', or fixed annual sum, in lieu of normal tithe payments.[17] Both the Postwick and the South Walsham marshes were, before the Dissolution, the property of St Benet's Abbey. Other areas in this northern section of the marshes had a similarly uncertain position within the parish system in post-medieval times, or even lay outside it altogether. In 1769 most of what was to become the easternmost of the detached portions of Acle, comprising the Fowlholme and Skeetholme Marshes around Scaregap Farm near Yarmouth, was described as paying no parish rates, 'being Extraparochial'.[18] Also known as 'Nowhere', the area was returned with Runham in the Census of 1851 and its attachment to the adjacent, existing detached portion of Acle occurred only following the passing of the Poor Law Amendment Act of 1868.[19] The area of Runham parish lying to the south of the Bure, known as Chambers or Chamberer's Marsh, was likewise described as 'extra-parochial' on maps from the 1820s surveyed in connection with the proposed new turnpike road (the modern 'Acle Straight') and, while it was considered as part of the parish when the tithes were commuted, was said to have had anciently paid a 'modus' in lieu of tithes.[20] Both of these areas of marsh had also, before the Dissolution, been monastic property: Fowlholme and Skeetholme part of the estates of the Cathedral Priory, Chambers Marsh belonging

---

17   NRO DN/TA 610.
18   NRO DCN 59/15.
19   NRO DN/TA 194.
20   NRO C/Scf 1/500. NRO C/Scf 1/502. NRO DN/TA 276.

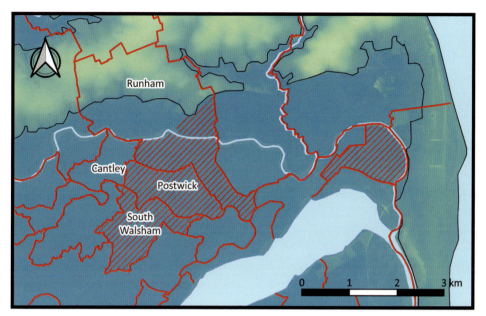

Figure 3.7 The holdings of St Benet's Abbey and Norwich Cathedral Priory preserved as detached parochial areas, and extra-parochial areas, in the northern section of the Halvergate Marshes. The unnamed shaded area to the east is 'Nowhere'.

to St Benet's (Figure 3.7).[21] As noted earlier, St Benet's already owned South Walsham before the Norman Conquest but the marshes in Postwick Detached, then known as Fuelholm, were granted to the monks in 1147 by Phillip Basset 'of Postwick'.[22] Chambers Marsh was also a post-Conquest acquisition, and the Cathedral Priory marshes must have been obtained at or after its foundation at the end of the eleventh century but probably before the start of the thirteenth. Other monastic houses held land elsewhere on the marshes and in at least one case – the detached portion of Langley parish on Haddiscoe Island, once the property of the Premonstratensian abbey of Langley and acquired some time after its foundation at the very end of the twelfth century – this was later tithe free.[23] But what is striking is the concentration of the holdings of the early, Benedictine houses towards the northern edge of the marsh, accounting for some but not all of the most distantly located of the detached sections of parishes, which were mostly clustered in the same area.

This pattern is almost certainly associated with salt production, for most of the places in which Domesday records salt-houses were (as already noted) found in this same area. The salt-houses it records in North Burlingham and Cantley must,

---

21   NRO DN/HAR 3/1. Tithe-free status is not an infallible indication of former monastic ownership. The southernmost section of Mautby, immediately to the east of Chamber's Marsh, paid no tithes but appears always to have been in lay hands.
22   West, *St Benet of Holme*, p. 54.
23   Blomefield and Parkin, *Topographic history*, vol. 10, pp. 148–50. NRO DN/TA 211.

like those in South Walsham, have been located in what became those parishes' detached marshland holdings. Blofield's tiny detached portion, it is true – 14 hectares of land more than 11 kilometres from the parent parish – was located further to the south, but still within the northern section of the marsh, at the end of the Halvergate Fleet. Its size makes it hard to believe that its primary function was the exploitation of the saltmarsh grazing. It was adjoined to the north by the second, smaller, of Cantley's detached portions, which covered around 130 acres (c.50 hectares) and likewise fronted on the Fleet. The more remote detached parochial properties were, in other words, probably particularly associated with salt production; the other, more local detachments mainly reflect a broader desire to exploit the resources of the marshes, especially the summer grazing.

Early medieval exploitation of the marshes is represented in archaeological form by a number of low mounds, generally 1.5 metres or less in height, occurring alone or in concentrations of up to six. Most examples are amorphous or irregular in form but a few are more neatly ovoid or circular. A small number have signs of enclosures or other associated features. They vary greatly in size, although most extend for less than 75 metres in their longest dimension. Many have disappeared over the last half century or so, levelled by temporary or permanent conversion of areas of the marsh to arable, or simply bulldozed away as inconveniences, and are thus known only from old aerial photographs or descriptions. These, as well as examples still extant, are included in Figure 3.8. Many, but probably not all, of the mounds represent piles of waste produced by salt-making. This process was undertaken in a variety of ways in medieval England.[24] One method, known as *'muldefang'* in Lincolnshire, involved digging salt-impregnated sand from the foreshore and placing it in a trench together with sea water. The salt-rich solution was then extracted and heated, in ceramic or metal containers, and the crystals skimmed from the surface. The waste sand was dumped next to the processing site, creating substantial mounds. This method does not appear to have been employed in Broadland, presumably because the salterns were located in a landscape of marshes and muddy creeks, rather than beside the sandy foreshore. The mounds of waste material here are much smaller than those in Lincolnshire or west Norfolk, which can be as much as six metres in height. An alternative approach involved allowing seawater to flow at high tide, via a channel and sluice, into a shallow 'pan', and then successively into further pans, the brine becoming ever more concentrated through evaporation. It was then, as in the previous method, heated in containers and the salt crystals removed. It was, perhaps, a variant of this second method that was employed on the Halvergate Marshes, whereby seawater was collected in

---

24 A.M. and A.P. Fielding, *Salt works and salinas. The archaeology, conservation and recovery of salt making sites and their processes* (Marston, 2005). D.M. Grady, 'Medieval and post-medieval salt extraction in north-east Lincolnshire', in R.H. Bewley (ed.), *Lincolnshire's archaeology from the air* (Lincoln, 1998), pp. 81–95.

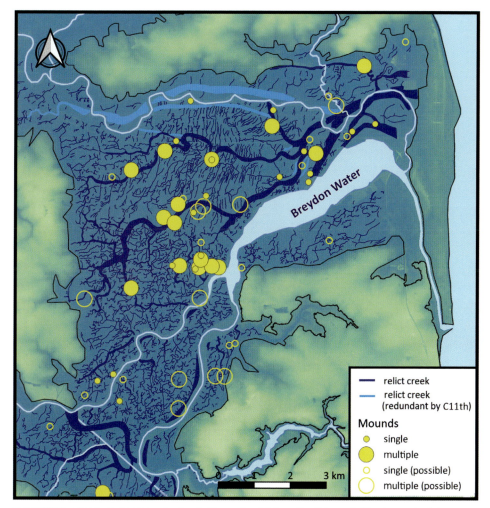

Figure 3.8 The distribution of mounds of probable medieval date on the Halvergate Marshes, and relict saltmarsh creeks and channels.

a single pan and allowed to partially evaporate. The brine, containing much silt, was then removed and heated in containers and the salt crystals skimmed off. This would explain both the lack of clear evidence, comparable to that from parts of Cumbria, of series of settling pans, and also the modest scale of the waste produced, as suggested by the size of the mounds. These were built up from the relatively small amounts of silt suspended in the brine, and discarded once the salt had been removed, accompanied by such things as vessels broken in the heating process. Burnt material and fragments of unglazed pottery have been recovered from some of the Halvergate sites. It seems likely, although unproven, that peat brought by boat from pits located higher up the rivers provided the fuel required by the industry.[25]

---

25 Campbell, 'Domesday herrings', pp. 9–10.

122 BROADLAND

Figure 3.9 The medieval mound near Ash Tree Farm, beside the A47, surmounted by a First World War pillbox.

It should, however, be emphasised that not all of the mounds on the marshes necessarily represent early salterns. Some seem to have been constructed as farm sites, to give residents and livestock a measure of protection from flooding when particularly high tides overtopped the creeks and flowed freely across the surface of the marsh. Such an interpretation is, perhaps, more likely in the case of single mounds, than the groups. Some sites may have had dual functions, as farms *and* as salterns. We should also note that some mounds on the marshes may not be medieval features at all, instead representing no more than dumps of material slubbed out from dykes during routine maintenance, or the waste produced by localised clay extraction. Probable examples have been omitted from Figure 3.8. Others are of uncertain status, and these we have mapped as 'possible' sites. It is noteworthy that a clear tendency for mounds to cluster towards the north of the marshes, where Domesday suggests most salt production occurred, is increased when only the more certain examples are considered, and increased still further if we omit 'single' mounds.

Only two mounds have been the subject of limited archaeological excavation. The single large ovoid example at Ashtree Farm – a metre high, 96 metres long, very visible from the A47 and now topped by a First World War pillbox – was dug into in 1948 (Figure 3.9).[26] It was found to be largely composed of clay and overlay an area of burning associated with pottery of eleventh- to thirteenth-century date. Further sherds of similar date were found beneath this layer, at around a metre below current sea level. One of three irregularly shaped mounds near Berney Arms Reach (TG 4677 0532) was excavated in 1999 by the Norfolk Archaeological Unit.[27] It measured *c.*35 by 20 metres and contained burnt material and twelfth- and thirteenth-century pottery, but none of pre-Conquest date. In addition, some dating evidence has come from pottery and other artefacts recovered, usually with quantities of animal bone, from the sites of levelled mounds, or from examples during their disturbance or destruction, including from that on which Six Mile House on the river Bure (formerly in Cantley Detached) now stands. One site produced thirteenth-century sherds, one unspecified 'medieval' material and five pottery of eleventh-, twelfth- and thirteenth-century date, in two cases accompanied by late medieval and post-medieval material.[28] Even if the latter examples originated as salt-making sites, these finds do not necessarily indicate that they continued to function as such into the sixteenth or seventeenth centuries. Dual-use sites, functioning as both salterns and farms, may have continued to serve as farms alone long after salt-making had

---

26   Lambert *et al.*, *Making of the Broads*, p. 131.

27   NHER 24208.

28   Information from Norfolk Historical Environment Record. The site of a levelled mound some 600m north-east of that at Ashtree Farm allegedly produced only pottery of fourteenth- to eighteenth-century date, but there are grounds for believing that this material in fact came from a nearby hollow, which had been filled with refuse brought out from nearby Great Yarmouth. NHER 4323.

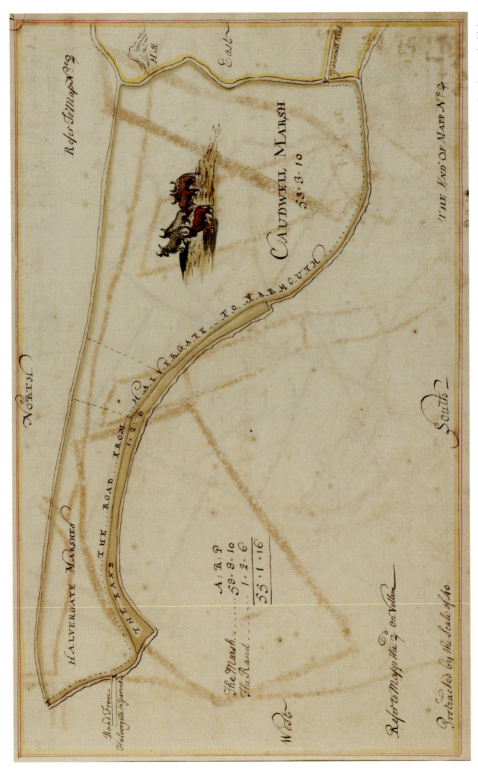

Figure 3.10 Estate map, surveyed in the 1730s, showing land in Halvergate parish lying to the north of the Halvergate Fleet. Note the 'hill' (top right), a medieval mound which has since been levelled.

ceased, while abandoned saltern mounds made convenient places on which to build farms or on which to place other structures. Six Mile House, for example, stands on a mound, roughly a metre and a half in height and incorporated into the 'wall' beside the river Bure, which was used as a site for brick-making in late medieval times.[29] Lockgate Farm beside Breydon Water, demolished in the 1980s, stood on a probable saltern mound, as does a yard and cattleshed, perhaps all that remained of a farm site, in the detached portion of Great Moulton parish, at TG 46291 05689, some 600 metres north-west of Berney Arms.[30]

Such as it is, the archaeological evidence suggests that salt-working began on the marshes perhaps a century before Domesday and came to an end in the thirteenth century. It did not entirely cease in the area but thereafter took place close to the outfall of the Yare, where the water was most saline, rather than being widely scattered: William Harborne appears to have been producing salt in Yarmouth in the 1590s and Samuel Doubleday just outside the town in the 1620s, while in the following decade Nicholas Murford established an extensive works on Cobholm Island covering some 24 acres (10 hectares), on which brine was evaporated and then heated. The latter works continued to operate into the eighteenth century and are shown on James Corbridge's 1724 *Prospect of Yarmouth*.[31]

As noted earlier, many of the medieval mounds have been levelled in the past, often leaving no clear surviving traces. The sites of some examples may be indicated by the name 'Hill Marsh', which appears on a number of early maps and which, in this level terrain, must almost certainly refer to a lost saltern or farmstead mound. It is no coincidence that a map of the Dean and Chapter's estate of Fowlholme and Skeetholme, drawn up in 1733, describes the field lying next to the mound at Ashtree Farm as 'Hill Marsh' (the tithe map of 1838 labels the mound itself, with some exaggeration, the 'Great Hill').[32] Occasionally, eighteenth-century maps depict 'hills' in elevation. A survey of Miles Branthwaite's marshes in Halvergate parish, for example, drawn up in the 1730s, depicts and labels a 'Hill' on the property lying adjacent to the east (Figure 3.10).[33] A mound is shown here on the 1946 RAF aerial photographs but was levelled in the post-war period. Its site has produced Late Saxon and medieval pottery.[34]

A map of the detached portion of South Walsham parish, surveyed in 1768, names two portions of marsh – lying a short distance to the south of the 'Northern

---

29 NHER 21103.
30 NHER 42174. NHER 42215.
31 J.K. Gruenfelder, 'Nicholas Murford, Yarmouth salt-producer', *Norfolk Archaeology*, 41/2 (1991), pp. 162–70. Albone *et al.*, 'Coastal Zone', p. 119.
32 NRO DCN 127/19.
33 NRO HNR 15/5.
34 NHER 22349.

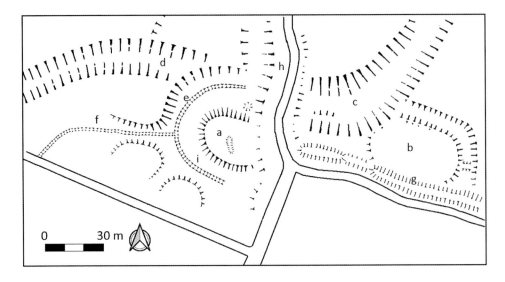

Figure 3.11 Earthworks of probable medieval saltern, located in the far north of what was formerly the detached portion of South Walsham parish (TG 4666 0824). See text for key.

Rond' – as 'Great Hill Marsh' and 'Little Hill Marsh'.[35] They lie to the north and south of a complex of earthworks located some 800 metres to the south-west of Britannia Farm at TG 4666 0824 (Figure 3.11). The site, which is bisected by a north–south drainage dyke, was surveyed by a team of volunteers in the winter of 2019. To the west is a low but well-defined platform ('a' on Figure 3.11) from which a single piece of thirteenth-century pottery was retrieved from a molehill. To the east is another low platform, less well defined, perhaps the 'hill' referred to in the names, partially levelled at some unknown date. What is particularly interesting, however, is the wider context of the earthworks. Features 'e' and 'f' are comparatively modern, perhaps nineteenth-century, surface drains, while 'h' and 'g' appear to be long mounds of material cleared from the adjacent drainage dykes; but the great curving depressions 'c' and 'd', which evidently once formed a single, continuous feature, appear to represent a natural saltmarsh channel that was deliberately blocked when the site was established. This was presumably to divert the saltwater flowing along it at high tide into area 'i', where evaporation took place. Further processing, involving direct heating, may have been carried out on the adjacent platform 'a', with waste material being dumped to the east. As we have seen, Domesday lists four salt-houses in its entries for South Walsham, and this is almost certainly the site of one of them.

The natural channel with which the site is associated flows into the Northern Rond just over 200 metres to the north. A number of other mounds are similarly

---

35 NRO MS 4553.

THE MARSHES 127

Figure 3.12 Lidar image showing the 'Northern Rond' and medieval mound sites. The latter typically lie a little back from the former watercourse ('a' and 'd'), or stand on its levee banks ('b' and 'c'). 'd' is the probable saltern shown in Figure 3.11; 'b' is the lost farm illustrated in Figure 3.21.

located, set back between 100 and 200 metres from the Northern Rond, the Halvergate Fleet or one of the other major relict creeks (Figure 3.12), and they presumably functioned in a similar way, making use of water flowing up the minor channel at high tide, but removed from the full force of water surging up the main channel. A few examples are, however, located immediately adjacent to major creeks, and were presumably equipped with sluices in the levée bank to control the ingress of saltwater. Either way, almost all the mounds are positioned close to one of the major, double-sided creeks; names such as 'Hill Marsh' are, perhaps unsurprisingly, similarly located. Not all the mounds, as already emphasised, necessarily represent salt-making sites, and in some cases proximity to a creek may reflect the ease of access to isolated farms by small boats that this provided.

What is also striking is that parish boundaries, which form such a complex pattern across the marshes, often follow these major creeks, sometimes crossing at intervals from one side to the other; such features made obvious lines of division in this open landscape. As a result, almost all the mounds, and certainly all of those likely to mark salt-production sites, lie on or within *c.*200 metres of a parish boundary (Figure 3.13). The major creeks, the parish boundaries and the saltern sites all seem to represent elements of the same relict landscape, dating to the period between (perhaps) the tenth and the thirteenth centuries. There are nevertheless hints that some of the major creeks were stable features in the landscape for a rather longer period. It is, for example, noticeable that the main channel of the Halvergate Fleet has its origins less than 400 metres from Wickhampton church, which presumably marks the original Middle Saxon focus of settlement in the parish, suggesting that the site was chosen because of the access so provided. The name Wickhampton means something like 'home farm at the *wic*'. This latter element has a number of meanings, one of which is 'trading place', so it may be significant that metal-detector finds from the area near the church include eighth-century coins, one a gold dinar of the Abbasid Caliphate, based in Baghdad.[36]

Yet, as suggested earlier, we should not exaggerate the stability of the saltmarsh landscape. The relict channels visible on lidar and aerial photographs display evidence of change over time, with some examples rather less visible than others, and some appearing to overlie others. Indeed, major changes in the pattern of creeks and watercourses seem to have continued long after the Norman Conquest. In particular, there seems little doubt that, until the fifteenth century, the river Bure did not turn south after Scaregap Farm to join the Yare as it does today, but instead continued due east (through what is now the North Denes race course), entering the sea to the north of Yarmouth at a place called Cockle Water or Grubb's Haven. Manship, writing in 1619, first recorded this tradition, and the way in which that

---

36 NHER 24595.

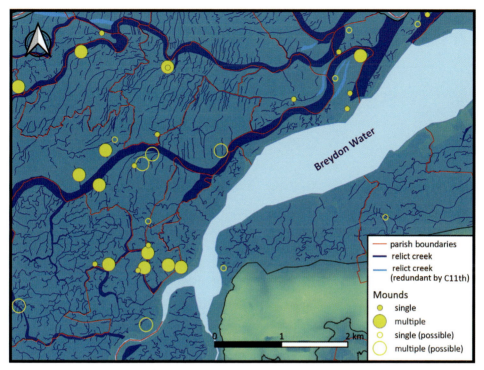

Figure 3.13 The relationship between former creeks, medieval mounds and parish boundaries in the area lying to the north-west of Breydon Water.

outfall was 'long since, by sand heaps ... dammed up'.[37] He implies that this happened around 1346.[38] Aerial photographs, lidar and the character of the topography all support the suggestion. Its outfall blocked, the Bure was diverted southwards, joining the Yare as it does today. Their combined waters then flowed for more than four kilometres south before reaching the sea (at a point some way to the south of the present outfall). This change probably had another important effect. Breydon Water is sometimes described as the 'remains' of the 'great estuary', its history by implication one of steady contraction. But the configuration of relict creeks suggests a more complex picture, for the Halvergate Fleet did not, as we have seen, originally drain into Breydon Water but instead skirted its northern margins, an unusual relationship between a tidal creek and an estuary, even one surviving in truncated form. Breydon looks, instead, to have expanded north across an earlier pattern of creeks, a process which may have been continuing as late as 1742, when 'Mr Turner's heirs' successfully appealed to the Sea Breach Commission against the rates charged on 160 acres of land in Halvergate parish on the grounds that 'twenty acres parsell

---

37   C.J. Palmer (ed.), *Henry Manship: the history of Great Yarmouth* (Great Yarmouth, 1854), pp. 171–5.
38   *Ibid.*, p. 78.

130 BROADLAND

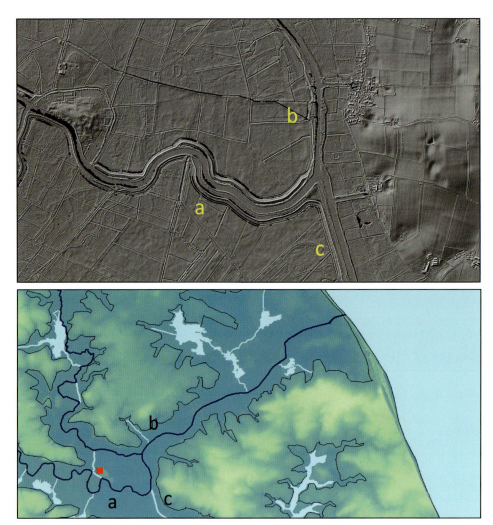

Figure 3.14 Above: lidar image of Thurne Mouth; the earthworks of St Benet's Abbey, on the island of Cow Holm, left centre. Note how the Bure ('a') here appears to flow *into* the Thurne ('b'), in a smooth curve. Its course below Thurne mouth ('c'), in contrast, is ruler-straight for a kilometre and looks remarkably artificial. Below: shown in dark blue, possible courses of the rivers Ant and Bure before changes in the thirteenth century; 'a', 'b' and 'c', as above; red square, site of St Benet's Abbey. According to this interpretation, the Thurne then formed the lower reaches of the Bure. Joined by the Ant, which at this time flowed east along the Hundred Dyke, it flowed north to the sea, following the line of what is now the Hundred Stream.

thereof are nowe some years since swallowed up by Braydon'.[39] Breydon's expansion was almost certainly the result of the enforced confluence of the Bure and the Yare, and a consequent increase in the amount of water ponded back along the latter at high tide. The long, constricted channel to the outfall to the south of Great Yarmouth was now taking the waters of the Bure as well as those of the Yare.

---

39   NRO EAW 1/2.

It is just possible that, perhaps a century or so before the closure of Grubb's Haven, there had been a more dramatic change in the course of the Bure. The apparent concentration of medieval salt-making on the northern margins of the marshes, mainly in parishes (or detached portions of parishes) bordering the Bure, is surprising, for it would be hard to make salt in these locations today because of the volume of fresh water flowing down the river.[40] Even when it had an outfall at Grubb's Haven conditions would have been more brackish than saline even at high tide, as indeed was clearly the case along the lower reaches of the Yare and the Waveney, to judge from the meagre evidence for early salt-working in the central and southern sections of the Halvergate Marshes. This in turn raises the possibility that, until some time in the thirteenth century, the Bure did not flow across the north of the marshes at all. Indeed, its course appears, as we have seen, to overlie a pattern of purely tidal creeks in the area immediately to the north-west of Great Yarmouth (Figure 3.4).

We noted in Chapter 1 how the river Ant originally flowed into what is now the Thurne along the Hundred Dyke, and then into the sea along the Hundred Stream, and hypothesised that the gradual blocking of the outfall here led to flooding, obliging St Benet's Abbey to redirect the Ant along its present course and to create what is now the river Thurne (see above, pp. 27–8). It is possible, however, that the changes made were even more radical, and that before the outfall became blocked it may have taken not only the waters of the Ant but also those of the Bure: that is, the Thurne may at this time have been the lower course of the Bure (Figure 3.14). One indication of this is the curious configuration of waterways in the vicinity of Thurne Mouth. Examined on a map, or indeed on the ground, the Bure ('a') here appears to flow *into* the Thurne ('b'), in a smooth curve. Its course below Thurne Mouth ('c'), in contrast, is ruler-straight for a kilometre and looks remarkably artificial. It appears to have been dug to divert the Bure southwards, thereby turning its old lower course into a new river, the Thurne, flowing in the reverse direction. Beyond the end of the straight new channel, the redirected waters may have been left to pick their own way through the marshes before following the line of an existing minor watercourse, a continuation of the Muck Fleet. This redirection of the Bure along its present course, perhaps in the thirteenth century, may have drastically reduced the viability of salt production on the marshes. There are, we admit, a number of difficulties with this theory, but it would account for a number of otherwise puzzling features about the configuration of the river system, the relationship of the Bure to the pattern of relict creeks and the distribution of early salt-making activity on the Halvergate Marshes.

---

40   M. Pallis, 'On the causes of the salinity of the Broads of the River Thurne', *The Geographical Journal*, 37/3 (1911), pp. 284–91.

The draining of the marshes

Much uncertainty surrounds the question of when the Halvergate Marshes were drained. In part, this reflects the fact that, even within a single block of land, drainage was more of a process of progressive improvement than a single 'event'. Moreover, the rate of that progression – towards a well-drained sward, protected from flooding, which could be safely grazed for six months or more of the year – was not uniform throughout the area of the marshes. There was never a unified scheme to drain the area or an official body to oversee the process, although it often involved cooperation between neighbouring landowners, sometimes in large groups. Instead, improvement occurred in a gradual, piecemeal manner.

The most important, and initial, stage was the conversion of saltmarsh, subject to periodic inundation by the sea, to fresh marsh, with a sward dominated by grass species rather than by salt-tolerant, less nutritious or less palatable herbage. As noted earlier, this change was brought about by raising earth 'walls' or embankments along the edges of the rivers, and beside Breydon Water, to prevent the ingress of saltwater. It is possible that the construction of embankments was initially stimulated by rising sea levels, increasing incidence of storm surges and a need to protect livestock from floods. Either way, natural channels to the rear of embankments were then repurposed as drainage dykes and where one of them met the wall a 'flap sluice' was installed, comprising a hollowed trunk of elm at the end of which was a wooden flap. Water could drain away from the marsh at low water but at high tide the pressure sealed the sluice, preventing saltwater flowing back onto it. Walls were also raised which ran back from the river frontage, to guard against flood waters flowing in laterally, from areas yet to be embanked. These were sometimes raised on the levée banks of former creeks, sometimes beside tributary streams, like the Pickerill Holme on the boundary between Mautby and Caister, draining off the adjacent uplands. Less substantial 'walls', again often following the levées of old creeks, were usually raised to the rear of the embanked area. As we have seen, such features had long been used to define major boundaries in the open landscape of the saltmarsh.

The Halvergate Marshes cover an extensive area of land and some portions lie more than three kilometres from a river or from Breydon Water; thus, once the openings of major creeks had been sealed, neither Halvergate nor Wickhampton, the parishes with the largest shares of the marsh, would have had direct contact with tidal water. The same was true of several of the detached portions of parishes, such as that belonging to South Walsham. Where marshes lay remote from the rivers, protected from saltwater floods by the defences of other proprietors, there was less immediate need to raise embankments. 'Walls' were raised in such areas, but usually at a later stage in the drainage process, and with a slightly different purpose.

There are only scattered and often ambiguous references to embankments or flood defences before the seventeenth century. A lease of marshes in Raveningham and Thurlton, drawn up in 1493, thus notes the tenant's obligations to maintain the *fossata* marshes, although whether this means 'ditched marshes', 'embanked marshes' or both is uncertain.[41] Another lease, dating to the 1550s, for the Dean and Chapter's marshes at Fowlholme and Skeetholme 'with all the ditches and stremys Fleetis and Fysshyng to the same marryshes and pastures belonging', bound the tenant to the task of 'drawynge skowryng rearyng and matyng [maintaining] off the diches ffences stremes and Fleets and Bridges'.[42] 'Fences' may or may not be a reference to embankments, although the more general attention paid to the maintenance of dykes probably suggests drained rather than saltmarsh. The process of embanking the principal watercourses may have continued into the sixteenth century – in the 1580s and 1590s there was a legal dispute over whether the reclamation of Lodsco Marshes, beside the river Waveney in Raveningham Detached, should mean an increase in tithes paid.[43] But it must have been largely complete by 1608. In that year the whole of the Halvergate Marshes were devastated by a great flood caused, as several later ones were to be, by the sea breaking through the dunes around Happisburgh, sea water flowing down the Thurne and then along the Bure. The following year a parliamentary act was passed to establish a Sea Breach Commission to deal with the problem – a body charged with the task of surveying the breaches in the sea defences, levying a rate on those affected in order to repair them and undertaking the necessary works. The preamble to the Act noted the damage sustained by:

> The greatest parte of the marshes and Lower Groundes within the Townes and Parishes hereinafter mentioned (the same conteyning many Thousand Acres) upon whch a great part of the Wealth of the said Counties doth depend, being grounde of themselves very ritch, and without wch the Uplande, specially of the Countie of Norff, being of themselves for the most Parte vy dry and barren, cannot be so well husbanded or ymployed.[44]

The very fact that all this land could be so damaged by the temporary ingress of sea water suggests that it must have been embanked ground with an improved sward, rather than saltmarsh subject to frequent inundation. After this date references to river walls become more common in the documents. In 1636, for example, Richard Jenkinson leased to John Baker of Upton and Thomas Coats of

---

41 NRO DCN 49/57.
42 NRO DCN 49/66B.
43 TNA C 2/JasI/C6/47.
44 7 James I CAP XX.

Acle 'the reed rond called Childes Marsh in Tunstall lying between Childes Marsh wall … on the south and the common river', the Bure, on the north.[45] In 1649 the parliamentary surveyors, making their report on the Dean and Chapter's estate on Fowlholme and Skeetholme, included an estimate of the cost of maintaining the river embankments.[46]

The conversion of the saltmarshes to fresh thus appears to have largely occurred in the fourteenth and fifteenth centuries, continuing perhaps in some areas into the sixteenth. Investment in embankments and sluices is superficially surprising, given that this was generally a period of plague and demographic decline, followed by only slow recovery. But, while grain prices certainly stagnated, lower rents and higher wages increased disposable incomes and thus spending on meat, dairy produce and items made of wool and leather. This was a good period for livestock farmers, one in which the conversion of arable to pasture led, in the Midland counties especially, to the contraction or even disappearance of villages. In such circumstances, large-scale investment to improve and protect the marshes should, perhaps, be expected.

Yet even when the marshes were sufficiently embanked to prevent the regular ingress of saltwater, they remained poorly drained in comparison to today, with areas of standing water and waterlogged, reed-infested ground in the old relict creeks. A document of 1580, describing land in Stergott Marsh in the detached portion of Postwick parish, thus refers to a 'gill [small stream or watercourse] called Stergott gill and in the same estward is a flashe of water called Stergott flashe'.[47] As Marshall put it in 1787, 'the individual marshes are far from being level; they being more or less scooped out into hollows; where the water lodges a considerable time after the higher parts are dry'.[48]

The initial embanking of the marshes was therefore followed by several centuries of attempts to improve their drainage. But such efforts were more necessary in some areas than others. Water was constantly flowing into the area of the marshes not only along the now embanked rivers but also along minor streams, from peripheral springs and seepage lines, and as surface run-off from the farmland on the adjacent uplands. In general, the areas of marsh furthest from the rivers therefore tended to suffer more from seasonal waterlogging than those lying close to them, from where water had only to flow a short distance to reach the sluices. An undated seventeenth-century document describes 18 acres of the marshes in the detached portion of South Walsham parish as being 'of late much prejudiced for want of drayning and may be improved and made worth 10s

---

45 Sheffield City Archives, BFM/1234.
46 NRO DCN 52/1, p. 127.
47 NRO Hansell 12/1/71 R 187B no. 12.
48 Marshall, *Rural economy*, vol. 2, p. 278.

per acre'.[49] In 1616, in order to calculate the amount to charge for repairs to the breaches in the Happisburgh dunes, the Sea Breach Commission undertook a comprehensive assessment of the various parcels of marsh, listing the 'trewe yerely vallewe of them by the acre as they are undrowned'. Values recorded varied greatly, with some portions worth only a few pence but a few as much as 5s per acre, but with most assessed at between 3s and 4s. Those in Wickhampton and Halvergate, lying far from the rivers, were the exceptions, with most parcels valued at 2s 6d or less per acre.[50] Yet even lands lying close to the rivers and sluices could benefit from increased attention to drainage works. Owners were everywhere keen to extend the growing season and to expand the area of good-quality marsh at the expense of the 'ronds' and other places where the water collected. In 1728 it was said that the Dean and Chapter's marsh at Skeetholme, beside the river Yare, was 'in a Wett season … for half a Yeare together a Meer Puddle notwithstanding its fine Appearance in Summer'.[51]

Attempts to improve conditions in the course of the seventeenth century – a period in which major drainage projects were under way in other wetland areas of England, most notably the Fenlands of Cambridgeshire, Lincolnshire and western East Anglia – may be reflected in rising land values. By 1702, when the Sea Breach Commission drew up another valuation list, most marshes were thought to be worth between 5s and 7s an acre *per annum* and even those in Halvergate and Wickhampton were generally valued at around 6s. Even allowing for inflation, this represents a significant increase.[52] Land closest to the rivers nevertheless continued, on the whole, to be valued most highly and other sources suggest it commanded the highest rents. In 1672 70 acres of marsh in Runham were rented for £28, or 8s an acre.[53] It is possible that the apparent increases in land values were in part caused by the erection of the first drainage mills, which were certainly being employed on a large scale from the 1660s in the more extensive wetlands of the Fens on the western side of Norfolk. These raised water over a river wall, allowing the water table within embanked areas to be maintained at a lower level than when drained by gravity alone through a sluice. They could also be used to drain new areas, away from the main rivers, moving water from blocks of land sealed from the surrounding marshes by embankments into relict creeks or minor streams distantly connected to the sluices beside the tidal waters.

There is firm evidence that drainage mills or 'engines' were being erected in Broadland by the start of the eighteenth century, but so far this comes from

49   NRO Clayton Mss Ms 3354.
50   NRO C/Scf 6/1.
51   NRO DCN 9/15/2.
52   NRO EAW 1/3.
53   NRO Clayton Mss 3329 4B2.

Figure 3.15 Detail from a map of 1721, showing the drainage windmill erected following the enclosure of Stokesby Common in the previous year.

places just outside the Halvergate 'triangle', in areas of alluvial marsh lying in the lower reaches of the river valleys feeding into it. One example is shown beside the Bure on a map of St Benet's Abbey, surveyed in 1702, standing some way from the iconic tower later built into the old gatehouse. Another is depicted on a map of Colonel Cope's Marshes, later Peto's Marsh, in Oulton on the river Waveney in 1723. The existence of other early examples is suggested by minor place-names. The 1702 map of Benet's Abbey labels a portion of marsh, lying at a distance from the drainage mill, as 'Mill Brigg Marsh' (the same name is recorded as early as 1617). It is therefore possible that mills were also being erected on the Halvergate Marshes in the seventeenth century, and the list of land drawn up by the Sea Breach Commission in 1715 does indeed include a reference to 'parte of Merrie Marsh called the Mill Marsh' in Halvergate parish.[54] But so far we only have certain evidence for their construction from the eighteenth century.

One was built in 1720 following the enclosure of Stokesby Common, which occupied one of those pockets of particularly damp, peaty land that, as already

---

54 NRO DN HAR 3/3. NRO EAW 1/8. NRO EAW 1/8.

noted, are dotted around the margins of the Halvergate 'triangle' (Figure 3.15). The next known example was erected in the 1760s by William Windham, a major landowner, to drain 225 acres (91 hectares) of marsh in Norton Subcourse and Raveningham, a document drawn up in 1768 listing 'The Contents of ye several Marshes lying in Norton belonging to Wm Windham Esq wch are Drain'd by ye New Engine'.[55] In 1769 he, John Berney of Bracon Ash, John Fowle of Broome and Dionissa his wife agreed jointly to erect a mill to drain their lands in the neighbouring Thurlton Marshes, which were described as being 'Subject to be overflowed and have been freqtly damaged by Floods and Inundations of water for want of a Mill or Engine and other proper Works Cuts Drains Dams Sluices and Outlets to carry off the same'.[56] The four parties also agreed to share the costs of ancillary features – 'Bridge Trunks Arches Dams Sluices and the Great drain leading towds the River' – between them, 'rateably and in Proportion to ye Number of Acres wch Each of them ... have or hath in the sd parcells of Mars'es'. The new mill was to be built on Berney's property and he was to be paid yearly for the loss of land, the cost of the works and the costs of their maintenance. Around the same time, John Houghton of Bramerton erected a 'Windmill or Water Engine' on Scarsdale Marsh in Halvergate parish and in 1769 drew up an agreement with the owners of adjacent lands allowing them also to make use of it in return for a yearly payment.[57] The very same year a very similar contract was made between William Fisher and his neighbours holding land in the marshes in and around that portion of Cantley Detached later absorbed into Halvergate parish, less than a kilometre south-west of Scarsdale Marsh.[58] It is possible that this apparent flurry of mill-building activity in the 1760s is an illusion, caused by the chance survival of evidence. But it would perhaps explain why William Marshall, writing in 1787, believed that the first drainage mills had appeared on the marshes only two decades earlier.[59]

By the mid-1790s, to judge from the evidence of William Faden's 1797 map of Norfolk and Joseph Hodskinson's 1783 map of Suffolk, there were around 32 drainage mills within the Halvergate 'triangle', of which a quarter lay at a distance of more than 200 metres from a river, draining water instead into minor watercourses or relict creeks such as the Halvergate Fleet.[60] The figure had risen to around 37 by the 1880s, but by this time some areas of the marshes were being drained by steam. Already in 1844, Bacon could describe how Sir William Beauchamp-Proctor,

---

55   NRO MEA 2/53, 651X8.
56   NRO MEA 3/578, 659 X2. NRO MEA 2/53, 651X8.
57   NRO FEL 154, 549X 8.
58   NRO MC 2000/1, 898X7.
59   Marshall, *Rural economy*, vol. 2, p. 277.
60   NRO KNY 27.

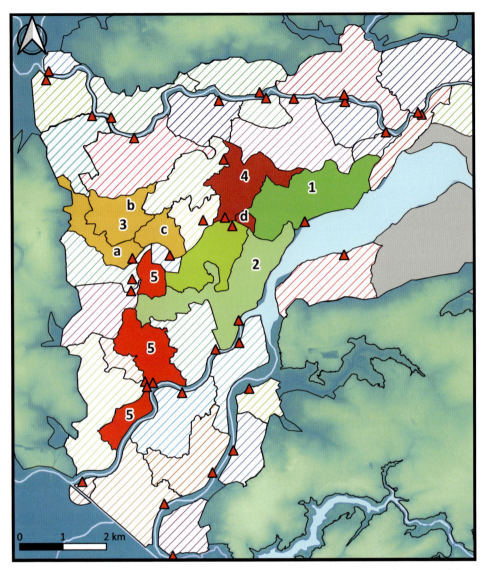

Figure 3.16 The pattern of drainage 'Levels' on the Halvergate Marshes in the late nineteenth century, and the mills or steam pumps that drained them. Areas in light grey, on the right of the map, were drained by gravity alone. See text for key.

owner of the Langley estate, had erected a 'steam mill' that was draining a wide tract of land to the south-west of the New Cut (and extending up the Yare valley), while another was operating 'near Yarmouth', the tithe map of 1838 showing it beside the river Bure near Scaregap Farm in the detached portion of Acle parish.[61] Steam pumps proliferated through the second half of the nineteenth century but, as we shall see, never replaced windmills.

---

61   R.N. Bacon, *The report on the agriculture of Norfolk* (London, 1844), p. 294.

By the nineteenth century the marshes were divided into embanked areas called 'Levels', each usually drained by its own mill, although only in the last decades of the century do the sources allow us to reconstruct their configuration with confidence (Figure 3.16).[62] Their embankments followed the edges of rivers, former creeks or 'ronds' or – especially in areas lying at a distance from the rivers – smaller relict channels, and were embanked to varying degrees. The pattern was a complex one that seems to have developed over time. An individual level typically covered around 1.5 square kilometres but some were more extensive. That drained by Berney Arms Mill ('1' on Figure 3.16) covered 2.7 square kilometres and that served by Lockgate Mill ('2' on Figure 3.16) more than three. Conversely, a few were significantly smaller, that drained by North Mill in the south of Wickhampton parish, for example, extending over little more than 0.4 square kilometres. There is little doubt that the larger levels emerged through the progressive amalgamation of smaller ones. What late-nineteenth-century sources describe as 'Howard's Level' in Halvergate ('3' on Figure 3.16), drained by Mutton's Mill, for example, the 1839 tithe map still describes as three separate levels – Frothelms ('a'), Mants ('b') and Scardell ('c') – albeit already drained by the one mill. The same source shows a tiny embanked area called Little Thuston Level ('d') that, by the late nineteenth century, had been incorporated with the adjacent South Walsham Level ('4'). Levels usually formed unitary blocks but that drained by Cadge's Mill lay in three separate sections, one lying at a little distance ('5').

Some levels appear to have originated as the property of a single proprietor, drained by its own sluice and eventually acquiring a mill. Some, such as Mautby Level, remained like this into the nineteenth century. But in others ownership fragmented, gradually or suddenly, so that a number of different proprietors came to contribute to the maintenance of the mill and other drainage works. South Walsham Level, coterminous with South Walsham Detached – the old St Benet's holding, 390 acres (158 hectares) in all – still formed a single property until at least 1768.[63] But by the time the tithes were commuted around 1840 it was divided between 13 different owners, the tithe apportionment noting that the marshes were 'formerly the property of one individual and have since been divided and sold'.[64] Kerrison's Level, coterminous with the detached portion of Acle lying between Halvergate and South Walsham Detached, was owned as one block in the early eighteenth century and had almost certainly been embanked as such, but by 1840 contained the lands of 14 proprietors.[65]

---

62 The levels have been reconstructed from a large number of nineteenth-century sales particulars, mainly deposited in the NRO, supplemented with later Internal Drainage Board data.
63 NRO MS 4553.
64 NRO DN/TA 610.
65 NRO AG 86, 233X3. NRO PD 164/16.

Some levels, in contrast, probably comprised the lands of numerous owners from the start. This was almost certainly the case with that comprising the detached portion of Raveningham parish fronting on the Yare opposite Reedham, a document of 1675 describing: 'The Severall Marshes with theire Quantities which have theire Drayn through the Sluice Lyinge between Glover Denny gent. and Francis Langley and ought to be Chargeable toward the Renewinge and repayers of the Sayd Sluice.'[66] Fourteen different landowners are listed holding a total of 174 acres (70 hectares), each paying 6d per acre towards the cost of the works. A similar document, drawn up in 1694, records the payments due from the same area as well as receipts for the 11s 6d paid 'for ye Damming worke to the Sluice' and for the 'use and carriage of ye Planks and Rafters about ye said Sluice'. Another document in the same collection records 'the names of ye Persons for the Repayr of the Head Damm in Norton Subcors', the adjacent level of marshes lying immediately to the west.[67] In such cases groups of proprietors, often perhaps agreeing to an initiative spearheaded by one or more leading landowners, had jointly paid for the construction of banks, sluices and other works, perhaps as early as the fourteenth century, with their successors continuing to share responsibility for their maintenance. It is likely that some of the properties thus combined in a level had previously been protected by their own smaller embankments. Certainly, the early 6-inch Ordnance Survey maps and lidar images sometimes reveal stretches of embankment – often in the form of discontinuous fragments – lying within the area of later levels.

The joint funding of sluices and main drains within particular levels, once these had been established, was easily extended to the erection of drainage mills. In 1778 an agreement was drawn up to drain 'certain marshes in Raveningham and Towns adjoining', almost certainly the same level drained by the sluice in the 1675 agreement.[68] The document points out that, for want of drainage work, the marshes in question had become 'of little value' and that, in consequence, two of the principal owners, Jane Welham and E. Clarke, 'are come to a resolution of Erecting a Mill for Draining the same'. There were now eight other proprietors in the level, who agreed to pay 2s per acre every year for the next 20 years towards the costs of the mill and associated works. But in areas of the marsh lying at a distance from the rivers, where embankments were not required to exclude tidal waters, levels as such may not have existed before and may only have come into existence with the erection of mills. Sometimes single landowners raised embankments around their lands and erected a mill to

---

66   NRO KNY 27.
67   NRO KNY 27.
68   NRO KNY 27.

drain water into an adjacent 'rond'. But sometimes levels were created as two or more landowners jointly funded a mill and hydrologically sealed their collective lands from the surrounding marshes. The agreement drawn up in 1769 between Miles Branthwaite of Gunthorpe and John Houghton of Bramerton concerning the 'Windmill or Water Engine' on Scarsdale Marsh in Halvergate, already referred to, is of particular interest in this respect. This had already been erected by Houghton, 'for the better Improvement of his said Marsh Lands', partially obstructing an 'old way or Road there leading through his marsh to the said Marsh of the said Miles Branthwaite'. Houghton had constructed a replacement road and, by the terms of the agreement, Branthwaite and his heirs were to pay 10s yearly for its maintenance and for the use of the mill to drain their own land 'During all such time as the said Windmill or Water Engine shall continue to work and the said marsh called Scarsdale Marsh shall be drained by means thereof'. Branthwaite agreed to make 'sufficient' banks and walls against the Halvergate Fleet and all other dykes and drains 'except against the marshes of the said John Houghton and others agreed to be drained by the same mill'.[69] In the same year and less than a kilometre away on the Cantley Marshes, now in Halvergate parish, the situation was similar. William Fisher had already erected a 'Water Engine or Mill' on his own land and six neighbours, 'owners, tenants and occupiers' holding a total of 80 acres, agreed to contribute 2s 6d per acre *per annum* to have it take the water from their own marshes.[70] This was the origin of the level drained by what we now know as Stone's Mill, near the western end of the Halvergate Fleet, although it was later expanded, after 1805, to incorporate land enclosed from Halvergate Common.

The erection of drainage mills thus served to create levels, as well as taking place within levels already long in existence. And from the later eighteenth century levels gradually increased in size, as areas formerly drained by gravity alone or by some diminutive form of 'engine' were progressively amalgamated with neighbours and drained by tower mills and ultimately, in some cases, by steam. This process went further in some parts of the marshes than others, leading by the late nineteenth century to the emergence of the complex pattern shown in Figure 3.16. Even at this time, however, some areas were still drained by gravity alone – without the assistance of a mill or a steam pump – in the lower reaches of the rivers, where the tidal range was greatest.

The adoption and then the increasing sophistication of drainage 'engines' led to other changes, relating in particular to the 'ronds' marking the former creeks of the saltmarsh. These had always played a role in marsh drainage, lying as they

---

69   NRO FEL 154, 549X 8.
70   NRO MC 2000/1, 898X7.

did slightly below the level of the surrounding land. As mills were erected in areas lying at a distance from the river walls, some ronds came to have an increased importance as receptacles for the water they moved off the adjacent levels. By the 1790s the Halvergate Fleet in particular was flanked by a string of mills draining the marshes in Wickhampton, Halvergate and South Walsham Detached; the banks beside it were heightened, as we have seen in the case of Scardell Marsh in the 1760s, and the water moved into it flowed via a sluice into Breydon Water. Haddiscoe Thorpe Mill discharged its water, via a short channel, into the Thorpe and Haddiscoe Fleet, and Kerrison's Level Mill likewise into the Northern Rond. But as larger areas came to be more efficiently drained by wind many of the ronds began to be removed: their banks were neglected or levelled and they were incorporated into the adjacent areas of marsh. The process was, once again, gradual and piecemeal. The section of the Northern Rond marking the northern boundary of South Walsham Detached remained intact in 1768, to judge from an estate map of that date, but it had gone by the time the tithe map was surveyed in 1839.[71] The section lying further to the west, forming the boundary between Tunstall and Halvergate, in contrast, was still in existence when the tithe maps for the two parishes were surveyed, in 1838 and 1840 respectively.[72] By the time the first edition 6-inch Ordnance Survey map was made in 1884 this had also largely disappeared. Indeed, by this stage, although some lengths of its banks remained (and still remain), the Northern Rond had ceased to be a continuous ribbon of damper land physically divided from the surrounding marsh. The same was true of most of the major ronds, with the obvious exception of the Halvergate Fleet, although several minor examples still survive.

The disappearance of ronds was accompanied by significant changes in the pattern of drainage dykes. Numerous new channels were dug, thus producing the complex mixture of serpentine and straight dykes that now characterises the marsh landscape. In some cases these simply served to tidy up older, more sinuous channels, the traces of which can sometimes be seen on lidar images or aerial photographs, weaving to either side of them. Nearly half of the dykes shown on a map of 100 acres (40 hectares) of land lying to the south and east of Halvergate Manor Farm, surveyed in 1733, had been replaced by the time the tithe map was made in 1839, with little change in the size of the individual land parcels.[73] In most cases, however, the creation of new dykes was associated with the subdivision of larger parcels of ground, especially in areas lying at a distance from the principal rivers. Here, it appears, much of the marsh initially lay in very extensive blocks,

---

71 NRO MSS 4553. NRO DN/TA 610.
72 NRO DN/TA 595. NRO DN/TA 950.
73 NRO FEL 1068.

only minimally subdivided by dykes, between the 'ronds'. A survey of the Branthwaite estates drawn up in the 1730s shows Cauldwell Marsh in Halvergate, for example, as a single area, undivided by dykes, covering more than 55 acres (22 hectares (Figure 3.10)).[74] By the time the tithe map was surveyed, a little over a century later, ruler-straight dykes separated it into five portions ranging in size from 5.5 to nearly 12 acres. An undated map of the detached portion of Acle parish lying to the south of Cantley and Postwick, probably drawn up around 1700, shows in a schematic manner 14 parcels of marsh, the largest extending over some 40 acres (16 hectares), with an average size of around 24 acres (10 hectares).[75] By the time the tithe map was surveyed in 1838 the same area was divided into no fewer than 21 individually dyked areas, averaging just over 16 acres (6.5 hectares),[76] and when the first edition 25-inch Ordnance Survey map was surveyed in 1884 it lay in no fewer than 30 separate blocks. In a similar manner, in 1768 the marshes in South Walsham Detached, excluding the ronds and farmyards, lay in 12 parcels with an average area of around 33 acres (13 hectares), but the tithe map of 1839 shows 28 parcels with an average area of around 14 acres (6 hectares) and the 6-inch Ordnance Survey map of 1884 no fewer than 31 with an average area of less than 13 acres (Figure 3.17).[77] The progressive subdivision of large blocks of marsh probably explains many of the cases where eighteenth- and nineteenth-century maps show four, five or more separate parcels bearing the same, often archaic-sounding, name lying adjacent or in close proximity. Often, as with the 6 'Landry Marshes' in Chedgrave Detached, the 4 'Hulver Coat Marshes' in Wickhampton or the 11 'Dirt Holmes' in the same parish, they are separated by straight dykes and collectively enclosed, in whole or part, by serpentine ones following the course of major relict creeks or subsidiary saltmarsh channels.

The proliferation of dykes was, to an extent, associated with changes in patterns of ownership. In the cases of both Acle Detached and South Walsham Detached it accompanied the subdivision of large, unitary properties between a large number of smaller landowners. It was primarily, however, an aspect of a more general improvement in the condition of the marshes. Increasing the density of dykes of itself improved drainage. In 1825 Robert Fellowes was informed by his agent: 'I have taken … view of your Halvergate Estate and I find every thing is in good order and going on in a proper manner except some small drains is wanted to be cut in the different Marshes, this will be of great use to take the water from the marshes.'[78] Combined with the removal of the more serpentine elements of the dyke network,

---

74 NRO HNR 15/5.
75 NRO AG 86, 233X3.
76 NRO DN/TA 208.
77 NRO MSS 4553. NRO DN/TA 610.
78 NRO FEL 387.

144 BROADLAND

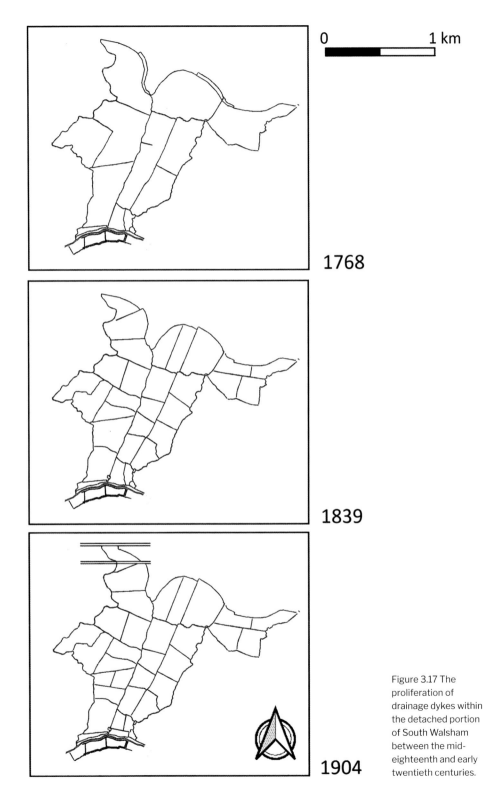

1768

1839

1904

Figure 3.17 The proliferation of drainage dykes within the detached portion of South Walsham between the mid-eighteenth and early twentieth centuries.

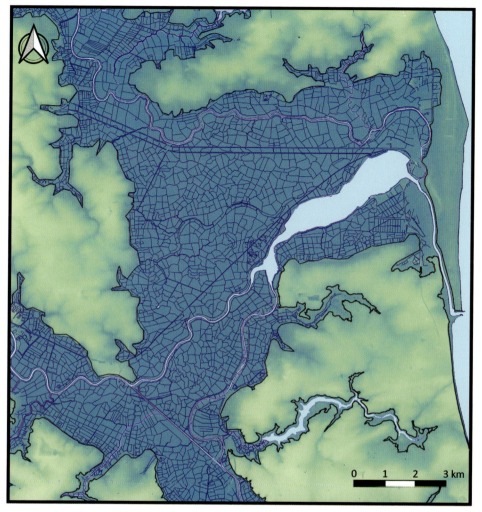

Figure 3.18 The modern pattern of drainage dykes on the Halvergate Marshes. Note the dominance of straight dykes towards the margins of the marshes, and the mixture of 'straight' and 'serpentine' examples elsewhere. The long, straight features running east–west across the north of the marsh are the 'Acle Straight' and the Norwich–Yarmouth railway line.

it facilitated the movement of water to the main drains, and so to the drainage mills. Indeed, some of the changes were directly associated with the erection of new mills. When the proposals for building one to drain the marshes in Thurlton were drawn up in 1769 it was agreed that the 'Great Drain' leading to it would be funded jointly, but that the individuals concerned were to pay for 'all such Cuts Drains and Outlets as shall be necessary to be made on any of ye Marshes or Marsh Lands of or belonging to the sd Proprietors … for the Convenience of conveying away the Water to the Great Drain'. Not surprisingly, as a consequence of all these changes the value of the marshes increased steadily. At the start of the eighteenth century even the best areas were let for 8s or 9s an acre *per annum*, but by the early nineteenth century, according to Arthur Young, many were fetching 30s (at a time when average rents for pasture in the county were around 20s), an increase that was nearly twice the rate of inflation.[79]

The great historical ecologist Oliver Rackham once suggested that the landscape of the Halvergate Marshes was dominated by serpentine, curvilinear dykes that had developed directly from the natural channels of the former saltmarsh. 'There has been some local tidying-up; but the chief monuments to the Age of Straight Lines are the Acle New Road (1835), New Cut (1833) … and railways (1843, 1845, 1882).'[80] In reality, this rather underplays the number of straight dykes that were added to the landscape in the course of the later seventeenth, eighteenth and nineteenth centuries (Rackham's 'Age of Straight Lines'). Across most of the marsh the two types are inextricably mixed, with 'linear' usually slightly more numerous than 'serpentine' examples (Figure 3.18). In a number of areas, however – mainly towards the margins of the marshes – all, or almost all, of the drainage dykes are of linear form. These mainly represent places where patches of undivided common land once existed. Early documents, such as the 1616 Sea Breach Commission ratings list, show that while some small areas of common were present in the interior of the marshes, in the marshy ronds, the largest areas were located near the edges. As we have seen, the margins of the marshes tend to be damp and peaty, due to the presence of springs and the constant inflow of water draining off the higher ground. A few of these peripheral commons were removed by private agreements but most, like the majority of common fens in the valleys, were enclosed by parliamentary enclosure acts (see pp. 185–91). Stokesby was enclosed as early as 1720 but there were no further acts affecting the marshes until 1797, when one was passed affecting 2,646 acres (1,071 hectares) of open fields and commons, including common marsh, in the parish of Acle, with the actual award coming two years later. They then came thick and fast, with acts including common marshes being passed for Halvergate and Runham in 1802, Thurlton, Haddiscoe and Haddiscoe Thorpe in 1809, Hardley in 1810, Caister in 1815 and Norton Subcourse in 1817. This spate of enclosure was shared by eastern England as a whole, as the high agricultural prices of the Napoleonic War years ensured the optimism and resources required to undertake such schemes of 'improvement'. The patches of planned rectilinearity thus created stand in sharp contrast to the complex, multi-layered and generally much older landscape of the rest of the Halvergate Marshes.

---

79 A. Young, *General view of the agriculture of the county of Norfolk* (London, 1804), p. 373.
80 Rackham, *History of the countryside*, p. 381.

The economy of the marshes

by Jacky Heath and Tom Williamson

As we have seen, in the early Middle Ages the marshes were mainly grazed by flocks of sheep, although these were sometimes accompanied by other livestock. In the thirteenth century horses and bullocks were pastured with sheep on the Norwich Cathedral Priory marshes of Fuelholm, for example.[81] During the fourteenth and fifteenth centuries the place of sheep appears to have been taken, as on many other marshes in England, by cattle, which by the sixteenth century loom large in the inventories drawn up at the deaths of local farmers. The change may, in part, reflect the fact that as drainage and embanking transformed the environment from saltmarsh to 'fresh' marsh it became more suitable for cattle and less so for sheep, which tended to suffer from foot rot where conditions were damp but not saline; however, other developments, including the emergence of a more integrated national economy, were also important. This was the great age of the drovers. Cattle one or two years old were walked all the way from Scotland and sold to local farmers at fairs held at Horsham St Faiths, Hopton or Harleston, fattened for a year or 18 months and then sold for slaughter, either locally or, after one last trek, at Smithfield in London. They were grazed on the marshes for much of the year and in the winter kept in farmyards on the 'uplands' and fed on hay or fodder crops such as turnips.

The essentials of the system seem to have remained stable for perhaps 400 years. The presence of store cattle on local farms (bought young to be fattened for market) is well attested in the sixteenth century – like the '5 bullockes boughte at Hopton fayre' mentioned in the probate inventory of John Dymonde of Halvergate, who died in 1590.[82] In 1722 Daniel Defoe described how

> In this vast Tract of Meadow are fed a prodigious Number of Black Cattle ... and the Quantity is so great, as that they not only supply the City of Norwich, the Town of Yarmouth, and the Country adjacent, but send great Quantities of them weekly, in all the Winter-season, to London.

He described how 'These Scots Runts, as they call them, coming out of the cold and barren Mountains of the Highlands ... feed so eagerly on the rich pasture of these marshes, that they thrive in an unusual manner, and grow monstrously fat.'[83] Marshall in 1787 described how the stock on the marshes comprised 'principally young cattle, lean "Scots", albeit accompanied by some horses and sheep.'[84] In

---

81 Cornford, 'Past water levels'. Campbell, 'Agricultural progress', p. 37.
82 NRO DN INV 7/197.
83 D. Defoe, *Tour through the whole island of Great Britain*, 2nd edn, vol. 1 (London, 1738), p. 64.
84 Marshall, *Rural economy*, vol. 2, pp. 279–80.

1844 Bacon similarly mentions sheep, but cattle – locally bred animals, Scots and now Irish – were the most important animals, purchased at the Harleston and St Faiths fairs and at 'other country fairs'.[85] Much the same system continued into the twentieth century, now with more emphasis on Irish stores, with Mosby in 1938 noting how, while horses and some sheep were grazed on the marsh and a few dairy cows were kept on the marsh farms, the most numerous stock were 'Irish short-horned cattle … bought in the Norwich market'.

> These Irish cattle thrive straight away on the outdoor feeding of the marshes. They make good shape and progress and fetch good prices from the local and London butchers. Scotch Angus … are good stock, but by no means so numerous as the Irish store cattle. English cattle are also grazed here: on the whole they are inferior to the Irish and Scotch, but Devon and Cumberland cattle are quite good.[86]

The names of the various parcels of marsh, as recorded on eighteenth- and nineteenth-century estate maps – and most comprehensively by the tithe maps and apportionments drawn up around 1840 – clearly reflect the importance of cattle in the local economy. Of the names recorded by the last of these sources which either directly or indirectly reference domestic livestock – that is, for example, including 'Bullock Shed Marsh' as well as 'Bullock Marsh' – only 3 per cent relate to sheep and 33 per cent to mares and horses, but 58 per cent to cows and bullocks. It is noticeable, but perhaps unsurprising, that those referencing bullocks are scattered fairly evenly across the marshes, while those relating to cows tend to occur towards the margins or, if found in the interior, close to marsh farms, reflecting the practicalities of milking. The name 'Mowing Marsh' has a similar distribution, presumably because grass managed as hay meadow needed to be easily accessible. 'Fatting' and 'Fattening' Marsh occur frequently. Other names on the tithe maps refer to the quality of the vegetation, with 'Reed Marsh' and 'Rush Marsh' widely scattered, although with a tendency to cluster behind embankments, presumably reflecting seepage from adjacent watercourses. References to shape, such as Three Corner Marsh, Roundabouts and Heater (the last a reference to a triangular warming iron); to adjacent structures like drainage mills; and, less informatively, to former owners or the area of the parcel in question account for most of the other names.

Agricultural exploitation took place within a framework of ownership structures and tenurial arrangements of some complexity. In theory the Sea Breach Commission rating lists for 1616, 1702 and 1716 should provide useful

---

85   Bacon, *Report on the agriculture of Norfolk*, p. 26.
86   Mosby, *Norfolk*, p. 198.

information about patterns of ownership on the marshes, but these seem to provide rough estimates, and often gross underestimates, of the areas of marsh owned by different individuals, while problems are also posed by the way that detached areas of parishes seem to be grouped, sometimes clearly but sometimes in an uncertain manner, with neighbours for the purpose of assessment. They do, however, suggest that already, by the start of the seventeenth century, the size of marsh properties displayed a great range of variation. The 1616 rating book thus shows that all but 28 of the 448 assessed 'acres' in Mautby were owned by the Paston family, albeit let on long leases to a number of different 'fermors', whereas in Stokesby with Herringby 165 'acres' were divided between 11 proprietors, with others owning pieces of 'rushie ground', and with 77 'acres' of common.[87] It is, once again, not until the tithe maps and apportionments were drawn up around 1840 that we obtain a clear view of ownership patterns in the Halvergate Marshes.

These sources exist for almost all parishes having a share of the marshes and reveal a highly splintered and complex pattern of ownership. Around a third of the land area was owned in very small blocks, continuous or discontinuous, extending over 50 acres (c.20 hectares) or less (Figure 3.19), around a third comprised properties of between 50 and 200 acres (c.80 hectares) and a third lay in larger blocks.[88] Many properties were owned by members of the local gentry or freehold farmers dwelling on the adjacent uplands, sometimes in parishes lying a little way back from the marsh edge, but a significant proportion belonged to individuals or institutions who were based much further away. Sixty-five acres (26 hectares) of marshes in Norton Subcourse, for example, were owned by Lord Berners of Wolverstone, near Ipswich; Magdalen College in Oxford held 90 acres (c.36 hectares) of marsh in Beighton Detached; while King's College and Peterhouse College in Cambridge owned 225 acres and 263 acres (91 and 106 hectares) in Toft Monks Detached and Chedgrave Detached respectively. Some small parcels of marsh were owned by charities and a few formed part of the glebe land not of the parish in which they lay but of ones in the City of Norwich (St Michael at Plea, St Margarets, St Stephens) or scattered widely across East Anglia, such as Ashley in Cambridgeshire, Corton in Suffolk and Sheringham, Tuttington and Corpusty in Norfolk. This land had been acquired under the provisions of 'Queen Anne's Bounty', a scheme launched in 1703 to raise the incomes of the poorer parish

---

87   NRO C/Scf 6/1.
88   This account is based on an analysis of the tithe maps and apportionments of Norfolk parishes holding land on the marshes: Acle, Beighton, Blofield, Burlingham St Andrew, Caister, Cantley, Chedgrave, Freethorpe, Halvergate, Langley, Loddon, Mautby, Moulton, Norton Subcourse, Postwick, Raveningham, Reedham, Runham, South Walsham, Stockton, Stokesby, Toft Monks, Tunstall and Wickhampton. The copies held at TNA were accessed during 2020 and 2021 via The Genealogist, Tithe apportionment data, https://www.thegenealogist.co.uk/search/advanced/landowner/tithe-records/.

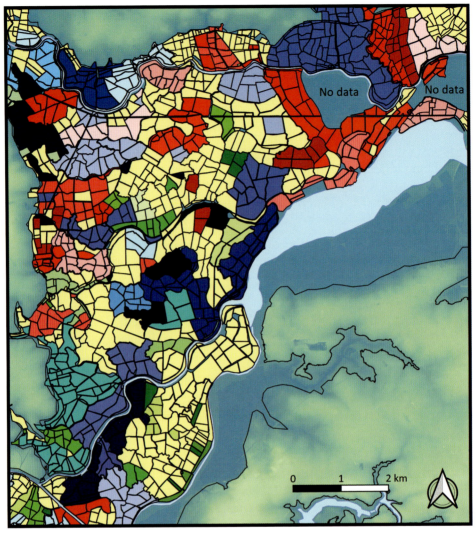

Figure 3.19 Patterns of ownership in the Norfolk section of the Halvergate Marshes in c.1840. Properties in shades of blue comprise more than 200 acres (c.80 hectares) of marsh; those in shades of red 100–200 acres (c.40–80 hectares); green, 50–100 acres (c.20–40 hectares). The remainder, less than 50 acres.

clergy by augmenting their glebe land and thus their rental income.[89] Acquisitions under the scheme continued into the nineteenth century. The terrier of St Michael at Plea in Norwich records in 1801 the purchase of 11 acres, 3 roods and 3 perches of marsh and 'a certain piece of Rond or coarse Marsh containing five acres one rood and thirteen perches', all part of East Bullen marsh in the detached portion of Acle lying to the north-east of Halvergate parish.[90] A few small parcels of land were

---

89   W.R. Le Fanu, *Queen Anne's Bounty: a short account of its history and work* (London, 1921).
90   NRO PD 66/32.

also owned by private individuals widely scattered across East Anglia. Land was the main form of investment in the seventeenth, eighteenth and early nineteenth centuries, for the wealthy, for institutions and charities and for people of moderate means, many of whom regarded banks, bonds and shares with a measure of justified suspicion. Land was a secure investment that brought in a regular income and its value could be realised as opportunity offered or circumstances dictated. There was no shortage of potential tenants, for grazing marsh was a highly prized commodity in a district in which pasture was in short supply. For the same reason local farmers were keen to acquire a portion of land on the marshes. The result was a very active market in land and a highly complex, and constantly changing, pattern of ownership.

Some of the largest marsh properties formed, in effect, distant outliers of large landed estates. The main possessions of Sir Edward Stracey, who owned just over 300 acres (*c*.120 hectares) of marshland in Tunstall and Burlingham St Andrew Detached, lay around his home at Rackheath Hall to the north of Norwich, more than 16 kilometres away, with outlying lands a little to the north, in Buxton and Oxnead.[91] Thomas Trench Berney's marshes in Reedham and Wickhampton, over 480 acres (*c*.190 hectares) in all, were more than 30 kilometres from most of his other properties, which were clustered around his residence at Morton Hall near Attlebridge (a branch of the family had owned much of Reedham before the early eighteenth century and the core of Berney's marshland holdings seem to represent the inherited rump of this estate).[92] In other cases the individual's seat and principal properties were even more distantly located. Lord Calthorpe owned extensive areas of marsh near Acle and, while he possessed some other land in East Anglia, most of his estates lay in Warwickshire and Hampshire and his seat was at Elvetham in the latter county. Sir Edward Bowyer Smyth, who owned large tracts of marsh in Norton Subcourse and the adjacent parts of Raveningham Detached – as well as some in Wickhampton, just to the south of the Halvergate Fleet – also owned property in the area around Attleborough and Old Buckenham in central Norfolk but he lived at Hill Hall near Epping in Essex, where the rest of his lands were located.

Rather more of the larger marsh holdings, however, simply formed parts of gentry estates that extended down onto the marshes from the neighbouring uplands. The 180 acres (72 hectares) of marsh owned by George Copeman in Stokesby, for example, formed part of a 415-acre (168-hectare) property which included arable land on the higher ground. Typically for the area, Copeman was lord of the manor and lived in Stokesby Hall, a 'neat house', but farmed the land

---

91   NRO PD 160/31. TNA IR 30/23/413. NRO PD 625/15. TNA IR 30/23/515. TNA IR 30/23/434. W. White, *History, gazetteer, and directory of Norfolk, and the city and county of Norwich* (Sheffield, 1845), p. 784.
92   Blomefield and Parkin, *Topographical history*, vol. 11, pp. 124–30. NRO BER 117, 687X1.

himself: the line between a large freehold farmer and minor gentleman was a blurred one in Broadland.[93] Similar was the extensive block of marshes in Reedham owned by John Leathes, lord of the manor of Reedham, which formed part of an estate based on Reedham Hall, although in this case the entire property was leased to tenants, except for the woodland; Leathes resided at the family's main residence of Herringfleet Hall, on the other side of the marshes, in Suffolk. The line between a large, isolated marshland property belonging to a major landowner whose main estates were located elsewhere and one which formed part of a gentry estate on the adjacent upland was also, however, a fuzzy one. Andrew Fountaine's extensive marsh holdings in Tunstall formed part of a 444-acre estate in that parish, where he was lord of the manor. But he lived at Narford Hall in west Norfolk, surrounded by more extensive lands. Similarly, Robert Fellowes owned over 850 acres (344 hectares) of marsh in Runham, Halvergate and Mautby, as well as most of the 'upland' in the latter parish, where he was lord of the manor. But he lived 20 kilometres away on his home estate in Shotesham to the south of Norwich. How far the acquisition by such men of estates in parishes bordering the marsh was fortuitous, how far motivated by the value of the marshes for grazing, and perhaps by the sporting opportunities they provided, remains unclear.

Quite how the complex pattern of ownership shown in Figure 3.19 came into existence also remains uncertain. In many parishes marshes were originally divided between a number of holdings – copyhold or freehold farms and the demesne of the manorial lord, or lords. In some, such as Wickhampton or Halvergate, significant numbers of small proprietors survived into the nineteenth century, but in others most of the smaller holdings were gradually absorbed, from the late Middle Ages, by one or more of the manorial demesnes, through purchase or other means. In some cases local lords eventually acquired all or almost all of the property in a parish, 'upland' as well as marsh. When, in 1616, the Paston family were recorded as sole proprietors of the marshland in Mautby – mainly comprising the Shortrack Marshes – they were already also owners of much of its upland portion.[94] The property passed to Lord Anson in 1742, and subsequently to the Fellowes family of Shotesham, forming, as we have seen, an outlier to their main estate. In 1839 Robert Fellowes possessed 1,562 of the 1,646 acres in the parish, most of the rest being glebe.[95] But some large marsh holdings had already, in medieval times, comprised extensive properties, the demesne lands of powerful lords, especially monastic houses. Marsh estates of the latter kind generally survived the Dissolution intact, such as the St Benet's Abbey marshes in

---

93 TNA IR 30/23/527. White, *Directory of Norfolk*, p. 299.
94 NRO C/Scf 6/1. NRO Lucas and Wyllys 09/04/1975.
95 Blomefield and Parkin, *Topographical history*, vol. 11, pp. 228–9. NRO MC 488/1–16, 747X7. NRO DN/TA 337.

South Walsham Detached, which by the start of the seventeenth century were in the hands of the earl of Arundel; or the abbey's marshes in Postwick Detached and Runham, both of which came into the possession of the Pastons, who had leased them from the abbey since the fifteenth century.[96]

Whatever their precise origins, the many extensive estates that appear to have existed on the marshes by the end of the sixteenth century tended to fragment in the course of the seventeenth, eighteenth and nineteenth centuries. In 1768 the whole of South Walsham Detached, covering some 390 acres (158 hectares), was still owned as a single property, by one James Arden,[97] but by 1840 it was divided between 13 owners.[98] The Postwick marshes remained in the hands of the Paston family until 1674, when Clement Paston defaulted on a mortgage he had taken out on them with Thomas Windham of Felbrigg.[99] They passed to John Windham, but were sold off in the course of the eighteenth century and by 1838 were in the hands of ten different owners.[100] The 17 acres acquired by St Michael at Plea in Norwich in 1801 under the terms of the Queen Anne's Bounty scheme seem to have formed part of a block of marshes that, when mapped in c.1700 'as they are in the original lease', evidently formed a single property embracing the whole of this detached portion of Acle parish.[101] By c.1840 it had become divided between no fewer than 14 different proprietors.[102] The problems with the early Sea Breach Commission rating lists have already been emphasised but it is nevertheless noteworthy that while the list for 1616 suggests the marshes in Halvergate parish were almost entirely owned by just two individuals – the earl of Arundel (the lord of the manor) and Richard Jenkinson – the 1715 list shows them divided between 18 proprietors, with five large holdings of 104, 120, 127, 160 and 200 'acres', but with some people owning as little as 6.[103] By 1839, to judge from the tithe apportionments, no fewer than 36 men and women owned portions of marsh in the parish.[104] Fragmentation affected smaller land parcels as much as larger ones. It could result from a simple need to liquidise assets but also, among minor local gentry and freehold farmers especially, from divided inheritance. It is striking how often the tithe maps show individuals with the same surname owning adjacent parcels of land on the marshes. Those owned by Cyrus, William and Richard Gillett in Halvergate and Tunstall, for example, often lay adjacent,

---

96   NRO C/Scf 6/1. NRO DN HAR 3/1.
97   NRO MS 4553.
98   NRO DN/TA 610.
99   NRO WKC 1/370.
100 NRO DN/TA 194.
101 NRO AG 86, 233X3.
102 NRO PD 164/16.
103 NRO C/Scf 6/1. NRO EAW 1/3.
104 NRO DCN 127/79.

probably indicating those parts of their respective portfolios of property that had been inherited from their father John.[105] Above all, fission was fuelled by the high demand for marsh properties, especially among local farmers and investors of moderate means, private or institutional.

The overall direction of travel through the post-medieval period was not, however, uniformly or inexorably in the direction of smaller units of ownership. Large holdings in the hands of permanent institutions were, on the whole, more resistant to fragmentation than those owned by private individuals. The 225-acre property held in 1840 by King's College in the detached portion of Toft Monks, which had originally belonged to the abbey of Préaux, appears to have survived unchanged from the time it was donated to them by Edward IV in the fifteenth century, following the suppression of the alien houses.[106] The Norwich Cathedral Priory lands on Fowlholme and Skeetholme passed intact at the Dissolution to its successor body, the Dean and Chapter, and continued with the same boundaries into the twentieth century, although they were held on long leases by a succession of 'farmers' who sublet to one or more tenants: the 1616 Sea Breach rating list thus records one 'Mr Fachard' holding 300 'acres' there, which were let to 'George Wells and others'.[107] Those large marsh holdings that formed outlying portions of aristocratic estates based elsewhere were also relatively immune from the forces of fission, for great landowners followed strict rules of primogeniture and were generally prevented from alienating portions of the family patrimony by 'strict settlements', legal agreements designed to ensure its passage undivided from one generation to the next. But, in addition, some new examples of large marsh holdings were built up over time through sustained policies of purchase. In c.1840 Sir Edward Stracey owned over 300 acres (c.120 hectares) in the north-west of the marshes. Most (c.245 acres) lay in a continuous block straddling the parish boundary between Tunstall and Burlingham Detached; a further 50 acres lay a short distance to the north, entirely in Tunstall; and another 20 acres around 500 metres to the east, in Acle Detached. Lying in three different parishes and two different Levels, the Stracey holding had clearly been assembled from at least four separate properties in the course of the post-medieval period. A similar process of accumulation must have created many of the properties extending over 100 acres (c.40 hectares) or more shown on the tithe maps. The overall consequence of the interaction of these various processes of division and accumulation was the highly complex pattern of ownership that existed when the tithes were commuted around 1840, with no very obvious structure beyond a slight tendency for these

---

105 NRO DCN 127/79. NRO PD 354/27(M).
106 Blomefield and Parkin, *Topographical history*, vol. 8, pp. 61–2.
107 NRO C/Scf 6/1.

larger holdings of more than 100 acres (*c.*40 hectares) to be clustered towards the margins of the marsh (Figure 3.19).

Patterns of tenancy were as complex as those of ownership. William Marshall described in 1787 how 'The inclosures, or "marshes", run from ten to fifteen to forty or fifty acres each; belong to a variety of owners; and are rented by a still greater number of occupiers; almost every farmer, within fifteen or even twenty miles, having his marsh'.[108] By *c.*1840, to judge from the tithe maps and apportionments, most of the marshes – around 75 per cent – were occupied by tenants (Figure 3.20). Many held land from more than one owner, while even relatively small owners might have several tenants – the 75 acres (30 hectares) owned by Samuel Bignold in Halvergate in 1840, for instance, were rented out to four different farmers.[109] In general, the larger units of ownership were divided into fewer, larger tenancies. The 315 acres (127 hectares) owned by the Straceys, for example, were leased to only 12 tenants, the 440 acres (178 hectares) owned by Thomas Trench Berney to 6, both estates keeping a portion 'in hand'. There was a clear tendency for owner-occupation to be more important towards the north of the marsh, where, for example, all 12 of the owners in the 390 acres (158 hectares) of South Walsham Detached occupied their land themselves. But the overall explanation for this pattern, if indeed there is one, remains elusive.

The larger landowners in particular usually made strenuous attempts to preserve the value of property leased to tenants. To avoid 'poaching' the grass sward, leases restricted grazing to spring, summer and early autumn – often to the period between May 1 and October 24; stocking densities were carefully regulated, generally restricted to five sheep, one fat bullock, or two neat stock per acre; and the taking of a hay crop, widely believed to adversely affect the long-term condition of the sward, was often prohibited or restricted. A lease for Mautby New Farm, drawn up in 1825, typically bound the tenant not to 'cut or mow any part of the meadow or marsh land ... without the consent in writing of the Lessor'.[110] None of this applied to the ronds, however, which were regularly mown for rough hay or cut for reeds.

Leases also prohibited the ploughing up of portions of marsh and their conversion to arable; that for New Farm in Mautby, just mentioned, instructed the tenant not to 'plough or otherwise break up any of the pasture or marsh ground'.[111] Ploughing reduced the value of the land because it would take many years to re-establish pasture of such quality, but as grain prices rose towards the end of the eighteenth century, and especially during the French Revolutionary

---

108 Marshall, *Rural economy*, vol. 2, p. 278.
109 NRO DN/TA 595.
110 NRO FEL 387.
111 NRO FEL 387.

156 BROADLAND

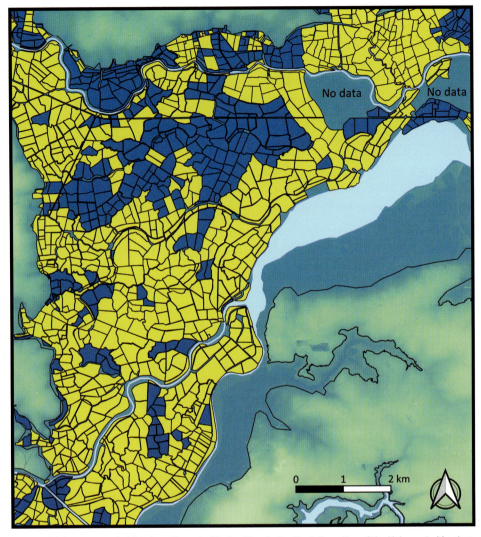

Figure 3.20 Owner-occupied (blue) and tenanted (yellow) land in the Norfolk section of the Halvergate Marshes in c.1840.

and Napoleonic Wars, the pressure to plough increased significantly for, as Armstrong put it in 1781, the marshes 'sometimes, when ploughed, afford greater crops of corn than any other land'.[112] Interestingly, most references to arable use come from marshes near Yarmouth, perhaps because these could be accessed easily from roads and cultivations and harvest thus posed fewer organisational problems than elsewhere. In 1790 the agent for the Norwich Dean and Chapter examined the Fowlholme and Skeetholme Marshes and described

---

112 M.J. Armstrong, *The history and antiquities of the county of Norfolk* (London, 1781), vol. 2, p. 93.

how some were under cultivation. 'Can Lessee breake them up without consent of the Lessors? they ought to be Covenanted against it under a penalty of five Pounds an Acre for every Acre yearly so converted into Tilth.'[113] The 1805 enclosure award for Runham refers to a boundary in the detached section of the parish 'taking in about an acre of an arable marsh' near Southtown in Yarmouth, while in 1803 a marshman reported that marshes near Yarmouth had been so much damaged by saltwater flooding in the 1790s 'that they have not since been ploughed', and that other pieces of marshland 'in this part of the district were also cultivated prior to the great Flood which was occasioned by overflowing of the Sea at Horsey'.[114] Only small areas of marsh appear to have been used as arable even in this period, however, and most had returned to pasture by the time the tithe maps were surveyed around 1840. These show only small areas under cultivation, mainly towards the north-western fringes of the marshes, on peaty soils in Tunstall and Acle, although a few parcels on the alluvial clays lying at a distance from the 'upland' were also under the plough, most notably in the area to the east of Stracey Arms Mill, to either side of the Acle Straight turnpike road. It is possible that arable land use increased once again after this time. Richard Bacon in 1844 thought that since the commutation of the tithes several areas of marsh had been ploughed up, and that more would soon follow (the higher tithe charge imposed on arable had previously discouraged cultivation).[115] He was confident, however, that most of the marsh would remain as pasture, and any renewed expansion in the ploughed area was certainly reversed when the agricultural depression began in the late 1870s, ushering in a sustained period of low grain prices. Mosby in the 1930s noted how 'Up to about 50 years ago quite a number of the marshes grew crops of mangolds, wheat and oats, but, with the exception of a few areas in the immediate neighbourhood of Yarmouth and Horsey there is no arable land now.'[116]

Cattle grazing thus formed the main activity on the marshes from the late Middle Ages onwards and, given the fragmented patterns of ownership and tenancy and the considerable distances often separating farmers and their stock, this presented a number of obvious management problems. The solution, as described by Marshall in 1787, was to place the animals 'Under the care of marshmen, who live in cottages scattered over the Marshes: – each having his district, or "level of marshes", to look after. His perquisite is a shilling upon the pound-rent, which is sometimes paid by the landlord but more generally by the

---

113 NRO DCN 52/2.
114 NRO C/Sca 2/235. NRO EAW 2/118.
115 Bacon, *Report on the agriculture of Norfolk*, p. 295.
116 Mosby, *Norfolk*, p. 198.

tenant.'[117] The same system was described, although by then in decline, by Mosby a century and a half later:

> Almost every marshman inherits his job, and certain areas have been in the hands of one family for many generations. One marshman may look after as many as 1,000 acres of marshes. During the grazing season he looks after the cattle of a number of different owners, and this keeps him very busy for he counts the cattle every day and sorts them out if need be ... in the winter he is busy repairing fences and gateways, cutting and 'croming' drains, 'bottomfying', etc ... The marshman lives near his work ... often miles away from a town or village.[118]

Such individuals, occupying remote marsh farms or cottages, usually kept some livestock of their own, Marshall describing how they 'also keep cows, which pick about in the swamps, roads and unenclosed parts, in summer; and for which they mow winter fodder from the reed-ronds, &c., They carry the butter to Yarmouth ... '.[119] The system, or some version of it, must have existed from an early date, and a survey of Stergott Marsh, the remote detached portion of Postwick parish, drawn up in 1580 states that the bounds had been given by Thomas Harvey and John Daymes, 'bothe marsh men'.[120] It must be emphasised, however, that the term was a broad one, evidently encompassing labourers skilled in constructing or maintaining the facilities necessary for successful water management. An early-nineteenth-century account book for the Langley estate records the payments made to 'William Crisp Marshman', working alone or with others, for 'drawing' and 'slubbing' dykes and digging new ones, repairing 'walls' and sluices, cutting reed and 'gladdon', maintaining causeways, digging fishponds and working the drainage mill, but not for work with livestock.[121]

Even before the draining of the marshes, when sheep had grazed over the saltings, isolated farms had existed to facilitate livestock management. Most of the detached portions of parishes and extra-parochial areas had their own marsh house, although where a parish possessed two detached portions in reasonable proximity one farm might perhaps have served both. Many survived into the late nineteenth century, appearing on the first edition 25-inch Ordnance Survey maps. Some remain, although no longer fulfilling their original function. Five Mile House seems to have served the detached portion of Postwick; Six Mile

---

117 Marshall, *Rural economy*, vol. 2, p. 280.
118 Mosby, *Norfolk*, pp. 198–9.
119 Marshall, *Rural economy*, vol. 2, pp. 280–1.
120 NRO Hansell 12/1/71, R 187 B No. 2.
121 NRO BEA S 196 D.

House that of Cantley; Scaregap Farm the extra-parochial estate of the Dean and Chapter on Skeetholme; Lockgate Farm (now demolished) the detached portion of Freethorpe beside Breydon Water; Raven Hall, Langley Detached; Seven Mile House, Toft Monks Detached; and Upper Seven Mile House, the isolated portion of Chedgrave parish on Haddiscoe Island. The unnamed house and associated outbuildings shown on the 25-inch map in South Walsham Detached are marked as a farm on earlier maps. Parishes that simply extended down onto the marsh likewise possessed one or more isolated farms, at least if their marshland section was extensive. Examples include Seven Mile House on the Yare in Reedham and Manor Farm in Halvergate.

Most of these farms stood beside river walls or on the margins of relict creeks, and some of the surviving examples clearly occupy low mounds. Many probably originated in the eleventh or twelfth centuries; medieval finds have been made on the site of the demolished Lockgate Farm, during building work at Six Mile House in Cantley detached and as stray finds in gardens elsewhere.[122] It is possible that some post-medieval farms simply reoccupied old saltern mounds because of the safety from floods these provided, but in most cases direct continuity of occupation seems likely, either from a medieval farm or from a combined farm and salt-making site.

The number of marsh farms seems to have dwindled over time, although with an uncertain chronology. The isolated portion of Acle parish lying to the south of Cantley and Burlingham Detached had, by the nineteenth century, a single farm, standing in its north-eastern corner. Located beside a relict creek and around 100 metres to the south of the Northern Rond, it almost certainly occupied a medieval site. But lidar images show a complex of small enclosures, indicating another possible farm, standing on the bank of the Northern Rond, on the western boundary of the detached parish area (TG 45301 08572).[123] It had disappeared by the nineteenth century, but an undated map of c.1700 shows it clearly, drawn in elevation (Figure 3.21).[124] Where detached portions of parishes lacked a farm by the time the earliest maps were made it is often possible to suggest that they once had one and where it might have been located. That for Burlingham Detached, for example, may well have stood at TG 44339 08020, where two mounds and associated enclosures stand a little way back from the southern tributary to the Northern Rond; while that for Moulton Detached is probably represented by an early-nineteenth-century barn and associated yard that, until recently, stood on a low mound at TG 46308 05688, c.500 metres north-east of Berney Arms station.[125]

122   NHER 24208. NHER 21103.
123   NHER 42195.
124   NRO AG 86, 233X3.
125   NHER 42215.

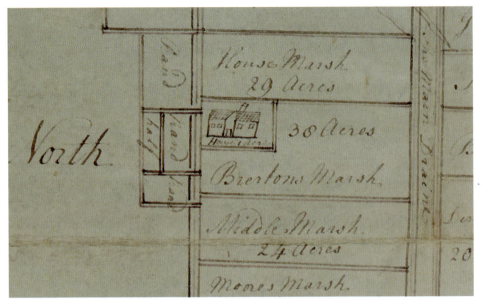

Figure 3.21 A lost marsh farm in the portion of Acle parish lying to the south of Cantley and Burlingham Detached, shown on a map of *c*.1700 but now surviving only as a complex of earthworks beside the Northern Rond (see Figure 3.12, 'b').

The surviving farmhouses vary greatly in age and character. Some, in their present form at least, are clearly nineteenth-century in date, but several, such as Seven Mile House in Reedham Detached, Ashtree Farm near Berney Arms or Raven Hall in Chedgrave Detached, are brick-built structures from the eighteenth or later seventeenth century, in the latter case perhaps incorporating fragments of an earlier building (Figure 3.22). These are all substantial houses but some examples are smaller and, at the lower end of the scale, the category of 'marsh farm' merges with what the early Ordnance Survey maps describe as 'marsh cottages'. Indeed, some of the latter may once have been – or may occupy the sites of former – farms, although others were evidently erected to provide accommodation for the individuals responsible for looking after drainage windmills.

Recent history

The landscape of the marshes has continued to develop since the Second World War, the most dramatic change perhaps being a further reduction in the numbers of marsh farms and the conversion of most of the survivors to purely residential use or, in a number of cases, holiday accommodation. In 1950 an article in the *Yarmouth Mercury* described Lockgate Farm, close to the northern edge of Breydon Water, as 'One of the most isolated houses in Norfolk, where … life is a hundred years behind the times … It has no electricity, modern plumbing

Figure 3.22 Raven Hall, a seventeenth-century farmhouse standing beside the Yare at the northern end of Haddiscoe Island.

or radio, and no newspapers or mail are ever delivered.'[126] It was still a working farm: Gordon Addison, the marshman, kept horses, cows, pigs, chickens, ducks and geese. But after his death in 1967 the house was left empty and gradually deteriorated until it was demolished in 1981. An article in the *Eastern Evening News* reported in 1971 that 'all but one' of the marsh farms in the area to the west of Yarmouth stood 'empty and derelict'.[127] While this may have been an exaggeration, in the later decades of the twentieth century many other places shared the fate of Lockgate Farm, including Six Mile House and Upper Seven Mile House in the detached portion of Chedgrave parish on Haddiscoe Island, Tunstall Marsh Farm, Bailey's House in Postwick Detached and Scaregap Farm near Yarmouth, as holdings were progressively amalgamated. The most recent loss has been the marsh house near Kerrison's Level Mill, demolished in 2018. Marsh cottages, such as that near High's Mill on Halvergate Fleet, have also disappeared

---

126 *Yarmouth Mercury*, 17 February 1950.
127 *Eastern Evening News*, 30 December 1971.

Figure 3.23 Cattle grazing on the marshes near Manor Farm, Halvergate parish.

on a significant scale, being no longer required for the accommodation of millmen or other workers.

In spite of the pressure to increase arable production during the Second World War, the 1946 RAF aerial photographs suggest that almost the entire area of the marshes still lay under pasture and, for the most part, except in some peripheral areas, this continued to be the case into the 1970s. The main changes to the character of the marshes in the immediate post-War decades, other than the steady attrition of farms and cottages, were limited and subtle: the levelling of some of the surviving settlement and saltern mounds and of most of the remaining embankments lying away from the river walls. But from the mid-1970s changes in the prices for farm produce and the availability of grants to improve drainage led to a rapid increase in the area of land under the plough. In the early 1980s this provoked a carefully orchestrated campaign by environmentalists, led by Friends of the Earth, which involved an element of direct action. Protesters chained themselves to the mechanical diggers excavating new drains and deepening existing ones. It was not just the beauty of the landscape which was at stake. The changes caused immeasurable damage to a wide range of flora and fauna. The dispute culminated in 1987 with the establishment of the marshes as the first Environmentally Sensitive Area, within which farmers were paid to maintain the land as pasture and to follow 'traditional' agricultural practices favourable to conservation.[128] Over the following three decades or so many of the arable marshes reverted to pasture, partly as a consequence of agro-environmental initiatives, although some new areas were ploughed. Today, away from some marginal areas, especially in the north-west of the 'triangle', the majority of the marshes are under permanent grass and still mainly grazed by cattle although, over the last few decades, with increasing numbers of horses (Figure 3.23).

As late as 1980 ownership of the marshes was still divided between around a hundred farmers, over half of whom held less than 25 acres (*c.*10 hectares).[129] But now large, consolidated holdings predominate, although most of these – and particularly Beckhithe Farms, probably the largest landowner on the marsh – use the land for grazing and maintain the landscape on broadly 'traditional' lines. In addition, the Royal Society for the Protection of Birds now owns 550 hectares in the area around Berney Arms to the north of Breydon Water, around 84 hectares of which had formerly been arable; within five years of its reversion to grass 'plant communities had shifted towards those characteristic of lowland wet grassland'.[130] The impact on the landscape of the RSPB's management, which also embraces the land of some neighbouring owners, is subtle, but noticeable. Instead of strenuous attempts being made to remove water from the surface of the marshes in the early spring, water is moved back onto it with the aid of small windpumps, creating shallow surface pools to attract wading birds, while in other places deeper scrapes and ponds have been created. Nevertheless, the land is grazed and under pasture and, in broad terms at least, looks much as it has done for centuries.

The needs of nature conservation now shape the landscape to an extent that would have bewildered farmers and landowners only a few decades ago. While this chapter primarily concerns the history of the marsh landscape, its ecological character, critically shaped by that history, also needs to be briefly noted. The Halvergate Marshes in their unploughed state provide a range of important habitats for wildlife. Firstly, there are the vast areas of unimproved or minimally improved grassland, with a high water table and dissected by a network of drainage dykes containing water that ranges in character from fresh to brackish. Secondly, this

---

[128] George, *Land use*, pp. 277–312. J. Purseglove, *Taming the flood: a history and natural history of rivers and wetlands* (Oxford, 1988), pp. 268–73.
[129] Purseglove, *Taming the flood*, p. 269.
[130] G. Lyons and M. Ausden, 'Raising water levels to revert arable land to grazing marsh at Berney Marshes RSPB Reserve, Norfolk, England', *Conservation Evidence*, 2 (2005), pp. 47–9.

essentially artificial landscape has at its heart the entirely natural Breydon Water, with its extensive tidal mudflats and shallows. There are also scattered areas of reedbed and scrub and, towards the margins of the marshes, numerous areas of alder carr. Crossed by only a small number of roads and containing only a handful of inhabited houses, it is a remarkably remote and undisturbed area, in spite of the proximity of Great Yarmouth.

The marshes are most noted for their bird life. Resident breeding populations of birds such as gadwall, shoveller, redshank, lapwing and the rare Bewick's swan are augmented in winter by a massive influx of arrivals from elsewhere. Some are species of duck, attracted to Breydon and, to a lesser extent, the marsh dykes. Teal and wigeon, thinly scattered across northern Britain for most of the year, congregate here and are joined by continental migrants. Others are waders, such as the pink-footed goose, redshank, lapwing, golden plover and black tailed godwit, attracted in part by the character of the grass sward maintained by cattle grazing, and in part by the fact that a high water table ensures that worms and other invertebrates are concentrated in the upper levels of the soil, within easy reach.[131] A high water table and areas of standing water of various depths are thus critical factors and, while we have no detailed records or observations pre-dating the middle decades of the nineteenth century, there can be little doubt that the progressive improvements in drainage which occurred during the previous century and a half – the erection of drainage windmills, the eradication of most of the marshy 'ronds', the adoption of steam drainage – all made the marshes drier. Late-nineteenth-century writers certainly saw the decline in the numbers of snipe on the marshes as a consequence of continued improvements in drainage; in the twentieth century falls in the numbers of wigeon and both pink-footed and white-fronted geese were similarly explained.[132] The RSPB's management regime on their reserve near Breydon Water thus represents, in large measure, a return to earlier conditions.

Of equal conservation importance are the flora and the invertebrate fauna of the drainage dykes. The distinctive flora associated with the 'broads' themselves declined, as we shall see, from the middle decades of the nineteenth century, largely as a consequence of 'eutrophication', or nitrogen enrichment, but survived to varying extents in Broadland's numerous drainage dykes.[133] This was particularly the case on the vast expanse of the Halvergate Marshes, because of

---

131 E.L. Turner, *Broadland birds* (London, 1924).
132 Lord Walsingham and R. Payne Galley, *Shooting: moor and marsh* (London, 1889), pp. 136, 142. M. Bird, 'Bird life', in W.A. Dutt, *The Norfolk Broads* (London, 1905), pp. 215–31, at p. 230. Moss, *The Broads*, p. 251.
133 Moss, *The Broads*, p. 252. R.J. Driscoll, 'Broadland dykes: the loss of an important wildlife habitat', *Transactions of the Norfolk and Norwich Naturalists' Society*, 26/3 (1983), pp. 170–2.

the large number of dykes and the considerable distance that so many lie from the main sources of nutrient enrichment – agricultural land on the uplands. Many are also remote from the tidal rivers that provide the other main threat to floral diversity: high levels of salinity. The freshwater-plant communities of Halvergate are accordingly recognised as being of international importance, featuring such nationally rare or scarce species as whorled water milfoil (*Myriophyllum verticillatum*), water soldier (*Stratiotes alludes*), fen pondweed (*Potamogeton coloratus*), hairlike pondweed (*Potamogeton trichoides*) and greater water-parsnip (*Sium latifolum*). The dykes lying close to Breydon Water are more brackish and their flora less diverse, but they nevertheless contain important species such as soft hornwort *(Ceratophyllum submersum)* and the nationally scarce stiff saltmarsh-grass (*Puccinellia rupestris*).[134] This rich diversity, commonly featuring more than 20 species for every 100 metres of dyke, is maintained only by regular management. Where dykes are not regularly slubbed out, reeds gradually shade out many submerged and emergent species, and the dyke itself can become shallow and silted, and ultimately disappear altogether. Moreover, it is only the kind of dyke characteristic of a traditionally managed grazing marsh that provides really valuable habitats, featuring high water levels and gently sloping sides that, trampled by cattle, afford opportunities for a wide range of invertebrates, including numerous dragonflies. When marshes are converted to arable and the water table is lowered, both the flora and the fauna of the reprofiled, deeper, V-shaped ditches are greatly impoverished.[135] As so often, in Broadland as elsewhere, biodiversity and the survival of rare species is sustained by the continuation of traditional but intensive management systems within essentially artificial landscapes, rather than by leaving nature to its own devices.[136]

Perhaps the greatest change to the Halvergate landscape over recent years has been the massive Broads Flood Alleviation Project, undertaken by the civil engineering firm Broadland Environmental Services Ltd and funded by the Environment Agency. The project began in 2001 and has involved widening and marginally raising the river walls, and in places realigning them further back from the rivers, creating wider ronds and areas of reedbed. The changes have been particularly dramatic beside Breydon and along parts of the Yare; here in particular much of archaeological interest was destroyed and the new

---

134 C. Doarks, 'Ecology and management of marsh dykes in Broadland', MPhil thesis (University of East Anglia, 1986). C. Doarks, *A study of the marsh dykes in Broadland* (Norwich, 1984).
135 Doarks, 'Ecology and management'.
136 R.J. Fuller, T. Williamson, G. Barnes and R. Dolman, 'Human activities and biodiversity opportunities in pre-industrial cultural landscapes: relevance to conservation', *Journal of Applied Ecology*, 54 (2017), pp. 459–69.

embankment still looks raw and new. But, overall, the new works are gradually merging into the landscape. In an environment critically shaped by reclamation and artificial drainage, criticism of new flood defences perhaps makes little sense. The alternative – of leaving the marshes unprotected in the face of continuing changes in relative land/sea levels – would eventually have led to the destruction of this immensely important, yet fragile, historic landscape.

4

THE VALLEYS

Before the nineteenth century

The landscape of the river valleys differs significantly from that of the Halvergate Marshes, although the two merge seamlessly in the lower reaches of the Bure, Yare and Waveney. Halvergate is a wide, ancient, level landscape of grazing marsh, devoid of woodland except towards its margins. Moving up the valleys the wetlands narrow, the prospects become more bounded and enclosed, and the landscape is often wilder, with areas of open water, reedbed and valley-floor woodland (Figures 4.1 and 4.2). Where the land comprises open pasture, moreover, the dyke pattern is usually rectilinear, with few of the sinuous channels we find on Halvergate (Figure 4.3). Underlying these differences are the geological patterns discussed in Chapter 1. Progressing up the valleys the extent of estuarine clays gradually falls and that of peat increases, completely covering the valley floors of the Ant, of the Yare above Claxton and the Bure above Ant Mouth, although always accompanied by areas of clay on the floodplains of the Thurne and the Waveney.

In all the valleys the silts and clays were, as on Halvergate, traditionally used as grazing marsh. The peats, in contrast, were associated with areas of *fen*. As William Marshall helpfully explained in 1787:

> The produce and principal use of a fen are totally different from those of a grazing marsh. The profits of a fen arise, in general, from Reed and gladdon, cut for thatch for buildings. Sedge and rushes, for litter; and thatch, for hay and corn-ricks, and sometimes for buildings. Coarse grass, for fodder, and sometimes for pasturage; – and Peat for fuel.[1]

---

1 Marshall, *Rural economy*, vol. 1, pp. 319–20.

168 BROADLAND

Figure 4.1 Dawn at Upton Broad. The landscape of the river valleys is generally wilder, wetter and more wooded than that of the Halvergate Marshes.

Figure 4.2 Extensive beds of reed (*Phragmites australis*) on the edge of Hickling Broad.

Figure 4.3 Where grazing marshes exist in the river valleys, as here at Thurne, the pattern of drainage dykes displays the rectilinear pattern characteristic of eighteenth- or nineteenth-century enclosure and reclamation. Looking north along the river Thurne, with Thurne Mill, or Morse's Mill, in the foreground.

Figure 4.4 Typical fen vegetation at Catfield Fen in the Ant valley, with encroaching alder carr in the far distance.

The distinction between the two kinds of land was always, in reality, more blurred than Marshall implies, especially where the peat lay thinly over clays and silts or was significantly raised above the summer water table. Local terminology was, moreover, usually looser than Marshall's, referring (for example) to the rough fodder cut from fens as 'marsh hay'. But the broad division – between wetlands primarily used for grazing and those mainly cut for a range of products – remains a useful one.

In late prehistoric times, to judge from the character and composition of the 'brushwood peat', the floodplains in the upper reaches of the valleys had been occupied by extensive tracts of wet woodland. But the *Phragmites* peat that formed after the Romano-British marine transgression suggests a landscape of more open fen (Figure 4.4). The change has never been fully explained, but must presumably reflect more intensive use of the valley floors resulting from higher population densities and limited reserves of woodland on the surrounding uplands. Alder and willow were perhaps cut for fuel (although neither makes very serviceable firewood) and regeneration was suppressed by the grazing of livestock and regular cutting of the fen vegetation. Whatever the explanation, by the time local records become abundant, from the thirteenth century, the valley-floor peats mainly comprised open fen, exploited in the ways described by Marshall.

Even in the Middle Ages there were numerous areas of private marsh in the valleys, much of it manorial demesne, such as the extensive holdings of St Benet's around the site of the abbey in the valley of the Bure. There were also some areas of private fen, such as the 'reed ground' in Surlingham that Robert of Surlingham conveyed to Norwich Cathedral Priory in 1260.[2] But a high proportion of the silt marshes and the overwhelming majority of the peat fens were common land and remained as such well into the post-medieval period: that is, land that was technically owned by the lord of the principal manor in a parish but over which the local inhabitants enjoyed rights to graze livestock and extract useful commodities. Some commons were shared between the lords and tenants of two or more adjoining parishes; large tracts of fen in the valley of the Ant were thus jointly exploited by Irstead and Neatishead.[3] Common rights were not usually enjoyed by all the inhabitants of a place, but were instead attached to particular properties, usually only those that had been in existence since the early Middle Ages ('none but ancient tenants shall presume to reap any profit', as seventeenth-century regulations for the commons of Ludham and Potter Heigham put it).[4]

---

2   NRO DCN 44/105/5.
3   NRO MC 36/123.
4   NRO Ms 19424, 103X4.

In 1682 the commoners in Irstead and Neatishead – in dispute with their manorial lord, the bishop of Norwich – claimed the right to 'Take cut and carry away Fodder Rushes Reed and Sedge growing in any of the said Fenns for their cattle and repairing the said messuages and also Liberty of Fishing in a certain water there called Alder Fenns and in all other the Broads and Waters in Irstead aforesaid'.[5] They also claimed rights of 'Common of Pasture of all Commonable Cattle', but grazing was a secondary use of fens, generally limited to particular times of the year. This was partly because the ground might be too waterlogged to safely bear the weight of horses and cattle (sheep were seldom pastured on such damp land because of the danger of foot rot). But it was mainly because livestock would eat and trample the vegetation that, as Marshall's account makes clear, was the main produce and chief value of these areas.

In particular, the better draining areas of fen were cut annually for 'marsh hay', a mixture of fen grasses and rushes (principally *Juncus subnodulosus* and *Juncus effusus*), which was used as winter fodder for cattle. Cutting took place in the summer, usually from the end of June (the regulations for the management of the Potter Heigham and Ludham commons, for example, drawn up in 1671, prohibited cutting 'till the day after Midsummer' (24 June)).[6] Areas for cutting were usually allotted annually to common right holders: a lease for a property in Rockland St Mary, drawn up in 1744, thus described how it came with the right to cut a '19th part of the vestergrass or marsh hay in Rockland Marsh'.[7] In addition, rougher areas, where the vegetation contained a high proportion of rush, were mown in late summer for 'litter', principally used for cattle bedding, in place of the more usual straw. Mixed with dung and urine, it made excellent manure for arable land, contributing 'to the great fertility of much of this country'.[8]

The fen vegetation was exploited in other ways. In the sixteenth and seventeenth centuries rushes were routinely used for covering the floors of houses, at least by the poorer members of society. In Beccles in 1544 it was ruled 'lawfulle to all women inh[abit]yng wythyne the seyd towne of Becclys att all tymes mete and convenyent to go into the sayd fen lands … to shere and gather wythe thyr sykkle … for the dressyng up of thyr houses'.[9] Soft rush (*Juncus effusus*) and, to a lesser extent, compact rush (*Juncus conglomeratus*) were also used to make 'rush lights'. The rushes were harvested by hand and piled in heaps until they became soft and pliable; the outer green skin was then largely removed to leave only a thin strip on each side of the soft white pith, to provide rigidity. They continued to be used

---

5   NRO MC 121/238.
6   NRO Ms 19424, 103X4.
7   NRO MC 1569/7–8, 815X6.
8   Young, *General view*, p. 76.
9   TNA E 163/11.4.

as a form of domestic lighting by the poor into the early nineteenth century, and were sold in bundles called 'whips' at the Norwich Rush Fair, held at the Artichoke Inn near the Magdalene Gates.[10] 'Bolder' or bulrush (*Typha latifolia*), 'gladdon' or lesser reedmace (*Typha angustifolia*), club-rush (*Schoenoplectus* spp.) and yellow flag (*Iris pseudacorus*) were woven into baskets, mats and horse collars, for sale as much as for domestic use.[11] In *c*.1803, during an investigation into common rights in Irstead, John Morton of Ludham claimed 'He had always cut Boulder and Gladding [gladdon] on Irstead Broad for a Right of a Cottage he was owner of at Irstead'; he was described as a 'bedmat and collar ma'er'.[12]

More importantly, permanently waterlogged areas of peat fen were harvested for thatching materials. Reed (*Phragmites australis*) was widely used as a roofing material. It was generally preferred to the alternative, wheat straw, because it lasted almost twice as long and was accordingly used some distance from the places it was actually harvested. Marshall believed a reed roof would last for 50 years, 'and thirty or forty more, with … levelling the hollows with a little fresh reed'.[13] Reeds, in contrast to hay and litter, were cut in the winter and spring. The regulations for managing the commons of Ludham, Catfield and Potter Heigham, drawn up in 1677, typically ordered that 'no reed be cut upon any of the said commons before the day after St Andrew [30 November] under penalty of 6sh 8d for every fathom so cut'.[14] It was the dead stems of the plant, rather than the young growth, that were harvested; cutting after the end of March would cause damage to the emerging reed colts and reduce the following year's harvest. Reed can be cut either annually or every other year; the latter produces a greater length of reed, but mixed with larger quantities of unwanted plant material that must be removed. Several biennial fen species flourish under this form of management.[15]

Reeds were cut using a 'maigue' or 'meek', a sickle with a long, curved blade. Marshall described how the reed-cutters worked from wide, flat-bottomed marsh boats, or from planks suspended over the surface of the water, or – where the water was relatively shallow – by wading. The reeds were cut below the surface of the water, as close to the roots as possible: 'It being an idea, even unto a proverb, that one inch below the water is worth two above it; for the part which now appears green changes to a blackish brown, and becomes as hard as horn; whereas that

---

10   M.C.H. Bird, 'The rural economy, sport and natural history of East Ruston Common', *Transactions of the Norfolk and Norwich Naturalists' Society*, 8 (1909), pp. 631–66.
11   Malster, *The Broads*, p. 29. W. Weaver, 'The bulrush in commerce', *The Country Home*, 1 (1908), pp. 326–8.
12   NRO MC121/238–40.
13   Marshall, *Rural economy*, vol. 1, p. 88.
14   NRO Ms 19424, 103X4.
15   C.J. Hawke and P.V. José, *Reedbed management for commercial and wildlife interests* (Sandy, 1996).

which grows above the water is brittle, and of a more perishable nature.'[16] By post-medieval times the reeds were tied in bunches called 'shooves' and sold by the fathom – that is, in bundles of shooves, usually five or six in number, with a combined circumference of around six feet (*c*. two metres).[17]

'Sedge' – that is, saw-sedge (*Cladium mariscus*) – was also harvested, principally for making the ridges of roofs – it is extremely pliable when dry – although it was also used on its own to thatch hay and corn ricks and poorer dwellings and also in other ways, most notably as cattle bedding (as indeed were poor-quality reeds). Suffling, writing in the 1880s, also recorded that local labourers made leggings 'of twisted sedge, to keep off the weather'.[18] Sedge was cut on a longer rotation than reed, usually at intervals of three or four years, in order to obtain the long stems required for ridging, and in the summer months rather than in the winter and spring. The two plants tended to grow in different parts of the fens. This was mainly because the regular cutting of an area for one plant tended, over time, to suppress the growth of the other. But it was also because, while reeds will flourish in a wide range of conditions and will tolerate the brackish or even saltwater flowing at high tide along rivers in their lower reaches, saw-sedge grows best in fresher conditions, towards the margins of floodplains.

Given that thatching was a skilled task, mainly carried out by professionals, it is not surprising that many reedbeds were on private land rather than commons, like the 'piece of reedbed' purchased in Gillingham in 1303, the one acre of reedbed in Scratby included in a conveyance of 1414 or the 'reed pond' leased by Francis Davis in Norton Subcourse in 1731.[19] Most private reed grounds were small and in some cases the required waterlogged conditions were encouraged by excavation or the construction of embankments or channels. Efforts were evidently made to manage the beds in other ways and, in particular, by dividing up mats of roots, spreading the fractions around the area of water and fixing them in place with stakes.[20] Lesser bulrush was also cut for thatching, as were some other fen plants, but only to cover ricks, outbuildings or the dwellings of the very poor.[21]

In addition to this diverse range of crops, the Broadland fens were also cut for peat, more usually referred to in the past as 'turf', which was used as a domestic fuel throughout the medieval and post-medieval periods and probably at times industrially, for metal-working and, as we have already noted, for producing salt.[22] As

---

16 Marshall, *Rural economy*, vol. 2, p. 89.
17 Malster, *The Broads*, pp. 28–9. Marshall, *Rural economy*, vol. 2, p. 89.
18 E.R. Suffling, *The land of the Broads* (London, 1885), p. 211.
19 NRO GIL 1/34, 716X5. NRO DCN 44/95/39. NRO KNY 27, 369X4.
20 Marshall, *Rural economy*, vol. 2, p. 89.
21 *Ibid.*
22 Campbell, 'Domesday herrings', pp. 5–17.

most readers will be aware, and as discussed in more detail by Jarvis in a subsequent section of this book (below, pp. 198–9), large-scale extraction in the Middle Ages of the so-called 'brushwood peat', lying two metres or more below the surface, led to the formation of the lakes or 'broads' for which the area is famous, and which have given it its modern name. But, in addition, in all periods peat was extracted from relatively shallow workings, between a metre and a metre and a half deep. Cutting usually took place in the summer, when the ground was drier; manorial courts commonly restricted it to the months of May, June and July. Marshall in 1787 described how the individual blocks of peat ('turves'), when first cut, were 4 inches square, drying to 3¼ inches, and 'from two to three feet long, or of a length equal to the depth of the moor'.[23] Environmental evidence suggests that as much as 75 per cent of surviving undrained fens in the Ant and Bure valleys have at some stage been dug for peat.[24] Such shallow cuttings, like the deep medieval pits, soon flooded, but the resulting 'turf ponds' were more rapidly colonised by vegetation and filled with new peat at a rapid rate, perhaps accumulating as much as 15 millimetres a year. Indeed, in some places, such as the Reedham Marshes in the Ant valley, this less consolidated peat was itself extracted within a century or so, although its calorific value was generally low.[25] The cheapest firing was provided by the unconsolidated fibrous vegetable material on the surface of the fen, often described as 'flag' rather than 'turf', which was scraped off before the true peat was extracted.[26] But even the consolidated humified peat, as opposed to the brushwood peat found at depth, was essentially a cheap fuel, certainly in comparison to firewood. By the time Marshall was writing, its use was largely restricted to the poor, although in earlier periods it was more widely employed. He estimated the value of all the peat in an acre (0.4 hectares) of fen at only £78[27] – roughly £7,000 in modern money.

Marshall also noted how, after the peat had been removed, reed ('that valuable aquatic') regenerated 'spontaneously'.[28] Many of the cuttings, or 'turbaries', had an active after-life as managed reed beds and it is possible that this was anticipated, and partly explains their relatively consistent depth of c.1.0–1.5 metres. The shallow ponds so formed, in contrast to the areas of water created by deeper excavations, would have been colonised by reeds after only a few years. More rapid reed growth would have resulted from shallower cuttings, for these would have allowed regeneration from the rhizomes lying at a depth of 0.5 metres or less below

---

23 Marshall, *Rural economy*, vol. 2, p. 98.
24 J.M. Parmenter, 'The development of the wetland vegetation of the Broadland region', PhD thesis (University of East Anglia, 2000), p. 176.
25 *Ibid.*, p. 184.
26 C. Wells, 'Post-medieval turf-digging in Norfolk', *Norfolk Archaeology*, 43/3 (2000), pp. 469–82, at pp. 470–1.
27 Marshall, *Rural economy*, vol. 2, p. 98.
28 *Ibid.*

the surface of the fen, but this would have produced little peat. A more important influence on the depth of cuttings was, perhaps, the fact that, below a metre or so, the use of a spade was rendered increasingly difficult by the pressure of the water.

It has been suggested that, following the peak in peat-digging that created the 'broads' in the early and high Middle Ages, the scale of extraction declined, and that there was a hiatus throughout East Anglia that lasted from the late fourteenth until the later eighteenth century.[29] This argument should not be taken too far. It may in part be an illusion created by the character of the surviving documents, and it underestimates the extent to which turbaries *are* mentioned in the records, including examples at Stokesby in 1428 and 1443, Lowestoft in 1460 and Chedgrave in 1637. In 1527 Robert Clere was said to own, among other property, 40 acres of turbary in Ormesby and 50 acres in Reedham; in 1682 a dispute over the use of Neatishead Common included the right to cut turves.[30] Nevertheless, the scale of peat-digging in Broadland, as elsewhere in East Anglia, does appear to have increased significantly from the middle of the eighteenth century as a result of a rapidly growing population and increasing rural poverty.[31]

Where, as was usually the case, the valley-floor fens were common land, regulating the exploitation of all the varied resources they provided could prove challenging. Stock had to be excluded from the fen each season prior to cutting fodder, litter or marsh hay, to ensure a reasonable harvest. More importantly, the unrestrained extraction of peat, even from shallow excavations, created extensive areas of open water, reducing the amount of grazing that was available and the quantity of hay that might be cut. At Martham in 1404 two men were fined by the manorial court for digging peat from part of the parish common land which should have been left for hay; in 1509 the court forbade the extraction of turves from all the commons in the parish, except Cess Heath and parts of South Fen.[32] Manorial courts worked hard to ensure that the various resources, especially peat, were exploited only to support the domestic economy of commoners, prohibiting, in particular, the sale of peat to outsiders.[33] They also attempted to allocate resources fairly and to prevent commoners taking more than was due to them.

One solution was to divide part of the common into strips called 'doles', allocated to individual commoners, from which they could cut peat and other things. The practice was not confined to wetland commons: it was also a way of regulating the cutting of gorse and heather, likewise used as fuel, on common

---

29   Wells, 'Post-medieval turf-digging', pp. 476–7.
30   NRO MC 2488/1/1 and 2488/4/1. NRO PD 589/142. NRO BEA 435X3. TNA C131/269/4. NRO MC 36/123.
31   Wells, 'Post-medieval turf-digging'.
32   NRO DCN 60/22. B. Cornford, 'The commons of Flegg in the Middle Ages and early modern periods', in M. Manning (ed.), *Commons in Norfolk* (Norwich, 1988), pp. 14–20, at pp. 18–19.
33   NRO Ms 19424, 103X4.

heaths. A list of the doles on the commons of Hemsby, drawn up in 1639, included both 'whin [gorse] doles' on the upland commons and wetland doles like those which 'abutteth upon Smale fenn towards the south & begineth within Dole of the lady of this Mannor', the latter also an indication that some doles formed part of the manorial demesne.[34] In theory the doled land remained part of the common land of the manor, and the strips were unbounded so that livestock could still roam freely across them; in the case of the Hemsby list, the doles were said to be 'Common of Hemsby as concerning the feed Thereof', but the 'sweepedge', or cut material, was considered 'the freehold of the persons hereafter named'. Peat was the main fen commodity allocated in this way but other resources, especially reeds – sometimes but not always from flooded cuttings – were also extracted from doles. In the manorial records of medieval Hemsby there are references to 'reed doles', 'rush doles', 'moor doles' and 'flag doles'.[35] In nearby Fleggburgh a document of 1588 describes the layout of the reed doles within Reed Fen.[36] Doling was well established by the fourteenth century – there is a reference to a 'turbary called West Dole' in Gillingham in 1316[37] – but peat-digging, and the cutting of reeds and other commodities, also continued on open commons, as the evidence from Martham mentioned in the previous paragraph attests.

Doles seem initially, like common rights, to have been attached to particular properties, passing with them as they changed hands through sale or inheritance, but they soon began to be separated from them and treated as parcels of private land. As early as 1394 John Roth granted 'a parcel of marsh called a fendole' in Gillingham.[38] Doles could then be accumulated – in the early sixteenth century William Docking of Dilham bought two acres in 'Twelve Men Dole' from Robert Eche and five acres from William Blome – and amalgamated into larger blocks of private fen or marsh.[39] Progressive amalgamation and privatisation served to remove most systems of doles from the landscape by the nineteenth century, leaving only a few survivors. The tithe map of 1839 shows that the whole area of 'Upton Doles', now 40 hectares of open reedbed and wet woodland lying to the north-east of Upton Broad and managed by the Norfolk Wildlife Trust, was then divided into a mass of strips, without physical boundaries, the narrowest less than seven metres wide (Figure 4.5).[40] Similar arrangements are depicted by the tithe maps in Surlingham, in the area around Surlingham Broad and (less well

---

34   NRO MC 1559, 1, 815X4.
35   Cornford, 'Commons of Flegg', p. 16.
36   NRO Ms 2506 2F1.
37   NRO GIL 1/67, 716X6.
38   NRO GIL 1/17, 716X3.
39   NRO KC 1/105, 391X5.
40   NRO PD 255/29.

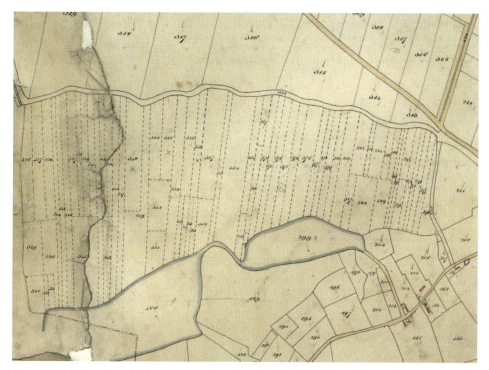

Figure 4.5 'Doles' – unfenced strips of common fen allocated to individual commoners – at Upton in the Bure valley, as shown on the 1839 tithe map.

preserved) in Rockland St Mary and Honing, but elsewhere only the occasional example of a single open strip, or a small groups of strips, survived to suggest their former presence.[41]

In a number of places, however, the practice of doling had left a distinctive mark on the patterns of land division recorded on the tithe maps. At Rockland St Mary the land parcels lying adjacent to the doled area, each enclosed by water-filled dykes, have a 'strippy', parallel, slightly sinuous appearance suggesting that they evolved through the consolidation and enclosure of bundles of narrower, unfenced doles, with the land subsequently being upgraded to grazing marsh or meadow (Figure 4.6). Similar patterns are apparent in areas of marsh shown on the tithe maps for Langley, Worlingham, Barsham and Gillingham, the latter perhaps representing the 'turbaries of divers men' referred to in a deed of 1391.[42] They can also be discerned, less clearly, in parts of Aldeby, Hardley, North Cove and Strumpshaw. In most cases these arrangements continue to be apparent in the landscape today.

While the doles shown on the tithe maps lying within what are still areas of undrained fen have largely become filled with plant debris over the last two

---

41   NRO PD 611/33; NRO PD 256/16.
42   NRO GIL 1/15, 716X3.

Figure 4.6. Narrow strips of grazing marsh lying to the south of Rockland Broad probably developed through the amalgamation and privatisation of fen doles.

centuries and are invisible on the ground, at both Upton and Rockland, and to a lesser extent at Surlingham, they can still be seen on lidar images as networks of close-set parallel lines running through the fen. Similar patterns appear in the area between Ranworth and Malthouse Broads and the river Bure. Common land in Ranworth disappeared at an early date and there is no surviving map earlier than the tithe map of 1839, but this shows two long, narrow strips of 'marsh or turf ground' on the same alignment as the lines on the lidar images, surviving within larger blocks of property that had presumably been consolidated from groups of doles.

Not all parallel, narrow peat diggings were necessarily doles. On private areas of fen extraction might also take this form, which made it easier to place the blocks of cut peat or 'hovers' on adjacent firm ground where they would be left to dry. For private turbaries also existed, even in the Middle Ages, alongside those on commons and doles, although the small size of many of the examples described in early documents suggests that they may have originated as doles, or at least formed fractions of larger workings: half an acre at Scratby in 1260, one acre at Ormesby in the early fourteenth century, three roods in Gillingham in the mid-fourteenth century, even a single rood in the same parish in the mid-thirteenth century.[43] By post-medieval times, to judge from the configuration and size of turf ponds shown on early maps, peat was often extracted from larger pits, but even then many private turbaries remained small.

Whether doled or otherwise, common fens usually lacked embankments or drainage dykes. The exceptions appear to have been 'fen meadows' found in slightly drier areas of the peat, where waterlogged conditions did not persist all year and where the quality of the herbage could be significantly improved through relatively limited drainage works. At Beccles in the sixteenth century the dykes in the 'comen fenne' were regularly 'drawne and skorrede', the causeways providing access repaired and gravelled and the 'dams' and walls reinforced with faggots, many cut from a particular area of the common, Oxholmes, in which large numbers of pollarded willows and alders grew.[44] At Fleggburgh in the seventeenth century a rate was charged for 'casting, carting, or other repairing or drayning of the common', apparently meaning the fen meadow still known as Burgh Common.[45] Where, as was more usually the case, the deposits of peat were thicker and more waterlogged, the fens were simply dissected by a complex network of channels that provided access for small flat-bottomed boats to areas dug for peat or cut for reed, sedge or litter. In many cases these channels, as shown on the earliest maps, have an irregular or serpentine appearance, suggesting a natural origin. Some, however, follow a relatively straight course, indicating that they were intentionally created, like that running roughly north–south through the middle of Ward Marsh in Horning. In some fens, most notably in Ranworth, patterns of parallel channels are present that may have developed along the boundaries of doles.

Where the floodplain deposits comprised estuarine clay, common land was mainly used for grazing, rather than being mown and cut. Many communities had access to both kinds of common. At Carlton Colville in the Waveney valley, for example, there were three wet commons in the seventeenth century. The 40-acre Redefenne and 10-acre Slypp Marsh were essentially peat fens, of which it was said that the commoners 'doe use to mowe in somer and wth in some tyme after

---

43   NRO DCN 44/95/22. NRO GIL 1/22, 716X5. NRO GIL 1/23, 716X5. NRO DCN 44/95/28.
44   Beccles Fen Reeves' Account 1552: transcript by the Beccles branch of the Workers Educational Association, 1977, Beccles Town Hall.
45   Cornford, 'Commons of Flegg', p. 20.

mowinge the grass being growne … doe feade wth there cattall'. The 50-acre Horde Marshe, in contrast, overlay estuarine clay, and this they used for 'pasturing there horsebeasts and other cattall all the year'.[46] More usually, grazing was restricted to the dry summer months, to avoid 'poaching' the land and damaging the sward, as at Heigham Holmes in Potter Heigham, where it was stated in 1632 that 'the saide inhabitants … do feede it as their common or waste from the 24th day of June yearely till the eighth day of September'.[47] The productivity of common marshes was often enhanced by the construction of drains and embankments, at least by post-medieval times and where they lay in the lower reaches of the rivers, where there was a significant tidal range. At Cantley in the early eighteenth century a rate was levied 'for the repairs of the Walls, Banks, Sluices, Ditches, Drains, Gates and Fences of the Said Common'. Commoners had to pay 3s a year for each bullock grazed on the marsh, a custom changed in 1728 to a more flexible system, by which a committee of five, chosen by the commoners, decided what works were required and fixed the yearly rate accordingly.[48] Common marshes were often embanked not only where they fronted a river but laterally, along their boundaries with adjacent parishes. Flood banks or 'dams' were, in particular, often raised on either side of a stream draining off the uplands that was already being used to demarcate a parish boundary. Good examples of such embanked watercourses exist between Worlingham and Beccles (the 'Worlingham Wall') and between North Cove and Barnby, in the Waveney valley, and between Buckenham and Hassingham in the valley of the Yare.

Private marshes in the valleys, where they existed, were also embanked from an early date. The 'wall' protecting Oulton Marshes was, by 1700, already 'so out of repair and the ditches so filled up that the grass it produces … [is] full of flaggs and so of little value'.[49] It is from these areas of private marsh in the valleys, moreover – rather than, as we have seen, from the more extensive area of estuarine clays in the Halvergate Marshes – that we have our earliest evidence of drainage mills, some erected on land anciently owned as private property, some on land enclosed from commons in the course of the sixteenth and seventeenth centuries. A map of 1702, of the Norwich Cathedral Dean and Chapter's lands at St Benet's Abbey 'with the marshes belonging to the same', shows a small drainage mill in elevation, although not the famous brick structure that now sits within the medieval gatehouse and which had itself been constructed in the 1720s (see below, pp. 231, 261).[50] Another

---

46   R. Sweet, 'Beccles to Burgh St Peter: a landscape history of the marshes', MA dissertation (University of East Anglia, 1989), p. 27.
47   NRO DN HAR 3/1, p. 31.
48   NRO MC 76/1.
49   NRO DCN 59/47A/1–2.
50   NRO Snelling 11/12/73 (P150 B5).

Figure 4.7 Typical 'carr' or wet woodland, dominated by alder, in the Ant valley.

drainage mill is depicted on a map of 1723 showing 'Colonel Cope's Marshes', now Peto's Marsh, in Oulton, while a further example was constructed in 1740 by the Langley estate to drain the Round House Marshes in Langley.[51] By c.1761 the latter had been joined by another example, further upriver in the marshes at Buckenham.[52] It is noteworthy that the only surviving mills that can be securely dated to the eighteenth century by datestones, extant or recorded – Wiseman's Mill in Oby (1753) and Brograve Level Mill in Waxham (1771) – are likewise located in valley marshes, rather than on Halvergate.

Today, large areas of peat in the river floodplains, especially those of the Bure and Ant, are occupied by wet woodland or 'carr', dominated by alder, with smaller quantities of willow, birch and, in some cases, oak (Figure 4.7). Most of this woodland developed, as we shall see, in the course of the twentieth century, but smaller blocks, usually managed by coppicing, have a longer history. Alder was a valuable wood, used to make high-quality charcoal (for manufacturing gunpowder) and scaffolding poles, and – because it rots slowly if kept wet – for constructing the jetties and river revetments needed in large numbers in Broadland. Alder carrs are often mentioned in deeds and other documents. A mid-thirteenth-century grant of a turbary in Gillingham, for example, refers in passing to the 'alder carr

---

51 NRO BEA 337/ 1–6, 438X7.
52 Both are shown on a map by Joseph Rumball, showing a section of the river Yare, of c.1761; NRO NCR 16c/108.

of Fayergate'.[53] There were other small carrs in the parish: an 'alder carr near the common river and Clementisyerd', covering two acres, is referred to in 1304 and 1457, while in 1310 John, son of William de Gapetone, granted to Lawrence de Huntingfield a 'pightle called Gaptunesherd with alder carr adjoining'.[54] There are many other examples. In 1530 Robert Longe, alderman of Norwich, granted an estate including 'a piece of alder carr in Whitlingham', while in 1645 an 'alder carr' in Langley was among the property divided, following the death of John Heathe, between his four daughters.[55]

Alders and other trees existed on some of the peat commons, but not in dense stands. The grazing of livestock and cutting of hay and litter presumably suppressed the regrowth of trees felled or fallen in the damp ground; any significant level of grazing would certainly have made management by coppicing difficult, because the livestock would browse off the regenerating stools. Alder carrs, like other forms of coppiced woodland, were thus usually private property. Before the twentieth century those in Broadland were mainly found on the margins of the floodplains, or on patches of particularly damp and boggy ground around the fringes of the great level of the Halvergate Marshes. Carrs were, and indeed still are, often to be found where tributary streams enter the floodplains, as at Buckenham in the valley of the Yare, or on the boundary between Gillingham and Aldeby in the Waveney valley. For the most part, carrs were long-lived features of the landscape, although they were sometimes cleared and drained to create fen meadow or grazing marsh, as on the bishop of Norwich's lands at Horning in the sixteenth century.[56] Conversely, deteriorating drainage, causing a reduction of grazing or cutting, sometimes led to the spontaneous development of carr and its subsequent management by coppicing. In this and other ways the landscape of the valleys in the period before the nineteenth century was characterised as much by change and dynamism as by stability.

Through the fifteenth, sixteenth and seventeenth centuries the proportion of the fens and marshes managed as common land was gradually reduced through the privatisation and consolidation of doles and small, piecemeal encroachments, such as the half rod of marsh, 'some time parcel of the Common Pasture called Clynt Fenn Well', referred to in a terrier for Horning in the reign of Edward IV.[57] But some larger areas were also enclosed – that is, converted to private property – by formal agreements, as at Aldeby in 1614, where lord and tenants agreed to enclose 'all such marshes rushe grounds and reede grounds … as nowe bee or are reputed to bee or

---

53   NRO GIL 1/23, 716X5.
54   NRO GIL 1/32, 716X5. GIL 1/115, 716X7.
55   NRO COL 1/183. NRO BEA 16–17, 433X9.
56   NRO DN HAR 3/3, p. 214.
57   NRO DN HAR 3/3.

might be used or fedd in common'. When this aim was finally achieved, in 1635, most although not all the common was allotted as private parcels to the lord, and to the landowners in proportion to the commonable rights claimed on the basis of land held on the adjacent 'upland', with 20 acres being set aside 'for charitable and good uses to and for ye benefitte of ye said towne only'.[58] In 1676, similarly, an agreement was made to enclose the Great Marsh in Langley, while a document of 1678 refers to 'one marsh late parcell of the Common called East Marsh' in the adjacent parish of Hardley.[59] Early enclosures were not always amicable. At Clippesby in 1573 there were disputes when the lord of the manor fenced off part of the common and took it into private ownership. In 1589 six Ormesby yeomen brought a legal action against Sir Edward Clere, lord of the manor, for obstructing their access to the common and enclosing 30 acres for his own use.[60]

The extent and character of early enclosure in the Broadland valleys remains poorly understood and it is often unclear whether particular pieces of private land referred to in our documentary sources represent land that had always been private property, usually ancient demesne, or were the consequence of early enclosures from commons, such as the 'marsh or moor' called Crabbetts Marsh in Hoveton St John, already held in severalty by 1551.[61] What is clear, however, is that early enclosure tended to affect common marshes more than fens, and that a high proportion of the latter, in the valleys of the Ant, Thurne and Bure especially, survived until they were enclosed by parliamentary acts in the late eighteenth or early nineteenth centuries.

The impact of enclosure
by Keith Bacon and Tom Williamson

The sixteenth- and seventeenth-century enclosures of marsh and fen just discussed, carried out by formal agreements between lords and tenants, were part of a much wider process that affected not only the marshes and fens in the river valleys but also much of the intervening uplands. Enclosure was the process of turning land subject to common rights into privately owned land, and involved not only areas of common land but also open-field arable. It could be achieved by several methods, in addition to formal agreement. Enclosure by unity of possession was where one person, usually the lord of the manor, acquired ownership of all of the parish by buying up the property of any other owners possessing common rights. These rights could then be extinguished and the layout of the land rearranged at the will of the sole owner. Piecemeal enclosure, in contrast, was

---

58 NRO MS 7458, 736. NRO MS 19913, 123X1.
59 NRO BEA 72–4, 435X6. NRO BEA 76/1.
60 Cornford, 'Commons of Flegg', p. 16.
61 NRO ACC 2019/228 BOX 1.

where individual owners acquired bundles of contiguous arable strips through sale or exchange, surrounded them with a hedge and, with the agreement, usually undocumented, of their neighbours, withdrew the land from common grazing and communal management. This form of enclosure could, over time, largely or completely remove the open fields in a parish.[62] By its very nature, it could have no impact on common land, comprising areas of shared use-rights rather than intermixed property. Commons were, however, often subject to minor piecemeal encroachment, in Broadland as elsewhere. As the lord of the manor was the legal owner of the soil of the common wastes, he could grant permission for individuals to enclose small areas, provided that other commoners did not suffer significant loss of grazing or other rights. At least three such grants were given in Catfield, for example, and recorded in the manor court books, for parishioners to take in very small plots along the edge of the heath and then build cottages on them.[63]

There are a number of examples of enclosure by unity of possession in Broadland, especially in the north of the district. Waxham, in the Thurne valley, for example, was entirely in the hands of successive single owners for centuries and its upland arable enclosed and reorganised at an early date. Sir Berney Brograve, who inherited in 1753, drained a large area of fen and marsh, the Brograve Level, by a network of drains leading to Brograve Mill, built in 1771, one of the oldest surviving drainage mills in Broadland. The parish of Ashby was owned by the bishop of Norwich (it had previously formed part of the estate of St Benet's Abbey), except for a few small pieces of land in the south-east of the parish belonging to 'outsetters' from Clippesby and Rollesby. The bishop enclosed areas of fen near Shallam Dyke and the parish's portion of Stevenheath on the highest land where the parishes of Ashby, Rollesby, Repps and Clippesby meet. The remaining open fields were removed in the eighteenth century and the parish reorganised, mostly as one large farm – Manor Farm – although with some fields attached to the holdings of the bishop's tenants in other parishes, mainly Thurne. Other Broadland parishes that had their fens and marshes, as well as their upland heaths and open fields, enclosed by sole or dominant owners include Oby, Clippesby and Mautby in Flegg, as well as Coltishall, Horstead and Wroxham in the Bure valley.[64]

All Broadland parishes underwent piecemeal enclosure of their arable fields to a greater or lesser extent, a process spread over several centuries but which probably accelerated after *c*.1700. By the eighteenth century the typical farm in most parts of Broadland was a mixture of small private closes and tiny open 'lands'

---

62 J.A. Yelling, *Common field and enclosure in England, 1450–1850* (London, 1977). G.E. Mingay, *Parliamentary enclosure in England: an introduction to its causes, incidence and impact 1750–1850* (London, 1997), pp. 11–13. Williamson, 'Understanding enclosure', pp. 56–79.
63 NRO P 187E/6–15 Purdy & Holley.
64 Bacon, 'Landholding and enclosure', pp. 208–9, 233–40.

all intermixed with those of other farms. Only in parishes on the heavy clay soils around the Waveney valley had this form of enclosure sometimes succeeded in removing all the open arable. A survey of Catfield, drawn up around 1761, shows that the parish's farmland (excluding woodland, heath or fen) consisted of 965 acres (390 hectares) in 425 pieces, a mixture of private closes and open 'lands'.[65] The average parcel size was 2.27 acres (0.9 hectares) and *c*.56 per cent of parcels covered less than 2 acres (0.8 hectares), although amounting in total to only 18 per cent of the farmland. Around 38 per cent of pieces covered between 2 and 6 acres (0.8–2.4 hectares), accounting for 61 per cent; and while only 24 of the 425 total, under 6 per cent, extended over more than this, they collectively made up 22 per cent of the farmland.

These various forms of enclosure continued in Broadland right to the end of the eighteenth century. As late as 1790 most of the common marsh of Carlton Colville was enclosed by agreement and became Share Marsh, now the western section of the Suffolk Wildlife Trust Carlton Marshes reserve. A map in the Suffolk Record Office shows that the new grid of drainage dykes enclosed parcels covering around 7.5 acres (*c*.3 hectares, the majority) or multiples or fractions of this area, presumably representing the 'shares' allotted in proportion to the number of stock the commoners were each permitted to graze before enclosure.[66] Access tracks were created, flood banks constructed and a mill erected to drain the area.[67] A document of 1816 describes how, at Easter each year, the holders of land on the marsh elected two reeves who supervised the maintenance of roads, fences, dykes and access ways.[68] Three parts of the marsh were not individually owned but were instead the joint property of the 'Share Marsh proprietors', remaining so until sold by auction in 1909.[69]

By the 1790s, however, parliamentary enclosure was becoming the preferred method of removing open fields, heaths and perhaps especially the common fens and marshes of the floodplains, which had been only marginally affected by earlier forms of enclosure. This method required a private act of parliament to be passed, ordering the land in a specified area to be allotted or reallocated to private owners by an enclosure award, and for common rights such as grazing to be abolished.[70] Most acts applied to just one parish but a few covered two or more. Sometimes this was because one landowner was dominant in both parishes, even when they

---

65 NRO STA 761. Bacon, 'Landholding and enclosure', pp. 241–3.
66 SRO 1117/91/1.
67 This stood at TM494928, some 110m to the north-east of the steam mill shown on the first edition Ordnance Survey 6-inch map of 1882.
68 SRO 1146/1.
69 SRO 1146/1.
70 M. Turner, *English parliamentary enclosure: its historical geography and economic history* (Folkestone, 1980).

lay several miles apart. This was the case with Eccles and Repps-with-Bastwick, in both of which John Lombe was principal landowner.[71] More usually it was two or more adjoining parishes with major landowners in common that shared an act: examples include Winterton with East and West Somerton; Cantley with Hassingham; and Haddiscoe with Thurlton and Thorpe.[72] Of particular interest is an act of 1812 covering areas of marsh and fen in Hempstead, Eccles, Palling, Lessingham, Happisburgh and Ingham, all of which also had their own individual enclosure acts, which was in effect a joint drainage scheme embracing much of the upper Thurne catchment.[73]

Most parliamentary enclosures in Broadland occurred after the passing of the General Enclosure Act in 1801, which laid down standard procedures for the process.[74] Firstly, there had to be agreement from the owners of four-fifths of the land in the parish, *not* four-fifths of the owners by number. This could mean a few owners or even just one. Owners, moreover, were not necessarily residents of the parish, nor were they the people who actually farmed the land. Much of this, in Broadland as elsewhere, was cultivated by tenant farmers who had no say in the enclosure process. Three commissioners were appointed to carry out the enclosure, usually members of the local gentry and solicitors. They invited owners to state what they claimed to own, in terms of both land and the rights attached to it. These 'statements of claims' were printed and made available for public scrutiny and any disputed claims were settled. A surveyor was then appointed who mapped the land in the parish, usually both the private farmland and the common waste. The rental value per acre of every piece of land was established and marked on a map, sometimes employing a code based on the word 'CUMBERLAND', with each letter representing a number, starting with 1 and ending with 0 (so that 'ud', for example, equals 20). This provided a measure of secrecy perhaps intended to prevent onlooking owners disputing the surveyor's valuations. The valuations for all owners were collated and the total values of common fields and wastes were calculated. Incidentally, these maps show that in most cases the small closes that had been enclosed piecemeal during previous decades or centuries were valued in a similar manner to adjoining open-field strips, suggesting that the main motive for enclosure was not, as some historians have suggested, an anticipated increase in land values.

The land was allotted in surveyed parcels bounded by straight new hedges or, in fens and marshes, water-filled dykes (Figure 4.8). The lord of the manor was given a substantial proportion of the newly enclosed land in compensation for his losses

---

71 NRO NCR 25b/21/13.
72 NRO MC 3231/3/44, 1066X. NRO PD 291/20. NRO MS 10859.
73 NRO C/Sca 2/147.
74 Mingay, *Parliamentary enclosure*, pp. 55–82.

Figure 4.8 Detail from the enclosure map for Thurne, 1820. The former common is shaded in green. Note the main drain, running north–south, and the drainage mill, its site now occupied by Morse's Mill, which replaced it in 1836 (bottom centre). Figure 4.3 shows the same landscape as it is today.

as the owner of the soil of the common waste, and some was used for a variety of public purposes. In particular, an allotment was usually made for the parish poor, a recognition of the benefits they had derived from the commons, albeit usually on sufferance rather than by legal right.[75] From the very start such 'poor's allotments' seem to have constituted a normal, expected part of a parliamentary enclosure. In Stokesby the principal landowner, Major England, was obliged to provide one at his own expense following the enclosure of 1720 because 'The poor inhabitants finding that no allotment was set out for their benefit under the Inclosure Act … proceeded in a riotous manner and insisted upon having some allotment given to them.'[76] Poor's allotments were not administered by the poor themselves but by the parish overseers or by trustees drawn from the wealthy or middle-class residents. Most were used by the poor (generally classified as those owning property worth less than £10 *per annum*) primarily as a source of fuel, which in Broadland meant

---

75 S. Birtles, 'The impact of Commons Registration: a Norfolk study', *Landscape History*, 20/1 (1998), pp. 83–97. S. Birtles, 'Common land, poor relief and enclosure: the use of manorial resources in fulfilling parish obligations 1601–1834', *Past and Present*, 165 (1999), pp. 74–106. S. Birtles, 'A green space beyond self-interest: the evolution of common land in Norfolk, c.750–2003', PhD thesis (University of East Anglia, 2003).

76 NRO P/CH 1/19.

peat – many were described in enclosure acts as 'fuel allotments'.[77] In addition, an allotment was made to the parish Surveyor of the Highways for digging sand and gravel to repair the roads, which often incorporated an existing pit, long used for the purpose, on one of the commons. Areas were often allocated for use as public 'staithes' or landing places. New drainage works were undertaken and new roads laid out, either public or private, the latter in modern times often the subject of disputes as to their ownership and status.

The land remaining after all such subtractions had been made was allotted to individual landowners in proportion to the rights and property they had possessed in the pre-enclosure landscape, with small amounts of land going to owners of tenements with ancient common rights attached, but no farmland. Thus the whole process was regarded as being scrupulously fair, at least from the viewpoint of landowners. There must have been informal negotiations between the commissioners and individual proprietors so that particular preferences of location and types of land could be taken into account. Of two landowners entitled to 300 shillings-worth of land, one might desire 10 acres of good arable land in the former open field while the other might prefer 300 acres of open water. The wealthier gentry, especially resident squires, often chose to receive large areas of water and fen, probably for its sporting value but in some cases perhaps because they hoped to make a good profit by investing in its 'improvement'. Because the awards generally valued arable land at between 20s and 30s per acre, fen at around 5s and open water at only 1s, this can make their allotments appear disproportionately over-generous. Very small owners often preferred to have allotments near to their cottages, or sometimes small blocks of fen on which they could continue customary practices such as peat-digging; the owners of eight very small farms thus each received allotments of about five acres (*c.* two hectares) in Catfield Fen.[78]

After an enclosure award had been finalised, those in receipt of allotments received a bill for their share of the costs, including those relating to road building, drainage and other public works. These were allocated fairly in proportion to the value of the allotments; often the smaller allottees were excused payment. Each landowner then had to pay the costs of, or themselves undertake the work of, hedging or dyking their allotments and, in many cases, converting former waste into farmland. It has often been argued that parliamentary enclosure brought about a rapid decline in the numbers of small landowners particularly because of the costs involved. This does not appear to have been the case in most Broadland parishes, where there was often some selling and buying of land and small farms for a few years following enclosure awards, but not on a large scale. The most

---

77 C. Wells, 'The role of turf and associated fuels in the nineteenth-century rural economy of Norfolk', *Norfolk Archaeology*, 43/4 (2001), pp. 630–42, at pp. 631–3.
78 NRO C/Sca 2/67.

noticeable trend in the land market of the early nineteenth century in this area, coinciding with parliamentary enclosure rather than caused by it, was in fact the selling of farms by absentee owners to their tenants.[79]

There are clear chronological, and to some extent spatial, patterns to the incidence of parliamentary enclosure within the Broads area, although it should be noted that the timing of an enclosure can be measured either by the date when the act was passed or by that when the award actually reorganising the landscape was made, allocating land and terminating established rights. In Broadland the gap between the two dates might range from less than a year to over ten years, although in most cases it was just a few years – three years or less in 60 per cent of examples, with only 20 per cent separated by more than five years. The exceptional ones were Horning (11 years), Hoveton St John (9 years) and the joint enclosure of Surlingham and Strumpshaw (in different hundreds and on opposite sides of the river Yare), which took 13 years to complete. At a national level, parliamentary enclosure occurred in two main waves. The first, in the 1760s and 1770s, was particularly associated with the Midlands, and with the enclosure of open fields and their conversion to pasture. The second wave broadly coincided with the French and Napoleonic Wars from 1793 to 1815 and, while also dealing to some extent with open-field arable, was more concerned with the enclosure and reclamation of common wastes, whether upland moors or lowland heaths and fens.[80] The wars increased still further the prices of wheat and other agricultural commodities that were already rising as a result of population growth and the expansion of industrial towns. Buoyant prices encouraged landowners to boost agricultural output by enclosing and reclaiming common land, although it has also been suggested that the increasing availability of borrowed money further incentivised them to undertake such endeavours, and that to some extent agricultural improvement was a fashionable activity, encouraged by writers such as Arthur Young and the example set by prominent aristocratic estate owners. Either way, Broadland enclosures fall firmly within this second wave. The 1720 act for Stokesby was the earliest in Norfolk and many decades ahead of any others in Broadland: the principal owner was an MP and the act involved only an area of common marsh. The next act, for Woodbastwick in 1779, was still over 20 years ahead of the bulk of parishes in the area. About two-thirds of the acts were passed between 1797 and 1812, with the rest coming after the latter date. The latest were for Bramerton's 102-acre (*c.*41-hectare) common, awarded in 1852, and for Thorpe Low Common, comprising 62 acres (25 hectares) of marsh or fen, in 1863.[81]

---

79   Bacon, 'Landholding and enclosure', pp. 118–24.
80   Turner, *English parliamentary enclosure*. Turner, 'Parliamentary enclosure'.
81   TNA MAF 1/859. NRO BR 90. NRO MC 1395.

Although parliamentary enclosures in the Broads area often dealt with the small residues of open-field arable left after centuries of piecemeal enclosure, together with more extensive tracts of common land, in a few parishes, especially in Flegg, such as Somerton, Runham, Fleggburgh, Billockby and Hemsby, rather larger areas of open arable were removed. Some of the commons enclosed were heaths, either occupying areas of glacial gravel on high ground, like that in Filby enclosed in 1802, or associated with outcrops of Crag at lower levels, such as Cess Heath in Martham, on the edge of the Thurne valley ('Martham Common' on William Faden's 1797 map of Norfolk), which was enclosed and converted into private arable land by the Martham award of 1812.[82] In the parishes of Hickling and Catfield a heath of the latter type, covering several hundred acres, was enclosed in 1808 and mostly converted into rectangular arable fields, although in both parishes sections allotted as fuel allotments to the poor survived for a while. Other examples depicted on Faden's map but enclosed within decades or years of its publication were located around the Trinity Broads in Hemsby, Ormesby and Rollesby, at Lessingham in the Thurne valley, in Ludham, and in Belton and Burgh Castle near the river Waveney.[83] The largest area of heathland enclosed was the great Mousehold Heath, covering nearly 18 square kilometres in the area between Norwich, Woodbastwick and Blofield on the interfluve between the Bure and the Yare, which was enclosed by a series of separate acts, affecting the various parishes with rights to its use, between 1799 and 1810.[84]

While parliamentary enclosure removed large areas of heathland, its environmental impact on the fens and marshes was more complex. Most Broadland enclosure awards made provision, alongside other public benefits, for drainage works. They often established Drainage Commissions, with members drawn from the parish's wealthier landowners, and allotted them land for the construction of embankments, drains or dykes, and drainage mills. No fewer than 17 such commissions were set up between 1800 and 1820, some embracing (like the awards themselves) a single parish, some two (such as Catfield and Sutton, 1808) and a few several (Winterton and East and West Somerton, 1805). The water in the drains surrounding and within the new private allotments and in the landspring dykes running along the margin of the floodplain flowed into major drains – still often referred to as 'Commissioners' Drains' – which ran, ruler-straight, across the enclosed land or into the 'soke dykes' behind the river embankments. From there the water was lifted over the bank into the river by a

---

82 NRO FX 385, 1030X4. NRO PC 125/9. W. Faden, *A topographical map of the county of Norfolk* (London, 1797).
83 Faden, *Topographical map*.
84 Faden, *Topographical map*. Enclosure acts for: Rackheath 1799, Salhouse 1800, Thorpe 1800, Sprowston 1800, Little Plumstead 1800, Blofield and Hemblington 1801, Great Plumstead and Postwick 1810.

new drainage mill. Even when a mill was not immediately erected, and drainage initially made by gravity and sluice alone, one was often subsequently built. When Thurlton, Haddiscoe and Haddiscoe Thorpe were enclosed in 1806 a piece of land was awarded to the drainage commissioners 'as an outfall to the river in case they should find it necessary or expedient to erect a Mill thereon for the better drainage of the said Lands and Grounds'.[85] Most Drainage Commissions continued to function until the passing of the Land Drainage Act of 1930, when their properties and duties were split. Their windpumps and drains were transferred to the new Internal Drainage Boards, each covering several parishes. The river embankments, in contrast, went to the new East Norfolk Rivers Catchment Board, which, after several reorganisations and mergers, is now part of the Environment Agency. In the early twentieth century drainage commissioners in parishes such as Martham, Repps and Potter Heigham subsidised their drainage rates by leasing riverbank plots for moorings or the erection of bungalows, the freehold owner of which is now the Environment Agency (see below, p. 351).

The construction of a mill and associated drainage works signals that a significant proportion of the enclosed land was to be used as grazing marsh. Most of the reclaimed areas were on estuarine clays, overlain at most by only thin layers of peat, especially in the Thurne valley: they had mainly been used as common grazing marsh before enclosure, or else as fen meadow. The aim was to improve the quality of the sward and extend the length of the grazing season. But in a few cases, as with Eastfield Mill in Hickling, commissioners erected mills that mainly or even entirely served to drain areas of peat, true fen. It is, in fact, unclear how ambitious the large landowners who led the enclosures may have been in their plans for the wetlands. Some may have hoped to emulate the achievements in the peat Fenlands of Cambridgeshire, where even the great Whittlesey Mere near Peterborough was drained and ploughed. Indeed, in 1804 William Smith, the prominent geologist and civil engineer, drew up a scheme for improving the upper Thurne valley that included the draining of Hickling Broad.[86] It is even unclear how most of the enclosed fens were initially used. While the tithe maps and apportionments drawn up in *c*.1840 record land use, they do so in rather vague terms, and many of the private parcels described as 'pasture' were probably still primarily mown for rough marsh hay and litter. They also show, however, that some landowners had by now erected mills to better drain their allotments and sometimes those of neighbours, such as the predecessor of the present Hunsett Mill in Stalham, or the lost Barton Turf Mill.[87] Many more drainage mills were constructed within the

---

85   NRO C/Sca 2/294.
86   NRO DN/Msc 6/6.
87   NRO PD 262/60(H). TNA IR 30/23/41.

area of the enclosed fens, especially in the valleys of the Ant and the Upper Yare, in the middle and later decades of the nineteenth century. While a few of these, such as Moys Mill in Smallburgh, were – like the majority of the 'Commission' mills – brick towers, most were relatively light wooden structures – hollow post mills or trestle mills, relatively cheap devices used to drain limited areas of land (see below, pp. 245–6). Such attempts to improve the quality of the herbage of the former fens rarely met with long-term success. The first edition 6-inch Ordnance Survey maps from the 1880s mark much of the reclaimed land as only 'rough pasture', liable to floods. Some, especially in the Ant valley, had already reverted to reedbed and fen. Indeed, in a few places the erection of drainage mills and pumps may signal not the reclamation of fens but the better regulation of water levels within them, to facilitate the continuation or intensification of established modes of exploitation such as peat-digging or reed-cutting.

For many of the fen allotments appear, in fact, to have been used in traditional ways, as turbaries and reed or sedge beds. Before enclosure, as we have seen, the common fens had been exploited in a variety of ways and attempts were made to limit those activities that might, in particular, reduce the area available for cutting marsh hay and litter. Private land, in contrast, could be used in whatever way owners saw fit, and the late eighteenth and early nineteenth centuries saw an increasing local demand for peat, as both the rural population and the numbers of the rural poor rose rapidly. The scale of peat-digging escalated accordingly. In Irstead and Catfield Fens, for example, more than half the fen surface has been removed to a depth of 0.50–0.8 metres (in some places more), the cuttings following the boundaries established at the enclosure of 1808.[88] Some of the land here comprised poor's allotments but much was private property and, while the digging of peat in such contexts may sometimes have been for personal use, there was also a significant commercial trade, organised by people such as Henry Debbage of South Walsham, who is described as a 'coal and turf dealer' in White's *Directory* of 1845.[89] In some places large-scale peat extraction led to the formation of areas of open water as extensive as, although shallower and therefore less permanent than, the broads themselves. Following the enclosure of Woodbastwick in 1779 a turf pond ('Broad Waters') developed in Woodbastwick Fen which, by 1839, covered more than 40 hectares. It then rapidly terrestrialised, effectively disappearing by 1905 (Figure 4.9).[90] Flooded peat cuttings made good reedbeds, and similar conditions were created on some private allotments by making shallow excavations, *c*.0.5 metres deep and three

---

[88] K.E. Giller and B.D. Wheeler, 'Past peat cutting and present vegetation patterns in an undrained fen in the Norfolk Broadland', *Journal of Ecology*, 74 (1986), pp. 219–47.

[89] White, *Directory of Norfolk*, p. 500.

[90] 1773 map, private collection. NRO PD 259/55. Ordnance Survey 6-inch maps.

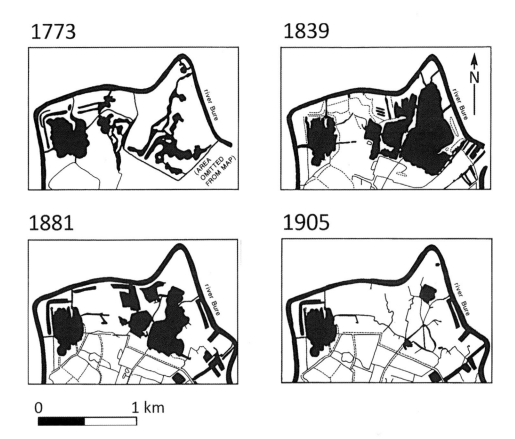

Figure 4.9 The development of 'Broad Waters', Woodbastwick Fen, between 1773 and 1905.

metres wide, a practice known as 'turfing out', which continued into the twentieth century.[91] Although clay pantiles came into widespread use in East Anglia in the course of the eighteenth century, reeds remained in high demand not only for repairing or renewing existing thatched roofs but also because they were used as lining beneath pantiles, to provide a firm base and insulation: 'Having nailed on the pan-tile laths, the tiler distributes reeds … Upon the reed he spreads a coat of mortar, and on this lays the tiles.'[92] It was a practice that seems to have become more common in the course of the nineteenth century and continued into the twentieth, as did the use of reed in the lath and plaster of ceilings. Continuing demand for peat and reeds, in short, militated against wholesale attempts at drainage and reclamation in private allotments.

---

91 C. Wells, 'Historical and palaeoecological investigations of some Norfolk Broadland flood-plain mires and post medieval turf cutting', PhD thesis (University of Sheffield, 1988), pp. 141–2, 215–16. K.E. Giller, 'Aspects of the plant ecology of a flood-plain mire in Broadland, Norfolk', PhD thesis (University of Sheffield, 1982), pp. 58, 199.

92 Marshall, *Rural economy*, vol. 1, p. 65.

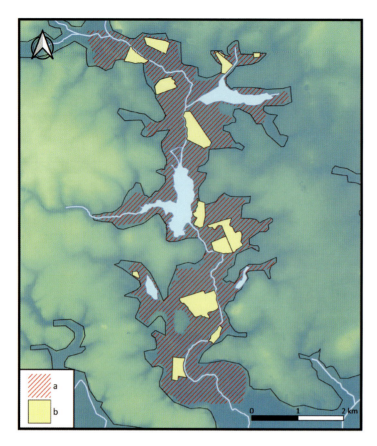

Figure 4.10 The distribution and extent of poor's allotments, established by parliamentary enclosure acts, in the valley of the river Ant ('a', areas of fen enclosed by parliamentary acts; 'b', allotments).

Not all of the enclosed wetlands, moreover, were allotted to private landowners. It was here that the majority of poor's allotments were to be found and on these, too, traditional forms of land use continued (Figure 4.10). The most important was peat-cutting, the Trustees often setting quotas for the number of turves each household could extract annually: 3,000, for example, at Horning and Hickling, 5,000 at East Ruston.[93] They often struggled, however, to enforce such rules and control the scale of removal.[94] Arrangements were generally made to provide for those unable to dig the peat themselves and in some cases all the peat was dug by paid labourers and distributed to recipients. Not all fuel allotments provided firing directly in this way. In some parishes they were rented out, in whole or part, for shooting, grazing or the cutting of sedge, reed or peat, and the income used to buy supplies of coal. A few were managed in this way from the start but they were joined by others as the price of coal gradually fell in the course of the nineteenth century. Such arrangements were favoured by some Trustees because they avoided

---

93 C.F. Carrodus, *Life in a Norfolk village: the story of Old Horning* (Norwich, 1949), p. 19. NRO KIM 5/13/9. Wells, 'The role of turf'.
94 Wells, 'The role of turf', pp. 432–3.

the trouble of administering direct exploitation – making sure that the peat was removed in an appropriate and tidy fashion, and that nobody took more than they were entitled to – or of organising labourers to dig on the behalf of recipients. They were usually able to make the change without difficulty because the section of the enclosure award dealing with the allotment included a clause stating that it was to be used as a source of fuel for the poor or 'otherwise appropriated, and the Produce and Profits arising therefore applied for their use and benefit'.

Many poor's allotments in Broadland were also used in other ways. This, indeed, was a characteristic feature of the allotments in the area, distinguishing them from those found elsewhere in East Anglia. They were also among the largest in the region. Both circumstances reflected the particular importance the informal use of the common fens had, prior to enclosure, possessed in the lives of the local poor. Parishes in the Thurne valley were particularly well endowed. At Thurne in 1832 there was a fuel allotment of 18 acres, partly rented out on a three-year lease and partly 'appropriated to the purpose of cutting fuel and fodder to be distributed amongst the ... poor', but also another, slightly larger, which was 'depastured by the cows of poor inhabitants of the parish ... They pay 10s each and if they have a second cow they pay £1.10s in addition for the second. No person having an allotment sufficient to keep a cow is allowed to turn them out.'[95] At Martham in 1845 the 'Poor Marsh', covering more than 41 acres (17 hectares), was 'a pasture for the cows of the poor inhabitants', while at Burgh St Margaret 40 acres (16 hectares) were rented and the remaining 106 acres (43 hectares) 'used for cutting fuel, reeds etc, but the poor cottagers are allowed to turn cows on it'.[96] The most extensive provision was at East Ruston, where the enclosure award of 1810 set out 300 acres (121 hectares) of poor's allotment in five contiguous blocks extending out from the valley-floor wetlands onto the adjacent uplands (thereby serving to save a large area of heathland from the fate shared by most of its neighbours in Broadland).[97] By the rules drawn up the following year certain areas were reserved for digging fuel and the rest for other uses.[98] The 'poor' were divided into three categories: those with a cottage and less than an acre; those renting property worth less than £5 per annum, or between one and ten acres; and those *owning* such property. Members of the first group could turn 'three head of stock and two brood geese and goslings, reared by them, unto the said allotments'; could dig up to 2,000 'upground flags' – heather – and up to 3,000 'fenground flags' – peat – each year; and could mow fodder on Burnt Fen for one day a year. Those in the median category were allowed to graze 'two head of stock, and two brood geese

---

95 NRO P/CH1/51.
96 White, *Directory of Norfolk*, pp. 301, 303.
97 NRO C/Sca2/236.
98 NRO KIM 5/13/9.

Figure 4.11 Barton Broad from the air, looking north-west. The river Ant now runs through the broad (entering top right of photo, exiting bottom centre) but originally bypassed it to the east. The wide embayment on the far (western) side of the broad is the entrance to Lime Kiln Dyke.

Figure 4.12 Rockland Broad, one of only a handful of broads surviving in the Yare valley.

and goslings, reared by them' and to cut the same number of flags, but not to mow fodder. Those in the third category could graze only 'one head of stock and one brood goose and the goslings reared by it', and could cut only a thousand of each type of 'flags' each year.[99] Such ample provision was unusual and a reflection of particular social and tenurial circumstance, but more generally in Broadland, and in the Ant valley parishes especially, poor's allotments accounted for much of the land enclosed by parliamentary acts from the wetland commons (Figure 4.10).

Parliamentary enclosure had a major impact on the landscape of the 'uplands', removing the remaining areas of open-field arable and destroying thousands of hectares of heath. Its effects on the valley-floor wetlands were more mixed. On the estuarine clays a mesh of rectilinear drainage dykes was established across the open marshes and the quality of the grazing was significantly improved. But on the deep peats most of the fens remained largely undrained. And where schemes of 'improvement' were successfully implemented they were often soon abandoned, a subject to which we will shortly return.

The making of the Broads
by Charlotte Jarvis

The 'broads' from which Broadland takes its name are a collection of shallow freshwater lakes situated in the valleys of the rivers Yare, Bure, Ant, Thurne and Waveney and in the valleys of streams draining into them. They vary in size from the 154-hectare expanse of Hickling Broad to small pools of water such as Hassingham and Buckenham Broads or Sprat's Water in Carlton Colville (Figures 4.11, 4.12 and 4.13).[100] A globally important habitat for numerous species of flora and fauna, they have been managed by the Broads Authority since 1988.

The origins of this unusual collection of lakes, tightly concentrated and all situated within the floodplains of river or stream valleys, has prompted debate and speculation for more than a century and a half. In 1871 the geologist J.E. Taylor wrote that the Broads were originally glacial hollows that had become filled with water.[101] This theory was countered by other geologists, such as J.W. Robberds and J.W. Gregory, who believed them to be the remnants of an estuary or estuaries that had otherwise since silted up.[102] Geomorphologist Joseph Jennings also ascribed a natural origin to the Broads following his 1952 study, in which he undertook a number of hand bores and analysed the resulting cores. These revealed two distinct layers of clay separating

---

99   NRO KIM 5/13/9.
100 Broads Authority, *Hickling Broad Dossier: part of the review of lake restoration practices and their performance in the Broads National Park, 1980–2013* (Norwich, 2016), p. 3.
101 J.E. Taylor, 'The Norfolk broads and meres geologically considered', *Transactions of the Norfolk and Norwich Naturalists' Society*, 1 (1871–2), pp. 30–40.
102 Robberds, *Geological and historical observations*, pp. 3–22.

Figure 4.13 Sprat's Water, Carlton Colville, one of the smallest of the broads.

the peat deposits in the river floodplains, leading Jennings to conclude that the Broads had formed as a result of two marine transgressions.[103] There were, however, from the very beginning, some who argued that the broads were the result of human activity. Naturalist Samuel Woodward's study of Barton Broad in 1834 convinced him that it, and probably other broads, had been dug to extract peat.[104] This idea was further endorsed by his son, Horace B. Woodward. A geologist of repute and Fellow of the Royal Society, he argued that the flooding of some other peat excavations, made in the eighteenth and nineteenth centuries, suggested the 'seemingly very recent origin of our broads'.[105] Even Jennings in 1952 noted that peat-cutting had occasionally been extensive in the past and that some of the broads may have originated in this way, although he did not believe that this provided an acceptable general explanation for their formation.[106] Until the middle decades of the twentieth century prevailing opinion remained firmly on the side of natural origins.

However, in the late 1950s Jennings joined forces with ecologist Joyce Lambert and the man-made origin of the broads became firmly established. Together they undertook a substantial fieldwork project during which over 2,100 bores were

---

103 J.N. Jennings, *The origin of the Broads* (London, 1952), p. 49.
104 George, *Land use*, p. 79.
105 H.B. Woodward, 'The scenery of Norfolk', *Transactions of the Norfolk and Norwich Naturalists' Society*, 3 (1882–3), pp. 439–66, at p. 458.
106 Jennings, *Origin*, pp. 3–4.

taken at various locations throughout the Broadland river valleys.[107] These revealed several features indicating that the Broads were a result of large-scale human intervention. Many possessed vertical or, less commonly, stepped sides, as well as parallel lines of islands or underwater ridges running through them from where the peat and clay had not been extracted, representing the boundaries of individual cuttings. These were often surrounded by patches of clay that appeared to have been redeposited, presumably representing overburden that had been removed to reach the deposits of peat.[108] Horizontal floors were recorded in most of the basins.[109] All the broads, moreover, had a remarkably similar depth, of between three and four metres.[110] In 1960 *The Making of the Broads: A Reconsideration of Their Origin in the Light of New Evidence* was published. Co-authored by Lambert, Jennings, historical geographer C.T. Smith, archaeologist Charles Green and engineer J.N. Hutchinson, it argued convincingly that the Broads were flooded pits resulting from the large-scale extraction of peat in the Middle Ages. Their depth was attributed to a desire to exploit the 'brushwood peat' of the Middle Peat deposits, the high wood content of which provided a better quality fuel than the Upper Peat, which consisted almost entirely of sedge, reed and other water plants.[111] The excavations, and thus the resultant broads, were carefully sited a little back from the major rivers, or in side valleys, in order to reduce the risk of flooding or the rate of seepage. Lambert and colleagues' findings were supported with a detailed review of historical documents and archaeological records, with Smith in particular presenting evidence for extensive peat extraction in the thirteenth and fourteenth centuries drawn from account rolls, court rolls and registers.[112] He also noted that during the late fourteenth and fifteenth centuries the turbaries from which peat had been extracted began to be recorded as water and marsh.[113] This change, it was argued, coincided with a period of high tides, great storms and flooding, which rendered the extraction pits unusable.[114]

The publication made an immediate impact and effectively settled the argument as to the origins of the broads. Interest in the subject tailed off and little further work was undertaken over the following decades. It was not until 40 years later that new investigations into the history of local peat extraction were undertaken by Jo Parmenter as part of her PhD thesis 'The development of the wetland vegetation

---

107 Lambert et al., *Making of the Broads*, p. 4.
108 Ibid., pp. 6–7.
109 Ibid., pp. 23 and 31.
110 Ibid., p. 23.
111 Ibid., p. 58.
112 Ibid., pp. 70–7.
113 Ibid., p. 77.
114 Ibid., pp. 101–2.

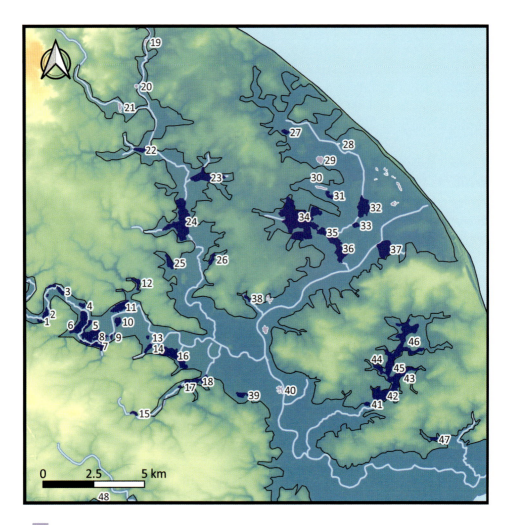

Figure 4.14 The location of broads, lost or extant: northern Broadland. Names of principal examples given where known. Broads are found in either side valleys or the main valleys, where they are set back a little way from the rivers. 1. Norton Broad 2. Belaugh Broad 3. Bridge Broad 4. Snape's Water 5. Hudson's Bay 6. Wroxham Broad 7. Salhouse Broad 8. Hoveton Great Broad 9. Devil's Hole 10. Decoy Broad 11. Hoveton Little Broad 12. Burntfen Broad 13. Cockshoot Broad 14. Ranworth Broad 15. Pedham Lake 16. Malthouse Broad 17. Sotshole Broad 18. South Walsham Broad 19. Crostwight Water 20. Honing Broad 21. Dilham Lake 22. Dilham Broad 23. Sutton Broad 24. Barton Broad 25. Alderfen Broad 26. Crome's Broad 27. Calthorpe Broad 28. Waxham Decoy 29. Wigg's Broad 30. Hare Broad and Gage's Broad 31. Chapman's Broad 32. Horsey Mere 33. Blackfleet Broad 34. Hickling Broad 35. Whiteslea 36. Heigham Sound 37. Martham Broad 38. Womack Water 39. Upton Broad 40. Old Upton Broad 41. Little Broad 42. Filby Broad 43. Ormesby Little Broad 44. Lily Broad 45. Rollesby Broad 46. Ormesby Broad 47. Mautby Decoy.

THE VALLEYS 201

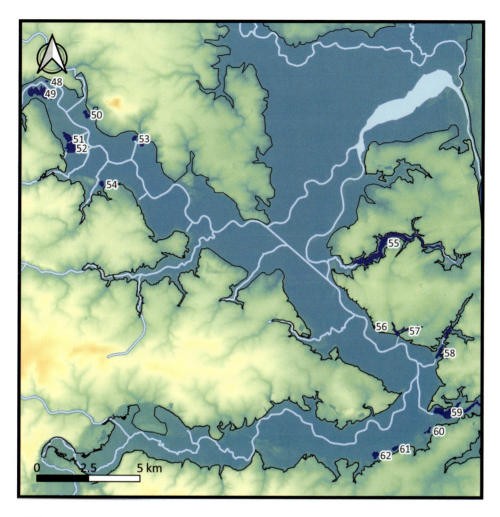

extent of known broads c.1840.

Figure 4.15 The location of broads, lost or extant: southern Broadland. Names given where known. Broads are found either in side valleys or the main valleys, where they are set back from the rivers. 48. Brundall Broad 49. Surlingham Broad 50. Strumpshaw Broad 51. Wheatfen Broad 52. Rockland Broad 53. Buckenham Broad 54. Carleton Broad 55. Fitton Water 56. Wicker Well 57. Summer House Water 58. Flixton Decoy 59. Oulton Broad/Lake Lothing 60. Sprat's Water 61. Barnby Old Broad 62. Barnby Broad.

of the Broadland region'. Parmenter made a detailed study of the socio-historical factors that influenced the development of Broadland wetland vegetation, including historic land use and patterns of ownership. She demonstrated that, although deep-level peat extraction may have ceased in the late Middle Ages, shallower peat deposits were still being exploited until the nineteenth century and that up to 75 per cent of the land on the middle and upper floodplains of the principal rivers appears to have been cut for peat (see below, p. 225).[115] Parmenter's scholarship opened up a new avenue of investigation into the evolution of the broads, raising the possibility that the idea that the broads were all, of necessity, flooded peat pits of medieval date might obscure a more complicated history. Accordingly, in 2017/18 a GIS mapping project was undertaken to examine the morphology of the broads and investigate other possible factors influencing their evolution.[116]

GIS is a powerful spatial database application that can provide a medium for identifying and visualising changes to the landscape over an extended period of time, and for comparing and contrasting different kinds of spatial data. The study was restricted to the county of Norfolk but the omission of the small number of Suffolk broads from the analysis is unlikely to have significantly affected the overall conclusions. A database was compiled that contained the changing outlines of all known broads, lost or still existing, based on a wide range of early maps. For it must be emphasised that many broads have, over time, been lost from the landscape. As soon as they were created they were quickly colonised by a variety of plants, and as these died they formed new layers of peat at the bottom of the basin. This in turn allowed rooted plants to spread across the shallowing water, leading to further accumulations of peat.[117] The rate of contraction and terrestrialisation is largely related to extent and to depth – rapid contraction of a body of water suggests shallower extraction – but a number of extensive broads, including Honing Broad and Crostwight Water, have disappeared entirely since the eighteenth century, while the overall number of water bodies covering more than *c*.2 hectares has fallen from at least 87 to around 48 (Figures 4.14 and 4.15).

GIS allows the locations of the known broads to be related to the complex patterns of geology and soils described in Chapter 1. Overlaying geo-referenced outlines of the broads onto a copy of the National Soil Map (NATMAP) confirms that the majority of the Norfolk broads (81 per cent) were, as we might expect, located on peat soils. These broads clearly were, in the words of the Broads Authority, 'the flooded sites of former great peat pits, made in the natural fenland

---

115 Parmenter, 'Development of the wetland vegetation', p. 176.
116 C. Jarvis, 'The Norfolk Broads: a reappraisal of their origins through geospatial analysis', MA dissertation (University of East Anglia, 2018).
117 Ellis, *The Broads*, pp. 86–7.

in medieval times'.[118] Altcar 2 is the dominant soil association, characterised by deep fen peat soils and accounting for 88 per cent of all peat-based broads; 12 per cent are found on Hanworth soils, which consist of a mixture of non-calcareous loam and peat.[119] The remaining 19 per cent of broads, however, are located not on peat but on deposits of estuarine clay. These are associated exclusively with the Wallasea 1 soil association, comprising clayey soils with only a peaty surface horizon.[120] Most of these clay-based broads, including Heigham Sound, Blackfleet Broad and Martham Broad, are located towards the northern end of the Thurne valley. Interestingly, Little Broad, the southernmost broad of the Rollesby Broad complex, also appears to be a clay broad despite the rest of the complex being situated on peat. In short, while the broads may all be artificial, around a fifth of known examples appear to have been largely or entirely dug to extract clay rather than peat. Broads of this latter type are, moreover, more prone to disappearance through terrestrialisation, silting or deliberate drainage than those on peat. Only 44 per cent of known examples located on Wallasea 1 survive as open water today, compared with 75 per cent of those on Altcar 2 peat soils (those on Hanworth soils have a 50 per cent survival rate).[121] The difference may in part reflect the greater depth of pits dug to reach the brushwood peat. Lambert noted that the Thurne floodplain broads were often shallower than average.[122] Shallower depth, as noted, militates against a broad's long-term survival.

While dug to exploit peat and clay, the size, configuration and location of the various broads were not simply a function of geology and topography. They were also influenced by socio-economic factors. The digging of the broads in the twelfth, thirteenth and fourteenth centuries coincided with a period of rapid demographic expansion, the national population peaking at approximately 5.5 million in the early fourteenth century.[123] This, in turn, led to a corresponding increase in competition for resources, perhaps especially fuel. The local population, and that of the city of Norwich, had limited access to coal and supplies of firewood, gorse and heather were restricted. Vast amounts of peat were accordingly consumed, with Norwich Cathedral Priory alone receiving 400,000 turves per year in the fourteenth century.[124] During the same period the turbaries at Hoveton, belonging to St Benet's Abbey, were

---

118 Broads Authority, *Broads Plan 2017: partnership strategy for the Norfolk and Suffolk Broads* (Norwich, 2017), p. 7. J.M. Lambert, J.N. Jennings and C.T. Smith, 'The origin of the Broads', in E.A. Ellis (ed.), *The Broads* (London, 1965), pp. 37–68, at p. 65.
119 *Ibid.*
120 *Ibid.*
121 Jarvis, 'The Norfolk Broads', pp. 22–3.
122 Lambert *et al.*, *Making of the Broads*, p. 44.
123 M. Bailey, *After the Black Death* (Oxford, 2020), p. 4.
124 I. Rotherham, *Peat and peat cutting* (Princes Risborough, 2009), p. 22.

producing 260,000 a year.[125] It is within this context, of large-scale extraction and competition for resources, that we also need to consider the location of the broads.

It is noticeable that a significant number of broads are located on parish boundaries. This is best demonstrated by the Rollesby Broad complex, the waters of which divide the parishes of Rollesby, Burgh St Margaret, Ormesby St Michael, Filby, Hemsby and Martham. Lambert and Jennings noted how, in Barton Broad, the parallel lines of uncut peat baulks changed direction where they met the parish boundary between Barton and Irstead, while in other locations baulks were observed to follow the line of parish boundaries.[126] GIS allows a more systematic exploration of this relationship and reveals that, of the 75 broads, both extant and extinct, that can be located with sufficient accuracy for the relationship to be examined, no fewer than 35 (45 per cent) cross a parish boundary. Martin George argued that the relationship reflected the way in which peat resources had been divided between neighbouring communities when the boundaries were laid out.[127] Williamson, in contrast, suggested that it was an accident of 'local administrative topography', noting that rivers and streams running along the valleys from which peat was extracted provided convenient features with which to demarcate a parochial boundary.[128] However, GIS analysis suggests a more complex situation, highlighting not only the close relationship between broads and parish boundaries but also the association of both with areas of common land.

Commons, as discussed earlier (above, p. 170), were areas of uncultivated land owned by manorial lords but used by a defined group of commoners for grazing and as a source of fuel and raw materials. William Faden's county map, published in 1797 before the great wave of parliamentary enclosure removed most remaining Broadland commons, is not entirely reliable as a guide to their numbers or distribution, sometimes categorising known examples not as common land but as 'fen and marshes'.[129] It also, of course, shows them at a late stage in their development, already much reduced by piecemeal enclosure and 'doling' (above, pp. 175–8). GIS mapping reveals, nevertheless, a clear correlation between broads that cross parish boundaries and areas of common land. Only six single-parish broads, or 14 per cent of the total, appear to be located on, or adjacent to, common land. But cross-parish broads demonstrate an almost 50:50 split between common and non-common locations.[130] Commons tended to occupy land that was marginal not only agriculturally, such as the wet peats where the broads were dug, but also spatially, towards the outer edges of parish territories, introducing another

---

125 Jennings, *Origin of the Broads*, p. 61.
126 Lambert *et al.*, *Making of the Broads*, p. 49.
127 George, *Land use*, p. 87.
128 Williamson, *Norfolk Broads*, p. 85.
129 *Ibid.*, p. 102.
130 Jarvis, 'The Norfolk Broads', pp. 25–8.

factor behind the association of broads and boundaries. A further explanation for the relationship between broads, parish boundaries and common land may be suggested by the depth of the excavations, generally in excess of three metres, required to reach the brushwood peat.[131] The affected land could not subsequently be used in any other way and so the siting of pits on the most remote areas of common land, where the grazing of livestock or the harvest of marsh hay were particularly difficult to manage, may have made good practical sense.

After centuries of intense extraction the deep pits fell out of use and, during the later fourteenth and fifteenth centuries, documentary references to turbary begin to be superseded by ones to 'fen', 'water and fen' or 'water and marsh', suggesting that many of the pits were at least partially flooded.[132] In addition to the severe weather events and flooding highlighted by Smith, wider economic factors may have rendered deep-level excavations unviable.[133] After the Black Death England lost as much as 50 per cent of its population, taking centuries to return to its early-fourteenth-century peak, both reducing the market for peat and increasing the cost of the labour required to extract it.[134] However, peat continued to be exploited for fuel, as we have seen, from shallower cuttings, and at a rate that seems to have increased markedly from the eighteenth century. This renewed exploitation was driven by the rapidly rising population and its increasing need for fuel. Although coal was gradually becoming cheaper and more readily available, peat remained an important fuel for Broadland's poor until the mid-nineteenth century.[135] Some examples of how this resurgence of peat-digging could produce extensive but shallow and short-lived water bodies have already been described, but others could be given. An area of water covering nearly 12 hectares thus developed in the fens to the south-east of Horning church some time between 1838, when the tithe map was surveyed, and the early 1880s, when the first edition 6-inch Ordnance Survey map was produced. Still extant around 1905, when the second edition was surveyed, it had become extinct by the time the area was photographed from the air by the RAF in 1946.

Considering the impact of eighteenth- and nineteenth-century peat-digging on the landscape of the Broadland valleys, a pertinent question is whether all the broads are medieval. Generally, documentary evidence suggests so. Numerous references to turbaries appear in deeds, court rolls and account rolls dating from the twelfth, thirteenth and fourteenth centuries. Smith's research uncovered records of their existence at 20 locations in the thirteenth century, rising to 29

---

131 Lambert et al., *Making of the Broads*, p. 58.
132 Jennings, *Origin of the Broads*, pp. 77–8.
133 *Ibid.*, p. 78.
134 J. Hatcher, 'England in the aftermath of the Black Death', *Past and Present*, 144 (1994), pp. 3–35, at pp. 8–9. Bailey, *Black Death*, p. 4.
135 Wells, 'The role of turf', p. 639.

in the fourteenth. These demonstrate a striking correlation with the location of extinct or surviving broads, including Hickling Broad, Ormesby/Rollesby/Filby Broad, Rockland Broad, South Walsham Broad and Barton Broad.[136]

Yet, while it seems unlikely that any existing broads have post-medieval origins, some were significantly modified by this much later phase of peat extraction. A major example of this is the eastern extension of Hoveton Little Broad into Crabbett's Marsh, covering some 4.5 hectares. This first appears on the Ordnance Survey preliminary drawings of 1816, although with a more sinuous outline than later. It features prominently on the first edition 6-inch Ordnance Survey map of 1881, but had virtually disappeared by the time the second edition was surveyed in 1907. There is no discernible trace of it on the 1945 RAF air photographs. The extension to the broad was therefore cut, abandoned and became extinct within the space of a century or so. At nearby Hoveton Great Broad a geoarchaeological survey carried out in 2016, extracting samples of material by boring with an auger, revealed evidence of medieval peat extraction to a depth of about four metres at a number of locations across the broad, as well as areas of post-medieval digging rarely exceeding one metre.[137] Some of the baulks that had separated the original pits had subsequently been dug away during the second phase.[138] If post-medieval peat extraction altered both Hoveton Great Broad and Hoveton Little Broad, there is potential for the same to have occurred at many other locations, although the shallow depth of the later cuttings will in most if not all cases have ensured rapid terrestrialisation and a return to something close to the broad's original, medieval outline. This said, deep medieval broads also experience contraction (as well as total disappearance), and it is sometimes hard to determine the true status of areas of open water that have been lost since a particular broad was first mapped.

Surlingham Broad, first referred to in 1608, is a particularly interesting example.[139] The tithe map of 1840 and, more schematically, an undated late-eighteenth-century map of the parish, show an area of open water extending over nearly 30 hectares.[140] But by the time the first edition 6-inch Ordnance Survey map was produced in the 1880s its central and western sections had become a series of small, separate ponds that dwindled still further over subsequent decades, Marietta Pallis describing in 1911 how 'the existing remnants of free water remain merely water-holes surrounded by fen and entirely unconnected with each other'.[141] The

---

136   Jennings, *Origin of the Broads*, p. 59; Lambert et al., *Making of the Broads*, pp. 73–6.
137   Wessex Archaeology, 'Bringing the Bure back to LIFE', pp. 11–12.
138   *Ibid.*, pp. 11–12.
139   Ellis, *The Broads*, p. 57.
140   NRO BR 276/1/1082. NRO PD 611/33.
141   L. Cameron and D. Matless, 'Translocal ecologies: the Norfolk Broads, the "Natural", and the International Phytogeographical Excursion, 1911', *Journal of the History of Biology*, 44 (2011), pp. 15–41, at p. 37.

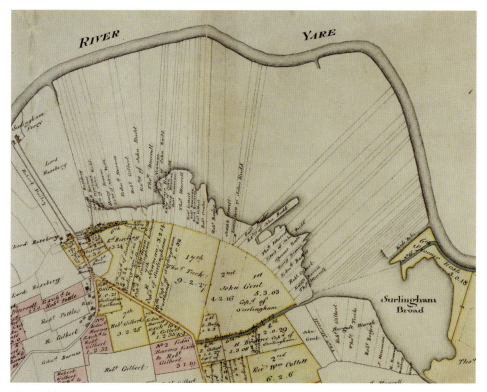

Figure 4.16 Surlingham Broad, as depicted on the enclosure map of 1822.

only part of the broad to remain largely unchanged was, and remains, the eastern section, covering around four hectares, which the undated map appears to label separately as 'The Broad'. Lambert and colleagues' core samples indicate that this part of the broad was dug to a uniform depth of 2.5–3.0 metres, but elsewhere it was shallower, around 2.0–2.5 metres, comparable to the deeper post-medieval cuttings in Catfield Fen (above, p. 191).[142]

The enclosure map of 1822 does not depict the northern edge of the broad but shows its western and central sections divided into numerous parallel dole strips that extended out from the drier ground to the south, unlike the eastern section, which is shown as undivided open water: the ruler-straight character of the boundaries suggests, perhaps, relatively recent allocation (Figure 4.16).[143] The tithe map, in contrast, also shows the eastern section divided into doles but here the layout is less regular and the boundaries have broken lines, rather than the solid ones used to demarcate the doles shown in the central and westerns sections. The difference may indicate a distinction between a more intangible right to the use of deep water

---

142 Lambert *et al.*, *Making of The Broads*, pp. 5–9.
143 NRO C/Sca 2/278.

and the actual ownership of ground that was in part more shallowly flooded and in part dry. It is noteworthy that a map of the estate of J. Tuck, dated *c*.1820, similarly delineates only his strip in the eastern section of the broad using a dashed line, those elsewhere being bounded by unbroken ones. In the accompanying list of his holdings, the former is recorded as 'water' while the others are described as 'water and marsh'.[144] It is thus possible that only the easternmost part of Surlingham Broad is of any great age, and that the rest is not actually a 'broad' at all but was instead created, at least in part, by shallower post-medieval turf-cutting.

While it is thus clear that no 'true' broads originated in the post-medieval period, the possibility that some were dug significantly *earlier* than Lambert and her colleagues suggested, in the pre-Conquest period, also needs to be considered. Some light can be shed on this, and on other issues, by nomenclature. None of the broads possesses a name suggesting its existence in the Anglo-Saxon period.[145] The majority are named after the parish in which they lie, or after some former owner. The first use of the word 'broad' comes in a reference to 'Brodingge' in South Walsham in 1315 and by the Elizabethan period 'brode', which originates from Middle English, seems to have been used relatively frequently.[146] The use of 'broad' as a noun to refer to a wide body of water appears to be derived from local dialect, like the use of 'water' or 'tarn' in the Lake District. The term does appear to specifically denote those water bodies that were created by the deep-level extraction of peat or clay during the medieval period, although it has occasionally been used more widely in recent times as a term for a lake nominally located within Broadland. The University of East Anglia Broad was dug in the 1970s as a means of extracting the sand and gravel required during the building of the university. The Whitlingham Broads were also dug for gravel extraction in the 1990s. Catfield Broad, located to the south-east of Barton Broad, is another small body of water that has picked up the 'broad' moniker, but which originated from the extraction of peat between *c*.1880 and 1946.[147]

Lambert *et al.*'s hypothesis that the broads originated in the medieval period from the deep-level extraction of peat remains compelling. However, more recent research suggests that the situation is more nuanced than originally thought. In particular, many broads were dug to extract clay rather than peat and the shape and size of some were radically if temporarily modified by much later phases of peat-cutting. Since their origin, hundreds more years of human exploitation of and interaction with the Broadland landscape have continued to leave its mark on the broads, something which will no doubt continue for many years to come.

---

144 NRO NRS 4050.
145 Jennings, *Origin of the Broads*, p. 58.
146 Lambert *et al.*, *Making of the Broads*, pp. 65–6. Smith, *English Place-Name Elements*, pp. 45, 52.
147 Jarvis, 'The Norfolk Broads', p. 37.

Figure 4.17 The drainage mill erected in Catfield Middle Fen was already disused, and surrounded by fen and flooded turf cuttings, by the end of the nineteenth century.

The recent history of the fens

The history of the peat fens during the last century and a half has, in general, been a steady progression towards a wilder, wetter, more wooded and less managed landscape. With the onset of agricultural depression from the late 1870s, and increasingly from the 1890s as livestock prices declined, most of the areas reclaimed from the deeper peats, and their attendant drainage mills and windpumps, were progressively abandoned as landowners reduced their expenditure on drainage works. In some cases, this was finally precipitated by some natural event or accident that caused damage to the drainage works which the owner was simply unable or unwilling to repair. The greatest retrenchment occurred where the most reclamations had been made, in the valley of the Ant, where Hunsett Mill, Catfield Middle Marsh Mill, Boardman's Mill and Turf Fen Mill now stand in landscapes of reedbed, fen and secondary woodland (Figure 4.17). Some of this land had probably been abandoned before the onset of depression. Middle Marsh Mill may already have stopped working by 1884, when the first edition 6-inch Ordnance Survey map shows all the surrounding land in Catfield Fen as open water, reedbed and swamp; it is possible that it may always, in part, have served to regulate water levels in land cut for peat but it had certainly been abandoned by 1905, when the second edition 6-inch Ordnance Survey map marked it as 'disused'. Abandonment of management usually occurred rather later. The first edition 6-inch map shows the land immediately to the south of Turf Fen Mill in the Ant valley as waterlogged – it was described as 'turf ground' in the tithe apportionment of 1838 – but the land that it drained lay to the north and north-west, and this is depicted as grazing marsh. The second edition map of 1907 shows a similar situation but aerial photographs suggest that the mill was derelict in the 1920s and the 1946 6-inch map shows the area it drained as reeds and swamp and marks the mill itself as 'disused'.

More striking than the re-expansion of fen at the expense of drained marsh, however, was the steady encroachment of fen by alder carr. From the late nineteenth century the various traditional practices that had held the otherwise inexorable succession to wet woodland in check went into decline. Regular cutting of peat came to an end first. On some poor's allotments this was because the accessible peat had been removed. Indeed, as early as the 1830s there was reported to be 'very little remaining' at Sutton, while the fuel allotment at Stalham was 'nearly cut up'.[148] But, more importantly, the availability of cheap coal ensured that more and more allotments were, by the end of the century, being rented out – especially for shooting, to judge from the Charity Returns made around 1900.[149] By this stage, moreover, few private turbaries appear to have been operating, as the market for peat steadily contracted. Dutt in 1903 reported that 'turf or peat cutting, which formerly found employment for many of the marshmen, can hardly now be called a profitable business', although there were still 'a few men who cut and dry the riverside hovers'. There is little evidence for the continuation of peat-cutting on a significant scale into the inter-war period.

Marsh hay and litter were still being harvested from the fens at the time Dutt was writing. Indeed, he reported a recent increase in the scale of litter-cutting. Large quantities of the material were being transported to London, where there was huge demand due to the numbers of draught horses. But this market shrank as the use of motorised vehicles increased rapidly in the first decades of the twentieth century, and at the same time local use was steadily reduced as the number of cottagers and small landowners keeping their own cattle declined. Only the cutting of reed and sedge continued on a significant, if reduced, scale, photographs from the 1920s and 1930s echoing Dutt's accounts of river banks 'almost covered' with reed-stacks in early spring, and of boats laden with reeds being 'continually rowed or quanted [punted] down the dykes'.[150] But by the middle decades of the century much of the crop of sedge and reed was being cut from new areas, more accessible than the flooded turbaries in the heart of the fens – from new beds established on former fen meadows, wet and waterlogged, rather than from permanently flooded ground.

---

148   NRO P/CH1/10. NRO P/CH1/29.
149   NRO P/CH2.
150   W.A. Dutt, *The Norfolk Broads* (London, 1903), pp. 140, 161.

These changes had a profound effect on the appearance of the fens. Turner in 1922 described how areas of fen and meadow, once mown for hay or litter or grazed by cattle, had 'reverted and their rough herbage is stronger and coarser than ever'.[151] Decline continued over the following decades, and in 1939 T. Boardman bemoaned how: 'Now, since acres upon acres of this material remain uncut and the vegetation gets into such a terrible tangle, the marshes have to be burned. Alders, birch and sallows are taking possession … . When the marshes were mown regularly all the young trees were kept under … .'[152] The speed with which woodland spread across the open fens should not be exaggerated, however. The vertical aerial photographs taken by the RAF in the immediate aftermath of the Second World War show some new areas of woodland, but mainly a thin and intermittent scatter of trees, in the areas most affected by this development – the floodplain of the Bure between Ant Mouth and Wroxham, and (to a lesser extent) that of the Ant between How Hill and Wayford Bridge. To judge from the evidence of aerial photographs, regeneration was most rapid in the 1950s and 1960s. Nor, indeed, should we exaggerate its extent, for – as we shall see – large areas of open fen, managed for nature conservation or as commercial reed and sedge beds, still remain in Broadland. Nevertheless, the change was a profound one, in the Bure valley especially, although to some extent it was an intensification of existing patterns in the environment. The small, discrete areas of carr woodland that had been a feature of the Broadland landscape for centuries appear to have been particularly numerous in the areas most affected by regeneration. There was continuity in another way. The composition of the new woodland was to some extent influenced by previous patterns of land use and management, with that developing over solid peat generally containing a significant proportion of grey willow (*Salix cinerea*) and downy birch (*Betula pubescens*), while that growing over former peat cuttings has a greater dominance of alder (*Alnus glutinosa*) (Figure 4.14).[153]

The making of the Broadland fens

by Jo Parmenter and Tom Williamson

Broadland constitutes an internationally important complex of wetland habitats, with around 25 per cent of the area of the National Park currently protected by national designation as SSSIs on the basis of biological and geological or physiographical interest. The *c.*1,700 hectares of fen that are our focus here are of

---

151 E.L. Turner, 'The status of birds in Broadland', *Transactions of the Norfolk and Norwich Naturalists' Society*, 11 (1922), pp. 228–40, at p. 231.
152 E.T. Boardman, 'The development of a Broadland estate at How Hill, Ludham, Norfolk', *Transactions of the Norfolk and Norwich Naturalists' Society*, 15 (1939), pp. 5–21, at p. 14.
153 A. Burrows and G. Kenyon, 'A woodland resources survey of the Bure Broads and Marshes Site of Special Scientific Interest', report (English Nature and the Broads Authority, 1985).

Figure 4.18. Crested buckler-fern (*Dryopteris cristata*), one of several nationally endangered plants found in the Broadland fens.

particular conservation importance.[154] They support 13 Red-Listed species based on the 2001 International Union for the Conservation of Nature Guidelines, including three – fen orchid (*Liparis loeselii*), crested buckler-fern (*Dryopteris cristata*) and greater water-parsnip (*Sium latifolium*) – that are considered 'Endangered' under the most recent Joint Nature Conservation Committee guidelines on species status (Figure 4.18).[155] A number of uncommon and rare species of bird, including Cetti's warbler (*Cettia cetti*), bearded tit (*Panurus biarmicus*) and marsh harrier (*Circus aeruginosus*), are closely associated with the fen vegetation; the bittern (*Botauris stellaris*) is now once again relatively common as a breeding species; and many other birds use the fens for breeding, resting and feeding during the spring or autumn passage or for overwintering. The otter (*Lutra helvetica*) has become common in recent decades; water vole (*Arvicola terrestris*) occurs quite frequently; and the fens also provide valuable habitat for amphibians and reptiles, such as common toad (*Bufo bufo*), adder (*Vipera berus*) and grass snake (*Natrix natrix*). In addition, the fens support rich invertebrate populations, including such rare or endangered species as the swallowtail butterfly (*Papilio machaon*), which benefits from the abundance of its larval food-plant, milk-parsley (*Thyselium palustre*), and Fenn's wainscot (*Photedes brevilinea*) and the reed leopard moth (*Phragmataecia castaneae*), both of which are closely associated with reedbeds.

'Fen' vegetation encompasses a range of successional vegetation types, which together may be referred to as a 'fen system'. The term 'successional' means that, without regular intervention by human or natural influences, these communities will develop into something else and, eventually, in the context of the Broadland fens, into wet woodland or 'carr'. Traditional management of the fens – mainly, as we have seen, involving the removal of vegetation for fodder, litter and thatching materials – arrested this progression, holding the habitat in what is referred to as a 'plagioclimax', or artificially stable state. These various types of management also, more immediately, shaped the character of the vegetation. In general, the denser and taller the growth of vegetation, the more species-impoverished the fen flora is likely to be. Accumulation of a dense litter layer has a similar effect. Regular management reduces the height and density of the taller elements within the vegetation and reduces litter build-up through removal of standing biomass. Over time, this leads to a lowering of nutrient levels and, by reducing the vigour of the larger and more robust species and increasing light penetration to the ground

---

154 Broads Authority, 'Managing land and water'. https://www.broads-authority.gov.uk/looking-after/managing-land-and-water/ (accessed 18 April 2023).

155 International Union for the Conservation of Nature Standards and Petitions Committee, 'Guidelines for Using the IUCN Red List Categories and Criteria. Version 15.1', 2022. https://www.iucnredlist.org/documents/RedListGuidelines.pdf (accessed 4 April 2023). Joint Nature Conservation Committee, 'Conservation designations for UK taxa – collation updates', 2023. https://jncc.gov.uk/our-work/conservation-designations-for-uk-taxa-updates/ (accessed 10 April 2023).

Figure 4.19 A fine example of fen meadow on the Norfolk Wildlife Trust's Upton Marshes nature reserve.

surface, allows low-growing species to survive and hence a wider diversity of flora to develop, along with a wider range of host-specific fungi and invertebrates.

The vegetation of the peatlands displays much variation. 'Fen' vegetation, which includes tall-herb fen (mixed fen) and reed and sedge beds, develops where the water table remains at or above the ground surface for much of the year. These communities are irrigated from river water and run-off from adjacent areas of higher ground, as well as by precipitation and, to varying extents, groundwater. Where the summer water level is greater than 0.2 metres above the ground surface the vegetation is termed 'swamp' rather than 'fen'. 'Fen meadow', in contrast, typically has much lower water levels than either, the water table usually falling below the ground surface in summer (Figure 4.19). 'Mire' communities are different in that a greater proportion of their irrigating water comes from groundwater – they are irrigated mainly from springs and seepage lines – their particular character accordingly reflecting the water's acidity or alkalinity.[156] Most are found in side valleys or on the extreme margins of the river floodplains. Different again, and relatively rare in Broadland, are *ombrogenous* mires, which are raised above the surrounding landscapes and receive a majority of their water from precipitation.

---

156 B.D. Wheeler, 'The wetland plant communities of the river Ant valley, Norfolk', *Transactions of the Norfolk and Norwich Naturalists' Society*, 24 (1978), pp. 153–87.

Several researchers, most notably Wheeler and Giller, but more recently, *inter alia*, Parmenter and Harding, have undertaken detailed studies of the botanical diversity of the Broadland fens.[157] A majority of surveys and studies have been restricted to single sites or to small areas of wetland, making it difficult to assess the status of the fen resource as a whole, or the threats to community types or to individual species. In 1990 a strategy for a resource survey of botanical interest of the Broadland fens was proposed by the Broads Research Advisory Panel. This was undertaken in the early 1990s and was based on the detailed investigation of the vegetation of 57 sites.[158] It formed the basis for a more complex and granular Broads-specific system for classifying the fen vegetation. Using the widely adopted National Vegetation Classification (NVC) scheme, which describes and classifies the types of semi-natural vegetation present in Great Britain as a whole, a total of 17 swamp and tall-herb fen communities, 1 woodland community, 9 fen-meadow and mire communities and 4 saltmarsh communities can be identified in the Broadland valleys.[159] The Broads-specific classification resulting from this survey allowed a more detailed subdivision that served, in particular, to replace the three NVC categories that account for the majority of stands of tall-herb fen vegetation (S24, S25 and S26) with no fewer than 28 structurally and floristically distinct communities. It identified, in addition, 16 fen-meadow and mire communities, 8 saltmarsh and saline communities and 1 ombrogenous mire community. The full range and complexity of the Broadland fen vegetation, in other words, is not fully represented by the necessarily coarser framework of the NVC.

Undrained fens are not found to the same extent in all the Broadland river valleys, and the types of fen community found in each also displays much variation. The Ant valley floodplain supports the greatest number of fen communities, often occurring in close proximity, including a number of less common types of vegetation. It is also notable for the high number of nationally and locally rare and scarce plant species present. As a unit, the Ant valley fens represent one of the best remaining examples of lowland wet fen habitat in Great Britain and one of the most important wetland areas in western Europe. This said, a large area of land that was formerly open fen was lost to carr woodland and scrub as a result of

---

157 Wheeler, 'Wetland plant communities'. B.D. Wheeler, D.J.G. Gowing, S.C. Shaw, J.O. Mountford and R.P. Money, *Ecohydrological guidelines for lowland wetland plant communities* (Peterborough, 2004). Giller, 'Aspects of the plant ecology'. B.D. Wheeler, 'Observations on the plant ecology of Upton Fen, Norfolk, with special reference to the doles', *Transactions of the Norfolk and Norwich Naturalists' Society*, 27 (1985), pp. 9–32. J. Parmenter, *The Broadland fen resource survey*, 11 vols (Norwich, 1995). ELP, 'Fen plant communities of Broadland: results of a comprehensive survey 2005–2009', report (Broads Authority, 2010, minor amendments in 2014).

158 Parmenter, *Broadland fen resource survey*.

159 J.S. Rodwell (ed.), *British plant communities. Volume 2. Mires and heaths* (Cambridge, 1991). J.S. Rodwell (ed.), *British plant communities. Volume 4. Aquatic communities, swamps and tall-herb fens* (Cambridge, 1995).

Figure 4.20 Tufted sedge (*Carex elata*), a prominent species in many of the fens of the Bure and Ant valleys.

neglect in the middle and later decades of the twentieth century. This has happened to an even greater extent in the valley of the Bure, where less than a quarter of the 1,500 hectares of open fen present in the early twentieth century still remains, although much of the carr woodland is itself of great ecological interest, with large areas of swamp carr, an unusual community virtually restricted to the Bure valley.[160] The remaining areas of open fen, moreover, have a diversity approaching that of the river Ant fens, and support strong populations of such rare or scarce species as marsh fern (*Thelypteris palustris*), milk-parsley (*Thyselium palustre*), marsh pea (*Lathyrus palustris*) and fibrous tussock-sedge (*Carex appropinquata*). In both valleys the most frequently occurring fen species are saw-sedge (*Cladium mariscus*), true sedges, including tufted sedge (*Carex elata*, Figure 4.20), blunt-flowered rush (*Juncus subnodulosus*) and common reed (*Phragmites australis*). Common reed and saw-sedge are the most commonly occurring dominants, although in places in the Bure fens they are replaced by smaller sedges, such as common sedge (*Carex nigra*), with species such as black bog-rush (*Schoenus nigricans*) also prominent.

Different again are the fens of the Thurne. These are mainly restricted to the areas around the various broads, much of the catchment comprising thin peat soils over estuarine clays, or formed in estuarine clays alone, which are exploited as grazing marsh or arable, but they constitute nevertheless the largest area of near-continuous open fen in Broadland, with a relatively small proportion of woodland. The vegetation mainly comprises extensive tracts of sedge beds and reedswamp, dominated by saw-sedge and common reed respectively, some still managed on a commercial basis. Some but not all of the sedge beds contain plants more familiar from coastal habitats than fens, such as brookweed (*Samolus valerandi*) and parsley water dropwort (*Oenanthe lachenalii*). A short distance to the south-east the valley of the Muck Fleet and the low-lying land around the Trinity Broads displays further variations. Here there are extensive tracts of species-rich fen meadow, most notably on Burgh Common, in Hall Farm Fen and around Lily Broad, which contain a number of species of interest, including narrow-leaved southern marsh orchid (*Dactylorhiza praetermissa* ssp. *schoenophila*), marsh pennywort (*Hydrocotyle vulgaris*), tormentil (*Potentilla erecta*), marsh valerian (*Valeriana dioica*) and devil's bit scabious (*Succisa pratensis*). One of the more unusual features of this area is the presence of an intact successional fringe of swamp vegetation around the margins of the broads, with concentric bands of species favouring progressively deeper water, from fen communities dominated by saw-sedge and common reed through to common club-rush (*Schoenoplectus lacustris*) and lesser reedmace (*Typha angustifolia*) swamp.

---

160 Burrows and Kenyon, 'A woodland resources survey'.

Most of the important fen habitats are thus to be found in the north of Broadland, in the valleys of the Bure and its tributaries, the Ant and Thurne. The Yare valley used to contain some of the most significant fens in Broadland,[161] but the quality of their vegetation deteriorated over the course of the twentieth century due to the combined effects of eutrophication (nutrient enrichment) and a lack of management. Those fens that survive in reasonable condition, and mostly under conservation management, are of note because of the relative abundance of greater pond sedge (*Carex riparia*) and reed sweet-grass (*Glyceria maxima*): in the other valleys, saw-sedge and common reed are usually the most frequently occurring dominants. In the Waveney valley most of the floodplain comprises grazing marsh and there are only three extensive areas of fen – Barnby Marshes, Stanley and Alder Carrs, and Sprat's Water – although a number of isolated parcels are scattered along the valley margins.

The Broadland fens appear to be an entirely natural landscape, but are in fact the result of centuries of interaction between humans and the environment. As noted, only regular management of the vegetation by mowing and cutting halts the inexorable succession of most fens to wet woodland, while the removal of areas of peat for fuel served in the past to disrupt and retard this process more radically, typically acting to 'reset' wetland succession altogether. A number of researchers have postulated models for the development of fen vegetation, but particularly useful is that formulated in the early 1990s by Van Wirdum *et al.* for fens in the Netherlands. This is based on three conceptual 'templates': the geological, historical and modern.[162] Van Wirdum *et al.* identified three main successional pathways in the development of fen vegetation. The 'standard' succession is based on the geological template: the characteristics inherited from the underlying strata, coupled with water chemistry and climate, combine to determine the initial development of the vegetation. Subsequent influences – elements of the 'historical template', which include traditional systems of management and peat extraction – determine how the succession deviates from the 'standard' successional pathway. In the modern period, factors such as anthropogenic changes in water quality, water abstraction and perhaps climate change have an increasingly significant impact and these combine to make up the 'modern template', which also embraces both the cessation of traditional management and management for conservation.

---

161 M. Pallis, 'The river-valleys of east Norfolk: their aquatic and fen formations', in A.G. Tansley (ed.), *Types of British vegetation* (Cambridge, 1911), pp. 214–45. J.M. Lambert, 'The distribution and status of *Glyceria maxima* (Hartm) Holmb. in the region of Surlingham and Rockland Broads, Norfolk', *Journal of Ecology*, 33 (1946), pp. 230–67.

162 G. Van Wirdum, A.J. Den Held and M. Schmitz, 'Terrestrialising fen vegetation in former turbaries in the Netherlands', in J.T.A. Verhoeven (ed.), *Fens and bogs in the Netherlands: vegetation, history, nutrient dynamics and conservation* (Dordrecht, 1992), pp. 323–60.

While the factors that determine the precise nature of each of these pathways in the Netherlands are not always applicable in the Broadland situation, numerous parallels nevertheless exist. Much of the diversity exhibited by the fen vegetation can thus be explained in terms of the 'geological template' – that is, as a consequence of the character of substrates, and of the water feeding the fen. The notable diversity of fen communities in the Ant valley, for example, owes much to geological and hydrological circumstance. Firstly, there is a distinction between the 'fen' communities of the floodplain, which derive a large proportion of their irrigating water from fluvial sources, and the 'mires', mainly found in side valleys and along the upland margin, which are irrigated by water from springs and marginal seepage zones, such as at East Ruston Common, Honing Common and Smallburgh Fen. Secondly, there are significant variations in character within both these broad types. Most of the floodplain communities grow in mesotrophic (moderately nutrient-rich) conditions and, while they take various forms, are generally dominated by saw-sedge and common reed. But where the influence of river water is less, areas of relatively oligotrophic (nutrient-poor) fen and mire have developed, most notably in the eastern part of Catfield Fen. Towards the floodplain margins the influence of groundwater character on the vegetation becomes greater than that of river water, although not to the same extent as with the valley mires. The latter are usually irrigated by water derived from the Crag and mildly alkaline, although in some cases, as in Smallburgh Fen, directly from the chalk, a difference clearly reflected in their respective vegetation. On the margins of both the side valleys and the main floodplain, local acidification may result from peat desiccation and oxidation, so that calcifuge communities – ones intolerant of alkaline conditions – develop, typically dominated by purple moor grass (*Molinia caerulea*), often with extensive patches of *Sphagnum* spp. Cross-leaved heath (*Erica tetralix*) is not uncommon in this habitat; other species found include meadow thistle (*Cirsium dissectum*), tormentil and devil's bit scabious. Some wetter areas support communities dominated by the locally scarce bottle sedge (*Carex rostrata*), growing with associated species including marsh cinquefoil (*Comarum palustre*) and bogbean (*Menyanthes trifoliata*).[163]

The particular character of the Bure valley fens is the consequence of a similar range of edaphic (soil-related) and hydrological factors. Here, however, many of them are highly calcareous, due to the influence of the underlying Chalk aquifer, and there are fen-meadow communities characteristic of lime-rich conditions on seepage lines on some of the steeper slopes. Decoy Carr near Acle and Upton Fen thus receive water from the Chalk aquifer, resulting in, predominantly, species-rich fen and fen-meadow communities suited to lime-rich conditions, including

---

163 Parmenter, 'Development of the wetland vegetation'.

a nationally uncommon habitat, *Schoenus nigricans–Juncus subnodulosus* mire, which has developed over an old decoy pool.

In the Thurne valley, proximity to the sea and incursion of saltwater into the groundwater table produce locally brackish conditions, leading to the development of communities that combine species typical of tall-herb fen with halophytes (salt-tolerant plants) of a kind not found in the other valleys. This is why the commercial sedge beds, in addition to supporting species such as black bog-rush, milk-parsley and hemp-agrimony (*Eupatorium cannabinum*), also include plants such as brookweed and parsley water-dropwort. The substrate over which the fens of the floodplain margins have developed, moreover, has an extremely low nutrient content and a pH within the range 3.5–5.5. The communities found in this acidic habitat are typically dominated by purple moor grass and often feature extensive patches of *Sphagnum* moss. The conditions enable a number of species that are unusual or even rare in Broadland to survive here. These include white sedge (*Carex canescens*), both common heather and cross-leaved heath, marsh violet (*Viola palustris*) and various bog mosses. In many places these two influences – brackish water and low pH – combine to produce an unusual array of fen communities, especially in the fens around Hickling Broad, the particular type being dependent upon their position along the two gradients. In addition, in places the fens overlie deposits of alluvial clay, supporting lesser-bulrush- or reed-dominated communities, along with grey club-rush (*Schoenoplectus tabernaemontani*).[164]

Much of the character of the fen vegetation can thus be explained in terms of Van Wirdum *et al.*'s 'geological template'. But many aspects are self-evidently related to their 'modern template': that is, to relatively recent change in the management of the fens themselves, or in their wider environmental context. The most important of these has already been noted: the way in which the decline in traditional forms of management – the mowing for litter and marsh hay, the cutting of reed and sedge – and the cessation of peat extraction led, in the course of the twentieth century, to the development of grey willow or downy birch scrub and extensive tracts of alder carr, particularly in the Ant, Bure and Yare valleys. The decline in management has had other, more subtle effects, including the wholesale loss of low-growing species from stands of fen vegetation that are no longer regularly mown. Other 'modern' influences are also significant, most notably nutrient enrichment of the water irrigating the fens as a consequence of run-off from the intensively farmed, heavily fertilised arable 'uplands', especially in the catchment of the Thurne; and pollution of the rivers, especially the Yare, with nutrients from human effluent. These encourage the development of a rather rank vegetation

---

164 Parmenter, 'Development of the wetland vegetation'.

dominated by the kind of more common, faster-growing plants that thrive in nitrogen-rich conditions, to the detriment of the typically lower-growing rarer species. The outfall of the Whitlingham sewage treatment works and a number of minor sewage works contributed significantly to the Yare's nutrient load during the twentieth century. Although levels of pollution have declined significantly over recent decades, the quality of the fen vegetation remains damaged even where, as is often the case, fens are now under some form of conservation management. Important plants recorded by early botanists have been lost and the vegetation in many of the fens is rather uniform in comparison with the northern valleys, although displaying nevertheless some features of interest (such as the abundance, already noted, of greater pond sedge and reed sweet-grass). Eutrophication and the proliferation of rank vegetation led to the general decline of plants such as marsh marigold (*Caltha palustris*) (Figure 4.21) and common meadow rue (*Thalictrum flavum*), which were formerly very common in the Yare valley, although both species still occur in profusion at a number of places, including Strumpshaw Fen. Water abstraction has also been a significant threat in some areas. King's Fen at East Ruston in the upper Ant valley, for example, suffered a rapid decline in its species and community interest when a public water-supply borehole was established on adjacent land, although the site had been suffering from the effects of desiccation before this time. Extraction for agricultural use has had a marked impact on the internationally important Catfield Fen, recently provoking a vocal and largely successful campaign. A further threat is posed by the increasing incursion of saline water into the rivers and thence the fen system as a consequence of sea-level rise, exacerbated by lower river flows due to water abstraction.

Mire communities appear to have suffered most from the decline in traditional fen management since the Second World War, with the complete loss of important acid-mire communities at Belton Bog, Ashby Warren, Worlingham Wild Carr and Honing Common. Not only are they prone to the ravages of neglect, but their constituent species demand a relatively high and stable water table, given that they are principally fed by groundwater. While other broad vegetation types, such as tall-herb fen communities, are still widespread and abundant, their area has been much reduced as a result of scrub invasion and the populations of a number of rare and scarce fen species have declined markedly.[165] Indeed, an examination of botanical records, local and national floras, and herbaria such as those held by the Natural History Museum and Norwich Castle Museum suggests that there has been a more general decline in the species diversity of the Broadland fen communities since the start of the twentieth century, with the greatest losses occurring since

---

165 G. Crompton, 'Rare species dossiers – *Dryopteris cristata* and *Liparis loeselii*', report (Nature Conservancy Council, 1977).

Figure 4.21 Marsh marigold (*Caltha palustris*), one of the plants which declined significantly in the Yare valley fens in the twentieth century as a result of eutrophication and the proliferation of rank vegetation.

the 1950s.[166] Low-growing species have suffered particularly badly as a result of scrub invasion or the proliferation of rank vegetation, or where desiccation or eutrophication have occurred. Several species that are rare and scarce at a national level and that were once widespread in parts of Broadland are now uncommon or declining here, such as fibrous tussock-sedge (*Carex appropinquata*) and round-leaved wintergreen (*Pyrola rotundifolia* ssp. *rotundifolia*). Positive conservation management of fens supporting fen orchid (*Liparis loeselii*) has, however, delivered a significant increase in the size of the population, so that, although it remains endangered, it is no longer considered to be at high risk of extinction.

For the 'modern' template, we should note again, also embraces such influences as current conservation management – whether this is simply replicating 'traditional' practices or specifically designed to benefit a particular species or community, and whether it is carried out directly by a conservation body or by a private landowner as part of a government-funded agro-environment scheme. Without such grant aid many fens would not be maintained. The 'modern' template is, indeed, more than a matrix of decay and decline. In large measure as a result of conservation initiatives, the Ant and Thurne valleys still have sizeable populations of most, if not all of the species that were recorded in the past; the Bure valley fens retain much of their species interest; and overall, as noted at the beginning of this section, the Broadland fens remain a habitat of international conservation importance.

The third of the 'templates' discussed by Van Wirdum *et al.*, that relating to historic land use, is arguably the most important for understanding the fen vegetation, and perhaps of greatest interest to readers of this book. Its influence is most obvious, perhaps, in the contrast between areas of fen reclaimed, drained and grazed following enclosure and then subsequently abandoned and reflooded, on the one hand, and those set out as poor's allotments or otherwise remained undrained, on the other. The former, for the most part, are characterised by a rather uninteresting flora, often heavily dominated by reed or coarse sedge species, in response to the higher nutrient levels resulting from drainage and consequent oxidation of the peat, while the latter – where the extraction of peat and the cutting of vegetation often continued into the twentieth century and water levels remained at or near the ground surface – today support some of the best wetland vegetation in Broadland, especially in the Ant valley. In part, of course, the distinction simply reflects the fact that poor's allotments were located on some of the wettest and most unproductive land in the parish. It is, nevertheless, part of a wider and usually more subtle pattern.

---

166 W. Wittering, *An arrangement of British plants* (Birmingham, 1796). J.E. Smith, *Flora Britannica* (London, 1800–4). J.S. Henslow and E. Skepper, *Flora of Suffolk: a catalogue of the plants found in a wild state in the county of Suffolk* (London, 1860). K. Trimmer, *Flora of Norfolk* (London, 1866). W.M. Hind, *The flora of Suffolk* (London, 1889). C.P. Petch and E.L. Swann, *Flora of Norfolk* (Norwich, 1968). G. Beckett, A. Bull and R. Stevenson, *A flora of Norfolk* (Norwich, 1999).

Traditional management did not simply create plagioclimax states, interrupting the progression to wet woodland. It shaped a complex range of distinct communities because various forms of management promoted the growth of particular species. Grazing, for example, results in the suppression of the taller or most palatable species, while allowing grasses, low-growing plants and coarse rushes and sedges to flourish.[167] More strikingly, regular winter reed-cutting supports and promotes the growth of reeds and thus encourages the development of a reed-dominated fen flora, while summer cutting of saw-sedge creates, over time, ever purer stands of that plant. Some commercial reed and sedge beds still exist in Broadland, examples of ongoing management maintaining plagioclimatic vegetation. Most fen community types, in contrast, are the result of the abandonment of economic management from the late nineteenth century – that is, of resumed natural development after an interruption in the succession – usually followed, more recently, by some measure of conservation management. What is particularly noteworthy is that many of these communities change slowly and follow, for a time, distinct paths of development, so that to a surprising extent the current mosaic of vegetation communities echoes spatial variations in past land-use systems. The reasons for such persistence are varied and complex but include the ability of some plant communities, particularly those dominated by dense reed or saw-sedge, to resist the colonisation of succeeding species. The most dramatic way in which past land use continues to influence the modern environment involves, however, not the historic management of vegetation but phases of its complete removal, by peat extraction, followed by recolonisation.

These correlations, it should be noted, which survive for only as long as fens remain free of scrub, are principally with patterns of land management recorded on nineteenth-century maps. Earlier cartographic coverage is too limited to establish longer-term relationships and, as we have seen, the management of the fens seems to have changed significantly with enclosure, and associated social and economic developments, from the later eighteenth century, often towards the more specialised use of particular land parcels. Yet one important habitat was, of course, the consequence of much earlier land-use patterns: the broads themselves, mostly created in the early Middle Ages, the depth of which has often precluded all but very limited colonisation by fen vegetation.

The continued dominance of reed in the vegetation of former reed beds long after regular cutting has ceased is particularly striking. This is most obvious in the case of beds created from pasture in the middle decades of the twentieth century and then abandoned, but much of the distribution of communities dominated by

---

167 J. Treweek, P. José and P. Benstead, *The wet grassland guide. Managing floodplain and coastal wet grassland for wildlife* (Sandy, 1997).

common reed more generally seems to relate to earlier areas of specialised reed-growing. Similarly, abandoned sedge beds usually remain dominated by saw-sedge because the dense litter mat inhibits invasion by other species.

Litter and fodder were cut mainly, although not exclusively, from fens on solid peat, an activity accompanied by usually limited amounts of summer and autumn grazing. Most of the areas exploited in this way before the decline in management are today characterised by the various forms of tall-herb fen vegetation that are widespread in Broadland, and most notably by communities in which mixtures of reed and blunt-flowered rush are accompanied by significant quantities of marsh valerian, or by marsh bedstraw (*Galium palustre*) and water mint (*Mentha aquatica*). Also prominent in such contexts are fens in which common reed is dominant, but with large amounts of blunt-flowered rush and marsh pennywort, or milk-parsley and marsh cinquefoil. This said, some tall-herb fen communities also seem to have developed where sedge- or reed-cutting were significant activities in the past.[168]

Peat-digging has probably had a greater impact upon the development of fen vegetation in Broadland than any other single factor. Over half of the present-day fens have developed over former turbaries, and in places this proportion rises to more than three-quarters. The relatively shallow post-medieval peat workings provided conditions that were ideal for rapid succession to reedswamp and fen. Common reed, saw-sedge and lesser bulrush were usually the first to invade the abandoned workings, and were joined, as terrestrialisation progressed, by various herbaceous species. These together produced fresh peat at a rapid rate – as much as 15 millimetres per year.[169] The nineteenth-century peat cuttings have now almost completely terrestrialised and the resultant fen surface is usually quite firm, but they still support vegetation that is markedly different from that growing over adjacent areas of solid peat, although taking a variety of forms due to variations in the way in which the terrestrialised areas were subsequently managed, coupled with local variations in the substrate and hydrological regime. Saw-sedge is often very abundant on such sites, especially in the Ant valley where it is accompanied by a large number of uncommon species, including lesser tussock-sedge (*Carex diandra*), fibrous tussock-sedge and slender sedge (*Carex lasiocarpa*), and a range of bryophytes, including pointed spear-moss (*Calliergonella cuspidata*) and yellow starry fen-moss (*Campylium stellatum*). Some of the most recently terrestrialised turf ponds support semi-swamp communities with species such as lesser bulrush, cowbane (*Cicuta virosa*), greater water-parsnip (*Sium latifolium*), greater spearwort (*Ranunculus lingua*) and great water dock (*Rumex hydrolapathum*),

---

168 Parmenter, 'Development of the wetland vegetation'.
169 J. Gunn, *A sketch of the geology of Norfolk* (Norwich, 1864), p. 20.

growing in abundance in reed-dominated vegetation. Indeed, such vegetation is almost exclusively found over former peat cuttings, as are a number of other communities. Lastly, we should note that fens in the downstream sections of most of the river valleys are underlain by estuarine clay, which in some places has been exposed by peat-cutting. These locations often support lesser-bulrush- or reed-dominated communities, with a number of species tolerant of the slightly brackish conditions created by the clay substrate – again, very different from those on adjacent, uncut ground.[170]

The Broadland fens are not 'natural', although their existence is unquestionably in part dependent upon, and their varied character in part shaped by, purely 'natural' factors. They were essentially created by practical, economic and agrarian activities that are now largely abandoned. Only by continuing or reinstating traditional practices, or forms of management that mimic their effects, can these important habitats survive. Even these, the wildest of the Broadland landscapes, are a product of human history.

---

170 Parmenter, 'Development of the wetland vegetation'.

5

DRAINAGE BY WIND AND STEAM

Drainage windmills are iconic features of the Broadland landscape, the subject of innumerable paintings and photographs over the last two centuries or more. The Broads would not be the Broads without them. No fewer than 70 remain in recognisable form, mainly brick tower mills. Some, such as that at Stracey Arms, beside the 'Acle Straight' (TG 4416 0897), are in a restored (although not a functioning) state. Many are derelict and ruined, albeit often with some attempts made, by the Norfolk Windmills Trust or the Broads Authority, to slow the rate of further deterioration by, for example, installing an aluminium cap. A few examples have been converted to other uses. The mills display much variation in other respects, not least in terms of size. While some, such as Swim Coots Mill, Catfield (TG 411 212), are scarcely more than 6 metres high, that at Berney Arms (TG 465 049) is a huge building, towering a full 22 metres above the surrounding marshes. This heritage of wind drainage has no parallel in England, but its importance should not be allowed to entirely obscure the various other mechanical methods of improving drainage that have been employed in the area over time, variously powered by horses, steam, paraffin, diesel and latterly electricity.

Almost all Broadland drainage windmills featured the same basic range of elements. The sails – four in number – turned an inclined shaft called the *windshaft* on which was mounted a large gear wheel, variously known as the *brakewheel* or the *headwheel*, located within the cap. This meshed with another large wheel, the *wallower*, which was mounted on the *upright shaft* running vertically through the centre of the mill from top to bottom. Mounted on this, towards the base of the mill, was the *crown wheel*, which meshed with the *pit wheel* and thus drove a horizontal shaft (Figure 5.1). Until the later nineteenth century, when turbine pumps began to be used in some mills, this served to turn a *scoopwheel*, with paddles that lifted water from a mill dyke – which was connected to the wider

Figure 5.1 Drawing of Herringfleet smock drainage mill, showing the internal workings of a typical early Broadland drainage mill, equipped with cloth or 'common' sails, tailpole-winded and driving a scoop wheel.

network of dykes – into a channel called a *raceway*, from which it was discharged into a river or other higher-level watercourse. The scoopwheel was usually housed in a *hoodway*, a tight-fitting semicircular weatherboarded cover adjoining, but outside, the structure of the mill itself.

Early mills were equipped with *common* sails, comprising a wooden framework over which a narrow sheet of cloth or canvas was stretched. They needed to be adjusted or 'reefed' to cope with different wind conditions, a task that could be carried out only when the sails were stationary, meaning that on some days the mill might need to be repeatedly stopped and an operative had to be in constant attendance. The wooden cap, which rotated on a greased wooden *curb*, had to be winched manually into the wind by means of a rope or chain attached to a sturdy *tailpole* which extended down from the rear of the cap and which was braced to the cap frame by two pairs of long braces – in the obscure language of millwrighting, early mills were *tailpole winded* or *manually winded*. This, too, was something that might need to be done frequently in changeable conditions. In the course of the nineteenth century more sophisticated forms of technology were developed. In particular, cloth sails were replaced by *patent sails*, consisting of a large number of parallel shutters arranged widthways across the sails. These were weighted, allowing the wind to 'spill' in gusts, and could be opened or closed to allow for changes in wind speed using a complex system of rods and chains. In addition, mills were now equipped with a *fantail*, a small vaned wheel attached to the back of the cap at right angles to the sails. This was connected through gears to a winding mechanism. As the wind changed direction, the fantail rotated and turned the cap, and therefore the sails, automatically into the wind. Such mills were thus *self winding*, and could respond almost instantaneously to quite minor changes in wind direction.

The chronology of and extent to which these and other technological improvements were adopted, and in some cases their full purpose and impact, are still not entirely understood, in spite of the fact that a number of researchers have investigated the subject.[1] Documentary evidence is patchy, and while, as noted, the mills have been painted on numerous occasions, most importantly by members of the Norwich School of artists in the early nineteenth century, such visual representations need to be treated with caution and understood within the context of contemporary artistic conventions. Particular problems attend the

---

[1] The principal studies are: R. Wailes, *The English windmill* (London, 1954); R. Wailes, 'Norfolk windmills part II: drainage and pumping mills, including those in Suffolk', *Newcomen Society Transaction*, 30 (1956), pp. 157–77; A.J. Ward, Archive held by Norfolk Windmills Trust; A.C. Smith, *Drainage windmills of the Norfolk marshes: a contemporary survey*, 2nd edn (Stevenage, 1990); S. Wade Martins, 'The study of the drainage windmills of the Norfolk Broadlands', *Norfolk Archaeology*, 35 (1970), pp. 152–4; A. Yardy, 'The development of the Broadland drainage windmills with particular reference to the firm of Englands of Ludham', MA dissertation (University of East Anglia, 2004). Unreferenced statements and information included in this chapter, if not from these sources, is based on observation and survey by the authors.

investigation of the surviving buildings themselves. It might be thought that the best way to understand the development of mill technology would be to compare the features of a number of dated examples, but this is difficult for two main reasons. Firstly, a significant proportion of surviving mills cannot be closely dated: mills were frequently rebuilt on the same spot so references to construction at a particular date, or indications of a mill's existence on maps or in documents, do not necessarily relate to the structure that stands on the site today. Secondly, mills were frequently updated, with the addition of the latest technology, and their towers altered and rebuilt either to allow for this or for some other reason: when the mill erected following the enclosure of Burgh St Margaret Common in 1804 was badly damaged by a storm in 1840, for example, it was rebuilt 'from the top of the door' upwards.[2]

All this makes the systematic archaeological investigation of surviving mills problematic. Many of the structural variations they display, moreover, have little or nothing to do with chronology. The brickwork of most examples is laid in English bond, with alternate lines of 'headers' (ranged at right angles to the surface) and 'stretchers' (laid parallel with it), but some are built in 'header bond' (all headers), at least on the outside. But this seems to be largely related to the size of the mills in question (smaller examples being more likely to be built in header bond) rather than having any necessary chronological significance. Some mills have much longer raceways than others but this is largely a function of location. Those serving mills draining into the lower, tidal courses of the rivers needed to be long, to store water at high tide. There are many other examples. In spite of these difficulties, the broad outlines of the development of wind drainage in Broadland are now clear, even if some of the details remain uncertain.

Early drainage mills

We noted in the previous chapter that drainage mills were already being erected in Broadland by the end of the seventeenth century, and that sporadic documentary references suggest their proliferation in the course of the eighteenth. By 1787 William Marshall was able to describe the typical Broadland drainage mill as having 'a body of brick, about twenty feet high, with sails similar to those of a corn-mill, but somewhat smaller'. It drove a single scoopwheel, capable of raising water a little over a metre, which was like 'a small undershot watermill wheel', with flat radiating paddles or 'floats'.[3] Only eight of the surviving drainage mills in the Broads appear, however, to date from the eighteenth century. Two of these have (or had) dates inscribed on the towers: Brograve Mill on the Waxham Marshes (1771, TG 447 236, Figure 5.2) and Oby Mill on the river Bure (1753, TG 409 137).

---

2   NRO MC 554 16–19, 774X9.
3   Marshall, *Rural economy*, vol. 2, pp. 282–3.

Figure 5.2 Brograve Level Mill, one of the oldest in Broadland, was built in 1771.

The others – St Benet's Abbey Mill (TG 380 157), St Benet's Level (TG 399 156), Clippesby (TG 409 129), Mautby (TG 489 099), Kerrison's Level (TG 462 085) and Pettingill's on Haddiscoe Island (TG 458 016) – all occupy the sites of mills shown on eighteenth-century maps and display clear evidence of early brickwork.[4]

The eight are not a very helpful group with which to illustrate the typical features of early mills. The St Benet's Abbey mill, which dates from the early 1720s, is probably the oldest, but is certainly not typical.[5] It was built to grind coleseed, as well as to drain the adjacent marshes, and accordingly has a particularly large base diameter to accommodate oil-milling machinery and, being built into the ruins of the medieval gatehouse, a corresponding height that appears to have been greater than that of its contemporaries.[6] Moreover, only the shell of the tower survives. We do, however, know that when it finally ended work in the 1860s it was still manually winded, and the numerous early visual representations made of it show a multi-sided conical cap very different from those of surviving Broadland mills. As for the other

---

4 All but two have mills marked on their site on Faden's county map of 1797. The exceptions are depicted on other eighteenth-century maps. Pettingill's appears to be shown on Hodskinson's 1783 map of Suffolk, and a mill is referred to here in a lease of 1802, NRO MC 2575/4/5–7. Kerrison's Level is depicted on the Acle enclosure map of 1799, NRO PC 112/1. Sales particulars from 1938 state that the drainage mill rents were created from deeds dated from 1796, NRO BR143/113.

5 As described in A. Norris, 'An History of the Hundreds of East and West Flegg, Happing, Tunsted, and Part of North Erpingham', c.1782, unpublished ms., NRO RYE 3. See below, p. 261.

6 Ibid.

Figure 5.3 Pettingill's Mill, photographed by Hallam Ashley shortly before it finished work in the 1940s. The mill was still winded by a tailpole and, unusually, was fitted with one pair of common and one pair of patent sails. Note the low height, typical of early mills.

seven examples, all but one had their towers heightened and/or partially rebuilt, and patent sails and fantails installed, in the course of the nineteenth century and three – Oby, Brograve and St Benet's Level – had their scoopwheels replaced with turbine pumps, necessitating alterations to the lower gearing. The last of these, moreover, has suffered a series of catastrophic events in its long life, including a major fire in 1894 that destroyed most earlier internal features,[7] while the machinery and fittings were stripped out of Mautby Mill, seemingly with no formal record made, when it was converted to residential use in the 1980s. Only Pettingill's (Figure 5.3) seems to have survived to the end of its working life with little modification of its brickwork and still retaining one pair of its common sails and scoopwheel, although these, together with cap and internal machinery, have now largely gone, leaving an empty brick shell.[8]

Nevertheless, we can learn something from an examination of these structures. Most have been heightened, or 'hained', since originally built, as indicated by changes in the character of the brickwork and often the angle of the walls, more vertical in the addition than in the original structure. As the top courses were usually rebuilt ahead of heightening we cannot assume the current extent of the older brickwork precisely represents the former height, but it can provide some indication of this.

---

7   CERC ECE/7/1/32731.
8   Wailes, 'Norfolk windmills', p. 163.

Brograve Mill is just over 9 metres high to the curb but has probably been raised by around 1.5 metres; Oby Mill likewise around 9 metres high, of which perhaps 2.5 metres is rebuild and addition; Mautby around 8 metres, with a metre or so of addition; Kerrison's Level was around 6.5 metres high, before being raised by nearly 2 metres; while Clippesby, now around 10 metres in height, appears to have been raised by nearly 2.5 metres. All were thus originally rather low structures, perhaps 6.5–7.5 metres in height, excluding cap. Pettingill's, which apparently retains its original height, is a little under 8 metres to the top of the brickwork. It is a rather squat, stubby building, as apparently were Oby and Brograve, in particular, when originally constructed. It is worth noting, however, that the towers of all of these mills were slightly taller than the approximate 6 metres which Marshall described as typical in 1787, while the original height of the brickwork of St Benet's Level Mill appears to have been around 8.5 metres. Early mills, while lower (with the exception of that at St Benet's Abbey) than most nineteenth-century examples, were thus not quite, or at least not universally, the diminutive structures suggested by Marshall's description.

Oby and Clippesby Mills, which stand within a kilometre of each other on the river Bure, have retained some early internal features. In particular, the former until recently possessed a cap frame (that is, the framework of beams forming the base of the cap), which had been adapted from that of an earlier, perhaps original, cap, equipped with the typical long tailpole to the rear that allowed it to be turned into the wind from the ground. In both mills, moreover, the floor structure retains evidence for the former presence of upright posts forming part of a framework mechanism that kept the mill cap centred (in later mills this was achieved using truck wheels on the underside of the cap, running around the inside face of the 'curb' at the top of the tower). Pettingill's Mill retains traces of something similar.[9] At Kerrison's Level Mill much of the original tailpole-winded cap survives, while some of the roughly hewn timber floor joists likewise appear original. The only surviving internal machinery of probable eighteenth-century date is, however, to be found reused in High's Mill in Halvergate (TG 457 071). This was completely rebuilt in the nineteenth century, although with the low height (just over seven metres to the curb) presumably displayed by the previous mill, which Faden's map of Norfolk, published in 1797, shows on the site. The machinery was, almost certainly, originally installed in this earlier mill and reused when it was replaced. The upper gearing – that is, the wallower and headwheel – are of wood, the former with pegs that project upwards to engage with the latter; we may assume that the lower gearing, now of iron, was similarly constructed. The horizontal scoopwheel

---

[9] Wailes, 'Norfolk windmills', p. 161. V.G. Pargeter, Heritage Statement, Pettingill's Mill, Toft Monks, 2015, archived with the Norfolk Windmills Trust, Norwich, pp. 3–4.

shaft and the multi-sided upright shaft, both of timber, also survive. In addition, although, as noted, no machinery now survives at Pettingill's Mill, Wailes suggested that it similarly had a wallower with vertical pegs that meshed with the headwheel.[10]

Mill technology did not change significantly in the first three decades of the nineteenth century, a period from which rather larger numbers of drainage mills – probably around 15 – appear to survive. Herringfleet Mill (TG 465 976), built around 1820, working into the 1950s and then immediately preserved, is the most complete survival, although unusual in that it is a low, wooden, octagonal 'smock' mill rather than a brick tower (above, Figure 5.1).[11] The lower gearing has been replaced in cast iron but otherwise the early wooden machinery survives and it retains a sturdy tailpole to the rear and 'common' or cloth sails. Several other mills erected before *c*.1830 continued in this archaic, unmodernised form until they ceased working, including High's Mill, Chedgrave Detached Mill on Haddiscoe Island (TG 452 033), Old Hall Mill in Stokesby (TG 436 094), Womack Mill in Ludham (TG 399 174) and Middle Marsh Mill, Catfield (TG 372 211).[12] All were probably, like their predecessors, originally fitted with wooden shafts and gearing; Chedgrave Detached Mill retains, like High's, its horizontal timber scoopwheel shaft, but none now possesses a timber windshaft (the last to survive were in Pettingill's Mill and Womack Mill). Like those just discussed, all these mills are, or were before subsequent heightening, fairly low structures, less than *c*.8.5 metres to the curb, and the same is true of other examples that have undergone a greater degree of later modernisation but were probably first built in this period, including Upton Black Mill (*c*.1800, TG 404 141); Repps Level Mill in Repps-with-Bastwick (probably *c*.1807, TG 416 179); Swim Coots Mill in Catfield (between *c*.1824 and 1839, TG 411 212); and Belton Black Mill and Fritton Marshes Mill (both *c*.1830, TG 467 034 and TG 450 997).[13]

---

10   Wailes, 'Norfolk windmills', p. 163.

11   The mill is not present on the 1819 Herringfleet enclosure map, NRO PD 126/1, but is shown on Bryant's 1824 map of Suffolk.

12   Tailpole winding, common sails and other features indicate that these buildings represent the structures whose origins are indicated by map or documentary evidence, rather than later replacements, *viz*: the building of Catfield Middle Marsh Mill was directed by the enclosure award of 1808, NRO C/Sca 2/67. Stokesby Hall is absent from Faden's map of Norfolk, published in 1797, but is shown on both the Ordnance Survey drawings of *c*.1816 in the British Library and Bryant's Norfolk map of 1824. Womack is absent from the latter two sources but appears on the tithe map of 1842, NRO PD 653/48.

13   Dating based on aspects of physical structure, coupled with the extent of subsequent heightening and other alterations, which suggest that these buildings represent the mills whose origins are indicated by map or documentary evidence, rather than later replacements. Fritton is described as newly built in an advert in the *Norwich Mercury* in 1832; Repp's Level is absent from Faden's county map of 1797 but shown on both the Ordnance Survey drawings of *c*.1816 and Bryant's county map of 1824, and was probably built following the enclosure in 1807. Swim Coots is absent from the latter two sources but appears on the Catfield tithe map of 1839, NRO PD 531/37. Upton Mill has a damaged datestone, on which the figures '00' are discernible, suggesting it was built in 1800, following the enclosure act of 1799. For Belton, see Wailes, 'Drainage mills'. It was in fact rebuilt in the early twentieth century, but in its original form: see below, p. 252.

Figure 5.4 The archaic lower gearing at Tunstall Black Mill – a 'lantern gear' or 'trundle pinion', comprising vertical staves enclosed by a disc top and bottom, which engaged with the pitwheel – photographed while still in use in 1938.

We have rather more information about the character of the wooden machinery employed in these slightly later early-nineteenth-century mills. Tunstall Black Mill, which stood near to the point where Tunstall Dyke meets the river Bure, was demolished in the 1950s but was still working in 1938 when it was, fortunately, recorded by H.O. Clark and George Watkins.[14] A mill is marked on the site on William Faden's 1797 map of Norfolk, but was presumably replaced by this structure, which bore a datestone showing 1818. Here, as at Pettingill's, the crownwheel took the form of a wooden 'lantern gear', with vertical staves running between solid wooden discs, while the wallower again had vertical pegs that projected upwards to engage with the headwheel (Figure 5.4). Old Hall Mill, immediately across the river in Stokesby, seems to have had very similar gearing, as did Swim Coots Mill,

---

14 Mills Archive, Reading, AMLS-A-121. G. Watkins, *Stationary steam engines of Great Britain* (Bath, 1993), vol. 9, pp. 144, 147–9.

Figure 5.5 'Mill at Reedham' by Thomas Lound (1802–61). A small brick tower with common sails, turned into the wind via a long braced tailpole and displaying the very low height described by William Marshall as typical of marsh mills.

Catfield.[15] The terminology used for such arrangements varied. Clark, writing about Tunstall, described the wallower as a 'pinwheel' and the lantern gear as a 'trundle pinion';[16] one of the last traditional millwrights at work in the Broads, Arthur Thrower, referred to 'whole and half lantern gears'.[17] In 1827 the Potter Heigham drainage commissioners ordered that 'new staves or gears should be made to the trundle' and in 1835 that 'new staves should be put in the trundle of Grapes' Mill'.[18]

We should not under-estimate the effectiveness of these apparently archaic structures or the wooden machinery they contained. Until recently Six Mile House Mill in Cantley Detached (TG 461 098) retained the remains of a pegged wallower gear but this was evidently reused in a much later mill, described in 1875 as a 'brick tower drainage mill, with patent sails, built a few years since'.[19] Despite its primitive form and the installation of steam-drainage engines on either side

---

15 Wailes, 'Norfolk windmills', p. 163.
16 Mills Archive, Reading, REXW-11856, H.O. Clark, 'Notebook on Norfolk drainage windmills'.
17 A. Thrower, 'East Anglia's Mills', *Eastern Daily Press*, 6 June 1945.
18 NRO ACC 2010/243.
19 *Norwich Mercury*, 10 July 1875.

of Tunstall Dyke, Tunstall Black Mill continued in service until at least 1938. The equally archaic Stokesby Old Hall Mill was still working in 1929, by which time a steam pumping engine had come, and gone, beside it.[20]

We suggested earlier that not all early drainage mills possessed brick towers that were quite as low as Marshall described in 1787. His account needs to be qualified in another, more important way. The paintings made by the nineteenth-century Norwich School artists, especially Thomas Lound, Henry Bright, John Sell Cotman and Alfred Stannard, depict low brick tower mills with common sails, substantial braced tailpoles and a variety of cap shapes (Figure 5.5). But they also show numerous wooden 'smock' mills, which – with the notable exception of Herringfleet Mill, already mentioned – have since disappeared from Broadland (Figure 5.6). Allowance must be made for artistic preferences – mills such as these may have been deemed more 'picturesque' subjects than brick towers – and for the fact that, for a variety of reasons, not least ease of access by boat downriver from Norwich, the endeavours of these artists were geographically focused on the mills of the river Yare (with the notable exception of the St Benet's Abbey mill on the Bure, which was a perennial favourite). But, this said, it is clear that smock mills did initially play an important role in early marsh drainage.

Most of the wooden mills painted by Norwich School artists, which come in a variety of sizes, cannot now be located, but a number are explicitly identified as being on the Reedham marshes. These include an example painted by Lound that boasts a multi-sided conical cap similar in form to that of the St Benet's Abbey mill, one by Bright with a vertically boarded cap and a small example depicted by Cotman with simple conical cap. One of these may have been the structure that eighteenth- and early-nineteenth-century maps show on the site now occupied by the late-nineteenth-century brick tower mill at Seven Mile House on the river Yare called Polkey's (TG 444 034), as restoration work in 2002–5 revealed a variety of reused and adapted material within it, including parts from the floor of a substantial octagonal wooden mill, recycled as floor beams.[21] What is particularly interesting is that these display a complex form of construction found in the Dutch and Fenland mills in which the floor beams are a structural component of the 'smock' and are tenoned into the *cant* (corner) posts, creating a strong framework. The carpentry techniques involved, not least working with eight cant posts arranged in an octagonal plan at the angle necessary to create the sloping walls or *batter* to the tower, were considerably more complicated than those employed in the 'English' form found in Herringfleet Mill, where the floor beams are independent of the wall framing. Other wooden mills of 'Fenland' type are known to have existed in

---

20   Letter from Arthur E. Smithdale, *Eastern Daily Press*, 31 August 1929.
21   'Former Smock Mill at Seven Mile House', Letter from Vincent Pargeter, millwright, to Norfolk Windmills Trust, 6 November 2004. Archived with the Norfolk Windmills Trust, Norwich.

Figure 5.6 Herringfleet Mill, built around 1820, is the only smock drainage mill surviving intact in Broadland. It continued to work into the 1950s.

Broadland, such as the small example that stood in Barton Turf until the early 1900s and which was purchased in Lincolnshire in 1811 by a Mr Perowne of Stalham, 'who had considerable experience in such matters'.[22] Certainly, the paintings, while they do show small smock mills similar to that which survives at Herringfleet, also depict larger examples that were perhaps of 'Fenland' type.

Timber smock mills, especially small ones of the Herringfleet type, were cheaper than brick towers – that erected for Colonel Preston in Neatishead in 1810 cost £226 10s, less than £15,000 in modern money – and could be erected more quickly, and also more successfully on unstable ground.[23] They could also be prefabricated and could clearly be treated as moveable structures. However, they were renowned for problems with rotting cant posts and distorting curbs.[24] They were also particularly vulnerable to gale damage, which could be catastrophic, George Christopher Davies describing in 1884 how he 'once saw a fine wooden tower-mill blown clean over during a heavy gale'.[25] That on Beccles Fen was blown down in 1836.[26] So, too, was that on Heigham Holmes in Potter Heigham in 1810, although it was not so badly damaged that it could not be reinstated, for the millwright William England of Ludham was contracted 'to repair and set up the mill in a workmanlike manner and provide good Baltic timber for the same', putting down 'proper posts and Tyes to secure the mill on the Foundation'.[27]

Smock drainage mills were steadily taken down in the course of the nineteenth century, replaced by other forms of windmill or rendered redundant by the installation of steam drainage, with owners often attempting to sell them for use elsewhere. The process began quite early. In 1827 'a small weatherboarded drainage mill … now standing on the marshes belonging to the Fishley estate' was advertised for sale in the *Norwich Chronicle*;[28] the following year the Yarmouth millwrights Huke and Flatman were selling a marsh mill described as a 'strong wood tower' 27 feet (8 metres) high, that 'last year drained near 500 acres [*c.*200 hectares]'.[29] Removal continued through the middle decades of the century. In 1831 a 'wooden tower capable of draining 100 acres [*c.*40 hectares] of land' at Fritton was offered for sale;[30] in 1846 two mills at Hardley were advertised, one built of brick, the other a

---

22 *Eastern Daily Press*, 4 April 1903.
23 NRO MC 225/3–4, 674X6.
24 B. Flint, *Suffolk windmills* (Woodbridge, 1979), p. 44.
25 G. Christopher Davies, *Norfolk broads and rivers: or, the waterways, lagoons, and decoys of East Anglia*, 5th edn (Edinburgh and London, 1884), p. 109.
26 *Norwich Mercury*, 3 December 1836.
27 NRO ACC 2010/243.
28 *Norfolk Chronicle*, 11 August 1827.
29 *Norwich Mercury*, 28 June 1828.
30 *Norfolk Chronicle*, 9 July 1831.

'wood tower'.[31] The smock mill in Beccles Fen was sold in 1860, a few years after the installation of steam drainage there in 1857.[32] In 1866 the marsh mill at Worlingham ('composed of best Foreign Fir and Weather-board') was put up for sale, it likewise having been replaced by steam.[33] Nevertheless, while overall the number of smock mills seems to have steadily declined, a small number of new examples continued to appear, as we shall see, during the second half of the nineteenth century.

A third type of early wind-powered drainage 'engine' needs to be mentioned. Devices that have come to be called 'hollow post mills', but which early sources often describe as 'skeleton pump mills', were employed to drain limited areas of land. Smaller and cheaper than smock or tower mills, they were also less durable in the long term. Indeed, although they continued to be erected into the twentieth century, only two examples remain: Palmer's Mill, saved from dereliction on the Acle marshes, restored and re-erected beside Upton Dyke in 1978; and Clayrack, brought from Ranworth Marshes to How Hill on the river Ant in 1981. Both comprise a stout upright wooden post around four metres high supported by diagonal braces and mounted with a tiny 'buck' (that is, the body of the mill). The post is hollow and contains a vertical rod. At Palmer's Mill this was moved up and down, driven by the cranked windshaft. Clayrack, however, has two pairs of iron gears to produce a rotary motion. Palmer's Mill has twin winding vanes to ensure that the sails are kept facing into the wind (Figure 5.7), carries spring sails and originally drove a plunger pump. It has no associated brickwork and is fastened directly onto timber piles, discharging water into a timber trough. Clayrack, the former Ranworth mill, has the more familiar patent sails and fantail and drove a scoopwheel. Hollow post mills evidently took a variety of forms and Richard Noverre Bacon illustrated one in his *Report on the Agriculture of Norfolk* of 1844 with elements of both these surviving examples: a simple vane to turn it into the wind, but with two plunger pumps, which he described as an improvement on the 'single pump mills peculiar to this county', although even so it could only drain around 40 acres (*c*.16 hectares).[34] His wording implies that hollow post mills were by this time familiar features of the Broadland landscape and, indeed, an example on the river Bure was illustrated by John Sell Cotman in 1841, already looking rather old, while in March 1783 an advertisement in the *Norfolk Chronicle* offered for sale 'At Mawtby, in Norfolk, A skeleton Engine, which works by Wind, and is able to work two Pumps that will drain off thirty or forty Acres of Marsh Land; it is in good Repair'.[35]

---

31   *Norwich Mercury*, 1 August 1846.
32   *Norwich Mercury*, 23 June 1860.
33   *Norfolk Chronicle*, 23 June 1866.
34   Bacon, *Report on the agriculture of Norfolk*, pp. 293–4.
35   J.S. Cotman, *Mill on the Bure*, BM 1902, 0514.169, viewable online at https://www.britishmuseum.org/collection/object/P_1902-0514-169. *Norfolk Chronicle*, 15 March 1783.

Figure 5.7. Palmer's Mill, brought from the Acle Marshes and restored and re-erected beside Upton Dyke in 1978, is one of only two surviving examples of a 'hollow post mill' now remaining in Broadland.

We do not know how common such diminutive 'engines' may have been in Broadland or when they were first employed there. It is doubtful whether such structures would have been shown systematically, or even at all, on small-scale maps, which perhaps accounts for a number of known omissions. A map of the estate of the Rev. Wollaston in Aldeby, for example, drawn up in 1797, shows some kind of drainage mill omitted on William Faden's map of Norfolk, published in the same year; neither Faden nor Joseph Hodskinson's Suffolk map of 1783 show the mill depicted on a 1796 map of Worlingham by Isaac Johnson.[36] It is possible, however, that both represent particularly small examples of smock mills, equally likely to have been omitted from small-scale maps such as these.

In addition to drainage windmills, there are a few early references to the use of horses to drive scoopwheels. A 'horse mill' close to Decoy Broad is marked on a Woodbastwick estate map of 1845;[37] another is probably remembered in the name of 'Horse Mill Plantation' beside Ormesby Broad in Martham, marked on the 1884 Ordnance Survey map. Robert Bacon in 1844 described how a 'two horse draining mill' had been erected some 10 or 20 years earlier to drain marshes in Surlingham, but proved 'troublesome and expensive' to operate and had soon been replaced with a hollow post mill.[38] Nevertheless, there are a number of references to the use of horse mills in Broadland over the following decades, usually in association with drainage windmills. The 1852 sales particulars for the Ingham Hall estate refer to a 'Drainage Mill with Horse-works attached'; a 'Pump Mill for draining (complete), a twelve feet water wheel, with horse works (complete), and other property' were advertised for sale in Strumpshaw in 1860; in 1868 a 'MARSH MILL with both Horse and Wind power, nearly new' were offered for sale in South Burlingham; and the following year 'two skeleton pump windmills and one horse wheel with gear' were advertised in Great Yarmouth.[39]

The spread of mechanical drainage

The uneven nature of the documentary and cartographic evidence, coupled with the fact that some forms of drainage 'engine' were more visible and obvious to surveyors than others, makes it difficult to assess their number and distribution at any time before the later nineteenth century. The earliest period for which this can

---

36 NRO MC 2231/2, 942X7, Plan of the estate of Revd Francis Wollaston at Aldeby by Isaac Johnson, 1797. SRO HD 115, Survey and plan of Great Worlingham by Isaac Johnson, 1796/7.
37 Woodbastwick estate archives. Redrawn in George, *Land use*, p. 192. The building is still marked on the 1884 6-inch Ordnance Survey map, although not named.
38 Bacon, *Report on the agriculture of Norfolk*, p. 293.
39 NRO MS 18622/141, 477X1. *Norfolk Chronicle*, 31 March 1860. *Norfolk News*, 12 December 1868. *Ipswich Journal*, 18 December 1869.

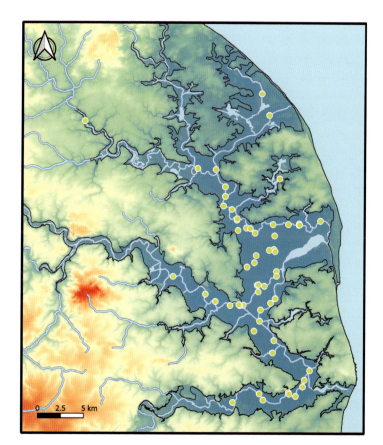

Figure 5.8 The distribution of drainage windmills in the late eighteenth century (for sources, see text).

be attempted is the late 1790s, using Faden's map of Norfolk, published in 1797, and Hodskinson's of Suffolk, which appeared in 1783; in a few areas, mainly in the Waveney valley, the information from these can be augmented with evidence from the kind of large-scale estate map likely to record the more diminutive varieties of mill.[40] These sources together suggest that in the late eighteenth century drainage mills were mainly a feature of the Halvergate Marshes and of the lower reaches of the Bure, Yare and Waveney rivers draining into them. Few had yet been built in the higher reaches of these rivers or in the valleys of their main tributaries, the Ant, the Thurne and the Muck Fleet (Figure 5.8). The tithe maps, mainly surveyed in the late 1830s and which are available for most Broadland parishes, suggest that the number of mills increased dramatically in the early nineteenth century, with the number of marked sites rising from 57 to around 105. Mills became more numerous in the areas where they were already present, but also now spread into the valleys of the Ant and the Thurne and, to a lesser extent, further along that

---

40   In addition to the above, the mill in Peto's Marsh, Aldeby, is shown on NRO MC 2677/3, PH13, map of the estate of Colonel Cope at Wheatacre Burgh, Norfolk and Oulton, Suffolk, and on a map of *c*.1825, NRO MC 103/2, so presumably remained in existence between these two dates.

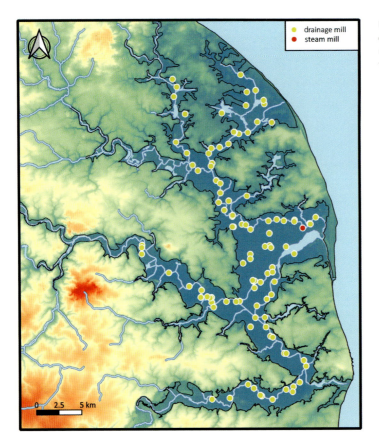

Figure 5.9 The distribution of drainage mills c.1840, based on the tithe maps.

of the Yare (Figure 5.9). The increasing density of mills may to some extent be more apparent than real, as the larger scale of the tithe maps ensured that a higher proportion of the smaller 'engines' were recorded. But their spread into the higher reaches of the river valleys unquestionably reflects the enclosure, by parliamentary acts, of large tracts of common fen and marsh in these areas in the first three decades of the nineteenth century. Many of these new mills, such as Upton Mill or Middle Marsh Mill in Catfield, were 'Commission' mills, erected by Drainage Commissions in accordance with the terms of particular enclosure acts.[41] Others, such as the predecessor of the present Hunsett Mill beside the Ant in Stalham, were built by individual owners within new blocks of private land allotted at enclosure. More than three-quarters of the new mills in these valley locations drained areas of alluvium, rather than peat – former common grazing marshes, rather than fens. While it is possible that some common marshes had already, before enclosure, been drained by forms of diminutive 'engine' invisible to the kinds of source used to construct Figure 5.8, it is likely that in most cases the new mills mapped in

---

41   Catfield enclosure award, 1808, NRO C/Sca 2/67.

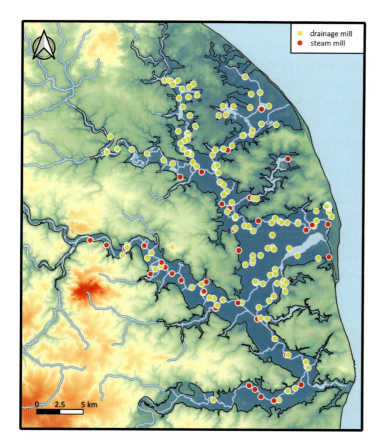

Figure 5.10 The distribution of drainage mills c.1885, based on the first edition 6 inch Ordnance Survey maps. NB: only 'stand alone' steam mills, unaccompanied by windmills, are mapped as such.

Figure 5.9 were the first forms of mechanical drainage to be established within the areas in question.

The first source that appears to systematically record every drainage mill in Broadland, including examples marked as 'disused', is the first edition 25-inch Ordnance Survey of c.1885 (Figure 5.10).[42] This series of maps shows the sites of around 180 examples, variously labelled as 'draining pump', 'windmill (pumping)', 'mill (pumping)' and 'engine house' – the last two terms references to steam-drainage engines but the first seemingly applied in an arbitrary manner to a variety of wind- and steam-powered machines (only steam pumps standing alone, unaccompanied by a windmill, are separately mapped on Figure 5.10). This further rise in numbers, compared with the situation depicted by the tithe maps, again involved both higher densities in areas where mills were already present and their spread into new ones, especially the higher reaches of the Yare, Bure and Ant valleys. But there were some areas, most notably the Waveney valley, where a

---

42   Figures 5.8, 5.9 and 5.10 do not collectively show every example known to have existed in Broadland. New mills on new sites continued to be erected well into the twentieth century, and a number of examples seem to have come and gone from the landscape in the four and a half decades separating these 'snapshots'.

comparison of the two map series suggests a reduction in the number of sites, the reasons for which we shall return to shortly.

It is striking that most of the new sites appearing in the period c.1840–85 were in areas of peat, rather than alluvium, not only in the higher reaches of the principal river valleys but also in places on the fringes of the Halvergate Marshes and in the valleys of minor watercourses such as the Muck Fleet. Most were associated with attempts by private landowners to reclaim peat fens or fen meadows, changing their character to grazing marshes. This was the period of Victorian 'High Farming', in which landowners everywhere invested heavily in the latest technologies in attempts to improve areas of marginal land. It is, however, possible that some of the new mills were used to regulate water levels in fens which continued to be exploited in traditional ways, for reeds or peat.

Of the 75 sites that appear for the first time on the 25-inch maps fewer than ten, and possibly as few as six, appear to have been brick tower mills. This is in spite of the fact that numerous existing mills, on established sites, were rebuilt or replaced with new brick tower mills in this period. The new sites mainly comprised other kinds of 'draining pump' and, while their precise character is often unclear from the maps, surviving remains and references in documents suggest that most were various kinds of wooden structure, cheaper to erect than brick towers but less durable in the landscape: smock mills, hollow post mills or the wooden 'trestle mills' which were developed in the late nineteenth century, all of which were used to drain relatively small parcels of land generally of less than c.20 hectares. The remaining new sites were steam pumps and while some of these were substantial engines in large brick engine houses, like those widely installed beside or on the sites of existing drainage windmills in this same period, most were much smaller affairs, often housed in sheds of corrugated iron. The more ephemeral nature of the drainage mills and, to an extent, steam pumps installed in the areas of peat in the higher reaches of the rivers in the second half of the nineteenth century largely explains why the overwhelming majority of those shown on the 1880s Ordnance Survey maps have since vanished, a rate of attrition greater than on the Halvergate Marshes, where sturdy brick tower mills always predominated.

Nineteenth-century improvements: patent sails and fantails

The steady increase in the number of drainage mills in the course of the nineteenth century was accompanied by the progressive replacement of existing 'engines' with new, improved forms, or their wholesale modernisation. Such changes might be carried out by private individuals or by Drainage Commissions established by enclosure acts; or, on occasion, they might be jointly funded by proprietors of a particular 'level' as when, in 1831, 11 owners of land in the 350-acre (c.140-hectare) Limpenhoe and Southwood Level paid a contractor to erect a new mill,

DRAINAGE BY WIND AND STEAM 247

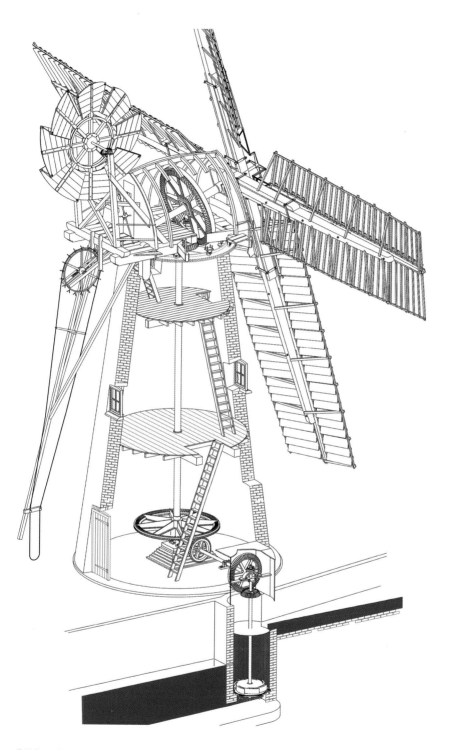

Figure 5.11 Drawing of Stracey Arms drainage mill, showing features typical of the later Broadland mills. The mill, built in 1883, has patent sails, a fantail and self-winding mechanism, and drives an external turbine pump.

with sluices, drains and a millman's cottage, at a cost of £744.[43] As a consequence of this great wave of building and rebuilding, the majority of Broadland's drainage mills post-date *c.*1830 and most earlier ones have been very extensively modified. They are essentially a Victorian and Edwardian heritage. The most important development was a shift from labour-intensive manual mills, tailpole winded, to ones fitted with patent sails and fantails, providing a degree of automation. In addition, iron increasingly replaced wood for the manufacture of shafts and gears, with components initially comprising rather rough blacksmiths' work but soon cast, although wooden teeth slotted into an iron wheel were often still used for the larger gears. Lastly, new methods of lifting water were adopted involving changes in the placement (and number) of scoopwheels and, ultimately, the adoption of turbine pumps (Figure 5.11).

In 1807 William Cubitt, the 22-year-old son of a Norfolk miller, patented his design for self-regulating windmill sails. Patent sails are generally regarded as a combination of two existing technologies, the so-called 'spring' and 'roller reefing' types of sail, which had been developed, but sparingly adopted, in the previous century.[44] Spring sails comprised rows of shutters or *vanes*, arranged in bays, that were connected together by a *shutter bar*, allowing them to be opened or closed all at once. In gusty conditions they could open to 'spill the wind', but they still had to be manually set, one sail at a time, to suit the prevailing wind strength. As with cloth sails, the mill needed to be stopped and the sails adjusted when the wind speed changed significantly. Patent sails introduced the remote-control element of the roller reefing sails by allowing adjustments to be made to the shutters by varying the amount of weight attached to an endless chain at the rear of the mill. The chain passed around the *Y wheel*, so called because it had 'Y' shaped guides fitted to its circumference, and via a pinion gear engaged with a horizontal rack attached to the *striking rod*. This passed through the centre of the windshaft, now usually made of cast iron, and was connected at the front to an arrangement of cranks and levers set at the junction of the sails, known as the *spider*. This transferred the in-and-out movement of the striking rod to an up-and-down motion in the shutters, thus allowing the sails to be adjusted without stopping the mill.

Because patent sails were heavier and allowed more air to leak than the lightweight, canvas-covered common sails, they were less efficient and turned more slowly. The sails of the mill therefore needed to be longer in order to maintain the same output of power, and this in turn meant that the mill tower needed to be heightened, or 'hained'. Evidence of heightening can, as we noted earlier, be clearly seen on a number of early broads mills, the new section of brickwork tending to

---

43   NRO BR 90/47/19.
44   Wailes, *English windmill*, p. 95.

maintain the same diameter as the original curb rather than continuing the batter of the tower. The distinctive profile so produced is most familiar, perhaps, from the much-photographed Morse's Mill at Thurne (TG 401 159, Figure 5.12). But the change is not always clearly apparent. In the case of Polkey's Mill, for example, the heightening is disguised by continuing the batter and by the tarring of the exterior of the mill. From the interior, there is clear evidence that the mill has been heightened by around a metre and the timber upright shaft has been reused by letting in an iron section of approximately the same length. It is often suggested that the adoption of automatic sails made it possible to build taller mills with longer sails that were more powerful and better able to catch the wind. Before their introduction, mill heights and sail lengths had been limited by the need to regularly adjust the sails from the ground. In reality, mills were increased in height when fitted with patent sails because they had to be, in order to maintain the same level of power. The main reason for installing such sails was not that they allowed the construction of more powerful mills but that they reduced labour costs by removing the need for constant supervision.

Installing patent sails also made the adoption of the fantail, or *flyer*, the other significant innovation of the period, a more viable proposition. This was a device designed to keep the sails of the mill facing squarely into the wind and, like the patent sail, was essentially a labour-saving invention that removed the need to turn the mill manually whenever the wind direction changed. A small 'fan wheel' with an iron hub and between six and ten wooden blades set at an angle of between 20 and 30 degrees was mounted on a projecting stage at the rear of the cap, at 90 degrees to the sails. With the wind direction constant, the fantail remained still. When the wind changed direction it turned, in most local mills then driving, via a downshaft and two pairs of bevel gears, a worm gear. This engaged with a gear rack on the circumference of the curb at the top of the tower and turned the cap until the sails were once again facing squarely into the wind.

Although the fantail had been patented by Edmund Lee as early as 1745, there was little point in using it as long as sails still required manual setting. The adoption of fantails and patent sails therefore usually occurred together. In advertising his new sails in the *Norfolk Chronicle* on 13 June 1807 Cubitt emphasised how they would be 'extremely useful in draining of marshes'.[45] Yet, while their use soon became widespread for corn mills throughout eastern England, their employment in Broadland drainage mills was gradual and never universal. Patent sails and their associated machinery were significantly more expensive than 'common' ones and converting an existing mill from the one to the other required major structural alterations including, in addition to raising the tower, the installation of a new,

---

45   H. Apling, *Norfolk corn and other industrial windmills* (Norwich, 1984), p. 22.

Figure 5.12 Thurne Mill or Morse's Mill, originally built in 1836, displays the characteristic profile of a mill subsequently heightened or 'hained' when patent sails were fitted.

hollow windshaft or the boring out of an existing wooden one. Because patent sails were much heavier, moreover, they required a strong cap frame. At Kerrison's Level Mill and Oby Mill the old frame was strengthened when the change was made by strapping on additional timber supports and at Polkey's Mill, similarly, the old frame, already a fairly substantial one, was utilised.[46] But, more usually, an entirely new cap was needed. The slower turning speed of the sails also meant that changes to the upper gearing of the mill were required, usually with a smaller cast-iron wallower being fitted to 'gear up' the drive. To fit a fantail to an older mill likewise demanded significant alterations. A new curb with toothed rack had to be installed and, in most cases, the old form of curb, with cap turning on greased wooden blocks, would be replaced with a 'live' curb, whereby it would rotate on a series of cast iron rollers. The cap frame would also need to be replaced or adapted to allow for the main longitudinal timbers, known as *sheers*, that supported the *fanstage* at the rear, on which the fantail was mounted.

The adoption of patent sails and fantails in Broadland seems to have occurred only from around 1830, usually perhaps taking place as mills needed to be rebuilt, repaired or reconditioned for some other reason. The predecessor of the present mill at Berney Arms was described as a 'powerful patent sail mill' in 1836;[47] two years later orders were given to repair Horsey Mill with patent sails; while a reference in the Winterton and Somerton drainage board's records to 'harp irons to vanes' shows that by 1840 the nearby Somerton Mill was also provided with them.[48] Fantails appear on a mill included in an undated view across the river Yare at Reedham by James Stark, apparently painted before the construction of the New Cut began in 1832,[49] and on two of John Preston Neale's Horsey drawings from 1835.[50] As just noted, mills with patent sails needed to be taller than those with common sails and the height of two examples that we can be confident were built in the early 1830s – Limpenhoe Mill (*c.*1832, *c.*11 metres to curb, TG 394 018) and Mutton's Mill on the Halvergate Marshes (*c.*1833, *c.*10 metres, TG 441 063) – indicates that both were equipped from the start with patent sails.[51] The new technology soon became widely adopted. In 1840 the drainage mill at Burgh St

---

46   Richard Seago and Vincent Pargeter, pers.comm.
47   *Norfolk Chronicle*, 6 August 1836.
48   *Norfolk Chronicle*, 8 December 1838. WMA, Winterton and East and West Somerton Drainage Commission minutes 1812–1860.
49   Haworth Art Gallery HAG162 (ArtUK.org); an 1830 engraving of Stark's painting produced by James Burnet is reproduced in *Scenery of the rivers of Norfolk comprising the Yare, Waveney and the Bure* (Norwich, 1834). The accompanying text fixes the location of the mill.
50   John Preston Neale, *Views in Norfolk*, vol. 1, Duleep Singh Collection, Norfolk Library and Information Service NMS NWHCM: 1957.356.109 and NWHCM: 1957.356.105.
51   The contract for Limpenhoe Mill was drawn up in 1831, NRO BR 90/47/19. For the dating of Mutton's Mill see below, p. 253).

Margaret, built following the enclosure of the commons there in 1804, was blown down in a storm, and the drainage commissioners

> Resolved and agreed that a new Tower should be erected and that the same should commence from the present Foundations of the old mill at the top of the door … the tower shall be built on the best and most improved principle so as to carry the machinery with self acting winding tackle and patent sails.[52]

The two Ludham enclosure mills, Bridgefen and Horsefen, were both modernised in the 1850s, the former around 1856 and the latter around 1859.[53] In Potter Heigham one of the enclosure mills, High's Mill, was updated in 1853 and the other, Heigham Holmes Mill, was rebuilt in modern form in 1860.[54] Major repairs and alterations were ordered at Stubb Mill in Hickling in 1856 (TG 437 219) while in 1860 the cap of Eastfield Mill, in the same parish (TG 438 233), was blown off and 'several yards of the tower were blown down', prompting plans for repairs and improvements.[55] But a few tower mills were still being newly built in the older form, tailpole winded and with common sails, into the middle decades of the nineteenth century, including Thurne Mill, erected in 1836, and Reedham Ferry Mill, which appears to post-date 1840; while many existing mills, erected in the eighteenth and early nineteenth centuries – including High's Mill on Halvergate Fleet, Chedgrave Detached Mill, Stokesby Old Hall Mill, Catfield Middle Marsh Mill and Womack Water Mill in Ludham – remained unmodernised and ended their working lives in the twentieth century still in their manual form.[56] Ashtree Farm Mill was a manually winded mill with cloth sails until it was rebuilt in 1911–12; Belton Black Mill was rebuilt slightly earlier, but remained tailpole winded and with cloth sails.[57]

Scoopwheels and turbine pumps

There were other important innovations in the course of the nineteenth century. Most mills experience some degree of subsidence and this can make them lean away from the scoopwheel side, where the volume of brickwork required for the

---

52   NRO MC 554 16–19, 774X9.
53   WMA Thurne DC Minute book 1820 to 1866.
54   *Norfolk Chronicle*, 7 June 1856. *Norwich Mercury*, 28 May 1859. NRO ACC 2010/243.
55   WMA Hickling Drainage Commission Minutes 1801–74.
56   Reedham Ferry Mill has been significantly 'hained' since first built, yet appears to be absent from the tithe map of 1840, TNA IR 30/23/441. It was provided with patent sails and fantail by Englands in the 1890s, NRO MC 165/13, 628X7. Thurne Mill replaced an earlier mill, shown on the enclosure map. Its construction in 1836, by James Rust of Martham, is recorded in WMA Thurne DC Minute book 1820 to 1866. For the dating evidence for the other mills see above, p. 234.
57   CERC ECE/7/1/37240. Flint, *Suffolk windmills*, pp. 94–5. Flint gives a date of *c.*1910 for its rebuilding but Wailes, 'Norfolk windmills', p. 175 says 1907.

scoopwheel channel provided additional structural support. Internal scoopwheels, placed centrally within the mill and with the water entering and leaving via low arched openings, were probably an attempt to deal with this problem. Most Broadland examples can be connected with the Norwich millwright and engineer William Thorold. What we now know as Mutton's Mill was probably built by him some time around 1833 as part of a wider reorganisation of drainage in the area lying to the north of the Halvergate Fleet in Halvergate parish: in 1833 the materials from what seems to have been the former mill here were being offered for sale, and in 1836 he cited drainage mills in Limpenhoe and Halvergate as examples of his work.[58] The tiny Swim Coots Mill in Catfield, built some time before 1838, is also possibly by him, while Child's Mill in Runham (TG 470 160) was constructed after the Runham Drainage Commission advertised in 1851 for tenders for the erection of a 'tower mill to the Plans and Specifications of Mr Thorold'.[59] Cadge's Mill on Reedham Marshes (TG 446 035) was built to Thorold's specification by Thomas Smithdale and Sons in the early 1870s.[60] All these mills have a more pronounced batter than is usual, caused by the large diameter base required to house the scoopwheel.

Three mills are known to have been built with two external scoopwheels, one at either side of the tower, which was presumably another way of addressing the problem. The earliest was the Coldharbour Mill at Ludham of *c.*1840 (TG 397 169, now demolished), the builder of which is unknown. Hunsett Mill, beside the river Ant in Stalham (TG 364 237), was built in 1860 by William Rust, the Stalham millwright, to replace an earlier mill on the site. Turf Fen Mill, a few kilometres downstream in Irstead (TG 369 188), was also built by Rust and is very similar and so presumably similar in date (Figure 5.13). The surviving machinery at Turf Fen gave the option of using one or both scoopwheels, with high and low gears also offering two different speeds. Why these varied modes of operation, which would have added to the costs of the mill, were provided remains unclear. Ingham Marsh Mill (TG 410 263) – formerly a large tower mill, now truncated – is unusual in having had two scoopwheels of differing sizes, both of which appear to have been housed within the mill tower. It was built in 1827–8 by Norwich millwright and engineer Henry Lock, with William Thorold engaged to supervise the completion of the works to specification.[61]

Until around 1870 all Broadland drainage mills (other than some hollow post mills, equipped with plunger pumps) drove one or more scoopwheels, but over the next four decades a number were fitted with centrifugal impellor pumps,

---

58   *Norfolk Chronicle*, 20 October 1832. *Norwich Mercury*, 15 June 1833. *Norfolk Chronicle*, 28 September 1833. NRO MC 2525/3, 979X6.
59   *Norfolk Chronicle*, 12 July 1851.
60   *Norwich Mercury*, 19 January 1870. NRO BR 136/2–4.
61   WMA Hempstead Drainage Commission Minutes 1812–1883.

Figure 5.13 Turf Fen Mill, beside the Ant in the parish of Irstead, was built around 1860 by the millwright William Rust. With patent sails and fantail, and around 10 metres in height, it is typical of mid-nineteenth-century Broadland drainage mills but, unusually, drove two external scoop wheels.

Figure 5.14 Hardley Mill on the river Yare, built in 1874, has an internal turbine pump, the water passing through the mill via low arches in the walls (visible bottom left).

more generally known as 'turbines'. These comprised a cylindrical brick or metal casing containing a vertical spindle with a horizontal impeller of curved vanes at the base, sandwiched between two metal plates. Water entered through a hole in the base plate and was then centrifuged by the spinning vanes, causing it to travel upwards and spill out through a non-return door in the side of the casing, passing from there into a higher-level outfall waterlane. A version of such a pump was developed by the engineer and inventor J.C. Appold and exhibited at the Great Exhibition of 1851. Turbines were initially used with steam engines, and first in the Cambridgeshire Fens, where one was installed at Whittlesey Mere as early as 1852, although they never became popular there.[62] The first to operate in the Broads was probably at the new Easton and Amos steam-drainage plant at Beccles in 1857.[63] Another had been installed on the Lessingham House estate at Surlingham by 1860, described when the property was sold in 1866 as the 'Superior Iron Appold Centrifugal Drainage Pump'.[64] Within a few years, however, they were being fitted to windmills. Daniel Chasteney England, of Ludham, fitted one inside the tower of the new Hardley Mill (TG 387 024) in 1874 and the Waxham drainage commissioners called for tenders for the installation of a turbine in Brograve Mill, then known as Bishop's Mill, in 1874 and 1875.[65]

Turbines were often, although not invariably, fitted in mills newly built, or very substantially rebuilt, in the period after 1870, in which case they were often placed within the body of the tower, with the waterlane passing through it via arched openings, as at Lambrigg Mill (c.1873, TG 437 252), Somerton Mill (1898, TG 464 202) or Hardley Mill (1874, Figure 5.14).[66] This was presumably, as with internal scoopwheels, to avoid uneven settlement. But they were more usually added to existing mills, displacing scoopwheels, in which case they were usually placed outside the mill, although occasionally (as at Brograve Level) inside it.

Turbines needed to turn at much higher speeds than scoopwheels, necessitating changes to the lower gearing of the mill. No pitwheel was now needed, but a new, larger crownwheel was installed that meshed instead with a counterwheel small enough to generate the required speed. Where the pump was located beside the mill this meshed with a bevel gear fitted onto a shaft that passed out through the wall to another pair of bevel gears at the top of the turbine housing; where placed internally, the turbine could be driven off a large spur gear that engaged with a very

---

62 K.S.G. Hinde, *Fenland pumping engines* (Bath, 2006), p. 30.
63 Easton and Amos were known collaborators with J.C. Appold. D. Eaton, *Easton and Amos: a brief history of a Victorian engineering company* (Westonzoyland, 2002).
64 *Norfolk News*, 11 August 1866.
65 *Eastern Daily Press*, 15 July 1874. *Norwich Mercury*, 14 August 1875.
66 Hardley Mill has a datestone. For Somerton, see NRO DB2/14–19. The present Lambridge Mill must have been built around 1872, when its predecessor's machinery was being offered for use in repair of the other Waxham mill. *Norwich Mercury*, 29 June 1872.

small gear ('mortice pinion') in place of a bevelled crownwheel, thereby requiring one less pair of gears (another reason, perhaps, for adopting such an arrangement). Surviving drawings and correspondence relating to Somerton Mill show that Daniel England designed four different methods of gearing internal turbines and claimed to have all versions at work in the Broads in the 1890s.[67] His firm, based in Ludham, and the Norwich firms Smithdale's and Holmes and Sons all developed their own versions of the turbine. Most of those installed in windmills were, however, the work of England's firm; those produced by Smithdale's and Holmes's were generally used in conjunction with steam and internal combustion engines, and even in a few cases early electric motors.

Only a minority of drainage windmills came to be fitted with turbines, most of them located in the northern parts of Broadland, the area in which England's of Ludham was the dominant millwrighting business, and on the Langley estate on the river Yare. On Halvergate and Haddiscoe Island, where the Yarmouth and Reedham millwrights worked, they were largely absent, although Richard Barnes of Southtown Ironworks built Stracey Arms Mill with a turbine in 1883 and may have fitted that in nearby Perry's Mill in Runham around the same time. Turbines were not necessarily superior to scoopwheels. They could achieve greater lifts and performed well at low water levels because their vanes were always set below the surface; they were also less susceptible to windfrost damage. But scoopwheels performed better in gusty winds and where a lot of water needed to be moved, and they were much easier to maintain.[68] As late as 1932 Daniel England stated that he was not averse to the use of scoopwheels, especially if well-fitted in culverts, and claimed to have recently installed a number of examples.[69] In 1912 the mill at Ashtree Farm on the Bure, the last to be comprehensively rebuilt in Broadland, was fitted with one.

The diversity of later mills

There were other ways in which Broadland mills displayed significant levels of structural and technological diversity in the middle and later decades of the nineteenth century, in addition to the adoption or non-adoption of patent sails, fantails and turbines. We noted earlier that mills fitted with patent sails needed to be taller than those with common sails because the former, being heavier and more prone to leak the wind, needed to be longer than the latter to provide the same amount of power. Mills that were certainly, or probably, built before 1830 were usually less than eight metres in height to the curb. Most built after this date were

---

67   NRO DB2/16.
68   A.J. Ward, 'The wind and the water', unpublished typescript, copy held by Norfolk Windmills Trust, Norwich, p. 46. R. Hills, *Power from wind: a history of windmill technology* (Cambridge, 1994), pp. 162–3.
69   Unpublished notes of an interview with Dan England, 1932, by H.O. Clark, Mills Archive, Reading, REXW-11856, H.O. Clark, 'Notebook on Norfolk drainage windmills'.

Figure 5.15 Berney Arms Mill, the tallest in Broadland, also drove machinery for the adjacent cement works.

taller. The majority – such as Limpenhoe Marshes (*c*.1832, TG 395 019); Mutton's Mill in Halvergate (*c*.1833); Burgh St Margaret Mill (1840s, TG 418 119); Dilham Dyke Mill, Smallburgh (1847, TG 344 248); Runham Child's Mill (early 1850s); Hunsett Mill (1860); Turf Fen Mill (*c*.1860); Cadge's Mill in Reedham (1870s); Stracey Arms Mill (1883) – were between 9 and 11 metres to the curb, also the height to which the majority of earlier mills were 'hained' when modernised.[70] But a small number are noticeably taller: Runham Five Mile House (1849, TG 478 098), which stands over 12 metres to the curb; Hardley Marshes Mill (1874), over 13 metres; and Berney Arms Mill (1865), which has a total height of 22 metres (Figure 5.15).[71] The size of Hardley Marshes Mill may reflect the flamboyant extravagance of its aristocratic owners, the Beauchamp-Proctors of Langley Hall. Berney Arms had particularly large sails, around 3 metres wide, perhaps because it powered a particularly large (7.3-metre diameter) scoopwheel and drained a particularly extensive area of marsh – around 2.7 square kilometres. But other mills draining very extensive areas, such as Cadge's or Lockgate Farm by Breydon Water, also carried such sails yet were of normal height. Berney's unusual stature probably reflects the need to accommodate a range of industrial machinery, for as well as serving as a drainage mill it also functioned as part of the adjacent cement works. It is noteworthy that the only pre-1830 mill taller than 9 metres to the curb – the anomalous Benet's Abbey Mill, built into the medieval gatehouse – likewise also drove industrial machinery. Conversely, a few brick tower mills well below the average height were also erected. That standing just to the north of Ludham Bridge on the river Ant (TG 372 172), for example, 6 metres to the curb, was constructed in 1877.[72]

The middle and later decades of the nineteenth century also saw the installation of various kinds of small, cheap wooden mill, mainly by private landowners, where only small areas needed to be drained. Small smock mills were still sometimes built. A short-lived example, known as the Butterfly Mill, draining 68 acres (*c*.28 hectares) owned by the Lowestoft Improvement Commissioners, was built by Reedham millwright James Barnes in 1869 on the south side of the Halvergate Fleet in Wickhampton parish (TG 450 063). The tenant had given up the marshes in 1866, claiming that the two existing pump mills were not of sufficient power to drain the marshes properly and water was destroying the grass. The new 'smock timber water mill' was erected soon after these had been toppled by gales.[73] Another example

---

[70] *Norwich Mercury*, 19 January 1870. NRO BR 136/2–4. The Dilham date is etched into a brick near the entrance door. Smith, *Drainage windmills*, p. 59. For the others see above, pp. 251–3, 256.

[71] Runham Five Mile House Mill has a datestone. For Berney Arms see Apling, *Norfolk corn and other industrial windmills*, pp. 42–5.

[72] The Ludham Bridge mill is dated from a lost Ludham Drainage Commission minute book accessed by A.J. Ward: A.J. Ward Archive, held by Norfolk Windmills Trust, Norwich.

[73] *Ipswich Journal*, 13 March 1869. *Norfolk News*, 10 July 1869.

Figure 5.16 Boardman's Mill, beside the Ant at How Hill in Ludham, is one of only three 'skeleton' or 'trestle' mills surviving in Broadland.

was built at North Cove in 1869–70 by the new estate owner, perhaps because of the ready availability of timber on the property, although extracting it from one of the carr woodlands led to a legal action by the shooting tenant.[74] Others were built at Horning Ferry, some time between 1882 and 1891, at the request of the landlord of the Ferry Inn;[75] and on Tunstall Dyke (TG 422 092), probably around 1897 when Daniel England referred in a letter to the installation of a new turbine pump somewhere in Tunstall.[76] Its truncated remains still survive; the Horning Ferry mill survives in part within a 1930s residential conversion; the others have vanished.

Hollow post mills also continued to be erected in some numbers throughout the nineteenth century – the two surviving examples, Palmer's and Clayrack, both probably post-date c.1870. But they were now joined by 'trestle' mills, also confusingly described as 'skeleton' mills but a new type mainly associated with, and probably developed by, England's of Ludham. These were towers of open wooden framing, surmounted by a cap with fantail and vaned sails – essentially, a low-cost, diminutive version of a tower mill (Figure 5.16). They drove either scoopwheels or turbines and were used to drain relatively small areas of between 100 and 150 acres (c.40–60 hectares). Only three examples survive, as mills of this type usually deteriorated

---

74 *Bury Free Press*, 2 December 1871.
75 The mill is not shown on the 1882 Ordnance Survey map but a photograph of it does appear in John Payne Jennings' *Sun Pictures* of 1891.
76 NRO MC 165/13, 628X7.

rapidly once they became redundant, leaving at most only the scant remains of their bases, comprising four piers of brick: while we know the sites of at least a dozen examples, they probably account for several others among the numerous 'draining pumps' marked on the early 6-inch Ordnance Survey maps, but which have since vanished, although the majority of these were probably hollow post mills. Trestle mills were a particular feature of the northern parts of Broadland, where they seem often to have replaced small smock mills. They first appeared in the 1870s and new examples continued to be built into the twentieth century: one at Barton Common was built c.1906, replacing the smock mill erected by the drainage commissioners following the enclosure of 1810; Hobbs Mill in Horning (TG 347 163) was built the year after the 1912 floods; while St Olaves Mill (TG 456 997) dates from 1915.[77] Both of the latter mills survive, have parts cast from the same patterns and boast identical, simple, flat-sided caps. But St Olaves was less solidly built. Its skeleton framework was subsequently boarded over to stiffen it and the brick piers encased in concrete to enlarge them. The only other remaining example is Boardman's Mill, beside the Ant at How Hill (TG 370 192), erected in 1897 and again the work of England's of Ludham (Figure 5.16).[78] Not all mills of this general type were made by them. A six-sided steel skeleton mill thought to have been built by Smithdale's stood on the Caister Marshes, while an example with a distinctive, rather elongated cap and six-bladed fantail that stood near Long's Corner at Rockland Broad likewise appears to have been the work of another firm.[79]

Living and working with mills

The Broadland mills were built, modified and maintained by a number of local millwrighting and engineering firms, most of which have been mentioned over the course of the previous pages.[80] In the early part of the nineteenth century Norwich millwrights clearly played a significant role in the area. They included Nathaniel Lock of Norwich, who built the smock mill at Neatishead in 1811; Henry Lock, his son, who built Ingham Mill in 1827–8; and William Thorold, noted, as we have seen, for his use of internal scoopwheels. Yarmouth millwrights were also prominent, including Thomas Norton, who built the two mills at Ludham following the

---

[77] In 1903 the old mill at Barton was stated to be 'on its last legs' and means were to be taken for its repair or replacement. By 1906 the Norwich Corporation, as owners of the Berry Hall estate, had it taken down and a new one erected. *Eastern Daily Press*, 4 April 1903 and 17 August 1906. A decision to build Hobbs Mill, Horning, in 1913 is recorded in the Church Commissioners estate management files, CERC ECE/7/1/32731. St Olaves Mill replaced a smock mill taken down in 1898 after a period of lapsed drainage. The construction of the new mill was photographed by Annie Grant of The Priory, St Olaves, NRO MS 21477/21.

[78] The drawings for the 'How Hill Skeleton mill' survive, NRO ACC 2011/10.

[79] Wailes, 'Norfolk windmills', p. 175. Yardy, 'Development of the Broadland drainage windmills', p. 84.

[80] Wailes, 'Norfolk windmills'. M. Fewster, 'Thomas Smithdale and Sons: a study of a Victorian ironfounder', *Journal of the Norfolk Industrial Archaeology Society*, 3/1 (1981), pp. 25–33. Yardy, 'Development of Broadland drainage mills'.

parliamentary enclosure in 1800, and they continued to be important during the Victorian period, when most Broadland mills were built or modernised, with the Stolworthy family, Richard Barnes of Southtown Ironworks and W.T. England all building and maintaining, in particular, mills on the Halvergate Marshes. Another Barnes family of millwrights was based in Reedham, and different branches of the Rust family operated independently from Martham and Stalham. Thomas Smithdale started in Norwich, then worked also in Panxworth from 1869, before relocating to Acle in 1889. The England family based at Ludham were related to but professionally unconnected with the Yarmouth England and, like most of these firms, continued to trade over several generations.

There are differences, some subtle and others less so, between the work styles and choices of these various firms. England's of Ludham favoured fantails with ten blades, for example, while Rust's usually fitted six and Smithdale's and the Yarmouth millwrights preferred eight; there were different ways of constructing scoopwheels and managing how the cap rotated on the curb. The most important of these firms was probably England's of Ludham, who dominated the trade in the northern parts of Broadland. They claimed to have pioneered the use of patent sails and developed the distinctive boat-shaped cap that, by the mid-nineteenth century, had become universal in the eastern areas of East Anglia, for corn mills as much as drainage mills. They fitted turbine pumps to mills more often than the other firms and, in the late nineteenth century, Daniel England appears to have developed the skeleton tower mill.[81]

As already intimated, some of the brick tower drainage mills had other uses. The St Benet's Abbey mill, built into the gatehouse of the monastery, is one example. Anthony Norris, writing around 1782, described how, shortly after 1722, 'the Gate Way was converted into a mill, to serve the double purpose of dreyning the Fens and grinding cole seed for oil; the necessary alterations and buildings made on that occasion has totally disfigured and obscured this building'.[82] The Ludham parish registers include a series of entries referring to an 'Oylman of St Benet's' in the period between 1725 and 1735, and an elevation included on an estate map of 1731 shows the mill with a long industrial building, complete with cowl chimneys, attached to it.[83] Berney Arms Mill was originally built in the 1860s, for both drainage and grinding cement clinker; only from 1883 was it used for drainage alone.[84] The mill it replaced had similarly served more than one function, being described in 1836 as a powerful patent sail mill that worked with a 10-hp steam engine to drive a saw mill

---

81   Yardy, 'Development of Broadland drainage windmills', pp. 54–65.
82   A. Norris, 'An History of the Hundreds of East and West Flegg, Happing, Tunsted, and Part of North Erpingham', c.1782, unpublished ms., NRO RYE 3.
83   NRO PD 653/2. NRO HNR 15/5.
84   Apling, *Norfolk corn and other industrial windmills*, pp. 42–5.

and cement-works machinery, as well as serving to drain the marshes.[85] Perhaps less surprisingly, a number were also used to grind corn. That standing just to the west of Wayford Bridge briefly doubled as a corn mill. The Knights family were recorded as millers there in trade directories between 1850 and 1863,[86] and some of the milling apparatus remained *in situ* into the 1940s.[87] Sales particulars for the Horsey estate, drawn up in 1863, tell us that one of the two drainage mills adjoining Horsey Mere was fitted with millstones.[88] So, too, was the tiny Swim Coots Mill beside Hickling Broad, according to Rex Wailes, although they were perhaps used only occasionally, to grind animal feed (if the report is correct: in both 1847 and 1866 it was described in sales particulars simply as a 'brick tower marsh mill').[89]

Unlike some of the larger Fenland mills, the Broadland mills were not generally lived in and the individual charged with looking after one was usually accommodated in an associated cottage or nearby marsh farm. But there were some exceptions. Stubb Mill and Eastfield Mill in Hickling, large mills built with plenty of windows, had their pitwheels partitioned off and Stubb Mill still boasts a large fireplace on the first floor where the remains of partitions and cupboards can also be seen. Until recently Clippesby Mill contained the remains of rush-plastered ceilings, stairs with full-size treads let into the wall and recesses that probably accommodated bunks.[90] All three of these mills seem to have been permanently occupied by a millman and his family but elsewhere there was, at most, only an attempt to provide some basic comfort for when the mills were being worked at night. Many of the earlier mills, including High's Mill on the Halvergate Fleet, Polkey's Mill in Reedham, Middle Marsh Mill in Catfield and Chedgrave Detached Mill on Haddiscoe Island contain a small fireplace, although even this may have been mainly to prevent the damage that frost might cause to machinery, especially to wooden cogs in the headwheel or pitwheel (it is noteworthy that Cadge's Mill on the Reedham Marshes, with its internal scoopwheel, has two fireplaces, perhaps because the through-draft created by the internal waterlane made frost damage more of a problem). Horsey Mill, built in 1912, contains a small wooden cubicle or millman's cabin, a feature clearly retained from the earlier mill, where Suffling in 1892 noted 'the arrangements for sleeping that the mill-tender has made for himself; quaint to a degree'.[91] In 1840 the Somerton millman was supplied with a

---

85 *Norfolk Chronicle*, 13 August 1836.
86 E. Hunt and Co., *Hunt's directory of east Norfolk with part of Suffolk* (London, 1850). J.G. Harrod and Co., *Harrod's directory of Norfolk and Norwich including Lowestoft* (London, 1863).
87 A.J. Ward Archive held by Norfolk Windmills Trust, Norwich. Wailes, *English windmills*, p. 81.
88 British Library, 137.a.12,(3).
89 NRO MC 527/27, 761X2. *Norfolk News*, 7 July 1866.
90 Vincent Pargeter cited in Smith, *Drainage mills of the Norfolk marshes*, pp. 17–18.
91 Ernest R. Suffling caption to image in J.P. Jennings, *Sun pictures of the Norfolk Broads*, 2nd edn (Ashstead, 1892), p. 47.

box to sleep in which was deemed 'necessary whilst working the mill at night'.[92] Similarly, in 1843 the Potter Heigham drainage commissioners ordered that 'a box or place of shelter be made for the millman'.[93]

The lives of marshmen and millmen were lonely ones and drainage mills, especially ruined ones in remote locations, are lonely and evocative places. Not surprisingly, a number have attracted folk stories. Several are said to be haunted by millmen killed or injured in accidents with internal machinery; Dydall's Mill in Hoveton is said to be haunted by the ghost of a millman's daughter, killed by the sails. Brograve Level Mill leans because the Devil, annoyed by attempts to drain the land, tried to blow it down. Mill names, while sometimes mundane references to the administrative geography of drainage, can also have a certain romantic quality, commemorating past owners or operators – High's, Mutton's, Polkey's, to name only three. Since the nineteenth century, as we have seen, artists have been drawn to them, writers have described their picturesque qualities. Dramatic landmarks in this level landscape, especially in the open expanses of the Halvergate Marshes, drainage mills have acquired a significance well beyond the practical purposes for which they were built.

Drainage by steam

In a landscape so closely associated with windmills the contribution of steam drainage is easily overlooked, not least because the remains of steam installations have not survived well. No engines have been preserved *in situ* in Broadland – they were systematically scrapped as they became redundant – and there are only two examples of engine houses, at Strumpshaw (TG 340 057) and on the Wheatacre Marshes (TG 477 959) that still retain full-height chimneys, with a third, at Seven Mile House in Reedham (TG 444 035), surviving in truncated form (Figures 5.17 and 5.18). Steam drainage never came to dominate in Broadland as it did in the Fenlands of western East Anglia, where wind drainage had effectively been abandoned by the late nineteenth century. But it was deployed in a variety of ways at around 70 locations and played an important part in marsh drainage.

The earliest known steam-drainage engine in Broadland was installed by Benjamin Heath Baker of Acle Hall on the Scaregap Marshes near Great Yarmouth, where the 1838 Acle tithe map marks a 'Steam Engine'.[94] Its builder is unknown, but a number of other early sites were associated with William Thorold, the notable Norwich-based millwright, iron founder and engineer already mentioned in connection with internal scoopwheels. In 1841 he advertised that

---

92 WMA Winterton and East & West Somerton Drainage Commission Minutes 1812–1860. NRO ACC 2010/243.
93 NRO ACC 2010/243.
94 NRO/BR 276/1/1131.

Figure 5.17 The steam-engine house at Strumpshaw was built by Smithdales for the Strumpshaw estate in 1882 in expensive white brick and features decorative cast-iron windows, tie plates and chimney top.

Figure 5.18 Polkey's Mill and steam-engine house, Reedham Marshes. Typically, wind and steam worked together: the steam-engine house dates from 1880 and until the 1960s contained a steam engine built by Richard Barnes of Southtown Ironworks; the mill was extensively modernised in the 1890s.

he was installing a 16-hp 'Drainage Engine' for Sir W. Beauchamp-Proctor on the Langley Park estate, and that he had already provided a similar engine for R. Hanbury Gurney the previous year.[95] The latter replaced a windmill on the Wheatacre Marshes (Thorold advertised for sale 'the materials of a windmill lately used for drainage, in consequence of a steam engine being about to be erected' in September 1839).[96] He also supplied a steam engine at Cantley in the 1840s, part of a scheme to drain both the marshes there and the new railway line.[97] It is shown on a map of the Yare Navigation drawn up in 1847, together with two on the nearby Langley estate marshes.[98] Confusingly, an earlier map of the Yare Navigation of 1845 fails to mark any of these sites, but the accompanying schedule does record an engine at Reedham, owned by the Rev. Emmett (TG 4474 0363).[99] It did not last long, 1879 sale particulars referring to the foundations of buildings 'formerly used for a Steam Engine'.[100] These remains were finally lost when the riverbank was rolled back as part of the Broadland Flood Alleviation Project in 2003.[101]

Several other steam-drainage schemes were initiated in the 1840s. White's *Directory* of 1845 refers to the Caister Marshes 'for the better draining of which a steam-engine was erected in 1841', while part of the Yarmouth Southtown Marshes, owned by Lord Anson, were steam-drained from 1843.[102] When the Hilborough estate in Stokesby was put up for sale in 1852, special mention was made of the

> Steam Drainage Mill ... built in 1844 in the most substantial manner, no expense having been spared in the Mill-house or Machinery. The Steam Engine is capable of draining a thousand acres; the boiler was purchased in 1850 of Pontifex and Wood, Farringdon Works, London, and erected under their direction.[103]

There may have been another early example on the Claxton marshes. Richard Lubbock, lamenting the loss of land suitable for snipe-shooting grounds in 1847, described how the land there had been rendered 'as dry as Arabia' as a consequence of steam drainage.[104]

---

95 *Cambridge Chronicle and Journal*, 22 May 1841.
96 *Bury and Norwich Post*, 18 September 1839.
97 *Eastern Daily Press*, 22 July 1899.
98 NRO/C/Scf 1/454.
99 NRO C/Scf 1/455.
100 NRO MC 527/47, 761X2.
101 A. Yardy, *Mills of the Halvergate Marshes: Reedham Marshes and Ashtree Farm* (Norwich, 2008), p. 34.
102 White, *Directory of Norfolk*, p. 294. *Norwich Mercury*, 9 October 1880.
103 *Norfolk Chronicle*, 7 August 1852.
104 T. Southwell, 'Introduction', in R. Lubbock, *Observations on the fauna of Norfolk, and more particularly on the district of the Broads*, revised edn (Norwich, 1879), p. iii.

All these early steam engines were installed by private owners, often those of quite extensive estates. Drainage Commissions seem, at least initially, to have been less interested in the new technology. In 1846 the Runham drainage commissioners built a new steam-engine house, having invited tenders for repairing their existing mill or 'for erecting an engine to be driven by steam or wind, of sufficient power effectually to drive a waterwheel of not less than 18 feet diameter with scoops 15 inches wide'.[105] In 1848 the Winterton and Somerton Drainage Commission engaged Norwich millwrights Howard and Gaze to supply a steam engine to act as auxiliary to their windmill.[106] But these were unusual cases, and the proposals made in 1844 for uniting Martham, Thurne, Repps and Oby 'in one general Steam Drainage' came to nothing.[107]

By 1850 there were perhaps a dozen steam-drainage engines at work in the Broads. Most were beam engines – that is, relatively simple devices in which a pivoted overhead beam was used to apply the force from a vertical piston to a vertical connecting rod; a flywheel converted this up-and-down motion into a rotational movement on a crankshaft, ultimately powering the scoopwheel. When the Winterton and Somerton engine was put up for sale in 1867, however, it was described as an 8-hp 'frame engine'.[108] This type likewise had a simple, vertical cylinder but it drove an overhead crankshaft supported by two A-shaped frames.

The 1850s and 1860s saw a significant expansion of steam drainage, especially on the Suffolk side of the Waveney, upstream of Oulton, something that explains the reduction in the number of drainage windmills there which, as we have already noted, occurred between c.1840 and c.1885. In 1852–3 a steam engine was built in Carlton Share Marshes (TG 493 927) – the second on the river Waveney – to drain the new 'Oulton Level' created by uniting three contiguous levels (Carlton, Barnby and Oulton) formerly drained by wind.[109] A survey of the river Waveney made in 1854 confirms that this and the engine at Wheatacre were the only examples in place in the valley at that date.[110] But in 1857, after much local opposition, it was agreed to erect a steam mill on Beccles Fen (TG 437 927). George Fenn, the town surveyor, who had campaigned for the scheme for nine years, declared in a speech given at the launch of the new engine that windmills were 'sources of the greatest annoyance and disappointment, at the moment you require their services they are utterly helpless. But steam, mighty

---

105 *Ipswich Journal*, 6 June 1846.
106 WMA Winterton and Somerton Drainage Commission minutes 1812–1860.
107 *Norfolk Chronicle*, 26 October 1844.
108 *Norfolk News*, 18 May 1867.
109 *Norfolk Chronicle*, 21 August 1852.
110 NRO Y/PH/1803. *Norfolk Chronicle*, 21 August 1852.

steam, will effect such a revolution in this noble property that the most sanguine amongst us can hardly calculate.'[111]

By 1861 the 800 acres (c.325 hectares) of the Corporation's marshes were reported to have sunk by ten inches as a result of drainage and the company responsible for the engine, Easton and Amos, were back to carry out alterations, adjusting the height of the scoop wheel in line with the new water levels. The engine was, however, considered a success, Fenn claiming that for an outlay of £2,000 the value of the property had been increased by about £10,000.[112] George Fenn was involved in other steam-drainage projects. His name appears in connection with the earlier Carlton Share Level scheme, advertising the redundant windmill on Carlton Marshes for sale, and in 1854 he was involved in plans for a broader scheme of steam drainage in the Waveney valley.[113] He was also surveyor to the board establishing a Haddiscoe-area scheme in the 1860s that joined up several existing levels into one 1,600-acre (c.650-hectare) steam-drained level.[114]

The proliferation of steam-drainage engines through the 1850s and 1860s was accompanied by significant changes in their technology, as slow-running beam engines driving scoopwheels were superseded by more sophisticated engines with horizontal rather than vertical cylinders, capable of the greater speed required to power the new centrifugal impellor pumps, or by other more modern types. Easton and Amos's distinctive overhead-crank 'grasshopper' engines, popular in the Somerset Levels, were installed at Somerton, Haddiscoe and Beccles, the latter with the Appold turbine pump constructed as an integral part of the engine frame. A local variant of the type, made by Holmes of Norwich, was established at the Waxham Lambridge site (TG 431 251), where it worked in partnership with a windmill.[115] In addition, Smithdale's developed a small single-cylinder vertical engine with a curved framework, known as a 'humpback vertical'.[116] One example was installed in a purpose-built engine house near the windmill at Toft Monks on Haddiscoe island (TG 448 009) and another was housed within the tower of the still-functioning Stokesby Commission Mill (TG 422 104), with the boiler placed in a corrugated-iron shed adjoining.[117] But, alongside these new forms, some beam engines continued to be installed. Halvergate Steam Mill (TG 426 069), a small beam engine, was established on the former wet common to the west of Halvergate

---

111 *Norwich Mercury*, 14 November 1857. E.A. Goodwyn, *A Suffolk town in mid-Victorian England* (Beccles, 1965), pp. 52–3.
112 *Ipswich Journal*, 19 April 1862.
113 *Norfolk News*, 30 July 1853.
114 NRO DCN 54/9.
115 R.H. Clark, 'Early engines of the Eastern counties', *English Mechanics*, 20 November 1936, p. 137.
116 R.H. Clark, *The steam engine builders of Norfolk* (Yeovil, 1988), pp. 203–4.
117 R.H. Clark 'Early engines of the Eastern counties', *English Mechanics*, 23 October 1936, p. 40.

Marshes in 1861 and was used for grinding animal feed as well as for drainage; adding to its unusual qualities, the waterwheel was also used to fill a brick-lined sheep dip.[118] Another example was installed at Ingham as late as 1872 (TG 410 264), acquired secondhand from the Grout and Co. silk factory in Norwich.[119]

After the 1860s fewer new engines were installed but a number of early examples were replaced with more modern types. The brickwork of the engine house on the Upton Marshes (TG 405 141), latterly fitted with a turbine, still shows the scar of the former scoopwheel housing. In 1882 the beam engine and scoopwheel 'of the old type' and the chimney which had long been leaning at an alarming angle on the Wheatacre Marshes were replaced by a new compound horizontal engine and turbine fitted by Holmes of Norwich.[120] The derelict remains of this installation, most notably the fine octagonal chimney, survive today. Early beam engines on the Southtown marshes and at Langley were also replaced in the 1880s and that at Cantley in 1899.[121]

In all there were probably more than 30 areas in Broadland, of varying extent, at some time drained by steam engines placed in purpose-built engine houses, either alone or in association with windmills. A significant number were the work of Smithdale's. The engine house façade facing the river was often constructed of high-quality white brick, with decorative ironwork, as at Strumpshaw. In the case of Herringby (TG 447 100), the building was also finished with decorative crow-stepped gables. But many surviving engine houses, reflecting more limited budgets or the caution of drainage commissioners, are more rudimentary affairs. Castle Mill in North Cove (TM 479921) lacks any decorative features and combines walls made of local brick with a roof of corrugated iron. The engine house at Boyce's Dyke, Norton Subcourse (TG 401 008), was formed from a truncated windmill tower with a corrugated-iron extension. Part of the reason that the surviving evidence for steam drainage is so poor is that engines were frequently housed in lightweight timber and corrugated-iron engine houses that have now vanished.

Figure 5.10, based on the evidence of the 1880s first edition 25-inch Ordnance Survey maps, underplays the extent of the land drained by steam in Broadland. This is partly because we have mapped only those examples of engine houses that stood alone, unaccompanied by windmills with which the work of drainage might still, as in the case of the Lambridge site, be shared. But it is also because, in addition to places drained by steam engines housed in engine houses, there were many where portable wheeled steam engines were employed as a cheaper option, brought in

---

118 NRO MC 14/9 388X3. R.H. Clark 'Early engines of the Eastern counties', *English Mechanics*, 24 April 1936, p. 41.
119 WMA Hempstead Drainage Commission minutes 1812–1883. R.H. Clark, 'Early Engines of the Eastern Counties', *English Mechanics*, 31 July 1936, p. 371.
120 *Norwich Mercury*, 16 September 1882.
121 *Norwich Mercury*, 9 October 1880. *Eastern Daily Press*, 22 July 1899.

when there was insufficient wind to power windmills or when additional capacity was required. These could be hauled into place and, with drainage being seasonal, could theoretically be moved and used for other purposes at other times of the year. Such engines were certainly in use by the 1850s – one made by Norwich firm Riches & Watts was installed on the Limpenhoe Marshes in 1855.[122] They could be used to drive pumps and scoopwheels directly, as on the Dean and Chapter properties on Skeetholme in 1889, where one part of the marshes was 'at present drained by a scoop wheel in connection with a portable engine'.[123] Alternatively, a portable engine could be connected to a mill's lower gearing via a bevel gear (windmills usually had provision to disengage the crownwheel and pitwheel gear and in doing so disconnect the wind drive, which allowed this to take place). Pulley wheels attached to mill towers (as at Hunsett Mill in Stalham and Stubb Mill in Hickling) are evidence of such arrangements, showing that power was transmitted from portable engines standing outside.

It is important to emphasise that steam engines, whether portable or stationary, usually worked alongside windmills; steam engines working alone were mainly used by private landowners to drain small areas of land, except in parts of the Waveney valley, where entire levels came to be drained by them. Most fixed engines were located beside windmills and, even where they were not, the work of drainage was usually shared. A report on the drainage of the marshes in Horning, carried out in 1876 for the Church Commissioners by William Rich of Easton's, thus described the use of five windmills and one fixed steam installation, with the work of the former being supplemented with portable steam engines hired in as required.[124] Many areas, large and small, continued to be drained by wind alone, especially where mills lay at a distance from good roads and navigable rivers (as on parts of the Halvergate Marshes), making the movement of coal problematic. Steam-engine plants were expensive to build and to run; they increased land values, but also raised drainage rates.

There was thus no simple, inexorable progression from wind to steam. As early as 1851, only four years after having a new steam-engine house erected, the Runham Drainage Commission was advertising for a new windmill to be built, to the plans and specification of William Thorold, albeit one 'to which auxiliary power could be applied'.[125] At Martham, the Drainage Commission decided to build a new windmill as late as 1908, despite having operated steam since the 1850s. This led to local protests, and a petition signed by 39 out of 50 ratepayers was forwarded to Mr R.J. Price MP for presentation to the Board of Agriculture.

---

122 Testimonial in *Illustrated catalogue, Howard, Riches and Watts, Engineers, Millwrights, Iron and Brass Founders and General Machinists, Duke's Palace Iron Works, Norwich*, 1859, private collection.
123 NRO DCN 59/15.
124 CERC ECE/7/1/32731.
125 *Norfolk Chronicle*, 12 July 1851.

As a result, the site originally selected on the staithe had to be filled in and a new one, acquired from one of the drainage commissioners, used instead.[126] At nearby Somerton the steam engine installed in 1848 was replaced in 1866 with an Easton and Amos grasshopper unit with turbine pump. Despite this, by 1886 the erection of a new windmill was being discussed by the drainage commissioners, and in 1896 the millwrights Smithdale's were asked to 'form some conclusion as to the cost of Wind Power to be applied to [the] existing steam mill at the same place'.[127] In 1899 the foundations for the new mill were dug and in 1900 the mill, a tall brick tower, was connected to the steam engine's main dyke. Both mill and engine were then used together until they were replaced by an electric pump in the 1930s.

The cost of building, maintaining and operating a steam engine and engine house, compared with that of a drainage windmill, was clearly the key factor in such decisions, especially as agriculture moved into depression from the late 1870s, with livestock prices falling significantly from the 1890s. The correspondence associated with the tenders for the Somerton mill shows that the drainage commissioners carefully reviewed the previous five years' running costs of the mill, described as being 40 years old, and agreed to borrow the money needed to build a new mill only when they had satisfied themselves that it should not need any major repairs for around 20 years.[128] In 1873 the Burgh and Billockby drainage commissioners met to determine 'Whether it would be expedient that Steam drainage should be carried out in connection with the existing Drainage … inasmuch as the present drainage by means of the existing mill is inadequate'. Tenders were put out for a steam engine and turbine pump, but when the bids came in at between £878 and £1007 the plan was dropped, and instead the millwright Daniel Rust was instructed to provide an estimate for the 'cost of a new wheel of 3 feet increased diameter and to raise the laying shaft 6 inches, and also to give an estimate for constructing a rigger to turn such Wheel by means of a portable engine'.[129] Steam engines could be much more expensive than this. That installed at Beccles in 1857 cost around £2,000, while the Haddiscoe, Thorpe and Aldeby Drainage Board spent £2,534 on a steam engine and its housing in 1869.[130] In comparison, the surviving tenders submitted for building the smart new mill constructed at West Somerton in 1895 range from £900 to a little over £1000.[131]

Steam engines required fuel in a way that a windmill did not, as well as skilled operatives and almost continuous attention when working. Robert Stone, the

---

126 *Norfolk News*, 2 May 1908.
127 NRO DB 2/16.
128 NRO DB 2/14–19.
129 NRO MC 554/19, 774X9.
130 NRO PD 208/83. *Ipswich Journal*, 19 April 1862.
131 NRO DB 2/16.

Figure 5.19 A mixture of drainage technologies captured in an undated late-nineteenth-century photograph by William Henry Finch. In the foreground is Calthorpe Mill in Acle, still tailpole-winded and equipped with common sails. Behind it stands Calthorpe Steam Engine House and beyond this, on the far side of the river Yare, Stokesby Commission Mill has recently been fitted with fantail and patent sails.

operator of South Walsham steam engine (TG 385 151), a Smithdale's horizontal engine, described lighting the fire the night before the engine was to be used, then 'firing her up hard' the next morning. From this point, depending on the weather, it could take anything from two to five hours to get up to the correct steam pressure. It might then take ten hours to clear the level and more if it was raining or snowing. He also referred to the tendency of the engines to get rid of the water 'more quickly than it could come down the dykes'.[132] This meant the dykes immediately around the engine house would be dry while those further away in the level were still full. The turbine would therefore be running with nothing to move. Salt water getting into the boilers was also a frequent problem. Smithdale's were obliged to remove two steam engines from a site at Limpenhoe due to saltwater damage.[133]

But perhaps the most important reason why steam did not take over from wind was simply that, in contrast to the situation in the Fens of western East Anglia, the organisation of drainage in Broadland remained highly fragmented, the individual drainage levels small. Windmills, when in good condition, were therefore usually

---

132 A.J. Ward, 'The wind and the water', unpublished typescript, copy held by Norfolk Windmills Trust, Norwich.
133 Presumably relating to the boilers. NRO HNR 401/2.

adequate for the task required of them, particularly if there was some kind of auxiliary engine available at times when there was no wind or particularly high water levels. The continued use of the land for grazing allowed a higher water table to be maintained than was the case in the largely arable Fenland, while the alluvial clays and silts that characterised most of the drained areas did not contract on drainage to the same extent as the Fenland peat, where water had to be lifted an ever greater height as subsidence progressed. Wind power therefore endured, with steam only one part of the technology mix, until both approaches were superseded by other methods in the first half of the twentieth century (Figure 5.19). The last all-new brick tower mills were Somerton, already described, and Martham, completed in 1908. Both were by England's of Ludham and fitted with internal turbines.[134] Ashtree and Horsey mills are later, dating to 1911–12, but both were rebuilt on existing sites, reusing much of the old machinery; Belton Black Mill was similarly rebuilt with its old gearing, some time around 1907, and even retained its original tailpole-winded form.[135]

Oil, diesel and electricity

Steam engines continued to be used to power pumps and scoopwheels, alone or in combination with windmills, well into the inter-war period – a portable engine at Horsey was replaced by a secondhand Robey steam engine as late as 1926. But they were gradually superseded by internal combustion engines, initially in the form of the 'hot-bulb' paraffin engine. In 1895 the engineers Holmes of Norwich exhibited an example powering one of their turbine pumps at the Norfolk Agricultural Association show, the press account suggesting that it was 'the first time an oil engine has been applied to such a purpose'.[136] The earliest to be deployed in Broadland was probably that manufactured by the Birmingham engineering firm Tangye in 1906, which was used to power the scoopwheel in a former steam-engine house on the Whitlingham/Kirby Bedon parish boundary belonging to the Crown Point estate until 1931.[137] The retention of the scoopwheel here was unusual and necessitated a gear reduction: the speed of oil engines meant they were best suited to work with centrifugal pumps. In the period leading up to the First World War their use gradually increased, with the majority being manufactured by Tangye, or by Richard Hornsby of Grantham in Lincolnshire.

Oil engines were smaller and simpler than steam engines. The buildings to house them could be fairly basic and there was no need for boiler rooms, coal

---

134 Mills Archive, Reading, REXW-11856, H.O. Clark, 'Notebook on Norfolk drainage windmills'.
135 Wailes, 'Norfolk windmills', p. 175.
136 *Eastern Evening News*, 4 July 1895.
137 Letter from H.C. Rowley, City Engineer, to A.J. Ward 24 January 1963. Copy held by Norfolk Windmills Trust, Norwich. Following demolition of the engine house in 1989, the scoopwheel was salvaged and later powered by electricity at the Wind Energy Museum, Repps-with-Bastwick.

storage or problematic chimneys. Several were installed in redundant (sometimes truncated) mill towers or in former steam-engine houses, as at Fishley, where, by 1914, the estate had replaced the old steam engine with a Hornsby patent safety oil engine and turbine pump.[138] Alternatively, they could be housed in lightweight timber and corrugated-iron structures (an advantage on less stable ground), like that which contained the Tangye engine installed beside the Heigham Holmes drainage windmill on the Eelfleet dyke at Potter Heigham in 1913.[139] The mill and engine here continued to work in partnership until the 1940s, and it is clear that oil engines were often used as auxiliary plant to windmills, in much the same way as steam engines had been. In 1907 the Church Commissioners replaced a portable steam engine on their estate in Acle Detached near Great Yarmouth with a 7-bhp oil engine and turbine. This quickly proved inadequate to cope with the drainage requirements; in 1910 it failed to clear the winter flood waters, reducing the value of the summer grazing. It was decided, however, that before the oil engine was replaced the drainage windmill on the property (which had been in use 'time out of mind') should first be rebuilt and modernised. This done, a new 16-bhp engine was installed and the original engine moved to the Church Commissioners' Horning estate, where it replaced an ageing steam engine as auxiliary power for another windmill.[140]

The First World War interrupted the spread of oil engines as many of the firms involved in their production and supply were engaged in war work. In 1915 the Runham Drainage Commission sought a quotation from Walsh and Clark of Guiseley for a Victoria Oil Engine, but could not be supplied because of the war; Smithdale's of Acle were then approached, but said they could not fulfil the order without permission from the Ministry of Munitions. Finally in 1916 a Tangye hot-bulb paraffin engine was installed inside Runham mill tower, which allowed the mill's internal scoopwheel to run when there was insufficient wind: a half-glazed entrance door was installed to provide light for working the engine.[141] Landowners elsewhere managed to get engines installed in spite of the war. In 1915 C.A. Fellowes instructed his agent to accept the quotation from Smithdale's for installing an oil engine beside his drainage windmill in the detached part of Mautby, south of the river Bure, believing that the improved drainage would increase the value of the marshes and was necessary 'now that the bar at the mouth of the river had been dredged away'. He insisted on an engine house of brick and slate, rather than the timber and corrugated-iron structure proposed by Smithdale's. When the property was sold in

---

138 NRO MC 14/67, 388X5. The 1914 sale particulars describe this as 'practically new'.
139 R.H. Clark, unpublished report for East Norfolk Rivers and Catchment Board, 1941. Private collection.
140 CERC ECE/7/1/37240 Acle Estate files. NRO MC 14/190, 388X8. The 1923 Horning Hall estate sale particulars describe this installation as a 7-hp oil engine by Tangye.
141 Wailes states that the engine was manufactured by Tangye ('Norfolk windmills', p. 167), but the Drainage Board Minutes do not specify the make: WMA, Runham DB Minutes, 1889–1936.

1917 the particulars boasted of the 'Excellent Drainage Plant comprising Brick and Slated Engine House with 20-h.p. Hornsby's Horizontal Oil Engine and "Smithdale" Turbine Pump with the necessary Tanks and Fittings, erected new in August 1915'.[142]

After the war a wide range of manufacturers began to supply oil engines for drainage in Broadland, including Crossley, Blackstone, Worthington and Torbinia. As in the Fenland of western East Anglia, however, most were made by the firm of Ruston & Hornsby, for whom Smithdale's of Acle acted as local agents.[143] In 1919 they installed a Ruston & Hornsby engine for the Yarmouth brewers Lacon and Son, the new owners of the Mautby estate, across the river from the site just described, after the windmill there (which had worked alongside a steam engine) was struck by lightning. Through the 1920s they provided numerous others, including examples at Claxton (in a former steam-engine house); at Limpenhoe (upgrading an earlier oil engine, after the windmill it had worked with suffered storm damage); at Ludham Bridge (in place of an auxillary steam engine); and on the Carlton Marshes (replacing a steam engine).[144]

While windmills continued, often with the help of oil engines, to play a role in drainage, their importance was now waning, in part as a consequence of the wider abandonment of wind power. When Arthur Smithdale was asked in 1929 if the windmill at Ingham was repairable, his response was that 'the windmill is done with'. He thought it might be repaired for £400, or renewed for around £800, but there were no millwrights being trained for future work so maintenance would be problematic. Instead he proposed replacing it with an oil engine and turbine pump, at a cost of £995.[145] This was agreed, and the mill tower was reduced in height and fitted with a conical roof to form the engine house. The decline of the windmills accelerated over the following decades, for a number of reasons. In 1930 the Land Drainage Act brought major changes to the organisation of drainage. The East Norfolk Rivers Catchment Board was established in 1931 and Drainage Commissions were gradually amalgamated into larger Internal Drainage Boards (IDBs) under its overall control. Grants of 50 per cent for drainage improvement schemes were now being provided by the Ministry of Agriculture and Fisheries. Perhaps of more importance, the spread of the National Grid meant that electricity was now becoming available as a potential power source. The 1930s accordingly saw the start of a major change in drainage technology, with the increasing use of fewer, more powerful diesel or electric pumps, draining larger areas of land.

---

142 NRO FEL 1151, 559X9. NRO MC 14/88, 388X5. NRO PD 246/33.
143 The Lincolnshire firms Ruston, Proctor and Co and Richard Hornsby merged in 1918 to form Ruston and Hornsby.
144 A.J. Ward, 'The wind and the water', unpublished typescript held by the Norfolk Windmills Trust, Norwich. NRO HNR 401.
145 WMA Hempstead Drainage Commission Minutes 1884–1935.

As early as 1932, following much discussion about the future of their gale-damaged drainage mill and associated steam engine, the Repps Drainage Commission decided to install an electric motor, which was belted to the existing steam-turbine pump (the following year the salary of Johnson, the millman, was lowered by £5, on the grounds that his workload had been significantly reduced).[146] This arrangement did not last long, as there was a fire at the site in the autumn of 1936, but the following year a new updated electrical installation was fitted by Smithdale's that allowed the turbine to be directly driven, eliminating the need for belts and gear wheels.[147] More ambitious schemes could be undertaken by the new IDBs. In 1936 the Muck Fleet and South Flegg Internal Drainage Board decided to drain the whole of their 'No. 2 Sub District', which covered the Runham, Herringby and Stokesby Hall marshes, with a new electric pump installed at the site of the Herringby steam plant. Mr Childs, who looked after the Runham windmill and oil engine, then also became responsible for the new electric plant.[148] By 1937, when the Yarmouth Corporation Electricity Commission toured the local installations, the Board had also installed electric pumps at Clippesby and Stokesby.[149]

Internal combustion engines, now in the form of diesel installations, continued to have a role in marsh drainage, especially where distance from existing power lines or other factors rendered them a cheaper option. In 1941 the Lower Bure Internal Drainage Board adopted an ambitious scheme to replace the three windmills and steam engine near Seven Mile House on the Reedham Marshes with two Ruston & Hornsby engines and a starter engine powering two centrifugal vortex pumps manufactured by Gwynnes Pumps Limited.[150] These drained a newly rationalised and enlarged level of over 2,000 acres (800 hectares) and, together with the steel-clad engine shed in which they were housed, still survive beside the Bure, albeit relocated in 2003 as a result of the Flood Alleviation Project. They continued to operate, overseen by an operative housed in the nearby cottage, until the fully automatic electric pump was installed nearby in 1984. Electricity had originally been considered as an option for the site – the Board's other schemes in the 1940s, at Tunstall and Stracey Arms, employed electric pumps – but diesel was chosen here on the grounds of running costs.[151]

---

146 NRO HNR 406/3/3.
147 NRO 406/3/3.
148 WMA Muck Fleet and South Flegg Internal Drainage Board Minutes 1936–1943.
149 *Yarmouth Independent*, 29 May 1937.
150 WMA Lower Bure Internal Drainage Board Minutes 1937–1944.
151 The drainage here was not electrified until 1985 and, even then, the diesel engines were retained on standby. The engines and housing were relocated slightly upriver in 2003 as part of the Broadland Flood Alleviation Project. They are in the care of Norfolk Windmill Trust and form part of a group with two windmills and the former steam engine house that are periodically opened to the public.

Through the 1940s and early 1950s the adoption of electric or diesel pumps draining extensive areas finally rendered the remaining windmills redundant. Among the last to operate were the six privately owned mills that drained water into the Halvergate Fleet, which in turn emptied via a sluice into Breydon Water. Longstanding problems with the sluice and silting led the mill owners to propose installing a new pump at the Breydon end of the Fleet to help get their water away. A new Internal Drainage Board had been formed, and diesel plant was installed in 1934.[152] In 1944 the Board met to consider a scheme proposed by the East Norfolk Rivers Catchment Board to deepen the Fleet, draining water into it by gravity alone and dispensing with the services of the mills altogether. A new enlarged Drainage Board for the Lower Bure, Halvergate Fleet and Acle Marshes was created, and in 1946 construction began on a new large-capacity electric pumping station at Breydon. The Fleet windmills ceased to operate soon afterwards. A few others on private estates elsewhere in Broadland continued into the 1950s; the last to work were probably Ash Tree Farm Mill on the Bure near Yarmouth (1953) and Herringfleet Mill and St Olaves Mills on the Waveney (1955).

Conclusion

The history of mechanical drainage in Broadland is long, complex and in some respects surprising, especially perhaps the continuing vitality of wind drainage. It comes as something of a shock to discover that some drainage windmills continued to work more or less within living memory and that substantial brick towers such as Somerton or Martham were built in the twentieth century. As we have emphasised, most surviving mills are largely or entirely the creations of Victorian or Edwardian millwrights. We always, it seems, want these essentially practical structures to be older and more romantic than they really are. The various examples that appear in pictures painted by Norwich School artists seem already picturesquely dilapidated, although in most cases they were then less than a century old. By the end of the nineteenth century their more sophisticated replacements were themselves being described by writers as timeless and iconic adornments of the Broadland landscape. Yet this understandable fascination with windmills, more perhaps than with the often scant, less visually prominent physical remains left by other, less picturesque forms of drainage, has been allowed to obscure the importance of the latter in the history of Broadland, a neglect we have tried to remedy in the course of this chapter.

---

152 WMA Halvergate Fleet IDB Minutes 1934–1944.

WATERWAYS AND INDUSTRY

Visitors come to Broadland because of its rural landscape. Most seek tranquillity, and relish the area's sense of remoteness and its abundant wildlife. But, as commentators have repeatedly observed since tourism began in the nineteenth century, there is a paradox here. Visitors in large numbers destroy the very peace they have come to enjoy, while the facilities they require have a significant, and to many an unwelcome, impact on the environment. Yet commercial boatyards and riverside bungalows are themselves now a part of the cultural landscape, worthy of the historian's attention. Tourism, moreover, is not the only or the first industry to shape the local landscape. Our modern construction of Broadland as a quintessentially rural world ignores the importance of its industrial heritage, created and structured – like its modern leisure industry – by the intricate network of navigable waterways. In this chapter we will examine the vessels that sailed the rivers and dykes, the cargoes they carried, the places they landed and the industries they serviced, before going on, in Chapter 7, to consider the landscape history of tourism itself.

Wherries, keels and cargoes

by Ann and Michael Nix and Tom Williamson

By the nineteenth century the most important type of craft plying the Broadland rivers was the wherry. This was (and is) a broad, shallow-draughted clinker-built vessel, with a mast located towards the bow and a single large sail (Figure 6.1).[1] The hull, of oak but usually tarred, was divided into three unequal sections by substantial transverse beams. The largest section comprised the hold where the cargoes were

---

[1] R. Clark, *Black-sailed traders: keels and wherries of the Norfolk Broads* (Newton Abbot, 1972). M. Kirby, *Albion: the story of the Norfolk trading wherry* (Norwich, 1998). Malster, *Wherries and waterways*.

Figure 6.1 A wherry under sail on the river Yare at Reedham, c.1910, with the railway swing bridge open.

Figure 6.2 A keel, laden with timber, on the river Yare in Norwich. Engraving of 1829, after a painting by James Stark.

carried, which was securely covered with cambered water-tight hatches. The small rear section contained the cabin, or 'cuddy', from which the tiller was operated. The third section, in the bow, accommodated the 'tabernacle', the housing for the 40-foot mast of larch or pine, which had a lead weight at its foot to serve as a counter-balance; this, combined with the fact that the mast had only a single 'stay' of rope, running from the bow, to stop it from falling backwards, allowed it to be raised or lowered quickly, and with relative ease, even with the sail unfurled. Wherry sails were large – some covering as much as 1,200 square feet by the end of the nineteenth century. By then they were usually coated in a mixture of tar, oil and lamp-black, although paintings from the early nineteenth century generally show tanned, red-brown sails. In the shallow Broadland rivers the wherryman was not wholly dependent on the wind. When becalmed, the wherry could be quanted, or punted. The essential features of the wherry may have developed by the start of the seventeenth century, its distinctive rig perhaps reflecting the influence of the Protestant 'Strangers' from the Low Countries who settled in Norwich in the sixteenth century.[2] By 1789 the craft had certainly attained its fully developed form, one example being clearly illustrated on a horn cup of that date in Norwich Castle Museum.

Wherries joined, and eventually replaced, vessels called 'keels', which had sailed the Broadland rivers since medieval times. No keel now exists. What seems to have been the last surviving example, the *Dee-Dar*, was deliberately sunk at Postwick to strengthen the river wall in 1912. Its remains were excavated and raised in 1985 and then stored in a succession of places, but they were inadequately protected from the elements and sporadically vandalised; it proved impossible to obtain the funds required for conservation and restoration and they gradually disintegrated, finally being destroyed in 2012.[3] From the drawings made of these remains, but mainly from nineteenth-century descriptions and illustrations, we know that the keel was in some respects similar to the wherry. It was a shallow-draughted, usually clinker-built craft with a single sail and, at least by the nineteenth century, many (although not all) had a hold covered over and accessed by hatches (Figure 6.2). But it differed from the wherry in having its mast centrally placed, rather than towards the bow, and in having the cabin – which might accommodate not only the keelman but his entire family – placed in the bows rather than in the stern, near the tiller.[4] The sail, moreover, was a simpler affair, a square of canvas hung from a single transverse spar, or gaff, that was raised and lowered by a winch located in the stern. Another winch, in the bows, was used to raise and lower the mast itself, to allow the vessel to pass under bridges.

---

2   Clarke, *Black-sailed traders*, p. 42.
3   NHER 20492. Rob Driscoll, pers. comm.
4   T.E. Douglas-Sherwood, 'The Norfolk keel', PhD thesis (University of St Andrews, 1988).

Keels, as Douglas-Sherwood has demonstrated, increased steadily in size and capacity over time: recorded examples from the seventeenth century could carry a maximum load of around 20 tons, but by the 1720s the figure was 40–50 tons and by the 1760s 50–60 tons, while in the 1790s some examples had capacities of as much as 97 tons.[5] The latter figure comes from a remarkable document, a register of commercial vessels plying the Broadland rivers drawn up in 1795–8 in accordance with a parliamentary act.[6] This lists no fewer than 156 vessels but, as Margaret Bird has pointed out, the act required the registration only of those carrying more than 13 tons, and wherries carrying as little as 7 or 8 tons are referred to in contemporary advertisements and other sources, so there were probably significantly more trading craft than this figure suggests.[7] The Register shows that at this point wherries were fast replacing keels: there were 117 wherries listed but only 36 keels (as well as 3 'boats'). By the middle of the nineteenth century only a few keels were still operating, now mainly transporting timber, and by the 1880s they had effectively disappeared.[8]

The triumph of the wherry was not due to the fact that it could carry larger cargoes. As Bird has shown, the 36 keels in the 1790s Register could carry an average of 63 tons, more than twice the 26 tons that was the average figure for the 117 listed wherries (with the keels accounting for 42.7 per cent of the overall tonnage and wherries 57.3 per cent). Instead, it may have eventually eclipsed its rival because of the superior design of its sail, which made it better able to cope with changes in wind direction, a particular advantage on the more winding sections of the Broadland rivers. Indeed, the 48 berths of the vessels listed in the 1795–8 register indicate, strikingly, that by this stage most keels were to be found on the Yare, the least tortuous of the Broadland rivers, and none on the Ant, the most tortuous.[9] More important, perhaps, was the fact that the character of the wherry's mast and sail, and other features, meant that it required a smaller crew and was thus cheaper to operate.[10] Its taller sail, more capable of catching the wind above the height of riverside trees, may also have been in its favour.[11]

In addition to keels and wherries, newspapers and documents from the eighteenth century also refer to 'barges' on the Broadland rivers, especially the Yare. It is unclear exactly what this term refers to, although it frequently occurs in

---

5   Douglas-Sherwood, 'Norfolk keel', pp. 23–4.
6   NRO Y/C 38/3.
7   M. Bird, *Mary Hardy and her world 1773–1809, volume 4: under sail and under arms* (Kingston upon Thames, 2020), p. 186.
8   Douglas-Sherwood, 'Norfolk keel', pp. 97–100.
9   Bird, *Mary Hardy*, p. 199.
10 Douglas-Sherwood, 'Norfolk keel', pp. 97–100.
11 M. Stammers, *Norfolk shipping* (Stroud, 2002), p. 73.

the context of reports or advertisements relating to passengers, or to the carriage of 'parcels' and 'goods'. One possibility is that it may have described a small wherry adapted for transporting people, their luggage and small packages. But Palmer, writing in 1809, drew a sharp distinction between barges and wherries, which suggests that they were a different form of craft, while in 1791 Pickers & Co. of Norwich, describing themselves as a 'barge company', advertised the services of both their barge, for the carriage of goods, passengers, parcels, etc., and their wherry, for bale goods (textiles).[12] Barges may have been relatively small vessels with a flat-bottomed hull but the question remains unresolved.

Some keels and wherries were operated by individuals whose only occupation was the movement of goods by water. But many were run as part of larger businesses, by people who needed to move their own products but who might often have spare capacity to offer to others. Kelly's *Directory* of 1904, for example, lists Harry Burton at Stalham Staithe as a 'Corn and coal merchant, miller (wind), brick and tile manufacturer, and carrier by water'.[13] Even some of the larger farmers kept their own vessels. John Repton, brother of the landscape gardener Humphry, who farmed at Oxnead on the river Bure near Aylsham, had a wherry which he sold in 1828 for £50.[14]

We have only snippets of information about what was carried by water before the seventeenth century, and have detailed information only from the eighteenth. The most useful sources are the local newspapers, such as the *Norwich Mercury*, the *Bury and Norwich Post*, the *Norfolk Chronicle* and the *Ipswich Journal*.[15] These contain numerous accounts of events relating to vessels and staithes that mention cargoes, usually in the context of accidents or thefts. They also include advertisements that refer to goods transported by river or sold at staithes. Around 70 per cent of the goods mentioned comprised grain (usually unspecified 'corn', but clearly dominated by wheat and barley), coal and coke (the latter usually described as 'cinders') and building materials, including bricks, pamment tiles, oak and fir timber, 'yew firs', mahogany planks, boards, deals, laths and plaster, flagstones and Dutch, English and 'Hull' pantiles. A further 20 per cent comprised lime, flour or malt. Other sources suggest a similar range. The 1791 toll book for the Aylsham Navigation – the canalised section of the river Bure opened in 1773, which allowed wherries and other vessels to sail as far as Aylsham – listed the charges levied on bricks and tiles, coal, timber, wheat and other grain, although in this case there is no specific mention of lime.[16] When parliamentary enclosure acts established or

---

12 Maltster, *Wherries and waterways*, pp. 58–9. *Norwich Chronicle*, 23 July 1791.
13 Kelly's Directories, *Kelly's directory of Norfolk* (London, 1904), p. 443.
14 W. and M. Vaughn-Lewis, *Aylsham: a nest of Norfolk lawyers* (Itteringham, 2014), p. 177.
15 The following analysis is based on a survey of these four titles across the period 1740–1800.
16 S. Spooner (ed.), *Sail and storm: the Aylsham Navigation* (Aylsham, 2012), pp. 108–9.

recognised public staithes within particular parishes they generally stipulated that these were 'to be used by the owners and occupiers of Estates in the said parish … for laying and depositing corn, manure, and other things thereon', or 'for the conveyance of corn, manure and other goods to and from the river by owners and occupiers of the Parish'.[17] The term 'manure' probably referred not to farmyard dung (farms would have produced their own) but to urban refuse from Norwich and Yarmouth, and in particular to marl and lime, which were used to neutralise the natural acidity of the local soils (although lime was also used for making mortar and lime plaster for buildings). What these documentary sources fail to mention are the loads of marsh produce – reeds and sedge, litter and marsh hay – that a number of early-nineteenth-century sketches and paintings suggest were carried on the smaller wherries (as well as on yet smaller, clinker-built, shallow-draughted boats called 'reed lighters').

All the main cargoes carried by wherries and keels were thus heavy or bulky in nature, much more easily transported by water than overland at a time when even the main roads were often poorly surfaced. Some were brought from elsewhere in England, especially London, or even from abroad, the newspaper reports and advertisements referring to items coming from France, Holland and Ireland. Probably the most important of such cargoes was the coal brought down the coast from the mines in north-east England. All these commodities came by sea-going ships to Great Yarmouth and were then transhipped onto the smaller river craft for transport to Norwich or other destinations. The dominance of the river over the road system in the movement of goods between Norwich and Yarmouth is clearly shown by the list of carriers included in the Norwich directories. The 1783 edition lists only one road carrier operating between the two places; none at all are listed in those for 1822 or 1836. Vessels did not make their return journeys empty, but laden with cargoes, especially Norwich textiles, malt and grain, which were transhipped at Yarmouth and taken by sea to some more distant destination in England or beyond. A substantial proportion of the material being moved by water, however – most of the bricks and tiles, and lime – was both produced and used locally. In 1750, for example, the owner of a lime kiln just outside Conesford gate in Norwich advised readers of the *Ipswich Journal* that it was positioned 'very convenient for delivering Lime for Water-Carriage to Yarmouth, and up Beccles River, and also up the North River to Catfield, Ludham, Horning &c'.[18] It is a testimony to the effectiveness of the wherry hatches that lime, which reacts with water and gives off considerable heat, could be transported in this way, and wherrymen evidently had no difficulty with other similarly vulnerable commodities, including flour and even

---

17   As, for example, in the awards for Catfield, 1802 (NRO C/Sca 2/67) and Martham, 1812 (NRO C/Sca 2/193).
18   *Ipswich Journal*, 29 September 1750.

Plaster of Paris.[19] Timber was another important commodity both produced and used locally, although a proportion was also imported from abroad via Yarmouth. Newspaper advertisements often emphasised that trees to be felled and sold for timber were located close to the Broadland rivers, and make it clear that oak bark for tanneries was also customarily transported along them.

Other heavy items moved by water included the millstones required by the many wind and water mills in this intensively arable region. In August 1749, for example, John Reyner of the Music House Staithe in Conesford Street, Norwich, advertised that he was selling 'peak stones' (alongside Dutch and English pantiles and Portuguese cork).[20] Peak stones were millstones made from the Millstone Grit of the Peak District, but the softer, better-quality burr stones from France were also transported from there and transhipped onto river vessels at Yarmouth.[21] Other heavy or bulky goods that eighteenth-century reports or advertisements associated with wherries or keels, or with staithes and their warehouses, include hay, tar, cheese, iron gates and fencing, tallow, hides brought from as far afield as Ireland, and textiles, although the latter are recorded only at Norwich staithes, or on ships that were probably coming from them. Norwich, of course, was still at this time a major centre of textile production.[22] Indeed, the evidence suggests that all the Norwich textiles shipped from Great Yarmouth were carried there in keels and wherries. Given that, between 1760 and 1820, more than 1,750 ships loaded with textiles left the port bound for destinations in Europe, these must have accounted for a high proportion of the cargoes carried down the Yare by these much smaller craft.[23] Many of the raw materials required by the industry also appear to have been moved up the river to the city, having been transhipped at Yarmouth, including yarn from southern Ireland, alum from Yorkshire, fuller's earth from Kent, fustic (grown in Italy, Spain or New England), madder from the Austrian Netherlands and Yorkshire, and long-staple wool from Lincolnshire and Yorkshire.[24]

More surprisingly, the newspapers indicate that lighter and more exotic cargoes were sometimes carried on the rivers. In March 1754 tobacco and 'mountain wine' were stolen from a wherry moored at Bungay, while in 1756 there were complaints about the damage done by watermen on the Waveney to 'casks of liquor'.[25] There are references to gin, unspecified 'spirits', vinegar, Herefordshire cider and 'London goods', probably a vague term for luxury items. Passengers were

---

19   The latter brought from France via Great Yarmouth: *Ipswich Journal*, 10 June 1775.
20   *Ipswich Journal*, 12 August 1749.
21   *Ipswich Journal*, 30 June 1770. *Ipswich Journal*, 10 June 1775.
22   M. Nix, *Norwich textiles: a global story 1750–1840* (Norwich, 2023).
23   Nix, *Norwich textiles*, pp. 368–72.
24   Nix, *Norwich textiles*.
25   *Ipswich Journal*, 16 March 1754. *Ipswich Journal*, 27 November 1756.

also regularly carried by water, at least 22 per vessel in some cases. Regular services were advertised from Norwich to Yarmouth and they also feature in reports of accidental drownings, as in 1776 when an unknown man, thought to be 'about 23 years in age', was knocked overboard 'by jibing of the sail'; or the 'three poor women, a girl, and a boy' who were drowned when the barge *Royal Charlotte* capsized in the Yare in 1782.[26] More fortunate were the 18 passengers of a barge that overturned on Breydon Water three years later, for thanks to 'two keels passing by nearly at the same time, they were all taken up without any lives being lost'.[27] Particularly numerous are the reports of the individual keelmen, wherrymen and watermen who were drowned in the rivers in a variety of ways.

The early nineteenth century was probably the heyday of the wherries. Thereafter their trade was gradually eroded: first by improvements to the local road network, especially the construction of the Norwich–Yarmouth turnpike in 1834; then by the construction of the rail line from Norwich to Yarmouth, via Reedham, in 1844; and finally by the development, through the 1870s and 1880s, of a mesh of local rail lines linking the main market towns and many of the principal villages. In 1890, the year that Aylsham South Station was opened, the income from tolls on the Aylsham Navigation fell by 24 per cent; three years later the company issued an apology to shareholders for the lack of dividends, a consequence of 'the depressed state of trade and the falling off of tonnage dues'.[28] In 1900 the Wherry Owners' Insurance Friendly Society, formed in 1880, still had no fewer than 67 vessels on its books, and others were insured with different companies.[29] But by this time wherries such as *Zulu* on the Bure were largely carrying a limited range of bulk cargoes – mainly grain and flour downriver to Yarmouth, coal (and some gravel) on the return.[30] Rather less valuable bulk goods were now more likely to feature as cargoes, especially litter and thatching materials cut from the local fens, which photographs and postcards from the early twentieth century often show, piled high beside staithes. The table of tolls from the public staithe at Repps-cum-Bastwick in the collection of the Norwich Museums Service, probably from the 1920s, mentions only three commodities – reeds, litter and corn.[31] The continuing importance of river transport for certain commodities is attested by the construction in 1909 of the large modern corn mill and granary by Harry Burton beside the public staithe at Stalham. Nevertheless, the last trading wherry, the *Ella*, was launched from John

---

26 *Norwich Chronicle*, 5 October 1776. *Ipswich Journal*, 2 November 1782.
27 *Norwich Chronicle*, 13 August 1785.
28 Spooner, *Sail and storm*, p. 127.
29 Malster, *The Broads*, p. 49.
30 Spooner, *Sail and storm*, pp. 134–5.
31 The wooden sign is now in the Norfolk Museums Service store at Gressenhall.

Allen's boatyard at Coltishall in 1912.[32] Both corn and coal, and to an extent bricks, continued to be moved by water into the inter-war years, but on a dwindling scale, and by small steamboats (on the main rivers) or by wherries that were increasingly fitted with petrol engines.[33] Only two trading wherries now exist, saved from redundancy or restored from dereliction: the *Albion*, built in 1898, and the *Maud*, built in 1899.

Canals and improvements
by Keith Bacon and Tom Williamson

Given the critical economic importance of water-borne trade, it is unsurprising that numerous attempts were made to improve the Broadland waterways and extend their navigability (below, Figure 6.20). The former began in medieval times; the latter only in the seventeenth century, with the partial canalisation of the Waveney between Beccles and Bungay. This occurred following a parliamentary act of 1670 and involved the construction of locks at Geldeston, Ellingham and Wainford. The improvements probably represented a restoration of recently lost navigability, for before the early seventeenth century it had been possible for keels to reach Bungay along the river.[34] A more significant extension of the waterways occurred a century later with the construction, following a parliamentary act in 1773, of the Aylsham Navigation. This improvement of 15 kilometres of the Bure between Coltishall and Aylsham was opened six years later and for the most part followed the old course of the river, deepened where appropriate.[35] But there were diversions, each provided with a lock, around the mills at Horstead, Buxton, Oxnead and Burgh-next-Aylsham, while the last 2.4 kilometres comprised a true canal (again with a lock) running parallel to the river and terminating at a staithe at 'Dunkirk', just north of Aylsham town.[36] In contrast, the North Walsham and Dilham Canal, which extended navigation on the Ant for 14 kilometres above Wayford Bridge, had the character of a real canal for its entire length – it represented a re-engineering and straightening of the old course of the river and was provided with a towpath and six locks, all again associated with the sites of mills. The works were initiated by an act of 1812 but only begun in 1825 owing to local opposition and other difficulties, although they were then completed in little over a year.[37] There were a number of staithes along the navigation's length, one – at the hamlet of Meeting Hill, just south of North Walsham – reached via a boat dyke 300 metres long. The canal

---

32 Malster, *The Broads*, p. 53.
33 Malster, *Wherries and waterways*, p. 144.
34 E.W. Paget-Tomlinson, *The complete book of canal and river navigations* (Albrighton, 1978), p. 237.
35 J. Boyes and R. Russell, *The canals of eastern England* (Newton Abbot, 1977), p. 123.
36 Spooner, *Sail and storm*.
37 NRO C/Scf /667. R. Russell, *The lost canals of England* (Newton Abbot, 1971), pp. 249–51.

ended near Antingham, north of the town of North Walsham, at a large bone mill that was a major destination for wherries. All three of these navigations were provided with locks larger than those on conventional canals – 50 feet (15 metres) long and 12 feet 4 inches (3.8 metres) wide – as many wherries were significantly larger than normal narrow boats.

The Aylsham Navigation and the North Walsham and Dilham Canal were relatively short-lived. Both were experiencing financial difficulties by the 1880s; the former was abandoned after a disastrous flood in 1912, the latter declined more gradually. In 1886, with trade dwindling, it was sold to one Edward Press, a North Walsham miller, who hoped to develop it for pleasure boating, but without success.[38] The first 1.5 kilometres, from Antingham to Swafield lock, were abandoned in 1893; the section between Swafield and Bacton Wood slowly slid into dereliction in the early years of the twentieth century; and the main stretch, between Honing Lock and Bacton Wood Lock, was closed in 1937. The lower three kilometres, as far as Honing Lock, were navigable as late as 2003, but no longer. The navigation between Beccles and Bungay likewise became financially unviable around the start of the twentieth century and was finally closed in 1934.[39]

One other, less ambitious, extension to navigation needs to be mentioned. The Waxham New Cut ran from Horsey Mere for 5.5 kilometres as far as Lound Bridge in Sea Palling. Passing through level marshes around the headwaters of the Thurne, it was a simple affair, constructed without the need for locks. It was apparently dug between 1795 and 1816, perhaps originally to facilitate drainage, but subsequently providing access to the brickworks at Lound Bridge (it has left little obvious trace in the documentary record).[40] It remained largely navigable until 1953 when – following changes to the drainage system on the Brograve Level – it was closed above Bridge Farm, Waxham. Today it is just navigable, for small boats, between Horsey Mere and Brograve Mill.

Attempts made to improve rivers where they were already navigable have a rather longer history than extensions to navigation and, often poorly documented, pose a number of questions in terms of both their date and their purpose. Cuts and diversions can be identified in some cases by the line of parish boundaries, which usually follow rivers but sometimes deviate from them, running along some minor, meandering dyke marking an earlier course. The most obvious example is perhaps the straight cut on the Bure, 480 metres long, near St Benet's Abbey, made to avoid a 1.9-kilometre-long loop to the south of Ward Marsh, still surviving as a channel and followed by the Horning parish boundary. The cut was already

---

38 NRO BR 208.
39 Paget-Tomlinson, *Canal and river navigations*, p. 237.
40 It is absent from Faden's county map of 1797, but is clearly shown on the draft Ordnance Survey drawings of 1816 in the British Library, London.

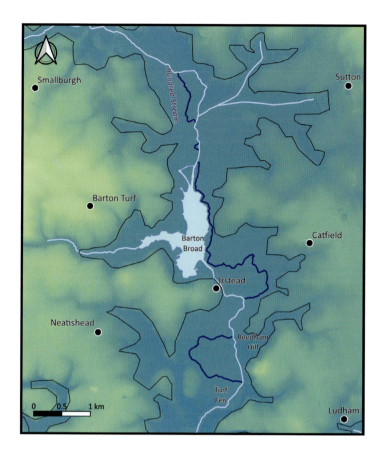

Figure 6.3 Principal improvements made to the course of the river Ant (in dark blue).

in place when a map of the demesne lands of the abbey was surveyed in 1700, and almost certainly in 1617, when a document appears to refer to the original meander not as the river Bure but as 'Ward Dyke'. It may well have been dug in the Middle Ages.[41] More complex and extensive are the many changes made to the course of the Ant (Figure 6.3). Firstly, the configuration of the parish boundary between Catfield to the east and Barton Turf and Irstead to the west indicates that the course of the river was diverted to flow through Barton Broad at some unknown date, but presumably not before its formation in the late Middle Ages. To the south of the Broad the river once again forms a parish boundary, between Irstead and Catfield, until the small island of higher ground called Reedham Hill is reached, where another deviation begins, picking out a meandering loop running to the west of Reedham Marsh as far as Turf Fen Mill. North of Barton Broad the boundary between Sutton and Barton Turf mainly follows the river for some 700 metres but the boundary between Stalham and Barton Turf again leaves it, running instead along a minor watercourse described as the 'Hundred Stream' on various

---

41 NRO Snelling 11/12/73 (P150 B5). NRO DN HAR 3/3.

nineteenth-century maps for some 1.2 kilometres before returning to the Ant at a point *c.*1.2 kilometres downriver of Wayford Bridge.[42]

From here the river forms the boundary between Stalham and Smallburgh, but a map of the latter parish, made in 1582, shows that this section then had numerous small meanders. However, the map carries later amendments, dated '1762', which show the river straightened and meanders removed.[43] In contrast, the much larger alterations to the course of the Ant just described were all in place by the time the earliest maps were surveyed. Many appear to be cuts made to avoid large loops of the river. However, in many cases the saving in distance and time for vessels was unlikely to justify the scale of the work and costs involved when boat travel was slow and manpower was cheap. This explanation might make sense in the case of the Ward Marsh cut on the Bure, which is only 23 per cent of the length around the original loop of the river. But on the river Ant, the diversion through Barton Broad is 66 per cent the length of the old course, that around Reedham Marsh 43 per cent, while the Stalham cut is actually longer, at 124 per cent. If shortening the distance to be travelled was not the main motivation, it is possible that the poor quality of the old river was. The old courses, as represented today by dykes and parish boundaries, were in most cases tortuous, with many small meanders, and often appear to have been quite narrow. These conditions would have encouraged the accumulation of both silt and vegetation, problems alleviated by creating a new wider, deeper and straighter course.

Making new courses to the river would have required the consent of the landowners and, given that the floodplain was common waste, the permission if not the active involvement of the lord of the principal manor. In most if not all of the townships concerned this was the abbot of St Benet's Abbey before 1540 and the bishop of Norwich after this date. The abbey, which was sited at the lower end of the river Ant, received significant income from properties in the Ant valley and the capital and political clout to make such changes to the river. The bishopric had less direct local involvement and much of the estate was let on long leases for lives, while many of the manorial dues and rentals were fossilised at sixteenth-century values, decreasing over time because of inflation, and the bishopric tended to be conservative in its policies of land management. All this strongly suggests that the major changes to the course of the Ant pre-date the Dissolution in 1539.

The most visually dramatic improvement to navigation on the Broads is much more recent in date: the New Cut, which runs, ruler-straight, through the Halvergate Marshes for a distance of four kilometres from St Olaves on the

---

42   NRO PD 189/78.
43   NRO ACC 2004/167.

WATERWAYS AND INDUSTRY 289

Figure 6.4 The New Cut, connecting the Yare at Reedham to the Waveney at St Olaves, was dug in 1832–3.

Waveney to Reedham on the Yare (Figure 6.4). Dug in 1832–3, it was part of an ambitious scheme that, in contrast to those just described, was not intended to facilitate transport by keel or wherry but instead to allow direct access to Norwich by sea-going vessels, avoiding the necessity of transhipping cargoes at Yarmouth.[44] Norwich merchants and businessmen had long been concerned about the inconvenience of this, as well as the high tolls charged at Yarmouth, and in 1814 the Norfolk engineer William Cubitt was engaged to prepare plans for a new shipping route to the city, coming via Lowestoft. In 1821 he unveiled his ambitious proposals, which met with considerable opposition from wherry owners, the port of Yarmouth and the proprietors of both the North Walsham and Dilham Canal and the Aylsham Navigation. The Norwich and Lowestoft Navigation Bill was defeated in parliament in 1826 but a revised bill was passed in 1827 and the works were executed between 1827 and 1833. They involved extensive dredging, a host of minor works and three major projects. First, a new 400-metre-long channel was dug linking the interconnected Oulton Broad and Lake Lothing, just to the south of Lowestoft, to the sea. Second, Oulton Dyke, which connected Oulton Broad with the Waveney, was widened, deepened and in part straightened. These changes created a situation in which Oulton Broad,

---

44   NRO BL 38/4. NRO BR 276/1/857. NRO MC 103/2, 542X9. NRO MS 1244–1252, 2B4. Boyes and Russell, *Canals of eastern England*, pp. 111–19.

290 BROADLAND

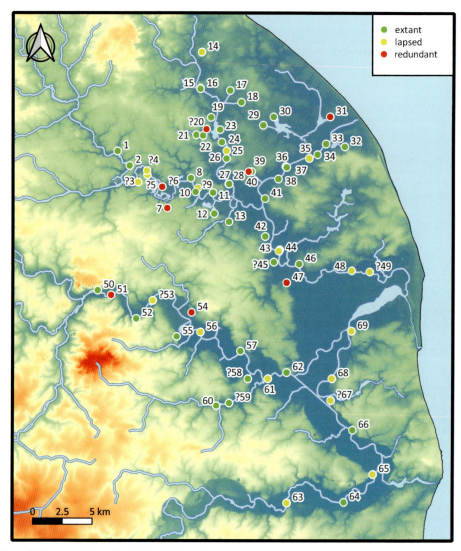

Figure 6.5 Known public staithes in Broadland and current status. 'Lapsed' staithes are those which might be reinstated; 'redundant' examples are those where this would not be possible due to loss of navigable watercourses. '?' denotes status or existence uncertain. 1. Coltishall Common 2. Commissioners' Staithe, Belaugh 3. Malthouse Lane, Wroxham 4. Wroxham Bridge, Wroxham 5. Wroxham Bridge, Hoveton St John 6. Hudon's Water (Haugh End Road) 7. Salhouse and Woodbastwick 8. Horning Lower Street 9. Ferry, Horning 10. Horning Ferry, Woodbastwick 11. Horning Upper Street 12. Ranworth 13. South Walsham 14. East Ruston 15. Wayford Bridge, Smallburgh 16. Wayford Bridge, Stalham 17. Stalham 18. Sutton 19. Barton Turf 20. Callow Green, Barton Turf 21. Neatishead 22. Gay's Staithe, Irstead 23 Wood End Staithe, Catfield 24. Church Staithe, Irstead 25. Johnny Crowe's Staithe, Catfield 26. How Hill, Ludham 27. Ludham Bridge, Ludham 28. Ludham Bridge, Horning 29. Hickling Staithe 30. Common Staithe, Catfield 31. Horsey Mere 32. West Somerton 33. Damgate Staithe, Martham 34. Boatdyke Staithe, Martham 35. Cess Staithe, Martham 36. Potter Heigham 37. Repps 38. Bastwick 39. Womack Water, Ludham 40. Ludham Staithe 41. Thurne 42. Upton 43. Burgh St Margaret, Acle Bridge 44. Acle Bridge, Fishley 45. Acle Dyke 46. Stokesby 47. Tunstall 48. Runham Swim 49. Marsh Farm, Mautby 50. River Green, Thorpe St Andrew 51. Whitlingham 52. Woods End, Bramerton 53. Surlingham Ferry 54. Strumpshaw 55. Rockland 56. Buckenham 57. Cantley 58. Langley Staithe 59. Chedgrave Common 60. Loddon 61. Norton 62. Reedham 63. Beccles 64. North Cove 65. Burgh St Peter 66. Somerleyton 67. St Olaves 68. Fritton 69. Burgh Castle.

Lake Lothing and the new channel connecting the latter to the sea were tidal in two directions, necessitating the construction of a lock – Mutford Lock – at the junction of lake and broad, with two sets of gates arranged to cope with the alternating water pressure. Third, the New Cut was dug connecting the Waveney at St Olaves to the Yare at Reedham, allowing boats to reach Norwich without passing through Breydon Water and Yarmouth.[45]

In March 1833 the first ships reached Norwich using the new navigation and ten years later a further modification was made when another 'New Cut' 950 metres long was made at Thorpe St Andrew, just to the east of Norwich, to avoid the necessity of building swing bridges where the new Norwich–Yarmouth railway made two successive crossings of the Yare.[46] But the size of commercial sea-going vessels was increasing rapidly at this time and the New Cut, Oulton Dyke and Mutford Lock were soon too narrow for many to navigate. A proposed new harbour at Norwich was never built, maintenance costs soon outstripped the revenue from tolls and by 1847 the navigation was bankrupt. It was bought by the entrepreneur Sir Morton Peto of Somerleyton Hall, mainly to facilitate his plans for expanding Lowestoft harbour. The New Cut was badly damaged by the great floods of 1953 and very nearly closed. Like the rest of the 'navigation', it is no longer used by ocean-going vessels, although these continued to dock at Norwich well within living memory.

Staithes

All the varied cargoes carried on the Broadland rivers had to be loaded and unloaded somewhere and by the eighteenth century, and presumably long before, there were innumerable landing places or *staithes* – a word with Scandinavian origins – along the rivers, or at the end of long dykes running back from them (Figure 6.5). Many examples still exist, others have disappeared over time. Some were private, others were public and associated with particular parishes, some of which possessed more than one; Catfield had three public staithes on the river Ant and one accessed, via Hickling Broad, from the Thurne. Public staithes were places where people had a right to moor boats for the purpose of depositing cargoes. Private ones were for the use of particular residences or industrial premises such as brickworks. But the line between the two categories was blurred. Public staithes often had private staithes beside them, or privately owned buildings standing on them; some public staithes seem to have become private over time, and (to a lesser extent) *vice versa*; and a few privately owned staithes had some public rights of use and access.

---

45   Boyes and Russell, *Canals of eastern England*, pp. 111–19.
46   Malster, *Broads*, p. 53. NHER 28920.

It is sometimes thought that village staithes were generally established by parliamentary enclosure acts in the late eighteenth or early nineteenth century, as defined areas of ground, allotted to some public body, where goods could be loaded and unloaded. It is certainly true that enclosure awards often did allocate an area 'as a public staithe to be used by the owners and occupiers of Estates in the said parish'. But many staithes did not originate in this manner; rather, they came about by customary use over a long period, and their origins are lost in the mists of time.[47] Few of the staithes allotted by enclosure awards, moreover, were really new. Those so established at West Somerton, Upton and Thurne, for example, are all shown on William Faden's 1797 map of Norfolk, surveyed some time before the enclosure of the places in question.[48] In most cases enclosure commissioners simply recognised and regularised customary landing places that had existed 'time out of mind', just as they formalised and regularised much of the existing road network. Public staithes developed, for the most part, organically, where places with public access met navigable waterways, with rights gradually being asserted through regular use. Many were thus to be found on common land and a few still are, as at Coltishall or Stokesby; but more usually the common disappeared at enclosure and a village staithe was formally established by the enclosure commissioners in the same or a neighbouring place. This close association with common land explains why some staithes were 'public', yet had an owner – as at Ranworth or Surlingham.[49] The individuals in question were the manorial lords, technically the owners of common land. Other 'customary' staithes, as at Bramerton or Thorpe St Andrew, grew up where roads ran alongside rivers for a considerable distance, or where roads, and especially major roads, crossed rivers at fords or bridges. In the latter case the road often widened just before the bridge, as a fan or triangle running down to the water on either side of it, as at Wey Bridge and Wayford Bridge.[50]

There was a legal logic to all of this, although few of those involved were perhaps aware of it. Tidal rivers and other navigable watercourses are in legal terms highways: 'the right of navigation … is a right of way for all the public for all purposes of navigation, trade, and intercourse.'[51] This does not mean that individuals using the waterway have an equivalent right to moor, or to load and

---

[47] T. Williamson, P. Parker and I. Ringwood, 'The staithes of the Broads: a history and assessment', report for the Broads Authority (2017). https://www.broads-authority.gov.uk/__data/assets/pdf_file/0030/260499/The-Staithes-of-the-Broads.pdf (accessed 21 May 2024). R.A.F. Kemp, *Staithes: a survey and register* (Norwich, 1986).

[48] NRO C/Sca 2/331 and 332. NRO C/Sca 2/306 and 7. NRO C/Sca 2/296. Faden, *Topographic map*.

[49] NRO DN/TA 151. NRO NRO DN/TA 610. TNA IR/58, 1910 Finance Act field books and maps.

[50] NRO C/Sca 2/273. NRO DN/TA 363.

[51] A.S. Wisdom, *The law of rivers and watercourses* (London, 1979), p. 58.

unload, on its banks.[52] However, there are places 'appropriated by usage, grant or statute' for the purposes of landing or embarking, and among the first of these categories roads and commons were evidently the most important. Where a public highway or a common to which there was *de facto* public access met a navigable river, there would need to be a place, and a public right, to tranship goods and people, given that both road and river were effectively highways (at least for local inhabitants), and that a boat cannot navigate a road, nor a vehicle drive along water.

Many public staithes lay not on rivers but some way back from them, and were accessed via broads or along narrow boat dykes. Some of the latter, such as that at Thurne, appear entirely artificial in character, but most were clearly adapted from a natural watercourse, the staithe growing up where this met a public road. A landing place for small boats, picking their way along a small stream, gradually developed, with the stream itself being artificially widened at a later stage, although only as far as the landing place, to allow the passage of larger vessels such as keels. The natural origins of these access dykes explains why many – such as those leading to the staithes at Dilham, Neatishead, South Walsham and Catfield Common, and the lost Salhouse staithe – are followed by parish boundaries. Natural streams were often used to fix parochial limits.

As already noted, many public staithes have been lost with the decline in river-borne trade that has occurred since the late nineteenth century. Some, such as Strumpshaw Staithe, were abandoned because the channel leading to them became silted up. Others, such as Buckenham Staithe on the Yare, have simply been forgotten about. Several examples, following a tradition stretching back centuries, have been converted to private staithes or otherwise taken into private ownership. Indeed, there is now much confusion over the legal status of particular staithes and who might be responsible for their upkeep. Where village staithes were formalised by parliamentary enclosure acts provision had to be made for their future management and maintenance. Parish councils did not exist before 1894, so they were generally allotted to some other local body. Some were entrusted to Drainage Commissions, bodies which, as we have seen, were also often established by enclosure awards to maintain the flood banks, principal drains and arterial watercourses within a parish. Others were allotted to the Surveyors of the Highways, who were responsible for maintaining the parish roads (partly because staithes were part of the local transport infrastructure but also because they were used to bring in the materials, especially gravel, required for road maintenance). More rarely, as with Church Staithe at Irstead, they were given to the Trustees for the Poor; or, as with Bastwick Staithe, Barton Turf Staithe and Gay's Staithe at

---

52   *Ibid.*, pp. 5 and 9.

Irstead, to named individuals who were to act as trustees, maintaining them into the future for the public good.[53]

In general, staithes allotted to the Surveyors of the Highways had devolved, by the start of the twentieth century, to parish councils, but not always. The staithe at Horning Lower Street, for example, although listed as the surveyors' property when the tithe map was drawn up in 1839, was simply included as part of the road network on the Finance Act maps of c.1910. The other two public staithes in this parish, at Upper Street and Ludham Bridge, likewise allotted to the surveyors, were by 1839 in the hands of a different body, the 'Trustees of the Public Staithes'. By 1910 one was considered part of the adjacent public road and the second had been absorbed into a neighbouring property, but in the 1970s was declared a piece of common land, with the parish council as owner![54] Those staithes allotted to the drainage commissioners usually remained with them into the twentieth century. But, again, not always. At West Somerton, while the staithe still belonged to the drainage commissioners in 1841, by 1910 it was considered the property of the parish council, as were those at Thurne and probably at Repps.[55] Crowes Staithe at Catfield, in contrast, was allotted to the drainage commissioners at the enclosure in 1802, but by 1840 was recorded as common land, and is so registered today.[56] Ownership of those staithes that remained with the drainage commissioners into the early twentieth century, moreover, then developed in diverse ways. As a result of the 1930 Land Drainage Act the banks and flood walls owned by the drainage commissioners beside the rivers and around the broads passed to the East Norfolk Rivers Catchment Board (ENRCB), while the main drains and drainage mills devolved to the new local IDBs. Staithes that were on, or cut into, the river banks went to the ENRCB while some staithes lying off the main rivers, either on broads or at the ends of boat dykes, went to the IDBs. The former then passed in the late 1940s to the East Suffolk and Norfolk Rivers Board and subsequently (after 1977) to the Anglian Water Authority, before devolving in 1989 to the National Rivers Authority and, finally, in 1996, to the Environment Agency.

Given all this, it is hardly surprising that uncertainty often surrounds the question of who is now responsible for maintaining the staithes established

---

53   NRO C/Sca 2/177. NRO C/Sca 2/223. NRO C/Sca 2/18.
54   NRO C/Sca 2/167. NRO DN/TA 368. TNA IR/58 1910 Finance Act, maps and field books. Commons Registration Act, decision reference 25/d/2, https://acraew.org.uk/sites/default/files/uploads/Norfolk/THE%20STAITHE%20-%20LOWER%20STREET%20-%20HORNING%20NO.CL.116.pdf (accessed 25 July 2022).
55   TNA IR/58 1910 Finance Act, maps and field books.
56   NRO C/Sca 2/67. NRO DN/TA 722.

by enclosure acts. Nevertheless, a very high percentage of such staithes have survived, now used for leisure and holiday craft, while 'customary' staithes, in contrast, unprotected by any kind of formal documentation, have been much more vulnerable to neglect and encroachment. To take one of several examples, the 6-inch Ordnance Survey map of 1884 marks 'Staithe House' in Ludham, at the end of a short inlet that extended west from Womack Water to the road leading south from the village, itself still known as Staithe Road. William Faden's county map of 1797 marks a 'staithe' at this point and the 6-inch Ordnance Survey map shows how the road widened at the end of the dyke into a broad rectangle that evidently represents the staithe itself. But during the twentieth century the channel was neglected and use of the staithe dwindled. Later Ordnance Survey maps show that by the 1930s the rectangle of open ground had been fenced off from the public road and was soon afterwards incorporated into the grounds of Staithe House. Other customary staithes, lacking any kind of permanently constituted body to maintain them, have simply been lost since the nineteenth century through neglect. The tithe maps for Woodbastwick and Salhouse, for example, show a long boat dyke running along the boundary between the two parishes, extending south from the end of Salhouse Broad and terminating a few hundred metres to the east of the main concentration of houses in Salhouse parish with a 'turning circle' for boats.[57] Faden's map suggests, typically, that this was an area of common land. Sheds or small warehouses seem to have been erected beside the staithe between 1839 and 1881 and the access channel remained navigable into the 1930s, but not beyond that, and it has now largely disappeared.[58]

Alongside the many public staithes numerous private ones existed, as noted above. Some fronted directly on the river, especially in towns and larger villages such as Wroxham or Beccles, but others were reached along boat dykes. Both Caister Castle, built in the 1430s and 1440s, and Claxton Castle, erected in the mid-fourteenth century, were accessed by long channels running back from the Bure and the Yare respectively. Manor houses such as that at Clippesby were similarly accessed and, by the post-medieval period, even large farms sometimes had their own boat dykes and staithes, such as Boundary Farm in Ashby, reached from the Bure along the 200-metre long Boundary Dyke. Large landowners sometimes created staithes and boat dykes for the use of their tenants, and as a commercial investment. The Beauchamp-Proctors of Langley probably dug the 480-metre-long ruler-straight dyke to Langley Staithe some time in the eighteenth century, although it may be earlier; there was certainly a 'Stathe and

---

57   NRO DN/TA 254. NRO DN/TA 716.
58   Ordnance Survey first edition 6-inch map, Norfolk Sheet LII, surveyed 1881. C. McCormack, *The book of Salhouse & Woodbastwick* (Wellington, 2016), p. 51.

Stathehouse with a warehouse and stables new built' here in 1736.[59] They also, by the nineteenth century, owned Hardley Staithe, likewise accessed by the ruler-straight Hardley Dyke from the Yare. It is possible that the latter, in particular, originated as a public village staithe, but both seem to have been appropriated by the estate, which certainly invested significantly in their improvement. Both Faden's 1797 map of Norfolk and the enclosure map of 1810 show Hardley Dyke as a much more meandering watercourse. The tithe map of 1840 shows the present watercourse in place, but also the line of the older, and recently redundant, boat dyke.[60]

A number of private dykes were dug to provide access to staithes associated with industries or businesses. Tyler's Cut in Dilham now branches off the boat dyke leading from the river Ant to Dilham village staithe, although it originally led off from the lost Dilham Broad. A kilometre long and still navigable, it appears to have been created in the early nineteenth century by adapting a natural watercourse in order to serve a small brickworks located some 500 metres to the north of Dilham village. In 1840 the 'brickground, kiln, cottages, staithes etc' here were owned by a Thomas Shephard Taylor, and the dyke's name may be a corruption of his own. The 1910 Finance Act documents show that it was then the property of H.M. Taylor, although occupied by 'George Walker and others'.[61] Some of these 'industrial' dykes, and the premises to which they led, could be substantial. Geldeston staithe is accessed from the river Waveney by a boat dyke, ruler-straight for much of its course and over 800 metres long, that terminates at a large basin, now used by a boatyard but accompanied by four cottages and some converted industrial buildings, the remains of a more extensive collection. In 1776 a newspaper advertisement announced the sale of 'Geldeston staithe etc.', described as 'All that well-known staithe and wharf with the sole and exclusive right of navigation belonging thereto.' It was accessed along a 'fine navigable canal cut from the River Waveney half a mile up to it' and included 'a small town of warehouses, malthouses, granaries, etc. all adjoining to the land and locked up every night: with an exceeding fine coal wharf, capable of containing 2000 chaldron of coal, which are landed with little or no expense, with a very quick sale for the same'.[62]

Many public staithes were also provided with warehouses, in which coal and other commodities could be kept secure and dry. A number of eighteenth- and nineteenth-century examples survive: small brick-built sheds on the waterside, such as the 'Black Shed' at Barton Turf or the examples at Stokesby

---

59   NRO BEA 9/7, 433X5.
60   NRO C/Sca 2/184. NRO DN/TA 362.
61   NRO DN/TA 394. TNA IR 58/62418.
62   *Ipswich Journal*, 6 January 1776.

and South Walsham (Figure 6.6). Others, incorporated into private gardens, await identification. Mundane and in most cases resolutely unpicturesque, they are nevertheless an important part of Broadland's historic landscape. Granaries, where grain could be loaded onto wherries, were also a common feature of staithes, both public and private, although few survive. That erected at Stalham in 1808, a magnificent three-storey structure, remains, the boat dyke passing beneath it via a low entrance so that grain could be dropped directly into the wherries below (Figure 6.7). It was built by (and its datestone carries the initials of) Samuel Cooke, who also built and owned the ten-sided smock mill in Stalham, reputedly the tallest smock mill in Norfolk. The granary adjacent to Grove House in Irstead – also known as the 'Wherry Arch', and of early-nineteenth-century date – is built across a rather wider boat dyke, running in from Lime Kiln Dyke, with a storage chamber over a high arch through the floor of which grain was similarly loaded.

Some warehouses on public staithes, usually those established by enclosure acts, were erected and owned by the public body responsible for maintaining them. But many, especially on 'customary' staithes, were privately owned. They were built for the use of an individual proprietor or as an investment, with local people being charged for storing goods there. Manorial lords were happy to give permission for their erection on common land or roadside waste as they could charge the owner an annual 'quit rent' for the land occupied. Such arrangements often caused confusion and arguments in later decades; so, too, could the tendency of local landowners to misunderstand the role of their ancestors as trustees for public staithes, as in the case of Barton Turf. When the Barton Hall estate was offered for sale in 1935 the auction catalogue included 'the large shed on the public staithe' as lot number 2.[63] Local people believed that the Black Shed belonged to the parish, employed a solicitor to press their case, and managed to have it withdrawn from the sale.[64] But its ownership was again contested in 1979, when workmen started to put new windows and a floor into the shed for someone who thought they had bought the building. A long dispute ensued, lasting ten years, before the Commons Commissioners ruled both that Barton Turf Parish Council was the owner of the staithe, which was declared common land, and that the Black Shed was part and parcel of it.[65]

---

63 NRO MC 14/351, 389.
64 Barton Turf Parish Council Minute Book, 1894–1959 (held by the parish clerk: not yet deposited at the NRO).
65 Barton Turf Parish Council Minute Book, 1959–1987. Commons Registration Act 1965 ruling on Barton Turf, ref. no. 225/U/253, 790. https://acraew.org.uk/sites/default/files/uploads/Norfolk/THE%20STAITHE%20-%20BARTON%20TURF%20NO.CL.356.pdf (accessed 22 June 2023).

Figure 6.6 Former warehouse, early- to mid-nineteenth century, at Stokesby Staithe.

Figure 6.7 The granary at Stalham Staithe, built in 1808 for Samuel Cooke. The building was accessed to the rear by a boat dyke; wherries entered the building via a low entrance, to be loaded through hatches in the floor of the chamber above.

Some individual staithes

by Keith Bacon, Michael Brandon-Jones, Di Cornell, Carol Horner, Ann and Michael Nix and Claire Penstone-Smith

More detailed discussions of some individual examples of staithes, all lying in parishes located in close proximity within the valleys of the Ant and the Thurne, may make the key features of the history of Broadland's staithes rather clearer. We may begin with Gay's Staithe, one of two public staithes in Irstead, the other being located beside the parish church of St Michael (Figure 6.8). A map of 1790 shows the land now occupied by the staithe as 'Part of Irstead Common', with a dyke running through it, and Faden's county map of 1797 shows how the latter quickly widened towards the east as it joined the watercourse called Lime Kiln Dyke and entered Barton Broad.[66] Such an arrangement would have made this an ideal place for unloading cargoes brought by water and when the enclosure award of 1810 allotted a staithe here to 'Thomas Preston and Jared Horner [lords of the manor] and their heirs forever in trust for the use of the owners and occupiers of lands and tenements in Irstead and Neatishead', it was almost certainly ratifying and formalising an existing landing place.[67]

The Irstead tithe apportionment and map of 1839 describe the staithe as being owned and occupied by Irstead Trustees of the Poor, a classic example of how responsibility for staithes tended to shift over time.[68] Two buildings are shown: one a boathouse beside the dyke and one probably a small warehouse. To the south, in a separate parcel of land, stood a 'cottage and gardens', owned and occupied by John Allen. This is the building now known as Wherry Cottage, evidently built after the enclosure, as it is absent from earlier maps and stood on what had formerly been common land. Around 85 metres to the south, on Lower Road, was another cottage, occupied by Samuel Canham.

The census of 1841 records John Allen, living at the 'Staithe' in Irstead, as 'merchant', but his real profession is clearer in White's *Directory* for 1845, which describes him as 'wherry owner'. It also lists Samuel Canham, an 'Ag[ricultural] Lab[ourer]', as dwelling 'near Staithe', with his wife and seven children. In November 1848 one of these children, Sarah, married John Gay 'boatman', of Barton Turf, at Irstead Church and the 1851 census shows them living on Lower Road. By 1856 he, too, is listed as a wherry owner in *Craven's Commercial Directory*. The couple are described as living at 'the staithe' in the 1861 census, presumably having replaced Allen at Wherry Cottage. They shared it with another family and were still there in

---

66   NRO MC 337/121–24, 709X6. Faden, *Topographic map*.
67   NRO C/Sca 2/177.
68   NRO DN/TA 129.

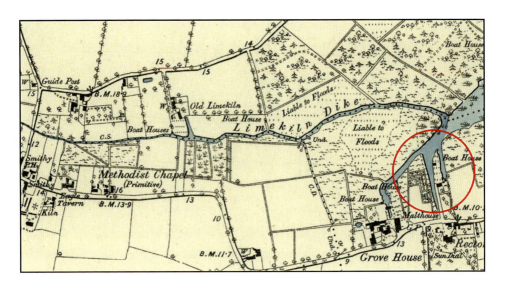

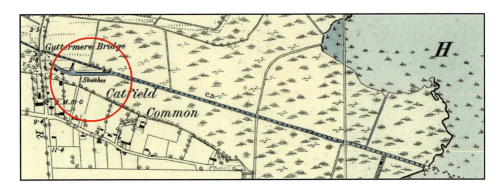

Figure 6.8 The staithes discussed in this section, as depicted on the first edition 6-inch Ordnance Survey maps from the 1880s. Top: Gay's Staithe, Irstead. Centre: Barton Turf Staithe. Bottom: Catfield Common Staithe.

Figure 6.9 Gay's Staithe, Irstead, from Payne Jennings' *Sun pictures of the Norfolk Broads* (1892).

1871, this time accompanied by two families, both of agricultural labourers, and in 1881 and 1891, now again accompanied by one family. Evidently, Wherry Cottage – a not insubstantial house – was divided into a number of residences, Gay living cheek-by-jowl with others in spite of the fact that the *Post Office Directory* of 1879 describes him as 'Coal Merchant and Wherry Owner' (John Allen was still living locally, now listed as a Reed Merchant).

A photograph taken by John Payne Jennings and published in 1892 neatly captures the transition of this part of Broadland from a world of farming and industry to a holiday destination (Figure 6.9). It shows 'Wherry Cottage', the boathouse and stacks of reed and marsh hay awaiting transportation. But the caption reads:

> Gay's Staithe, Barton Broad. – The advent of a yachting party or canoe club makes the Staithe still more gay; but on a brilliant summer's day, such as that depicted in this view, one's spirits are, like the barometer, so high that everything around seems gay. We see everything through rosy glasses, and even the commonest scenes are then imbued with an interest and peacefulness that

we do not see on a dull or wet day. A stroll through the village and chat with the natives gives one a good insight into their manners, customs and speech, which will be found highly interesting.[69]

Jennings was obviously ignorant of the real derivation of the staithe's name, even though John Gay, now aged 74 and described as a general labourer, was still living here when the 1901 census was taken. His wife Sarah died on 14 July 1906 aged 79; he died the following year on 14 May. They were buried in Irstead churchyard, a stone monument attesting a middle-class status more in keeping with earlier, than with later, descriptions of his occupation.

To the north, Irstead parish is bordered by Barton Turf, the boundary between the two following Lime Kiln Dyke. This is a natural watercourse, artificially widened in its lower reaches to improve navigability, which begins in Tunstead and then flows south and east to enter Barton Broad, joining the dyke from Gay's Staithe in Irstead, just described, as it does so. At the modern head of navigation, close to where the dyke meets the Smallburgh Road, there was a private staithe serving an adjacent tannery. The tannery itself was in existence by 1775, when Joshua Bacon purchased the 'tan yard and other yards and gardens' from Thomas Cooper of North Walsham.[70] Almost certainly there was already a staithe of some kind here. None is shown on the 1810 enclosure map for the parish, but there is clearly a channel leading off the main dyke close to the tannery, while a short stretch of the main channel nearby had been widened, presumably to enable wherries to pass or to tie up while waiting to load or unload. The tannery was still operating in 1821, when Sir Thomas Preston of nearby Beeston Hall tried to purchase it from Mrs Bacon, but it seems to have disappeared soon afterwards and is not mentioned in the tithe award of 1838.[71]

By the nineteenth century a number of other properties seem to have possessed staithes on Lime Kiln Dyke, usually on short boat dykes running back from it, including the house called The Limes and Iken's Farm, but of particular importance was the industrial site that gave the watercourse its name. In 1840, when the tithe map was surveyed, there was a lime kiln, with its own staithe and associated cottages, some 250 metres to the east of the tannery.[72] It is not marked on the enclosure map of 1810 so was presumably created between these two dates.[73] The chalk required was not dug on site – here it was too deeply buried beneath later deposits – but brought by wherry, probably from pits in the Bure valley at

---

69   Jennings, *Sun pictures*, p. 7.
70   NRO MC 337/49–51, 709X4. NRO D73.
71   NRO DN/TA 205. NRO MC 121/247. NRO D1470–4.
72   NRO DN/TA 205.
73   NRO C/Sca 2/18.

Horstead and Coltishall (see below, pp. 312–13). The cheap transport provided by wherries meant that kilns could be constructed some distance from the chalk quarries. The finished lime, as already noted, could be distributed by water with ease and economy throughout the Broadland area. In 1840 the kiln was owned by Sir Jacob Preston (Sir Thomas's son) but operated by Abraham Webster and John Cobb, who lived in the adjacent cottage. Various trade directories list Abraham Webster and his son William as 'limeburners' in Barton Turf from 1836 to 1854. The kiln may have stopped operating soon after the latter date: it is marked as 'old limekiln' on the first edition 6-inch Ordnance Survey map, surveyed in 1881.

As well as these various landing places strung out along the north side of Lime Kiln Dyke there were, by the nineteenth century, at least three staithes in Barton Turf parish, lying on the margins of Barton Broad. Barton Hall had its own staithe, clearly shown on an estate map of 1830.[74] Callow Green Staithe was also private by the nineteenth century and reserved for the use of Hall Farm, but it may well have had public origins, being accessed by a public road leading from the parish church. The third staithe, located in the hamlet of Barton Turf itself, was and is public. A parcel of land covering around 0.25 hectares was allotted by the enclosure award of 1810 as a staithe for the use of the 'owners and occupiers of lands and tenements' in the parish, with three trustees appointed: Revd William Gunn, the incumbent, Revd James Wiggett, and Thomas Preston of Beeston Hall.[75] The tithe apportionment shows that by 1840 it was owned and occupied by the Surveyors of the Highways, and was now provided with a shed or warehouse.[76] The latter, which had been built at least ten years earlier (it is marked on a map of 1830) is the 'Black Shed' already referred to, a small red-brick building with a tiled roof. It may have been built in stages, the original eastern section being given an extension later in the nineteenth century, of timber with a thatched roof, which was itself subsequently rebuilt in brick (Figure 6.10).[77]

By the later nineteenth century this staithe was administered by trustees appointed annually by the parish vestry, which included the Overseer of the Poor and the Surveyor of the Highways, but in 1894 management devolved to the new parish council, who discussed its poor condition on a number of occasions. In 1924 the Port and Haven Commissioners at Great Yarmouth agreed to clean out the channel by the side of the staithe and in 1937 Mr Lewis Storey of Horning, who also owned property in Barton Turf, offered to pile round the staithe free of charge

---

74 NRO MC 337/267, 710X3.
75 NRO C/Sca 2/18.
76 NRO DN/TA 205.
77 The building has a butt joint showing that it was built in two stages. The section to the west appears to have replaced a thatched wooden range shown on a photograph by G. Christopher Davis, but the view is obscured by a wherry. Malster, *The Broads*, Plate 47.

Figure 6.10 The 'Black Shed', a nineteenth-century warehouse, on Barton Turf Staithe.

if the parish would pay to back fill behind the quay heading, but the plan was abandoned as too expensive and the staithe continued to pose problems.[78] By the 1950s private boats were being offered for hire from the staithe without permission and several half sunken hulks were causing an obstruction and posed a danger to children bathing. There were also arguments about the precise boundary with the land of an adjacent boatyard. Various plans for improving the staithe came to nothing and while further dredging was carried out in 1957 by the Port and Haven Commissioners it was said that more work was required 'in order that in future there would still be a staithe'.[79] In 1958 a Staithe Restoration sub-committee of the council was formed and donations invited, but the staithe continued to suffer damage from lorries collecting reed and sedge, the Black Shed was now in a dangerous condition and on the point of falling down, soil and rubble were being dumped and boats illegally moored.[80] By 1963, however, the Barton Turf Staithe Restoration Fund had received £120 in donations, enough to pay for 20 yards of quay heading and other improvements, and through the 1970s the dyke to the north of the Black Shed was dredged to provide better moorings for parishioners and the quay heading was extended.[81] Now, with the Black Shed protected and repurposed for communal use, the staithe is an attractive and well-used area.

---

78 Barton Turf Parish Council Minute Book 1894–1959 (held by the parish clerk: not yet deposited at the NRO).
79 *Ibid.*
80 *Ibid.*
81 Barton Turf Parish Council Minute Book 1959–1987 (held by the parish clerk: not yet deposited at the NRO).

Catfield parish, as noted earlier, had no fewer than four separate staithes, one of which, Common Staithe, in the far north-east of the parish, exemplifies many of the themes outlined earlier. It is very probable that a customary staithe existed here before the enclosure of 1808. The site is situated on a stream called Guttermere, just below the lowest bridging point, Guttermere Bridge, originally where it flowed into an embayment of Hickling Broad. No staithe was formally established here by the enclosure commissioners or is mentioned in the enclosure award. Instead the staithe lay within a tract of fen covering 11 acres (4.5 hectares) called The Smee, which was allotted to the Trustees of the Poor as a poor's allotment.[82] The parish boundary between Catfield and Hickling, as described in the parish register in 1610, followed a straight line sighted from Guttermere Bridge to Winterton church tower, across reedbeds and open water.[83] Today the staithe is reached along the ruler-straight Catfield Dyke, which follows this same boundary, but this seems to have been created only in the course of the nineteenth century, as the natural embayment gradually terrestrialised.

In 1859 a petition was sent to the Trustees of the Poor, the rector, the churchwardens and the Overseers of the Poor bearing the signatures or marks of 43 pauper householders and requesting that the Trustees accept an offer of £8 per annum from Richard and William Riches, wherrymen, to lease 'the canal and staithe on our common rights', with the proceeds being distributed to the poor.[84] Many of the paupers were Primitive Methodists, as were the Riches family, who had paid most of the money for the erection of a chapel in Catfield in 1838; William was the leader of the chapel.[85] The request was agreed to and the Riches family continued to lease the staithe until 1964, apparently without opposition. They paid £8 per year for the staithe and £5 per year for The Smee, the area of reed and sedge beds to the east, rents that remained almost unchanged for the next century.[86] The Riches family were soon treating Catfield Dyke as a private waterway with no public right of navigation, a view supported by several witnesses at a public inquiry in 1971.[87] That opinion was rejected, the channel was judged to fall under the Port and Haven Commissioners, and it is today maintained by the Broads Authority as part of the public navigation.

Public rights over the staithe were eroded in another way. Between 1822 and 1827 Robert Pollard, a wherryman, occupied a portion of the poor's allotment and

---

82 NRO C/Sca2/67.
83 NRO PD531/1.
84 CUC Trustees papers (held locally).
85 T. Overton, *A programme of events to celebrate 150 years of Catfield Methodist Chapel* (Catfield, 1986). NRO FC16/335.
86 CUC Accounts Books 1861–1918 and 1941–1971 (held locally).
87 Department of the Environment, APP/2374/C/17452-5, Planning Appeal Inquiry by Inspector M. Adamson, January 1971. Appeal by Catfield Parish Council, CUC and Messrs Buck.

built a thatched clay cottage on it.[88] Unopposed, the land became his by adverse possession, the rector of the parish describing in 1881 how it had been 'successfully abstracted by encroachment years ago, the Trustees being asleep'.[89] Most of the land was subsequently sold to Richard Riches, Pollard retaining only the cottage and a small garden. It was one of several buildings that gradually gathered around the staithe in the middle and later years of the century. By 1883 a pair of semi-detached cottages had been built by the Riches beside Pollard's cottage, which were used to house their employees.[90] By 1905 the family had erected a brick warehouse against the road. Across the road from the staithe, on land allotted in the enclosure, Staithe House was built in 1830 by John Bird Crowe.[91] It was constructed of quarry flint with white-brick quoins, materials typical of those being brought in by wherries in the early nineteenth century. Richard Riches tenanted the house in 1839; in the 1841 and subsequent censuses Richard Riches 'corn merchant' and William Riches 'waterman' were recorded as sharing it.[92] In addition, to the south of the staithe there was an ice-house where ice, cut from Hickling Broad in winter, was stored and then taken by wherry to Yarmouth to be used in the fishing industry. In 1971 William Riches' widow, then aged 83, told the public inquiry how the building had ceased to be used for this purpose around 1892/3 and was then used to store about 7,000 sacks, with two men employed 'to mend the rat-holes in them'. In 1939 the ice-house was converted into a dwelling.[93] It seems to have occupied another piece of land filched from the Trustees.

Richard Riches died in 1870 and his son William in 1879, the business passing to William's son John George Riches and, subsequently, in 1911, to his son William Riches, who moved away from Staithe House to live at Sutton Lodge near Catfield railway station.[94] By this time much of the trade in corn, animal feed, coal and so on was carried by train and William Riches had a coalyard and other facilities at the station. But he continued to be based at the staithe and to operate wherries until 1936, when, following the loss of *The Brothers*, his remaining wherries – *Zulu* and *Violet* – were sold.[95] Trading, though reduced, continued by contractors' lorries and by rail until 1950. As commercial use of the staithe declined through the 1940s and 1950s it became a private mooring place

---

88 CUC papers, Correspondence between Trustees and Charity Commission, 1857.
89 NRO PD531/63.
90 Ordnance Survey first edition 6-inch map, Norfolk Sheet XLI SW, surveyed 1883. Ordnance Survey second edition 6-inch map, Norfolk Sheet XLI SW, surveyed 1905. TNA RG 12/1506, Census 1891.
91 Date and name plaque on Staithe House.
92 NRO DN/TA 722. TNA HO 107/775/16, Census 1841. TNA 107/1808, Census 1851. TNA RG 9/1197, Census 1861. TNA RG 10/1793, Census 1871.
93 APP/2374/C/17452–5 Inquiry, p. 20.
94 TNA RG 14/11124, Census 1911.
95 APP/2374/C/17452–5 Inquiry, pp. 19–20.

used by the Riches family and a few other people. But in October 1964 Catfield Parish Council leased the staithe for 21 years at £12 per annum from the Trustees (since 1916, Trustees of Catfield United Charities).[96] They let much of the staithe to Mr Buck as a boatyard while reserving part for public use. In 1997 Catfield United Charities did not renew the lease of the staithe to the parish council but instead took direct control of the public section, and leased the commercial part directly to Mr Buck.

Perhaps the most impressive staithe in Broadland is that at Stalham, with its particularly extensive collection of commercial riverside buildings, and which is now home to the Museum of the Broads. The enclosure map of 1807 shows a boat dyke running north from Sutton Broad that bifurcates at its end, thus forming a rough 'Y' shape (Figure 6.11).[97] Two public roads (now Staithe Road and East Staithe Road, but described on the map as 'Public Road Number 6' and 'Public Road Number 5' respectively) ran south from the village, towards the dyke; they were linked by a broad area coloured the same as the roads but unlabelled, which runs east–west just to the north of the 'Y'. This is clearly the public staithe, which still exists. An area similarly detailed, and containing two buildings, is shown running west from East Staithe Road along the southern side of the eastern arm of the 'Y', and then for some 40 metres south along the main boat dyke. The tithe map of 1841 shows the broad area running between the two roads as a 'staithe' owned by the Trustees for the Poor and occupied by John Burton and others. The north side of the second staithe, to the south, was partly marked as 'warehouses', partly now as private property, but both were likewise rented by Burton and associates.[98] The two small sheds had now been replaced by larger warehouses, one of which still survives as part of the museum. It is a single-storey red-brick building with a datestone inscribed '1820' and 'RB', presumably for Robert Burton, another family member. In addition, the tithe map marks a further private staithe on the southern edge of the western arm of the 'Y', owned by Susan Brooke and occupied by William Gaze 'and others', with a warehouse and boathouse; and also a new dyke, running north-east from the main channel some 60 metres to the south of the eastern arm of the 'Y' which terminated at a building on the roadside, owned, like the adjoining land, by William Cooke. This is the magnificent brick-and-flint granary that still survives beside the road leading to the staithe, built by Cooke's father, Samuel, in 1808 on land allotted at the enclosure the previous year (above, Figure 6.7). Beneath it, as already described, wherries would moor and be loaded through hatches in the floor of the building. The same buildings are shown on

---

96 APP/2374/C/17452–5 Inquiry. CUC papers, leases and correspondence.
97 NRO C/Sca 2/273.
98 NRO DN/TA 857.

308 BROADLAND

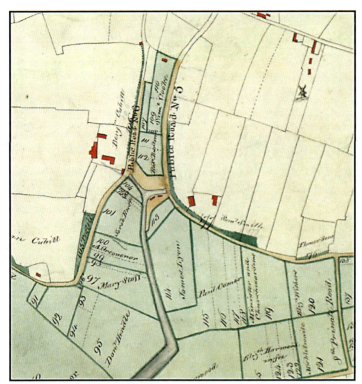

Figure 6.11 The development of Stalham Staithe. Above, as depicted on the enclosure map of 1807. Below, as shown on the first edition 6-inch Ordnance Survey map of 1884. a: warehouses; b: granary; c: Staithe House.

the 6-inch Ordnance Survey map of 1883, although additional houses had by now appeared on the approach roads to the staithe (Figure 6.11).

The Cooke family continued to flourish in the second half of the nineteenth century. Robert Cooke, farmer, merchant, brick-maker and miller, operated the wherries *William* and *Stalham Trader* out of Stalham.[99] But the history of the staithe is really dominated by the Burton family, who lived here from at least the start of the nineteenth century. The residence called Staithe House, which stands a little to the north of the staithe, bears Robert Burton's initials and the date 1813. As well as Robert Burton, the documents refer to Jonathan Burton, probably his son, who was born in 1811 and is recorded as a 'merchant' in the census of 1841, and as 'corn and coal merchant, and lime burner' in White's *Directory* of 1845.[100] He seems to have operated the mill on Mill Road as well as a number of wherries. When Jonathan died in 1871 he left his estate to his wife Sarah, who continued to trade as a 'Coal and Corn Merchant', helped by sons John and Harry.[101] In 1891 John was trading as an 'Oil Merchant'; Harry Burton operated the windmill but also owned at least three wherries trading from Stalham Staithe, *Cornucopia*, *Ceres* and *Dispatch*.[102] In 1909 he added the final building to the Stalham Staithe ensemble, a large steam-driven flour mill that still stands, now converted to residential use, on the eastern side of the staithe. At this time he was living with his family in Staithe House.[103]

Burton's *Cornucopia* had been built by the boat-builder Allen's of Coltishall. *Ceres*, however, was constructed by Josiah Cubitt Teasel, who from the 1870s had a yard on Stalham Staithe.[104] By the end of the century Teasel was hiring out wherries, yachts and small rowing boats to visitors from his yard and when he died in 1906 his wife, Sarah, continued the business. Later, she sold the yard to Edward (Ted) and George Southgate, who had built wherries with their father, Richard, at Sutton. The Southgates ran the boatyard up to the Second World War. It continued afterwards as Stalham Yacht Services, and is now operated and owned by the Simpson family.[105]

Staithes, in various forms, were thus a key part of the economic life of Broadland until the late nineteenth century, with public staithes then enjoying a new lease of life as places where holidaymakers could moor for the night, while

---

99 Malster, *Wherries and waterways*, p. 115.
100 TNA HO 107/775/27. White, *Directory of Norfolk*, p. 776.
101 TNA RG 12/108. Oral history interview, the late Michael Burton, Stalham.
102 Malster, *Wherries and waterways*, p. 115. Oral history interview, the late Michael Burton, Stalham.
103 TNA RG14 PN:11141 RD:221 SD:3 ED:2 SN:55, p. 109.
104 *Ibid.* P. Simpson, 'A brief history of Simpson's Boatyard, Stalham'. https://www.simpsonsboatyard.com/history (accessed 31 July 2021).
105 Simpson, 'A brief history of Simpson's Boatyard, Stalham'.

some private staithes embarked on new careers as boatyards. Yet not every staithe has early origins: some new public ones were created in the twentieth century to serve the needs of leisure craft and holidaymakers. Neatishead Staithe, located near the end of Lime Kiln Dyke and both owned and maintained by the parish council, was established in 1933 at a cost of £300.[106] It was completed within three months of the scheme receiving the unanimous assent of parish councillors. Indeed, within ten days of the meeting men on the unemployed list were busy clearing the banks of Lime Kiln Dyke. A dredger was used to deepen the dyke as far as the dock mouth, then local manual labour dug the dock, 150 feet long by 30 feet wide.[107]

These kinds of individual case study help to give a human face to the landscape, as a place where real people lived and worked in the past. They also bring into sharp focus some of the key themes in the history of the Broadland staithes and the activities associated with them. They highlight once again the sheer importance of the waterways as arteries of commerce before the twentieth century. They remind us of the role of local dynasties like the Burtons and the Riches. And they reveal the problems experienced in the past by public bodies trying to fulfil responsibilities that the public itself was reluctant to fund, and their understandable readiness to offload their obligations onto private individuals. This, however, is only one aspect of a more general shifting and blurring of the line between public and private ownership and use-rights that continues to cause problems to this day.

Industry

We have already noted how particular industries were drawn to the Broadland rivers, either locating close to public staithes or constructing their own, private ones. Raw materials, finished products and fuel were all, in many cases, moved more easily by water than by road. The number of riverside businesses seems to have increased steadily through the eighteenth and nineteenth centuries, as the local economy expanded. Their character mirrored, to a large extent, the principal cargoes carried by keel and wherry, as discussed earlier. Some have left no trace in the modern landscape, such as the timber yards that, by the late nineteenth century, were a particular feature of Norwich, Yarmouth, Beccles and Reedham. But three industries in particular have left a more enduring mark: malting, the production of chalk and lime, and brick-making.

Eastern Norfolk and north-east Suffolk were prime barley-growing areas and much of the crop was processed locally into malt. The barley was soaked for several days in tanks or 'steeps' and then spread onto a heated germination floor, where it was repeatedly turned. It was then placed in a kiln, where it was

---
106 *Eastern Daily Press*, 17 February 1933.
107 *Eastern Daily Press*, 9 March 1933.

Figure 6.12 Nineteenth-century malthouse near the public staithe at Ludham.

'cured', the temperature being gradually raised over a period of three or four days to around 210 degrees Fahrenheit.[108] The requirements of these two processes produced distinctive buildings – longer than they are wide and of two or three storeys, in order to provide an extensive floor area; and featuring a cube-shaped kiln at one end with pyramidal roof surmounted by a cowl or other covering. The small malthouse beside Womack Water in Ludham, erected in the middle decades of the nineteenth century by the Green family (who also ran the adjacent brickworks), still boasts its kiln roof, although it is now converted to residential use (Figure 6.12).[109] The huge maltings on Oulton Broad – erected in the 1890s and an example of how the scale of such businesses increased markedly in the course of the century – is also immediately recognisable, with its prominent cowls, although likewise now converted into apartments. Coltishall was a major centre of the industry, with around 18 working malthouses in the 1880s, and a particularly fine eighteenth-century example survives on Anchor Street.[110] But here, as in other places, conversion to new uses has often involved loss of kilns and cowls, rendering buildings' original purpose less immediately obvious. The large

---

108 J. Brown, *Steeped in tradition: the malting industry in England since the railway age* (Reading, 1983).
109 Norfolk Industrial Archaeology Society, 'A survey of Ludham', *Journal of the Norfolk Industrial Archaeology Society*, 3/1 (1981), pp. 34–51.
110 R. Bond, *Coltishall: heyday of a Broadland village* (North Walsham, 1986), p. 5.

example in Stalham, built in the late nineteenth century a few hundred metres north-east of Wayford Bridge and reached by a long boat dyke, has no visible kiln and is easily missed. Others have been extensively altered or severely truncated. Only a small part of that located beside the staithe at Ranworth, and which gave its name to both Malthouse Broad and the nearby Maltsters public house, survives, now incorporated into the modern visitors' centre. Many of those shown on the late-nineteenth-century Ordnance Survey maps, including that at Hardley Staithe, most of those in Beccles and all but a few of the examples in Wroxham, have simply disappeared without trace.

Lime was a major cargo carried on the waterways, as we have seen; it was mainly used agriculturally but also for making mortar and plaster. The raw material, chalk, was burnt to a high temperature in coal-fired circular kilns constructed of brick and/or flint. Chalk is exposed at the surface in the west of East Anglia, but dips towards the east and becomes buried beneath the Crag and later deposits. In Broadland it could be extracted only where, in the west of the district, rivers have cut deeply through the overlying geology: in the valley of the Yare around Thorpe St Andrew and Norwich; and in the valley of the Bure between Horstead and Wroxham. In these areas a substantial extraction industry developed, with chalk being taken by river to lime kilns at Acle Bridge, Barton Turf, Reedham, Ludham, Stalham, Dilham, Yarmouth and elsewhere. Keels or wherries also brought coal to these sites and carried away much of the finished lime.[111] Most kilns are now ruinous or inaccessible, or have disappeared, but that at Coltishall, located behind the Railway public house, has been restored and can be visited with permission. Not all the chalk that was excavated at the quarries was converted to lime. Some was suitable for use as a building material; much, softened by glacial action, could be applied directly to the fields as 'marl'. Again, the ease of transport provided by the rivers stimulated the scale of extraction. William Marshall in 1787 described how the farmers at Woodbastwick obtained their marl from the pits near Norwich by water, via Yarmouth – the distance was more than 40 miles (64 kilometres), although by road it was little more than 6 (*c*.9 kilometres).[112]

It is, in fact, not entirely clear what proportion of the chalk dug from the various pits was used in these different ways. Terms were often employed loosely, but it is noteworthy that the tithe apportionments generally use 'marl pit' to describe the principal extraction sites. They were already striking features of the landscape by the end of the eighteenth century. Those at Whitlingham were painted, as suitably dramatic and 'picturesque' subjects, by artists of the Norwich School such as

---

111 Norfolk Industrial Archaeology Society, 'Survey of Ludham', p. 41. J. Jones and M. Manning, 'Lime burning and extractive industries', in P. Wade-Martins (ed.), *An historical atlas of Norfolk* (Norwich, 1993), pp. 162–3. Jones and Jones, 'Lime burning in Norfolk'.
112 Marshall, *Rural economy*, vol. 2, p. 99.

Joseph Clover and John Sell Cotman in the 1810s and 1820s; by the 1850s the chalk was taken to the river's edge on a narrow-gauge wooden railway, loaded on trucks pulled by horses, although some was converted to lime on site.[113] Extraction also occurred on a large scale to the north of the river, in Thorpe, and in the west of that parish, around Gas Hill, although in these locations the density of modern housing makes the pits less obvious. More dramatic in many ways were the workings at what became known as 'Little Switzerland' in Horstead, the largest of several extraction complexes on the Bure.[114] The working faces of the pits were accessed by two boat dykes, approaching from the north and south, each over a kilometre long: the northern dyke was, and is, crossed by a substantial bridge, the 'High and Low Bridge'. Following their abandonment in the late nineteenth century the pits and associated waterways became something of a tourist attraction – hence the name 'Little Switzerland'. At least two other pits in the parish were similarly accessed by purpose-built channels. All are shown as 'marl pits' on the tithe map of 1841, and by implication were still functioning; all had probably begun to be worked in the eighteenth century, although extraction on a smaller but still significant scale may have begun in the locality much earlier, especially where the river came close to the upland, without much in the way of intervening marsh.[115] The seventeenth-century Horstead House appears to be built within a former chalk working.

By the later nineteenth century brick-making was another important Broadland industry, not so much because of the particular suitability of local clay (serviceable bricks could be fired from a wide range of geological materials available in East Anglia) but due, once again, to the ease of transport offered by the rivers. In the 1770s Mary Hardy of Coltishall described in her diary how her husband regularly brought bricks by wherry all the way from a brickworks at Strumpshaw, a distance by river of more than 70 kilometres, but around a third of this distance by road.[116] Even at this time wherries could carry loads of 7,000 bricks; by the middle of the nineteenth century cargoes twice this size were routine.[117] The brickworks shown on the 6-inch Ordnance Survey maps from the 1880s at Rockland, Surlingham, Aldeby, Neatishead, Dilham, Sutton, Stalham, Ludham, Reedham, Coltishall and Wroxham seem to have exploited the clays within the Crag formation, which also includes deposits of the sand that brick-making also required. But the yard at Martham exploited estuarine clays dug from the river floodplain, as did those at Lound Bridge in Sea Palling, and

---

113 C. Fisher, 'Early chalk tramways at Whitlingham', *Journal of the Norfolk Industrial Archaeology Society*, 3/2 (1982), pp. 89–91.
114 NHER 12554.
115 NRO DN/TA 922.
116 Bird, *Mary Hardy*, p. 153.
117 Bird, *Mary Hardy*, p. 202. A. and A. Butler, *Somerleyton brickfields* (Somerleyton, 1960), p. 5.

at Burgh Castle, while the Somerleyton works seems to have made use of both sources. Some of these brickyards lay a short distance uphill from the navigable waterway (as at Coltishall and Reedham) but others (Ludham, Surlingham, Sutton, Wroxham, Martham, Burgh Castle and Somerleyton) lay beside it or close by, accessed by boat dykes less than 200 metres in length. The yard at Aldeby, in contrast, was separated from the Waveney by a wide and marshy floodplain and reached along the 500-metre long Wherry Dyke or Carpenters Dyke, while the Dilham brickworks, as we have seen, was served by a dyke over 800 metres in length. Those at Ludham, Martham, Sutton and Rockland were located beside public staithes, the presence of which presumably explains the development of brick-making at these particular locations.

Up until the middle decades of the eighteenth century brickworks had been small, scattered and in some cases temporary, but larger units of production then began to develop, in East Anglia as elsewhere, a process that continued into the nineteenth century.[118] Even then, many brickworks were relatively short-lived affairs. Faden's 1797 map of Norfolk shows riverside examples at Brundall, Wroxham and Salhouse, all of which had ceased to operate by the time the tithe maps were surveyed around 1840. The same was true of that at Strumpshaw referred to by Mary Hardy in the 1770s. While some of the Broadland brickyards shown on the first edition 6-inch Ordnance Survey maps – at Surlingham, Neatishead, Dilham and Somerleyton – were already in existence when the tithe maps were surveyed around 1840, most – at Aldeby, Burgh Castle, Martham, Ludham, Reedham, Coltishall, Sutton, Wroxham – were not, while that beside Stalham Staithe developed between 1884 and 1903. It is true that some other Broadland brickworks had ceased to operate before the end of the nineteenth century, such as that on the Yare at Berney Arms. Nevertheless, there was apparently a significant expansion of the industry in Broadland during the middle and later decades of the nineteenth century.

By the late nineteenth century local brickyards varied greatly in character. Some were small family businesses, with one or two simple kilns, drying sheds and some settling tanks, and served a relatively local market. But others were large and complex affairs, owned by major landowners and leased to commercial operators, which, by the 1880s, were equipped with large modern Hoffman kilns – multiple kilns arranged in blocks that allowed for continuous firing. Those at Hoveton, Burgh Castle and Somerleyton all fall into this category. The latter was operated initially as the brickworks for the Somerleyton estate (it supplied the bricks for the rebuilding of Somerleyton Hall in the 1840s after the property was acquired by the

---

118 R. Lucas, 'Brickmaking', in T. Ashwin and A. Davison (eds), *An historical atlas of Norfolk*, 3rd edn (Chichester, 2005), pp. 162–3. K.A. Watt, 'Nineteenth century brickmaking innovations in Britain: building and technological change', PhD thesis (University of York, 1990).

Figure 6.13 The remains of Somerleyton brickworks, located at the end of a boat dyke leading off the river Waveney.

entrepreneur Sir Morton Peto). Between 1849 and 1873 it was leased by the firm of Lucas brothers and its bricks were used for a number of large projects, including the construction of Liverpool Street Station.[119]

Most of the brickworks shown on the first and second edition 6-inch maps disappeared over the next 40 years and were not replaced by new ones, as a further phase of centralisation concentrated brick-making in a small number of favoured areas – around Peterborough or in south Bedfordshire, for example.[120] The brickworks at Ludham, Sutton and Coltishall had disappeared by 1905; that at Surlingham was marked as 'old kilns' on the revised 6-inch Ordnance Survey map of 1912.[121] Burgh Castle closed in 1912 and Reedham around the same time. Those at Aldeby, Dilham, Hoveton, Lound Bridge and Stalham seem to have survived into the inter-war period but then ceased trading. The last to operate was probably that at Somerleyton, which closed down in 1939.[122] Most have left only subtle traces in the landscape; pits, and scant remains of a kiln, at Dilham; pits (or working faces cut into hillsides) only at Aldeby, Coltishall,

---

119 *Suffolk Industrial Archaeological Society Newsletter* 23 (September 1988).
120 A. Cox, *Royal Commission on Historical Monuments, England, survey of Bedfordshire. Brickmaking: a history and gazetteer* (Bedford, 1979).
121 Information from 6-inch and 25-inch Ordnance Survey maps.
122 *Suffolk Industrial Archaeological Society Newsletter* 23 (September 1988).

Figure 6.14 Early-twentieth-century postcard showing the cement works beside the river Yare at Berney Arm.

Neatishead, Surlingham and Reedham. At Hoveton and Stalham even the pits have been levelled and built on, while at Martham there are few indications of the origins of the water-filled hollows beside the Thurne. But the large brickyards at Burgh Castle and Somerleyton have left extensive remains (Figure 6.13). The latter site is publicly accessible and boasts the ruins of a 'Belgian' kiln (an improved version of the Hoffman), built in 1900.[123] The Burgh Castle works site was surveyed by the Norfolk Industrial Archaeology Society in the 1980s and includes the remains of settling ponds, a kiln, various buildings and two crushing plants.[124]

Some of these structures, however, relate to a rather different industry, based at the same site. The Burgh Castle Brick and Cement Company also made 'Roman' or Portland cement, using a mixture of chalk brought from Whitlingham and estuarine clay dredged from Breydon Water. It was opened in 1859, joining a similar works at nearby Berney Arms. The latter had closed by the 1880s, by then boasting an impressive range of buildings that included cottages for workers and the Berney Arms Mill, built in 1860, which was used to grind clinker as well as to drain the local marshes (Figure 6.14).[125] When advertised for rent in 1821 the business already included

---

123 Butler and Butler, *Somerleyton brickworks*.
124 NHER 10501.
125 Malster, *The Broads*, pp. 62–5.

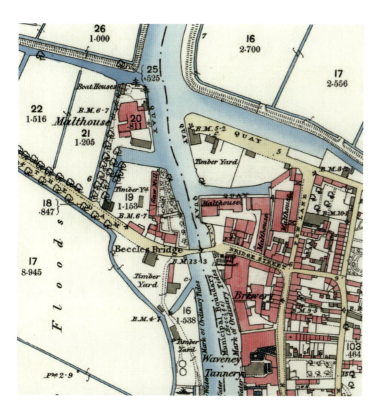

Figure 6.15 The Suffolk town of Beccles, as shown on the first edition 25-inch Ordnance Survey map. Private and public staithes, warehouses, timber yards, malthouses and a tannery line the banks of the river Waveney.

Figure 6.16 Sign on the wall of a house in Northgate Street, Beccles.

a Kiln, Windmill, and Warehouses, with every convenience for the manufactory of Roman Cement. Also an extensive Brick Ground, with an unlimited extent of brick earth, and most complete drying sheds, coal and sand houses requisite for making bricks. Also a Public House, the Berney Arms.[126]

By the time the 'Berney Arms Works' closed there were four kilns.[127] Now only the mill and the public house, currently closed, remain in what seems like a remote rural spot, untouched by modernity, a symbol of the more general deindustrialisation of Broadland that has taken place since the late nineteenth century. Indeed, the only significant riverside industrial site now remaining is the sugar factory beside the Yare at Cantley, opened by the Anglo-Netherlands Sugar Corporation in 1912, closed in 1915 but re-opened in 1920 by the English Sugar Beet Corporation.[128] Its presence had an almost immediate impact on the local landscape. In 1923 the Dutch industrialist J.P. Van Rossum began to purchase land in the parishes around Cantley for growing sugar beet and by 1939 the East Anglian Real Property Company owned 5,000 acres, across which the landscape was transformed. Large, regular fields were laid out and old buildings were replaced by substantial, brick-sided Dutch barns (it is said that these were suspected by the authorities of being secret airfields, to be used in a German invasion).[129]

River transport had a fundamental impact on the urban landscapes of Norwich and Yarmouth – a subject too large to be discussed here – and on that of the smaller riverside towns of Loddon, Bungay and, in particular, Beccles. Here nineteenth-century maps show a mass of private and public staithes, warehouses, timber yards, malthouses and tanneries lining the banks of the Waveney (Figure 6.15). Even today, a walk along Fen Lane and its continuation, Northgate Street – which run parallel to the river and are connected to it by numerous parallel alleys or 'scores' – reveals many traces of this industrial past. A converted malthouse lines one side of Fen Lane; another is visible on Bridge Street, which crosses it at right angles. Further south the huge nineteenth-century tannery survives, again converted into apartments. Brick storage sheds line some of the alleys running down to the river and, as the road gradually climbs towards the Old Market and the parish church, and immediately opposite Staithe House, a sign painted on the wall still advertises the staithe of Smith and Easthaugh, 'Corn and Coal Merchants, Dealers in Malt and Hops of the best quality. beans, peas, oats, pollard, cinders' (Figure 6.16). Reaching the church itself, with its unusual detached tower, we encounter another subtle sign of the river's influence. East Anglia lies far from sources of

---

126 *Norfolk Chronicle*, 10 February 1821.
127 First edition 6-inch Ordnance Survey map, Suffolk I NW, surveyed 1883.
128 A. Douet, 'Norfolk agriculture 1914–1972', PhD thesis (University of East Anglia, 1989), p. 157.
129 Douet, 'Norfolk agriculture', pp. 157–9.

good-quality stone and the region's churchyards boast few gravestones pre-dating the transport improvements of the late eighteenth century. Here, in contrast, there are many examples of late-seventeenth- and early-eighteenth-century date, crudely carved with gruesome death's heads. It is a pattern repeated, in more muted form, in several village churchyards in Broadland, including that at nearby Geldeston.

Bridges, roads and railways

The Broadland rivers were, for many centuries, vital arteries of trade and communication. Yet at the same time they, and the associated wetlands of the valley floors, provided obstacles to movement overland by road. Today, ignoring examples in the major urban centres of Norwich and Great Yarmouth, there are bridges on the Bure at Coltishall, Wroxham and Acle (Wey Bridge); on the Ant at Ludham and Stalham (Wayford Bridge); on the Thurne at Potter Heigham; on the Chet at Loddon; and on the Waveney at St Olaves and Beccles. The Yare, in contrast, has no bridges downstream of Norwich, probably a consequence of the fact that the river flows due east from the city, and the only significant settlements in this direction are reached by a road (the A47) running roughly parallel to it.

Most if not all these crossings seem to have developed from earlier fords (as indicated by the name Wayford Bridge) or, in the lower reaches of rivers, ferries, as at St Olaves or Wey Bridge in Acle.[130] Bridges began to be constructed in the Middle Ages, that at Wey Bridge perhaps as early as 1101. Those at Potter Heigham and Beccles are referred to in 1268, Wroxham was in place by 1320, St Olaves was built in 1509.[131] Initial construction and in some cases subsequent improvements were funded privately, thanks to individual benevolence or groups of benefactors. The bridge at St Olaves, for example, was paid for by Sir James Hobart of Hales Hall, attorney general to Henry VII, or more probably by his widow.[132] Several surviving wills include bequests for rebuilding the 'great bridge of Beccles' in the mid-fifteenth century.[133] Whoever funded their initial construction, responsibility for subsequent maintenance lay with local communities, as did that of roads more generally. Such a system was poorly suited to deal with major routeways, as the volume of traffic increased inexorably through the post-medieval period, even though the county Quarter Session magistrates sporadically forced parishes to fulfil their obligations (and could levy a county rate to pay for projects deemed essential to the county's economy, such as the rebuilding of Wroxham Bridge

---

130   C. Green, 'Broadland fords and causeways', *Norfolk Archaeology*, 32 (1961), pp. 316–31.
131   For Wey Bridge see above, p. 82. Blomefield and Parkin, *Topographical history*, vol. 11, p. 182. SHER BCC 022. NRO DN/EST 7/23. A.I. Suckling, *The history and antiquities of the county of Suffolk* (London, 1848), vol. 3, p. 19.
132   W.A. Smith Wynne, *St Olave's priory and bridge* (Norwich, 1914), p. 70.
133   SHER BCC 022.

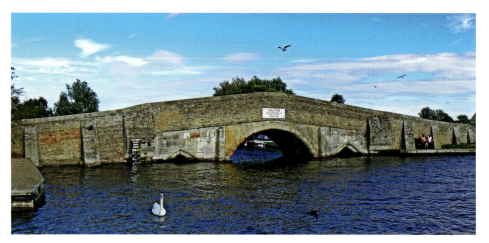

Figure 6.17 The late medieval bridge over the river Thurne at Potter Heigham.

in the 1570s).[134] But from the late seventeenth century many major transport routes began to be improved through the institution of 'turnpike trusts'. Created by individual acts of parliament, these comprised boards of trustees that would adopt sections of road, erect toll gates, charge tolls and use the proceeds (after a suitable cut had been taken as profit) to keep the route in adequate repair.[135] The bridges at Coltishall and Acle were thus taken into the care of turnpike trusts in the course of the eighteenth century, along with the roads they served, although they do not appear to have been significantly remodelled in consequence. In addition, urban communities could on occasions fund the construction of major bridges, as when Beccles Corporation rebuilt the town bridge in 1884 in elaborate wrought-iron form, replacing the three-arched masonry structure erected in the fifteenth century.[136]

All the Broadland bridges became the responsibility of the relevant county councils following their establishment in 1889. Ludham Bridge, described by Suffling in 1885 as 'a small, stone structure of one narrow, low arch', was replaced by Norfolk County Council in 1915 after its foundations, already weakened by floods in 1912, were further damaged when new pipes were laid by the Yarmouth Water Works Company in the following year. Most of the others were completely rebuilt in the course of the twentieth century in order to cope with the escalating volume of motorised traffic – often more than once.[137] As a result, only two early bridges now survive in Broadland. That at Potter Heigham, picturesque if routinely

---

134 NRO NCR 22a/5. NRO WKC 7/109/1–4, 404X5.
135 W. Albert, *The turnpike road system in England 1663–1840* (Cambridge, 1972). P. Langford, *A polite and commercial people: England, 1727–1783* (Oxford, 1989), pp. 391–408.
136 TNA MT 10/404/1.
137 NRO STA 872. Suffling, *Land of the Broads*, p. 153.

cursed by those using the river on account of its low central arch, is a fourteenth- and fifteenth-century stone structure with eighteenth-century brick additions (Figure 6.17); and Wroxham Bridge is a single-arch structure of brick with some stone dressings, originally built in 1576–9 but modified in the seventeenth century, widened in the eighteenth and partly rebuilt in the nineteenth, and with a modern superstructure.[138]

The bridges of Broadland have a range of distinctive landscape associations. With the exception of that at Coltishall they are approached by raised causeways running across the floodplains, which in the case of Wey Bridge and St Olaves Bridge, located where the rivers approach the great levels of the Halvergate Marshes, are of some considerable length. The south-western approach to the latter, along the Haddiscoe Dam, follows the levée of a former creek for most of its three-kilometre length. Many crossings, as we have already noted, were associated with public staithes, the road characteristically widening in a fan as it approached the bridge and continuing down to the water's edge to either side of it (as originally at Wroxham, Wayford Bridge, Wey Bridge and, to an extent, Potter Heigham and Ludham). Two – St Olaves and Wey Bridges – had minor religious houses located beside them in the Middle Ages, while Beccles Bridge had a chapel and hermitage at one end. These associations reflect the liminal character of these locations, the potential hazards of river crossings and the donations offered by thankful passengers on their safe completion, and probably also – in the case of St Olaves and Wey Bridges – the role of religious houses in the maintenance of bridges and ferries. Most Broadland bridges are, or were, also accompanied by public houses, either in immediate proximity – the Waterman's Arms at Potter Heigham, The Bell at St Olaves, the Angel at Wey Bridge, the White Horse at Coltishall – or set a little further back, on harder ground – as with the Dog at Ludham and the King's Head at Wroxham. These catered for travellers by road but, in particular, for the crews of passing keels and wherries. Lastly, most were considered strategically important during the First and (in particular) the Second World War. Pill boxes survive beside the bridges at Ludham and St Olaves, the former inserted into a drainage windmill, and there are concrete bases for mobile spigot mortars at Ludham and Wayford Bridge.[139] In fact, aerial photographs from 1946 show concentrations of defensive activity around most of the bridges and especially at Wey Bridge, Wayford Bridge, Potter Heigham and St Olaves.

Although major river crossings had all been provided with bridges by the end of the Middle Ages, many ferries survived, serving less important routes or particular local needs. Even in the late nineteenth century no fewer than six were

---

138   NRO WKC 7/109/1–4, 404X5. NHER 8425.
139   NHER 5235. NHER 15092. NHER 24411. NHER 35280.

Figure 6.18 Buckenham ferry, as painted by Joseph Stannard in 1826.

still operating on the Yare (at Surlingham, Coldham Hall, Buckenham, Cantley and two at Reedham); three on the Waveney (at Fritton, Somerleyton and Burgh St Peter); three on the Bure (at Stokesby, Upton and Horning); and one on the Thurne (at Martham).[140] Most, like bridges, were accompanied by public houses and some (Fritton, Somerleyton, Stokesby, Horning and Burgh St Peter) by public staithes.[141] Ferries formerly existed at other places. Faden's 1797 map of Norfolk marks one at Whitlingham on the Yare that continued to operate until at least 1845; references to a 'Ferry Close' in 1547 suggest that one existed a little upstream at Thorpe; and circumstantial evidence suggests the presence of one crossing the Bure at St Benet's.[142] Some examples appear to have always been for transporting pedestrians, using rowing boats, and these mostly connected only minor tracks or footpaths providing access to cottages and farms. But those at Horning, Surlingham, Buckenham and Martham, and one of those at Reedham, were vehicular crossings that, at least by the nineteenth century, took the form of chain ferries. These probably all had medieval origins: there are references to Horning ferry in the thirteenth century, while in 1372 a new ferry boat was built and launched by the manor of Claxton, part-owner of Buckenham ferry (Buckenham parish itself has

140 J. Points, *Floating bridges: ferries across the Broadland rivers* (Surlingham, 1994). Malster, *Wherries and waterways*, pp. 48–53.
141 Information from the first edition 25-inch Ordnance Survey maps, 1881–6.
142 White, *Directory of Norfolk*, p. 795. NRO DCN 41/107.

been known as 'Buckenham Ferry' since at least 1325) (Figure 6.18).[143] Pedestrian ferries were less profitable and may have been less long-lived. The example at Burgh St Peter is said to have been established as late as 1857, while that shown on the first edition 6-inch Ordnance Survey map of 1885 had disappeared by the time the second edition was surveyed in 1905.[144] Most of the ferries shown on the 1880s Ordnance Survey maps, however, and certainly all the vehicular ferries, survived up until the Second World War, although they then rapidly disappeared and only two now remain. These are the public chain ferry at Reedham and the unusual floating pontoon structure at Martham, which replaced the private chain ferry here in 1927, and which was itself replaced by more modernised versions in 1987, and again in 2012, by the National Trust (who had acquired most of the land on Heigham Holmes, to which it provides access).[145]

Almost all the public roads crossing the wetlands do so to reach bridging points, with only four real exceptions. One is the present B1159 between West Somerton and Horsey, running just inland from the sea, which was established only following the enclosure of the common marshes of the two parishes in 1811 and 1816 respectively.[146] More dramatic is the stretch of the A47 running across the Halvergate Marshes between Acle and Great Yarmouth, commonly known as the 'Acle Straight'. This was built as a turnpike road in 1834 to shorten the previous turnpike route, established in 1769, which ran from Acle, across Wey Bridge, through Fleggburgh and across Rollesby Bridge, and then on through Caister. Those unwilling to pay a toll on either route were obliged to use the public track that followed the embankment of the Halvergate Fleet, through the heart of the marshes to a ferry across the Bure on the edge of Yarmouth, just to the north of the present bridge on the A149 Acle New Road. The new turnpike road ran, and still runs, across the north of the marshes in two ruler-straight sections – one seven kilometres long, and one four – that join near Stracey Arms Mill. Close to this point another straight road, branching south-west towards Halvergate village, was laid out at the same time. The most recent is the Stokesby New Road, the minor road branching to the south-east off the modern A1064 a little to the north of Wey Bridge, which was constructed in the late 1930s by Norfolk County Council.[147]

All these roads are, or were within living memory, flanked by continuous lines of close-set willows pollarded at a height of between 1.5 and 2 metres,

---

143 Blomefield and Parkin, *Topographical history*, vol. 11, pp. 1–2. NRO MC 2945/1, 1026X. Blomefield and Parkin, *Topographical history*, vol. 10, p. 114. NRO NCR 25a/3/176.
144 Points, *Floating bridges*, p. 41.
145 Points, *Floating bridges*, pp. 43–4.
146 NRO C/Sca 2/331. NRO C/Sca 2/168.
147 NRO C/SR 4/22.

Figure 6.19 Low-cut, closely set willows lining the ruler-straight road, created in the 1830s, which leads from the 'Acle Straight' turnpike road to Halvergate village.

a distinctive feature of the Broadland landscape but perhaps not a very ancient or 'traditional' one (Figure 6.19). Similar lines of willows occur beside the roads leading across the marshes to the crossings at Reedham Ferry, Beccles, Wey Bridge and St Olave's Bridge; the first of these was realigned at enclosure in the early nineteenth century, while the others were all taken over by turnpike trusts in the second half of the eighteenth. A few willow rows are found lining older roads, such as that approaching Potter Heigham Bridge, but for the most part they are associated with examples that were either constructed or improved between the late eighteenth century and the 1930s. Whatever their date, their function is clear. The trees were planted to stabilise the sides of the flanking ditches and probably, their roots spreading inwards, to provide additional stability for the road surface itself. The trees were, and are, pollarded to keep them low and thus prevent them being toppled by the wind, and also to allow them to be narrowly spaced in order to better fulfil their purpose.

Railways arrived in Broadland with the construction of the line running from Norwich to Yarmouth, via Reedham, in 1844, and proliferated gradually through the second half of the nineteenth century (Figure 6.20). They still make a dramatic impact on the landscape, on the Halvergate Marshes especially, which are crossed both by the 1844 line and by a second, constructed parallel to and south of the Acle Straight in 1883. The trains seem surreal intruders in this flat green landscape, as they do in the more enclosed and wooded context of the Yare valley between

WATERWAYS AND INDUSTRY 325

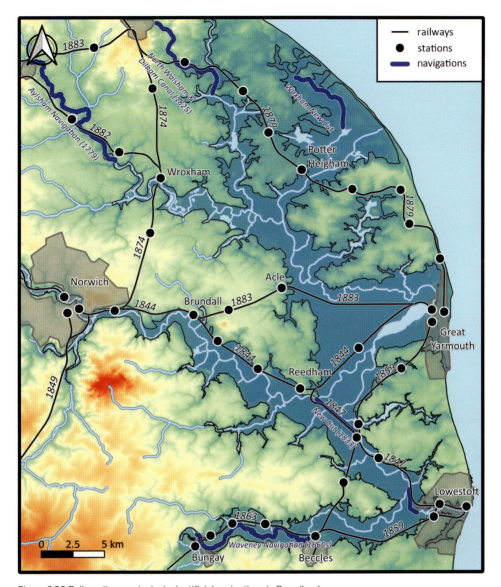

Figure 6.20 Railway lines and principal artificial navigations in Broadland.

Reedham and Brundall. Railways would have made a much greater impression before the 1950s and 1960s, when several local lines – most notably those opened between Yarmouth and Beccles in 1859 and between Haddiscoe and Lowestoft in 1847 – were closed.[148] In the level terrain of Broadland there was little need for dramatic schemes of engineering, although swing bridges were erected where the

---

148 R. Joby, 'Railways', in T. Ashwin and A. Davison (eds), *An historical atlas of Norfolk*, 3rd edn (Chichester, 2005), pp. 152–3. R. Joby, *Regional railway handbook 2: East Anglia* (Newton Abbot, 1987). D. Gordon, *Regional history of the railways of Great Britain volume 5. Eastern England* (Newton Abbot, 1977).

lines crossed the Norwich–Lowestoft navigation at Reedham, Somerleyton and St Olaves (the latter now destroyed), to facilitate the passage of sea-going ships, and also on the Waveney below Beccles (again, now destroyed, Figure 6.1). Much more important were the indirect effects of the railways, in both bringing about the decline, and eventual demise, of commercial wherry traffic and, as we shall see, initiating the emergence of the Broadland tourist industry.

7

RECREATION, TOURISM AND CONSERVATION

So far we have considered the landscapes of Broadland in essentially practical, economic and agrarian terms. We have discussed how fens and marshes were shaped by grazing and the extraction of fuel, fodder and a range of raw materials, and how the waterways served as a complex transport network that influenced commercial and industrial activities on the neighbouring 'uplands'. But from early times the rivers, broads and wetlands also afforded a number of rather different resources and provided opportunities for a distinct range of activities that were, if not always entirely recreational in character, certainly separate from the hard and humdrum toil of normal everyday life. Broadland teemed with wildlife, to be caught and shot; its waterways were a playground for sailing and boating, as well as serving as arteries for trade. The impact of such pursuits was initially slight, or at least subtle. Only with the rise of a significant tourist industry in the later decades of the nineteenth century did leisure activities come to have a major and enduring impact on the landscape. The result was a protracted conflict over how Broadland should be managed, and to what ends.

Sailing, trapping, shooting and fishing

To say that the writer George Christopher Davies, whose books served to popularise Broadland as a holiday destination in the 1880s, 'discovered' Broadland, or even its recreational potential, is like saying that Columbus discovered America. The broads and rivers had been used by local people for sailing and other pleasurable activities for centuries. By the eighteenth century many of the wealthier members of local society, including middle-class residents, owned sailing craft of various kinds, including punts and rowing boats, which they used in a variety of enjoyable ways, including as platforms for fishing. These are referred to in documents such as probate inventories – that drawn up in 1734 for Stephen Norris of Barton Hall,

Figure 7.1 Traditional Broadland boathouses at the northern end of Hickling Broad.

for example, included a boat, sail, oars and quant (punt pole) – and in newspaper advertisements and diaries.[1] Mary Hardy thus recorded how, on 2 July 1779, she and 'Mrs Neve drank tea with Mrs Starkey in their keel, went to Engall's garden after tea in Starkey's boat',[2] while on 30 June 1780 she and her family 'went down to Belaugh in Mr Palgrave's boat, drank tea at Mrs Prior's'.[3] Such vessels needed a place where they could be stored, especially during the winter months, and the first edition 25-inch Ordnance Survey maps surveyed in the 1880s label numerous 'boathouses', although some no doubt housed boats used more for work than for play. Most were to be found in the grounds of manor houses and 'halls', or were associated with parsonages, farms and other substantial middle-class residences, although a number were more remotely located. Some of the same buildings appear to be shown, although they are not named, on the tithe maps surveyed around 1840. Early photographs, such as those by Davies, suggest that local boathouses had a recurrent 'vernacular' appearance, featuring vertical or horizontal weatherboarding on a wooden frame and a reed-thatched roof, usually hipped (above, Figure 6.9). Examples of such structures survive in a number of places, perhaps most notably the picturesque cluster on the north-western edge of Hickling Broad, although most if not all appear to be of twentieth-century date (Figure 7.1).

---

1   NRO DN/INV 79D/16.
2   Bird, *Mary Hardy*, p. 412.
3   Bird, *Mary Hardy*, p. 409.

Those insufficiently wealthy to own their own craft could, at least by the eighteenth century, find many places to hire one. In 1794 Jacob Watson, publican of the King's Head in Coltishall, placed an advertisement in the *Norwich Mercury* describing how his establishment was:

> Very near (and from some parts there is a view of) a pleasing navigable river, where vessels are almost constantly passing, and for parties fond of fishing or sailing, proper boats can always be had. It will also be his practice to keep cold provisions and bottled beers in readiness to accommodate water parties.[4]

Waterside gardens, where boating parties might take refreshments, existed by the end of the eighteenth century at Thorpe St Andrew (Himsby's), Belaugh (Thomas Engall's), and elsewhere.[5] After *c.*1835 parties might visit Dilham Island, a 25-acre pleasure garden laid out beside the Ant by Sheppard Thomas Taylor, which by the 1850s featured a network of channels for boating and fishing, ornate swing bridges, walks, ornamental planting and a central two-storey summer house (the place became derelict in the early twentieth century but was partly restored in the early twenty-first).[6]

Already, by the late eighteenth century, 'water frolics' were being held at Hickling, Burgh Castle, Oulton, Hoveton and elsewhere – precursors of regattas, but also featuring rowing races and other forms of water-borne competition, as well as processions of decorated boats.[7] That held at Thorpe St Andrew, reputedly attended by 30,000 people, was painted by Joseph Stannard in 1824. In the middle decades of the nineteenth century the 'frolic' at Wroxham, in particular, came to emphasise yacht racing over other activities, and sailing craft became faster and more sophisticated. The races were dominated by craft funded by wealthy businessmen and landowners, such as *Maria*, acquired by Sir Jacob Preston of Beeston Hall in 1837.[8] But they continued to be attended by diverse social groups, and the waterways more generally continued to be enjoyed by a very wide range of local people.

The rivers and broads teemed with fish, particularly eel, pike, tench, bream, roach, rudd and perch. Although now considered 'coarse' fish, to be caught for sport rather than for food, most of these – especially perch, pike and tench – were regularly consumed well into the post-medieval period. The scale of the catches made in the local rivers in the Middle Ages is attested by the earthworks at St Benet's

---

4   *Norwich Mercury*, 9 August 1794: quoted in Bird, *Mary Hardy*, p. 411.
5   Bird, *Mary Hardy*, p. 412.
6   White, *Directory of Norfolk*, p. 478.
7   T. Fawcett, 'Thorpe Water Frolic', *Norfolk Archaeology*, 36 (1977), pp. 393–8.
8   P. Townley Clarkson, 'Yacht-racing', in W.A. Dutt, *The Norfolk Broads* (London, 1903), pp. 305–12.

330 BROADLAND

Figure 7.2 St Benet's Abbey from the air. The rectangular depressions behind the gatehouse represent a sophisticated fishpond complex. The remains of further fishponds exist in the south-east of the precinct (off-picture, top right).

Abbey, which include an elaborate arrangement of 'stews', or *servatoria* – shallow rectangular ponds used to keep fish prior to consumption or sale – immediately to the east of the gatehouse, and another group in the south-east of the precinct (Figure 7.2). A survey made in 1594, long after the abbey's destruction, described 'a howse of fiftie foote long & xxtie [20] foote wide by estimacon Wherein one Edmund Dye fisherman now dwelleth', while in 1617 Edmund Dey, presumably the same man, leased from Norwich Dean and Chapter 'the house called the ffishing house together with all the ffish pondes and holdes to the same belonging scituate and being within the late dissolved monastery of St Bennettes'.[9] After they had flooded, many broads became private fisheries: a survey of 1662 refers to 'one great water or ffishing knowne by the name of Brunn Fenn alias Burnt Fenn' – that is, Burntfen Broad – while Buckenham Broad was described as a 'large fishery' in 1736.[10] As late as 1832 payments were made by the Langley estate for 'Cutting fish

---

9   TNA 178/1667. NRO DN HAR 3/3, p. 204.
10 NRO CUL/1/44. NRO BEA 9/7, 433X5.

stews ... at Carleton Broad'.[11] Local landowners did not always manage to assert such exclusive rights and where they did they might be contested, as in Irstead and Neatishead in 1679, where the common rights claimed by the copyhold tenants of the bishop of Norwich included 'Liberty of Fishing in a certain water there called Alder Fenns and in all other the Broads and Waters in Irstead' (these and other rights continued to be disputed, on and off, into the nineteenth century).[12] Eels, too, were widely caught in rivers and dykes. Eel 'setts', comprising long, conical nets fixed in a river or stream and accompanied by a small hut providing overnight accommodation for the individual watching over them, were common features in the past. A lease of 1617 mentions several on the bishop of Norwich's land near St Benet's: 'a certain Elesett called Horning Elesett', the 'Elesettes ... called Thirne Settes', and 'Bacons Elesett'.[13] Only one example now survives in Broadland, on Candle Dyke in Potter Heigham, and even this is no longer used commercially.

Fishing was, at least by the sixteenth century, already a recreational activity as much as a way of procuring food. Initially, gentlemen enjoyed drawing their ponds with nets but by the seventeenth century angling with a rod was increasing in popularity. The Norfolk landowner and writer Roger North, in his book *A Discourse of Fish and Fish-ponds* (1712), described the benefits of fishing for the whole family:

> Young People love Angling extreamly; then there is a Boat, which gives Pleasure enough in Summer, frequent fishing with Nets, the very making of Nets, seeing the Waters, much Discourse of them, and the Fish, especially upon your great Sweeps, and the strange Surprizes that will happen in Numbers and Bigness, with many other incident Entertainments, are the Result of Waters, and direct the Minds of a numerous Family to terminate in something not inconvenient, and it may be divert them from worse.[14]

A map of the Somerleyton estate, surveyed in 1652, shows a detached area of gardens, with terraces and a viewing mount, lying well outside the park, some 1.25 kilometres to the south of the hall, traces of which survive as earthworks.[15] They were laid out around two small broads, one still known as Summer House Water, and are described in an accompanying survey as 'divers fish ponds gardens and walks'.[16] There were islands in each of the broads, occupied by small buildings,

---

11 NRO BEA (S 196 D).
12 NRO MC 36/123. NRO MC 121/238.
13 NRO DN HAR 3/3, p. 203.
14 R. North, *A discourse of fish and fish-ponds* (London, 1712), p. 73.
15 SRO 295.
16 SRO 194/A11/11.

Figure 7.3 One of the 'pipes' at Fritton Decoy, photographed by Payne Jennings, c.1890. The net supported on metal hoops and the reed screens arranged *en echelon* are clearly visible.

evidently fishing lodges. At the other end of Broadland, in Crostwight, an undated early-eighteenth-century estate map shows four conjoined fishponds, formed from an earlier broad, lying a few hundred metres to the north-east of the hall.[17] The ponds, clearly semi-ornamental in character, featured distinctive bastion-shaped projections in their sides, almost certainly for the accommodation of anglers. Casual fishing by the wider population, in rivers or in broads over which exclusive rights had not been successfully asserted, made no such impact on the landscape. But innumerable references make it clear that it was common, whether it was largely practical or largely recreational in character.

The undrained wetlands also provided habitats for huge numbers of waterfowl, both resident and migratory, and Broadland is closely associated with duck decoys, an ingenious method of trapping introduced into England from the Low Countries in the early seventeenth century. A decoy comprised an area of open water, the 'decoy pond', out from which ran a number of gently curving channels or 'pipes'. These were normally around 50–60 metres long, gradually tapered in width from around 20 metres to less than 0.5, and were covered with nets supported on a series

---

17 Private collection.

of curved hoops, which gradually reduced in height with increasing distance from the mouth, just as the channel itself narrowed (Figure 7.3). In early decoys the hoops were constructed of bent wood, commonly willow, but in many nineteenth-century examples they were made of wrought iron. Each pipe terminated in a detachable purse net. Along the outer edge of each pipe, set back by a metre or so, was a series of reed screens, each around 3 metres long and 1.5–2 metres high, which were arranged *en echelon* – that is, in an overlapping, staggered manner. The whole arrangement – pond, pipes, nets, screens – was surrounded by belts of trees or woodland, in order to provide the quiet and seclusion needed for successful operation.[18]

Wildfowl were attracted to the pond by the sight of specially trained decoy ducks, raised by hand, sitting contentedly on its surface. Once a sufficient number had joined them the decoyman would approach behind the reed screens and throw corn or hempseed into the pond near to the entrance to one of the pipes. Responding to his signs, the trained ducks would swim into the pipe, followed by their wild companions.[19] The decoyman would move along behind the screens, throwing food ever further along the pipe, drawing the birds after him. When they had progressed a sufficient way along it he would move back toward the mouth of the pipe and emerge from behind the screens. By this stage, any attempt to escape by flight was thwarted by the nets: the birds part swam, part flew down the pipe, the curving course of which obscured the fact that it was a dead end; they were then caught in the terminal purse net. The decoy ducks were marked in some way, and released from the net when the others were dispatched.[20]

Most seventeenth- and eighteenth-century decoys also used a dog called a 'piper' to entice the ducks into the pipe. It was trained to run around one of the reeds screens, a little way back from the entrance to the pipe, jumping over lower reed screens ('dog jumps') spanning the gaps with its neighbours. The wildfowl swam down the pipe towards it, encouraged by the tame decoy ducks and attracted to what must have appeared, from their perspective, to be an appearing and disappearing fox.[21] Presumably their intention was to keep a careful eye on a predator. As they progressed down the pipe, the dog would move ahead of them, running around the next screen in the sequence, and then the next. As with the method first described, the decoyman would then appear at the mouth of the pipe, scaring the birds into their doomed flight down towards the purse net.

It was essential that the wildfowl should remain ignorant of the decoyman's presence until he showed himself near the end of the pipe. But wildfowl have a

---

18   R. Payne-Gallwey, *The book of duck decoys: their construction, management and history* (London, 1886). A. Heaton, *Duck decoys* (Princes Risborough, 2001).
19   Payne-Gallwey, *Duck decoys*, p. 27.
20   Defoe, *Tour*, 2nd edn, vol. 3, p. 347.
21   T. Pennant, *British zoology*, vol. 2 (London, 1770), pp. 464–5.

good sense of smell, and it was important, if possible, to remain upwind of them. It was partly for this reason that decoys were generally equipped with more than one 'pipe', so that the decoyman had a choice of which to use. But this was mainly because the method worked best when the wind was blowing down a pipe, towards its mouth, for the birds 'swim most readily with their breasts to the wind' and, when scared into flight, tended to turn towards the wind, to give them better lift.[22] In addition, multiple provision ensured that there was a pipe entrance always close to that part of the pool where the birds were congregating.

Decoys were worked during the winter months, generally from the end of October until February. Indeed, an act of parliament passed in 1737 prohibited their operation in the period between 1 June and 1 October, an early example of a legally enforced 'close season' to maintain supplies of game.[23] Although examples could be found scattered throughout England they were mainly a feature, in Blome's words, of '*Moist, Marsh*, and *Fenny* Grounds' – of coastal marshes and of wetlands located at no great distance from the sea, especially in East Anglia, Cambridgeshire and Lincolnshire.[24] Here, local populations of waterfowl were augmented by an influx of winter migrants. Not surprisingly, decoys were a significant feature of the Broadland landscape, especially in areas of peat, where isolation and the shelter of alder carrs provided the tranquillity required.[25] Over half of the known examples, moreover, utilised an existing 'broad' as their decoy pond. This causes some problems in counting the total number of known decoys in Broadland, for it is a moot point whether broads such as Ormesby or Fritton, where pipes were constructed on different shores by different proprietors, should be considered as single or multiple examples. If the latter, then there were at least 17 examples, although not all were in operation at the same time (Figure 7.4). Because the birds could be scared away even by a passing wherry, most decoys were set back from the rivers and only one (Ranworth) was on a broad connected to the river system. A wide range of waterfowl, including pochard, pintail, mallard, shoveller, gadwall and wigeon (or 'smee', as they were known locally) was taken, but the Broadland decoys mainly trapped 'the common wild duck and the teal'.[26]

Henry Spelman described in *c*.1640 how Sir William Wodehouse had 'made among us the first device for catching Ducks, known by the foreign name of a koye

---

22   R. Lubbock, *Observations on the fauna of Norfolk, and more particularly on the district of the Broads* (London, 1845), p. 99.
23   10 George II, c. 32.
24   Payne-Gallwey, *Duck decoys*; Heaton, *Duck decoys*.
25   R.E. Baker, 'Norfolk duck decoys', *Transactions of the Norfolk and Norwich Naturalists' Society*, 27/1 (1985), pp. 1–8. T. Southwell, 'Norfolk decoys', *Transactions of the Norfolk and Norwich Naturalists' Society*, 2 (1879), pp. 538–55.
26   Lubbock, *Observations*, p. 99.

RECREATION, TOURISM AND CONSERVATION 335

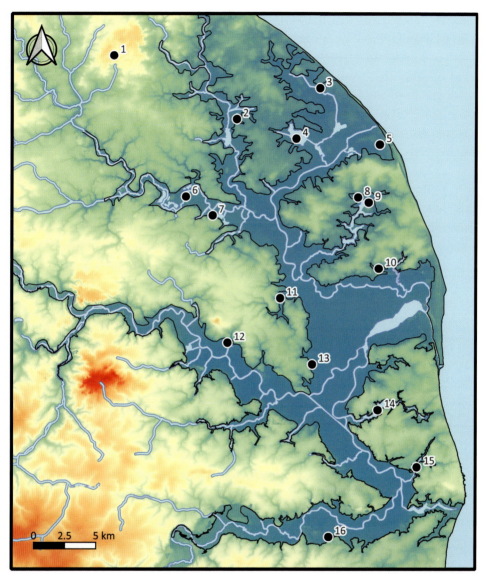

Figure 7.4 Wildfowl decoys in Broadland, with probable dates of operation. 1. Westwick, 1827–c.1880 2. Sutton, late nineteenth century 3. Waxham, early seventeenth century–late eighteenth century 4. Hickling, uncertain 5. Winterton, 1820s–1870s 6. Woodbastwick, ?seventeenth century–late eighteenth century 7. Ranworth, ?seventeenth century–1869 8. Rollesby, eighteenth century 9. Hemsby, ?seventeenth century–late eighteenth century 10. Mautby, early eighteenth century–c.1830 11. Acle, seventeenth century–mid-nineteenth century 12. Buckenham, seventeenth century–early eighteenth century 13. Reedham, eighteenth century 14. Fritton, early seventeenth century–early twentieth century 15. Flixton, early seventeenth century–1820 16. Worlingham, eighteenth century.

[decoy]', at Waxham.[27] In the 1670s this particular decoy became the subject of a bitter dispute, the then owner, Sir Peter Gleane, describing how his neighbour Thomas Smyth had 'caused shooting in every corner about it to fright the ffowl from it, when that would not doe, he sent his servants secretly in the morning when the ffowles came there to feed to frighten them out of the Quoy'; while 'persons imployed under the pretence of mowing ffodder in the ffenn' by the decoy had brought 'stones & slings to throw them into the decoy to fright the fowl'.[28] The decoy at Flixton also originated in the first half of the seventeenth century – it appears, complete with a dozen pipes, on an estate map of 1652[29] – while those at Acle, Fritton and on the Hemsby side of Ormesby Broad also seem to have been in existence by 1700.[30] The same may be true of a decoy at Buckenham, known only from a document of 1736 that describes Buckenham Broad as 'a large fishery … wherein lately a decoy was'.[31] There are hints of other early examples. The 'Duckoy' leased, together with an adjacent reed bed, in Tunstall in 1708 was probably (although not certainly) that already noted in Acle, which lay within 100 metres of the boundary between the two parishes; more intriguing is the will of John Thompson of West Somerton, 'decoy man', drawn up in 1690, as there are no other references to a decoy in the parish.[32] Other decoys, known to have been operating by the end of the eighteenth century, may likewise have had seventeenth-century origins, including those at Ranworth, Woodbastwick and Mautby. In the case of the latter, sales particulars from 1670 describe what became its site as 'about twelve acres of waters well stocked with fish and very convenient to make a decoy'.[33] Probably, although not certainly, of eighteenth-century date were the examples at Reedham and Worlingham. Most of these early decoys utilised existing broads as their ponds, ranging in size from Mautby, covering perhaps 4 hectares and with four pipes, which was shown on the tithe map of 1838, to Fritton, covering 130 acres and with 21 pipes, albeit not all in the same ownership.

Elsewhere in England many decoys were essentially commercial concerns, constructed by landowners and leased to professional operators. Those in the Lincolnshire and Cambridgeshire Fenlands supplied huge quantities of ducks to the London market.[34] But some were kept 'in hand' by owners and, while they might produce a surplus for sale, their main purpose was to provide birds for domestic

---

27 H. Spelman, *The English works of Sir Henry Spelman Kt. Published in his life-time; together with his posthumous works, relating to the laws and antiquities of England* (London, 1727), p. 153.
28 NRO BL/Y 2/21.
29 SRO 295.
30 Baker, 'Norfolk decoys'.
31 Baker, 'Norfolk decoys', p. 1. NRO BEA 9/7, 433X5.
32 NRO NCC original will 1690 no. 78. Payne-Gallwey, *Duck decoys*, pp. 137–9.
33 NRO MS 3329, 4B2.
34 Defoe, *Tour*, p. 344.

consumption and to serve as an object of interest on an estate. The 'mystery' of the decoy – the art of training the decoy ducks and dog, the skill of operation – clearly appealed to gentlemen, brought up to an appreciation of all things associated with fish, fur and feather. In Broadland some decoys were certainly leased out and even those retained in hand might be regarded in primarily commercial terms. Sir Peter Gleane, anxious to protect his Waxham decoy from difficult neighbours, managed it directly and primarily as a source of profit, describing how, 'although my Quoy is not a little help to me, yet that little is Grete where there is but a small estate'.[35] But Gleane lived far away in south Norfolk – the decoy was an isolated estate asset, hence his difficulty in protecting it. In contrast, most Broadland decoys formed part of a local estate and seem to have been primarily intended to produce birds for the owner's table or as gifts for his friends.[36] Particularly striking is the high proportion located within a short walk of the hall of the owner, including Woodbastwick (750 metres), Reedham (600 metres), Flixton (600 metres), Buckenham (560 metres), Mautby (400 metres), Ranworth (350 metres) and Worlingham (250 metres), a clear reflection of the decoy's esteemed position in the landscape of gentility.

By the last decades of the eighteenth century enthusiasm for decoys was waning. Those at Waxham, Hemsby, Woodbastwick and probably at Reedham and Worlingham had ceased to operate by 1800, followed by the demise of Flixton in the 1820s.[37] The Mautby decoy was in a state of disrepair by 1833 and plans to renew it were abandoned, 'Mr Fellows preferring the shooting'.[38] As Lubbock explained in 1845: 'A decoy mainly depends for its success upon its freedom from noise and disturbance … . Decoys which promised to be productive, have been abandoned just after formation, merely because shooting in the neighbourhood could not be prevented.'[39] By the middle decades of the nineteenth century only a handful of the old decoys – those at Fritton, Ranworth and probably Acle – were still functioning, although they had been joined by a new example, created at Winterton in the 1820s. Designed by the Lincolnshire decoyman George Skelton, it had, like many nineteenth-century examples, a highly regular plan, like a six-pointed star, ranged around a central pond, and was placed within a neat circle of woodland. By this stage, decoys were even more of a gentleman's hobby than a commercial endeavour, and one increasingly tied up with a burgeoning interest in natural history, not least because of the opportunities they provided for close ornithological observation. In Lubbock's words: 'Breaking the necks of forty or fifty unlucky ducks, consecutively, is not the main point of interest in the affair. It is perhaps the best place in which to

---

35   NRO BL/Y 2/21.
36   Lubbock, *Observations*, p. 96.
37   Payne-Gallwey, *Duck decoys*, pp. 137–9.
38   Payne-Gallwey, *Duck decoys*, p. 139.
39   Lubbock, *Observations*, p. 104.

speculate and gain knowledge on the habits of various birds.'[40] Decoys nevertheless continued to decline through the second half of the century. Acle disappeared in the 1850s (if it had survived that long), Ranworth was last worked in 1869, while Winterton disappeared soon after. In addition to competition from recreational shooting, the tranquillity required by decoys was now disrupted by the spread of railway lines through the area, something Dutt had 'little doubt' was the prime cause of their decline: 'The roar and rattle of the iron road drove the wild-fowl from many of their former haunts.'[41] Increasing numbers of pleasure boats sailing on the waterways further compounded these issues. By the 1880s only the two decoys on Fritton Decoy, owned by the Herringfleet and Somerleyton estates respectively, were still in use, although now with only 8 pipes between them, rather than the 21 maintained earlier in the century. Somewhat surprisingly, at some point between 1884 and 1905 the Fritton decoys were joined by a new example at Sutton, with a six-point 'star' plan similar to that at Winterton, but this was a short-lived affair, apparently already silted and reed-grown by the latter date. The Somerleyton pipes on Fritton Decoy continued to be worked into the twentieth century – in the winter of 1899–1900 no fewer than 2,721 wildfowl were caught there.[42] They appear to have been last used in the 1950s.

Decoys must have made a significant impact on the landscape experienced by people in the past, to judge from the number of Decoy Farms, Decoy Woods and, in particular, Decoy Carrs that still litter the map of Broadland. Their former presence is also recorded in the names of three broads – Decoy Broad in Woodbastwick, Mautby Decoy and Fritton Decoy. But they have left only meagre archaeological traces. The pipes, and the decoy pond itself if artificially constructed, were only around 0.6m deep and, once abandoned, were rapidly colonised by vegetation and subsequently filled with peat and silt. In a few cases, former entrances to pipes are still apparent as inlets in the sides of broads, as at the northern end of Flixton Water; and occasionally, most notably in the case of the decoys at Acle, Worlingham and Winterton, faint traces of ponds and pipes can be discerned on lidar images, but not really on the ground.

The popularity of recreational shooting on the Broads appears to have increased steadily from the late eighteenth century, and perhaps with particular rapidity from the middle decades of the nineteenth. A number of members of the local gentry, such as Colonel Henry Leathes of Herringfleet Hall, gained a national reputation for their sporting prowess, although some simply profited by leasing out the shooting rights to others.[43] An interest in shooting probably explains, as we

---

40   Lubbock, *Observations*, p. 94.
41   W.A. Dutt, *Highways, byways and waterways of East Anglia* (London, 1899), p. 117.
42   A. Patterson, *Nature in eastern Norfolk* (London, 1905), p. 56.
43   NRO HNR 196/6. NRO HNR 587/7.

have already noted, why local landowners were so keen to obtain allotments of fen and open water when parishes were enclosed by parliamentary act. Enjoyment of the local shooting, as much as a desire to profit from the grazing marshes, may also explain why wealthy families acquired properties in Broadland as outlying portions of their principal lands, whether full-sized landed estates such as Mautby, acquired by the Fellowes of Shotesham, or smaller units, such as the property on the north side of Hickling Broad owned by the Micklethwaites of Taverham Hall, to the west of Norwich.[44] Small sporting properties became an especially notable feature of the upper Thurne valley and included the Whiteslea estate, also in Hickling, which was acquired by the Liberal peer Lord Lucas in 1908 and passed, following his death in active service in 1916, to Ivor Grenfell, and was managed by Grenfell's father, Lord Desborough, of Taplow House in Buckinghamshire. Whiteslea Lodge, a thatched single-storey shooting lodge, was originally built at the eastern end of Hickling Broad in the late nineteenth century and extended for Lord Lucas, but further extended and largely rebuilt by Lord Desborough, who, inheriting on his son's death in 1926, expanded the estate from 97 hectares to 256.[45] The lodge contains painted friezes by the noted bird artist Roland Green.

The most important quarry for Broadland sportsmen were various kinds of wildfowl, and the most important areas for shooting them were the broads and wilder stretches of unreclaimed fen – especially in the valley of the Bure below Wroxham, and around the headwaters of the Thurne – and the mudflats of Breydon Water. These areas boasted, in particular, vast quantities of surface-feeding waterfowl such as wigeon, teal, pintail, shoveller and tufted duck, as well as divers such as the pochard (a noted feature of the area), and occasional rarities such as the scoter.[46] At the start of the nineteenth century small groups of sportsmen, or lone individuals, would shoot birds on the open water, either hidden in the reeds on the shore or – an old method – lying prone in a punt. With the development of lighter, more manoeuvrable guns, culminating in the 1860s with the appearance of breech-loading, double-barrelled shotguns, flight shooting – that is, the interception of flocks of birds on their morning or evening flights from pond or broad to feeding grounds – increased in popularity. Both forms of shooting also tended, in the last decades of the century, to become more organised, and to be undertaken by larger groups. Everitt described in 1903 how landowners erected small hides or shelters of reed screens around the margins of broads, raised on platforms above the high-water mark and reached from the shore by short banks or boarded plank-ways:

---

44 NRO MC 558/1, 774X5. TNA IR 30/23/283.
45 Matless, *In the Nature of Landscape*, p. 115. NHER 56243.
46 H. Stevenson, *The birds of Norfolk, with remarks on their habits, migration, and local distribution*, 2 vols (London, 1866). Walsingham and Payne Gallwey, *Shooting*, pp. 180, 186. Bird, 'Bird life', p. 228. A. Patterson, 'Wild life on Breydon', in W.A. Dutt, *The Norfolk Broads* (London, 1903), pp. 200–14, at p. 211.

Figure 7.5 Peter Henry Emerson, 'Snipe Shooting' (1886).

On the day of the shoot, before the party starts (for some prearranged place), a stated time is set and given to each shooter, and whatever happens no gun is allowed to be fired before the time agreed upon. This is done in order to give each gun a chance of getting to his stand before the fowl are alarmed … . At first gun-fire the fowl on the water rise and circle in all directions; possibly there may be only a very small quantity, possibly there may be from five hundred to a couple of thousand, and during the ensuing ten minutes every barrel may become uncomfortably warm. After this fusillade the birds leave the water for quieter and more secluded quarters; but within half an hour a great number will return, and if the shooter is still concealed and remains quite quiet, they will dip to the surface of the water and offer further opportunities.[47]

Not only waterfowl were shot. Large numbers of geese and waders such as plover and snipe were targeted (Figure 7.5). Some species more closely associated with woodland than wetland were also taken, where carrs were numerous: the name of Cockshoot Broad on the Ranworth estate is a reference to the woodcock, a favoured quarry in Norfolk more generally on account of the county's 'prominent position, having a great attraction for tired woodcock when arriving from the north'.[48]

Already, by the middle of the nineteenth century, most of the wilder areas

---

[47] N. Everitt, 'Wildfowling', in W.A. Dutt, *The Norfolk Broads* (London, 1903), pp. 323–30, at pp. 324–5.
[48] Walsingham and Payne Gallwey, *Shooting*, p. 125.

of Broadland were being very intensively shot. Colonel Leathes of Herringfleet reputedly won a bet that on one marsh 'if you sift three square feet of ground one spade deep … you will find three ounces of shot, dig where you will. The fact is: Fifty acres of this land has been shot over backwards and forwards for ages, and the whole surface of the ground is covered with shot'.[49] Whether shooting on this scale necessarily had a major impact on wild bird populations, and on biodiversity more generally, is less clear. It almost certainly served to preserve a range of wetland habitats. Sportsmen were well aware that improvements to drainage posed a threat to their activities. Many writers in the decades around 1900 bemoaned the decline in the numbers of snipe, so abundant at the start of the nineteenth century that Robert Fellows famously shot 158 in a single day, while on 11 December 1844 500 were brought for sale to a single Yarmouth game dealer.[50] In 1905 Maurice Bird observed that, while a 'good many' snipe still nested in Broadland, 'never again, perhaps, will it be possible for one gun in Broadland to kill thirty-three couple … in a day, and one hundred and sixty-six couple in a season, as my father did at Somerton in 1868'.[51] Their decline was principally attributed to improvements in drainage, and especially the use of steam pumps.[52] Snipe are birds of damp grazing marshes, rather than of fens, broads and reedbeds. They like land 'where, though the water splashes at every step, it rarely reaches the ankle', and in the first half of the century were particularly numerous around Hickling and Buckenham.[53]

Where land was owned by a keen sportsman, or by an individual deriving a decent income from leasing shooting rights, grazing marshes would be less intensively drained. More importantly, fens and reedbeds were more likely to survive intact. Sport may have played a particularly important role in conserving those in the upper Thurne valleys, where much of the land they occupied was capable of conversion to grazing marsh, but where some of the most important sporting properties were located. Nineteenth-century sportsmen certainly saw no necessary conflict, but instead a synergy, between the shooting of wildfowl and its conservation. Habitat preservation was essential to provide the large bags about which they boasted and in which they took pride, and to supply the rarer specimens that, if not treated as a culinary novelty, were stuffed by Norwich or Yarmouth taxidermists and proudly displayed – or sold to naturalist-collectors. Sportsmen did not dislike their quarry. Most were intensely interested in birds, and in wildlife more generally. Men such as Lord Lucas at Whiteslea were enthusiastic watchers of birds, as much as shooters and collectors of their eggs.

49   Walsingham and Payne Gallwey, *Shooting*, pp. 142–3.
50   Walsingham and Payne Gallwey, *Shooting*, p. 142.
51   Bird, 'Bird life', p. 230.
52   Walsingham and Payne Gallwey, *Shooting*, pp. 136, 142.
53   Walsingham and Payne Gallwey, *Shooting*, p. 136.

Figure 7.6 The naturalist Maurice Bird, punting on Hickling Broad in c.1900.

To an extent this was true everywhere – much of the ornithological information published in the *Transactions of the Norfolk and Norwich Naturalists* appears to have come from specimens that had been shot. But it was particularly true of Broadland, where truly wild birds, rather than the nurtured and cosseted pheasant, were the quarry. Most of the area's famous early naturalists were keen sportsmen. Many of the birds discussed by Richard Lubbock in his *Observations of the Fauna of Norfolk, and more particularly on the district of the Broads* (1845) he had himself shot.[54] At the end of the century Maurice Bird, rector of Brumstead between 1887 and 1924, prominent local naturalist and author of important papers on Broadland wildlife, happily recorded his sporting exploits in his diary: 'shot 37 Snipe, 2 Jack, a Heron (young bird) and Two Moorhens' (5 January 1887); 'Shot Somerton [Martham] Broad with George. 1 Teal, 1 Moorhen, 12 Jack and 1 full Snipe. Lovely hot still day (saw two Swallows)' (14 October 1890) (Figure 7.6).[55] Like many naturalists, he maintained an extensive collection of stuffed birds. By this time, it is true, such attitudes were being questioned by local naturalists such as Emma Turner and Arthur Patterson, but well into the twentieth century they remained dominant among most of those who actually owned and controlled the wilder parts of Broadland.

54 Lubbock, *Observations*.
55 Quoted in J. Parry, *Maurice Bird: The Gilbert White of the Broads*, Norfolk and Norwich Naturalists' Society Occasional Publication 20 (Norwich, 2024), pp. 51, 55.

The idea that conservation and shooting made ideal bedfellows, while perhaps not as unreasonable as modern sensibilities might suggest, should certainly not go unchallenged. The enthusiasm for collecting stuffed specimens encouraged, of necessity, the enthusiastic shooting of the rarer species, and also embraced the collection of and trade in eggs. In spite of attempts, local and national, to control all such activities – the 1880 Wild Birds Protection Act, in particular, establishing a close season between March and July – key species experienced an inexorable decline. That icon of Broadland, the bittern, had been reasonably common at the start of the nineteenth century (in 1819 Lubbock had 'killed eleven … without searching particularly hard for them'). By 1870 it was essentially a migrant visitor: 'Can we wonder if the Bittern's nest is robbed, when we consider the sum which a recently laid Norfolk example of its egg would command?'[56] But, while not unaware of such problems, most of those responsible for managing Broadland's wilder environments at the start of the twentieth century saw the greatest threat to wildlife as coming from a very different quarter – from the inexorable rise in the number of outside visitors.

Tourism and leisure

The development of Broadland as a tourist destination, visited by large numbers of people from outside East Anglia, began in the last quarter of the nineteenth century. The proliferation of rail lines, together with increasing levels of middle-class wealth, saw the development of a holiday industry in many parts of England. There had been railway connections to Norwich, Great Yarmouth and Oulton Broad from the 1840s: it was the construction of new lines, with stations in Wroxham (technically Hoveton) in autumn 1874 and Potter Heigham in 1880, that opened up the north of Broadland to visitors and really accelerated growth. This was where most of the broads were located, and where the scenery was most appealing to contemporary taste.

The development of tourism was not simply facilitated by the railways. It was actively promoted by the Great Eastern Railway and the Eastern and Midland, both keen to increase passenger numbers. The former engaged John Payne Jennings to produce photographs of Broadland scenery to advertise the area's attractions. In 1888 Jarrolds of Norwich began to sell 12 of the pictures, 'as seen in Great Eastern Railway Carriages', as loose prints in a cloth case. The following year customers were able to select from a choice of 100 of Jennings' photographs and in 1891 they became available in book form with the publication of the first edition of Jennings'

---

56 T. Southwell, 'Presidential address', *Transactions of the Norfolk and Norwich Naturalists' Society*, 1/3 (1872), pp. 7–19, at p. 18.

Sun Pictures of the Norfolk Broads.[57] The company also published, in 1893, its own *Summer Holidays in the Land of the Broads*, and actively promoted combined rail and pleasure steamer trips on two new vessels launched in 1889, *Pride of the Yare* and *Queen of the Broads*, each with capacity for 190 passengers. The former ran from the North Quay, Great Yarmouth to Foundry Bridge in Norwich, with return by train or river; *Queen of the Broads* travelled from Yarmouth to Wroxham and back.[58] Others organised similar combined rail/steamer trips. In 1886 Henry Keymer of Fisheries Ironworks in Gorleston built the steamboat *The Shadow*, especially adapted for the Bure and capable of carrying 40–50 passengers.[59] It was lengthened and relaunched in 1889 as *Lady of the Bure*, offering a new service operated in conjunction with the Eastern and Midland Railway. A second vessel, *Progress*, was soon acquired but the enterprise was short-lived, with the Eastern and Midland blaming the Great Eastern Railway for putting up bigger and better boats, and accusing them of encouraging hostile lawsuits concerning their authority to operate passenger steamers.[60]

Independently of the rail companies' endeavours, visitors were attracted to Broadland by a succession of books and articles extolling the attractions of the area. The most successful were George Christopher Davies' *Handbook to the Rivers and Broads of Norfolk and Suffolk*, and *Norfolk Broads and Rivers: or, the Waterways, Lagoons, and Decoys of East Anglia*, first published in 1882 and 1883 respectively, although the former in particular with numerous subsequent editions; and E.R. Suffling's *The Land of the Broads* of 1885.[61] But there were many others. Indeed, no fewer than 33 books on the Broads were received by the British Museum Library between 1880 and 1900, and one reviewer in 1897 commented:

> Surely no spot in the British Isles has been so 'be-guided' as the Norfolk Broads … hardly a magazine exists … which has not opened its pages to the flood of contributions on this apparently fascinating subject; and the whole has culminated in a shower of guide-books which enlivens the railway bookstalls with their gay exteriors … [62]

---

57 D. Clarke, *The Broads in print* (Norwich, 2010), pp. 45–6. *Eastern Daily Press*, 1 August 1888; 6 September 1889.
58 *Yarmouth Mercury*, 1 June 1889.
59 *Norfolk News*, 28 August 1886.
60 C. Beckett (ed.), *Forty years of a Norfolk railway: the reminiscences of William Marriott from 1884 to 1924* (Weybourne, 1999), p. 18. P. Allard, 'Henry Keymer of Gorleston, marine engineer', *Yarmouth Archaeology and Local History* (2014), pp. 108–11.
61 G.C. Davies, *The handbook to the rivers and broads of Norfolk and Suffolk* (Norwich, 1882). Davies, *Norfolk broads and rivers*. Suffling, *Land of the Broads*.
62 J. Taylor, 'Landscape and Leisure', in N. McWilliam and V. Sekules (eds), *Life and landscape. P.H. Emerson: art and photography in East Anglia 1885–1900* (Norwich, 1986), pp. 73–82, at p. 77. The quotation is from Malster, *The Broads*, p. 79.

Escalating visitor numbers increased the demand for boats. Before the 1880s the boatyards providing wherries for commercial operators and pleasure craft for private owners were mainly to be found in Norwich, notably around Carrow Bridge and King Street, as well as in Yarmouth and Lowestoft. There was also a thriving community at Anchor Street in Coltishall, where the transport needs of some 18 malthouses provided ample work for wherry builders and repairers, and a thinner scatter in other villages.[63] The growth of tourism, however, led to the wholesale migration of yards to new locations closer to the more scenic parts of Broadland and accessible by railway. While most continued to build boats, including racing yachts, for private owners, the emphasis was increasingly on providing vessels for hire.

The hire-boat industry was famously 'pioneered' by John Loynes, who from 1878 was building small boats in Norwich, initially to be hired for use on the river Wensum but soon on the Bure at Wroxham, transporting them there by handcart. He had clearly established a presence at Wroxham Bridge by 1882, when he advertised in Davies' *Handbook*, stating that 'some boats are stationed at Wroxham Bridge; others may be obtained at Elm Hill, Norwich'.[64] The landlord of the King's Head Hotel acted as Loynes' agent until he moved his business to Wroxham in the mid-1880s.[65] He was soon joined there by a number of boat-builders from Coltishall. Robert Collins had arrived by 1887, leasing a four-acre site from Robert Harvey Mason, owner of the Wroxham House estate, for £58 per annum; when the estate was put up for sale three years later the premises included 'newly and substantially erected boat houses' and three cottages.[66] On Collins' death in 1901 the yard was divided between his two elder sons, Ernest and Alfred, who from then on operated independently of each other. Collins was followed to Wroxham by Herbert Press, who was established on the Hoveton side of the river by 1889.[67] Another of the Coltishall boat-builders, Herbert Bunn, had also relocated to Wroxham by 1902, establishing a site near the railway bridge.[68]

By the early twentieth century the area around Wroxham Bridge had thus emerged as a major centre for boat-building and hire. But similar developments were occurring elsewhere. In 1882 H. Flowers and Co. established the Yare Yachting, Boating and Angling Station beside Brundall rail station. The enterprise

---

63 Bond, *Coltishall*, pp. 4–14.
64 Davies, *Handbook*.
65 C. Goodey, *A century of Broadland cruising* (Wroxham, 1978), p. 18.
66 NRO MC 3212/11 (36).
67 Collins was in Wroxham when advertising in the *Norwich Mercury*, 19 November 1887. Press and his sons were among the Wroxham boatbuilders to assist in a fire at Wroxham House in 1889: *Norfolk News*, 2 November 1889.
68 *Eastern Daily Press*, 27 March 1902. *Norfolk News*, 31 May 1902.

comprised a large boathouse for building and storing boats, refreshment rooms and 12 acres of ornamental grounds.[69] In 1884 George Mollett, a Carrow boat-builder, also moved his business to Brundall, offering 'boats of any description built to order'.[70] The first of these businesses was taken over by H.A. Little, a boatbuilder from Burgoines on the Thames, in 1893 and five years later the two were amalgamated as the Norfolk Broads Yachting Company, also acquiring Herbert Press's yard at Wroxham at around the same time.[71] Little was obliged to leave the company, which evidently did not initially flourish, the premises being offered for sale in 1901.[72] It was later taken over by C.J. Broom, a former employee of the company, and a substantial boat-hire business was established that continues to dominate the Brundall waterfront to this day.[73]

The Applegate family were key in the early development of the area around Potter Heigham Bridge, the third of the new tourist hubs. In January 1880 the new Potter Heigham railway station, on what was then the Yarmouth and North Norfolk Railway, was officially declared open.[74] As an access point to the waters of the upper Thurne, the location had a great appeal to anglers. By 1882 both the Applegates and the landlord of the Waterman's Arms were offering 'a capital service of boats'.[75] In 1886 George Applegate senior leased the exclusive fishing rights on Heigham Sounds and Whiteslea. For prospective visitors who hired one of his or his son's boats there was no further charge for fishing there.[76] When in 1892 Applegate Senior gave evidence in the famous legal case concerning navigation rights on Hickling Broad he described how, before the arrival of the railway, no pleasure boats had been kept at Potter Heigham, but no fewer than 40 were now available for fishing and sailing.[77] In 1899 the Norfolk Broads Yachting Company, having tried unsuccessfully to acquire the Applegate business, bought two sites below the bridge and one above it, and started to erect buildings, Walter Woods moving from Brundall to manage operations.[78] By 1902 it was said of Potter

---

69 *Yarmouth Independent*, 25 March and 22 April 1882.
70 *Yarmouth Mercury*, 10 May 1884.
71 *Norfolk Chronicle*, 27 February 1904. *Eastern Evening News*, 26 October 1898. Malster, *Norfolk and Suffolk Broads*, p. 161.
72 *Eastern Daily Press*, 20 May 1901.
73 B. Ayers and Brundall Local History Group, *The Book of Brundall and Braydeston* (Wellington, 2007), p. 51.
74 *Lowestoft Journal*, 24 January 1880.
75 *Yarmouth Independent*, 24 June 1882.
76 *Fishing Gazette*, 26 June 1886.
77 *Yarmouth Independent*, 18 June 1892.
78 A. Applegate, '"Boss of Broadland", the autobiography of Abiathar "Boss" Applegate, part 2', reproduced in *The Wherry*, Journal of the Norfolk Wherry Trust (1998), pp. 43–8. Walter Woods told a public meeting on the condition of the Upper Thurne in 1913 that he had been there 14 years; *Yarmouth Independent*, 5 July 1913.

Heigham that 'the number of yachts and visitors is only exceeded at Wroxham'.[79] In June 1920 it was agreed that the Norfolk Broads Yachting Company, then being wound up, would assign their lease to Walter Woods.[80] Walter then traded with his two sons Herbert and Walter as Walter Woods and Sons. Herbert also started up on his own account at a site above the railway bridge in 1925 and took over from his father in 1929, launching another well-known business that continues to this day.[81]

In addition to these new centres of boat-building, existing ones adapted to cater for the new market. Several of the Norwich boat-builders moved out to Thorpe, where riverside inns had long hired out boats to trippers. In the 1880s John Hart, who ran the Thorpe Gardens, developed an important business, having taken over the yard of another boat-builder, Stephen Field, and eventually moved the enterprise across the river to Thorpe Island.[82] W.G. Hazell was also hiring boats in Thorpe by 1885 and was one of the first to produce an illustrated catalogue, advertising his services as a yacht agent in the 1890s.[83] At Oulton Broad, similarly, the proprietors of riverside inns and others had long provided boats for hire, but activity expanded significantly in the last decades of the nineteenth century. In 1882 George Christopher Davies described Oulton Broad as 'populous with yachts lying at their moorings' and 'thickly clustered at the north east end of it', recommending one Mr Bullen as a likely man to have a yacht for hire. Robert and George Kemp were also both listed as boat-builders here by 1883.[84]

In the 1890 edition of Davies' *Handbook* 37 companies advertised boats for hire, ranging in size from 3 to 17 tons, and there were others who did not advertise. The craft provided for holidaymakers' accommodation were initially either large yachts or wherries converted on a permanent or temporary basis. Davies, discussing the latter, described how 'the hatches are raised a plank or two higher to give greater head-room, the clean-swept hold is divided into several rooms, and a capital floating house is extemporised'.[85] Press Brothers, millers from North Walsham, had 5 such vessels for hire in 1888, and two years earlier claimed that there were a total of 20 under sail in Broadland during the summer season, crediting their partner, Spencer Rix of South Walsham, with

---

79 *Eastern Daily Press*, 30 October 1902.
80 NRO HNR 406/3/3.
81 J. Woods, *Herbert Woods, a famous Broadland pioneer* (Tauranga, 2002), pp. 2, 25.
82 Malster, *Norfolk and Suffolk Broads*, p. 157.
83 *The Field*, 20 August 1892.
84 W. White, *History, gazetteer and directory of Suffolk* (London, 1874), p. 461. Davies, *Handbook*, p. 104; Kelly's Directories, *Kelly's directory of Suffolk*, p. 996.
85 Davies, *Handbook*, 17th edn (London, 1890), p. 167.

having converted the first, *Lucy*, in 1878.[86] In 1887, Halls of Reedham launched *Claudian*, the first wherry to be purpose-built exclusively for letting.[87] But soon new types of pleasure craft, designed for holidaying on the Broadland waterways, were being produced, especially by Loynes, whose four-ton boats were praised by Davies as 'beamy, of light draught – to enable them to visit the shallowest of the Broads'. The larger boats might be hired with a crew of 'watermen' who would, if required, also do the cooking. Even without a crew, a 'pleasure wherry' with 'ample accommodation for a party or a family' would cost, according to Davies in 1891, between 8 and 15 guineas a week, a not inconsiderable sum.[88] A Broadland holiday was essentially something to be enjoyed by the more affluent members of the middle class.

The industry continued to expand through the first half of the twentieth century, gradually broadening the social character of its customer base and bringing ever more visitors to the area. The first motor launches, powered by internal combustion engines, were developed in the 1910s and being hired out from the early 1920s.[89] Existing concentrations of boatyards expanded. At Thorpe Alfred Ward, the licensee of Thorpe Gardens, established the Yareside Yachting Station and became one of the first to hire motor cruisers, while in 1923 J.H. Jenner sold his Lowestoft fishing boats and bought the Town House, where he erected two two-storey boat sheds in what had formerly been its gardens.[90] At Hoveton, a number of new yards were established in the 1920s on land downriver from Wroxham Bridge, including those of A. Pegg and Son, E.C. Landamore and R. Moore and Sons. In Potter Heigham, Herbert Woods obtained permission in 1930 to breach the river wall south of the bridge to create his 'Broadshaven' yacht basin on adjacent marshes he had recently purchased, which was soon afterwards excavated by hand.[91] There was also further growth at Brundall, which, as at Wroxham, was part of a wider scheme of residential development. But the key rural hubs were now joined by another, at Horning, where the small yard of Smith and Powley near the Swan Hotel grew significantly after being taken over by H.C. Banham in 1925; the Chumley and Hawke Boatyard was established in 1922; Ernest Woods relocated his yard from Cantley in 1926; and H.T. Percival took over the Broads Motor Craft Company's site to establish a boatyard in 1929.[92]

---

86   Malster, *Norfolk and Suffolk Broads*, p. 156. *Evening Star*, 29 September 1886.
87   Malster, *Wherries and waterways*, p. 137.
88   Davies, *Handbook*, 17th edn (London, 1890), p. 167.
89   Malster, *The Broads*, pp. 91–2.
90   Malster, *Norfolk and Suffolk Broads*, p. 162.
91   WMA, Potter Heigham DC Minutes 1922–1935. Woods, *Herbert Woods*, pp. 39–52.
92   Cleveland, *A look back*, p. 205. *Eastern Daily Press*, 14 May 1931.

Although a number of distinctive centres developed, boatyards had always been widely scattered in Broadland villages and many of these refocused their businesses on the holiday industry. As early as 1890 Allen's, one of the Coltishall boatyards that did not move to Wroxham, were advertising seven yachts for hire from two to ten tons.[93] As we have seen (p. 309), Teasel's yard at Stalham similarly diversified into lettings by the 1890s. New examples of boatyards, moreover – isolated or in small clusters – continued to appear throughout Broadland in the first half of the twentieth century. E. Grottick and Son, for example, established a new yard at Acle Bridge after a fire in 1924 at their Hoveton premises. Sun Boats excavated the triangular basin in the 1930s and Eastick's, who otherwise operated from Acle Dyke, and Hazell from Thorpe also had bases there in the 1930s.[94] The number of boats for hire in Broadland rose from around 165 in 1920, of which only four were motor cruisers, to 547 in 1949, of which 301 were motor cruisers.[95] Moreover, as the industry expanded, its organisation became more complex. Agencies devoted to matching boats to customers emerged, with the establishment of Blake's in 1907 and Hoseason's in 1949.[96]

Many visitors, captivated by Broadland's scenery, wished to form a more permanent connection with the area by acquiring a holiday home, weekend retreat or place to retire. The influx of visitors was accordingly followed by a variety of speculative developments, concentrated especially in those places, easily accessible by rail, in which boatyards and hire companies were clustering. Oulton Broad saw much early development, encouraged not only by the presence of a rail station but also by the proximity of the seaside resort of Lowestoft. Dutt in 1903 thought that the 'red-brick villas and castellated houses which have sprung up on this side of the Broad have … robbed Oulton of what little beauty it once possessed'. Wroxham had similarly been ruined 'by the erection of unsightly modern houses for the accommodation of visitors'.[97] Here, following the death of his father in 1886 and a fire at Wroxham House in 1889, Robert Harvey Mason, the owner of the Wroxham House estate, embarked on a series of land sales. The first, in 1890, included a series of large plots with river frontages laid out in the area between Wroxham House park and the Bure.[98] A new road, Beech Road, was constructed and over the following 15 years a series of substantial residences were gradually erected above the floodplain with grounds extending down to the water's edge, where many had

---

93   *Eastern Daily Press*, 28 July 1890.
94   *Eastern Daily Press*, 18 September 1928. *Hamilton's map & chart of the Broads* (Norwich, 1935), p. 74. S. Hutchinson, *The Lower Bure: From Great Yarmouth to Upton* (Stoke Holy Cross, 2008), pp. 117–21.
95   George, *Land use*, pp. 366–7.
96   Malster, *The Broads*, pp. 92–100.
97   Dutt, *Norfolk Broads*, pp. 120, 121, 151.
98   NRO MC 3212/11 (36).

Figure 7.7 Riverside chalets on the Thurne, upstream from Potter Heigham Bridge.

water gardens and boathouses on inlets from the river. These houses, like those at Oulton, were substantial brick buildings with vaguely Tudor or Gothic detailing of the kind erected in late Victorian suburbs throughout England. But the second phase of development here, in the early 1900s, on land immediately downriver, was different. The plots were smaller and the houses, built on the floodplain and close to the river, took a form that was to become more typical of Broadland: thatched wooden riverside chalets, built in vaguely rustic style. By 1906 Dr W.A.S. Wynne of St Olaves was able to describe how

> the whole of that side has been quay headed and small weekend erections in the shape of Swiss Chalets have been built with smooth lawns in front of them and flowerbeds. The wild flowers, natural beauties of these shores, have been destroyed to make way for suburban gardens.[99]

Many people clearly disagreed with the doctor's judgement and a number of businesses were established locally to meet the rising demand for such riverside dwellings. By 1902 Boulton and Paul of Norwich, engineers and suppliers of

---

99 NRO/MS 21477/14.

glasshouses and garden buildings, had established a 'Rustic Works' branch at Wroxham advertising summerhouses, boathouses and pavilions. In 1906 it was taken over by Charles E. Curson, who in turn advertised the sale of 'Rustic Houses'.[100] He was soon followed by other Wroxham builders, including Robert Stringer and Arthur Taylor. Relatively insubstantial wooden structures (sometimes with a light iron frame), with roofs of thatch, shingles or occasionally painted corrugated iron, they were both cheap and light enough to be erected on the damp, unstable soils at the water's edge. Usually single storey, with low-pitched roofs, ornamental finials and, in many cases, verandas facing the river, they made ideal holiday homes or weekend retreats and were widely erected in Broadland in the first four decades of the twentieth century.

The largest collection of such wooden chalets developed on the banks of the Thurne, above and below Potter Heigham Bridge, on marshy land between the river wall and the water's edge rented from the Drainage Commissions (Figure 7.7). The first to appear was probably 'Bathurst', built near the railway bridge some time before 1901 and owned by Thomas F. Wright, a civil engineer from Norwich.[101] Here, however, development took more varied and on occasions eccentric forms. A houseboat known as the *Idler*, owned by William Kirby, the secretary of Great Yarmouth Piscatorial Society, was another early fixture. Arthur Patterson later recalled 'the old small house-boat, in a first cutting near the bridge, the pioneer of a new era in waterside delights, since then the little sentry box, so to speak has been replaced by a mile and more of barracks … .'[102] Indeed, by 1909 one observer was able to describe 'the floating village by Heigham Bridge', which included a 'converted lifeboat, a Yarmouth herringer and a Dutch smack.'[103] There were also land-based curiosities, including several converted railway carriages and a much-photographed house called *Dutch Tutch*, which began life as part of a helter-skelter on Britannia Pier in Great Yarmouth, was repurposed following a fire there in December 1909 and still survives on the banks of the Thurne downriver of Potter Heigham Bridge.[104] The Great Yarmouth connection with the community around the bridge was strong, with many members of the town's business and civic community owning a houseboat or bungalow there. The Great Yarmouth Yacht Club's Breydon Water course had been adversely affected by the construction of the Breydon viaduct and in 1911 Potter Heigham was described as 'practically now the headquarters of the club'.[105]

---

100 *Eastern Daily Press*, 11 January and 5 May 1906.
101 D. Cornell, *The history of the river Thurne bungalows* (Potter Heigham, 2018), pp. 8–9.
102 A.H. Patterson, *The cruise of the 'Walrus'* (London, 1923), p. 53.
103 *Morning Leader*, 24 August 1909.
104 *Norfolk News*, 25 December 1909. *Eastern Daily Press*, 21 January 1910. *The Era*, 12 March 1910.
105 *Yarmouth Mercury*, 1 April 1911.

After the First World War development around Potter Heigham Bridge intensified, with plots on the southern (Repps) bank now being built on (some plot-holders on the Potter Heigham side had initially leased the opposite bank to preserve their view). Already, by 1920, the spread of houses along both sides of the river had begun to frustrate the sailing community:

> Potter Heigham owes its prosperity entirely to yachtsmen; they discovered it; shops, stores, boatyards, and motor-bus service arose to meet their requirements. Later a few non-sailing people built riverside bungalows; others followed; the thing became fashionable; and the river is now a street. These bungalows shut off the wind; they have spoilt the sailing.[106]

By the late 1930s wooden dwellings of various kinds extended, almost without interruption, for more than two kilometres along the river, partly below but mainly above the bridge. After a gap of half a kilometre, another row lined the south bank in the parish of Martham.

The riverside ribbon-development along the Thurne was an example of a more general trend, one that was mirrored elsewhere in England – most notably, perhaps, on the Essex plotlands – before the planning reforms of the post-war years. Smaller collections of cheap dwellings appeared in a number of other Broadland locations where, as at Potter Heigham, almost anything could be adapted as a waterside residence. In 1919 'Two timber built portable bathing huts' and in 1920 a former 'Scotch fisher girls rest hut' were advertised for sale as being suitable for conversion into riverside bungalows.[107] Ex-army huts were also used, such as that set up near St Benet's Level Mill in the late 1920s or early 1930s. The parents of Phyllis Ellis, wife of famous Broadland naturalist Ted Ellis, also acquired such a hut to convert into a riverside bungalow (adding a verandah and a kitchen) at St Olaves in the 1920s. It was one of four neighbouring residences, the others being a railway carriage, a tiny wooden bungalow and an old gypsy caravan.[108]

But not all inter-war development in Broadland took this unplanned, individualistic form. Some was directed and organised by businessmen and property developers. The development of modern Horning owed much to the endeavours of Albert Ernest Oetzmann, a director of a large London furnishing company who, some time before 1916, built 'Riverholm', the first of the Horning riverside bungalows, using as a foundation the hull of an old wherry

---

106 *Eastern Daily Press*, 15 October 1924.
107 *Yarmouth Independent*, 14 June 1919; 7 February 1920.
108 P. Kelley (ed.), *From Osborne House to Wheatfen Broad: memoirs of Phyllis Ellis* (Surlingham, 2011), pp. 79–80.

houseboat.[109] In 1920 he purchased a farm on Lower Street from the Ecclesiastical Commissioners, established the Riverholm Estate Company and began to build a series of bungalows, all with water gardens and access to a new dyke cut parallel to the river, intended to provide quiet moorings and to preserve the riverbank and adjacent land in its 'natural' state.[110] He was one of the original directors of the Chumley and Hawke boatyard and built a large house for himself in the village, 'Roseway', later the Petersfield House Hotel. In 1923 he was negotiating to develop the Ropes Hill area of Horning, where he had plans for 40 more bungalows and a riverside club, when he rather abruptly departed for reasons unknown.[111] Abraham Lincoln Rhodes, a businessman and cinema owner from Doncaster, also made his mark on Horning. He built his own riverside property, 'The Pyramids' – the waterside entrance of which was flanked with two low pyramids – and in the early 1930s created a rather colourful development upriver of the Ferry Inn. It included the unlikely conversion of a slender timber smock mill into a more elaborate 'Dutch' mill residence, an accompanying 'Dutch' cottage and a substantial boathouse and clubhouse incorporating architectural salvage from his own collection.[112]

In Hoveton, downriver of Wroxham Bridge, a major development was begun around 1920, on land acquired from the Hoveton estate, by a consortium that included local land agent J.R.E. Draper and George Anderton, a retired architect from Preston, who was a specialist in building on wetland sites. A series of water cuts was made from the Bure, served by new access roads to either side of them. On his premature death in 1926 Anderton was described as the 'Man who transformed Wroxham Bureside'; 'his methods in cutting the inland waterways that now connect the river with every one of the bungalow plots were prompted by the desire for a pleasing natural effect'.[113] A number of the boatyards mentioned earlier also moved into the area: A. Pegg and Son, E.C. Landamore and R. Moore and Sons. Rustic bridges were built over the various waterways, revolving summer houses were erected at several points and, on a kind of promontory near the bend of the river, a large rock garden was laid out.[114] In the late 1920s the dredging contractor on the Hoveton project, J.S. Hobrough, went on to create his own riverside estate in Brundall on around 40 acres of 'wet and reedy marsh'.[115] It

---

109 Kelly's Directories, *Norfolk* (London, 1916), p. 202. W.L. Rackham, *Everybody's Broadland* (Norwich, 1927), p. 36.
110 *Eastern Daily Press*, 30 June 1920.
111 *Yarmouth Independent*, 2 June 1923. *Eastern Daily Press*, 30 October 1946.
112 *Eastern Daily Press*, 22 February 1932.
113 *Eastern Daily Press*, 21 June 1926.
114 *Eastern Daily Press*, 27 September 1956.
115 *Eastern Daily Press*, 31 May 1928.

comprised a new dyke 15 metres wide and nearly a kilometre long, boatyard sites with accommodation dykes and yacht basin, moorings for houseboats and a series of bungalows and holiday huts.

Not all developments progressed as envisaged. When the Cantley Grange estate was put up for sale in 1900 the land fronting the Yare was divided into 22 small building plots, the sales particulars claiming that 'undoubtedly this position will eventually prove to be the Head Quarters of the Boating and Yachting Interests in the County of Norfolk'.[116] On auction day the *Jenny Lind* steamer brought prospective purchasers from Norwich and a marquee was erected to accommodate them, but interest was limited and only four of the riverside plots were sold on the day.[117] One block of villas was subsequently built by the river and two boatyards established – by Henry Little and the firm of Woods and Newstead – around 1904. But they were soon overshadowed by the vast sugar beet factory constructed in 1912 and further development was stifled, with Ernest Woods finally moving his boatyard to a new location, downriver of Horning Ferry, at the end of the 1926 season.

By the 1930s the landscape around Wroxham, Hoveton, Brundall and to an extent Horning had been transformed, with new boat dykes running back from the river flanked by residential and holiday development in a variety of forms, and the timber and corrugated-iron sheds of numerous commercial boatyards; in 1937 there were more than a dozen firms in Wroxham alone building and/or letting boats.[118] Along the Thurne around Potter Heigham Bridge, in contrast, more individualistic, idiosyncratic development had erupted. Smaller-scale versions of both types could be found more widely scattered through Broadland, especially in places close to rail stations. In the immediate post-war decades new leisure and boating centres began to develop at places such as Stalham and St Olaves, while everywhere the visual impact of leisure boats, boat dykes and boatyard sheds seemed to increase inexorably.

Conflict and conservation

Late-nineteenth- and early-twentieth-century writers portrayed Broadland both as an essentially 'natural' world and as a timeless rural one, untouched by industry and modernity. The two approaches merged seamlessly. Patterson in 1902 described the typical local inhabitant – 'Broadland Man' – as 'so characteristic of the locality as to seem almost part and parcel of its indigenous *Fauna*'.[119] Marshmen and millmen in this remote area perpetuated, they

---

116   NRO MC 3212/11, (15).
117   *Eastern Evening News*, 23 June 1900.
118   Kelly's Directories, *Norfolk* (London, 1937), pp. 590–1.
119   Patterson, *Nature in Eastern Norfolk*, p. 37.

suggested, a way of life unchanged for centuries and had deep ancestral roots, several observers detecting clear signs of Viking ancestry. Dutt described the 'typical marsh farmer' as 'a tall, fair-haired, blue-eyed, ruddy-cheeked giant, who might have stepped out of the pages of the *Saga of Burnt Njal*'.[120] The isolated character of the local population was exaggerated, of course, given the proximity of Norwich and the vibrant port of Yarmouth. Patterson described one African or Afro-Caribbean waterman, and one of his Breydon punt-gunners was a German.[121] Like other rural landscapes in this age of urbanisation and industrialisation, Broadland was invested by contemporary commentators with qualities that enhanced its role as a calming refuge from an increasingly busy world, and obviously modern intrusions were regretted or ignored. Steam drainage in particular both destroyed habitats, threatening wildlife and shooting, and brought an inappropriate taste of the industrial. Dutt in 1902 worried that the work of the 'picturesque' old windmills 'will, at no very distant date, be done by ugly brick or corrugated iron housed steam-pumps'.[122] Dutt was a local man, born in Ditchingham; those newly settled in the area or visiting from outside often had even more romanticised views. The famous photographs taken by Cuban-born Peter Henry Emerson in the 1880s and 1890s show reedbeds and reed-cutters, rowing boats and wherries, but only very occasionally signs of the industries that clustered beside the waterways and only once a steam pump. The inhabitants of this bucolic world look remarkably clean, even when supposedly returning home from their labours (Figure 7.8).

The irony, of course, was that by describing and portraying this idealised rural world Dutt, Davies, Emerson and others encouraged an influx of visitors that undermined its isolation and threatened its tranquillity. And as larger numbers of people, from increasingly diverse social backgrounds, were drawn to the area, and as leisure activities came to have a greater and greater impact on the environment, the Broads became an increasingly contested landscape. The landowners and local residents who had formerly monopolised the sailing, fishing and shooting looked with unease at the influx of middle-class visitors brought by the railways, disturbing the peace and crowding the rivers. As early as 1882 Davies himself described being woken at 7 a.m., while moored on Wroxham Broad, by the occupants of a neighbouring boat loudly playing the piano.[123] Writers such as Dutt often describe Broadland as two separate and parallel worlds, defined by the seasons. In late summer:

---

120 Dutt, *Norfolk Broads*, p. 85.
121 A. Patterson, *Man and nature on tidal waters* (London, 1909), p. 41.
122 Dutt, *Norfolk Broads*, p. 170.
123 Davies, *Handbook*, pp. 40–1.

Figure 7.8 Peter Henry Emerson, 'Reed Cutters' (1892). After a day's hard work, these labourers look remarkably clean. Note the landscape, of open fen with few trees.

> The cruising yachts which have lingered late on the rivers disappear as if by magic, and at Oulton, Wroxham and Potter Heigham the fleets of white-winged craft are rapidly dismantled, drawn up on to the 'hard' or hauled in to the boat sheds … .
> For the next eight months the wherrymen, reed-cutters, and eel-catchers will have the rivers and broads to themselves.[124]

But this was not simply a clash between locals and outsiders. Many inhabitants of Broadland welcomed the commercial opportunities presented by the seasonal influx. Tourism offered alternative sources of employment at a time when traditional forms of employment on the rivers were under threat from the railways. Not only might boat-builders and wherrymen benefit from the demand for pleasure craft and crews. Riverside inns, many of which had long provided boats for hire, saw their trade expand and a number were extended or even rebuilt entirely to meet growing demand. At Potter Heigham Bridge in 1889 the Waterman's Arms was rebuilt, and soon afterwards renamed the Bridge Hotel, to serve the influx of yachters and anglers that followed the arrival of the Eastern

---

124 Dutt, *Norfolk Broads*, p. 56.

and Midlands Railway.[125] In Horning, the rather ancient-looking Swan Inn was rebuilt in 1897 as the Swan Hotel, while on the river Yare the Beauchamp Arms at Buckenham ferry was advertised to let in 1898, noting that 'the public house will shortly be entirely rebuilt'.[126] Tourism brought new life to the waterside, benefiting businesses, while rising disposable incomes, better transport and more leisure time meant that increasing numbers of local people, as well as outsiders, could enjoy the waterways.

As the landscape became more crowded, those in positions of local power, especially landowners, began to restrict access to the wetlands and waterways by locals, as well as outsiders, in order to preserve wildlife and protect shooting and fishing. They made particular efforts to curtail the 'free shooting' formerly enjoyed by both local people and visitors on sailing boats. As Nicholas Everitt noted in 1903,

> Speaking generally, it is not correct to say that wild-fowling in Broadland is practically a thing of the past; it is better to describe it as being more or less confined to private individuals. The rights of the public are being gradually curtailed to the narrowest possible limits, and so jealous is the game preserver, the Broad-owner, and the riparian proprietor, that the time when such rights will no longer exist seems to be drawing very near.[127]

It was no longer possible for anyone to just turn up and shoot 'on Hickling Broad, Horsey Mere, or Heigham Sounds; these happy hunting-grounds are all claimed as private property'.[128] Recreational fishing went the same way. There was 'very little bank fishing', according to Rudd in the same year, because the land bordering the rivers was private property, and while it was possible to fish the rivers from a boat, 'the fishing is preserved on the Salhouse Broads, Hickling, Horsey, Barton, Wroxham, Sutton, and Surlingham Broads, and part of South Walsham'.[129] Indeed, public access by boat for any purpose was now being denied to a number of broads. Davies bemoaned, in the revised and enlarged 1890 edition of his *Handbook*, how 'The old times when one could come and go upon the Broads as a matter of apparent right are now past.'[130] Rudd in 1903 claimed that access was currently denied to Hoveton Great and Little Broads, Decoy Broad in Woodbastwick, Belaugh Broad, to parts of Ranworth, Filby and Rollesby

---

125 *Norfolk Chronicle*, 25 August 1889.
126 *Downham Market Gazette*, 27 August 1898.
127 Everitt, 'Wildfowling', p. 330.
128 Everitt, 'Wildfowling', p. 326.
129 A.J. Rudd, 'Fishing', in W.A. Dutt, *The Norfolk Broads* (London, 1903), pp. 313–21, at p. 316.
130 Davies, *Handbook*, 17th edn (1890), p. 65.

Broads, and to South Walsham, Salhouse and Salhouse Little Broads, except along channels leading to public staithes. Landowners claimed these waters were private property, allotted to them by enclosure awards, and were beyond the reach of the tides – something that would otherwise, in legal terms, have ensured public navigation rights. Such claims were the subject of a number of high-profile legal cases. In 1892 H.S.N. Micklethwaite, the owner of Hickling Broad, attempted to stop the marshman Robert Vincent from sailing, shooting or fishing there, except within a prescribed channel. Part of the case was immediately thrown out and the rest failed on appeal, but other landowners had more success. In 1901, for example, the owner of Ranworth inner broad denied that there was even a right to sail the channel leading to the staithe, which he successfully claimed as private.[131] More celebrated was the dispute over Wroxham, where the High Court ruled that the broad itself was private property (although the victorious owner levied a charge only for fishing, and allowed continued access for sailing, although not for mooring).[132]

Such attempts to preserve Broadland's wildlife and tranquillity, fishing and sporting, through the assertion of private property rights – what Matless has characterised as 'private estate as sanctuary' – became increasingly difficult as visitor numbers soared in the inter-war years.[133] This was a time when – with further rises in disposable incomes, leisure time and car ownership – larger and more socially diverse groups flocked to the coast and attractive rural areas such as Broadland on holiday or for day trips. Regular middle-class visitors, as much as middle-class residents and landowners, regarded this wider influx with horror. Miller in 1935 described how

> Each year they had seen the crowds growing and the holiday season lengthening, until it seemed that the beautiful waterways would be turned into a Blackpool or a Brighton … great fleets of tripper-boats … hired yachts, floating ice-cream vendors, bum-boats and craft of every description, largely in the hands of people who had not the slightest knowledge of how to manage them.[134]

Local sailors were alarmed, as we have seen in the case of Potter Heigham, by the effects of uncontrolled riverside development (above, p. 352). In 1937 a proposed bungalow development on the north side of the Bure at Acle Bridge was opposed in part because the new residences would 'badly blanket what so

---

131 Dutt, *Norfolk Broads*, p. 139.
132 Dutt, *Norfolk Broads*, p. 147; Davies, *Handbook* 17th edn (1890), p. 70.
133 Matless, *Nature of landscape*, p. 115.
134 D. Miller, *Seen from a windmill: a Norfolk Broads revue* (London, 1935), pp. 12–13.

far has been one of the best sailing reaches on the north river'.[135] The advent of motor cruisers – slowly through the 1920s and 1930s, more rapidly in the post-war decades – added a further dimension to such conflicts. Sailing was a quiet pastime, one that seemed at home in this timeless world of reedbeds and windmills and which required a degree of acquired skill. Motor cruisers were loud, modern and intrusive – and did not.[136] The motor cruiser was 'simply an automobile that goes on water instead of tarmac'.[137] Their numbers increased inexorably through the post-war decades. As noted above, of the 547 boats for hire in Broadland in 1949, 301 were motor cruisers; by 1979 only 107 out of 2,257 were sailing craft.[138]

The 1947 Town and Country Planning Act allowed the designation of some extensive areas of rural land in Britain as National Parks, but, surprisingly given its acknowledged importance, Broadland was not among them, although such a move had been proposed as early as 1930.[139] Instead, conservation was initially piecemeal in nature. A number of areas of key environmental interest were thus acquired by the Norfolk Naturalist Trust (now the Norfolk Wildlife Trust): Starch Grass Meadow in Martham and Alderfen Broad in 1928; Barton and Hickling Broads in 1945; Ranworth and Surlingham Broads in 1948.[140] The Broads Society was founded in 1956, although, initially at least, it was primarily an interest group, protecting the rights of sailors, not least because navigation rights might on occasions still come under threat – as late as 1949 T.R.C. Blofield attempted to prevent public access to Hoveton Little Broad.[141] Concern about Broadland's fate was largely articulated through Norfolk County Council and national bodies such as the Nature Conservancy, and by vociferous individuals such as the naturalist Ted Ellis. Some measure of overall planning for the area began to emerge with the establishment in 1949 of the Broads Joint Advisory Planning Committee, with representatives from the local councils, but its powers were limited and, as the Nature Conservancy's 1965 *Report on Broadland* concluded, there was an urgent need for an overall plan to ensure the successful 'multipurpose use of land and water on a large scale'. It warned that 'To do nothing is to abandon the region to erosion, conflict and decay'. Further reports followed, but so too did proposals for unsuitable leisure developments, some on a huge scale: an 86-acre holiday complex with chalets, marina and restaurants on the Burgh Castle mudflats

---

135 *Eastern Daily Press*, 5 October and 11 October 1937.
136 Matless, *Nature of landscape*, p. 78.
137 R.H. Mottram, *The Broads* (London, 1952), p. 2.
138 M. George, *The land use, ecology and conservation of Broadland* (Chichester, 1992), pp. 66–7.
139 V. Cornish, *National parks and the heritage of scenery* (London, 1930), p. 60.
140 Norfolk Naturalists Trust, *Nature in Norfolk: a heritage in trust* (Norwich, 1976).
141 Matless, *Nature of landscape*, p. 90.

beside Breydon Water; a 100-acre development, complete with a five-storey modernist 'boatel' and golf course, beside Acle Dyke.[142] Finally, and fortunately, in 1978 the Broads Authority was established, initially as a coordinating body between district and county councils but from 1989 with statutory powers equivalent to those of a National Park. Belatedly, in 2015 the Broads Authority, after extensive consultation but not with universal support, assumed the status of a National Park for the area. By this time, moreover, large parts of Broadland had been acquired by conservation bodies, including Heigham Holmes beside the upper Thurne, bought by the National Trust in 1987, and/or were protected by national designations. No fewer than 29 areas had been declared SSSIs, extensive tracts of fen in the Bure and Ant valleys especially were National Nature Reserves and 4,623 acres of marsh and fen, together with 1,023 of mudflats and saltings on Breydon Water, were recognised as Wetlands of International Importance under the Ramsar Convention.[143]

Planning and management, culminating in the establishment of the Broads Authority, helped to save Broadland from inappropriate large-scale leisure development: riverside chalets, boatyards and other tourist facilities remained largely confined to particular locations, such as Wroxham, Brundall or Horning, rather than spreading like a contagion throughout the area (Figure 7.9). But the 'battle for the Broads' was in some ways resolved in an uneasy peace. The Broads Authority has always had a hard and often thankless task, balancing the competing demands of the holiday industry, local landowners, nature conservation bodies and local residents, of anglers, sailors, hire-boat users and birdwatchers. More importantly, some of the most serious threats to the landscape have come not from the number of outside visitors or development pressures but from more complex forces, difficult or impossible to control.

The Broads wetlands, as we have observed throughout, have never existed in isolation. Their character has always been critically shaped by developments on the surrounding uplands, largely lying outside the Broads National Park. In recent decades these have included a massive expansion in the number of houses and thus in the size of the local population, with all the associated issues of footfall and traffic volumes, and the construction of a variety of visually intrusive features, perhaps especially on the fringes of Great Yarmouth, visible for miles across the Halvergate Marshes. But more important are issues relating to water, through which the uplands and wetlands are inextricably connected. As early as the 1850s local naturalists were noting a marked change in the waters of the broads which, formerly crystal-clear, had become cloudy. Their vegetation, too, was changing.

---

142 *Eastern Daily Press*, 18 May 1965. *Eastern Daily Press*, 16 September 1965.
143 Matless, *Nature of landscape*, p. 125.

RECREATION, TOURISM AND CONSERVATION

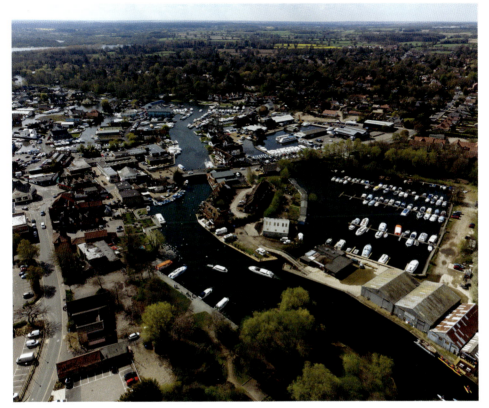

Figure 7.9 Wroxham and Hoveton from the air: the largest concentration of boatyards, holiday properties and visitor attractions in Broadland.

Plants such as horned pondweed (*Zanichellia palustris*), water soldier (*Stratiotes aloides*), hornwort (*Ceratophyllum demersum*) and water-lilies were suppressed by the growth of waterweeds such as the stoneworts and bladderworts.[144] The waterways were suffering from nutrient enrichment – eutrophication – caused by run-off from the surrounding higher ground, prime arable land that was now receiving ever higher doses of both fertiliser and dung from cake-fed cattle. Over the following century the problem intensified, not only because of continued agricultural pollution but also due to the effluent coming from innumerable septic tanks and from the sewage treatment plant at Whitlingham on the river Yare. While some of these problems have abated in recent years, water quality in Broadland remains a hot political issue, with the Environment Agency currently opposing the connection of new homes to the sewage mains (or to septic tanks) within the catchments of the Broads and the river Wensum. Water extraction from upland boreholes has also been a problem, as we saw in Chapter 4, threatening

---

144   George, *Land use*, pp. 105–12.

some key habitats – most recently Catfield Fen, with its rich butterfly population.

Others have written, with far more knowledge than we can muster, about these complex scientific matters.[145] Many of the key problems involved in the management of Broadland are, however, more closely related to the essentially historical themes that constitute the main focus of this book. They concern what we mean by a 'historic landscape' or, indeed, a 'natural' one. Such issues are raised, to some extent, by all valued landscapes, but perhaps, as we shall see in the Conclusion, with particular clarity in the case of Broadland.

---

145 See, in particular, George, *Land use*, and Moss, *The Broads*.

8

CONCLUSION

Society values particular landscapes, and attempts to conserve them, in part for their 'natural' and topographic qualities and in part for their cultural, historical characteristics, such as their legacy of vernacular buildings. These latter features do not usually date to a single period of time. They have built up over the centuries, each generation adding its own elements, as some of those established earlier gradually disappear through decay and redundancy. Such characteristic, defining features of a landscape were, for the most part, the product of practical, agrarian, economic activities. Particular forms of settlement and fields, characteristic buildings and the like were created as people struggled to make a living from the land, to prosper from trade and industry and to provide homes for their families. We now invest them with new meanings and values, as things that are important for our culture and identity; they are quaint and picturesque survivors from, and reminders of, simpler and perhaps more wholesome times. Not only do we try to preserve them, we also attempt to limit new additions to the landscape, even those that perform roles which are broadly similar to those undertaken by the 'traditional' features. Looking out across the vast green levels of the Halvergate Marshes, the brick drainage mills, in varying states of dereliction or restoration and all quite still, seem at one with the lonely landscape. The turbines of the Scroby Sands wind farm in the far distance, in contrast, blades glinting as they turn, will seem to many like an alien intrusion. The inherent illogicality of this approach is particularly clear when the iconic, 'traditional' features of a landscape are themselves not particularly old: the products of recent industrial history, rather than relics of the Middle Ages or of the remote prehistoric past. Most Broadland drainage mills, as we have seen, were built or very extensively modified in the middle or later decades of the nineteenth century. Writers on Broadland at the start of the twentieth century were able, nevertheless, to wax lyrical about the 'picturesque old mills'. Dutt claimed to have enquired of one old marshman, 'How old are the mills?' and to have received the reply: 'Ah, that I shouldn't like to say, but I've heard my grandfather say that they looked jist th' same as they did when he was an owd man three weeks off being a hundred.'[1] Yet West Somerton Mill, as we have seen, was built from scratch in the late 1890s, Martham Mill was constructed in 1908, while Horsey Mill and Ashtree Farm Mill were entirely rebuilt in 1912. In Broadland, more than in most landscapes, the new and the modern seem quite rapidly to become the picturesque and the traditional. The riverside chalets that filled conservationists with horror when first erected in large numbers in the first half of the twentieth century are now considered by the Broads Authority to make 'a significant contribution to the historic environment of the Broads'.[2] Fifty-eight examples have been given the status and protection of 'local heritage assets', and owners more generally are urged to make repairs, additions and alterations in a style and materials that enhance their 'traditional' appearance.

'Modern' intrusions into 'historic landscapes' are to be avoided, or at least concealed or disguised. And yet at the same time we know that everything was modern once and that some much-loved features of the landscape were, in the case of Broadland especially, raw and new almost within the reach of living memory. Of course, as we have seen, many key elements of the Broadland landscape are much older than this. The broads themselves are relics of a medieval peat-extraction industry; the Halvergate Marshes are still littered with the mounds created by medieval salt production, and with the remains of tidal creeks – either surviving as earthworks or incorporated into the modern dyke pattern – that are more than a thousand years old. Waterside buildings, boat dykes and innumerable drainage dykes, and much else, have been bequeathed by the post-medieval centuries. This is a complex, multi-layered historic landscape, the sum of changes and additions made by successive generations over an immense period of time – but now managed so as to limit the scale of further change. There is, indeed, something rather odd about landscape conservation.

Yet, like most people, we are more than happy to ignore such philosophical inconsistencies, and would be horrified if such efforts were to be abandoned, and in particular if planning controls were ever to be relaxed and unrestrained development allowed to rip through the area. For we are as embedded in contemporary society as everyone else, have absorbed the same attitudes to traditional rural landscapes and the threats they face, and happily embrace the preservation of this iconic example against the massed forces of change. This said,

---

1 Dutt, *Norfolk Broads*, pp. 36–7.
2 Broads Authority, 'Planning for waterside bungalows/chalets', pp. 6–8. https://www.broads-authority.gov.uk/__data/assets/pdf_file/0015/231054/Planning-for-Waterside-BungalowsChalets_18_11_2016.pdf (accessed 3 March 2023).

a historical perspective provides a useful reminder not only of what 'preserving Broadland' really involves but also of the fact that the complete freezing of any landscape at a particular point in its development is effectively impossible. We should not be too concerned about small-scale, piecemeal additions. We would not want Broadland to display the manicured, self-conscious, picture-postcard rurality of areas like the Cotswolds. A certain rough untidiness, even in places tackiness, is part of Broadland's character and charm. The aim should be managed change, allowing those necessary developments that do no great violence to the historic, inherited fabric. This, by and large, is the policy of the Broads Authority, and – with some exceptions – what it has successfully achieved.

Conserving Broadland's 'natural' heritage raises different and perhaps more intractable issues, for its wealth of habitats is threatened by a more complex range of forces. As we have emphasised throughout, while Broadland's wildlife and the wildness of its landscapes have long been appreciated, it is very much an assemblage of *semi*-natural habitats, shaped or created by human activities. The broads, most obviously, were a by-product of large-scale peat and clay extraction. But the reed and sedge beds, fens and fen meadows discussed in Chapter 4 were similarly formed, to a significant extent, by human action – by cutting, mowing, digging and grazing. As these practices have declined over the last century or so these habitats have changed, usually in ways that have had a negative impact on biodiversity. Natural processes no longer held in check, they have developed inexorably towards their climax vegetation of wet 'carr' woodland. For the most part, it is only where uneconomic or agriculturally redundant practices have been maintained, reinstated or mimicked that 'traditional' habitats are preserved. Sometimes this has been made possible by government agro-environment schemes and the enthusiasm of individual farmers and landowners, elsewhere it has been achieved through the activities of wildlife trusts, the RSPB or similar organisations on tracts of land principally dedicated to nature conservation.

This essential policy, of maintaining biodiversity through conserving habitats created by traditional management, is not, of course, unique to Broadland. It has, since the start of the twentieth century, shaped approaches to nature conservation in Britain more generally, for in this long-settled, crowded land there are few truly 'natural' places. Our valued habitats have in almost all cases been created by particular economic activities. Our heaths, for example, were formed and maintained by the intensive grazing of sheep and other livestock, and by the regular cutting of gorse, heather, broom and bracken for fuel and other purposes. It is the ambition of every heath to become a wood and this ambition has been widely achieved over the last century or so as, with a steady decline in use and management, thousands of hectares have tumbled down to secondary woodland of only limited ecological value. The distinctive flora of our ancient woods, and the invertebrate fauna that depends on it, have similarly declined dramatically with the cessation of coppicing and the resultant increases in shade. Meadows, moors and downlands, with their distinctive flora and fauna, were all likewise fundamentally shaped by centuries of human exploitation.

For many decades, nature conservation in Britain was accordingly based on the maintenance of what were essentially artificial habitats, in the face of the decline or disappearance of the practical, agrarian activities that had created and sustained them. But in recent years this approach has been increasingly questioned, characterised as 'wildlife gardening', by a new conservation philosophy. Proponents of 'rewilding' believe that biodiversity is best sustained and enhanced not by the management of particular areas of land, but rather by creating spaces, preferably extensive ones, in which nature can be left to its own devices – an approach put into practice most famously on the Knepp estate in Sussex.[3] On large tracts of land like this low-intensity grazing by cattle and pigs prevents the regeneration of dense secondary woodland, allowing the development of the kinds of more open wood-pasture environments that, according to ecologists such as Frans Vera, characterised the landscape of northern Europe before the adoption of farming.[4] Elsewhere, more 'hands-off' approaches to management often have less clearly defined objectives but might typically include the abandonment of man-made alterations to natural drainage systems and watercourses and the leaving of dead or fallen trees *in situ*, rather than their removal elsewhere.

There are, in reality, many problems with the idea that rewilding in its various forms offers a general remedy to the current crisis in biodiversity, problems that cannot be discussed in detail here.[5] While the approach clearly has a place in some contexts, the case of Broadland clearly indicates its redundancy in others. The broads themselves, left to the mercy of purely natural processes, contract and might disappear altogether. The Broads Authority has spent millions of pounds removing mud and silt from Barton Broad as well as on other measures. More importantly, for reasons discussed in Chapter 4, the intensive and essentially unnatural ways in which the peat fens were managed in the past served to boost biodiversity, allowing particular species to flourish that would have been only thinly distributed in purely 'natural' wetlands. And as wetlands of all kinds have disappeared through drainage over the centuries, the importance of these enhanced populations in managed sedge and reed beds, slowly terrestrialising turf ponds and regularly mown fens

---

3   G. Monbiot, *Feral: searching for enchantment on the frontiers of rewilding* (London, 2014). I. Tree, *Wilding: the return of nature to a British farm* (London, 2018). S. Carver and I. Covery, 'Rewilding: time to get down off the fence?', *British Wildlife*, 32 (2021), pp. 246–55.
4   F. Vera, *Grazing ecology and forest history* (Wallingford, 2002).
5   T. Williamson, 'Rewilding: a landscape-history perspective', *British Wildlife*, 33 (2022), pp. 423–9. R. Fuller and I. Gilroy, 'Rewilding and intervention: complementary philosophies for nature conservation in Britain', *British Wildlife*, 32 (2020), pp. 258–67.

and fen meadows has increased. These important species almost invariably decline with the cessation of traditional management and the ensuing development of scrub and woodland. The problem in Broadland is not too much management, but not enough of it. Nor should we imagine that this is simply a matter of obscure plants. Although, as we have seen, the bittern suffered badly from indiscriminate shooting and egg-collecting in the nineteenth century, the very slow recovery in its numbers in the course of the twentieth century was largely the consequence of habitat loss – the steady reduction in the extent of the managed reed beds in which it makes its nests. A range of other avian species are similarly dependent on such managed wetland vegetation, including the reed warbler and marsh harrier. The swallowtail butterfly is now largely confined to the managed fens of Broadland; Catfield Fen is the only place in Britain where *Trogus lapidator*, its Ichneumonid wasp parasite, has been recorded. Not surprisingly, the rewilding philosophy has had little impact on the management of the Broadland Fens. Instead, the Broads Authority, wildlife trusts and other conservation bodies have largely been concerned with the perpetuation of traditional management, not least through the encouragement of commercial reed-cutting, or else with the adoption of practices that mimic its effects or, at the very least, hold back the regeneration of woodland.

The situation is slightly different on the grazing marshes, where, as we have seen, extensive tracts of land have been acquired over recent decades by conservation bodies, to be managed for the benefit of wildlife. On the RSPB reserve beside Breydon Water the marshes are now maintained in a much wetter condition than formerly. Extensive shallow ponds have been created, most notably on Beighton Marshes, and deliberate pumping ensures the presence of standing water on some areas during the winter months. Such management benefits wading birds but runs against the current of history, reversing centuries of effort to remove water from the land. Nevertheless, the marshes here still look much as they have done for centuries, with extensive open panoramas across level, relatively close-cropped pasture, and the changes perhaps represent little more than a return to the conditions pertaining before the improvements in drainage that occurred in the course of the eighteenth and nineteenth centuries. Rather more radical are the changes taking place on the Suffolk Wildlife Trust's reserve at Carlton Colville, on more than 400 hectares of land beside the river Waveney and Oulton Dyke, acquired in stages between 2008 and 2019. Some of the area overlies peat, but most occupies alluvial clay and was accordingly used for centuries as grazing marsh until the northern portion – Peto's Marsh – was deep-drained and converted to arable in the 1970s. The Trust's aim has not been to conserve and restore the traditional landscape of the marshes but instead to create something much wilder. Water levels and stocking densities are managed so as to produce a rough sward, full of reed and sedge, and with areas of regenerating scrub (Figure 8.1). On Peto's

Figure 8.1 The Suffolk Wildlife Trust's Carlton Marshes reserve, deliberately managed to create a 'wilder' landscape than that of the traditional Broadland grazing marshes.

Marsh the changes have been particularly dramatic. Vast schemes of earthmoving have created extensive ponds, bounded by substantial dams, on land that had been kept free of water for centuries. All this constitutes, in effect, the creation of a new landscape, designed and engineered at vast expense, with little regard for what was here before. Although, of necessity, this complex and largely artificial mosaic of fen, marsh, scrub and water is fairly intensively managed, the Trust's publicity material is suffused with the fashionable rhetoric of rewilding:

> Thanks to the National Lottery Heritage Fund's investment of over £4 million in Suffolk Wildlife Trust's vision for 405 hectares (1000 acres) of wildness, the transformation of Carlton Marshes into the southern gateway to the Broads National Park is complete. As water flows back onto the land, nature is taking over once again.[6]

The undoubted success of this ambitious project in terms of nature conservation has tended to obscure its implications for *landscape* conservation: the violence that it has done to the distinctive character of this historic environment has

---

6   Suffolk Wildlife Trust, 'Carlton Marshes Nature Reserve'. https://www.suffolkwildlifetrust.org/carlton. (Accessed 3 June 2023).

gone largely unnoticed. Like more thorough-going examples of 'rewilding', and a number of other large-scale 'nature recovery' schemes, the Carlton Marshes pose a challenge for the landscape historian. On the one hand, such projects can be viewed as important twenty-first-century additions to the landscape, visually appealing and essential for the maintenance of biodiversity; they will be treated by historians of the future as examples of large-scale landscape design as typical of their time as 'Capability' Brown's manicured parklands, likewise vaunted as 'natural' by contemporaries, are of the eighteenth century. But, on the other hand, the creation of extensive 'wildscapes' erodes the historic fabric of the landscape and undermines the distinctive yet often fragile character of particular places. Broadland has a key role to play in the maintenance of biodiversity. But its open marshes should not be regarded by champions of nature conservation as a blank canvas on which to impose their particular visions of the 'natural'. They have an historical and cultural importance, and a place in the national psyche, which deserve respect. Given current pressures on wildlife, the design of areas specifically for conservation purposes has become a necessity. But we should perhaps be cautious about extending such 'natural' habitats too far, into further areas of Broadland, at the expense of landscapes created by centuries of human endeavour.

Whether the creation of this bold new landscape at Carlton Marshes signals the start of a more general shift in the development of Broadland is unclear. Hopefully nature conservation can mainly take place, as it has generally done in the past, within the framework of the historic landscape. There is no conflict between the two. But, even if one did exist, it would be only one of many in the long history of this contested landscape, which have ranged from legal disputes and riots over enclosure, through arguments over access, navigation and shooting rights, to clashes over the respective importance of conservation and the holiday industry. Balancing different interests will always be a challenge for the Broads Authority and others responsible for managing Broadland, and advances in one area often create problems in another. Thus, for example, hard-fought improvements in water quality since the 1970s, not least through a reduction in discharges from sewage works and septic tanks, have led to the more luxuriant growth of rare water plants, especially a range of stoneworts, which clog up navigation channels and snag the propellors of the motor cruisers.

Broadland's landscapes are not 'timeless' or 'traditional'. They have definable histories of change, the consequence of the complex interaction of social, economic and environmental factors operating on local, national and even global scales. And, however much we like to think of the area's wilder tracts as 'natural', even these have been shaped by the hand of man. Broadland's landscape is constantly changing and apparent successes in arresting its ongoing development are, in part, an illusion, as gradual alterations pass unnoticed and become the 'new normal'.

In particular, the higher reaches of the river valleys have almost everywhere seen an increase in the size and numbers of trees, steadily closing off formerly open vistas. Change and development are normal characteristics of all landscapes and will ultimately alter them all beyond recognition. Radical change may come to this fragile wetland sooner than to most. Already climate change is having an effect. The increased scale and duration of winter flooding disrupts the management of reedbeds, with negative effects on their associated flora and fauna, and impacts directly on important species such as the swallowtail butterfly. Tidal surges and storms bring saltwater ever higher up the rivers, threatening Broadland's freshwater ecosystems.[7] The human management and interventions that have shaped Broadland's habitats also render them uniquely vulnerable, for almost all of the National Park lies at or below sea level. If global warming continues unchecked, the sea will, perhaps within this century, reclaim the Halvergate Marshes, and tidal mudflats will replace the fens and the alders far up the river valleys.

---

[7] P. Barkham, 'An uncertain future for the Broads', *British Wildlife* 35 (2024), pp. 391–9.

BIBLIOGRAPHY

Books and articles

Abrams, L. and Parsons, D., 'Place-names and the history of Scandinavian settlement in England', in J. Hines, A. Lane and M. Redknap (eds), *Land, sea and home: settlement in the Viking period* (Leeds, 2004), pp. 379–431.

Albert, W., *The turnpike road system in England 1663–1840* (Cambridge, 1972).

Alcock, N., 'The Great Rebuilding in its later stages', *Vernacular Architecture*, 14 (1983), pp. 45–8.

Allard, P., 'Henry Keymer of Gorleston, marine engineer', *Yarmouth Archaeology and Local History* (2014), pp. 108–11.

Apling, H., *Norfolk corn and other industrial windmills*, Vol. I (Norwich, 1984).

Applegate, A., '"Boss of Broadland", the autobiography of Abiathar "Boss" Applegate, part 2', reproduced in *The Wherry*, Journal of the Norfolk Wherry Trust (1998).

Armstrong, M.J., *The history and antiquities of the county of Norfolk*, 10 vols (London, 1781).

Arthurton, R.S., Booth, S.J., Morigi, A.N., Abbott, M.A.W. and Wood, C.J., *Geology of the country around Great Yarmouth. Memoir for the 1:50,000 Geological Sheet 162 (England and Wales)* (London, 1994).

Ashton, N., Lewis, S.G., De Groote, I., Duffy, S.M., Bates, M., Bates, R., Hoare, P.G., Lewis, M., Parfitt, S.A., Peglar, S., Williams, C. and Stringer, C.B., 'Hominin footprints from early Pleistocene deposits at Happisburgh, UK', *PLoS ONE*, 9/2, e88329 (7 February 2014). https://journals.plos.org/plosone/article?id=10.1371/journal.pone.0088329.

Ashwin, T., 'Excavations at Harford Farm, Caistor St Edmund (Site 9794), 1990', in T. Ashwin and S. Bates, *Excavations on the Norwich Southern Bypass, 1989–91 Part I: excavations at Bixley, Caistor St Edmund, Trowse, Cringleford and Little Melton*, East Anglian Archaeology 91 (Dereham, 2000), pp. 52–140.

Ashwin, T., 'Neolithic and Bronze Age Norfolk', *Proceedings of the Prehistoric Society*, 62 (1996), pp. 41–62.

Astle, T., Ayscough, S. and Caley, J. (eds), *Taxatio Ecclesiastica Angliae et Walliae Auctoritate P. Nicholai IV c.1291* (London, 1802).

Ayers, B. and Brundall Local History Group, *The Book of Brundall and Braydeston* (Wellington, 2007).

Bacon, R.N., *The report on the agriculture of Norfolk* (London, 1844).

Badham, S., 'Beautiful remains of antiquity. The medieval monuments in the former Trinitarian Priory church at Ingham, Norfolk. Part 1: the lost brasses', *Church Monuments*, 21 (2006), pp. 7–33.

Bailey, M., *After the Black Death* (Oxford, 2020).

Bailey, M., '"Per Imperetum Maris": natural disaster and economic decline in Eastern England, 1275–1350', in B. Campbell (ed.), *Before the Black Death: the crisis of the early fourteenth century* (Manchester, 1991), pp. 184–209.

Baird, W. and Tarrant, J., *Hedgerow destruction in Norfolk, 1946–1970* (Norwich, 1970).

Baker, R.E., 'Norfolk duck decoys', *Transactions of the Norfolk and Norwich Naturalists' Society*, 27/1 (1985), pp. 1–8.

Barber, M. and Oswald, A., *An enclosure on Broome Heath, Ditchingham, Norfolk* (London, 1995).

Barkham, P., 'An uncertain future for the Broads', *British Wildlife*, 35/4 (2024), pp. 391–9.

Barnes, G. and Williamson, T., *Hedgerow history: ecology, history and landscape character* (Macclesfield, 2006).

Barnes, G. and Williamson, T., *Rethinking ancient woodland: the archaeology and history of woods in Norfolk* (Hatfield, 2015).

Batcock, N., 'The parish church in Norfolk in the 11th and 12th centuries', in J. Blair (ed.), *Minsters and parish churches. The local church in transition 960–1200* (Oxford, 1988), pp. 179–90.

Batcock, N., *The ruined and disused churches of Norfolk*, East Anglian Archaeology 51 (Dereham, 1991).

Beckett, C. (ed.), *Forty years of a Norfolk railway: the reminiscences of William Marriott from 1884 to 1924* (Weybourne, 1999).

Beckett, G., Bull, A. and Stevenson, R., *A flora of Norfolk* (Norwich, 1999).

Bird, M., *Mary Hardy and her world 1773–1809, volume 4: under sail and under arms* (Kingston upon Thames, 2020).

Bird, M.C.H., 'Bird life', in W.A. Dutt, *The Norfolk Broads* (London, 1903), pp. 215–31.

Bird, M.C.H., 'The rural economy, sport and natural history of East Ruston Common', *Transactions of the Norfolk and Norwich Naturalists' Society*, 8/5 (1909), pp. 631–66.

Birtles, S., 'Common land, poor relief and enclosure: the use of manorial resources in fulfilling parish obligations 1601–1834', *Past and Present*, 165 (1999), pp. 74–106.

Birtles, S., 'The impact of Commons Registration: a Norfolk study', *Landscape History*, 20/1 (1998), pp. 83–97.

Blair, J., *The church in Anglo-Saxon society* (Oxford, 2005).

Blake, J.H., *The geology of the country near Yarmouth and Lowestoft. Explanation of Sheet 67*, Memoirs of the Geological Survey (England and Wales) (London, 1890).

Bliss, W.H. and Johnson, C. (eds), *Calendar of papal registers: papal letters III 1342–62* (London, 1897).

Blomefield, F. and Parkin, C., *An essay towards a topographical history of the county of Norfolk*, 11 vols (London, 1805–10).

Boardman, E.T., 'The development of a Broadland estate at How Hill Ludham, Norfolk', *Transactions of Norfolk and Norwich Naturalists' Society*, 15 (1939), pp. 5–21.

Bond, F., *English church architecture*, 2 vols (Oxford, 1911–13).

Bond, J., *Monastic landscapes* (Stroud, 2004).

Bond, R., *Coltishall: heyday of a Broadland village* (North Walsham, 1986).

Bone, Q., 'Legislation to revive small farming in England 1887–1914', *Agricultural History*, 49 (1975), pp. 653–61.

Boulter, S., *Living with monuments. Excavations at Flixton Volume II*, East Anglian Archaeology 177 (Cirencester, 2022).

Boulter, S. and Walton Rogers, P., *Circles and cemeteries: excavations at Flixton Volume I*, East Anglian Archaeology 147 (Bury St Edmunds, 2012).

Boyes, J. and Russell, R., *The canals of eastern England* (Newton Abbot, 1977).

Bradley, R., *The prehistory of Britain and Ireland*, 2nd edn (Cambridge, 2019).

Broads Authority, *Broads Plan 2017: partnership strategy for the Norfolk and Suffolk Broads* (Norwich, 2017).

Broads Authority, *Hickling Broad Dossier: part of the review of lake restoration practices and their performance in the Broads National Park, 1980–2013* (Norwich, 2016).

Brown, J., *Steeped in tradition: the malting industry in England since the railway age* (Reading, 1983).

Brunskill, R., *Illustrated handbook of vernacular architecture* (London, 1971).

Butcher, D., *Norfolk and Suffolk churches: the Domesday record* (Oulton, 2019).

Butler, A. and A., *Somerleyton brickfields* (Somerleyton, 1960).

Cambridge, P.G., 'A section in the "Bure Valley Beds" near Wroxham (TG273158)', *Bulletin of the Geological Society of Norfolk*, 30 (1978), pp. 79–91.

Cameron, L. and Matless, D., 'Translocal ecologies: the Norfolk Broads, the "Natural", and the International Phytogeographical Excursion, 1911', *Journal of the History of Biology*, 44 (2011), pp. 15–41.

Cameron, T.D.J., Crosby, A., Balson, P.S., Jeffery, D.H., Lott, G.K., Bulat, J. and Harrison, D.J., *The geology of the southern North Sea* (London, 1992).

Campbell, B.M.S., 'Agricultural progress in medieval England: some evidence from eastern Norfolk', *Economic History Review*, 36 (1983), pp. 24–46.

Campbell, B.M.S., 'The complexity of manorial structure in medieval Norfolk', *Norfolk Archaeology*, 39 (1986), pp. 225–56.

Campbell, B.M.S., 'Medieval land use and values', in T. Ashwin and A. Davison (eds), *An historical atlas of Norfolk*, 3rd edn (Chichester, 2005), pp. 48–9.

Campbell, B.M.S., 'Population change and the genesis of commonfields on a Norfolk manor', *Economic History Review*, 33 (1980), pp. 174–92.

Campbell, J., 'Domesday herrings', in C. Harper-Bill, C. Rawcliffe and R. Wilson (eds), *East Anglia's history: studies in honour of Norman Scarfe* (Woodbridge, 2002), pp. 5–17.

Carrodus, C.F., *Life in a Norfolk village: the story of Old Horning* (Norwich, 1949).

Carver, S. and Covery, I., 'Rewilding: time to get down off the fence?', *British Wildlife*, 32 (2021), pp. 246–55.

Cattermole, P. and Cotton, S., 'Medieval parish church building in Norfolk', *Norfolk Archaeology*, 38 (1983), pp. 235–79.

Cavill, P., *A new dictionary of English field-names*, English Place-Name Society (Nottingham, 2018).

Chifferiel, A.H., *Records of Hickling Priory and Hickling district in the hundred of Happing* (privately printed, 1911).

Clark, R., *Black-sailed traders: keels and wherries of the Norfolk Broads* (Newton Abbot, 1972).

Clark, R.H., *The steam engine builders of Norfolk* (Yeovil, 1988).

Clarke, D., *The Broads in print* (Norwich, 2010).

Cleveland, D., *A look back at the Broads* (Manningtree, 2019).

Coles, B.P. and Funnell, B.M., 'Holocene palaeoenvironments of Broadland, England', in S.-D. Nio, R.T.E. Shüttenhelm, Tj.C.E. Van Weering (eds), *Holocene Marine Sedimentation in the North Sea Basin*, Special Publications of the International Association of Sedimentologists, 5 (Oxford, 1981), pp. 123–31.

Colgrave, B. (ed.), *Felix's life of Saint Guthlac* (Cambridge, 1956).

Cornell, D., *The history of the river Thurne bungalows* (Potter Heigham, 2018).

Cornford, B., 'The commons of Flegg in the Middle Ages and early modern periods', in M. Manning (ed.), *Commons in Norfolk* (Norwich, 1988), pp. 14–20.

Cornford, B., 'Past water levels in Broadland', *Norfolk Research Committee Bulletin*, 28 (1982), pp. 14–18.

Cornford, B., 'The Sea Breach Commission in east Norfolk 1609–1743', *Norfolk Archaeology*, 37 (1979), pp. 137–45.

Cornish, V., *National parks and the heritage of scenery* (London, 1930).

Cotton, S., 'Domesday revisited – where are the 11th-century churches?', *Norfolk Archaeological Research Group News*, 21 (1980), pp. 11–17.

Cox, A., *Royal Commission on Historical Monuments, England, survey of Bedfordshire. Brickmaking: a history and gazetteer* (Bedford, 1979).

Coxon, P., 'The geomorphological history of the Waveney valley', in P. Allen (ed.), *Field guide to the Gipping and Waveney valleys, Suffolk. May 1982* (Cambridge, 1984), pp. 105–6.

Crouch, D., *The reign of King Stephen: 1135–1154* (London, 2000).

Currie, C., 'Time and chance: modelling the attrition of old houses', *Vernacular Architecture*, 19 (1988), pp. 1–9.

Dallas, P., Last, R. and Williamson, T., *Norfolk gardens and designed landscapes* (Oxford, 2013).

Davies, G.C., *The handbook to the rivers and broads of Norfolk and Suffolk* (Norwich, 1882; 17th edn 1890).

Davies, G. Christopher, *Norfolk broads and rivers: or, the waterways, lagoons, and decoys of East Anglia*, 1st edn (Edinburgh and London, 1882; many subsequent edns).

Davis, R.H.C., 'East Anglia and the Danelaw', *Transactions of the Royal Historical Society*, 5 (1955), pp. 23–39.

Davison, A., *The evolution of settlement in three parishes in south-east Norfolk*, East Anglian Archaeology 49 (Dereham, 1990).

Defoe, D., *Tour through the whole island of Great Britain*, 2nd edn, vol. 1 (London, 1738).

Deslandres, P., *L'Ordre des Trinitaires pour le Rachat des Captifs*, 2 vols (Paris, 1903).

Doarks, C., *A study of the marsh dykes in Broadland* (Norwich, 1984).

Dodwell, B. (ed.), *The charters of Norwich cathedral priory*, Pipe Roll Society (London, 1974).

Driscoll, R.J., 'Broadland dykes: the loss of an important wildlife habitat', *Transactions of the Norfolk and Norwich Naturalists' Society*, 26/3 (1983), pp. 170–2.

Durandus, W., *The symbolism of churches and church ornaments*, 1286, trans J. Neale and B. Webb (London, 1906).

Dutt, W.A., *Highways, byways and waterways of East Anglia* (London, 1899).

Dutt, W.A., *The Norfolk Broads* (London, 1903).

Dyer, A. and Palliser, D. (eds), *The diocesan population returns for 1563 and 1603* (Oxford, 2005).

E. Hunt and Co., *Hunt's directory of east Norfolk with part of Suffolk* (London, 1850).

Eaton, D., *Easton and Amos: a brief history of a Victorian engineering company* (Westonzoyland, 2002).

Ekwall, E., *The concise Oxford dictionary of English place-names*, 4th edn (Oxford, 1960).

Ellis, E.A. (ed.), *The Broads* (London, 1965).

Ellis, H. (ed.), *Chronica Johannis de Oxenedes* (London, 1859).

Everitt, N., 'Wildfowling', in W.A. Dutt, *The Norfolk Broads* (London, 1903), pp. 323–30.

Eyre, S.R., 'The curving ploughland strip and its historical implications', *Agricultural History Review*, 3 (1955), pp. 80–94.

Faden, W., *A topographical map of the county of Norfolk* (London, 1797).

Fairweather, J. (ed.), *Liber Eliensis. A history of the Isle of Ely* (Woodbridge, 2005).

Le Fanu, W.R., *Queen Anne's Bounty: a short account of its history and work* (London, 1921).

Fawcett, T., 'Thorpe Water Frolic', *Norfolk Archaeology*, 36 (1977), pp. 393–8.

Fenwick, M., 'Langley', in S. Bate (ed.), *Capability Brown in Norfolk* (Aylsham, 2016), pp. 65–100.

Fewster, M., 'Thomas Smithdale and Sons: a study of a Victorian ironfounder', *Journal of the Norfolk Industrial Archaeology Society*, 3/1 (1981), pp. 25–33.

Fielding, A.M. and A.P., *Salt works and salinas. The archaeology, conservation and recovery of salt making sites and their processes* (Marston, 2005).

Fisher, C., 'Early chalk tramways at Whitlingham', *Journal of the Norfolk Industrial Archaeology Society*, 3/2 (1982), pp. 89–91.

Flint, B., *Suffolk windmills* (Woodbridge, 1979).

Fryer, V., Murphy, P. and Wilshire, P., 'Vegetation history and early farming', in T. Ashwin and A. Davison (eds), *An historical atlas of Norfolk*, 3rd edn (Chichester, 2005), pp. 10–11.

Fuller, R. and Gilroy, I., 'Rewilding and intervention: complementary philosophies for nature conservation in Britain', *British Wildlife*, 32 (2021), pp. 258–67.

Fuller, R., Williamson, T., Barnes, G. and Dolman, P., 'Human activities and biodiversity opportunities in pre-industrial cultural landscapes: relevance to conservation', *Journal of Applied Ecology*, 54 (2017), pp. 459–69.

Funnell, B.M., 'History and prognosis of subsidence and sea-level change in the lower Yare valley, Norfolk', *Bulletin of the Geological Society of Norfolk*, 31 (1979), pp. 35–44.

Funnell, B.M., 'The Palaeogene and Early Pleistocene of Norfolk', in G.P. Larwood and B.M. Funnell (eds), *The Geology of Norfolk*, Transactions of the Norfolk and Norwich Naturalists' Society, 19/6 (1961), pp. 340–64.

Gaffney, V., Fitch, S. and Smith, D., *Europe's lost world: the rediscovery of Doggerland*, Council for British Archaeology (York, 2009).

Gearey, B., Howard, A. and Chapman, H., *Down by the river: archaeological, palaeoenvironmental and geoarchaeological investigations of the Suffolk river valleys* (Oxford, 2016).

Gelling, M., *Signposts to the past: place-names and the history of England*, 3rd edn (Chichester, 1997).

Gelling, M. and Cole, A., *The landscape of place-names* (Stamford, 2000).

George, M., *The land use, ecology and conservation of Broadland* (Chichester, 1992).

Giller, K.E. and Wheeler, B.D., 'Past peat cutting and present vegetation patterns in an undrained fen in the Norfolk Broadland', *Journal of Ecology*, 74 (1986), pp. 219–47.

Gilmour, N., Horlock, S., Mortimer, R. and Tremlett, S., 'Middle Bronze Age enclosures in the Norfolk Broads: a case study at Ormesby St Michael, England', *Proceedings of the Prehistoric Society*, 80 (2014), pp. 141–57.

Goode, W.J., *East Anglian round towers and their churches* (Kings Lynn, 1982).

Goodey, C., *A century of Broadland cruising* (Wroxham, 1978).

Goodwyn, E.A., *A Suffolk town in mid-Victorian England* (Beccles, 1965).

Gordon, D., *Regional history of the railways of Great Britain volume 5. Eastern England* (Newton Abbot, 1977).

Goudie, A.S., *The landforms of England and Wales* (Oxford, 1990).

Grady, D.M., 'Medieval and post-medieval salt extraction in north-east Lincolnshire', in R.H. Bewley (ed.), *Lincolnshire's archaeology from the air* (Lincoln, 1998), pp. 81–95.

Green, C., 'Broadland fords and causeways', *Norfolk Archaeology*, 32 (1961), pp. 316–31.

Griffiths, S., Johnston, R., May, R., McOmish, D., Marshall, P., Last, J. and Bayliss, A., 'Dividing the land: time and land division in the English North Midlands and Yorkshire', *European Journal of Archaeology*, 25/2 (2022), pp. 216–37.

Groves, N., 'Two sisters: two churches', in A. Longcroft and R. Joby (eds), *East Anglian studies: essays presented to J.C. Barringer on his retirement* (Norwich, 1995), pp. 108–15.

Gruenfelder, J.K., 'Nicholas Murford, Yarmouth salt-producer', *Norfolk Archaeology*, 41/2 (1991), pp. 162–70.

Gunn, J., *A sketch of the geology of Norfolk* (Norwich, 1864).

Gurney, D., *Outposts of the Roman Empire: a guide to Norfolk's Roman forts* (Norwich, 2002).

Gurney, D., 'Roman Norfolk (c. AD 43–110)', in T. Ashwin and A. Davison (eds), *An historical atlas of Norfolk*, 3rd edn (Chichester, 2005), pp. 28–9.

Gurney, D. and Penn, K., 'Excavations and surveys in Norfolk 2003', *Norfolk Archaeology*, 44/3 (2004), pp. 573–89.

Hall, D., *Medieval fields* (Princes Risborough, 1982).

Hall, D., *The open fields of Northamptonshire* (Northampton, 1995).

Hamilton's map & chart of the Broads (Norwich, 1935).

Hart, C., *The early charters of Eastern England* (Leicester, 1966).

Hart, S., *The round tower churches of England* (Norwich, 2003).

Hatcher, J., 'England in the aftermath of the Black Death', *Past and Present*, 144/1 (1994), pp. 3–35.

Haward, B., *Master Mason Hawes of Occold, Suffolk and John Hore Master Carpenter of Diss* (Ipswich, 2000).

Hawke, C.J. and José, P.V., *Reedbed management for commercial and wildlife interests* (Sandy, 1996).

Head, M.J., 'Marine environmental change in the Pliocene and Early Pleistocene of Eastern England: the dinoflagellate evidence reviewed', in T. van Kolfschoten and P.L. Gibbard (eds), *The dawn of the Quaternary – proceedings of the SEQS-EuroMam Symposium, Kerkrade, 16–21 June 1996* (Utrecht, 1998), pp. 199–226.

Heaton, A., *Duck decoys* (Princes Risborough, 2001).

Henslow, J.S. and Skepper, E., *Flora of Suffolk: a catalogue of the plants found in a wild state in the county of Suffolk* (London, 1860).

Heywood, S., 'The round towered churches of East Anglia', in J. Blair (ed.), *Minsters and parish churches. The local church in transition 960–1200* (Oxford, 1988), pp. 169–77.

Heywood, S., 'Stone building in Romanesque East Anglia', in D. Bates and R. Liddiard (eds), *East Anglia and its North Sea world in the Middle Ages* (Norwich, 2013), pp. 230–56.

Hill, J.D., 'The dynamics of social change in later Iron Age eastern and south-eastern England *c*. 300 BC–AD 43', in C. Haselgrove and T. Moore (eds), *The later Iron Age in Britain and beyond* (Oxford, 2007), pp. 16–40.

Hill, J.D., 'Settlement, landscape and regionality: Norfolk and Suffolk in the pre-Roman Iron Age of Britain and beyond', in J. Davies and T. Williamson (eds), *Land of the Iceni: the Iron Age in northern East Anglia* (Norwich, 1999), pp. 185–207.

Hills, R., *Power from wind: a history of windmill technology* (Cambridge, 1994).

Hind, W.M., *The flora of Suffolk* (London, 1889).

Hinde, K.S.G., *Fenland pumping engines* (Bath, 2006).

Hinton, I. (ed.), *The buildings of Hempnall, Norfolk Historic Buildings Group Journal*, 7 (2020).

Historic England, *Causewayed enclosures: introductions to heritage assets* (Swindon, 2018).

Hodge, C.A.H., Burton, R.G.O., Corbett, W.M.C., Evans, R. and Seale, R.S., *Soils and their use in Eastern England* (Harpenden, 1984).

Höfele, P., Müller, O. and Hühn, L., 'Introduction: the role of nature in the Anthropocene – defining and reacting to a new geological epoch', *The Anthropocene Review*, 9/2 (2022), pp. 129–38.

Holman, I.P. and White, S.M., *Synthesis of the Upper Thurne research and recommendations for management: report to the Broads Authority* (Cranfield, 2008).

Holt-Wilson, T., 'Kirby Bedon slate roof', *Norfolk Historic Buildings Group Newsletter*, 46 (2022), p. 19.

Hooke, D., *Trees in Anglo-Saxon England* (Woodbridge, 2010).

Hooke, D., 'The woodland landscape of early medieval England', in N. Higham and M.J. Ryan (eds), *Place-names, language and the Anglo-Saxon landscape* (Woodbridge 2011), pp. 143–74.

Hoskins, W.G., 'The rebuilding of rural England, 1570–1640', *Past and Present*, 4/1 (1953), pp. 44–59.

Hutchinson, S., *The Lower Bure: from Great Yarmouth to Upton* (Stoke Holy Cross, 2008).

Isaacsons, R.F. (ed.), *Calendar of patent rolls, Edward III, volume 12, 1361-64* (London, 1912).

Jennings, J.N., *The origin of the Broads* (London, 1952).

Jennings, J.P., *Sun pictures of the Norfolk Broads*, 2nd edn (Ashstead, 1892).

J.G. Harrod and Co., *Harrod's directory of Norfolk and Norwich including Lowestoft* (London, 1863).

Joby, R., 'Railways', in T. Ashwin and A. Davison (eds), *An historical atlas of Norfolk*, 3rd edn (Chichester, 2005), pp. 152–3.

Joby, R., *Regional railway handbook 2: East Anglia* (Newton Abbot, 1987).

Johnson, M., *Housing culture: traditional architecture in an English landscape* (London, 1993).

Johnston, R., May, R. and McOmish, D., 'Understanding the chronologies of England's field systems', in S. Arnoldussen, R. Johnson and M. Løvschal (eds), *Europe's early fieldscapes: archaeologies of prehistoric land allotment* (New York, 2021), pp. 185–207.

Jones, J. and Jones, J., 'Lime burning in Norfolk', *Journal of the Norfolk Industrial Archaeology Society*, 2/2 (1977), pp. 21–31.

Jones, J. and Manning, M., 'Lime burning and extractive industries', in P. Wade-Martins (ed.), *An historical atlas of Norfolk* (Norwich, 1993), pp. 162–3.

Kelley, P. (ed.), *From Osborne House to Wheatfen Broad: memoirs of Phyllis Ellis* (Surlingham, 2011).

Kelly's Directories, *Kelly's directory of Norfolk* (London, 1904, 1916, 1937).

Kelly's Directories, *Kelly's directory of Suffolk* (London, 1883).

Kemp, R.A.F., *Staithes: a survey and register* (Norwich, 1986).

Kirby, M., *Albion: the story of the Norfolk trading wherry* (Norwich, 1998).

Knecht, T., *Histoire de L'Ordre de la Sainte Trinité et de la Rédemption Des Captifs* (Paris, 1993).

Knowles, D. and Hadcock, R.N., *Medieval religious houses of England and Wales* (Harlow, 1971).

Krawiec, K., Gearey, B.R., Chapman, H.P., Hopla, E.-J., Bamforth, M., Griffiths, C., Hill, T.C.B. and Tyers, I., 'A late prehistoric timber alignment in the Waveney valley, Suffolk. Excavations at Barsham Marshes', *Journal of Wetland Archaeology*, 10 (2011), pp. 46–70.

Kuhlmann, G., *High resolution stratigraphy and paleoenvironmental changes in the southern North Sea during the Neogene; an integrated study of late Cenozoic marine deposits from the northern part of the Dutch offshore area* (Utrecht, 2004).

Ladbrooke, J.B., *Views of Norfolk churches*, 7 vols (Norwich, c.1832).

Lambert, J.M , 'The distribution and status of *Glyceria maxima* (Hartm.) Holmb. in the region of Surlingham and Rockland Broads, Norfolk', *Journal of Ecology*, 33/2 (1946), pp. 230–67.

Lambert, J.M. and Jennings, J.N., 'Alluvial stratigraphy and vegetational succession in the region of the Bure valley broads: detailed vegetational and stratigraphical relationships', *Journal of Ecology*, 39 (1951), pp. 120–48.

Lambert, J.M., Jennings, J.N. and Smith, C.T., 'The origin of the Broads', in E.A. Ellis (ed.), *The Broads* (London, 1965), pp. 37–68.

Lambert, J.M., Jennings, J.N., Smith, C.T., Green, C. and Hutchinson, J.N., *The making of the Broads: a reconsideration of their origin in the light of new evidence*, Royal Geographical Society Research Series 3 (London, 1960).

Langford, P., *A polite and commercial people: England, 1727–1783* (Oxford, 1989).

Lee, J.R., Woods, M.A. and Moorlock, B.S.P. (eds), *British regional geology: East Anglia*, 5th edn (Keyworth, 2015).

Lennard, R.G., *Rural England, 1086–1135: a study of social and agrarian conditions* (Oxford, 1959).

Lewis, S.G., Parfitt, S.A., Preece, R.C., Sinclair, J., Coope, G.R., Field, M.H., Maher, B.A., Scaife, R.G. and Whittaker, J.E., 'Age and palaeoenvironmental setting of the Pleistocene vertebrate fauna at Norton Subcourse, Norfolk', in D.C. Schreve (ed.), *The Quaternary mammals of southern and eastern England: field guide* (London, 2004), pp. 5–17.

Licence, T., 'The origins of the monastic communities of St Benedict at Holme and Bury St Edmunds', *Revue Bénédictine*, 116 (2007), pp. 42–61.

Limpenny, S.E., Barrio Froján, C., Cotterill, C.J., Foster-Smith, R.L., Pearce, B., Tizzard, L., Limpenny, D.L., Long, D., Walmsley, S., Kirby, S., Baker, K., Meadows, W.J., Rees, J., Hill, J., Wilson, C., Leivers, M., Churchley, S., Russell, J., Birchenough, A.C., Green, S.L. and Law, R.J., *The east coast regional environmental characterisation*, Cefas Open Report 08/04 (Lowestoft, 2011).

Longcroft, A. (ed.), *The historic buildings of New Buckenham*, Norfolk Historic Buildings Group Journal, 2 (2005).

Lubbock, R., *Observations on the fauna of Norfolk, and more particularly on the district of the Broads* (London, 1845).

Lucas, R., 'Brickmaking', in T. Ashwin and A. Davison (eds), *An historical atlas of Norfolk*, 3rd edn (Chichester, 2005), pp. 162–3.

Lucas, R., 'Dutch pantiles in the County of Norfolk: architecture and international trade in the 17th and 18th centuries', *Vernacular Architecture*, 38 (1998), pp. 75–94.

Lucas, R., 'Some observations on descriptions of parsonage houses made in Norfolk glebe terriers', *Transactions of the Ancient Monuments Society*, 39 (1996), pp. 83–95.

Lucy, S., Tipper. J. and Dickens, A., *The Anglo-Saxon settlement and cemetery at Bloodmoor Hill, Carlton Colville, Suffolk*, East Anglian Archaeology 131 (Cambridge, 2009).

Lyell, C., *The student's elements of geology* (London, 1871).

Lyons, G. and Ausden, M., 'Raising water levels to revert arable land to grazing marsh at Berney Marshes RSPB Reserve, Norfolk, England', *Conservation Evidence*, 2 (2005), pp. 47–9.

McCann, J., 'Is clay lump a traditional building material?', *Vernacular Architecture*, 18 (1987), pp. 1–16.

Machin, R., 'The Great Rebuilding: a reassessment', *Past and Present*, 77 (1977), pp. 35–56.

McCormack, C., *The book of Salhouse & Woodbastwick* (Wellington, 2016).

Malim, T., Penn, K., Robinson, B., Wait, G. and Welsh, K., 'New evidence on the Cambridgeshire dykes and Worsted Street Roman road', *Proceedings of the Cambridge Antiquarian Society*, 85 (1997), pp. 27–122.

Malster, R., *The Broads* (Chichester, 1993).

Malster, R., *The Norfolk & Suffolk Broads* (Chichester, 2003).

Malster, R., *Wherries and waterways* (Lavenham, 1971).

Marshall, W., *The rural economy of Norfolk*, 2 vols (London, 1787).

Martin, E., 'Rural settlement patterns in medieval Suffolk', *Annual Report of the Medieval Settlement Research Group*, 15 (2001), pp. 5–7.

Matless, D., 'Checking the sea: geographies of authority on the east Norfolk coast, 1790–1932', *Rural History*, 30 (2019), pp. 215–40.

Matless, D., *In the nature of landscape: cultural geography on the Norfolk Broads* (Oxford, 2014).

Mayhew, D.F. and Stuart, A.J., 'Stratigraphic and taxonomic revision of the fossil vole remains (Rodentia, Microtinae) from the Lower Pleistocene deposits of eastern England', *Philosophical Transactions of the Royal Society of London, B*, 312 (1986), pp. 431–85.

Mercer, E., *English vernacular houses*, Royal Commission on Historical Monuments (England) (London, 1975).

Miller, D., *Seen from a windmill: a Norfolk Broads revue* (London, 1935).

Mingay, G.E., *Parliamentary enclosure in England: an introduction to its causes, incidences and impact 1750–1850* (London, 1997).

Monbiot, G., *Feral: searching for enchantment on the frontiers of rewilding* (London, 2014).

Moorlock, B.S.P., Hamblin, R.J.O., Booth, S.J. and Morigi, A.N., *Geology of the country around Lowestoft and Saxmundham. Memoir for 1:50,000 Geological Sheets 176 and 191* (London, 2000).

Morris, R., *Churches in the landscape* (London, 1989).

Mortimer, R., 'The family of Rannulf Glanville', *Bulletin of the Institute of Historical Research*, 54/129 (1981), pp. 1–16.

Mosby, J.E., *The land of Britain: Norfolk*, The Land Utilisation Survey of Britain No. 70 (London, 1938).

Moss, B., *The Broads: the people's wetland* (London, 2001).

Mottram, R.H., *The Broads* (London, 1952).

Murphy, P., 'Coastal change and human response', in T. Ashwin and A. Davison (eds), *An historical atlas of Norfolk*, 3rd edn (Chichester, 2005), pp. 6–7.

New, C.W., *History of the alien priories in England* (Chicago, 1916).

Nix, M., *Norwich textiles: a global story 1750–1840* (Norwich, 2023).

Norfolk Industrial Archaeology Society, 'A survey of Ludham', *Journal of the Norfolk Industrial Archaeology Society*, 3/1 (1981), pp. 34–51.

Norfolk Naturalists Trust, *Nature in Norfolk: a heritage in trust* (Norwich, 1976).

North, R., *A discourse of fish and fish-ponds* (London, 1712).

Norton, P.E.P. and Beck, R.B., 'Lower Pleistocene molluscan assemblages and pollen from the Crag of Aldeby (Norfolk) and Easton Bavents (Suffolk)', *Bulletin of the Geological Society of Norfolk*, 22 (1972), pp. 11–31.

Oswald, A., Dyer, C. and Barber, M., *The creation of monuments. Neolithic causewayed enclosures in the British Isles* (Swindon, 2001).

Overton, T., *A programme of events to celebrate 150 years of Catfield Methodist Chapel* (Catfield, 1986).

Page, W., 'Houses of Benedictine monks: the abbey of St Benet of Holm', in W. Page (ed.), *A history of the county of Norfolk, volume 2* (London, 1906), pp. 330–6.

Page, W. (ed.), *The Victoria history of the county of Norfolk, volume 2* (London, 1906).

Paget-Tomlinson, E.W., *The complete book of canal and river navigations* (Albrighton, 1978).

Pallis, M., 'On the causes of the salinity of the Broads of the River Thurne', *The Geographical Journal*, 37/3 (1911), pp. 284–91.

Pallis, M., 'The river-valleys of east Norfolk: their aquatic and fen formations', in A.G. Tansley (ed.), *Types of British vegetation* (Cambridge, 1911), pp. 214–45.

Palmer, C.J. (ed.), *Henry Manship: the history of Great Yarmouth* (Great Yarmouth, 1854).

Panter, C., Mossman, H. and Dolman, P.M., *Biodiversity audit and tolerance sensitivity mapping for the Broads*, Broads Authority Report (Norwich, 2011).

Parfitt, S.A., Ashton, N.M., Lewis, S.G., Abel, R.L., Coope, G.R., Field, M.H., Gale, R., Hoare, P.G., Larkin, N.R., Lewis, M.D., Karloukovski, V., Maher, B.A., Peglar, S.M., Preece, R.C., Whittaker, J.E. and Stringer, C.B., 'Early Pleistocene human occupation at the edge of the boreal zone in northwest Europe', *Nature*, 466 (July 2010), pp. 229–33.

Parfitt, S.A., Barendregt, R.W., Breda, M., Candy, I., Collins, M.J., Coope, G.R., Durbidge, P., Field, M.H., Lee, J.R., Lister, A.M., Mutch, R., Penkman, K.E.H., Preece, R.C., Rose, J., Stringer, C.B., Symmons, R., Whittaker, J.E., Wymer, J.J. and Stuart, A.J., 'The earliest record of human activity in Northern Europe', *Nature*, 438 (December 2005), pp. 1008–12.

Parmenter, J.M., *The Broadland Fen resource survey*, 11 vols (Norwich, 1995).

Parry, J., *Maurice Bird: The Gilbert White of the Broads*, Norfolk and Norwich Naturalists' Society Occasional Publication 20 (Norwich, 2024).

Patterson, A., *Man and nature on tidal waters* (London, 1909).

Patterson, A., *Nature in eastern Norfolk* (London, 1905).

Patterson, A., 'Wild life on Breydon', in W.A. Dutt, *The Norfolk Broads* (London, 1903), pp. 200–14.

Patterson, A.H., *The cruise of the 'Walrus'* (London, 1923).

Payne-Gallwey, R., *The book of duck decoys: their construction, management and history* (London, 1886).

Penn, K., 'The early church in Norfolk: some aspects', in S. Margeson, B. Ayers and S. Heywood (eds), *A festival of Norfolk archaeology* (Norwich, 1996), pp. 40–6.

Penn, K., 'Early Saxon settlement (c. AD 410–650)', in T. Ashwin and A. Davison (eds), *An historical atlas of Norfolk*, 3rd edn (Chichester, 2005), pp. 30–1.

Pennant, T., *British zoology*, 4 vols (London, 1768–70).

Pestell, T., *Landscapes of monastic foundation: the establishment of religious houses in East Anglia c.650–1200* (Woodbridge, 2004).

Pestell, T., 'Monastic foundation strategies in the early Norman diocese of Norwich', *Anglo-Norman Studies*, 23 (2001), pp. 199–229.

Pestell, T., 'Of founders and faith: the establishment of the Trinitarian Priory of Ingham, Norfolk (England)', in G. De Boe and F. Verhaeghe (eds), *Religion and belief in medieval Europe: papers of the Medieval Europe Brugge 1997 Conference 4* (Zellik, 1997), pp. 65–78.

Pestell, T., 'Using material culture to define holy space: the Bromholm Project', in A. Spicer and S. Hamilton (eds), *Defining the holy. Sacred space in medieval and early modern Europe* (Aldershot, 2005), pp. 161–86.

Petch, C.P. and Swann, E.L., *Flora of Norfolk* (Norwich, 1968).

Pettitt, P. and White, M.J., *The British Palaeolithic: human societies at the edge of the Pleistocene world* (Abingdon, 2012).

Pevsner, N., *The buildings of England: Cumberland and Westmorland* (London, 1997).

Pevsner, N. and Radcliffe, E., *The buildings of England: Cornwall* (London, 2002).

Pevsner, N. and Radcliffe, E., *The buildings of England: Suffolk* (London, 1991).

Pitts, M., 'Ceremony and settlement in rural Norfolk', *British Archaeology* (May–June 2021), pp. 9–10.

Plouviez, J., 'The Roman period', in D. Dymond and E. Martin (eds), *An historical atlas of Suffolk*, 3rd edn (Ipswich, 1999), pp. 42–3.

Points, J., *Floating bridges: ferries across the Broadland rivers* (Surlingham, 1994).

Pound, J., 'Sixteenth-century Norfolk: population and wealth', in T. Ashwin and A. Davison (eds) *An historical atlas of Norfolk*, 3rd edn (Chichester, 2005), pp. 100–2.

Preece, R.C. and Parfitt, S.A., 'The Cromer Forest-Bed: new thoughts on an old problem', in S.G. Lewis, C.A. Whiteman and R.C. Preece (eds), *The Quaternary of Norfolk and Suffolk: field guide* (London, 2000), pp. 1–27.

Purseglove, J., *Taming the flood: a history and natural history of rivers and wetlands* (Oxford, 1988).

Rackham, O., *Ancient woodland: its history, vegetation and uses in England* (London, 1980).

Rackham, O., 'The ancient woods of Norfolk', *Transactions of the Norfolk and Norwich Naturalists' Society*, 27 (1986), pp. 161–7.

Rackham, O., 'Grundle House: on the quantities of timber in certain East-Anglian buildings', *Vernacular Architecture*, 3 (1972), pp. 3–8.

Rackham, O., *The history of the countryside* (London, 1986).

Rackham, W.L., *Everybody's Broadland* (Norwich, 1927).

Rawcliffe, C., *The hospitals of medieval Norwich* (Norwich, 1995).

Reid, C., *The Pliocene deposits of Britain* (London, 1890).

Riches, P.F., Norton, P.E.P., Schreve, D.C. and Rose, J., 'Bramerton Pits SSSI', in I. Candy, J.R. Lee and A.M. Harrison (eds), *The Quaternary of East Anglia* (Cambridge, 2007), pp. 73–84.

Robberds, J.W., *Geological and historical observations on the eastern vallies of Norfolk* (Norwich, 1826).

Robertson, D., 'A Neolithic enclosure and Early Saxon settlement: excavations at Yarmouth Road, Broome, 2001', *Norfolk Archaeology*, 44/2 (2003), pp. 222–50.

Rodwell, J.S. (ed.), *British plant communities. Volume 2. Mires and heaths* (Cambridge, 1991).

Rodwell, J.S. (ed.), *British plant communities. Volume 4. Aquatic communities, swamps and tall-herb fens* (Cambridge, 1995).

Rogerson, A., 'Six middle Anglo-Saxon sites in west Norfolk', in T. Pestell and K. Ulmschneider (eds), *Markets in early medieval Europe: trading and 'productive' sites 650–850* (Macclesfield, 2003), pp. 110–21.

Rose, E., 'A linear earthwork at Horning', in Norfolk Archaeological Unit, *Trowse, Horning, deserted medieval villages, Kings Lynn*, East Anglian Archaeology 14 (Dereham, 1982), pp. 35–9.

Rose, J., 'Early and Middle Pleistocene landscapes of eastern England', *Proceedings of the Geologists' Association*, 120 (2009), pp. 3–33.

Rose, J., 'Palaeogeography of eastern England during the Early and Middle Pleistocene', in I. Candy, J.R. Lee and A.M. Harrison (eds), *The Quaternary of northern East Anglia: field guide* (London, 2008), pp. 5–41.

Rose, J., Candy, I., Moorlock, B.S.P., Wilkins, H., Hamblin, R.J.O., Lee, J.R., Riding, J.B. and Morigi, A.N., 'Early and Middle Pleistocene river, coastal and neotectonic processes, southeast Norfolk, England', *Proceedings of the Geologists' Association*, 113/1 (2002), pp. 47–67.

Rose, J., Gulamali, N., Moorlock, B.S.P., Hamblin, R.J.O., Jeffery, D.H., Anderson, E., Lee, J.A. and Riding, J.B., 'Pre-glacial Quaternary sediments, How Hill, near Ludham, Norfolk, England', *Bulletin of the Geological Society of Norfolk*, 45 (1996), pp. 3–28.

Rotherham, I., *Peat and peat cutting* (Princes Risborough, 2009).

Rowell, C.W., 'County council smallholdings, 1908–1958', *Agriculture*, 60 (1959), pp. 109–14.

Royal Commission on Historical Monuments (England), *An inventory of historical monuments in the county of Cambridgeshire, volume 2: north-east Cambridgeshire* (London, 1972).

Rudd, A.J., 'Fishing', in W.A. Dutt, *The Norfolk Broads* (London, 1903), pp. 313–21.

Russell, R., *The lost canals of England* (Newton Abbot, 1971).

Salzman, L., *Building in England down to 1540: a documentary history* (Oxford, 1992).

Saunders, H.W. (ed.), *The first register of Norwich cathedral priory* (Norwich, 1939).

Smith, A., 'The east', in A. Smith, M. Allen, T. Brindle and M. Fulford, *The rural settlement of Roman Britain*, Britannia Monograph Series 29 (London, 2016).

Smith, A.C., *Drainage windmills of the Norfolk marshes: a contemporary survey*, 2nd edn (Stevenage, 1990).

Smith, A.H., *English place-name elements*, 2 vols (Cambridge, 1956).

Smith, J.E., *Flora Britannica*, 3 vols (London, 1800–04).

Smith, J.T., 'Short-lived and mobile houses in late seventeenth-century England', *Vernacular Architecture*, 16 (1985), pp. 34–5.

Smith, P., 'Time and chance: a reply', *Vernacular Architecture*, 21 (1990), pp. 4–5.

Smith Wynne, W.A., *St Olave's priory and bridge* (Norwich, 1914).

Southwell, T., 'Norfolk decoys', *Transactions of the Norfolk and Norwich Naturalists' Society*, 2 (1879), pp. 538–55.

Southwell, T., 'Introduction', in R. Lubbock, *Observations on the fauna of Norfolk, and more particularly on the district of the Broads*, revised edn (Norwich, 1879), pp. i–xiii.

Southwell, T., 'Presidential address', *Transactions of the Norfolk and Norwich Naturalists' Society*, 1/3 (1872), pp. 7–19.

Spelman, H., *The English works of Sir Henry Spelman Kt. Published in his life-time; together with his posthumous works, relating to the laws and antiquities of England* (London, 1727).

Spooner, S. (ed.), *Sail and storm: the Aylsham Navigation* (Aylsham, 2012).

Stammers, M., *Norfolk shipping* (Stroud, 2002).

Stell, C., *Nonconformist chapels and meeting-houses in eastern England* (London, 2002).

Stenning, D., 'Small aisled halls in Essex', *Vernacular Architecture*, 34 (2003), pp. 1–19.

Stenton, F.M., *Anglo-Saxon England* (Oxford, 1943).

Stevenson, H., *The birds of Norfolk, with remarks on their habits, migration, and local distribution*, 2 vols (London, 1866).

Straw, A., 'The glacial geomorphology of central and north Norfolk', *East Midlands Geographer*, 5 (1973), pp. 333–54.

Straw, A. and Clayton, K.M., *The geomorphology of the British Isles. Eastern and central England* (London, 1979).

Suckling, A.I., *The history and antiquities of the county of Suffolk*, vol. 3 (London, 1848).

Suffling, E.R., *The land of the Broads: a practical guide* (London, 1885).

Taylor, H.M. and J., *Anglo-Saxon architecture* (Cambridge, 1980).

Taylor, J., 'Landscape and leisure', in N. McWilliam and V. Sekules (eds), *Life and landscape. P.H. Emerson: art and photography in East Anglia 1885–1900* (Norwich, 1986).

Taylor, J.E., 'The Norfolk broads and meres geologically considered', *Transactions of the Norfolk and Norwich Naturalists' Society*, 1 (1871–2), pp. 30–40.

Taylor, R., *Index monasticus* (London, 1821).

Taylor, R.C., 'On the Crag-strata at Bramerton near Norwich', *Transactions of the Geological Society*, Second Series, 1 (1824), pp. 371–3.

Taylor, R.C., *On the geology of east Norfolk; with remarks upon the hypothesis of Mr. J.W. Robberds, respecting the former level of the German Ocean* (London, 1827).

Thompson, M., 'Associated monasteries and castles in the Middle Ages: a tentative list', *Archaeological Journal*, 143 (1986), pp. 305–21.

Thurston, E., 'Neotectonics and the preglacial landscape of eastern Norfolk, UK', *Proceedings of the Geologists' Association*, 128 (2017), pp. 742–56.

Tizzard, L., Bicket, A. and De Loecker, D., *Seabed prehistory. Investigating the palaeogeography and early Middle Palaeolithic archaeology in the southern North Sea*, Wessex Archaeology Report 35 (Salisbury, 2015).

Tooley, B. and Hinton, I., *Barnby and North Cove: a history of two villages* (Barnby, 2002).

Townley Clarkson, P., 'Yacht-racing', in W.A. Dutt, *The Norfolk Broads* (London, 1903), pp. 305–12.

Tree, I., *Wilding: the return of nature to a British farm* (London, 2018).

Tremlett, S., 'Iron Age landscapes from the air: results from the Norfolk National Mapping Programme', in J. Davies (ed.), *The Iron Age in northern East Anglia: new work in the land of the Iceni*, BAR British Series 549 (Oxford, 2011), pp. 26–7.

Treweek, J., José, P. and Benstead, P., *The wet grassland guide. Managing floodplain and coastal wet grassland for wildlife* (Sandy, 1997).

Trimmer, K., *Flora of Norfolk* (London, 1866).

Tristram, E.W., 'The wall paintings at Horsham St Faith, near Norwich', *Norfolk Archaeology*, 22 (1926), pp. 257–9.

Turner, E.L., *Broadland birds* (London, 1924).

Turner, E.L., 'The status of birds in Broadland', *Transactions of the Norfolk and Norwich Naturalists' Society*, 11 (1922), pp. 228–40.

Turner, M., *English parliamentary enclosure: its historical geography and economic history* (Folkestone, 1980).

Turner, M., 'Parliamentary enclosure', in T. Ashwin and A. Davison (eds), *An historical atlas of Norfolk*, 3rd edn (Chichester, 2005), pp. 130–2.

Van Wirdum, G., Den Held, A.J. and Schmitz, M., 'Terrestrialising fen vegetation in former turbaries in the Netherlands', in J.T.A. Verhoeven (ed.), *Fens and bogs in the Netherlands: vegetation, history, nutrient dynamics and conservation* (Dordrecht, 1992), pp. 323–60.

Vaughn-Lewis, W. and M., *Aylsham: a nest of Norfolk lawyers* (Itteringham, 2014).

Vera, F., *Grazing ecology and forest history* (Wallingford, 2002).

Wade, K., 'The late Saxon period', in A.J. Lawson (ed.), *The archaeology of Witton near North Walsham*, East Anglian Archaeology 18 (Dereham, 1983), pp. 73–7.

Wade, K., 'A model for Anglo-Saxon settlement expansion in the Witton area', in A.J. Lawson, *The archaeology of Witton near North Walsham*, East Anglian Archaeology 18 (Dereham, 1983), pp. 77–8.

Wade-Martins, P., *Village sites in the Launditch Hundred*, East Anglian Archaeology 10 (Gressenhall, 1980).

Wade Martins, S., 'The study of the drainage windmills of the Norfolk Broadlands', *Norfolk Archaeology*, 35 (1970), pp. 152–4.

Wade Martins, S. and Williamson, T., *The countryside of East Anglia: changing landscapes, 1870–1950* (Woodbridge, 2008).

Wade Martins, S. and Williamson, T., *Roots of change: farming and the landscape in East Anglia, c.1700–1870* (Exeter, 1999).

Wailes, R., *The English windmill* (London, 1954).

Wailes, R., 'Norfolk windmills part II: drainage and pumping mills, including those in Suffolk', *Newcomen Society Transactions*, 30 (1956), pp. 157–77.

Wainwright, G.J., 'The excavation of a Neolithic settlement on Broome Heath, Ditchingham, Norfolk', *Proceedings of the Prehistoric Society*, 38 (1972), pp. 1–97.

Wainwright, G.J., 'The excavation of prehistoric and Romano-British settlements on Eaton Heath, Norwich', *The Archaeological Journal*, 130 (1973), pp. 1–43.

Walsingham, Lord and Payne Galley, R., *Shooting: moor and marsh* (London, 1889).

Warner, P., *Greens, commons and clayland colonization* (Leicester, 1987).

Warner, P., 'Shared churchyards, freemen church-builders and the development of parishes in eleventh-century East Anglia', *Landscape History*, 8 (1986), pp. 39–52.

Watkins, G., *Stationary steam engines of Great Britain*, vol. 9 (Bath, 1993).

Weaver, W., 'The bulrush in commerce', *The Country Home*, 1 (1908), pp. 326–8.

Wells, C., 'Post-medieval turf-digging in Norfolk', *Norfolk Archaeology*, 43/3 (2000), pp. 469–82.

Wells, C., 'The role of turf and associated fuels in the nineteenth-century rural economy of Norfolk', *Norfolk Archaeology*, 43/4 (2001), pp. 630–42.

West, J.R. (ed.), *St Benet of Holme 1020–1210: the eleventh and twelfth century sections of Cott.Ms Galba E ii, the register of the abbey of St Benet of Holme* (Norwich, 1932).

West, R.G., *From Brandon to Bungay. An exploration of the landscape history and geology of the Little Ouse and Waveney rivers* (Ipswich, 2009).

West, R.G., *The pre-glacial Pleistocene of the Norfolk and Suffolk coasts* (Cambridge, 1980).

West, R.G., 'Vegetational history of the Early Pleistocene of the Royal Society borehole at Ludham, Norfolk', *Proceedings of the Royal Society of London*, B, 155 (1962), pp. 437–53.

Wheeler, B.D., 'Observations on the plant ecology of Upton Fen, Norfolk, with special reference to the doles', *Transactions of the Norfolk and Norwich Naturalists' Society*, 27/1 (1985), pp. 9–32.

Wheeler, B.D., 'The wetland plant communities of the river Ant valley, Norfolk', *Transactions of the Norfolk and Norwich Naturalists' Society*, 24/4 (1978), pp. 153–87.

Wheeler, B.D., Gowing, D.J.G., Shaw, S.C., Mountford, J.O. and Money, R.P., *Ecohydrological guidelines for lowland wetland plant communities* (Peterborough, 2004).

White, W., *History, gazetteer, and directory of Norfolk, and the city and county of Norwich* (Sheffield, 1845).

White, W., *History, gazetteer and directory of Suffolk* (London, 1874).

Whitelock, D. (ed. and trans.), *Anglo-Saxon wills* (Cambridge, 1930).

Wight, J., *Brick building in England: from the Middle Ages to 1550* (London, 1972).

Williamson, T., *England's landscape: East Anglia* (London, 2006).

Williamson, T., *The Norfolk Broads: a landscape history* (Manchester, 1997).

Williamson, T., *The origins of Norfolk* (Manchester, 1993).

Williamson, T., 'Rewilding: a landscape-history perspective', *British Wildlife*, 33 (2022), pp. 423–9.

Williamson, T., 'Understanding enclosure', *Landscapes*, 1 (2000), pp. 56–79.

Williamson, T., Liddiard, R. and Partida, T., *Champion. The making and unmaking of the English midland landscape* (Liverpool, 2013).

Williamson, T., Ringwood, I. and Spooner, S., *Lost country houses of Norfolk: history, archaeology and myth* (Woodbridge, 2015).

Winchester, A., *Discovering parish boundaries* (Princes Risborough, 1990).

Wisdom, A.S., *The law of rivers and watercourses* (London, 1979).

Wittering, W., *An arrangement of British plants* (Birmingham, 1796).

Woods, J., *Herbert Woods, a famous Broadland pioneer* (Tauranga, 2002).

Woodward, H.B., *The geology of the country around Norwich* (London, 1881).

Woodward, H.B., 'The scenery of Norfolk', *Transactions of the Norfolk and Norwich Naturalists' Society*, 3/4 (1882–3), pp. 439–66.

Wormald, F., 'The rood of Bromholm', *Journal of the Warburg Institute*, 1 (1937), pp. 31–45.

Wymer, J.J., 'Late glacial and Mesolithic hunters', in T. Ashwin and A. Davison (eds), *An historical atlas of Norfolk*, 3rd edn (Chichester, 2005), pp. 15–16.

Wymer, J.J. *Palaeolithic sites of East Anglia* (Norwich, 1985).

Yardy, A., *Mills of the Halvergate Marshes: Reedham Marshes and Ashtree Farm* (Norwich, 2008).

Yelling, J.A., *Common field and enclosure in England, 1450–1850* (London, 1977).

Young, A., *General view of the agriculture of the county of Norfolk* (London, 1804).

Unpublished reports, dissertations and theses

Bacon, K.P., 'Landholding and enclosure in the hundreds of East Flegg, West Flegg and Happing in Norfolk, 1695 to 1832', PhD thesis (University of East Anglia, 2003).

Birtles, S., 'A green space beyond self-interest: the evolution of common land in Norfolk, c.750–2003', PhD thesis (University of East Anglia, 2003).

Boulton, D., 'Differing patterns of Viking settlement in East Anglia: an analysis of Scandinavian and Anglo-Scandinavian place-names in their geographical and archaeological contexts', PhD thesis (University of East Anglia, 2020).

Burrows, A. and Kenyon, G., 'A woodland resources survey of the Bure Broads and Marshes Site of Special Scientific Interest', report (English Nature and the Broads Authority, 1985).

Crompton, G., 'Rare species dossiers – *Dryopteris cristata* and *Liparis loeselii*', report (Nature Conservancy Council, 1977).

Doarks, C., 'Ecology and management of marsh dykes in Broadland', MPhil thesis (University of East Anglia, 1986).

Douet, A., 'Norfolk agriculture 1914–1972', PhD thesis (University of East Anglia, 1989).

Douglas-Sherwood, T.E., 'The Norfolk keel', PhD thesis (University of St Andrews, 1988).

ELP, 'Fen plant communities of Broadland: results of a comprehensive survey 2005–2009', report (Broads Authority, 2010, minor amendments 2014).

Giller, K.E., 'Aspects of the plant ecology of a flood-plain mire in Broadland, Norfolk', PhD thesis (University of Sheffield, 1982).

Godwin, M., 'Microbionization and microbiofacies of the Holocene deposits of east Norfolk and Suffolk', PhD thesis (University of East Anglia, 1993).

Hinton, I., 'Aspects of the alignment and location of medieval rural churches', PhD thesis (University of East Anglia, 2012).

Hoggett, R., 'Changing beliefs: an archaeology of the East Anglian conversion', PhD thesis (University of East Anglia, 2007).

Jarvis, C., 'The Norfolk Broads: a reappraisal of their origins through geospatial analysis', MA dissertation (University of East Anglia, 2018).

Parmenter, J.M., 'The development of the wetland vegetation of the Broadland region: a study of the sociohistorical factors which have influenced and modified the development of fen vegetation in Broadland', PhD thesis (University of East Anglia, 2000).

Riches, P.F., 'The palaeoenvironmental and neotectonic history of the Early Pleistocene Crag Basin in East Anglia', PhD thesis (University of London, 2012).

Rogerson, A., 'Fransham: an archaeological and historical study of a parish on the Norfolk boulder clay', PhD thesis (University of East Anglia, 1995).

Sweet, R., 'Beccles to Burgh St Peter: a landscape history of the marshes', MA dissertation (University of East Anglia, 1989).

Trimble, G., 'Land at North Rackheath, Norfolk. An archaeological evaluation', Pre-Construct Archaeology report R14843 (Pampisford, 2022).

Watt, K.A., 'Nineteenth century brickmaking innovations in Britain: building and technological change', PhD thesis (University of York, 1990).

Wells, C., 'Historical and palaeoecological investigations of some Norfolk Broadland flood-plain mires and post medieval turf cutting', PhD thesis (University of Sheffield, 1988).

Wessex Archaeology, 'Bringing the Bure back to LIFE: Hoveton Wetland Restoration Project', report no. 112861.01 (September 2016).

Yardy, A., 'The development of the Broadland drainage windmills with particular reference to the firm of Englands of Ludham', MA dissertation (University of East Anglia, 2004).

Online resources

Albone, J., Massey, S. and Tremlett, S., 'The archaeology of Norfolk's Broads Zone: results of the National Mapping Programme', 2007. https://historicengland.org.uk/research/results/reports/113-2007.

Albone, J., Massey, S. and Tremlett, S., 'The archaeology of Norfolk's Coastal Zone: results of the National Mapping Programme', 2007. https://historicengland.org.uk/research/results/reports/114-2007.

British Geological Survey, Borehole data, TG42 SE2. http://scans.bgs.ac.uk/sobi_scans/boreholes/519477/images/12117425.html.

British Listed Buildings, 'Listed buildings in Norfolk'. https://britishlistedbuildings.co.uk/england/norfolk.

Broads Authority, 'Managing land and water'. https://www.broads-authority.gov.uk/looking-after/managing-land-and-water/.

Broads Authority, 'Planning for waterside bungalows/chalets'. https://www.broads-authority.gov.uk/__data/assets/pdf_file/0015/231054/Planning-for-Waterside-BungalowsChalets_18_11_2016.pdf.

Commons Registration Act, decisions. https://acraew.org.uk/commissioners-decisions/norfolk.

Evans, C., 'Late Iron Age and Roman resource assessment', in *East of England Research Framework*, 2021. https://researchframeworks.org/eoe/resource-assessments/late-iron-age-and-roman/.

The Genealogist, Tithe apportionment data. https://www.thegenealogist.co.uk/search/advanced/landowner/tithe-records/.

Intergovernmental Panel on Climate Change, 'Summary for policymakers', in H.O. Pörtner *et al.* (eds), *IPCC special report on the ocean and cryosphere in a changing climate. Intergovernmental Panel on Climate Change*, 2019. https://www.ipcc.ch/srocc/chapter/summary-for-policymakers/.

International Union for the Conservation of Nature Standards and Petitions Committee, 'Guidelines for Using the IUCN Red List Categories and Criteria, Version 15.1', 2022. https://www.iucnredlist.org/documents/RedListGuidelines.pdf.

Joint Nature Conservation Committee, 'Conservation designations for UK taxa – collation updates', 2023. https://jncc.gov.uk/our-work/conservation-designations-for-uk-taxa-updates/.

Murphy, P., 'The archaeology of the Broads: a review', 2001. https://www.broads-authority.gov.uk/__data/assets/pdf_file/0021/198003/BroadsArchaeologyReviewFINALRptwithIll.pdf.

NHER. https://www.heritage.norfolk.gov.uk/.

Powell-Smith, A. (ed.), 'Open Domesday'. https://opendomesday.org.

The Round Tower Churches Society. https://roundtowers.org.uk.

Simpson, P., 'A brief history of Simpson's Boatyard, Stalham'. https://www.simpsonsboatyard.com/history.

Suffolk Wildlife Trust, 'Carlton Marshes Nature Reserve'. https://www.suffolkwildlifetrust.org/carlton.

Symonds, R., 'Bricks through history'. https://www.brocross.com/Bricks/Penmorfa/Bricks/Bits/BRICKS%20THROUGH%20HISTORY.pdf.

Thatch Advice Centre, 'Regional thatch – East Anglia'. https://www.thatchadvicecentre.co.uk/thatch-information/thatched-roofs/regional-thatching-styles/regional-thatch-east-anglia.

Williamson, T., Parker, P. and Ringwood, I., 'The staithes of the Broads: a history and assessment', report for the Broads Authority (2017). https://www.broads-authority.gov.uk/__data/assets/pdf_file/0030/260499/The-Staithes-of-the-Broads.pdf.

INDEX

Entries in italics refer to the Figures

Acle
  boatyards 349
  bridge 319, 320, 349
  church 55, 70, 71
  decoy 336, 337, 338
  Decoy Carr 219
  detached portions of 109, 114, 115, 118, 138, 139, 143, 150, 153, 154, 159, 273
  Domesday entry 108
  enclosure 146
  houses 96
  lime kilns 312
  lordship 117
  place-name 49
  staithes *290*
agricultural prices 62, 134, 146, 148, 155, 157, 162, 189, 209, 270
Aldeby
  brickworks 10, 313–15
  church 70–1
  cropmarks 44
  doles 177
  priory 83, *84*, 85
Alderfen Broad *200*, 359
amphibians 213
Anglo-Saxon archaeological remains 46–7, *47*
aquifers 23, 24, 32, 33, 56, 57, 219
arable agriculture 29, 33, 51, 56, 57–60, 62, 109, 120, 151, 155, 156, 157, 162, 165, 183–5, 188, 189–90, 197, 220, 283, 361, 367
artefacts, prehistoric 14, 17–18, 36–7 see also flint, worked

Ashby St Mary church 68
Ashby St Peter church 71, 73
Ashby Warren 221
Ashby with Oby 184
  cropmarks 40

Barnby
  church 68, 69, *69*, 70, 71
Barnby Broad *201*
Barnby Level 266
Barnby Marshes 218
Barnby Old Broad *201*
Barsham 43, 177
Barsham Marshes 18
Barton Broad *196*, 198, *200*, 204, 206, 287–8, 299, 302, 303, 359, 366
Barton Turf 97, 287
  church 53, 303
  lime kilns 302–3, 312
  mill at 191, 239
  staithes *300*, 302, 303, see also Barton Turf Staithe
  tannery 302
Barton Turf Staithe *290*, 293, 297, *300*, 302, 303
  'Black Shed' 296, *304*, 304
Bastwick
  church 55
  staithe *290*, 293
Beccles *317*, 318
  bridge 319, 320, 321
  church 69, 318
  hospital 77
  industry 318

malthouses 312
staithes *290*, 295, 318
timber yard 310
Beccles Fen
　smock mill 239, 240
　steam mill 255, 266, 267, 270
Beeston Hall 61, 303, 329
Beeston St Lawrence 79
　church 69
Beighton 116, 117, 149
　common land 61
　cropmarks 42, *42*, 43, 44, *45*
　detached portion 116
　place-name 49
Beighton Marshes 367
Belaugh 57
　church 55, 70
　pleasure gardens 329
　staithes 290
Belaugh Broad *200*, 357
Belton
　cottages 101
　cropmarks *39*
　enclosure 190
　heathland 190
　mire 190
Belton Black Mill 234, 252, 272
Belton Bog 221
Berney Arms 163, 318
　brickworks 314
　cement works 316, 318
　public house 318
Berney Arms Mill 139, 227, 251, *257*, 258, 261, 316, 318
Billockby 51, 190
Bird, Maurice 341, 342, *342*
birds 114, 163, 164, 213, 333, 334, 339, 340–3, 367
Blackfleet Broad *200*, 203
Blofield 49, 64
　detached portion 116, 118, 120
Boardman's Mill 209, *259*, 260
boat hire 329, 345–9, 356, 358–9, 360
boathouses 299, 301, *301*, 307, 328, *328*, 346, 350, 351, 353
boating see sailing and boating
boats see also cargoes; watermen; wherrymen
　barges 280–1, 284
　keels 97, *278*, 279–80, 281, 282, 283, 285, 289, 293, 310, 312, 321
　pleasure craft 338, 344, 345, 346, 348, 356
　reed lighters 282

wherries 97, 277, *278*, 279–82, 283–5, 286, 289, 297, 302–3, 306, 307, 309, 312, 313, 321, 326, 345, 347–8
boatyards 2, 277, 285, 296, 307, 309, 310, 345–6, 347–9, 353–4, 360, 361
Bramerton 7–9
　enclosure 189
　houses 97, 101
　staithes *290*, 292
Bramerton Pit, 9–10, *10*
Braydeston
　church 64, 70
Breydon Water 21, *23*, 43, 103, *106*, *112*, 129, *129*, 284, 291, 316, 339, 351, 360
　RSPB reserve 163–4, 367
brick
　as cargo 97, 281, 282, 285, 313
　in bridges 321
　in buildings 61, 71, 73, *73*, 92, 94, 96, 97, 98, *98*, 99–101, *101*, 160, 246, 296, 303, 307, 312, 318, 350 see also drainage mills, brick
brick bonds 97, 230
brickmaking 24, 310, 313–14
brickworks 10, 21, 125, 286, 291, 296, 311, 313–15, *315*, 316, 318
bridges 28, 82–3, 258, 274, 286, 292, 294, 313, 319–20, 320, 321, 323, 324, 326, 345, 346, 351, 356
　Wayford Bridge 292, 319, 321
　Wey Bridge 82, 292, 319, 321, 323, 324
Broadland 3
　landscape character 1–4, 366–7, 369–70
　literature and guidebooks 4–6, 344, 354–5
　National Park 1, 3, 63, 211, 359, 360, 370
　palaeoenvironment of 9–11, 14, 20–2
　perceptions of landscape 363–5
　research on 5–6
broads *200–1*
　access to 357–8
　contraction of 192, 202, 203, 206, 225, 305
　origins of 5, 22, 197–9, 202–3, 205–6, 208 see also peat extraction
　relationship with parish boundaries and commons 204–5
　term for 208
Broads Authority 197, 227, 305, 360, 364, 365–7, 369
Broads Flood Alleviation Project 165, 265, 275
Broads Society 359
Brograve Level 184, 286
Brograve Level Mill 181, 184, 230, *231*, 232, 233, 255, 263, 286
Broome Heath, prehistoric remains on 37–9

Brundall
  boatyard 346, 348, 354
  brickworks 314
  development 348, 353, 354
  houses 100
  railway station 345
  tourism 354, 360
Brundall Broad *201*
Buckenham
  carr woodland 182
  church 55, 67, 70, 71, 73
  decoy *335*, 336, 337
  ferry *322*, 322–3
  mills 181
  staithes *290*, 293
Buckenham Broad 197, *201*, 330, 336
building materials 8, 24, 73–4, 91, 92, 95–6, 97, 98, 99, 101, 102, 172, 193, 281, 282, 312 see also brick; plants, uses of; thatching; vernacular buildings
Burgh Castle 21
  brickyard 314–16
  cement works 316
  church 55
  heathland 190
  Roman fort 45, 105, *106*
  salterns at 107
  staithes *290*
  tourism 329, 359
Burgh St Margaret 204
  enclosure 230
  mills 230, 258
  poor's allotments 195
  salterns 107
  staithes *290*
Burgh St Peter
  church 55, 73, *73*
  ferry 322, 323
  staithes *290*, 322
Burlingham Hall 62, 97
Burlingham Old Rectory 93, 98, 100
Burlingham St Andrew see also North Burlingham; South Burlingham
  church 53, 55
  detached portions 151, 154, 159
Burlingham St Peter 51
  church 53, 55, 69, 71

Cadge's Mill, Reedham 139, 253, 258, 262
Caister Castle 295
Caister Marshes, drainage mills and engines 260, 265
Caister-on-Sea
  brickworks 21
  enclosure of marshes 146
  Roman fort 45, 105
  salterns and salt-houses 107, 119
Calthorpe Mill *271*
Cantley
  boatyard 348
  cropmarks 39, *42*, 43
  detached portions 116, 118, 120, 137, 159
  Domesday entry 108
  enclosure 186
  ferry 322
  place-name 49
  salterns 107
  Six Mile House 123, 125, 158–9
    Mill 234, 236
  staithes *290*
  sugar factory 318
Cantley Grange 354
Cantley Marshes 141
  steam engine 265, 268
cargoes 97, 277, 280, 281–4, 285, 289, 291, 299, 310, 312–13 see also staithes
Carleton St Peter 65
  church 68, 70
Carlton Colville
  common land 179, 185
  Sprat's Water 197, *198*, 218
Carlton Marshes 185, 266–7, 274, 368, *368*, 369
carr woodland see woodland
Catfield
  chapel 305
  church 55, 68
  common land 172, 190 see also Catfield Fen
  cottages 100, 184
  dykes 305
  enclosure 185
  mills *209*, 209, 227, 234, 235–6, 244, 252, 253, 262
  railway station 306
  staithes *290*, 291, 293, 294, *300*, 305–7
Catfield Broad 208
Catfield Fen *169*, 188, 192, 207, 209–10, 219, 221, 362, 367
cattle 33, 59, 104, 147–8, 157–8, 161, *162*, 163, 164, 165, 171, 195, 210, 361, 366
Cauldwell Marsh, Halvergate 143
cement works 258, 262, 316, *316*
Cess Heath, Martham 175, 190
chalk extraction 312–13
Chambers Marsh 118–19
Chedgrave

church 55
detached portions 115, 116, 143, 149, 159, 160, 161, 262
mills 252
Six Mile House 262
turbary 175
Child's Mill, Runham 253, 258
Church Commissioners' estates 269, 273
churches 49–50, *63*, 64–5, *115*, 116
  alignment 68
  architectural styles 71, *72*–3, *73*, 74
  building materials 73–4
  isolation from settlement 51, 53, *54*, 57, 62, 64, 75
  locations in landscape 55–6, *56*
  mentioned in Domesday Book 64, 65
  minsters 50, 64, 69, 78, 79, 81, 89
  multiple serving one settlement 51, *52*, 53–5, 65, 67
  number of 51, 62, 63–4, 65, 69, 74
  rebuilding and alteration 67, 68–73
  ruined, lost or redundant 64, 65, *66*, 67, 75
  size 69–70
  towers *70*, 70–2, 74
  urban 69
Claxton 53
  Castle 295
  church 68
  ferry 322
  marshes 265
  oil engine 274
clay extraction 96, 104, 123, 203, 208, 313, 316, 365
Clayrack mill, Ranworth 240, 259
climate 10, 13, 15, 18, 20, 24, 26, 33, 35–6, 59, 218, 370
Clippesby
  church 73
  drainage mills and pumps 231, 233, 262, 275
club-rush 172, 217, 220
coastal spit 21, 23, *23*, 25, 26, 43, 47, 106 see also coastline
coastline, changes in 9, 15, 21, 22, 26, 43
Coltishall 57
  boatyards 285, 309, 345, 349
  brickworks 313–15
  bridge 319, 320, 321
  chalk extraction 302–3
  church 68
  enclosure 184
  houses 99
  lime kilns 312
  malthouses 311
  public houses 321, 329
  staithes *290*, 292

common land 30, *54*, 56, 58, 104, 116, 146, 170, 175, 176, 179, 182, 184, 189, 190, 204–5, 292, 294, 297 see also fen, common; marshes, common; enclosure, of common land
common rights 171–2, 175, 183–4, 185, 188, 331
common-edge drift see settlement, mobility
creeks 21, 26, 30, 106, 107, 110, 113–14, 120, 123, 129, 132
  relict 21, 109–11, *111*–*12*, 113–14, *121*, 128–9, *129*, 131–2, 134, 135, 143, 159, 321, 364
cropmarks 37–9, *39*, 41–2, *42*, 43, 44, *45*
Crostwight 332
  place-name 50
Crostwight Water *200*, 202
Cubitt, William 248, 249, 289

Davies, George Christopher 2, 239, 327, 328, 344, 345, 347–8, 355, 357
Decoy Broad, Woodbastwick *29*, *200*, 242, 357
decoys, wildfowl *332*, 332–4, *335*, 336–8
development 349, *350*, 350–4, 358–60
Dilham
  brickworks 313–15
  lime kilns 312
  mills 258
  staithes 293, 296
  Tyler's Cut 296
Dilham Broad *200*, 296
Dilham Island 329
Dilham Lake *200*
Dobb's Plantation Pit, Wroxham 12
Doggerland 18, 20, 36
doles 175–7, *177*–8, 178–9, 182, 204, 207
drainage see fens, drainage of; marshes, drainage of
drainage channels see dykes
Drainage Commissions and commissioners 190–1, 192, 236, 244, 246, 252, 253, 255, 260, 263, 266, 268, 269–70, 273, 274, 275, 293, 294, 351 see also Internal Drainage Boards
drainage engines see drainage mills
drainage mills 135–8, *138*, 242–3, *243*–4, 244–5
  'Commission' 192, 244, 267
  accommodation at 160, 262–3
  brick 192, 227, 230–1, 231, 232–3, 237, 246, 248, 252, 255, 258, 261, 264, 268, 270, 272, 273, 276
  distribution 242–3, *243*–4, 244–5, *245*, 246
  electric 103, 227, 256, 270, 274–6
  engine houses 246, 263, *264*, 266–70, *271*, 272, 273–4
  hollow post 192, 240, *241*, 242, 246, 253, 259, 260
  horse-driven 242

internal combustion 103, 272–6
machinery 227, *228*, 229, 232, 233–5, *235*, 236, 240,
　247, 248–9, 251, 253, 255–6, 258, 262, 269, 272
other uses of 261–2, 268
perceptions of 363–4
sails 227, *228*, 229, *232*, 232, 234, *236*, 237, 240, 246,
　247, 248–9, *250*, 251–2, *254*, 256, 258, 259, 261,
　271
scoopwheels 227, *228*, 229, 230, 232, 233, 240, 242,
　248, 252–3, 255–6, 258, 259, 260, 261, 262, 266,
　267, 269, 272, 273
skeleton 260 see also drainage mills, hollow post;
　drainage mills, trestle
smock *228*, 234, 237, *238*, 239–40, 242, 246, 258,
　260, 297, 353
steam 137–8, 141, 164, 227, 236–7, 239, 240, *245*,
　245, 246, 255–6, 261, 263, *264*, 265–72, 275
tower 192, 227, 230, 233, *236*, 237, 239–40, 246,
　248–9, *250*, 252, 253, 255, 258, 259, 261, 270,
　272, 276
trestle 192, 246, *259*, 259–60
turbines 227, 232, *247*, 248, 252, 255–6, 259, 261,
　267, 268, 270, 271, 272–3, 274–5
upgrading or rebuilding of 230, 232–3, 246, 248–9,
　250, 251–3, 255–6, 260, 268, 273–4
wind 227–30, 240, 248–9, 263, 269, 271–2, 274, 276
Dutch Tutch 351
Dutt, W.A. 210, 338, 349, 355
dykes
　as fences 103
　boat 291, 293–6, 302, 313, 314, 354, 364
　drainage 26, 103, *105*, 109, 110–11, *111*, 132, 142–3,
　　144–5, 145–6, *169*, 177, 179, 185, 186, 190, 197,
　　229, 302, 307
　maintenance of 104, 123, 133, 158, 185
　value for nature 163, 164–5

early human activity 35–6 see also artefacts,
　prehistoric; prehistoric remains
East Norfolk Rivers Catchment Board 191, 274, 276
East Ruston 43, 194
　King's Fen 221
　poor's allotments 195
　staithe *290*
East Ruston Common 219
East Somerton
　church 53, *66*
Eastfield Mill, Hickling 191, 252, 262
Ellis, Ted 5, 352, 359
embankments 24, 103, 110–12, 132–4, 135, 139, 140,
　148, 162, 166, 173, 179, 180, 190–1

Emerson, Peter Henry 340, 355, 356
enclosure 177, see also Drainage Commissions
　by agreement 182–5
　by unity of possession 183, 184
　effects on environment 190, 223
　of common land 61, 104, 136, *136*, 146, 182–6, 190,
　　195, 244, 252
　parliamentary 59–60, 146, 157, 183, 185–7, *187*,
　　188–92, 197, *207*, 207, 244, 281, 292–3, 339
　piecemeal 59–60, 182–5, 204
　poor's allotments 187–8, 192, *194*, 194–5, 197, 210, 223
　staithes 292–3, 294–5, 297, 299, 303
engineering firms 165, 260, 274
　Ruston & Hornsby 274, 275
　Southtown Ironworks 261, 264, 256
　Tangye 272, 273
Environment Agency 165, 191, 294, 361
estuaries 25–8, 44 see also Great Estuary, the
estuarine conditions 15, 21–3, 24, 26–7, 44
estuarine deposits 6, 14, 20–1, 22, 23, 26, 29, 29–30,
　31, 105, 167, 179–80, 191, 197, 217, 203, 226,
　313, 316
eutrophication 24, 164–5, 218, 220–1, 223, 361

fen 21, 30, *169*, *356* see also doles; mires; peat
　extraction; reeds; turbaries
　access channels 179
　common 146, 170–2, 175–7, *177*, 177–9, 182, 185,
　　195–6, 204
　conservation value 360, 362, 365, 366–7
　drainage of 179, 190, 191–2, 209, 246 see also
　　Drainage Commissions; drainage engines;
　　drainage mills
　enclosure of see enclosure, of common land
　fen meadows 179, 182, 191, 214, *214*, 215, 217, 219,
　　365, 367
　private 173, 179, 182
　soils 21, 30, 167, 170, 203
　sporting value 188, 339, 341
　use and management 4, 167, 170–9, 191, 192–3,
　　195–6, 209–11, 218, 223–6, 366–7
　　decline in 4, 210–11, 220–1, 223, 225, 365–6, 367
　woodland encroachment 210–11
Fenland 30, 77, 80–1, 90, 135, 191, 255, 263, 272
ferries 82–3, 319, 321–3
　Buckenham *322*
　Horning 259, *290*, 322, 354
　Reedham 324
Filby 57, 204
　enclosure 190
　salterns 107

Filby Broad *200*, 206, 357
fish 329
fishing 83, 107, 171, 306, 327, 329–32, 346, 355, 357–8
Fishley
  mills 239, 273
  place-name 49
  staithes *290*
fishponds 330, *330*, 331–2
Flegg 16, 22, 32, 44, 50, 55, 107, 184, 190
Fleggburgh 176, 179, 190
  Burgh Common 22, 179, 217
flint 7, 8, *8*, 9, 12, 17
  in buildings 7, 8, 70, 71, 74, 92, 98, 306, 307, 312
  mining 38
  worked 7, 17, 36, 38 see also artefacts, prehistoric
flooding 28, 131, 132–3, 137, 157, 199, 260, 286, 291, 320, 370
footprints, human 14–15
fossils 9–12, 14
Fowlholme marshes 114, 118, 125, 133, 134, 154, 156
Freethorpe
  detached portions 111, 159
  prehistoric remains 40
Fritton
  church 69, *70*, 70, 71
  decoy *332*, 334, *335*, 336, 337, 338
  ferry 322
  mills 234, 239
  salterns 107
  staithes *290*, 322
Fuelholm marsh 109, 114, 119, 147
fungi 214

Geldeston 43, 285, 319
  Danegelt House 95, *95*
  Rush Fen Cottage 95
  staithes 296
Geographical Information Systems (GIS) 5, 202, 204
geology 6–7
  alluvial deposits 19, 21, 22, 26, 27, 29, 30, *31*
  Breydon Formation 20–3
    Lower Peat 26
    Middle Peat 26, 199
    Upper Peat 22–3, 199
  Brown Bank Formation 18
  Chalk 6–8, 21, 23, 30, *31*, 32, 33, 219, 312
  Corton Sands 16
  Corton Till 15
  Crag 8–10, 11–13, *13*, 14, 15, 16, 18, 23, *31*, 32, 33, 55, 56, *56*, 57, 190, 219, 313
  Cromer Forest Bed formation 14
  erosion 6, 8, 9, 15, 19, 22, 23, 24
  Happisburgh Formation 15, *16*, 22, *31*, 32, 56, *56*, 57
  Ingham Formation 14, 16
  loess 18, 32, 36, 51
  Lowestoft Formation 17, *31*, 32, 56, *56*
  Lowestoft Till 17, 23
  marine deposits 6–7, 21, 22, 23 see also marine transgressions
  river deposits 12–14, 17
  sands 9, 12, 14, *16*, 16–21, 23, 24, *31*, 32, 33
  Yare Valley Formation 18, 20
Gillingham 65
  carr woodland 182
  churches 65, 71
  doles 176, 177, 179
  reedbeds 173
  turbary 176, 181
glaciation 15, 16–17, 19
Gorleston
  hospital 77
  prehistoric remains 40
  salterns 107
granaries 284, 296, 297, *298*, 307, *308*
Great Estuary, the 21, 22, 23–4, 29, 43, 45, 47, 105–6, *106*, 129
Great Hautbois
  church 71
  hospital 77
Great Yarmouth 3, 23, *23*, 83, 105, 110, *112*, 282, 303, 323, 343, 344, 351, 360
  Southtown marshes 157, 265, 268
Gregory, J.W. 197
groundwater 23, 214, 219, 220, 221

Haddiscoe
  enclosure 146, 186, 191
  houses 93
  mills and engines 267
  Raven Hall 93, 100, 159, 160, 161
Haddiscoe Island 118, *119*, 159, 161, 231, 234, 256, 267
Haddiscoe Thorpe
  church 55, 73
  enclosure 146, 191
  mills 142
Hales 54
  church 67
  common land 58
Halvergate 115, 117, 132, 135, 137, 142, 150, 152, 153, 155
  church 68
  Domesday entry 108

enclosure 146
mills 267–8
Halvergate Common 141
Halvergate Fleet 110–11, *111–12*, 113, 128, 129, 137, 141, 142, 276
Halvergate Marshes *1*, 29, 30, 43, 103, *105–6*, *121*, 131, *150*, *156*, 243, 246, 256, 261, 323, 324, 364 see also marshes
Happisburgh 35, 133, 135, 186
 Camberley Cottage *101*
Hardley
 doles 177
 enclosure 146, 183
 malthouse 312
 mills 239–40
 staithes 296, 312
Hardley Dyke 296
Hardley Mill *254*, 255, 258
Hassingham
 church 16, 55
 common land 61
 enclosure 186
Hassingham Broad 197
heathland 32, 43, 58, 175–6, 185, 189, 190, 195, 197, 365
Heckingham 55
 church 55
 Domesday entry 108
Hemsby 204
 common land 176
 decoys *335*, 337
 doles 176
 enclosure 190
Herringby
 electric pump 275
 engine house 268
 hospital 77
 ownership of marshes 149
 salterns 107
Herringfleet Hills *19*, 19
Herringfleet smock drainage mill *228*, 234, 237, *238*, 239, 276
Hickling 53
 mills 191, 252, 262, 269
Hickling Broad *168*, 191, 197, *200*, 206, 220, 291, 305, 306, *328*, 328, 339, *342*, 346, 357–8, 359
High's Mill, Halvergate Fleet 110, 161, 233, 234, 252, 262, 263
Holverston 65
 church 67
Holverston Hall 67, 97

Honing Broad *200*, 202
Honing Common 219, 221
Honing Hall 61
Horning 29
 Anglo-Saxon linear earthwork 46
 boatyards 348, 354
 carr woodland 182
 church 55, 69, 79
 cottages 101
 development 352–4, 360
 enclosure 189
 ferry 259, 322
 hospital 77
 mills 259, 260, 269, 273
 peat-cutting 194
 place-name 79
 public houses 357
 staithes *290*, 294
horses 147–8, 161, 163, 171, 210, 227, 242, 313
Horstead 8, 9, 303
 chalk extraction 303
 church 55
 enclosure 184
 'little Switzerland' 7, 313
Hoveton
 boatyards 348–9, *361*
 brickyard 314, 315–16
 church 70
 development 353–4, *361*
 enclosure 189
 mills 263
 railways 343
 staithes *290*
 tourism 329, *361*
 turbaries 203
Hoveton Great Broad 29, *200*, 206, 357
Hoveton Little Broad 29, *200*, 206, 357, 359
How Hill, Ludham 12, 101, 260
 staithes *290*
Hunsett Mill, Stalham 191, 209, 244, 253, 258, 269
hunter-gatherer lifestyles 18, 36
hunting 35, 36

Ingham
 enclosure 186
 mills 242, 253, 260, 268, 274
Internal Drainage Boards 191, 274, 275, 276
invertebrates 164, 165, 213, 214, 366, 367
Irstead 204, 287, 302
 church 55, 299
 common land and rights 170–1, 172, 331

farmhouse 94
fishery 331
granary 297
mills 253, *254*
staithes *290*, 293–4, 299, *300–1*, 302
Irstead Broad 172
Irstead Fen 192
isostatic land movement 7, 14, 15, 20, 25

Jennings, John Payne 301–2, 343
Jennings, Joseph 5, 197–9, 204

Kerrison's Level 139
  Mill 142, 161, 231, 233, 251
Kirby Bedon
  churches 65, 67, 71, 74

Lake Lothing *201*, 289, 291
Lambert, Joyce 5, 198–9, 203, 204, 207, 208
Land Drainage Act, 1930 191, 274, 294
land market 151
land values 61, 135, 145–6, 269
landownership 51, 61–2, 118, 148–50, *150*, 151–5, *156*, 157, 163, 183, 184, 185–9, 194, 197, 202, 208, 288, 292, 293–4, 297, 310, 331, 357–8
Langley see also monastic houses, Langley Abbey
  detached portion 119, 159
  doling 177
  estate 61, 181, 256, 265, 330
  mills and engines 181, 256, 265, 268
  prehistoric remains 17, 41
  staithes *290*, 295
Langley Hall 61, 258
leisure pursuits 327–9, 331–2, 354–5 see also fishing; sailing; shooting
lesser bulrush 172, 173, 220, 225
lesser reedmace 172, 217
Lessingham
  enclosure 186, 190
lidar 5, *84*, *127*, *130*
Lime Kiln Dyke, Irstead *196*, 297, 299, 302, 303, 310
lime production 7, 24, 282, 302–3, 310, 312–13
  see also chalk extraction; Horstead, 'Little Switzerland'
Limpenhoe
  church 55
  marshes 246, 258, 269
  mills and engines 251, 253, 271, 274
litter 171, 172, 175, 179, 182, 191, 192, 210, 211, 213, 220, 225, 282, 284

Lockgate Farm, Freethorpe Detached 125, 159, 160, 161, 258
Loddon 55, 116, 318
  bridge 319
  church 50
  detached portions 116
  houses 93
  place-name 50
  staithes *290*
log boat, Middle Saxon *47*, 47
Lothingland 16, 22, 32, 44, 55
Lound 49, 50
Lound Bridge 313, 286
Ludham 51, 98, 100, 101
  church 50, 51, 55
  common land 170–2, 190
  brickworks 313–15
  lime kilns 312
  malthouse *311*, 311
  mills 234, 252, 253, 260, 261
  staithes *290*, 294, 295
Ludham Bridge 28, 258, 274, 294, 319, 320, 321
Ludham Research Borehole 10–11

malting and malthouses 296, 310–11, *311*, *317*, 318, 345
mammals 213
  fossils 9, 12, 14
manorial demesnes 107–9, 117, 152, 170, 176, 183, 287
manorial sites 51, 53, 55
manorialisation 50–1, 117, 152
marine transgressions 21, 22, 36, 43, 170, 198, 220, 221 see also geology, marine deposits
marsh farms 104, 110, 148, 158–60, *160–1*, 161–2, *162*, 262 see also marshes
marsh hay 170, 171, 175, 191, 192, 205, 210, 220, 282, 301
marshes 21, see also common land; fen; Halvergate Marshes; saltmarshes
  arable use 29, 103, 109, 120, 155–7, 163, 165, 367
  common 30, 104, 146, 170, 179–80, 182, 183, 185, 189, 244
  division between parishes 103, 107–9, 114–15, *115*, 116, 117–20, 128, *129*, 132 see also parishes, detached portions of
  drainage of 113, 132–8, *138*, 139–43, *144–5*, 145–6, 147, 164, *169*, 180–1, 184, 185, *187*, 197 see also Drainage Commissions; drainage engines; drainage mills
  enclosure of see enclosure
  freshwater 132

grazing of 107–9, 147–8, 157–8, *162*, 163, 164, 165, 167, 170, 177, *178*, 179–80, 182, 184, 185, 191, 195, 197, 210, 224, 225, 272
  leases on 133, 155, 171
  'levels' 139–41, 246, 267
  ownership and tenure of 148–50, *150*, 151–6, *156*, 157, 163, 170, 183, 202, 208
marshmen 157–8, 161, 210, 263, 354–5, 358, 364
Martham 61, 62, 204, 261
  brickworks 313–14, 316
  church 50, 69
  common land 175, 176, 190, 195
  development 352
  enclosure 190
  ferry 322, 323
  heathland 190
  houses 98, 100
  mills 269, 272, 276, 364
  poor's allotments 195
  staithes *290*
  Starch Grass Meadow 359
Martham Broad *200*, 203
Mautby
  church 69
  enclosure 184
  estate 339
  mills and engines 231, 232, 233, 273, 274
  ownership of marshes in 149, 152
  prehistoric remains 40
  salterns 107
  staithes *290*
Mautby Decoy *200*, *335*, 336, 337, 338
Mautby Level 139
Middle Marsh Mill, Catfield 209, 234, 244, 252, 262
millmen 162, 262–3, 275, 354
millwrights 236, 239, 253, 254, 256, 258, 260–1, 263, 266, 270, 274, 276
  England's of Ludham 239, 255–6, 259, 260, 261, 272
  Holmes and Sons 256, 267, 268, 272
  Locks of Norwich 253, 260
  Rust, William 253, 254, 261, 270
  Thomas Smithdale and Sons 253, 256, 260, 261, 264, 267, 268, 270, 271, 273–4, 275
  Thorold, William 253, 260, 263, 265, 269
mires 214, 219, 220 see also plant communities
monastic houses 47, 67, 75–90
  Aldeby *76*, 83, *84*, 85
  Bromholm *76*, 76–7, *84*, 88, 89
  Bungay *76*, 85
  colleges 77
  estates 79–80, 119, 152
  founders 81–2, 83, 85–9
  Great Yarmouth *76*, 83
  Herringfleet 82
  Hickling Priory *76*, *84*, 88–9, 90
  Horstead *76*, 77
  hospitals 77
  income *80*
  Ingham Priory *76*, 85–6, *86*, 87
  Langley Abbey *76*, 76, 119
  Lessingham *76*, 77
  locations in landscape 77, 78–9, 80–1, 83, 88–9
  Norwich Cathedral Priory 81, 85, 203
  relationship with water and crossing points 82–3
  St Benet's Abbey 28, 75, *75–6*, 77–8, *78*, 81, 130, 131, 329–30, *330* see also St Benet's Abbey
  St Olave's Priory *76*, 76, 82–3
  Toft Monks *76*, 77
  Weybridge *76*, 82–3
moorings 191, 304, 306, 353, 354
Morse's Mill see Thurne, Mill
Moulton 49
  church 67, 73, 116
  common land 61
  detached portions 116, 117, 159
  landownership 117
Mousehold Heath 18, 58, 59, 190
Mutton's Mill, Halvergate *1*, 139, 251, 253, 258

nature conservation 2, 4, 163–5, 211, 213, 221, 223, 224, 279, 341, 343, 359, 360, 365–9
  rewilding 366, 368, 369
Neatishead 171, 331
  brickworks 313–14, 316
  common land 170, 175
  houses 94
  mills 239, 260
  staithes *290*, 293, 310
nonconformism 67
nonconformist chapels 61, 83, 305
Norfolk Wildlife Trust 176, 359
North Burlingham
  detached portion 116
  salterns 107, 119
North Cove 18
  doles 177
  houses 98
  mills 259, 268
  staithes *290*
Norton Subcourse
  church 69
  enclosure 146

houses 100
landownership 151
marshes 137, 149, 151
mills and engines 268
quarry 14
reedbeds 173
Norwich and Lowestoft Navigation Bill 289
Norwich School of painters 2, 75, 229, 237, 276, 312

Oby Mill 230, 233, 251
Old Hall Mill, Stokesby 234, 235, 237, 252
Ormesby 7, 57
  churches 65, 71
  heath 190
  turbary 175, 179
Ormesby Broad *200*, 206, 242, 334, 336
Ormesby Little Broad *200*
Ormesby St Michael 40–1, 204
Oulton
  church 55, 71
  development 349
  malthouses 311
  mills and engines 136, 181, 266
  private marshes 180
  railway 343
  tourism 329
Oulton Broad 22, *201*, 289, 311, 347, 349
Oulton Dyke 289, 291, 367
Oulton Level 266

Palmer's Mill 240, *241*, 259
parish councils 294, 297, 303, 307, 310
parishes
  boundaries 28, 40, 49, 57, *63*, 111, 113, 118, 128, *129*, 180, 204–5, 286–8, 293, 305
  detached portions 107, 109, 111, 114–15, *115*, 116, 117–19, *119*, 120, 125, 132, 138, 140, 143, 149, 150, 153, 154, 157, 158–9, 161
  merged 53, 65, 137
  size 51
Parmenter, Jo 199, 202
peat extraction 22, 174–5, 178, 192, 199, 202, 206, 220
  see also doles
peats see Breydon Formation; soils
Peto's Marsh 136, 181, 243, 367
Pettingill's Mill *232*, 233, 234
pill boxes 321
place-names 47, *48*, 49, 50–1, 58, 79, 89, 114, 128, 136, 148, 338
plant communities 163, 211
  dykes 164–5

endangered *212*, 213
fen *169*, 171, 172, 173, 211, *212*, 213–15, *216*, 217–21, *222*, 223–6
fen-meadow 215, 217, 219
freshwater 165
mire 215, 218, 221
ombrogenous mire 215
saline 215, 220
saltmarsh 215
swamp 215, 217
tall-herb fen 215, 220, 225
woodland 215
plants, uses of 73, 100, 167, 172, 173, 179, 194, 210, 211, 220, 224–5, 282
Polkey's Mill, Reedham 249, 251, 262, *264*
pollution 24, 220, 221, 360–1 see also eutrophication
population 33, 46, 47, 49, 51, 53, 57, 68, 74, 94, 170, 175, 189, 192, 203, 205, 360
Port and Haven Commissioners 303, 304, 305
Postwick 7, 279
  church 73, 116
  detached portion 109, 114, 116, 118–19, 134, 153, 158, 161
Potter Heigham
  boatyards 346–7, 348
  bridges 319, *320*, 320–1, 324, 346, 351–2, 356
  church 55
  common land 170, 171, 172, 180, 239, 358
  development 351–2, 354
  Heigham Holmes 180, 323, 360
  mills 239, 252, 273
  railway station 343, 346
  staithes *290*
  tourism 346, 348, 356
prehistoric remains see also artefacts, prehistoric
  land division *40*, 40–1, *42*, 42–3
  monuments 37–9, *39*, 40
  settlements 41–2
public houses 96, *96*, 312, 318, 321, 322, 357, 356, 357

Queen Anne's Bounty 149, 153

railways 74, 104–5, *145*, 265, *278*, 284, 291, 306, 324–5, *325*, 326, 338, 343–4, 345, 346, 347, 356–7
  narrow-gauge 313
Ranworth
  church 55, 74
  Cockshoot Broad 340
  common land 178
  decoy 334, *335*, 336, 337, 338
  fens 179

malthouse 312
staithes *290*, 292, 312
Ranworth Broad *200*, 358, 359
Raveningham
    detached portions 115, 116, 133, 140, 151
    houses 96, 97
    marshes 133, 137, 140, 151
Raveningham Hall 62
Reedham 115
    brickworks 313–16
    church 49, 55
    decoy 335, 336, 337
    detached portion 111, 114, 160
    estate 152
    ferries 322, 323, 324
    lime kilns 312
    marshes 114, 151, 152, 174, 237, 262
    mills *236*, 237, 251, 252, 253, 258, 262, 263, *264*, 265, 275
    railway 284, 324–6
    Roman site 43, 45–6
    Seven Mile House 159, 160, 263, 275
    staithes *290*
    timber yards 310
    turbaries 175
Reedham Hall 152
Reedham Hill 287
reeds 73, 109, 155, 165, *168*, 172–3, 174, 176, 193, 195, 199, 210, 214, 224, 246, 282, 284
reedswamp 22, 112, 217, 225
religious estates
    bishop of Norwich's 184, 288
    Norwich Cathedral Priory 83, 85, 109, 119, 147, 154, 170
Repps 184
    church 73
    cottages 95, 100
Repps-with-Bastwick 266
    development 352
    landownership 186
    mills and engines 234, 275
    staithes 284, *290*, 294
reptiles 213
rights see also common rights
    fishing 331, 346, 357–8
    navigation 292, 346, 357–9, 369
    shooting 338, 341, 357–8, 369
    transhipment 293
river terraces 20, *31*
river transport 35, 74, 97, 109, 281, 282–4, 289, 303, 312, 313, 318–19, 327 see also boats; cargoes

river valleys 167, 180
    of the Ant 12, 32, 55, 167, *169*, 170, 174, 181, 183, 192, *194*, 197, 209, 211, 215, 217–21, 223, 225, 243, 299, 360
    of the Bure 7, 12, 23, *29*, 30, 32, 37, 55, *56*, 57, 167, 170, 174, 178, 181, 183, 184, 197, 211, 217–20, 223, 245, 302–3, 312, 339, 360
    of the Chet 55
    of the Thurne 55, 167, 183, 184, 186, 190, 191, 195, 197, 203, 217, 218, 220, 223, 243, 286, 299, 339, 341
    of the Waveney 10, 14, 16, 18, 19, 20, 21, 30, 37, 39, 43, 46, 55, 59, 89, 167, 179, 180, 182, 185, 197, 218, 243, 245, 267, 269
    of the Wensum 19
    of the Yare 7, 9, 17, 19, 23, 30, 32, 37, 38, 55, 138, 167, 180, 182, 192, 197, 218, 220–1, 243, 244, 245, 312, 324
rivers see watercourses and waterways
roads 44, 49, 57, 104, 164, 185, 188, 282, 284, 292, 293, 294, 295, 319, 320, 321, 323–4
    Acle Straight 104, 110, 113, 118, *145*, 323, 324
Robberds, J.W. 7, 197
Rockland Broad *178*, *196*, *201*, 206, 260
Rockland St Mary 65
    churches 51, 65
    doles 177
Rollesby 204
    bridge 323
    decoy *335*, 357
    detached portions 184
    enclosure 190
    heathland 190
    houses 98, *99*
    salterns 107
Rollesby Broads *200*, 203, 204, 206
    Lily Broad *200*, 217
    Little Broad *200*, 203
Roman remains 43–6
    Saxon Shore forts 45, 105, *106*
ronds 112–13, 135, 139, 141–3, 146, 150, 155, 158, 164, 165
    Northern Rond *111*, 113, 126, *127*, 128, 142, 159
Royal Society for the Protection of Birds 163, 164, 365, 367
Runham 118
    church 55, 74
    detached portions 115, 118
    Domesday entry 108
    enclosure 157, 190
    marsh 135, 146, 152, 153, 157

mills and engines 253, 256, 258, 266, 269, 273, 275
salterns 107
staithes *290*
rushes 109, 167, 171–2, 224

sailing and boating 327, 329, 346, 352, 354, 355, 357, 358, 359
St Benet's Abbey see also monastic houses
   estates 107, 108, 109, 118–19, *119*, 139, 152, 170, 180, 184, 203
   ferry 322
   mill at 75, *75*, 136, 231, 233, 237, 261, *330*
St Benet's Level mill 231, 232, 233, 352
St Olaves
   bridge 319, 321, 326
   development 352
   mill 260, 276
   staithes *290*
   The Bell *96*, 96
   tourism 354
Salhouse 295
   brickworks 314
   staithes *290*, 293
Salhouse Broad *29*, *200*, 295, 357–8
   saltern mounds 107, *108*, 120, 123, 125, *126–7*, 128, 159
salt-making 107–8, 108, 109, 119–21, 123, 125–6, 128, 131, 173, 364
saltmarsh 21, 26, 29, 106, 107, 109–10, *111*, 113–14, 120, *121*, 128, 132, 134, 147; see also marshes; salt-making; sheep
Scaregap Farm 118, 138, 159, 161
Scaregap Marshes 263
Scarsdale Marshes, Halvergate 137, 141
Scratby
   church 65
   reedbeds 173
   turbary 179
Sea Breach Commissions 28, 129, 133, 135, 136, 146, 148, 153
sea levels 7, 15, 18–19, *20*, *123*, 221, 370
sedge species 73, 100, 114, 173, 179, 192, 194, 199, 210, 211, 214, *216*, 217–18, 219, 220, 221, 223–5, 282, 365
settlement 30, 31–2, 33, 35, 53–4, *54*, 55–7, 60, 65, 88, 363
   Early Saxon 44, 46, 49
   Late Saxon 54–5, 64
   medieval 51, 55–6
   Middle Saxon 47, 49–50, 54–5, 64, 128
   mobility 53–4, 64
   patterns 33, 51, 53–4, 56–7, 60–1

post-medieval 60
prehistoric 37–8, 40–3
Roman 44, 46
sheep 107–9, 147–8, 155, 158, 171, 365
shooting 61, 194, 210, 265, 336, 337, 338–40, *340*, 341–3, 355, 357, 367, 369
shooting lodges 339
Skeetholme marshes 104, 114, 118, 125, 133, 134, 135, 154, 156, 159, 269
sluices 110, 114, 120, 132, 135, 139, 140, 142, 191, 276
Smallburgh
   mills 192, 258
   staithes *290*
Smallburgh Fen 219
soils 12, 18, 65, 202–3
   alluvial 21, 136, 157, 220, 244, 246, 272, 367
   brown-earth 17
   clay 32–3, 58–9, 94, 185, 203
   fertile 57, 58–9, 61, 94
   loam 32, 60, 203
   loess 36, 51
   peat 2, 27, 29, 30, 104, 136, 146, 157, 167, 170, 172, 181, 182, 191, 197, 202–3, 204, 211, 214, 217, 219, 223, 225, 244, 246, 334, 366, 367 see also peat extraction
   brushwood peat 22, 23, 170, 174, 199, 203, 205
   sands 16, 32, 19, 56, 58
Somerleyton
   brickworks 314–15, *315*, 316
   bridge 326
   estate 331, 338
   ferry 322
   houses 98
   staithes *290*
Somerleyton Hall 62
South Burlingham
   church 68, 73
   mills 242
South Burlingham Hall 97
South Walsham 107, 119, 208
   churches 51, *52*, 55, 65, 116
   detached portions 107, 116, 118, 125, 132, 139, 142, 143, *144*, 153, 159
   Domesday entry 107, 108
   dykes *144*
   landownership 153, 155
   marshes 108–9, 118, 134, 139
   mills and engines 271
   prehistoric remains 40
   salt-making 120, *126*, 126
   staithes *290*, 293, 297

South Walsham Broad *200*, 206, 358
Southwood 49, 51
staithes 188, 281, 282, 283, 284, 285, *290*, 291–97,
    298, 299, *300*, 302–4, *304*, 305–7, *308*, 309–10,
    312, 314, *317*, 318, 321, 322, 358 see also
    warehouses
  private 291, 293, 295–6, 302, 303, 306, 307, 310
  public 291–4, 296, 297, 299, 303, 305, 307, 309, 310
Stalham 18, 62, 261
  boatyards 309, 349, 354
  brickworks 313–16
  bridge 319
  granary 297, *298*
  lime kilns 312
  lordship 51
  malthouse 311–12
  mills 191, 244, 253, 269, 297
  staithes 284, *290*, 307, *308*, 309
  tourism 354
Stergott Marsh 114, 134, 158
Stockton
  detached portions 115, 118
  landownership 117
Stokesby 61
  church 51, 57
  Domesday entry 108
  enclosure 136, 146, 149, 187, 189
  ferry 322
  houses 98
  landownership 151, 187
  marshes 151, 275
  mills and engines *136*, 136, 234–5, 237, 252, 265, 267, *271*, 275
  staithes *290*, 292, 296–7, *298*
  turbary 175
Stokesby Hall 151
Stone's Mill, Halvergate Fleet 110, 141
Stracey Arms mill 104, 157, 227, *247*, 256, 258, 275
Strumpshaw
  brickworks 313–14
  church 68
  doles 177
  enclosure 189
  engine houses 263, *264*, 268
  mills 242
  place-name 49
  prehistoric remains 44
  staithes *290*, 293
Strumpshaw Broad *201*
Strumpshaw Fen 221

Stubb Mill, Hickling 252, 262, 269
Surlingham
  brickworks 313–16
  churches 51, 55, 71, 73
  doles 176, 178
  enclosure 189
  ferry 322
  mills and engines 242, 255
  prehistoric remains 17
  private fen 170
  staithes *290*, 292
Surlingham Broad 176, *201*, 206–7, *207*, 208, 359
Surveyors of the Highways 293–4, 303
Sutton
  boatyard 309
  brickworks 313–15
  church 55
  decoy *335*, 338
  houses 97
  poor's allotment 210
  staithes *290*
Sutton Broad *200*, 307, 357
Swim Coots Mill, Catfield 227, 234, 235, 253, 262

tenure 51, 116–17, 133, 148, 151, 155, *156*, 157, 170, 186
thatching 73–4, 99–100, 172, 173, 193
Thorpe St Andrew
  boatyards 347
  chalk extraction 312
  'New Cut' 291
  pleasure gardens 329, 347
  staithes *290*, 292
  'water frolics' 329
Thurlton
  enclosure 146, 186, 191
  marshes 133, 137, 145, 146
Thurne
  bridge *320*
  church 51
  development *350*
  enclosure *187*
  Manor *98*, 98
  Mill *169*, 249, *250*, 252
  poor's allotments 195
  staithes *290*, 292, 293, 294
tithe apportionments and maps 139, 153, 210, 243, 299, 303, 312
tithes 67, 83, 118, 133, 139, 154, 157
Toft Monks
  church 70, 71

detached portions 115, 116, 118, 149, 154, 159
mills 267
topography 6–7, 15, 17, 19–20, 22
tourism 277, 327, 343–9, 355–7, 360, *361* see also development; leisure pursuits
trees 11, 58, 182, 211, 370
  alder 9, 11, 170, 181, 182, 211 see also carr woodland
  birch 11, 181, 211
  oak 9, 14, 181
  pine 10, 11, 14
  willow 170, 211, 324
Trinity Broads 190, 217
Tunstall
  arable 157
  decoy 336
  Domesday entry 108
  landownership 61, 151–4
  marshes 151–4
  mills and engines *235*, 235, 237, 259, 275
  staithes *290*
Tunstall Black Mill *235*, 235, 237
Tunstall Dyke 235, 237, 259
turbaries 174–5, 176, 179, 181, 192, 199, 203, 205, 210, 225 see also peat extraction
Turf Fen Mill, Irstead 209, 253, *254*, 258, 287
turf ponds 174, 179, 192, 225, 366
  terrestrialisation of 174, 192, 225, 366

University of East Anglia Broad 208
uplands 6, 16, 17, 22, 31–3, 35, 38, 42, 44, 62, 147, 149, 151, 165, 170, 183, 195, 197, 327, 360
Upton
  doles 176–7, *177*
  ferry 322
  mills 234, 244
  staithes *290*, 292
Upton Broad *168*, 176, *200*
Upton Dyke 240
Upton Fen 219
Upton Green 61
Upton Marshes *214*, 268

valleys, dry 19–20
vernacular buildings 16, 61, 90–4, 102
  cottages 90, 91, 96–100, *101*, 101, 102, 157, 158, 160, 161, 162, 184, 248, 262, 299, 301, 302, 303, 306, 316, 322, 345
  farm buildings 96
  farmhouses 90, 91, 96–9, 101, 160, *161*
  houses 94–102

Ward Marsh, Horning 179
warehouses 283, 295–6, 297, *298*, 299, 303, *304*, 306, 307, *308*, *317*, 318
water abstraction 24, 218, 221, 361
water supplies 32–3, 55, 57
watercourses and waterways 1–2, *3*, 4, 18, 24, *27*, 47, 49, 97, 109, 110, 114, 128, 131, 132, 133, 137, 148, 180, 246, 277, 285, 292, 293, 310, 313, 327, 328, 361, 366 see also creeks; dykes; river valleys
  alterations and improvements to 27, *27*, 28, *130*, 131, 281, 285–7, *287*, 288, 296, 302
  Ant, river *27*, 28, 30, 38, 43, 47, 78, 88, *130*, 131, 196, 240, 244, 253, 258, 260, 280, 285, *287*, 287–8, 291, 296, 319, 329
  artificial 265, 285–9, 291, 296, *325*
    Aylsham Navigation 281, 284, 285, 286, 289
    New Cuts 113, 138, 251, 288, *289*, 291
    North Walsham and Dilham Canal 285–6, 289
    Waxham New Cut 286
  Bure, river 1, 12, 17, 22, *27*, 27–8, 30, 43, 75, 78, 82, 103, 113–14, 123, 125, 128–30, *130*, 131, 132, 134, 136, 138, 230, 233, 237, 243, 256, 275, 276, 281, 284, 285–6, 288, 295, 319, 322, 323, 344, 345, 353
  Chet 1, 50, 319
  Hundred Dyke *27*, 28, 130, 131
  Hundred Stream 22, *27*, 27–8, *130*, 131, 287
  Muck Fleet 1, 22, 131, 217, 243, 246
  outfall of Broadland rivers 3, 25, *27*, 27–8, 103, 125, 128–31
  palaeo-rivers 12–13, *13*, 14, 16, 20
  Thurne, river 1, 22, 23, *27*, 27–8, 32, *130*, 131, 133, 291, 316, 319, 322, 346, 351, 352, 354, 360
  Waveney, river 1, 17, 22, 29, 82, 83, 103, 113, 131, 133, 136, 243, 266, 276, 285, 296, *317*, 318, 319, 322, 326
  Wensum, river 36, 345, 361
  Yare, river 1, 17, 24, 28, 29, 103, 113, 125, 128, 129, 130, 131, 135, 165, 167, 237, *278*, 280, 283, 284, 291, 295, 296, *316*, 318, 319, 322, 354, 357, 361
watermen 283, 284, 348, 355
Waxham 28 184, 255
  Decoy *200*, *335*, 336, 337
  enclosure 184
  Marshes 230
  New Cut 286
West Somerton
  church 70, 71
  enclosure 186, 190
  hospital 77

mills 270, 364
  staithes *290*, 292, 294
Wheatacre
  church 69
  mills and engines 263, 265, 266, 268
Wheatacre Marshes *19*, 265, 268
Wherry Cottage, Irstead 299, 301
wherry owners 289, 299, 301
wherrymen 28, 279, 282, 284, 305, 356
Whitlingham 7, 8, 17
  chalk extraction 312, 316
  ferry 322
  staithes *290*
Whitlingham Broads 208
Whitlingham sewage treatment works 221, 361
Wickhampton 132
  chapel 61
  church 55, 128
  Church Cottages 97
  landownership 61, 152
  marshes 114, 115, 135, 143, 151
  mills 139, 142, 258
  place-name 128
  wildlife habitats 163, 165, 197, 211, 213, 215, 217–20, 223, 224, 226, 332, 341, 362, 365–6, 367, 369 see also amphibians; birds; invertebrates; mammals; plant communities; reptiles
Winterton 22–3, 28, 107, 190
  decoy *335*, 327, 338
  enclosure 186
Womack Mill, Ludham 234, 252
Womack Water *200*
Woodbastwick 61
  decoy *335*, 336, 337, 338
  enclosure 189

heathland 190
  mills 242
  staithes *290*
  turf pond 192, *193*
Woodbastwick Fen 192, *193*
woodland 11, 36, *48*, 49, 58, 95, 116, 152, 167, 170, 182, 209, 333, 337, 340
  carr 22, 104, 164, *169*, 176, 181, *181*, 182, 210, 211, 213, 215, 217, 220, 340, 365
  swamp 21
Woodward, Horace B. 10, 198
Woodward, Samuel 198
Worlingham
  church 71
  decoys *335*, 336, 337, 338
  Magna 65
  marsh 177
  mills 240, 242
  Parva 65
Worlingham Wall 180
Worlingham Wild Carr 221
Wroxham *361*
  boatyards 345–6, 347, 348, 349, 354, 360, *361*
  brickworks 313–14
  bridge 319–20, 321, 345
  church 55
  development 348, 349–51, 353, 354, 360
  landownership 184
  malthouses 312
  prehistoric remains 17
  railway station 343
  staithes *290*, 295
  tourism 2, 360, *361*
  'water frolics' 329
Wroxham Broad *29*, *200*, 357, 358